Springer Texts in Business and Economics

More information about this series at http://www.springer.com/series/10099

Michael Kleinaltenkamp • Wulff Plinke •
Ingmar Geiger
Editors

Business Project Management and Marketing

Mastering Business Markets

Springer

Editors
Michael Kleinaltenkamp
Freie Universität Berlin
Berlin
Germany

Wulff Plinke
European School of Management and Technology
Berlin
Germany

Ingmar Geiger
Freie Universität Berlin
Berlin
Germany

Translation from German language edition:
Auftrags- und Projektmanagement
by Michael Kleinaltenkamp, Wulff Plinke and Ingmar Geiger

ISSN 2192-4333 ISSN 2192-4341 (electronic)
Springer Texts in Business and Economics
ISBN 978-3-662-48506-4 ISBN 978-3-662-48507-1 (eBook)
DOI 10.1007/978-3-662-48507-1

Library of Congress Control Number: 2015954664

Springer Heidelberg New York Dordrecht London

Printed on acid-free paper

Springer-Verlag GmbH Berlin Heidelberg is part of Springer Science+Business Media (www.springer.com)

Preface

"Closing a deal" is for many sales managers the ultimate goal of their daily business. For repeat purchases of more or less commoditized goods and services, closing a deal may mean one among many others. If one order is lost, another may just line up. In the business type we are focusing on here, the project business, such a view is certainly not warranted. Rather, in order to close a deal for a large-scale construction project or a high-volume consulting project, many people on both the supplier and the customer side will have been involved before a transaction is sealed. From a supplier's perspective, winning one order may secure employment and profits for quite some time, whereas losing one may have devastating consequences.

Marketing and managing these types of large business-to-business projects is the focus of this book. It completes our four book series "Mastering Business Markets", which also encompasses "Fundamentals of Business-to-Business Markets", "Developing Marketing Programs for Business Markets" and "Business Relationship Marketing and Management".

The book features eight different chapters which try to give a holistic perspective of business project marketing and management. In chapter "Order Management", Frank Jacob gives an overview of order management in supplier companies, based on various theoretical paradigms and focusing on the transaction as the central object of reference. Ingmar Geiger and Sarah Krüger take a look at how companies can decide which customer inquiries are worth following and how the proposal preparation process can be structured. Price and financing related issues, often the make-or-break criteria for a successful proposal, are discussed in chapters "Pricing and Revenue Planning in the Project Business" and "Order Financing and Financial Engineering". The chapters "Contract Management" and "Negotiation Management" provide an overview of contract and negotiation management. Finally, Wolfgang Rabl and Bernd Günter focus on the implementation phase of business projects when they discuss the project management process and project cooperation between different supplier firms.

As with every book, we owe a big thank you to a number of people whose work was invaluable in finalizing this work. We thank all authors who contributed to this volume. Our sincere gratitude goes to our research associates Silvia Stroe and Ilias Danatzis who managed the whole translation and editing process. The original translation of the

German language book “Auftrags- und Projektmanagement” was provided by A.C.T. Fachübersetzungen GmbH. At Springer, Dr. Prashanth Mahagaonkar served as our publishing editor. Finally, our research assistants Corinna Ebert and Bianka Marquardt rendered outstanding service to all layout works. Of course any remaining inconsistencies or mistakes are the lone responsibility of the editors.

Berlin, Germany
July 2015

Michael Kleinaltenkamp
Wulff Plinke
Ingmar Geiger

Contents

Order Management

Frank Jacob

1 Introduction

The market transaction is a constituent feature of a market and the elementary object of trade and investigation of marketing. A market transaction is described by the fact that a supplier and a purchaser mutually make an agreement about the exchange of rights of disposal to goods or services (Plinke 2000, p. 9)—in the simplest form: 'Goods for money'. Market transactions; however, do not materialize due to overriding plans and they also are not bound to a process prescribed 'from above'. On the other hand, it fsealso does not make sense from a company perspective to leave its development as well as its process to chance. Rather transactions must be actively prepared and governed. This range of tasks can be referred to as order management. Modern markets are mostly characterized as buyer's markets, i.e., the offerings exceed the demand. Customers thus arrive at a situation of choice, i.e., they can select between various offers or suppliers and in some cases set conditions. By contrast, suppliers are competing with each other to the benefit of the customers. In this respect, order management is primarily a task of the supplier. This statement is qualified by the meaning which is assigned to acquisition as an independent management task in the company and market practice (Günter and Kuhl 2000). This perspective shall also be taken in the current piece.

A systematic consideration of order management can take two different points of view: a theoretical perspective and a management perspective. The theoretical perspective intends to (only) explain the events within market transactions. It searches for the formulation of cause/effect relationships. By contrast, the management perspective takes the position of the company decision maker and strives to provide decision support to him for attaining his goals. However, without a theoretical foundation the validity of management approaches often remains limited.

F. Jacob (✉)
ESCP Europe, Berlin, Germany
e-mail: fjacob@escpeurope.eu

M. Kleinaltenkamp et al. (eds.), *Business Project Management and Marketing*, Springer Texts in Business and Economics, DOI 10.1007/978-3-662-48507-1_1

In this respect, both perspectives shall be taken in this piece whereby the management perspective shall; however, remain the focus.

2 The Theory of Transaction

A selection of theoretical approaches will be presented in the following, which exhibit a connection to order management. This selection does not claim completeness. The connection to the management approaches presented subsequently also cannot always be shown explicitly. The company decision maker, who is charged with the management of orders, can always then employ the theoretical approaches meaningfully if he must modify and adapt management approaches for concrete and specific use cases. The theory will then—in addition to the concrete conditions of use—supply him the reference framework.

2.1 Exchange Theory

The *exchange theory* would be referred to as an interactive and economic perspective for the purpose of a classification of approaches in marketing, as they were made by *Sheth, Gardner and Garrett* (Sheth et al. 1988, p. 19 et seq.). The statements by Plinke (2000) can be drawn on for the classification as a fundamental economic perspective. The topic under examination is the exchange in the sense as it was defined above (Sect. 1; Plinke 2000). A basic statement now exists in the fact that such an exchange only comes into existence if it is seen as beneficial by all those involved. As consequence, a significant task must be seen therein to explain how a benefit arises and from which elements it is composed (Thibaut and Kelley 1959). The exchange is based on reciprocity in this respect as it is associated with benefits as well as with sacrifices (costs) for all those involved. The supplier and the customer compare and evaluate benefit and costs from their respective perspectives. The benefit as well as the costs can be based on the object of the contract itself, on the transaction as a process and on the consequence of the exchange. The classification develops according to Table 1 in this sense.

If the benefit exceeds the costs for the supplier as well as for the customer and if this difference is larger than for all alternatives, which are available to the customer and the supplier at the given time, then the requirements for the establishment of a market exchange are given.

Each participant in the market, who is interested in the establishment of an exchange, or would like to structure it as beneficially as possible from his perspective, can benefit from this connection. The approach as an analysis matrix for the evaluation of the probability of an exchange is helpful in any case. However, in addition it also provides clues to how this probability increases by taking measures, or how the exchange relationship can be further improved for one's own benefit.

Table 1 Benefit and cost elements of the exchange in an overview (Plinke 2000, p. 50)

Benefit elements			
	Benefit from the object of the contract	Transaction benefit	Benefit from the consequences of the exchange
Buyer viewpoint	Product benefit bundle	Know-how increase security	Security Reduction in costs
Supplier viewpoint	Fee	Know-how increase	Reference benefit Cooperation benefit
Cost elements			
	Costs from the provision	Transaction costs	Costs from the consequences of the exchange
Buyer viewpoint	Purchase price Operating expenses	Procurement costs	Suppliers-switching costs
Supplier viewpoint	Manufacturing costs	Sales costs	Stand-by costs Cooperation costs

2.2 Principal Agent Theory

The *Principal Agent Theory* must be allocated to the additional field of New Institutional Economics (Fischer et al. 1993; Jacob 1995, p. 145 et seq.). Its considerable attention is given to the circumstance that the level of information of those involved in a transaction is not only incomplete but is also still mostly distributed asymmetrically. Hence there are inherently participants with an information advantage (agents) and with an information disadvantage (principals). In the scope of order management for business-to-business markets this involves the purchaser for the principals as a general rule and the contractor for the agents (Fließ 2000, p. 262 et seq.). The principal's information disadvantage manifests primarily in so-called endogenous uncertainty, i.e. incomplete information about the agent's cooperation input. If this disadvantage is known to a principal and he is furthermore unable to inherently rule out opportunistic behavior, this leads to so-called behavioral uncertainty, thus the fear that the agent is using his discretionary room for maneuver for his own benefit and to the detriment of the principal. Depending on the time in which the behavioral uncertainty refers, from the possibility to still wield influence on the behavior and from the observability of the behavior by the principal, typical agency problems can now be distinguished upon which; however, shall not be gone into detail at this point (Spremann 1990; Jacob 1995, p. 146 et seq.).

If a transaction situation is characterized by high behavioral uncertainty then this can absolutely lead to market failure in this way, thus to the circumstance that no transactions whatsoever will actually be concluded. Such a fundamental market failure is; however, neither in the interest of the agent nor the principal as a general rule. Various transaction designs are available to reduce behavioral uncertainty and hence to avoid market failure. For example, the principal can demand formal warranties from the agent, he can increase his observation efforts or he can offer incentive systems to the agent which steer his behavior in a certain direction. On the other hand, the agent can also offer warranties, he can send out clear and obvious signals which improve the principal's level of information or likewise work on the development of incentive systems (Spremann 1988; Jacob 1995, p. 147 et seq.).

It is now important for the management of transactions, particularly in the business-to-business sector that the roles of the principal and of the agent must not be clearly assigned to the supplier or to the customer. Instead the assignment changes depending on the special behavioral facts and depending on the phase in which the transaction is situated. However, the buyer's market situation implies that the initiative for the overcoming of behavioral uncertainty—either one's own or that of the customers—must always emanate from the supplier. In this respect, order management requires a permanent analyses of the given agency circumstances and the taking of corresponding measures.

2.3 Transaction Costs Theory

The foundation of the transaction costs theory (e.g. Kühne 2008) is the awareness that not only the object of exchange itself is associated with the benefit and costs for the supplier and the customer but also the process of the exchange. So-called factor specificity is a crucial dimension for the characterizing of the exchange processes according to *Williamson* (Williamson 1990, p. 59). Factor specificity exists when one factor allows optimum benefit only within a certain reference context. A reduction of the factor benefit had to be accepted outside of this reference context. Investments in specific factors always have the character of 'sunk costs' in this respect. If a decision maker does not accept this benefit reduction he is bound to the original reference context in this way. If a transaction partner knows about this commitment he can thus exploit it for his own advantage. Factor specificity was originally only based on certain factors and belonging among these are locations, real capital, human capital and appropriated assets (Williamson 1990, p. 49 et seq.). The application framework can, however, be expanded absolutely. Initial investments are typically also specific investments which a supplier renders in business-to-business markets in or to increase his chances for an order with the customer (e.g. Jacob 1995, p. 165). If the customer's decision is omitted namely to the benefit of another supplier these initial investments are no longer valuable in this way as a rule because other customers require other initial investments. However, a customer can also make specific investments as related to a supplier roughly by catering to internal procurement processes specifically for the circumstances with one single supplier. If he changes the supplier later the efforts for the orientation of these procedures will lose their value.

The theory can now be postulated that transactions with a desired partner become all the more likely the more one succeeds in moving the partner to specific investments. To put it the other way round, market degrees of freedom can be only maintained by the supplier and the customer if the specific investments remain in certain boundaries. Hence the management of orders is always also a management of specific investments. Specific investments, which have already been made constitute the basic conditions and future investments must be evaluated based on their specificity.

2.4 Interaction Approach

The interaction approach in business-to-business marketing can be understood as the answer to problems that develop during the transmission of the SOR paradigm (stimulus organism response), which is very widely distributed in the consumer goods sector (Plinke 1991, p. 176). The supplier as the acting party subsequently sends out stimuli to the customer via the formation of its marketing tools during market transactions. The customer as the reacting party processes this stimuli under the influence of many behavior-relevant factors (organism). This processing leads to a behavior (response), under which in general the purchase decision or decision not to purchase is to be understood. This point of view is generally not tenable in the business-to-business sector. In particular, the clear classification as an exclusively acting or exclusively reacting party does not correspond to the reality of the markets. The supplier and customer act and react mutually to a greater degree and are equipped with a number of alternatives for action (e.g. Gemünden 1980, p. 21). The interaction approach takes the perspective of the mutual influence and potential to exert influence in this respect. The reciprocity of the influence; however, not only refers to both supplier and customer parties but also to interactions within the groups and committees on both sides. In addition, the interaction is not only limited to paired constellations (dyads) but can absolutely affect multi-staff or multi-organizational constellations (Gemünden 1985, also see chapter "Project Cooperation" of this book).

From an interaction-oriented perspective of market transactions, the consequence must initially be drawn that neither the supplier nor the customer can unilaterally formulate goals for a market transaction independent of each other. Goals are only meaningful if both partners find consensus about it. This does not mean that goal-setting must always be performed cooperatively. It can absolutely be delegated to one party. However, the prerequisite remains that both partners are in agreement with the delegation and are aware of it. Mutual goal-setting with the customer thus becomes an important task for the supplier's transaction management. The interaction approach furthermore teaches that the course of the transaction must always be guided under the aspect of the pursuit of these goals. Backhaus and Günter have demonstrated in a very descriptive piece how a model can look for this governance (Backhaus and Günter 1976).

2.5 Market Transaction and Integrativity

Approaches, which dedicate themselves to the fundamental researching of market transactions, now explicitly take account of the circumstance that market transactions comprise the exchange of a concrete object as well as the rights of

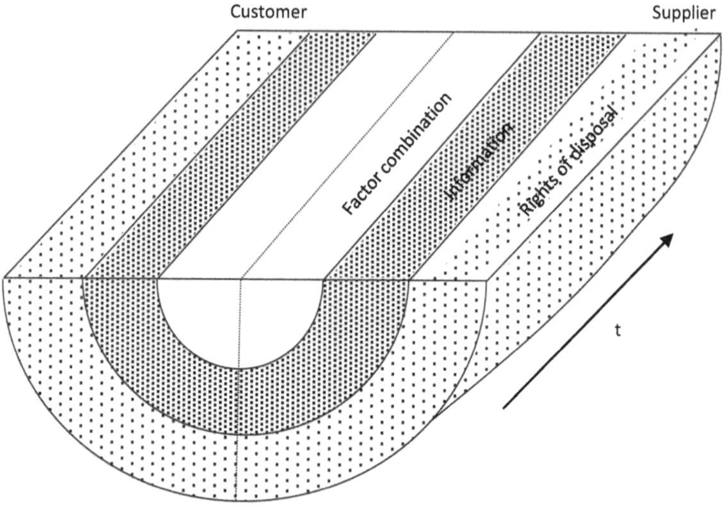

Fig. 1 Spheres of a market transaction (Kleinaltenkamp 1997, p. 89)

disposal over it as well as the relevant information (Kleinaltenkamp 1997). Hence a market transaction has a physical sphere, an information sphere and rights of disposal sphere (Fig. 1).

The complexity of the overall exchange and of the individual spheres is primarily dependent on the extent of the so-called integrativity, thus the degree of the individuality of a market transaction and of the influence of the customer on the result of the service. Alderson has already pointed out the meaning of this integrativity, particularly in the business-to-business sector in a piece from the year 1957 (Alderson 1957, p. 334). The more customized the need of a customer is, the more the necessity arises to also include the physical combination of factors into the concrete market transaction. The percentage of production factors also increases which are not contributed by the supplier but rather by the customer (e.g. information, however, the concept of information must be regarded as differentiated in the process (Kleinaltenkamp 1997, p. 92 et seq.). However, should uniform needs be covered for a number of customers the factor combination can take place—for example, on hand or according to a uniform standard—independent of individual transactions. However, influences on the management of information flows and the information processing also arise from the influence of the customer on factor combination processes. Information flows, which serve the definition of performance guidelines independent of individual transactions (potential information), namely require another management than such information flows that accompany or only make possible the integrative factor combination (episode information, Jacob and Weiber 2015). Special problems now arise from this for the integrative factor combination as well as for the management of transaction-related information and that the rights of disposal over the contribution of the customer shall remain with him. From this results the question, how the rights of

Table 2 Theory/approaches of transaction in an overview

Theory/approach	Focus
Exchange theory	Subjectively perceived net benefit of those involved
Principal agent theory	Information asymmetry and opportunistic behavior of those involved
Transaction costs theory	Commitment due to specific investments of those involved
Interaction approach	Mutual influence and the potential to exert influence of those involved
Integrativity	Physical integrativity, informative integrativity and integrativity of the rights of disposal

disposal shall be allocated to the result of the service, which indeed came about integratively. The supplier as well as the customer has an interest in these rights of disposal and they still constitute a substantial influencing factor for the agreement on a price between the supplier and the customer. Both also have knowledge of the problems of the distribution. The management of the rights of disposal also constitutes a substantial challenge within the management of transactions or orders in this respect.

2.6 Theory of Transaction in an Overview

In Table 2 the theories, which can be used as reference frameworks for a consideration of the order or of the market single transaction at the level of causes and effects, are summarized once again with their focus areas.

The company or market decision maker can set priorities during the selection of his reference framework depending on the decision making situation or given basic conditions. Concrete models and approaches for decision support are dealt with in the following sections.

3 The Management of the Transaction

Management as activity is the systematic use of instruments, models and methods (summarized: resources) for the achievement of company goals. The objectives for order management are effectiveness and efficiency in the pursuit of individual market transactions. The management process can generally be divided into the following substeps (e.g. Staehle 1994, p. 78 et seq.):

- Analysis,
- Planning,
- Implementation and
- Controlling.

For the order management, analysis means that all facts, which may be relevant for the development and course of a single transaction are compiled and systematized. Planning means that the supplier decides on a certain approach while order tracking with due regard to the analysis results. This plan is implemented in the execution phase. In contrast to the three substeps mentioned, controlling is not a sequential association but rather constitutes a task accompanying all phases. It shall be ensured via controlling that all other single steps of order management build upon each other and changes in facts can particularly be taken into consideration immediately. The outline of the following statements follows this scheme.

3.1 The Analysis of the Transaction

Orders or transactions have been defined above as the mutual agreement between the supplier and the customer in markets concerning the transfer of rights of disposal to goods or services. In this respect, in the case of the facts from the analysis of transactions or orders this involves ones from the customer's sector, ones from the competition's sector and ones from other involved party's sectors in the respective market (third parties).

3.1.1 Customer Analysis

In view of the customer analysis for the purposes of order management we are able to initially establish that investing customers always consciously or unconsciously perform procurements or investments with the goal of either directly or indirectly maintaining or improving their own position on the markets dealt with by them. In this respect, an 'objective' problem always underlies a procurement or investment decision. However, the procurement or investment decisions of individuals, are as a rule made even by groups which on the other hand relieves them of the sphere of the 'objective' and leads them to the 'subjective'. In this respect the problem itself as well as the individuals involved in the procurement are the subject of the analysis task for the management of orders.

Problem Analysis

Order-related problems of customers on business-to-business markets may be systematized according to various criteria, including according to

- the structure,
- the evidence,
- the scope and
- the institutional basic conditions.

If you intend to depict and analyze the objective **structure** of the order-relevant problem of a customer, then the value chain approach according to Porter (2008) offers itself as an analysis instrument. Thus every company can—and hence every customer on business-to-business markets—be understood as an accumulation of

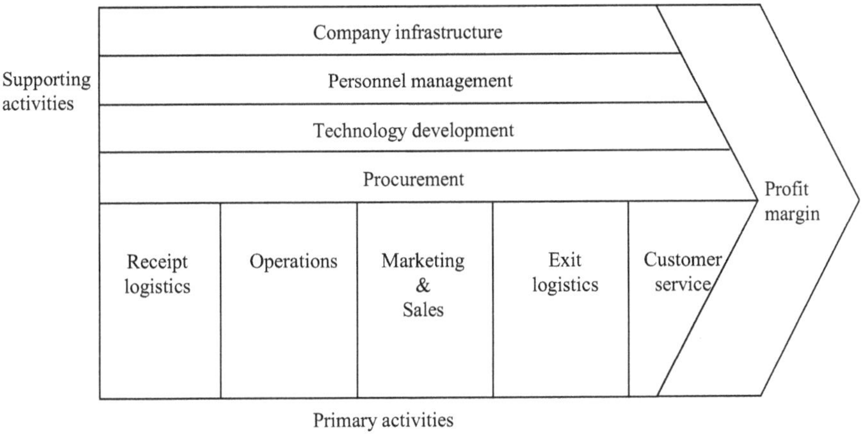

Fig. 2 Value chain model according to Porter (2008)

activities, via which a product is drafted, manufactured, distributed, delivered or supported. All these activities can be represented in a value chain. Value chain activities can be divided into primary and supporting activities: Primary activities are those involved in the physical creation of the product, its marketing and delivery to buyers, and its support and servicing after sales. Support activities provide the inputs and infrastructure that allow the primary activities to take place (Porter 2008). Figure 2 illustrates these correlations.

Problem structuring can now take place by anticipating and tracing the 'strand' of value chain activities, which is involved due to an order with the customer. An example shall make this clear:

Example 1

A manufacturer of pharmaceutical products wants to equip its field service with an information system of a newer kind. So-called 'doctor's visitors' are employed in the field service who as a rule are let in for very short discussions with physicians. Within the scope of these visits providing the doctors with new information and developments and obtaining information from the doctors about experiences with their own products belongs to their tasks. The information system shall consist of tablet computers that the field service employees take along to their visits. An app software specifies the information and questions and serves the gathering of answers. Permanent data synchronization with a central server can take place via a mobile Internet connection. A faster transmission of information to the field service employees, a systematization of data collection by the field service employees and an enhanced image at the doctors can be expected due to this information system.

A supplier of corresponding information systems would like to systematically ensure its acquisition success and therefore traces the pharmaceutical manufacturer's value chain strand that is affected by this investment:

- The doctor's visit sub-process is initially affected. The tablet computer along with the application software must be easy to operate and safe in operation for this purpose. In addition the aesthetics won't hurt in the appearance if a corresponding image effect shall actually be achieved.
- Furthermore, the system affects the 'server operating' area at the corporate head office. This area will if necessary focus on the compatibility between various tablet computer operating systems on the one hand and the server system on the other hand.
- The pharmaceutical manufacturer's 'sales management' area would like to in some cases manage data for the logistics of the visit via the system, which affects the scope and form of the application software. Furthermore, it may be assumed that trainings and help desk offers for the user (field service) by the suppliers are important.
- By contrast, possibilities for the acquisition or transmission of product-related information is the focus for the 'product management' area. These must also be taken into consideration for the application design.
- Finally the investment also affects the procurement area, which must decide if it will divide the aggregated order into individual batches (e.g. central server hardware, tablet computer, application software) or will assign as a 'turn-key' project.

This type of problem structuring applies to a customer's usage processes (Ehret 1996). Usage processes form a central procurement motive on business-to-business markets, whereupon it must be still agreed upon later (Sect. 3.1.2).

If the supplier conceived an idea of the structure of the problem in the literal sense this does not mean by a long stretch that this complies with the perception of the customer. It is also absolutely conceivable that the customer does not at all recognize the problem as such. A further analysis task of the supplier consequently exists therein to collect and classify the extent of the evidence on the customer's side. We can assume in the process that this involves a multi-level construct in the case of the demand evidence (Engelhardt and Schwab 1982, pp. 503–513; Ernenputsch 1986).

The starting point of a complete demand evidence is initially the problem itself, thus the deficit in the customer's value chain. The conception for the solution of this problem aligns itself here in an objective respect. However, complete demand evidence also comprises the possibilities for the procurement of this problem solution via the market. We are able to furthermore now differentiate between the consciousness and the transparency for the problem as well as for the solution and for the market. In this context, consciousness means that the customer basically recognizes the existence of a problem, a solution process or market procurement routes. Transparency is given if this knowledge can also be converted into a structured description and evaluation. Neither awareness nor transparency is discrete magnitudes to the effect that they are given or not given. Rather they can be more differently pronounced and thus respectively move on a continuum. The demand evidence in the manufacturer's example of pharmaceutical products is structured as follows:

Continuation Example 1
Awareness of the problem is given if the corporate or sales management determines that their field service works less efficiently and/or effectively than roughly the field services from affiliated companies in the same corporation or from competitors. The transparency of problems can be assumed if this deficit of those who are responsible can be traced back to an inadequate flow of information between the field service and the central office. The awareness of solutions exists, e.g. if the corporate or sales management knows that their concrete deficit must be solved roughly via the use of mobile and Internet-based information systems. The more alternative technical solution processes the customer is aware of the greater his awareness of solutions may be estimated. Solution transparency now means that the customer can systematize the solution process or solution processes and can thereby evaluate. The pharmaceutical manufacturer knows, for instance that a corresponding information system consists of the components 'server system', 'Internet integration', 'application software' and 'tablet computer'. Market awareness is the degree with which a customer recognizes if the required service can be externally sourced from the market. If the pharmaceutical manufacturer's corporate or sales management does not have any distinct market awareness, it will thus likely consider the make decision the only option on its own, thus the acquisition of individual components and the programming of a corresponding application software. Market transparency now means that the customer can assess and evaluate completely different offers from various market partners—roughly offers for partial services or the offer of a system ready for use.

Deficits in demand evidence can be traced back to various causes (Fig. 3). Exogenous causes do not stem from the customer's order-related problem as such but rather have an impact on it from the outside. Counted among these, for example are barriers to the will and capability on the customer's end as well as a general lack of information. The time plays a role to the extent that the demand evidence increases due to the experience collected with the repeated occurrence of a problem with an individual customer. If a special problem does not repeatedly occur with the individual customer, the customer can, however, revert to similar problems and solution experiences with other customers and thus an increase in demand evidence must likewise be expected (Marra 1995; Kleinaltenkamp and Marra 1995). The complexity of the problem itself, the technical and organizational potential

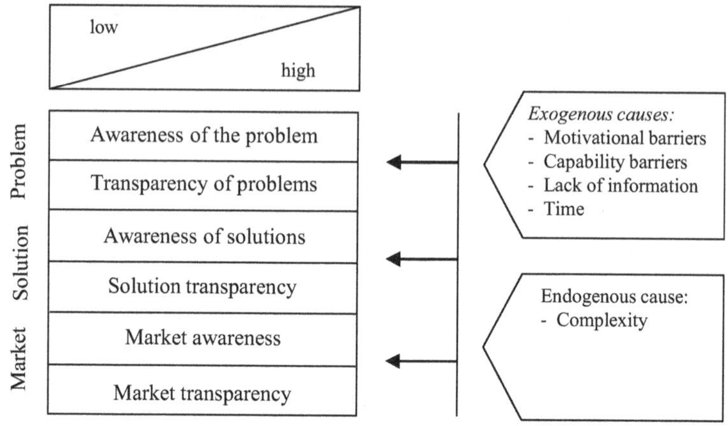

Fig. 3 Structure and causes of lacking evidence of the demand

solutions as well as the market constellations contribute to the reduction of the demand evidence as an endogenous cause.

In each case, it is important that the supplier is able to classify the demand evidence. The problem evidence on the customer's end is the fundamental requirement for any transaction. A maximum of problem evidence is thus in the interests of the supplier. It is also beneficial for the supplier with respect to the solution evidence, if the supplier can have an influence on its development. It will thus become more easily possible for him to steer this problem evidence in the direction of his own potentialities. According to the approach by Plinke for the modeling of the competitive advantage (Plinke 2000, p. 66 et seq.), the perceived benefit of an offer is determined via the solution evidence. However, with respect to the market evidence it must be noted that essentially all differentiation strategies in fact aim at reducing the market evidence. Differentiation ultimately aims at achieving a type of uniqueness in the customer's eyes. According to Plinke the market evidence has an influence in the formation of the net benefit.

Even in the case of broad demand evidence the customer maintains decision-making autonomy about which parts of an order-related problem he would like to actually solve via the market ('buy') or which ones he intends to overcome with his own resources ('make'). The fragmentation of a service into its parts must, however, not only follow its physical structure in doing so. The term **subtask** must be further comprehended. To characterize this aspect in more detail the overall problem offers itself, as it concerns the order, to be construed as follows:

- the procurement task,
- the financial task,
- the project management task,
- the integration task,
- the implementation task,

- the technical and economic benefit task and
- the competition task.

The procurement task effects the analysis of the market from the demand side point of view, the evaluation of the alternative decisions and the implementation of the market transaction itself. The financial task comprises the provision of financial resources for the payment of service. Project management is the scheduling of appointments and of resource utilization with the customer associated with procurement tasks. It shall be ensured via integration that a problem solution, which is procured within the scope of a transaction, is also actually technically and organizationally compatible with the other components of a customer's value chain. This integration is actually performed within the scope of the implementation task. The technical and economic benefit task affects the fundamental maintenance of the functionality of a customer's value chain during the ongoing usage. However, a value chain must not only be functional but also competitive which likewise constitutes a separate scope of duties (Fig. 4).

The customer can now either fulfill each of these tasks itself or contract out to one or a number of suppliers. Procurement may typically be a task that the customer takes on itself. At the moment, in the industrial plant and system business but also

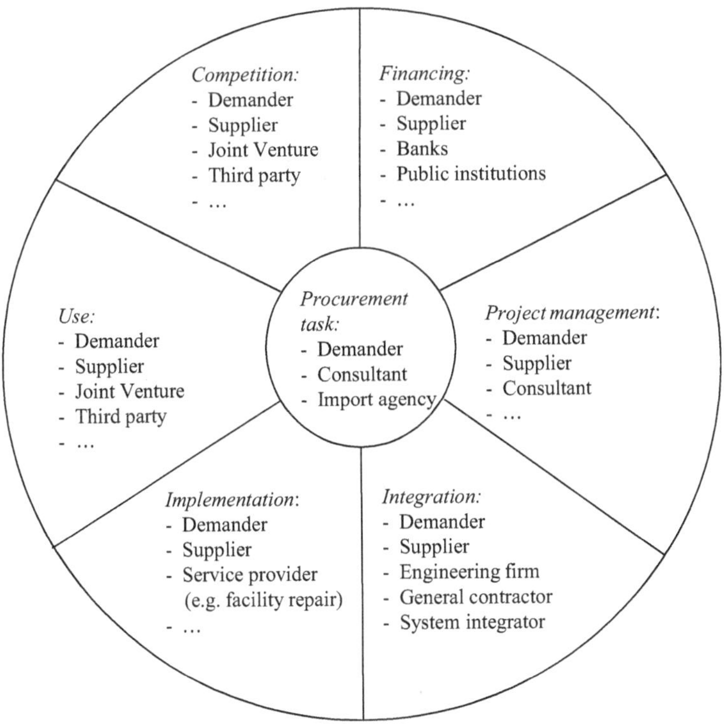

Fig. 4 Subtasks and possible person responsible for a task

with public contracting entities it is nevertheless not unusual to contract out the procurement task externally—for instance, to independent consultants. In the international industrial plant business, the financial task is likewise increasingly shifted to the supplier, which is then assigned the term 'financial engineering' (Backhaus and Voeth 2010, p. 375 et seq.; also see chapter "Order Financing and Financial Engineering" of this book). Project management can also be shifted to the supplier, however, project management as a separate service is likewise offered by independent service providers (Schulte and Stumme 1997). The integration task is primarily of outstanding importance in the system business where an individual supplier is often generally not in the technical position to offer all components from a single source. In this respect, the corresponding service providers have also developed so-called system integrators (Kleinaltenkamp 1993, p. 182 et seq.). Normally it may be assumed that a customer would like to use his value chain himself. However, aspects of risk may motivate him to involve the supplier also beyond the transaction. So-called 'Build Operate Transfer (BOT)' projects, within the scope of those of the supplier also remain technically and organizationally bound to the operation of the value chain, are therefore primarily no rarity in major plant engineering and construction. If an economic inclusion within the meaning of an involvement in profits and losses from the operation of the value chain is explicitly included this also concerns the competition task ('Build Operate Own Transfer (BOOT)'-Projects).

It can be said that an appropriate gathering and classification of the division of labor, as the customer imagines for itself, is of outstanding importance within the scope of order management for the decision maker on the supplier side. On the one hand, it enables him to formulate a suitable offer; however, it also reveals ways in which the customer can possibly be made aware of the benefits of another division of labor.

However, the option last mentioned in itself then always limits the customer if he himself formulates **institutional basic conditions** for an order or a transaction. Such basic conditions occur in the market practice roughly in the form of tenders and tender terms. These terms are defined very precisely and explicitly formulated for the field of public procurement (Robl 1995). Tenders from non-public customers are; however, basically subject to the freedom of action of independent market participants. They, however, often follow the procedure for public tendering.

The EU has stipulated binding guidelines for its member states, which contain, when public institutions must write out orders and how the tender process must proceed. In the process a clear and exhaustive specification of services is normally required based on a detailed list of the services to be rendered (specification of services with specifications) as the central element of the tender. Hence, the legislature hopes for a comparability of offers and a high profitability via the awarding of a contract to the supplier with the lowest asking price. The public tender, in which every supplier is called to submit a bid, and the limited tender, in which only a limited number of suppliers are invited to participate, must be distinguished (Günter and Kuhl 2000; Engelhardt and Günter 1981). A so-called awarding of contract in the open market can only take place in exceptional cases roughly if generally applicable market prices exist or roughly reasons of military secrecy require this. The principle of the awarding of the contract to the lowest offer may for example, be deviated from if the service still cannot be specified a priori and the service therefore has a more or less innovative character. Then the so-called cost price may be agreed upon in which it is invoiced at cost. However, in the recent past tenders also occur which no longer contain a specification but merely functional requirements. Every bidder must then develop a specification itself.

It is basically at the discretion of non-public customers to make use of the same methods. The so-called 'supplier qualification' constitutes a specific development in this context. In so doing, the customer formulates—normally non-public—terms, which the suppliers must fulfill, in order to come into question as suppliers or to be 'listed' at all. The fulfillment of these basic conditions is then checked within the scope of so-called 'audits' on a regular basis. These audits may go so far that the customer demands a view into the supplier's calculation and actively intervenes in its pricing policy.

These institutional basic conditions must be analyzed very closely within the scope of order management and they determine the supplier's scope of action in the market transactions too. If these basic conditions are actually very restrictive the market power of the corresponding customer is very high and if the general capacity utilization in one branch is temporarily low then actually only the price will remain as the parameter of the differentiation from the competition. Any such small space for other types of differentiation that the customer gives is thus assigned even more importance.

Individuals Involved

Purchasing processes on business to business markets are as a rule multi-personnel processes, i.e. groups of individuals play a part in them. All individuals, who are involved in a purchasing process on the customer's side, are named as 'buying center'. Substantial influences on the course of a transaction spring from the type of the composition of the buying center and hence on a supplier's acquisition success or acquisition failure. In any case, it is important for order management to know how the roles are allocated in a buying center. Only in this way can the behavior of the buying center be predicted and correctly classified. Indicators for targeted measures of the buying center influence can likewise be derived from this analysis. Different approaches exist for the analysis of this buying center. Because these were also already covered in detail in the current sequence (e.g. Fließ 2000, p. 251 et seq.; furthermore Mayntz 1980, col. 2044; Webster and Wind 1972; Witte 1973, 1976), they shall not be discussed in detail here.

Only a few suggestions for the treatment of so-called opponents in a buying center shall be pointed out (Klöter 1997). The term of opponents was originally introduced and thematized by Witte who identified various roles during the introduction of innovations in companies within the scope of a comprehensive empirical examination (Witte 1973, 1976). These roles allow themselves to also be used for the analysis of purchasing processes in general. Opponents develop in the process due to the resistance of individual ones against a purchase decision, which is either accounted for by motivational or capability barriers. Capability barriers concern the 'ability' of the individuals affected and by contrast motivational barriers concern the 'willingness'. It can now be furthermore subsequently distinguished whether the resistance is based on a loyal effort for the prevention of the negative consequences of procurement or if it is based on self-serving motives for prevention of exclusively personal disadvantages for the individual ones (Klöter 1997, p. 191). Opponents of the first-mentioned type are referred to as loyal resistance and by contrast the opponents of the second type are referred to as egocentric resistance. Loyal resistance shall cause the supplier to above all consider the offering presented by him for the specific order. Starting points for the structuring of this process are the performance program itself, the distribution performance, the communication performance and the compensation (Kleinaltenkamp et al. 2006). In this respect, resistance is not destructive anyway (Klöter 1997, p. 197) but rather may absolutely constitute a source for procuring information for the formation of competitive advantages.

Rational deliberations of this type fail; however, if this involves the overcoming of egocentric resistance. Therefore the following additional measures are suggested:

The adaptation of the problem solution to individual preferences of participants:
This path is practicable if the opponents' resistance is not the fundamental nature but rather only affects partial aspects of the offering. *Klöter* mentions the example of the assistant who indeed does not oppose the procurement of a new workstation computer in principle but for prestige purposes insists on a screen size that would actually not be necessary upon 'objective' consideration. The supplier as well as the customer can now get involved with a compromise if the transaction is thereby saved and the reduction of benefit for both sides is reasonable (Klöter 1997, p. 200 et seq.). However, the leeways for such measures are sinking with increasing performance complexity.

Use of individual power foundations:
The opponent can only cancel its effect if the corresponding individuals are equipped with sufficient power foundations. If these are not present the opponent thus remains irrelevant. If they are present the power of additional buying center members, who are positively positioned with respect to the procurement and the supplier, can be exploited. The possibility fails if the opponent is all-powerful.

Use of network-specific power foundations:
Project and order specific power in particular often is not based on the power positions of individuals but rather on relationships and interactions of a number of individuals amongst themselves. This process can be referred to as 'networking' (Fließ 2000, p. 341 et seq.). Opposing gatekeepers can be identified and specifically circumvented; via participants with a central position, i.e. many communication relations, information can be scattered; originally isolated participants with a high power base and a positive position to the order or supplier are more strongly incorporated into the network; cliques and coalitions

can bundle their power; the number of network members is increased or decreased; emerging coalitions are promoted or suppressed.

However, the list already makes clear that the possibilities for the overcoming of egocentric resistance are limited in particular. The extent of the input in resources in such measures should not be made lastly contingent upon the value of an order for the supplier affected.

3.1.2 Competitor and Third Party Analysis

Competitive advantages in modern business to business markets can always only be of a relative or comparative nature. Primarily the relative net benefit of a given offer perceived by the customer only arises via the comparison with other offers (Plinke 2000, p. 33 et seq.). Thus great importance is assigned to the analysis of the competition as a management task of a supplier. If the analysis is performed for the purposes of the development of marketing programs for comprehensive markets or more comprehensive market segments it is thus chiefly potential-oriented (Kleinaltenkamp 2000, p. 219 et seq.). Competition analysis in the context of individual orders has, however, more of an episode character (Jacob and Weiber 2015). Therefore within the scope of order management which suppliers are perceived as at all suitable by the customer in a given transaction situation must be initially limited. Primarily in the consumer goods sector, one speaks of the so-called 'evoked set' concerning this matter and designates a scope of seven offers which this 'evoked set' does not exceed for certain purchase types (Kroeber-Riel et al. 2009, p. 425 et seq.). In Fig. 5 it is schematically shown how the limitation of one such evoked set can proceed via the customer.

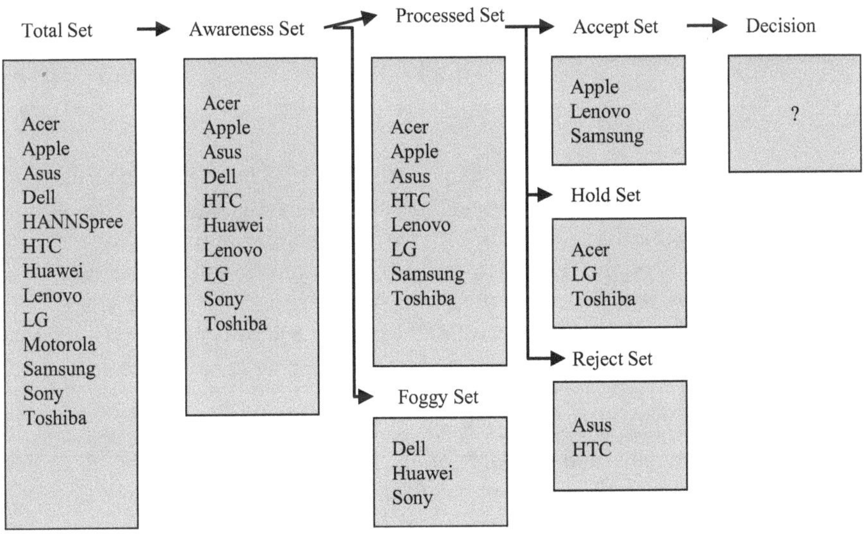

Fig. 5 Limitation of the relevant competitor (Kotler et al. 2007, p. 297)

Example 2
The starting point is initially the actual quantity of all suppliers who can offer services for the solution of a certain application problem (Total Set). For example, suppliers are specified in the figure who manufacture the tablet computer for the pharmaceutical company's (partial) need described above. However, it must not be assumed that every customer can render a complete overview of the overall offer for a certain need. The information costs for this are prohibitively high as a rule. The quantity of those suppliers who are actually perceived as such are referred to as 'Awareness Set'. Since the pharmaceutical manufacturer cannot possibly correctly estimate if the product of individual manufacturers actually corresponds to the criteria of a tablet computer or preferably must not be classified as a laptop after all it will in its awareness split the remaining suppliers into such with which it will continue to concern itself with ('Processed Set') and such which initially will be excluded ('Foggy Set'). If explicit reasons against the selection of certain suppliers already exist, e.g. an impending departure from a market or deficiencies in distribution and sales-related presence then the supplier will reach the 'Reject Set' in the next step. Suppliers, for which sufficient information exists and against which no upstream exclusion criteria are given, reach the 'Accept Set'. An insufficient information base leads to the fact that the corresponding suppliers are initially set up in a 'Hold Set'. The final supplier selection is ultimately made from the 'Accept Set'. However, it must be taken into consideration that this constellation can also change during the course of an acquisition. This means due to changes in the information base or in the target system suppliers, who originally were looked upon as 'foggy', can suddenly become absolutely acceptable, or suppliers who were explicitly rejected will be rerated. In addition to the acquisition the supplier must consequently keep its level of information about the customer's 'Evoked Set' up to date constantly.

Attention must also be paid that the pre-selection of suppliers in the business to business sector often takes place very deliberately and systematically. The concept of 'Supplier Qualification' must be referred to again within the scope of the selection criteria that the customer explicitly formulates and of its fulfillment which he formally reviews at the suppliers. A corresponding 'listing' constitutes a protection for those suppliers who fulfill the criteria and by contrast constitutes an obstacle for all others of which its overcoming is often associated with substantial efforts.

If the supplier has limited the 'Evoked Set' then the next task consists in assessing the strengths and weaknesses of all relevant competitors. A profile comparison of the competitors is methodically offered for this purpose with the aid of individual-order-related criteria that is represented in Fig. 6 by way of example.

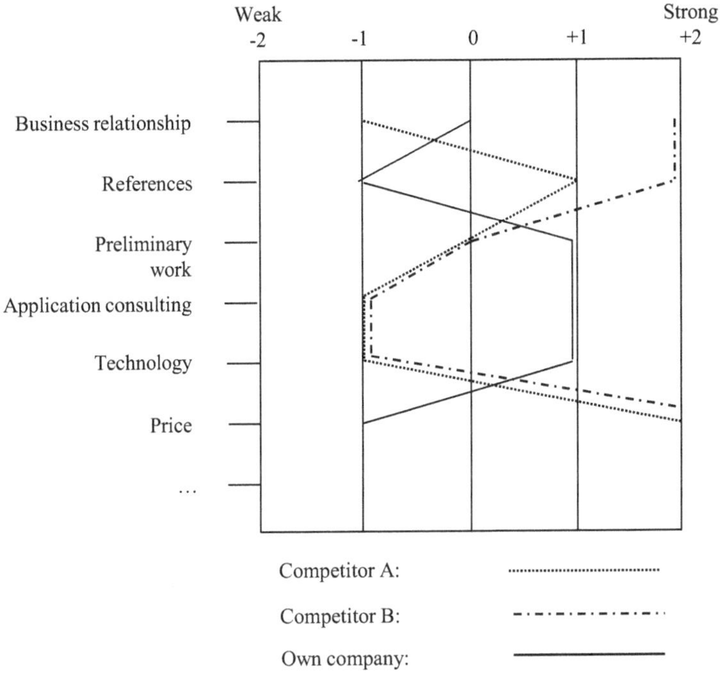

Fig. 6 Individual-order-related profile comparisons for the competition analysis

The business relationship plays a prominent role to the extent that it provides the so-called 'In-Supplier' opportunity to construct entry barriers for the 'Out-supplier' (Kleinaltenkamp et al. 2011). References are especially a substantial decision criterion for the customer for new types of problems and problem solutions (Sect. 3.3.2). If a competitor has already rendered initial investments within the scope of a pending transaction then this as a rule enhances his chances for acquisition success. In the majority of cases, customers can already be bound at an early stage or steered in a certain direction by such initial investments. All other competitors must take into consideration that competitors who have rendered initial investments are often prepared to make prices concessions due to their character as 'sunk costs'. A customer can also be subsequently prompted to formulate the awarding of the contract criteria in accordance to the wishes of a certain supplier via early and targeted application consulting concerning its own specifications. A great influence also emanates from the technological strength of a competitor and its pricing policy.

It must also be stressed again that this comparison must also be anticipated such as it will be performed by the customer. Since a customer benefit will only come about in the customer's subjective perception.

3.2 The Planning of the Transaction

Every analysis by its nature can indeed never be more than the foundation of a planning. Substantial deficits still exist in the operational use currently in the realm of the planning of orders or in particular in the acquisition of orders.

Example 3
An investigation by Kienbaum management consulting for the business to business sector revealed that indeed in 60 % of all companies more than 20 % of employees have direct customer contact and that, however, there is no binding procedural instructions for dealing with customers for three-fourths of companies. Missing procedures indicate a fundamental planning deficit. All employees are trained for customer contact for 20.7 % of companies, a few for 47.3 % and none for 30.4 % (Kienbaum 1996).

In Sect. 3.1.1 the evidence of a customer's problem and possible solution processes were introduced as a substantial analysis object. However evidence of the order progression also plays a large role with respect to order planning. It must initially be determined if or which perceptions the supplier as well as the customer have about the progression of an order. If we assume the three areas of offering potential, offering creation process and offering outcome (Kleinaltenkamp 2000, p. 219 et seq.) we can in this way speak of process evidence in this context (Fließ 1996). Two sources must also be distinguished for the process evidence, namely process awareness and process transparency. Process awareness describes the fundamental knowledge of an involved party that an order requires contributions from all who are involved and proceeds interactively. Process transparency describes the level of exact knowledge about contributions and processes in detail. Deficits may now exist for the customer as well as for the supplier. Four types of transaction situations must accordingly be distinguished dependent on the process evidence as they are presented in Fig. 7.

In the case of type I, there is neither process evidence on the supplier side nor on the customer side. The danger of this type of procedure consists in the fact that it is highly inefficient and an actual problem solution is unlikely for the customer. Type II occurs in situations in which the customer practices an active procurement management and specifies the proceeding. The supplier's task consists of balancing its evidence deficit as quickly as possible and adopting the customer's specifications into its own planning. The exact reverse constellation occurs in type III. The supplier can obtain competitive advantages for itself in this situation by enlightening the customer about its own planning and thereby encouraging the customer's willingness to cooperate. By contrast, in the case of type IV the willingness to cooperate may be assumed as given for both participants.

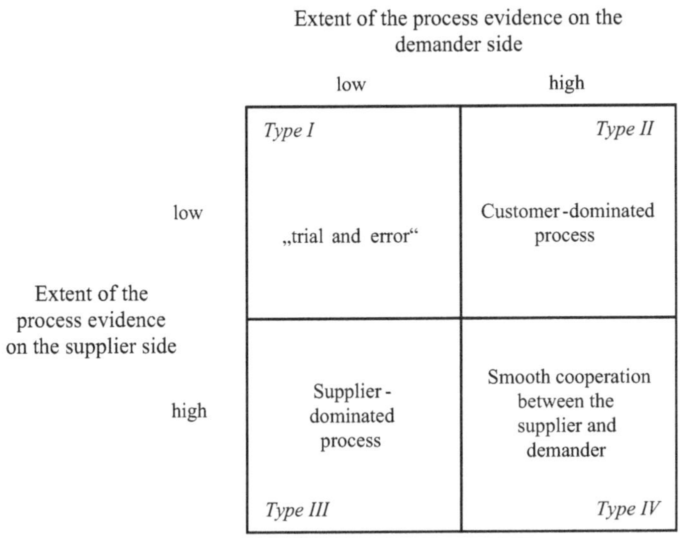

Fig. 7 Types of integration processes (Fließ 1996, p. 95)

In any case, it appears useful for the supplier to determine the planning status or the process evidence in its own ranks as well as with the customer in order to make further planning dependent on it.

The 'blueprinting' instrument offers itself for the detailed planning of an order progression from the supplier's perspective (Jacob and Weiber 2015, p. 578 et seq.). Blueprints present a schematic flow chart of the individual phases of a process—in this case of an order or of an acquisition of orders.

In addition to the chronological sequence it can be illustrated which corporate sectors are involved for the supplier and how these sectors must be classified in the perception of the customer. Therefore in a blueprint

- a 'line of interaction', the supplier and the customer sectors are separated,
- a 'line of visibility', the supplier sectors, which are visible for the customer, are separated from such which are concealed from the customer,
- a 'line of internal interaction', supplier's function separated with direct order reference from such without direct order reference and
- a 'line of implementation', which separates executive from regulating sectors for the supplier,

are listed. In Fig. 8 such a blueprint is described by way of example.

Blueprints serve as the structuring aid for the order progression as well as the planning of the utilization of resources over time and of the visualization for company employees and customers. If orders always proceed in a relatively similar form for a supplier a corresponding 'model progression' can be developed in the blueprint in this way. If individual orders are different according to their type and

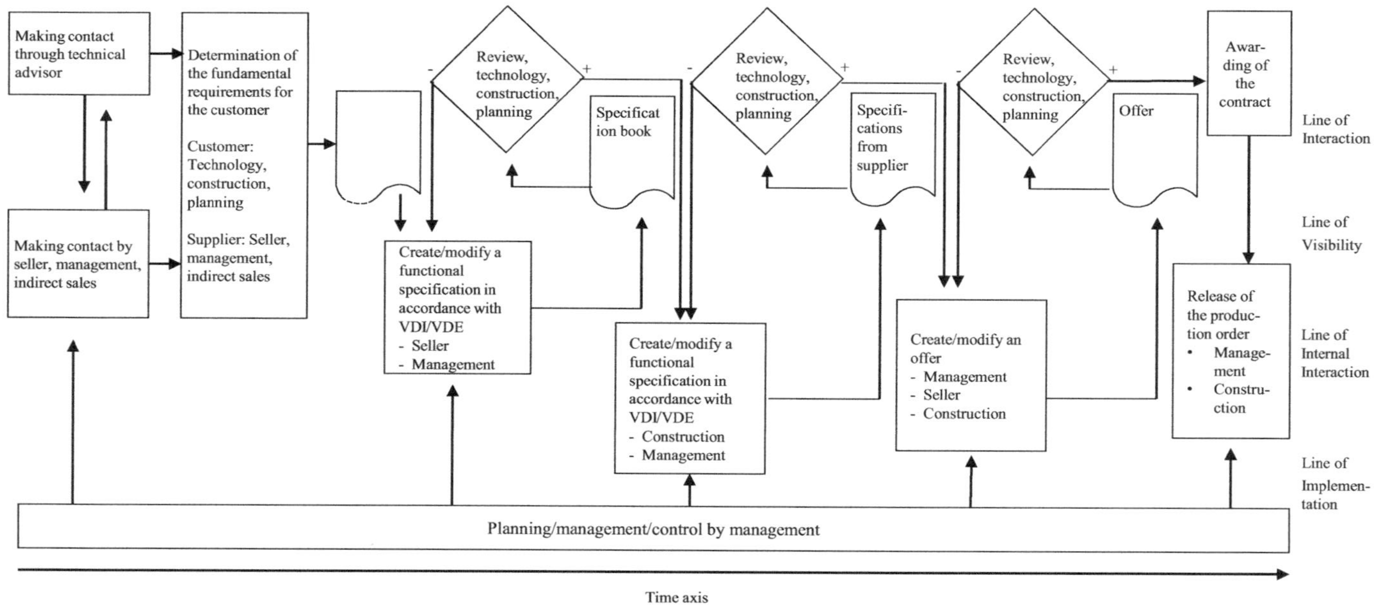

Fig. 8 Blueprint for the acquisition of orders (Jacob and Weiber 2015, p. 583)

requirements and a high profit contribution is additionally attributed to them then if need be blueprints must be specifically developed for each order.

3.3 The Implementation of the Transaction

Acquisition successes for individual orders are the fundamental success units in business to business marketing. A thorough analysis of transaction situations and a systematic planning of the transaction take place so that these successes can be ensured. If the execution of the transaction takes place for the purpose of planning then a receipt of order and a successful implementation of the order will in any case acquire likelihood.

However, this mostly involves interactive processes particularly for transactions in business to business markets (Sect. 2.4). This means the partners involved perform interactively and they also react to each other within individual transactions under exploitation of degrees of freedom. This fact again sets the predictability of transaction limits. "There are some activities which are only semi-routine and which cannot be fully prescribed and controlled by regulations. This is particularly true in such marketing activities as personal selling" (Alderson 1957, S. 82). The interactive character of the transactions often requires from the participants very quick and immediate adaptations to situations, which thus were not or could not be anticipated during the planning.

3.3.1 Sales Psychology and Salesmanship

Instruments were developed in connection with sales psychology and salesmanship that support a mastering of this challenge. Due to the fact that in spite of enormous efforts a unified, unchallenged and consistent theory of sales psychology is lacking, managers and the head of HR nevertheless see a substantial qualification field in this for employees in the marketing/sales sectors and the area is dominated by sales trainers and management consultants. Their abilities and achievements shall not be diminished. The methods are, however, very different and partially very strongly characterized by the trainer's or consultant's personality. At this point a limitation on such statements shall be made which is mentioned by various authors in the same way and for which a certain foundation exists (Bänsch 2006).

Approaches to sales psychology assess the phases of the sales process in most cases. Prominent among them is the AIDA approach signifying a sequence of attracting customer Attention, raising customer interest, convincing the customer to Desire the product, and leading the customer towards taking action.

Three phases of the sales process shall be distinguished for the systematization of statements for sales psychology, which are initially schematically represented in Fig. 9.

However, with this summary it already becomes clear that the approaches remain incomplete. Currently in the business to business sector the conclusion of negotiations namely cannot be considered the chronological endpoint of a transaction. The order manager also remains in an interaction with the customer after the

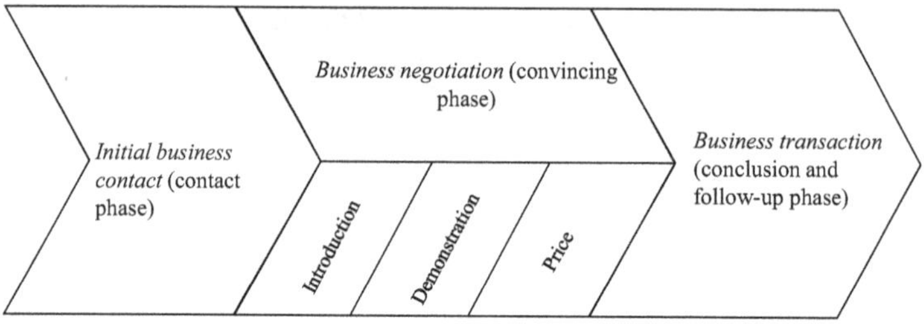

Fig. 9 Phases of the purchasing process

order completion. The task often even falls upon him to ensure the success of the order also during the execution of the order. In this respect, the statements concerning the sales psychology must be expanded accordingly.

Initial Business Contact

In general, three different initial situations can be distinguished for the first phase of a sales process:

- the customer takes the initiative and contacts the supplier on its individual initiative,
- the supplier is requested to make contact by the customer, or
- the supplier pursues making contact on its own.

The challenge for the seller increases in the order of naming. As a rule it is recommended to conduct appointment arrangements with the customer by telephone. However; in Germany the legal regulations must be noted which in principle only allow telephone contact if the supplier and the customer are already in a business relationship or the supplier can rightfully assume that the customer desires such a contact (e.g. Ahlert and Schröder 1989). The seller should proactively mention several alternatives in order to not abort the initial business contact on the customer's appointment calendar. If the first contact takes place on the supplier's premises then the spatial surroundings can be influenced. The receiving of visitors constitutes a separate scope of duties today in many companies, which is assumed by specially qualified employees. Something similar applies for switchboards or 'call centers'. It must be said with respect to the impact of colors that it is generally determined in a comparison test that the most pleasant effect springs from the color blue. By contrast, white has a boring effect and red has an aggressive effect (e.g. Houben 1971). In spite of the progressive development in almost all cultures into leisure societies regarding the seller's outfit it remains to be recorded that in all encounters between people a dominating and sustained effect springs from the first impression (Mann 1972, p. 151). The so-called 'primacy effect' is spoken of. Therefore, the following applies in case of doubt: 'Overdressed' trumps 'underdressed'. Correctness should initially really be paid attention to even in the salutation and in the spelling of names.

The American author Wroe Alderson writes in his early fundamental text book about marketing: "Among good salesmen, as well as among diplomats, a premium is placed on good manners and agreeable personality. While extending all possible courtesies to his opposite number, it may be the function of a representative to be pushing the other side constantly a little further in the direction of the arrangements which his side is trying to effect." (Alderson 1957, S. 134).

It is in the seller's interest for visitors at one's own company as well as at appointments away to offer a seat as quickly as possible or to receive an invitation to sit down. Discussions while standing tend to hint at a non-binding nature. As a rule, the initial contact between the supplier and the customer are characterized by mutual uncertainty. In this respect, an initial task of the seller exists in reducing the customer's corresponding fear of embarking on something new. Even if the customer explicitly points out the scheduling tightness the conversational gambit should contain elements of 'small talk' (Bänsch 2006)—for the necessity of a joke about the scheduling tightness. However, the following likewise already applies for the initial business contact: "Talk is silver, silence is gold!" Alderson pointed out the particular meaning of communication with self-purpose to which 'small talk' also belongs. He uses the term 'phatic communication', which particularly during the initial contact between individuals serves the exploration of mutual positions via communication about apparently trivial topics (Alderson 1957, p. 49). If the customer does not have his say then no activation takes place on his side. Activation is, however, a necessary requirement of learning. If the customer does not speak himself then the danger exists that he will forget the discussion and the discussion partner again very quickly. The seller should therefore activate—in some cases yes/no questions—even very reticent partners from the beginning on via questions.

Business Negotiations

The discussion content, which more easily points at the atmosphere, follows what is termed in German as the 'Verhandlung' or in English as the negotiation. The origin of the English term as it is elucidated by Alderson is quite amusing:

> The term for business in Latin language is *negocio*. This word is related in its original significance to the word *negation*. In classical times anyone who was in government or the army, in philosophy or the arts, had a recognized occupation. Businessmen were not engaged in any of these recognized occupations, so they were regarded as occupied with negotiating—in other words, doing nothing (Alderson 1957, p. 130).

Business negotiation means that the seller is 'coming to the point'. However, in any case the impression of a 'high pressure sale' must be avoided. The introduction of the second phase of the sales process should therefore emanate from need and not from the offer. The offer as an instrument for the coverage of this need should be demonstrated 'tangibly' later at any rate. Trial product samples, catalogs and presentation maps fulfill this function in a traditional way. Today presentation technology, however, develops parallel to computer technology that permanently leads to corresponding innovations. In principle it remains to be said that the seller should always carefully handle 'his' product or 'his' service in the buyer's presence. It is necessary to ensure intelligibility during the verbal explanation of a product or service demonstration. Intelligibility is generally attached to four dimensions (e.g. Langer et al. 1974, p. 11 et seq.):

- simplicity,
- classification and order,
- brevity and conciseness and
- additional stimulus.

Simplicity is achieved e.g., via the use of shorter sentences, the use of common words and the clarification of technical terms. It is furthermore known that a lot of informational appeal proceeds from nouns and adjectives. Intelligibility likewise decreases in words with increasing number of syllables (Hermann and Stäcker 1969, p. 432). Classification and order creates a recognizable 'common thread'. Brevity and conciseness are achieved by concentrating on the information goal and avoiding digressions. Additional stimulants are achieved during the oral presentation via all non-verbal elements of communication. Belonging to this, for example is the demonstration object already mentioned but also, for example an engaged gesture or dosed humor. Activation can proceed from the sensory perception of the product or of the service. However, activation also arises when the seller provokes the buyer to mutually make an outline, prepare a cost overview or to even perform an economic feasibility calculation. The greater the expenditure of time is for such activities the more bonding effects emanate from them.

Contributions to consumer behavior stress the meaning of purchasing motives for purchase decisions. A motive is an individual's willingness for a certain behavior. Motives are hence dispositions or latent behavior (also Kroeber-Riel et al. 2009, p. 170 et seq.). The buyer shall comprehend motives and address them in his sales reasoning. The profit motive or the reduction in costs or revenue increase motives is certainly valid in all market sectors. Something similar applies for time saving and security. However, motives such as convenience, validity instinct, imitative instinct or the variety motive are rather typical for consumer markets. Motives for procurement decisions in the business to business sector by contrast may have also been derived from the circumstance that each participant must first and foremost search for competitive advantages in its own markets (Sect. 3.1.1). If the supplier knows the competitive advantage of its customers on its downstream markets, he can thus derive its market motives. The investive customer's usage processes, (Sect. 3.1.1) in which its own product or its own service is included, consequently corresponds to the behavior structures of the consumptive end user.

Price reasoning also belongs to the reasoning phase. Recommend articles about sales psychology and push the price question as far as possible to the end of the negotiations (Bänsch 2006). At any rate an emphasis on benefits shall be made before the price naming. If the buyer insists on an early naming of the price then the seller can argue that he still needs further information about this from the customer and will thus pursue his emphasis on benefits. However, the price should not constitute the conclusion of a negotiation. Since just as the first impression persists, the last word also persists. In particular, professional buyers from the industrial sector derive their right to exist, however, from the circumstance of provoking the seller to price concessions. The principle is true though that discounts must always be objectively connected—for example, that the supplier agrees to assume the transport or assembly costs that bulk discounts will be given or compensating measures must be rendered by the customers. The impression with the buyer, that a price reduction only serves the increase of the likelihood of an order for the seller, must be avoided.

Business Transaction

The naming of a price by the supplier and a subsequent agreement about the price; however, still did not mean that the customer will actually buy. At the moment it is even typical in the business to business sector that negotiations for the ordered item, price negotiations and final negotiations are chronologically separated from each other. In this respect an additional task entails actually bringing about the conclusion. In the case of pure or modified repurchases, purchase decisions are often embedded in a formal process. However, if the risks associated with a purchase increase for the customer, these routines will lose importance in this way. The seller's task now entails inducing the customer to overcome his risk threshold. Sales psychology also offers certain techniques for this (Bänsch 2006).

A so-called 'risk boost phenomenon' can emanate from group effects in such situations according to pertinent examinations (Argyle 1972, p. 253 et seq.). In principle, this phenomenon says that groups have a disposition to riskier decisions than individuals. This phenomenon is explained by the fact that the individuals in the group can assume to be less affected by the negative consequences of a risk. In this respect, during the conclusion phases the seller should try to promote communication between buying center members and to influence in his interests. In general, the seller should; however, only apply closing techniques if the buyer signals that he considers all upstream phases of the purchasing process as terminated.

3.3.2 Management of Trust

The meaning of uncertainty as the central determinant of the purchase behavior in the business to business sector was already addressed in the previous section (Plinke 2000; Fließ 2000; Preß 1997). This meaning in the individual project or in the individual order actually arrives as the elementary trade and success unit of business to business marketing for the development. The customer's trust in the supplier is very often mentioned as a possibility to reduce uncertainty in the course of the sales reasoning. Trust is understood as the expectation with respect to a person or a group of persons that they have not or will not act in an opportunistic manner in regard to a deliberate event, at least not towards the person extending the trust (Plötner 1995, p. 36; Plinke 2000; Fließ 2000; Kühne 2008).

Above all, the question is posed for the company decision maker which instruments he can utilize for the creation, promotion and guarantee of customer trust.

References

As the first category of such trust-building measures any information shall be mentioned here which does not directly affect the adjoining transaction but makes clear to the customer that the supplier has already given proof of his trustworthiness within the scope of previous transactions. The maximum trust appeal surely emanates from such transactions in the process in which both partners were involved and which affected the same or a similar customer procurement problem—so in the case of pure or modified repeat purchases. This case; however, is currently less and less often given in the business to business sector due to the high technological development tempo and the increasing trends for the customization of the demand as well as the offer (e.g. Jacob and Kleinaltenkamp 1994). If this applies or absolutely no common transaction experiences exist between the supplier and the customer, the customer can try to seek experiences of others made with the supplier. The supplier can promote this information substitution via a targeted launching of references.

References are facilities/systems/projects from already completed orders or projects, to which reference is made after their completion and/or their sale for sales and/or procurement policy decisions within at least an additional purchase/sales process (Günter 1979). The construct of the reference omits modeling analogous to the description in Fig. 10.

The reference object initially stands at the center of the reference construct. In the process, this involves the specific facility/system/project that is realized together with a user for reference purposes and from which the reference effect shall emanate. This can concern an individual solution, a representative application or a pilot project in the process. The partner on the user side is identified as the reference carrier who uses the reference object. The reference subject is the manufacturer or marketer of the reference object that promises a reference effect for the follow-up projects. As a rule this will concern one's own company as well. However, the reference subject can also be the offer partner in addition, namely then when the market performance is created cooperatively. The reference targets are now those market partners whose (future) purchase decisions shall be influenced by the existence and activation of the reference. This usually concerns the customers in a special project or concerns the corresponding buying center members as well. It must be noted that a reference can only develop its effect if it is consistent. This means the application problem from the reference carrier and the reference target must match. The reference object must actually contribute to a solution for the application problem. Furthermore, the reference carrier as well as the reference target must be ready for making contact. For example, bilateral competitive relationships may be an obstacle to it.

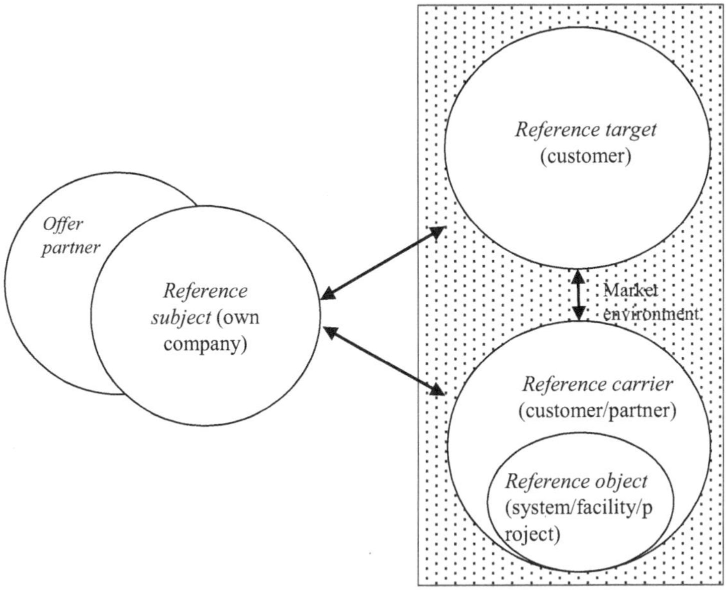

Fig. 10 Modeling of the reference

In summary, we can formulate the following requirements for a good reference:

- A fundamental similarity between the past and the planned transaction is required.
- The provider of the reference must be credible.
- The provider of the reference must furthermore be ready to give information about his experiences with the supplier.

Similarity

An additional category of trust building stimuli are such characteristics which imply an existing similarity between the suppliers. The results of an entire sequence of examinations namely support the hypothesis that a customer preferably shows trust to a supplier who is similar to him than on the other hand to such a one he increasingly detects differences to himself (e.g. Evans 1963; Schoch 1969; Crosby et al. 1990). In doing so the construct 'similarity' can be absolutely considered differentiated. In general similarities at the individual and at the organizational level must be distinguished.

At the level of individuals a further distinction can be made between the following types of similarity:

- status-related similarities,
- similarities in external appearance and
- lifestyle similarities.

It appears to be trust fostering if the similarity in these dimensions is highly pronounced as possible between dedicated contact partners on the provider and customer sides. The selection of one's own contact persons may not be regarded as an independent decision area. The supplier should instead utilize such personnel who come closest in status, in appearance and to the circumstances on the customer side with respect to the lifestyle.

Example 4
The following quote from experience shows that even similarities at the organizational level can have a trust-fostering effect: "Our strengths are the companies which have a similar structure like us, where the contractor personally takes the blame. The contractor loves that he also has a contractor on the other side. . . . In addition, one has the same societal interests. . . . This appears different for corporate enterprises. They prefer to take to the Big Boys." (Loose and Sydow 1994, p. 185)

Various dimensions of similarity can be distinguished again, for example:

- structural similarities (size, legal form, organization etc.),
- similarities in corporate and market strategy and
- similarities in the corporate culture (risk appetite, manners, shared values etc.).

For small and medium-sized suppliers these structural features must be generally regarded as a given and do not exhibit any degrees of freedom particularly in the 'projects and orders' marketing arena. Consequently, only the option remains for the order manager to concentrate his activities on such customers from the start for which a minimum of similarity exists. Big firms and companies, however, often have entity types of a different structure at their disposal in their area portfolios. In this respect it may absolutely be advisable in many cases to make the selection of the business unit, which is responsible for the project management, dependent on the customer's structures, thus for example to also serve a medium-sized customer via a medium-sized subsidiary.

Currently in the business to business sector similarity must indeed be additionally considered at an additional level between the individual employees and the corporation as a whole, namely the level of the buying center on the customer side and the level of the selling center on the supplier side. If the supplier takes the aspect of building trust into consideration during the formation of his selling center and if he appropriately heeds the similarity of the center structures then this can be declared as center matching in this way.

Self-Confidence

A general requirement in accordance with consistent behavior can be derived from the above-mentioned definition of trust. Trust can only develop if the behavior of

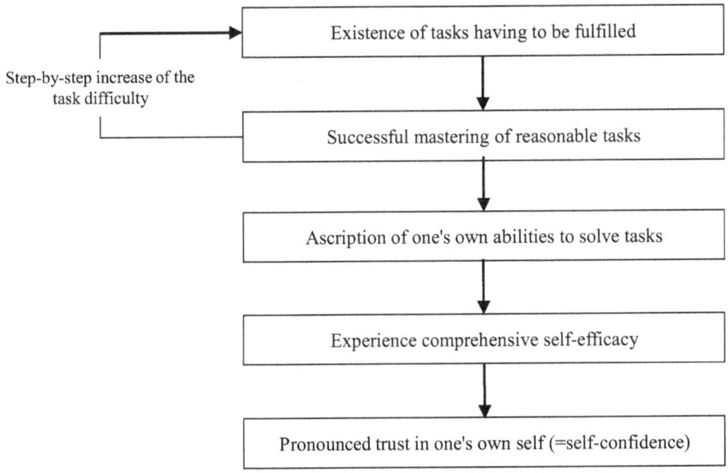

Fig. 11 Model for the establishment of self-confidence (based on Petermann 1992)

those whose trustworthiness is under high scrutiny can be regarded as consistent and hence predictable. If an individual does not have any self-confidence then he/she will be regarded as temperamentally unstable if it is not possible to extrapolate his/her future behavior with the aid of previously known status and behavioral characteristics. In fact, it must be feared that this individual has already changed his/her behavioral plans that are implicitly or explicitly shared with the counterpart if its implementation encounters relatively minor resistance in his/her social environment. Hence self-confidence is a necessary requirement for the creation of trust for the counterpart. The basic structure of the origination process of self-confidence is summarized in Fig. 11.

In a company which would like to promote customer trust through a promotion of self-confidence of its own employees incentive systems for example must be installed within the meaning of this model which enables the employee to perceive a behavior reinforcing correlation between his/her own actions and the environment's reactions. Performance or success-related reward and/or personal development systems shall be consistent with it. An additional starting point for the strengthening of the employee's self-confidence entail promoting or improving his/her skills. He/she will thus be placed in the position to successfully fulfill the tasks assigned to him/her. At the same time, the varied opportunities for further education must of course initially be thought of for the support of his/her technical and social competency.

Reciprocity

'Do ut des', 'tit for tat', 'Wie du mir, so ich dir'—such or similar proverbs nearly exist in every language or in every cultural circle respectively. They describe a fundamental reciprocity of behavior, i.e., behavior as action triggers the same behavior as reaction. To select a term we may identify this mutuality as reciprocity.

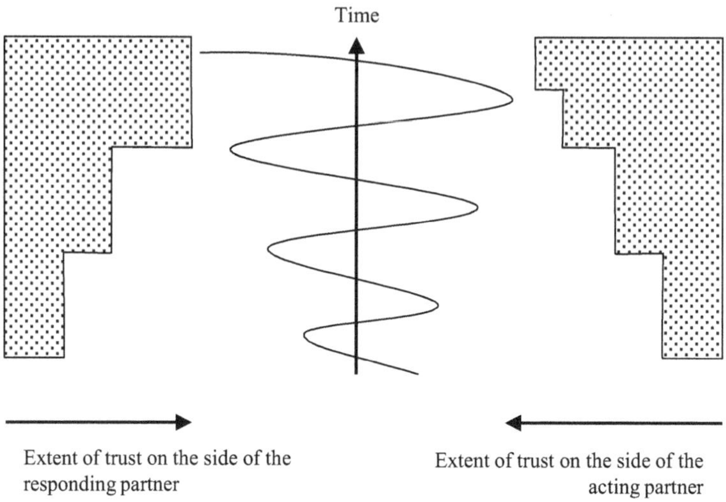

Fig. 12 Spiral of trust

The principle of reciprocity also now allows itself to be used as the principle for the management of trust. An entire sequence of studies even makes reciprocity into the constitutive element of trust (e.g. Blau 1964; Rößl 1992). Vivid examples for trust or distrust effects of reciprocity are surely the armament and disarmament spirals between the super powers at the time from the 1970s and 1980s (e.g. Osgood 1959).

The reciprocity of the building of trust will become apparent from Fig. 12. It will likewise become clear that the impetus to building trust must proceed from an acting partner. This impetus leads to the fact that a leap of faith must always be issued on his side. However, with the advancing building of trust this head start is nevertheless watered down.

Program suggestions for the initiation of such spirals stem from the field of sociology, which can be summarized in the following four steps (Plötner 1995, p. 149 et seq.):

1. formulation of one's own interests in a trusting cooperation within the scope of a general explanation,
2. announcement of a specific initiative with which one's own willingness to trust is demonstrated,
3. implementation of the initiative,
4. invitation to reciprocal behavior.

The formulation of one's own interests should preferably take place 'openly' in the process in order to emphasize credibility and seriousness. They can hence be called upon as the reference frameworks for the interpretation of subsequent negotiations. Publicity can be established in the business to business sector roughly via congresses, conventions or statements in advertisements. However, the multi-personality of a buying center also already constitutes a certain publicity. During the individual transaction, it should always be ensured that all members of the buying center actually reach step 1. The explicit announcement of a specific confidence-building measure in step 2 shall ensure that all parties affected also subsequently perceive the activity and form a corresponding target expectation. The supplier can, for example offer to render initial investments already before the conclusion of a contract. With the implementation of the measure in step 3, the supplier voluntarily delivers the risk that his leap of faith will be misused. At the same time, a policy of the small steps certainly appears to be suitable which makes this risk predictable. An excessive leap of faith could also ask too much of the partner since the logic of reciprocity implies a right to counter performance. Such a right can absolutely be misinterpreted as undesirable forcing of one's hand. This also corresponds to this argument if only an invitation to reciprocal behavior shall take place in the next step that clearly follows the character of voluntariness. Reciprocal behavior of the customer would, for example be given if that supplier who has rendered an advance payment is involved in the formulation of order specifications. The supplier concerned may basically promise an advantage since he can influence the specifications in its meaning and to the disadvantage of possible competitors. If success is achieved in preserving the necessary 'political sensibility' for the interests of all participants during the implementation of these four steps then justified probabilities shall exist considering that a spiral of trust can be successfully set in motion.

Table 3 once again shows the trust management toolbox.

3.3.3 Intercultural Aspects

The statements about sales psychology as well as the management of trust in the previous sections are qualified if cultural limits are exceeded. Thus, for example the color blue, which was mentioned above as generally still beneficial, is absolutely considered as the color of mourning in certain cultural circles. Cultural differences as the object of the management of individual transactions are not only limited to marketing activities which exceed continental borders but rather, for example must already be taken into consideration within Europe: "Indeed there is roughly

Table 3 Instruments for the management of trust in an overview

References	Identification 'opinion-leading lead user' Cooperation with 'opinion-leading lead user' Assurance of 'opinion-leading lead user' to provide information
Similarity	Similarity at the individual level Center matching Similarity at the organizational level
Self-confidence	Self-confidence as trait required of new recruits Establishment of incentive systems that reinforce behavior Measures to increase the professional and social competence of employees
Reciprocity	4-point program for the initiation of spirals of trust Promotion of leverage symmetry in the supplier/customer relationship

something like a common European tradition and 'framework culture'; however the manner in which to conduct business dealings clearly distinguishes itself from country to country" (Wever 1989, p. 23). The national and cultural differences may thus not currently be underestimated in the marketing arena of individual orders and projects. The introduction to the cultural idiosyncrasies of certain countries and nationalities likewise belongs to the standard program of sales trainers and management consultants today whereby branch differences are also able to find consideration. However, the work by *Hofstede* is considered a 'milestone' in comparative culture and management research in this context, in which 117,000 questionnaires from IBM company employees from 67 countries had an influence on its studies during the period from 1967 to 1973 (Hofstede 1984). The depiction of Table 4 arose from a compression of this data, which distinguishes the various cultural regions with the aid of four cultural dimensions that are relevant for transactions between suppliers and customers (Scholz and Hofbauer 1990, p. 88 et seq.).

Table 4 Cultural regions and countries (Scholz and Hofbauer 1990, p. 100)

Cultural region	Cultural dimension				Selected countries
	Power gap	Uncertainty avoidance	Individualism	Masculinity	
Germanic countries	●	●●●●	●●●	●●●●	Austria, Germany, Switzerland
Anglo-American countries	●●	●●	●●●●●	●●●●●	USA, England, Canada, Australia
Nordic countries	●	●●	●●●●	●	Denmark, Finland, Norway, Netherlands, Sweden
Less developed Romance countries	●●●●●	●●●●●	●	●●●●●	Mexico, Venezuela, Portugal, Chile
Higher developed Romance countries	●●●●●	●●●●●	●●●	●●●	Belgium, France, Spain, Brazil, Italy
Asian countries (except Japan)	●●●●●	●●	●	●●●	Thailand, Pakistan, India, Hong Kong
Japan	●●●	●●●●●	●●●	●●●●●	Japan
Near East	●●●●●	●●●●●	●	●●●	Greece, Iran, Turkey

High: ●●●●●; low: ●

The power gap shows to which extent a society accepts unequal distributions of power in organizations. If the power gap in a cultural region is highly pronounced this indicates a high importance of status that an individual possesses. In the case of order management, it must be taken into account while particular care is displayed in the hierarchical composition of the selling center. In countries with a minor power gap the selling party should by contrast deny their own status symbols.

If in one cultural circle the aspiration to avoid uncertainty is slightly pronounced then as a rule only a few formal rules exist, which particular managers think of as 'strategic' and person-oriented and are in the position to make individual and risky decisions. On the other hand if the aspiration to avoid uncertainty is high, then a number of written rules, 'detailed thinking' for managers, task orientation and management style faithfulness may be expected. The decision-making takes place collectively and results in less risky decisions.

Individualism expresses the importance of the individual in contrast to the group or to the collective. In countries with high individualism values the self-orientation of the individual is highly pronounced. Managers make sole decisions but they likewise are prone to high labor mobility, i.e., to company switching. Low individualism values by contrast involve a high moral obligation of the individual towards his company. Group decisions and the seniority principle dominate.

Masculinity is synonymous for terms such as assertiveness, achievement, ambition, material success and competition as opposed to professional security, maintenance of social contacts as well as quality of life. Business partners from countries with high masculinity are often very management oriented. They have a high stress tolerance and also transfer the principles of competition to the level of personal relationships. The percentage of women in management positions is rather low in countries with high masculinity. Low masculinity is associated with the propensity for cooperation and for group awareness. Innovations and reorganizations may be implemented easier in this environment.

3.4 Order Organization

The success of the management of orders substantially depends on the existing organizational basic conditions of a supplier. The requirements for a systematic and hence successful management of projects and orders are created by the formation of organizational structures.

3.4.1 Alternatives of the Organizational Structure

Basically three alternatives for the organizational structural design are available:

- Functional structuring: Relatively similar tasks are summarized at spots (Kieser and Kubicek 1992, p. 86).
- Object-oriented structuring: Tasks are bundled according to affiliation with certain objects (Diller 2001).
- Process-oriented structuring: Tasks are bundled according to affiliation with corporate processes (Picot et al. 2003; Jacob 1996).

Table 5 Structural alternatives in marketing and sales

	Structuring criteria	Structural units
Functional	Tasks	Sales force (acquisition) Internal sales (order logistics) Salesperson support Communication (advertising/trade fairs) Information (market research/EDP) ...
Object-oriented	Products	Product field A Product field B ...
	Regions	Region A Region B ...
	Groups of customers	Segment A Segment B ...
	(Key)customers	Key account A Key account B ...
	Projects	Project A Project B ...
Process-oriented	Core processes in marketing	Analysis and planning Distribution processes Innovation Management existing products ...

Specific manifestations of organizational structure may arise in the marketing and sales sectors as they are rendered in Table 5.

Functionally segmented marketing and sales sectors arise quasi organically when businesses are re-established and grow. In this sense functionally segmented organizations correspond to the principles of scientific corporate management as they were already formulated by Frederick Taylor at the beginning of the century and as the foundation of the industrial development in this century illustrates (Taylor 1913). However, studies have shown that this organizational form loses suitability as soon as certain phases of growth are achieved (Greiner 1972, p. 41). Then alternatives must be found. Product management makes products into the starting point for the formation of organizations and also plays an outstanding role in the consumer goods sector for the management of markets (Kotler et al. 2007, p. 1148; Wichman 1984, p. 27 et seq.). Regions and country markets then become relevant for the organizational structure when businesses expand regionally or even internationally (Köhler 1995, Col. 1644). If a supplier decides on a differentiated processing of its markets depending on the characteristics of certain market segments, then the summary of resources is obvious especially for the processing of this customer group (Meffert 1992). The knowledge that the company's success is often to a great degree dependent on merely a small number of so-called key customers has led to the development and prevalence of key account management and the corresponding organizational structures (Geiger and Kleinaltenkamp 2011; Rieker 1995). Product innovations in the product and system business as well as nearly all transactions in the industrial plant business are generally characterized as chronologically limited, complex and relatively new tasks. The corresponding projects then form the starting point of the organizational structure (see chapter "Project Management"; Urban and Hauser 1980, p. 65 et seq.; VDI 1995), the result is referred to as project management.

A rejection of forms of functional as well as of forms of object-oriented company structuring is generally stipulated in connection with the key word 'business reengineering' (Hammer and Champy 1994). Instead processes shall move into the center of the organizational structure (Homburg et al. 1997, p. 22 et seq.). Processes are thereby defined as "[..] activities, which taken together create a value for the customer" (Hammer and Champy 1994, p. 14). Figure 13 makes clear the fundamental paradigm shift between functional and object-oriented organization on the one side (vertical organization) and process-oriented organization on the other side.

At this point, it must be recognized that obviously none of the depicted organizational alternatives are specifically oriented to the management of orders and projects that do not fall within the innovation or industrial plant business sector.

However, studies show that businesses particularly in the marketing and sales sectors have a disposition to the combination of various structuring variants (Homburg et al. 1997, p. 27). In particular, object-oriented structures associated with a process organization, which places the market individual transaction in the center as the fundamental corporate process, appear to be very well suited for the management of orders and projects. See Homburg et al. (1997, p. 27) for the general meaning that is assigned to the process organization.

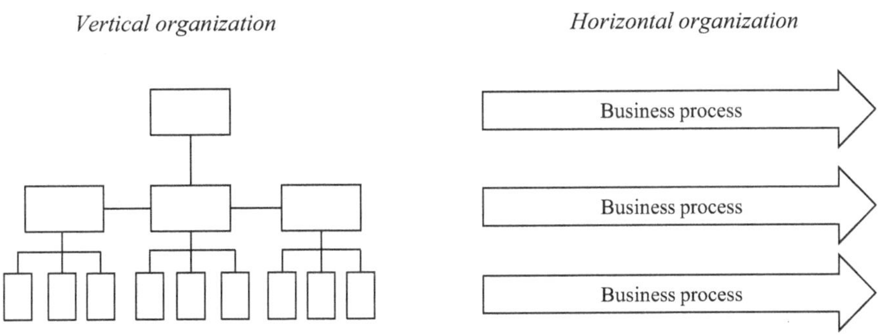

Fig. 13 Vertical and horizontal organization (Jacob 1996, p. 195)

3.4.2 Business Opportunity Management

An approach can be mentioned as exemplary in this context, which is currently introduced in day-to-day practice in companies under designations like 'Business Opportunity Management' or 'Opportunity Management'. The goals of these models are:

- to systematically recognize every resulting opportunity for the implementation of an order or of a project,
- to ensure the actual implementation of the order acquisition and order processing,
- to ensure transparency in orders and projects and thereby
- achieve customer satisfaction and customer benefits.

A 'job and task description' for the corporate process 'market individual transaction' can appear as rendered in Table 6.

The 'opportunity noticer' can be any employee in the company who obtains information about possibilities for the implementation of market individual transactions. His task would entail passing on this information to an 'opportunity identifier' who basically clarifies whether the business opportunity fits into the strategic framework of the company and passes on the information to that business unit which appears best suited for the order or project implementation. A 'resource coordinator' will allocate the information already expanded in this business unit to the area of responsibility of an 'opportunity owner'. He will in turn check if the feasibility is at all given on the supplier side and where starting points lie for customer and supplier advantages. The 'opportunity business manager' makes the final decision about the follow-up on a business opportunity or the termination.

Certain requirements must be fulfilled so that such a model can really be functional. It is initially clear that the fast information transfer and documentation is of outstanding importance. In this respect the models of 'business opportunity

Table 6 Classification and allocation of resources for the fundamental corporate process 'market individual transaction'

Sub-process	Contents	Resources
Knowledge	Recognition of opportunities for the implementation of market individual transactions	Opportunity noticer
Validate	Ascertaining of the fundamental need Assignment to a business unit	Opportunity identifier
Allocate	Allocation of an employee responsible for the order/project (of the opportunity owner)	Resource coordinator
Qualify	Check for feasibility, customer and supplier advantage If necessary, taking over of the complete responsibility for the order/project success	Opportunity owner
Selection	Prioritize and selection of opportunities Decision about the implementation Approval of resources	Opportunity business manager

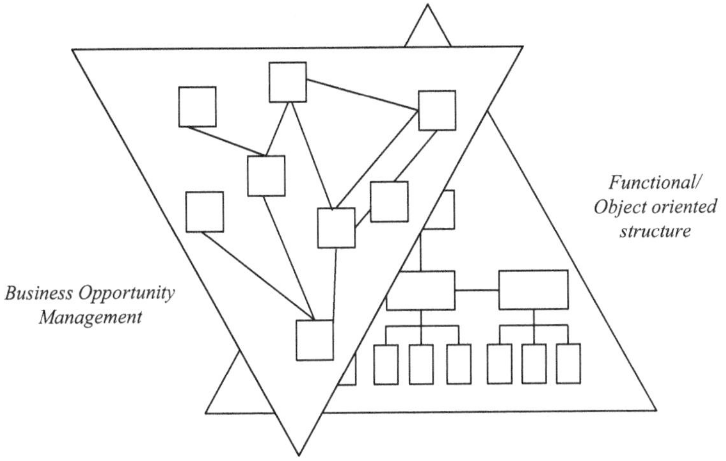

Fig. 14 Hypertext organization

management' are dependent on the use of modern and networked IT systems. Furthermore it becomes clear that these models are very dynamic and can hardly still be identified as a structure in the narrower sense. For example, it is stressed that actually every employee comes into question as an opportunity noticer. One can imagine that the entire system very quickly accepts random or even chaotic structures. In this context, a suggestion comes from Japan to view such structures only as a 'view' of a company structure (Nonaka et al. 1992). So-called 'hypertexts' are used as an analogy, which arise due to the decentralized storage of cohesive texts. The Internet is a known example for hypertexts, which exhibits very well definable structures for the user but appears chaotic and random. This means for the order or project-related structuring of the marketing and sales sectors that formal structures exist in the sense of a functional or object-oriented classification. Business opportunity management takes place within these structures via relatively spontaneous links. It ensures that the order and project orientation is guaranteed. Both dimensions exist in symbiosis and they don't impede themselves but rather mutually promote themselves. Figure 14 graphically summarizes the relationships again.

3.5 Controlling and Management of the Transaction

Controlling and management are mandatory components of each and every modern management. Controlling means that information is collected as soon as possible and made available. Management means that with the aid of this information the conformity of the implementation is continuously checked with the standards of the planning, deviations are recorded and starting points for countermeasures are revealed (Horváth 2003).

Order management also requires its own controlling. In connection with the individual order, the nature of controlling activities could be:

- preparatory,
- accompanying or
- subsequently evaluative.

3.5.1 Database Marketing for the Order Preparation

If customers do not themselves approach a supplier with an explicit request then a substantial task of order management entails systematically determining potential customers with a latent need and actively involving them (Adamson et al. 2012). The number of possible customers is often manageable in an industrial market which makes it possible to collect information about every single customer and thereby also about their latent needs. Conclusions can then be drawn from such an information inventory for targeted acquisition efforts. EDP technology makes the corresponding aids for this task available. The term 'database marketing' was introduced for the coupling of order management and in particular for the use of the corresponding database systems (Hildebrand and Link 1993, p. 29 et seq.).

In order to implement database marketing, it is initially necessary to clarify which types of information especially become important for this. Based on Hildebrand and Link (1993, p. 34) the following can be distinguished in this context:

- Basic data, which primarily contains longer-term, consistent and extensive non-order-related customer data,
- Potential data, which deliver order-related indications for volume of orders,
- Campaign data, which documents order-specific marketing measures and
- Reaction data, which records customer behavior and offers insight into the efficacy of the measures of one's own as well as competitor companies.

In Table 7, individual information fields from a customer database are derived from this coarse structure.

The goal of the database marketing is now based on a systematic acquisition, maintenance and evaluation of the databases "[. . .] to address the right customers at the right time with the right measures [. . .]" (Hildebrand and Link 1993, p. 30) and hence optimally prepare orders. If this, for example involves consumer goods in the case of one supplier's products then an approximate appointment for a renewed demand can be calculated from a comparison of quantities delivered and a number for consumption. The situation is similar to consumer goods that are subject to deterioration over time. If the supplier keeps a record of the procurement times of currently used facilities, machines, systems etc., he can thus roughly estimate when these must be replaced. If a supplier's R&D activities lead to innovations in his product and service range and this supplier is equipped with the most possible complete information regarding the utilization processes, technologies and/or production processes of his potential customers then he can relatively easily determine

Table 7 Information fields and contents of a customer database (according to Hildebrand and Link 1993, p. 36)

Basic data	*Potential data*
Company name	Product group specific total requirements
Address	Periods of specific demand situations
Telephone, fax, email	Current equipment (own products/ services and competitor products/-services)
Sales region	Delivery history
Supervising office	Position in the customer portfolio
Customer number	Competitive strategy of customer
Sector/branch	
Product-/performance program	
Size of enterprise	
Credit rating	
Ownership structure	
Complex relationships between companies	
Names and addresses of executives and contacts	
Structure and characteristics of buying center members	
Campaign data	*Reaction data*
Type of contact activity (mailing, catalog, telephone contact, field sales force visit)	Amount of turnover and structure of orders
Intensity of the contact activity (scope, value, duration)	Contribution margin amount of orders
Contact history	Total order backlog
Responsible customer advisor	Order history
	Inquiry status
	Complaint files
	Returns
	Lost orders
	Length of time of the customer relationship
	Customer loyalty

for which customers his innovation would endow the greatest benefit. The likelihood of the success of his acquisition efforts would be highly pronounced accordingly for these customers. A further example for the use of database marketing are the changes to legal basic conditions or other regulations which affect the customers. For example, the limit values for emissions from production processes may change. A comprehensive data base about the technologies used at the time with the individual customers would provide the opportunity to specifically point to amendments of the basic conditions and to begin acquisition efforts very early for a supplier of technologies for the reduction of these emissions.

3.5.2 Activity Based Cost Accounting for the Accompaniment of the Order

Order management will only then become a company organization task for the supplier in modern business to business markets if the execution of the order is correspondingly complex. This is consistently the case if market transactions are not uniform and similar but rather different and heterogeneous. This aspect currently; however, also leads to the fact that the determination of costs for the implementation of individual orders is designed extremely difficult. These costs must not be confused now with the costs for the manufacture of products and services which are exchanged within an order. Rather this concerns the costs for the analysis, planning, implementation and control of the order. With limitation, this is equivalent to the transaction costs as they are explained in other parts (e.g. Plinke 2000, p. 45). The representatives of the transaction cost analysis point out themselves how difficult it is in the operational use to determine these costs (Picot and Dietl 1990). Furthermore the fact must be considered that a great many costs positions arise through order management which are not clearly caused by individual orders, i.e., an overhead cost problem arises which must be used (Plinke and Rese 2000). Neither an order pre nor post calculation is then useful to perform. The company decision maker nevertheless actually requires the corresponding information. The results of a pre-calculation must have some influence on the deliberations for pricing and the results of a post-calculation must potentially have some influence on deliberations for the general formation of order management. An order-accompanying calculation can provide decision support for the question of whether the follow-up of an order is still even useful from a cost and income point of view or if a termination would be roughly more useful.

The explicit consideration of orders as independent cost units is surely a first step in the direction of the formation of a corresponding arithmetic unit. This practically means that a separate account is set up for every order in the cost accounting. Thus the clear direct costs of an order such as travel costs within the scope of acquisition efforts or costs for an advance payment can be allocated accordingly. The overhead cost problem is thereby however still not solved. A certain support for which its overcoming nevertheless promises the so-called ‘activity based cost accounting’ (Reckenfelderbäumer 1994). With it, the goal is pursued in explicit form to make overhead costs transparent and to also contribute to their reduction (Reckenfelderbäumer 1994, p. 26 et seq.). Figure 15 initially makes clear the fundamental establishment of activity-based cost accounting (hereafter referred to as ABC).

The starting point of ABC is the level of the cost center, roughly the sales/order processing sector. Which activities are specifically performed there is initially analyzed and which time requirement they require (Reckenfelderbäumer 1994, p. 35 et seq.).

In the sales/order processing sector this could thereby concern, for example:

- Making phone calls,
- Traveling,
- Processing of technical documents,

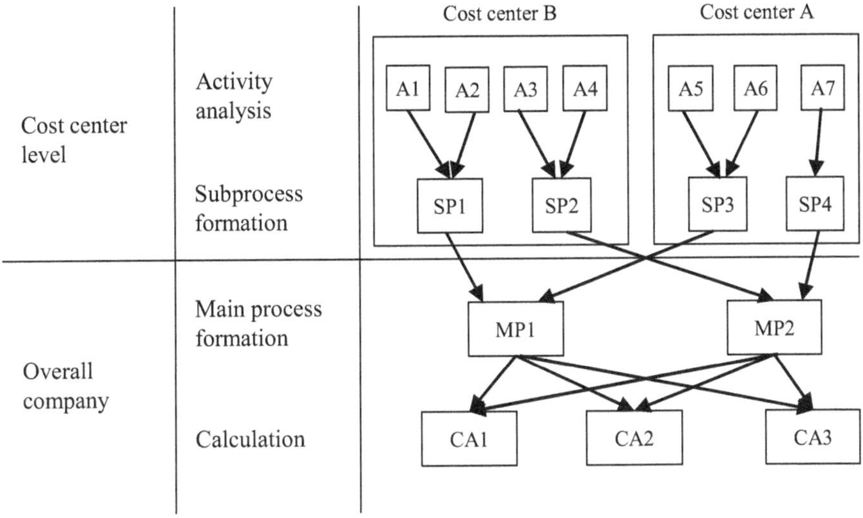

Fig. 15 Establishment of process cost accounting (Reckenfelderbäumer 1994, p. 34)

- Processing of business documents,
- Procurement of information,
- Plans etc.

Activities are then aggregated to sub-processes and the time requirement for the sub-processes likewise. Sub-processes for order management would typically be:

- Order analysis
- Acquisition planning
- Acquisition and order execution as well as
- Order controlling.

Those cost center costs, which cannot be assigned to the individual order directly as direct costs are then proportionalized with the aid of the time requirement for the individual sub-processes within the scope of an entire period. The time requirement is used as the key since it chiefly concerns personnel costs for the sales area overhead costs. For example, a situation is depicted in **Fehler! Verweisquelle konnte nicht gefunden werden.** in which the amount of 1,800,000 € within a cost center—must be considered as costs which cannot be directly further settled as the direct costs of orders. Altogether the cost center has 4.5 man-years per period at its disposal. Since 0.5 man-years is used for the sub-process 'order analysis', the amount of 200,000 €—is allotted to this sub-process.

Sub-process cost unit rates are determined with the aid of a benchmark from the overall period costs of a sub-process. In the example from Table 8 the number (symbol #) of order analyses is used as the benchmark for the sub-process 'order analysis', which were performed overall in one period. Thus a sub-process cost rate

Table 8 Exemplary determination of sub-process cost rates

		Sub-processes				
		Period costs		Benchmark		Sub-process cost rate
No.	Description	Base	Total	Type	Amount	
1	Order analysis	0.5 man years	200,000	# Order analyses	300	666
2	Acquisition planning	0.5 man years	200,000	# Acquisition planning	150	1333
3	Acquisition-/ order execution	3.0 man years	1,200,000	# Acquisition execution	100	12,000
4	Order controlling	0.5 man years	200,000	# Order controlling	25	8000
Σ		4.5 man years	1,800,000			

arises in the amount of 666 €. The sub-processes are then again consolidated into main processes. Examples of such main processes for the sales/order management sector would roughly be:

- Acquisition of a new customer,
- Acquisition within the scope of a new demand situation for a known customer,
- Transaction in the case of a known demand situation with a known customer.

Main process cost rates are determined via the number of sub-processes which each have an influence on a main process. In this way it is conceivable, for example that 50 % of the capacity of the 'order analysis' sub-process has an influence on the 'new customer acquisition' main process while for the 'routine transaction/pure repeat purchase' sub-process no capacity whatsoever from the 'order analysis' sub-process is required. It is also important in this context that sub-processes from various cost centers may have an influence on a main process. In some cases, for example sub-processes from the 'accounts receivable accounting' sector would have an influence on the acquisition of a new customer, roughly for the determination of the credit-worthiness of a customer. Sub-processes from the development/construction sector could also have an influence on the acquisition of a new demand situation for a known customer. Furthermore, so-called cost drivers must be determined for the main processes. These serve as the basis for the settlement of the overhead costs on the costing objects (Reckenfelderbäumer 1994, p. 62). The number of the respectively performed transactions is the respective cost driver within the scope of the main processes assumed here ('new customer', 'new demand for known customer', 'known demand for known customer'). Other main processes, which are assigned the same costing object—thus the orders may, however, show completely other cost drivers. Thus the number of orders would not be used as the cost drivers for the 'delivery' main process but rather roughly the need for tonne kilometers.

In particular the step from the sub-process formation to the main process formation, however, only makes sense if relatively rigid conditions exist between the sub-processes and the main processes—roughly in the sense of work plans. Since as a rule, this is not given in the case of order management, it is also partially recommended to conduct ABC only to the level of the sub-process (Reckenfelderbäumer 1994, p. 86). For example, if it is assumed that a 'man year' comprises 1000 working hours then a 'man hourly wage' of 200 € would yield from Table 8 for the 'order analysis' sub-process. Similar values may also be determined for the other sub-processes. Pre-calculations as well as order-accompanying calculations can now be performed for specific and unique order situations with these 'man hourly wages'. ABC can also provide a useful support for pricing as well as for order management in this context.

3.5.3 Order Loss Analysis for the Evaluation of the Acquisition

Process cost accounting allows its final assessment after the conclusion and the execution of an order in the sense of a post-calculation. However if one considers that the quota from the actual receipt of the order, so the number of orders for which a supplier actually receives the premium from the customer in proportion to the total number of orders for which he seeks to not exceed the value of 10 % in many businesses, it will very quickly become clear that substantial learning effects must also be expected from an analysis of those orders which were lost to the competition (Plinke and Fließ 1988a, b). They cause considerable losses due to high costs of the proposal preparation and unfavorable order rates. A goal must therefore entail perceiving all opportunities in order to increase the order rates and hence to reduce the offering costs.

However, not every loss of orders must absolutely be attributable to the supplier's errors. Table 9 summarizes possible reasons for a loss of orders.

An occasion is always then given for a systematic order loss analysis when an order has gone to another competitor despite acquisition efforts from one's own company. A systematic order loss analysis is characterized by the following characteristics:

Table 9 Possible reasons for a loss of orders

The customer's demand is no longer applicable ("project died"). The customer has deferred the demand. The customer business has been bought up or gone bankrupt ("customer died"). The customer is inhibited in the pursuit of the project ("force majeure").	Expression of changes and difficulties in the customer's sphere of influence ⇨ No indications for the review of one's own performance
A competitor received the order!	The business lost in the competition! ⇨ Systematic error search useful and helpful

- This concerns a systematic error analysis for the benefit of future acquisition efforts.
- It comprises activities which are primarily performed ex post facto for the customers, the competition as well as one's own potential, i.e. strengths and weaknesses.
- Usage should take place according to plan, i.e., not only in the case of an unexpected loss of orders. Businesses should already establish clarity about the value of an order sought during the offer phase and thus also about the type and scope of a possible order loss analysis.
- A systematic order loss analysis is a necessary component of an integrated acquisition planning and control.

Goals may be absolutely pursued at different levels with the order loss analysis:

- Appropriate actions can be taken at the operative level from the extensive analysis of the individual loss of orders for possible transactions with the same customer in the future.
- From a strategic point of view, the analysis allows a wide range of losses on orders and a comprehensive strengths and weaknesses evaluation of one's own company compared to the competitors in the same market.

Possible questions for the loss of orders analysis are summarized in Table 10.

To conduct the evaluation of loss of orders as efficiently as possible the analysis should be standardized to the extent possible. This is enabled if the form is suitable for an IT supported preparation. The expenditure of time for every single analysis is held as low as possible as a result. However, it must also be noted for the standardized evaluation that as a rule various orders also exhibit a different value for the supplying company. Therefore every lost offer should be subject to a moderately intense graduated loss of order analysis. The criteria of the order value can be determined already very early on within the scope of the inquiry evaluation, which should be still upstream of the actual offer phase (see chapter "Inquiry Evaluation and Proposal Preparation" in this book concerning this). The following elements can be differentiated as influencing factors of order value:

Table 10 Questions for the loss of orders analysis (Plinke and Fließ 1988a, p. 110)

⇨ Are there dominating reasons for the loss of orders?
⇨ Are there a bundle of reasons which imply deeper reasons for the losses of orders?
⇨ Are there typical constellations of reasons for the loss of orders?
⇨ Are there associations of typical constellations of reasons with certain competitors?
⇨ Do certain typical reasons for the loss of orders appear with certain facilities, systems or product types?
⇨ Are there associations of typical reasons for the loss of orders with certain customer groups or countries?
⇨ Do terminations of certain project types appear heaped in certain project phases?
⇨ Are there connections between the project duration and certain accompanying circumstances and causes of the loss of projects?
⇨ Do certain constellations of reasons appear for certain order size classes

- the offer benefit for the supplier (revenue, contribution margin, reference effect, ...),
- the offer expenditure for the supplier (time, effort and costs of the proposal preparation, ...) and
- the likelihood of an order.

The order value can be formally presented as follows:

$$Order.value = \frac{Offer.benefit}{Offer.costs} \cdot Order.propability$$

The offer benefit as well as the offer costs are multidimensional and partly qualitative magnitudes, which is why in most cases the use value models must be resorted to for their determination. Table 11 exemplarily constitutes such a use value model.

Dependent on such a determination of the order value a decision can then be made about the type and scope of the loss of order analysis. An appropriate allocation must be exemplarily inferred from Table 12.

Table 11 Use value model for the determination of the order value (Plinke and Fließ 1988b, p. 65)

Order characteristics	Weight	Characteristics	Input	Point value
Impact of results Radiating effect Reference customer Reference order Pre-qualification Cooperation partners	0.4 0.6 0.4 0.2 0.3 0.1	Weak = 1/medium = 3/strong = 5 Weak = 1/medium = 3/strong = 5 Weak = 1/medium = 3/strong = 5 Weak = 1/medium = 3/strong = 5 Weak = 1/medium = 3/strong = 5	3 2 5 4 1	1.20 1.86 0.8 1.0 1.2 0.1
Result benefit	1	1–5		3.06
Direct costs Acquisition intensity	0.4 0.6	Weak = 1/medium = 3/strong = 5 Weak = 1/medium = 3/strong = 5	1 3	0.40 1.80
Result expenditure	1	1–5		2.20
Likelihood of an order	4	Parallel offer = 0/low = 1/medium = 3/ high = 5	3	12.00
Order value		0–100		17.26

Table 12 Moderate intensity gradation of the loss of orders analysis (Plinke and Fließ 1988b, p. 66)

Index value	Measures for the loss of orders analysis
0–10	Standardized loss of orders analysis
11–20	Standardized + partially standardized loss of orders analysis
21–100	Standardized + individual loss of orders analysis

An individual loss of orders analysis is applied for all lost order with high and very high order value. As a rule these cases are of a heterogeneous nature so that the loss of order analysis approach entails that those who are responsible for orders and the corresponding line managers assemble in order to conceptually understand the chronological process of the acquisition and possibly search for recognizable weak spots. This process will be simplified if the acquisition process was accordingly documented beforehand. Two indications can be registered for the search for such weak spots:

1. The acquisition planning has proceeded from the false premises. The expectations of the customer were assessed incorrectly, the involved competitors and their conduct were not properly classified, the influence of third parties was over or underestimated. This basically points out the supplier's weaknesses during the analysis work for the preparation of the transaction.
2. False measures have been taken in the respective situation relating to the given goals. For example, the service offered was misinterpreted by the customer which points to an error in the communication policy. Or the offer does not solve the customer's problem wherein a flaw in product policy can be seen.

The basis for a standardized loss of orders analysis, which takes place computer-assisted, is the survey sheet in which all relevant evaluation categories are contained. Such a survey sheet should:

- Data categories for the identification of the project and of the project advisor,
- A list of typical reasons for the loss of orders,
- Data categories concerning the competitor who received the order and
- Receive data categories about the accompanying circumstances of the loss of the order.

A corresponding suggestion for the structuring of the information needs and of the acquisition of information was distributed by Plinke and Fließ and is rendered in Fig. 16.

A systematic loss of orders primarily serves to move those who are responsible away from the price as 'probates' alibi argument for the loss of orders. Employees in technical sales currently have a disposition to this way of behaving (Plinke and Fließ 1988a, p. 110). As was shown in this contribution, order management, however, far exceeds communication for pure price information. In this respect the price argument may provide the sole and substantial deflection for the customer's decision only in the most rare cases.

Loss of orders analysis			
Processor:	Date:	Distributor:	
Customer number:	Customer group:	Project number:	Project manager:
Order value:	Technology:		

Reason for the loss of orders:

Technical dimensions
☐☐☐ Know how
☐☐☐ Offered technology
☐☐☐ Compatibility
Economic dimension
☐☐☐ Price
☐☐☐ Profitability
Personal dimension
☐☐☐ Customer support
☐☐☐ Team composition
☐☐☐ Personal contacts
☐☐☐ Existing customer preferences
Country specific reasons
☐☐☐ Political changes
☐☐☐ Preferences for certain supplier countries
☐☐☐ Import-/export restrictions

Use of acquisitive instruments
☐☐☐ Image
☐☐☐ Customer information
☐☐☐ Offer documentation
☐☐☐ Offer presentation
☐☐☐ Defaults for submission of tender
☐☐☐ Financing terms
☐☐☐ Compensation transaction
☐☐☐ Additional services
☐☐☐ Contract terms
☐☐☐ Delivery dates
Preliminary work
☐☐☐ Error of previous orders
☐☐☐ Suppliers
☐☐☐ References
☐☐☐ Approbation

Legend: ☒☐☐ = no importance, ☒☒☐ = co-causal, ☒☒☒ = crucial

Remarks:

Date of submission of tender:	Date of project termination:

Phases of the project termination:			Order attractiveness evaluation:		
Inquiry	Offer	Negotiation	Price:	Contribution margin:	Likelihood:

Fig. 16 Questionnaire sheet for the standardized loss of orders analysis (Plinke and Fließ 1988a, p. 109)

Literature

Adamson, B., Dixon, M., & Toman, N. (2012). The end of solution sales. *Harvard Business Review, 90*(7), 60–68.

Ahlert, D., & Schröder, H. (1989). *Rechtliche Grundlagen des Marketing*. Stuttgart: Kohlhammer.

Alderson, W. (1957). *Marketing behavior and executive action*. Homewood, IL: R.D. Irwin.

Argyle, M. (1972). *Soziale interaktion*. Köln: Kiepenheuer & Witsch.

Backhaus, K., & Günter, B. (1976). A phase-differentiated interaction approach to industrial marketing decisions. *Industrial Marketing Management, 5*(5), 255–270.

Backhaus, K., & Voeth, M. (2010). *Industriegütermarketing* (9th ed.). München: Vahlen.

Bänsch, A. (2006). *Verkaufspsychologie und Verkaufstechnik* (4th ed.). München: Oldenbourg.

Blau, P. M. (1964). *Exchange and power in social life*. London: Wiley.

Crosby, L. A., Evans, K. R., & Cowles, D. (1990). Relationship quality in services selling: An interpersonal influence perspective. *Journal of Marketing, 54*(3), 68–81.

Diller, H. (2001). Marketingorganisation. In H. Diller (Ed.), *Vahlens Großes Marketinglexikon* (2nd ed., pp. 1006–1008). München: Vahlen.

Ehret, M. (1996). Nutzungsprozesse als Ausgangspunkt des Innovationsmanagements. In W. Engelhardt (Ed.), *Perspektiven des Dienstleistungsmarketing* (pp. 189–241, Focus Dienstleistungsmarketing). Bochum: Deutscher Universitätsverlag.

Engelhardt, W. H., & Günter, B. (1981). *Investitionsgütermarketing*. Stuttgart: Kohlhammer.

Engelhardt, W. H., & Schwab, W. (1982). Die Beschaffung von investiven Dienstleistungen. *Die Betriebswirtschaft, 42*, 503–513.

Ernenputsch, M. A. (1986). *Theoretische und empirische Untersuchungen zum Beschaffungsprozess von konsumptiven Dienstleistungen* (Bochumer wirtschaftswissenschaftliche Studien). Bochum: Brockmeyer.

Evans, F. B. (1963). Selling as a dyadic relationship—a new approach. *American Behavioral Scientist, 6*, 76–79.

Fischer, M., Hüser, A., & Mühlenkamp, C. (1993). Marketing und neuere ökonomische Theorie: Ansätze zu einer Systematisierung. *Betriebswirtschaftliche Forschung und Praxis, 45*(4), 444–470.

Fließ, S. (1996). Prozessevidenz als Erfolgsfaktor der Kundenintegration. In M. Kleinaltenkamp, S. Fließ, & F. Jacob (Eds.), *Customer integration* (pp. 91–103). Wiesbaden: Gabler.

Fließ, S. (2000). Industrielles Kaufverhalten. In M. Kleinaltenkamp & W. Plinke (Eds.), *Technischer Vertrieb—Grundlagen des Business-to-Business Marketing* (2nd ed., pp. 251–369). Berlin: Springer.

Geiger, I., & Kleinaltenkamp, M. (2011). Interne Umsetzung des Geschäftsbeziehungsmanagements. In M. Kleinaltenkamp, W. Plinke, I. Geiger, F. Jacob, & A. Söllner (Eds.), *Geschäftsbeziehungsmanagement* (2nd ed., pp. 208–255). Wiesbaden: Gabler.

Gemünden, H. G. (1980). Effiziente Interaktionsstrategien im Investitionsgütermarketing. *Marketing—Zeitschrift für Forschung und Praxis, 2*(1), 21–32.

Gemünden, H. G. (1985). Der Interaktionsansatz im Investitionsgütermarketing. *Lehrbrief des Weiterbildenden Studiums Technischer Vertrieb der Freien Universität Berlin*. Berlin.

Greiner, L. E. (1972). Evolution and revolution as organizations grow. *Harvard Business Review, 50*(4), 37–46.

Günter, B. (1979). Die Referenzanlage als Marketing-Instrument. *Zeitrschift für betriebswirtschaftliche Forschung, 31*, 145–151.

Günter, B., & Kuhl, M. (2000). Industrielles Beschaffungsmanagement. In M. Kleinaltenkamp & W. Plinke (Eds.), *Technischer Vertrieb—Die Grundlagen des Business-to-Business-Marketing* (2nd ed., pp. 371–450). Berlin: Springer.

Hammer, M., & Champy, J. (1994). *Business reengineering*. Frankfurt: Campus.

Hermann, T., & Stäcker, K. H. (1969). Sprachpsychologische Beiträge zur Sozialpsychologie. In K. Gottschaldt, P. Lersch, F. Sander, et al. (Eds.), *Handbuch der Psychologie* (Vol. 7, pp. 398–474). Göttingen: Hogrefe.

Hofstede, G. (1984). *Culture's consequences: International differences in work-related values* (2nd ed.). Beverly Hills: Sage.
Homburg, C., Gruner, K., & Hocke, G. (1997). Entwicklungslinien der Marketingorganisation: eine empirische Untersuchung im produzierenden Gewerbe. In *Arbeitspapier Nr. 2 des Zentrum für Marktorientierte Unternehmensführung*. Koblenz Wissenschaftliche Hochschule für Unternehmensführung Otto-Beisheim Hochschule.
Horváth, P. (2003). *Controlling* (8th ed.). München: Vahlen.
Houben, A. M. J. (1971). Farbwahl und Farbgestaltungsverfahren. In K. Gottschaldt, P. Lersch, F. Sander, et al. (Eds.), *Handbuch der Psychologie* (3rd ed., Vol. 6, pp. 744–769). Göttingen: Hogrefe.
Jacob, F. (1995). *Produktindividualisierung*. Wiesbaden: Gabler.
Jacob, F. (1996). Business reengineering und customer integration. In M. Kleinaltenkamp, S. Fließ, & F. Jacob (Eds.), *Customer integration* (pp. 193–201). Wiesbaden: Gabler.
Jacob, F., & Kleinaltenkamp, M. (1994). *Einzelkundenbezogene Produktgestaltung—Ergebnisse einer empirischen Untersuchung* (Vol. 4, Business-to-Business-Marketing). Berlin: Freie Universität Berlin.
Jacob, F., & Weiber, R. (2015). Business market research. In M. Kleinaltenkamp, W. Plinke, I. Wilkinson, & I. Geiger (Eds.), *Fundamentals of business-to-business marketing* (pp. 275–325). Cham: Springer.
Kienbaum Unternehmensberatung GmbH. (1996). *Wie managen Sie Ihre Kundenbeziehung*. Düsseldorf: VDI.
Kieser, A., & Kubicek, H. (1992). *Organisation* (3rd ed.). Berlin: Gruyter.
Kleinaltenkamp, M. (1993). *Standardisierung und Marktprozesse*. Wiesbaden: Gabler.
Kleinaltenkamp, M. (1997). Integrativität als Kern einer umfassenden Leistungslehre. In K. Backhaus, B. Günter, & M. Kleinaltenkamp (Eds.), *Marktleistung und Wettbewerb* (pp. 83–114). Wiesbaden: Gabler.
Kleinaltenkamp, M. (2000). Einführung in das Business-to-Business-Marketing. In M. Kleinaltenkamp & W. Plinke (Eds.), *Technischer Vertrieb—Grundlagen des Business-to-Business Marketing* (2nd ed., pp. 171–247). Berlin: Springer.
Kleinaltenkamp, M., & Marra, A. (1995). Institutionenökonomische Aspekte der Customer Integration. *Zeitschrift für betriebswirtschaftliche Forschung, 35*, 101–117.
Kleinaltenkamp, M., Plinke, W., & Geiger, I. (2011). *Geschäftsbeziehungsmanagement* (2nd ed.). Wiesbaden: Gabler.
Kleinaltenkamp, M., Plinke, W., Jacob, F., & Söllner, A. (Eds.). (2006). *Markt- und Produktmanagement* (2nd ed.). Wiesbaden: Gabler.
Klöter, R. (1997). *Opponenten im organisationalen Beschaffungsprozess*. Wiesbaden: Gabler.
Köhler, R. (1995). Marketingorganisation. In B. Tietz, R. Köhler, & J. Zentes (Eds.), *Handwörterbuch des Marketing* (2nd ed., pp. 1636–1653). Stuttgart: Schaeffer-Poeschel.
Kotler, P., Keller, K. L., & Bliemel, F. (2007). *Marketing-Management—Strategien für wertschaffendes Handeln* (12th ed.). München: Pearson Education.
Kroeber-Riel, W., Weinberg, P., & Gröppel-Klein, A. (2009). *Konsumentenverhalten* (9th ed.). München: Vahlen.
Kühne, B. (2008). *Asymmetrische Bindungen in Geschäftsbeziehungen: Einflussfaktoren im Business-to-Business-Bereich*. Wiesbaden: Gabler.
Langer, I., Schulz, V., Thun, F., & Tausch, R. (1974). *Verständlichkeit*. München: Reinhardt.
Hildebrand, V., & Link, J. (1993). *Database-marketing und computer aided selling*. München: Vahlen.
Loose, A., & Sydow, J. (1994). Vertrauen und Ökonomie in Netzwerkbeziehungen—Strukturationstheoretische Betrachtungen. In J. Sydow, & A. Windeler (Eds.), *Management interorganisationaler Beziehungen* (pp. 160–193, Schriftenreihe der ISDN-Forschungskommission des Landes Nordrhein-Westfalen). Opladen: Westdeutscher Verlag.
Mann, L. (1972). *Sozialpsychologie*. Weinheim: Beltz.

Marra, A. (1995). Marktprozess und Einzeltransaktion. In M. Kleinaltenkamp (Ed.), *Arbeitspapier Nr. 8 der Berliner Reihe "Business-to-Business-Marketing"*. Berlin: Freie Universität Berlin.

Mayntz, R. (1980). Rollentheorie. In E. Grochla (Ed.), *Handwörterbuch der Organisation* (2nd ed., pp. 2044–2052). Stuttgart: Poeschel.

Meffert, H. (1992). Organisation des Kundenmanagement. In E. Frese (Ed.), *Handwörterbuch der Organisation* (pp. 1215–1228). Stuttgart: Schäffer-Poeschel.

Nonaka, I., Konno, N., Tokuoka, K., & Kawamura, T. (1992). Hypertext organization for accelerating organizational knowledge creation. *Diamond Harvard Business*, August - September, 12–22.

Osgood, C. E. (1959). Suggestions for winning the real war with communism. *Journal of Conflict Resolution, 3*, 295–325.

Petermann, F. (1992). *Psychologie des Vertrauens* (2nd ed.). München: Quintessenz.

Picot, A., & Dietl, H. (1990). Transaktionskostentheorie. *Wirtschaftswissenschaftliches Studium, 9*(4), 178–184.

Picot, A., Reichwald, R., & Wigand, R. T. (2003). *Die grenzenlose Unternehmung: Information, Organisation und Management—Lehrbuch zur Unternehmensführung im Informationszeitalter* (5th ed.). Wiesbaden: Gabler.

Plinke, W. (1991). *Investitionsgütermarketing Marketing—Zeitschrift für Forschung und Praxis, 3*, 172–177.

Plinke, W. (2000). Grundlagen des Marktprozesses. In M. Kleinaltenkamp & W. Plinke (Eds.), *Technischer Vertrieb—Die Grundlagen des Business-to-Business Marketing* (2nd ed., pp. 3–99). Berlin: Springer.

Plinke, W., & Fließ, S. (1988a). Analyse von Auftragsverlusten im technischen Vertrieb erhöht Wettbewerbsfähigkeit. *Maschinenmarkt, 94*(13), 108–111.

Plinke, W., & Fließ, S. (1988b). Auftragsverlustanalyse im Anlagengeschäft senkt Angebotskosten. *Maschinenmarkt, 94*(4), 64–66.

Plinke, W., & Rese, M. (2000). Analyse der Erfolgsquellen. In M. Kleinaltenkamp & W. Plinke (Eds.), *Technischer Vertrieb* (2nd ed., pp. 691–760). Berlin: Springer.

Plötner, O. (1995). *Das Vertrauen des Kunden. Relevanz, Aufbau und Steuerung auf industriellen Märkten*. Wiesbaden: Gabler.

Porter, M. E. (1989). *On competition*. Boston: Harvard Business Press.

Porter, M. E. (2008). *On competition*. Boston, MA: Harvard Business School Publishing.

Preß, B. (1997). Kaufverhalten in Geschäftsbeziehungen. In M. Kleinaltenkamp & W. Plinke (Eds.), *Geschäftsbeziehungsmanagement* (pp. 63–112). Berlin: Springer.

Reckenfelderbäumer, M. (1994). *Entwicklungsstand und Perspektiven der Prozesskostenrechnung*. Wiesbaden: Gabler.

Rieker, S. A. (1995). *Bedeutende Kunden—Analyse und Gestaltung von langfristigen Anbieter-Nachfrager-Beziehungen auf industriellen Märkten*. Wiesbaden: Gabler.

Robl, K. (1995). Öffentliche Aufträge. In B. Tietz, R. Köhler, & J. Zentes (Eds.), *Handwörterbuch des Marketing* (2nd ed., pp. 74–82). Stuttgart: Schäffer-Poeschel.

Rößl, D. (1992). Die Funktion und die Bildung von Vertrauen in der unternehmerischen Partnerschaft. In U. Kleinbeck, H. Heil, & M. Lezius (Eds.), *Partnerschaftsmanagement in unternehmerischen Partnerschaften* (pp. 54–71). Dortmund: Betriebswirtschaftliches Institut für empirische Gründungs- und Organisationsforschung.

Schoch, R. (1969). *Der Verkaufsvorgang als sozialer Interaktionsprozess*. Winterthur: Verlag Hans Schellenberg.

Scholz, C., & Hofbauer, W. (1990). *Organisationskultur*. Wiesbaden: Gabler.

Schulte, H., & Stumme, G. (1997). Projektmanagement. In *Lehrbrief des Weiterbildenden Studiums Technischer Vertrieb der Freien Universität Berlin*. Berlin: Freie Universität Berlin.

Sheth, J. N., Gardner, D. M., & Garrett, D. E. (1988). *Marketing theory—Evolution and evaluation*. New York: Wiley.

Spremann, K. (1988). Reputation, Garantie, Information. *Zeitschrift für Betriebswirtschaft, 58*(5/6), 613–629.

Spremann, K. (1990). Asymmetrische Informationen. *Zeitschrift für Betriebswirtschaft, 60*(5/6), 561–586.
Staehle, W. H. (1994). *Management* (7th ed.). München: Vahlen.
Taylor, F. W. (1913). *Die Grundsätze wissenschaftlicher Betriebsführung*. München: VDM.
Thibaut, J. W., & Kelley, H. H. (1959). *The social psychology of groups*. New York: Wiley.
Urban, G. L., & Hauser, J. R. (1980). *Design and marketing of new products*. Engelwood Cliffs, NJ: Prentice Hall.
VDI. (1995). *Auftraggsabwicklung—Methodische Abwicklung von Aufträgen im Investitionsgütergeschäft* (Vol. VDI-Directive 4505). Berlin: VDI.
Webster, F. E., & Wind, Y. (1972). *Organizational Buying Behavior*. Englewood-Cliffs, NJ: Prentice Hall.
Wever, U. A. (1989). *Unternehmenskultur in der Praxis—Erfahrungen eines Insiders bei zwei Spitzenunternehmen*. Frankfurt: Campus.
Wichman, W. J. (1984). Product management—Lessons from the package goods industry. *Journal of Retail Banking, VI*(4), 27–34.
Williamson, O. E. (1990). *Die ökonomischen Institutionen des Kapitalismus*. Tübingen: Mohr.
Witte, E. (1973). *Organisation für Innovationsentscheidungen*. Göttingen: Schwartz.
Witte, E. (1976). Kraft und Gegenkraft im Entscheidungsprozess. *Zeitschrift für Betriebswirtschaft, 45*, 319–326.

Exercises

1. Isolate the purchase classes of the 'new purchase', of the modified repurchase' and of the 'pure repurchase' from each other.
2. Name and describe the individual dimensions of the demand evidence.
3. In which partial problems can the entire problem of a customer, as it concerns an order, be classified and how are these partial problems characterized?
4. Name various forms of the tender by public contracting entities. How are these forms distinguished?
5. Which roles distinguish the role model for the analysis of the buying center according to Webster and Wind? Which characteristics do these roles exhibit?
6. Explain a scheme for the limitation of the relevant competitors from the demand side point of view.
7. Explain typical constellations of the process evidence for suppliers and customers in individual transactions.
8. Explain how a blue print is constructed for the order planning.
9. How can a sales process by systematized?
10. Name fundamental rules which must be considered during the initial business contact.
11. How can 'intelligibility' be ensured during the business negotiation?
12. What must be considered during the naming of prices in a negotiation?
13. Name operative starting points for the management of trust.
14. Which parties and elements must be taken into consideration during the management of a reference?
15. Which cultural dimensions may be distinguished which must be considered for the classification of various countries and regions concerning its impact for order management?

16. How do functional, object-oriented and process-oriented forms of company structuring distinguish themselves?
17. Which functions can be distinguished in business opportunity management?
18. What is understood by database marketing?
19. Explain the fundamental establishment of process cost accounting for order management.
20. Which goals can be pursued with the loss of orders analysis?

Inquiry Evaluation and Proposal Preparation

Ingmar Geiger and Sarah Krüger

While research on organizational purchase behavior has been investigated in great detail (e.g. Backhaus and Voeth 2010; Bonoma et al. 1977; Kleinaltenkamp and Saab 2009; Parkinson and Baker 1986; Webster and Wind 1972), the opposite side, which deals with the selling behavior of companies, still displays a lot of gaps in the research. How firms process inquiries and tenders is of particular importance for the sales behavior of companies in the equipment and project business, as this aids order generation and is an important basis for a company's business activity.

The scope of the inquiries and tenders that a company is confronted with in the equipment and project business area during a financial year is extremely large and ranges from price information on a single machine through to the design and implementation of individually structured major projects or the construction of highly complex and customized machines or plants. A selection and prioritization of the plethora of inquiries is necessary as it is generally impossible to process all the inquiries received in the same manner. But which criteria can be used to ensure the most efficient implementation of this process?

This chapter presents and explains the models and selection criteria for successful inquiry evaluation that can be found in the literature as well as in practice in the equipment and project business. The proposal preparation process is then examined in greater detail. This chapter focuses on the first two steps in the proposal process (see Fig. 1).

As a result, it is important to first identify from which perspective, operational or strategic, the inquiry evaluation process can be considered and which objectives it pursues. This occurs in Sect. 1. Based on this, the following sections present the various models and approaches that help streamline and support the decision-making process with regard to the possible preparation of a proposal. It also investigates the extent to which the relevant approaches are used in practice and

I. Geiger (✉) • S. Krüger, BSc
School of Business and Economics, Freie Universität Berlin, Berlin, Germany
e-mail: ingmar.geiger@fu-berlin.de; sarah.krueger@fu-berlin.de

M. Kleinaltenkamp et al. (eds.), *Business Project Management and Marketing*, Springer Texts in Business and Economics, DOI 10.1007/978-3-662-48507-1_2

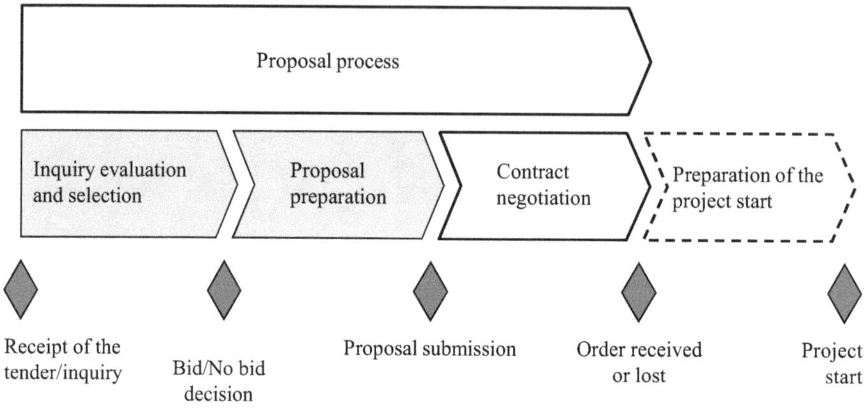

Fig. 1 The proposal process in the project business

whether they may represent an appropriate instrument within a company. Furthermore, the proposal preparation process, which builds on inquiry evaluation, is presented in more detail (Sect. 3). If, as part of the evaluation process, a decision is made to process the reviewed inquiry, the details of the order need to be clarified. We present an exemplary process model for proposal preparation for technical equipment, which distinguishes between the rough planning, detailed planning and conclusion phases.

The following deliberations are based on the existing B2B marketing literature on inquiry evaluation and proposal preparation. In this respect, it must be stated that, in the past 20–30 years, saturation has occurred in this field of scientific discussion and that many of the sources used may falsely give a somewhat 'outdated' impression. This is not the case; rather the number of more recent publications is simply limited. Our arguments are also based on numerous interviews with experts ($n > 25$) that we held with sales and contract managers from project and equipment business companies in the first half of 2012 in order to obtain a better insight into the corporate practice in relation to the outlined problem.

1 Principles of Inquiry Evaluation and Proposal Preparation

Before introducing individual inquiry evaluation and proposal preparation methods, it seems appropriate to first clarify the various perspectives from which inquiry selection and the resulting proposal preparation are to be considered. This should explain why a detailed evaluation is appropriate and what additional information can be acquired. According to Heger (1988, p. 153), an inquiry can be evaluated from a strategic or an operational perspective.

1.1 Strategic Perspective

A strategic perspective regarding the evaluation of inquiries primarily focuses on selecting and processing inquiries that are in the relevant market. According to Abell (1980, p. 169 et seq.), this can be determined based on three dimensions: based on the customer and target group ("*customer group*") under consideration, the functions to be fulfilled ("*customer function*") as well as based on the number of technologies available for solving the problem ("*alternative technologies*"). If these dimensions can be used to determine a company's relevant market and strategic business segment, every inquiry must be investigated for these points and classified accordingly. If the inquiry is in line with the strategic business segment in all three dimensions, the processing of the inquiry to achieve the strategic objectives can be considered appropriate. An evaluation based on Abell's concept can help to determine whether the processing of the relevant inquiry will help the company to pursue the objectives of the strategic business segment.

The topic of the strategic aspects of inquiry evaluation has not been adequately covered in the literature, even though this is required in practice. If inquiries are not selected so that only the relevant markets are targeted, this may have a negative impact on a company's competitiveness (Porter 1999, p. 33 et seq.).

Even if the criteria used for the evaluation frequently have more of an operational origin, in practice the strategic perspective still plays a significant role in the evaluation of inquiries. Frequently, the range of countries and customers that fall within a company's strategic target area is already restricted in advance. Individual factors, such as the hours of sunshine per day, limit the opportunity for a solar company to do business with some inquiring countries or make this entirely impossible. In this example, a strategic perspective of the inquiry evaluation allows for an early decision to be made on whether the inquiry should be pursued, as it helps to develop the strategic business segment, and/or whether a specific inquiry can be used as a reason to expand the strategic business segment to do business with additional target groups.

Based on previous experiences with certain countries, projects, products, or processes, many companies have established underlying principles based on which they can precisely determine their business segments using the three criteria mentioned above. From a strategic perspective, a selection then serves to "implement the marketing strategy based on a corresponding order structure" (Backhaus and Dringenberg 1984, p. 54).

1.2 Operational Perspective

Besides the strategic perspective relating to the decision on the potential submission of a proposal, an inquiry may also be evaluated from an operational perspective. In this case, the objective is to receive orders that lead to earnings for the company (Heger 1988, p. 160). To do so, an inquiry is evaluated based on certain minimum requirements. These may differ significantly between companies depending on their industry, but frequently include two identical criteria, namely the likelihood of receiving the order and the contribution margin (Heger 1988, p. 161). If both these criteria are adequately fulfilled, the submission of a tender is appropriate from an operational perspective.

Practical experience shows that a key focus is on minimum requirements with regard to various, relevant criteria. The company or the division establishes certain requirements that an inquiry must fulfill in order to be further processed. This particularly results in a review of criteria such as the feasibility, the presence of the necessary technologies and human resources or previous experiences with the inquiring party.

Objectives may also be set, which must be met by the proposal preparation and generation of orders. For example, if a division needs to finance all the orders independently, considering the order volume of an inquiry may take on greater importance while less consideration is paid to other aspects.

In order to optimize the inquiry evaluation from an operational perspective, establishing and nurturing a submission knowledge management system is paramount: It entails evaluating and documenting won and lost orders as well as central storage of the evaluation of previous inquiries. However, this approach is relatively time-consuming, as the terms and conditions of the individual inquiries vary greatly, but it is extremely helpful for future courses of action (Heger 1988, p. 164).

Although the separation of strategic and operational perspectives seems appropriate from a scientific perspective, it must be stated that, in practice, there is generally not a strict separation between the perspectives when evaluating inquiries. Rather, the decision and evaluation is based on an overall assessment that considers the criteria mentioned as well as the experience of individual employees. However, aspects of the strategic and operational objectives of inquiry evaluation can still be traced in the literature and are reflected in the decisions made in practice.

After presenting the intended tasks and objectives associated with the inquiry evaluation, the following sections introduce inquiry evaluation models that are used to improve "the decision in terms of a consistent alignment to the corporate objectives" (Heger 1988, p. 167).

2 Inquiry Evaluation Models

The objective of each inquiry selection process is to decide on whether a proposal should or should not be prepared based on the relevant circumstances. Within the scope of decision-making theory, this kind of decision-making situation is "defined by the uncontrollable possible states of the world [. . .], the possible actions [. . .] and the identified consequences of a decision" (Jungermann 1976, p. 7). In business decision-making research, providing processes and assistance that optimize the economic decision-making process is a key goal (Eisenführ and Weber 2010).

The decision-making process with regard to the possible preparation of a proposal should also have a rational basis (Heger 1988, p. 40).

In the literature, evaluation models are suggested as the basis for the decision on whether a company should or should not respond to an inquiry or tender with a proposal. These models can be used to evaluate an inquiry based on various criteria and derive the corresponding measures. However, in practice, companies differ significantly with respect to the extent and manner in which certain basic inquiry evaluation models are actually applied. Irrespective of this, we still consider it appropriate to provide an overview of the models that are generally available, as every individual model highlights various important aspects and different models can also be jointly applied.

The inquiry evaluation models currently provided by the literature can be distinguished by their quantitative and qualitative concepts (Backhaus and Dringenberg 1984, p. 59; Fischer and Minolla 1981, p. 21; Kuhlmann 2001, p. 253). For example, the checklist method is a qualitative process that enables a cost-efficient evaluation. However, it may also lead to different individuals coming to completely different conclusions in relation to the value of an inquiry, which can ultimately lead to diverging decisions on a proposal preparation. In contrast, quantitative processes may incur higher costs, but lead to a more reliable result (Kuhlmann 2001, p. 253). The literature also provides approaches with the objective of combining the benefits of both directions.

The structure of the inquiry evaluation process based on a model supports decision-making in several dimensions: Awareness of the problem is increased, the problem is better understood, and existing information can be better and more systematically used. A structured inquiry evaluation also allows information relevant to the decision to be stored, so that a specific evaluation process can be completed and assessed at any time. Ultimately, the information of a completed process is available for future inquiries and their evaluation (cf. Naert 1978, p. 450 et seq.; Naert and Leeflang 1978, p. 26 et seq.).

Although the processes presented below, which have been identified in the literature, can probably not be directly applied in practice, they should "[provide] heuristics that at least assist inquiry evaluation" (Heger 1988, p. 45) and ensure that certain criteria are always considered. The aim is to establish a systematic and standardized process that assists the decision-making process at an objective level. Thus, it is as rational and independent of the relevant decision-maker and their experience as possible (Heger 1988, p. 45). We start with the checklist method which, in our experience, is considered to be the most important in practice.

2.1 The Checklist Method

The evaluation and selection of inquiries using a checklist is the process that is most frequently applied in both the literature and in practice. A checklist primarily serves to "take stock of all of the perspectives relevant for the evaluation of a project" (Strebel 1975, p. 31). Although the evaluation of an inquiry based on a checklist

Table 1 Checklist for the global preselection of tendered projects (Barrmeyer 1982, p. 122)

Checklist items	Yes/No
Is the customer to be supplied in a position to meet its financial obligations?	
Do we have sufficient know-how to execute the order, or can this know-how be acquired in a timely manner?	
Are the technical risks arising as a result of the order manageable?	
Are the financial risks arising as a result of the order manageable?	
Are the political risks manageable? Are there any legal concerns?	
Can a potential capacity problem associated with the order be resolved?	
Are the qualitative requirements of the order feasible?	
Will the receipt of the order result in an unacceptable dependence on the principal?	
(For on-site fabrication:) Is the location acceptable?	
In view of the competition, is there a chance of receiving the order?	

creates a significant subjective scope of evaluation, it still ensures that all of the factors relevant for the evaluation are initially recorded, documented and considered (Strebel 1975, p. 32). In general, this relates to an initial acceptance and investigation of the general and technical project data. Frequently, evaluations such as "very good" and "good" through to "unsatisfactory" can be provided, similar to a grading scale, depending on the criterion. If the criterion does not allow for these gradual evaluations, a response of "Yes" or "No" is also possible (Strebel 1975, p. 31). A checklist for global preselection of tendered projects is displayed in Table 1.

For example, a checklist may be used as part of a "Bid/No-bid sheet". This lists the important criteria for the possible preparation of a proposal and can be evaluated by ticking "Yes" or "No". If a criterion receives a "No" response, there is still the option of submitting a subjective assessment and evaluating whether this point can be compensated for or specifying which measures can be taken to remedy a potential risk or weakness.

However, often it can also be an individual criterion whose positive evaluation results in the submission of tender. A possible example of this would be whether the inquiring organization is part of a group of regular customers, which can be of considerable importance when preparing a proposal. As soon as an inquiry can be allocated to the group of regular customers, a proposal is automatically generated, regardless of the capacity utilization and without any further checks. This occurs for two reasons, firstly due to a certain obligation and secondly, because positive experiences have already been gathered in this cooperation and it can be assumed that the submission of a tender is also associated with a higher probability of receiving an order. This does not define the level of detail of the proposal, which can vary greatly. But the decision to respond to an inquiry is self-evident.

When evaluating an inquiry based on a checklist, the individual points are not initially weighted or compared to each other; rather they are only used as a reminder for the processor so that every inquiry within the company can be checked based on the same criteria. Checklists may differ significantly, as every company classifies different criteria as relevant; but identical criteria can also be found in many cases.

The following section presents criteria and groups of criteria that have proven to be useful and helpful for decision-making in practice.

2.1.1 Customer Criteria

Criteria related to the customer are generally reviewed in order to obtain an overall impression of the inquiry received in advance. In this case the focus is primarily of the type of customer (new customer vs. regular customer), the reliability of the customer (if experience is available), the customer contact or project management, or the customer's credit rating.

2.1.2 Company Criteria

The next essential step is to check the criteria that relate to the company. This review includes important points, such as the availability of the requested products and the responsible individuals or the issue of feasibility. Are there any hurdles or scheduling bottlenecks that make implementation impossible? Project finance and liquidity planning is also relevant in this respect. In some cases, for large projects, the final payment is several months after the completion of the order and is linked to the success of the project. In particular, this point must be adequately considered for project costs that arise during the implementation of major projects. Capacity utilization is another important aspect. An inquiry is more likely to receive a response, with the resulting preparation of a proposal, in times of minimal utilization, than when capacities are fully utilized. In the event of full utilization, the focus tends to be on strategic perspectives, such as the development of strategic business segments. Even with full capacities a key customer may receive a proposal. In contrast, projects that are not strategically relevant may only receive a response when a large amount of capacity is available.

2.1.3 Environmental Criteria

The final group of criteria is the environment in which the inquiry company operates and the country of implementation. This includes the recording of ecological, social, and macroeconomic conditions that have the potential to significantly influence the decision on the submission of a tender. It requires a detailed assessment of the potential country risks (Backhaus and Meyer 1986, p. 43 et seq.). In many companies, a specially established database contains all the important information on feasible ordering countries, which helps to answer the following questions, among other:

- Is the country or the region in a crisis or war zone?
- What are the political, legal, and economic circumstances?
- Have there been recent social changes or changes to legislation?

For example, an inquiry from Greece regarding a major project in 2012 would have to be treated with care due to the currency crisis and potential bankruptcy of the government. The existing infrastructure and the presence of local cooperation partners also need to be checked. If restrictive export or customs provisions are in place, cooperation with local suppliers may be necessary. This then begs the question of whether such suppliers exist. The environmental conditions may also include a review of which licenses or authorizations are required in advance. In some cases, separate tools, computer programs and know-how databases are available, which store previously collected knowledge from completed orders, such as concepts or technical drawings, and make these available for future projects (Feuerbaum 1979, p. 5 et seq.; Gerke 1979, p. 88 et seq.; Steppan 1990, p. 43 et seq.). For example, for the acquisition of project-related information, the solar industry obtains information from government homepages, management consultancies, fairs and events or the German Energy Agency (dena) (information on the Germany Energy Agency at www.dena.de) in addition to their internal databases.

An allocation of criteria to groups seems to be appropriate given that many inquiries only require a partial review of the criteria catalog. For example, in the case of a regular customer or customers who have frequently been involved in cooperations in the past, with associated positive experiences, no further review of customer criteria is required. Skipping entire blocks of criteria allows a great deal of time to be saved.

Even if not all the criteria are of equal significance, it allows for an identification of whether a comprehensive criteria catalog is required for further action with respect to the preparation of a proposal. In this regard, a review using the checklist method provides an aid that is easy to use, even if the content and scope may vary.

As certain general and technical criteria need to be reviewed before every project, it can be assumed that a checklist method is applied in every sales department (an individual structure is certainly possible). At least, this is the result of our interviews.

These kinds of detailed and documented investigations are particularly intended to justify the relevant decision on further inquiry processing as well as to guarantee a certain degree of transparency (Heger 1998, p. 74). A topic to which particular attention has been paid in the past few years and which also requires the processes in the area of inquiry evaluation to be updated, is the criterion relating to compliance. Compliance refers to the fact that a company must ensure compliance with legal provisions as well as regulatory standards and that it establishes and complies with additional, important, and generally internal ethical standards and requirements (German Corporate Governance Code 2012). This criterion, which is being increasingly considered by companies, is used to identify and document which inquiries have been processed and which proposals have resulted in orders. It aims at preventing incidents in which companies receive orders as a result of corruption or bribery.

In practice, inquiries that are pursued are frequently initially reviewed and evaluated by a single person. If any uncertainty exists, or if additional opinions need to be obtained for a final decision, the checklist serves as the basis for discussion (Heger 1998, p. 75). The relevant inquiry is then once again submitted for an overall evaluation within a committee. The committee, consisting of employees from various departments and management if necessary, then decides on the submission of a tender. One option is that the contents of the inquiry and the associated project is described verbally and then discussed. In the event of larger and more complex projects, the project, including the opportunities and risks, is presented to the committee with the aid of a paper. The committee then takes a "Bid" or "No bid" decision.

Using the checklist criteria as a basis initially allows all the important information to be obtained and outlined in a clear representation. The decision reached as a result of the information provided, whether for or against the preparation of a proposal, remains the responsibility of the decision maker or the committee. The checklist does not provide a weighting of the criteria on whose basis a decision is to be made, so the decisions between the various stakeholders may differ despite having the same level of information.

2.2 Profile Comparison

Another tool to assist in the decision-making process when evaluating inquiries is profile comparison. Profile comparison expands the checklist method by way of a visual representation. The approach originated from the dissertation by Barrmeyer (1982) and provides for a two-stage review of the inquiry (p. 111 et seq.). It is specifically tailored to the possibility of sealed bid submissions. Sealed bids are a set process in which companies are required to submit a complete proposal in a sealed envelope. The principal opens all the envelopes on the submission deadline and accepts the bid by one supplier (Barrmeyer 1982, p. 2). In addition to the individual planning of tender submissions, the profile comparison approach also involves the option of preparing a program plan for the submissions of tender and an order of priority of the proposals to be processed, similar to that of scoring models (Barrmeyer 1982, p. 112 and 114).

The first of two stages is the preselection of all inquiries and submitted tenders based on the principle of a checklist, as already described in the previous section. Various questions, which cover the scope of the criteria specified in Sect. 2.1, are initially used to eliminate the inquiries with an excessive risk or which are simply not feasible (Barrmeyer 1982, p. 112). The inquiries for which a positive response can be provided for all the questions are transferred to the next step. This involves requesting the extensive tender documents based on which the detailed tender analysis is completed in the second step. The aim of the detailed analysis is to identify inquiries that meet and exceed certain minimum requirements so that the preparation of a proposal is appropriate and advisable. Inquiries that cannot meet the company's minimum profile must also be eliminated.

In order to prepare the minimum profile, Barrmeyer refers to the use of reservation criteria and success factors (Barrmeyer 1982, p. 125 et seq.). Reservation criteria refer to the minimum secondary conditions that need to be met in order to continue to pursue the proposal. The proposed reservation criteria are displayed in

Table 2 Catalog of reservation criteria (Barrmeyer 1982, p. 128)

Criteria	Evaluation grid 4 points	 0 points
I. Safety reservation		
1. Production risks	Not applicable: Production process is entirely manageable	Applicable: Order requires new construction with new production technology
2. Customer credit rating	Very good: Financial solvency ensured by 100 % guarantees	Critical: Customer's liquidity seems vulnerable
3. Securing liquidity	Payment of installments in advance	Installments after delivery/ construction
II. Independence reservation		
1. Maintenance of independence towards suppliers and subcontractors	No external procurement of materials or know-how required if the order is received	High proportion of external procurement inevitable; procurement price difficult to estimate
2. Maintenance of independence towards the customer	Small order for a "First-time customer"	Major order from a regular customer; other orders have already been completed
III. Employment reservation		
1. Securing employment/utilization of available capacities	Employment is ensured for a significant period if the order is received; idle capacities are utilized in an ideal manner	Order only leads to an employment overload

Table 2. These are not considered if the values significantly exceed the minimum requirements.

This is contrasted by success factors; criteria whose minimum requirements must be met, but whose value is included in the evaluation if these are exceeded and which receive positive consideration. A distinction can be made between sustainable and short-term success factors (Barrmeyer 1982, p. 129), which relate to the profit generation horizon. Table 3 provides an overview. The more comprehensively the criteria are met, the higher the score allocated to the criterion. Besides point values, verbal supplements are also included in the evaluation.

After determining all the necessary factors, an individual profile can be prepared for every existing inquiry. This is then compared with the minimum profile defined by the company. This also takes place graphically (cf. Fig. 2) so that it becomes clear at first glance whether an inquiry meets, or even exceeds, the minimum profile in all respects. If this is the case, the inquiry can be included for further processing. If the minimum profile is not achieved, these inquiries are initially shelved (Barrmeyer 1982, p. 112 et seq.). The minimum profile can be adapted by the company depending on the situation and the requirements can be increased or reduced, so the necessary minimum values do not have to be permanently fixed.

The process for evaluating inquiries developed by Barrmeyer has the benefits of a simple checklist method and also ensures that the assessment of inquiries, for which a proposal is prepared, is identical to the degree of fulfillment of the

Table 3 Catalog of success factors (Barrmeyer 1982, p. 130)

Success factors		Evaluation grid	
		4 points	0 points
Sustainable success factors in the sales area	1a. Development of new market segments—order-related	Installation of a completely new type of reference plant from a strategically important product area is possible; this relates to pioneering technology	The order cannot be used as a reference
	1b. Development of new market segments—regional	Delivery to an entirely new sales region of great strategic importance	Delivery to the main sales region
	2. Elimination of the competition	Order receipt results in complete market leadership and the sustainable elimination of the competition	Order does not involve any significant elimination or displacement of the competition
	3. Business relationship with the customer	The customer is extremely important; loss of the order may result in the loss of a dominant position	The customer was not known before and has no further importance
	4. Publicity	The order is extremely effective in terms of advertising; reports in various media are expected; improvement of the corporate image and level of awareness	Order is more likely to result in a loss of image
Sustainable success factors in the production area	1. Productivity improvement	Receipt of the order would result in the ideal implementation of synergies in production and procurement	The order "does not fit"; general productivity would suffer as a result
	2. Increase in technology and know-how	Order placement would lead to sustainable technological advancement and significantly improve the know-how of employees	The order is a standard product whose production has been understood and managed for years

(continued)

Table 3 (continued)

Success factors		Evaluation grid: 4 points	Evaluation grid: 0 points
Short-term success factors	1. Cost situation	The order would allow economies of scale to be implemented; low conversion costs; experience with comparable orders available	The order can only be completed by postponing other activities as well as implementing special shifts; significant conversions and instruction is necessary
	2. Competitive position	Company has a monopoly	Predatory pricing; competitors are offering dumping prices
	3. General profit expectation and comparable orders	Above average contribution margin realistic	Execution of the order is not likely to cover costs

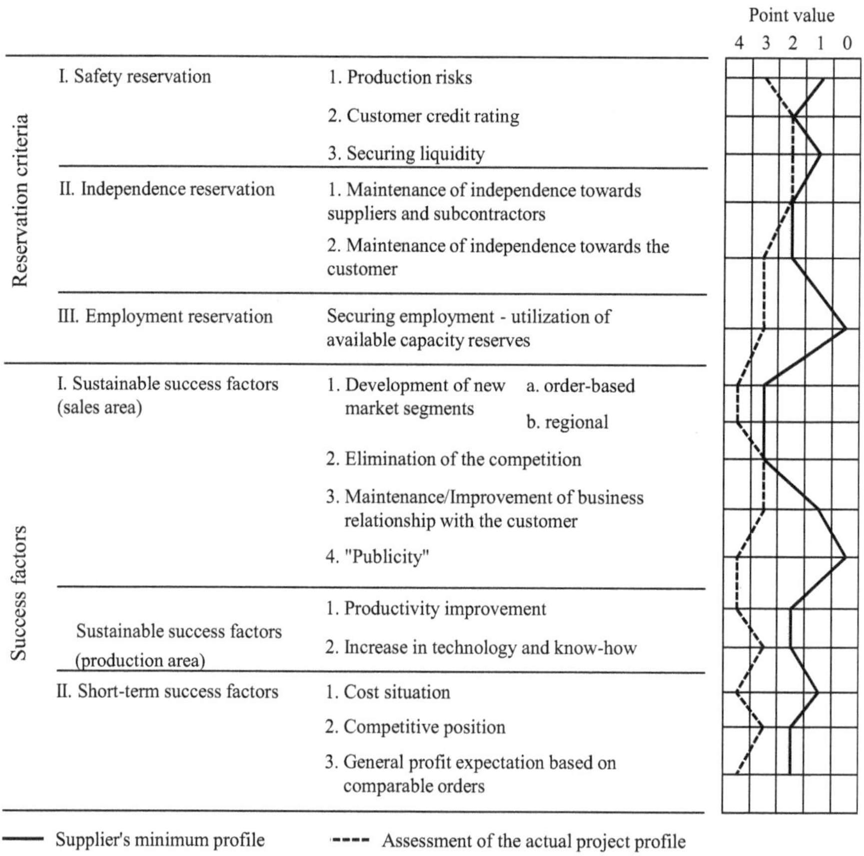

Fig. 2 Example profile comparison of a project (Heger 1988, p. 26)

important criteria. In contrast to other methods, which have relatively rigid requirements, Barrmeyer only provides suggestions for the selection of the criteria. The final structure of the individual criteria and the questions to be answered is left to the company. As a result, this approach is an appropriate basis with suggestions for a possible course of action, but can still be individually adapted so that sector- and company-specific characteristics are taken into account. However, the risk is that inquiries can be directly eliminated due to not meeting the minimum profile in a single, potentially less relevant, or compensable, criterion. The link to a centrally defined minimum profile has not been addressed in this respect, but it can be assumed that every evaluator of inquiries requires certain criteria to be met. From these perspectives, an inquiry evaluation using a profile comparison is a method which, apart from a pure checklist, is most likely to meet the associated practical requirements.

2.3 Additive Scoring Models

Scoring models, also referred to as point evaluation models or utility analyses in the literature, "are methods for arranging alternatives according to the decision-maker's preferences" (Heger 1988, p. 28). They represent a mixture between quantitative and qualitative concepts (Kuhlmann 2001, p. 253). A scoring model is generally applied in the following steps (Homburg and Krohmer 2009, p. 557):

- Definition of the relevant and sufficiently mutually exclusive evaluation criteria
- Weighting of the individual evaluation criteria
- Evaluation of the inquiry with regard to the fulfillment of the evaluation criteria
- Calculation of an overall value for an inquiry by adding up the individual, weighted values

With regard to the criteria to be selected, which are to be included in the evaluation of the inquiry, it must be ensured that they are sufficiently mutually exclusive and that they are in a compensatory relationship to each other: The results of a scoring model can only be valid if a criterion with a negative manifestation can be compensated by one with a positive manifestation. Consequently, it makes sense to check whether an inquiry fits minimum criteria, which are generally not compensatory, before applying a scoring model.

If various inquiries received over a period of time are compared against each other, it is also necessary to ensure that the criteria used in the scoring model are kept constant and define potential manifestations for the criteria. This provides an indicator of the attractiveness of an inquiry, which can be compared with the values of other inquiries (Kuhlmann 2001, p. 253). Scoring models allow an order of priority of the inquiries to be processed.

However, it must be stated that scoring models require the weighting of individual criteria as well as the evaluation of the manifestations of the criteria, both of which are subjective assessments by the user, so that there is significant potential for manipulation in the event of variable criteria and criteria weightings. On the other hand, most users are aware of this problem, so scoring models tend to be used as one of several bases for important decisions. Thus, they help obtain a consensus and contribute to the establishment of an informed and balanced decision.

An American extension and refinement of scoring models are the Analytical Hierarchy Process (AHP) approaches. In contrast to the simple scoring models, they include a hierarchy of the evaluation criteria used. In their pure form they also require the criteria to be weighted as well as a paired comparison of the criteria or alternatives to evaluate the alternatives, in our case the inquiries (Saaty 2006, p. 2). A series of matrix calculations are then used to determine both the criteria weightings as well as the alternative evaluations.

By linking AHP and utility theory, Dozzi et al. (1996) designed an AHP approach in order to determine the attractiveness of an inquiry or tender in the bidding process and to identify a correspondingly low or high markup on a proposal price depending on the attractiveness. The more unattractive the inquiry, the higher the markup determined by the process.

The process by Dozzi et al. (1996) is broken down into five steps:

1. The process starts by identifying and arranging the relevant evaluation criteria. Dozzi et al. (1996) propose 21 criteria, which they have taken from a study by Ahmad and Minkarah (1988) and which were determined from among 400 general contractors in the construction industry in the USA. They are then linked with regard to content and grouped before being arranged in a hierarchic order as displayed in Fig. 3.
2. Next, a utility function is established for each criterion. To do so, the first step is to identify the criterion's value range. Figure 4 shows an example of the value range for the criterion "2.5 Head Office share of work" along the x-axis: below 10 % and over 50 % of the work share by the company's head office are excluded. Next, the possible manifestations of the criterion must be transferred to cardinal utility values. The best manifestation should receive a utility value of 1. If a minimum manifestation exists for the relevant criterion, this should receive a value of 0. Any manifestations that do not fulfill the minimum requirements receive a negative utility value. In our example, the minimum requirement for a head office share of work was at 20 %, the best manifestation was 30 %. As shown for the 40 % and 50 % values, the transformation of attributable features in utility functions can also be used to model relationships that are not linear and display saturation effects or different risk tendencies.
3. In order to aggregate the individual assessments into an overall assessment, the relative significance values (weightings) of the individual criteria must also be determined. This is performed progressively at the individual hierarchy levels, so that the addition of the relative significance values in a group always amounts to 100 %. In our example in Fig. 3, these relative significance values are identified by a *. The relative significance values can either be determined directly (e.g. in a constant sum method) or indirectly (paired comparison of the criteria and subsequent arithmetic operations (Backhaus and Voeth 2010, p. 344).

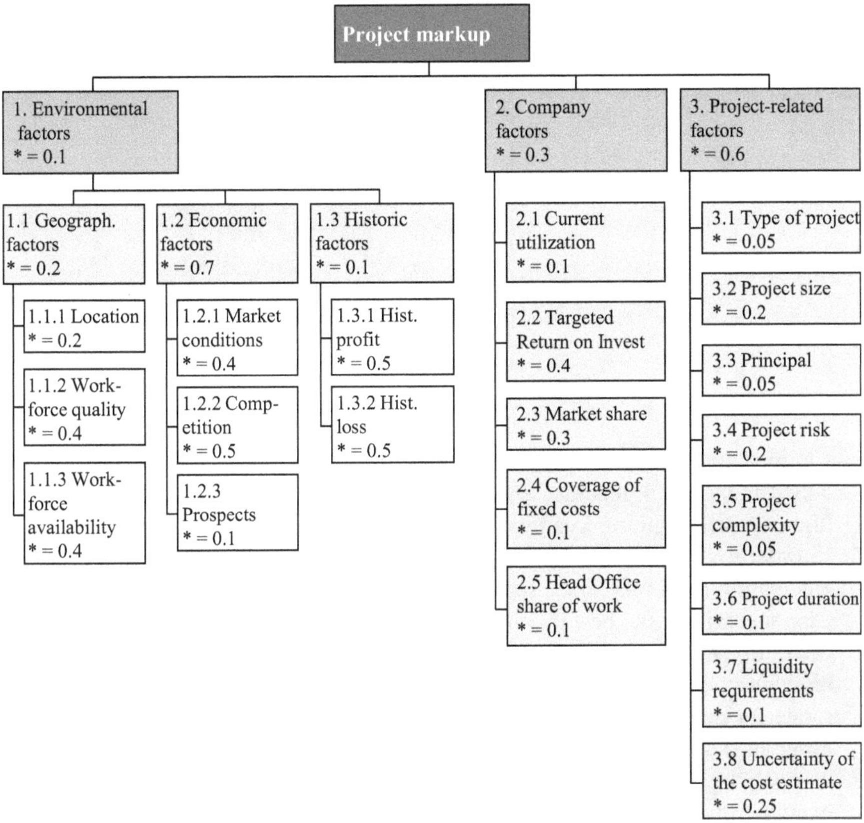

Fig. 3 Example of an AHP structure (based on Backhaus and Voeth 2010, p. 342)

Fig. 4 Example of a utility function for criterion 2.5

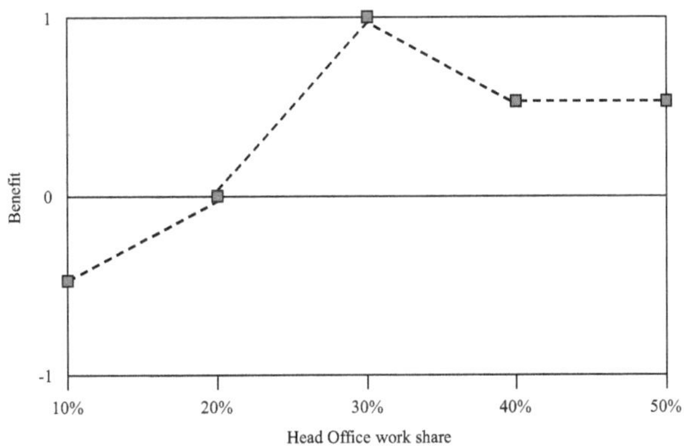

4. This model can now be used to calculate a total utility value for every inquiry. A utility value is determined from the criterion-specific utility functions for every criterion. The utility values of a group are then multiplied by the relative

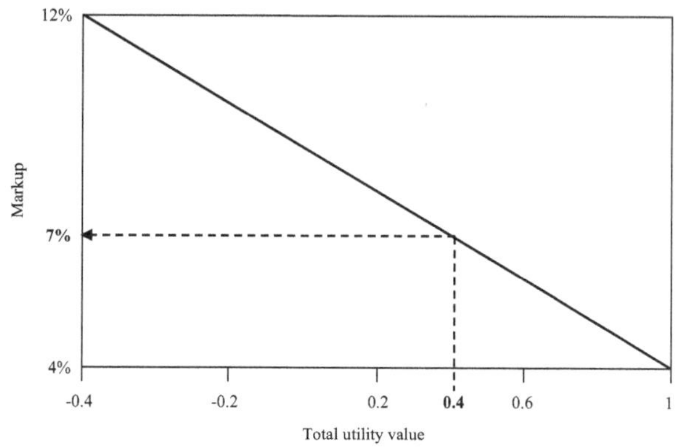

Fig. 5 Calculation of the markup for a known overall utility (based on Backhaus and Voeth 2010, p. 344)

significance values of the criterion and all these values within the group are added together to generate a group utility value. This also takes place at the higher levels resulting in a total utility value for an inquiry or tender.

5. In order to determine a markup using the relevant overall utility value, another calculation must take place for the entire model based on the theoretical worst case scenario. If the best manifestations of each criterion have always received the utility value of 1, the maximum overall utility value is also equal to 1. The relevant overall utility value for the worst and best case scenario provide the range for determining the markup. In our example in Fig. 5, an overall utility range of 0.4–1 is identified. The range of possible overall utility values is now compared to the markups usually applied by the company. As is the case in our example in Fig. 5 a linear relationship can be assumed; but other relationships may also be modeled. Assuming the evaluation of an inquiry using the criteria scheme displayed in Fig. 3 has resulted in a total utility value of 0.4, Fig. 5 shows that a markup of 7 % would need to be applied.

2.4 Other Models and Methods

2.4.1 "Wertziffernverfahren" (Significant Number Method) by Kambartel

A special scoring model is the significant number method by Kambartel (1973). In contrast to an additive scoring model, in which the individual criteria and their weightings can be freely selected by the user, the Kambartel model claims to define all the criteria relevant for inquiry selection as well as their weighting in a balanced manner. Kambartel depicts the total of 16 relevant criteria in a significant number W_{KI}, whereby the size of the significant number always depends on the degree of fulfillment of the relevant criterion. Multiplying the individual significant numbers ultimately results in an overall significant number that allows specific recommendations for action to be derived. A case handler responsible for evaluating an inquiry or tender then only has to review the degree of fulfillment

Table 4 Evaluation scheme for deriving the Kambartel significant value

Criterion	Value indicator depending on the evaluation					
	Very good	Good	Average	Poor	Very poor	No offer
Dominating criteria						
1. Reliability of the customer: $W_{K1} = (a + b)/4$ (a) Order-based (b) Project-based	(a) 30 (b) 10	(a) 21 (b) 7	(a) 18 (b) 6	(a) 12 (b) 4	(a) 6 (b) 2	(a) – (b) –
2. Customer credit rating: W_{K2}	10	8	6	4	2	0
3. Data use: W_{K3}	27,600	10	8	2.7	0.01	0
Supplementary criteria						
4. Technological risk: W_{K4}	1	–	0.9	0.5	0.01	–
5. Proposal deadline: W_{K5}	1	0.96	0.75	0.2	0.1	–
6. Government regulations: W_{K6}	1	0.98	0.9	–	0.005	–
7. Protective rights: W_{K7}	1	–	0.8	0.4	0.01	0
8. Political risk: W_{K8}	1	0.97	0.9	0.65	0.005	0
9. Average proposal capacity: W_{K9}	1	–	0.96	0.7	0.01	–
10. Technical capacity: $W_{K10} = (a + b)/2$ (a) Existence of production means (b) Availability of production means	(a) 1 (b) 3	(a) – (b) 2.6	(a) 0.4 (b) 1.2	(a) – (b) 0.1	(a) 0.02 (b) 0.06	(a) – (b) –
11. External procurement: $W_{K11} = (a + b)/2$ (a) Purchase prices (b) Procurement	(a) 1 (b) 1	(a) 0.96 (b) 0.96	(a) 0.8 (b) 0.8	(a) 0.25 (b) 0.25	(a) 0.1 (b) 0.1	(a) 0 (b) 0
12. Capital requirement: W_{K12}	1	–	0.7	–	0.01	0
13. Human resource requirement: $W_{K13} = (a + b)/4$ (a) Existence of specialists (b) Availability of specialists	(a) 1 (b) 3	(a) – (b) 2.6	(a) 0.4 (b) 1.2	(a) – (b) 0.1	(a) 0.02 (b) 0.06	(a) – (b) –
14. Target price: W_{K14}	1	0.96	0.8	0.5	0.4	–
15. Target deadline: W_{K15}	1	0.96	0.8	0.5	0.4	–
16. Investment period: W_{K16}	1	–	0.5	0.005	–	–

of the 16 criteria and subsequently receives a clear recommendation for action on the preparation of a proposal.

As the individual criteria are of varying importance, they receive different weightings with fixed significant numbers (cf. Table 4) so that the value of the inquiry can be expressed as precisely as possible. Figure 6 shows the calculation of an overall value indicator. The product is determined based on the individual significant numbers. In addition, the size of the overall value indicator provides

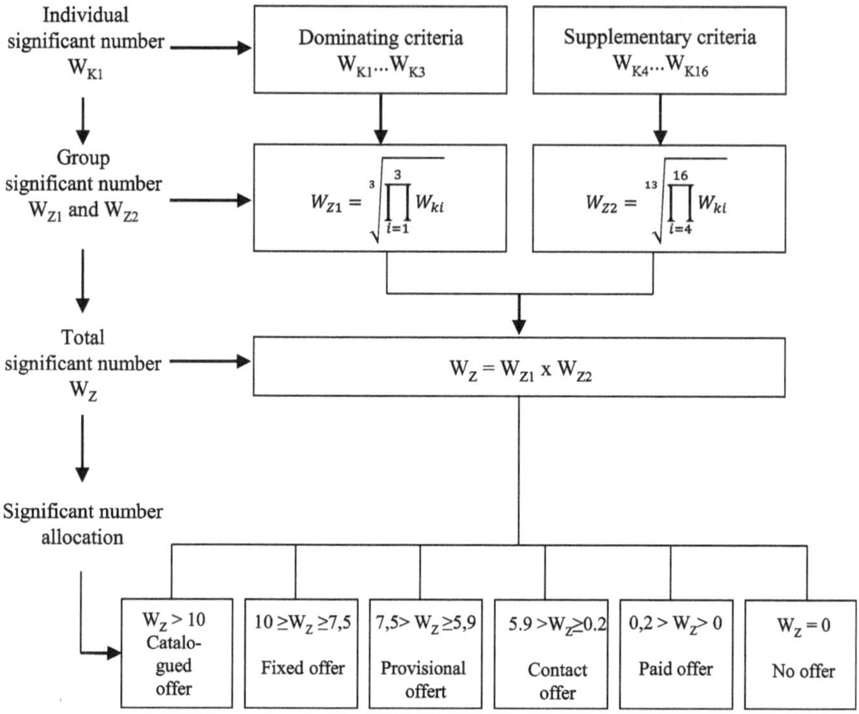

Fig. 6 Calculation and assertion of the overall significant number (Kambartel 1973, p. 72)

information on the type of proposal to be prepared. However, Kambartel's idea of a standard evaluation process for all inquiries and all companies is virtually impossible to apply in reality.

The requested products and projects are generally so individual and complex that a standardization of the evaluation criteria and their weighting would not be appropriate. In addition, Heger (1998, p. 84 et seq.) criticizes the fact that some of the criteria are interdependent, despite individual weightings, and that these still allow for subjective scope. Barrmeyer (1982, p. 172) also adds that this model for evaluating inquiries ensures that projects, which record an average performance throughout, are preferred over those which record very positive as well as very negative evaluations. This is due to the multiplicative link of the individual criteria. Thus, inquiries may potentially be neglected due to a negative evaluation in individual criteria, even though they may be extremely interesting for the company as a whole.

2.4.2 Proposal Success Indicator According to Backhaus

In order to counter the criticism of the subjective scope of evaluation, Backhaus (1980, p. 30 et seq.) proposed an inquiry evaluation using a proposal success indicator (PSI). This method is a quantitative concept of inquiry evaluation, as the decision is based purely on numbers. Given the fact that, in some cases, an inquiry can only be roughly specified and does not identify the entire scope of the relevant project and its components due to the low information potential, a calculation must be based on easily identifiable or already known parameters (Backhaus 1980, p. 31). The focus of this view by Backhaus is on the consideration of whether "the uncertainty [should] be accepted that the arising proposal costs/payments may not be covered by corresponding payment receipt [...]" (Backhaus 1980, p. 31). The proposal success indicator should provide a rough benchmark for the decision and can be determined as follows:

$$PSI = \frac{order\,receipt\,probability\,x\,price}{estimated\,proposal\,costs}$$

It is assumed that the price and order value can be closely estimated at an early stage of the evaluation process based on a few important reference points (Backhaus 1980, p. 32). The previously addressed wealth of experience of the responsible employee also plays a role in this respect. In order to calculate the additional variables in the equation, it is suggested that the estimated proposal costs are determined by a multiple regression analysis based on a proposal cost function. For example, the proposal value, the customer's country or the requested level of documentation for the proposal may represent influencing variables on the proposal costs. In contrast, the probability of the success of order receipt can be determined using indicators based on three types of uncertainty, which can either be found on the supplier's side or on the inquiring company's side. According to Backhaus, these include the uncertainty of the receipt of the order, the uncertainty of the performance by the supplier and the uncertainty of the receipt of payment (Backhaus 1980, p. 35). These three factors do not all need to flow into the calculation simultaneously, instead this may take place progressively (Backhaus 1980, p. 37).

Inserting the identified variables in the above equation then allows the user to obtain the proposal success indicator. However, this indicator does not answer the question of whether or not to prepare a proposal. At this point Backhaus suggests that the users defines a limit value based on their subjective experience, which must be met in order to prepare a proposal. If this is not met, a proposal should not be prepared.

Despite the initially seemingly straightforward calculation, the method has a few weaknesses that make it difficult to apply in practice (Heger 1998, p. 90 et seq.). For example, it mentions that potential follow-up orders are needed to be taken into account as part of the decision on further action regarding an inquiry. For example, in the area of technical plants there is the option of concluding contracts for employee training courses in addition to the requested construction and installation. This aspect, likely to be linked to earnings, which cannot be explicitly identified in an inquiry or tender in advance, may lead to the generation of additional earnings over the life of the project. These additional measures are not currently considered when calculating the proposal success indicator. This eventuality must at least be mentioned and allowed to flow into the calculation in order to structure the model more realistically and attractively for practical application. The subjective identification of the limit value as well as the indicators also need to be handled with care. In this case, the previous experience of the responsible processor play an important role. Furthermore, these limit values can differ significantly within a company and cannot be applied across the various projects.

Even if the process is not used by the managers we interviewed, it can be assumed determining a proposal success indicator would represent a helpful basis for an initial rough estimate (such as for the construction industry), as (especially in this industry) the cost and time expenditure for proposal preparation is extremely high while margins are low. The close cooperation with other companies often means that a large number of partners needs to be involved and proposals need to be obtained before a proposal can be submitted to the customer. In this situation, a quantitative concept as a decision-making basis would be appropriate to estimate whether the expense of preparing the proposal is justified.

2.5 Critical Assessment and Summary

Besides the benefits of inquiry evaluation models, the detailed investigation of the selected models also identified a number of weaknesses at both a theoretical as well as a practical level. The approach to and the process of inquiry evaluation differ for various companies and are primarily defined by the industry and the services offered. The overall inquiry evaluation and proposal preparation process, including the individual operations and tasks as well as the responsible employees and departments, is generally defined as part of a process instruction. The approach described in this process instruction should be complied with for every inquiry.

Admittedly, in principle, the inquiry evaluation approaches described, especially the evaluation process using a checklist, represent a tool that assists in a company's decision on whether or not to prepare a proposal and help to establish an order of priority for processing the inquiries. However, the actual practical implementation deviates significantly from theory. The decision-making models and methods established in the literature are poorly suited for the structures and procedures in many companies and do not enjoy a high level of acceptance among all users. Besides the checklist method and, in limited cases, the profile comparison our interviews did not identify the application of any other models. The following reasons were indicated for the non-application of the theoretical models:

- Lack of awareness,
- Insufficient flexibility of the models,
- High complexity of the projects, which is not reflected in the models, and
- Excessive expense or the lack of availability of data necessary for the calculation of forecast probabilities.

In addition, a practical application requires that a quick decision be made wherever possible, so that it is difficult to reconcile the theoretical models and their extensive calculations with the time pressure in everyday business; quite simply they take too long. As a result, companies often rely on the experience of individual employees and a decision is made intuitively rather than based on rules (Jungermann et al. 2005, p. 170). Only in exceptional cases does a detailed evaluation take place with the involvement of several individuals. The experiences of employees may be an essential component of the evaluation of inquiries, but they also allow for a large subjective scope (Heger 1998, p. 94) and may lead to a decision that is not based on a rational foundation. Employees make different decisions based on individual, positive or negative experiences. The scope of the investigated criteria also varies significantly. While some companies assess an inquiry based on about three key criteria, other companies review an inquiry based on an extensive catalog of criteria before making a decision (Backhaus and Dringenberg 1984, p. 88). Furthermore, many employees are frequently insufficiently informed of the existence of such tools, which leads to limited application.

Contrary to our initial suppositions, our practical inquiry has shown that, for many inquiries, a single person is responsible for the inquiry selection decision. This is particularly the case for routine projects and inquiries from countries with which the company is already familiar. Additional individuals are only included in the decision-making process in the case of extremely high order volumes as part of particularly complex projects, or for so-called flagship projects, which may potentially lead to the development of a new, strategically relevant market. In this case, a final decision is either submitted to another person for information purposes and confirmation, or the decision-making body is expanded. In the latter case, the decision-making body includes sales employees as well as engineers, lawyers or members of the Executive Board, who provide support in the event of the preparation of a proposal.

Another aspect of the theoretical decision-making models is not sufficiently taken into account with regard to its practical application: a clear distinction between inquiries that are received by companies without any active promotion and those that a supplier receives based on increased acquisition efforts. The literature notes that the order probability may potentially increase depending on the acquisition efforts (Albers and Krafft 2000, p. 1091). However, the extent to which this can or should be considered in the evaluation is not defined. It must be assumed that no additional decision is required in relation to the preparation of a proposal, if an inquiry or tender, which was obviously targeted, is submitted after a great deal of effort. It must be assumed that this possible order meets the minimum processing requirements, as a company has actively endeavored to obtain the inquiry, while less attention is paid to unforeseeable inquiries.

Some special practical requirements must be taken into account in order to clarify difficulties in applying the inquiry evaluation models and with regard to the modification of existing models as well as the generation of new models.

Backhaus (1980, p. 29) has already identified causes for the limited application. Firstly, the real process is much more complex than can be expressed by a model illustration. For example, unforeseeable environmental changes are difficult to represent. In addition, a clear distinction must be made between the order probability and the probability of implementation. The models frequently only contain the order probability. For example, the risk that a project cannot be implemented due to a lack of permits and licenses, or due to financing aspects, is only mentioned as an afterthought. However, this can frequently be the case in the project business and should be taken into account, especially in the construction industry, before a more detailed and costly proposal is prepared.

3 Proposal Preparation Process

As shown in the previous section, theoretical considerations and models and the practical application differ in relation to the evaluation of inquiries and tenders. However, our inquiries also showed that the proposal preparation process is assigned much greater importance in practice than has previously been described in the academic literature. Neither Backhaus and Voeth (2010) nor Kleinaltenkamp and Plinke (1998), as important representatives in German-speaking business-to-business marketing, have previously explicitly delved into the proposal preparation process in their writings on the equipment and project business. This is also due to the fact that many decisions in this process can be found at other points in the relevant texts, as well as in this book; for example, with regard to the structure of the service charges (see chapter "Pricing and Revenue Planning in the Project Business"), the financing concept (chapter "Order Financing and Financial Engineering"), a plant contract (chapter "Contract Management") or the project-related supplier organization (chapter "Project Cooperation").

On the other hand, besides our inquiries, a 2007 study on proposal management completed on behalf of The Association of German Engineers showed that great importance is assigned to the proposal preparation process in many companies and that there is also a significant need for optimization (Schmidt 2008, p. 5 et seq.). Besides the inadequate consideration of customer requirements in many proposals, such as by the representation of constructive alternatives, another reason for this is the lack of time to prepare these proposals (Krause et al. 2005, p. 7 et seq.). As a result, many companies place great importance on the fact that various activities need to run in parallel during the preparation of the proposal in order to deal with the factor of time. A prototypical course of a proposal preparation for a technical plant is displayed in Fig. 7. The starting point for the preparation of a proposal is the positive evaluation of the inquiry or tender. The process displayed here as an example is divided into three phases that are briefly introduced in the following section. The relevant departments that are involved are also assigned to the individual process steps.

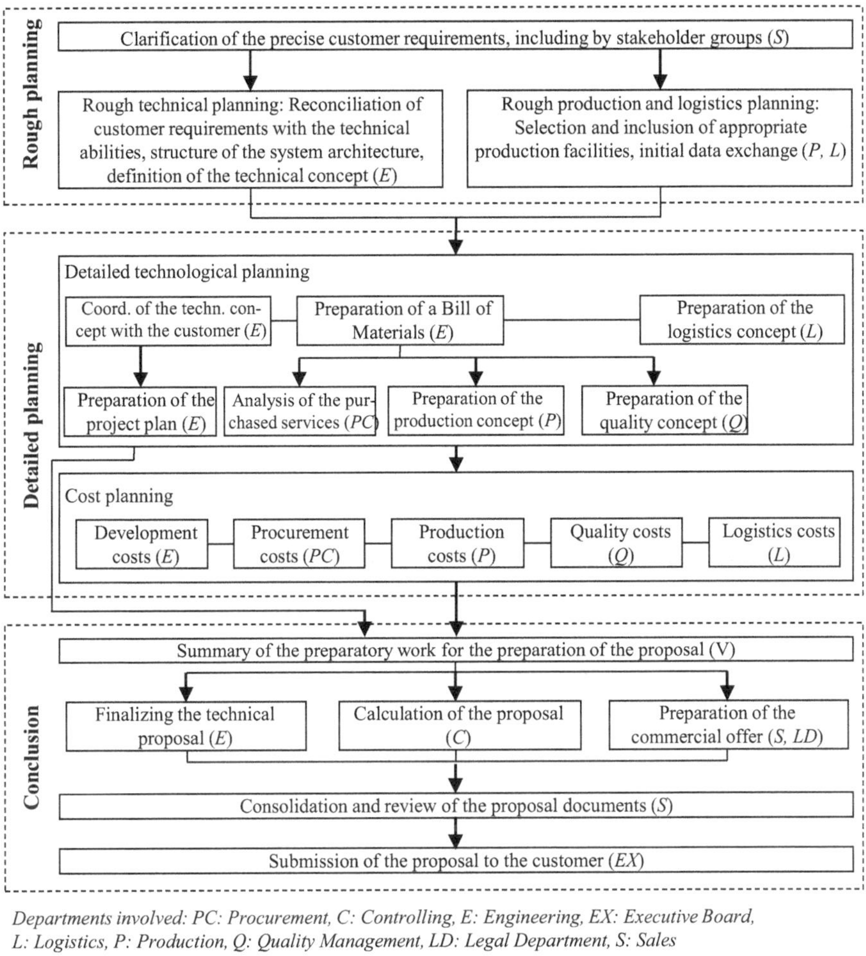

Fig. 7 Example of a proposal preparation process (technical plant)

3.1 Rough Planning

Oftentimes, a project team is established to evaluate an inquiry and prepare a proposal for larger technical plants or service projects, frequently headed by sales, which is responsible for the overall coordination of the preparation of the proposal. The first step in the rough planning stage is to clarify precise customer requirements. Various technological options frequently exist to meet the customer requirements, which may be evaluated differently by different members of the buying center in the customer organization. This means that a certain importance must also be ascribed to the consideration of the buying center structure. These clarification activities are often performed by sales.

Already in the following step, the actual rough planning, it is preferable to work on the proposal preparation in parallel for reasons of time. In this case, the Engineering or the Development Department is responsible for the rough technical planning. This includes the comparison of the customer requirements with the supplier's technical abilities, the drafting and structuring of a system architecture and the definition of a detailed technical concept. The structure of a modular design system for the preparation of customized plants is considered essential both in practice as well as in the literature (Krause et al. 2005, p. 8). The modular structure represents both an answer to the time problem in proposal preparation as well as to the increasing cost sensitivity of customer organizations. A modular structure allows for both a more quickly accessible diversity of options in design as well as a quicker cost transparency for the supplier (Körsmeier 1996, p. 10 et seq.).

Parallel to the rough technical planning, it also makes sense to implement a rough production and logistics planning. This clarifies issues, such as questions regarding the possible production facilities and their logistical connection. This step also involves an initial data exchange with the relevant units. While this step may not be applicable for a supplier with a centralized production facility, it is important for larger supplier companies if the potential customer includes local content requirements (for example). If the order cannot be managed as a general contractor, but rather in a consortium, this step should also involve the possible determination of the cooperation with consortium partners (cf. also chapter "Project Cooperation").

3.2 Detailed Planning

The rough planning results in both a defined technical concept as well as an initial representation of the required production and logistics capacities. The coordination of the detailed technical concept with the customer is vital before detailed planning can be commenced by the various roles. Otherwise the supplier runs the risk of failing to align their plans and proposal to the customer's requirements, which would almost certainly result in the loss of the order. This generally involves a discussion amongst technicians. The compilation of all the necessary resources, the so-called Bill of Materials, must take place in parallel to the coordination of the technical concept. This is a requirement for the preparation of a procurement, production and quality concept, which is prepared by the relevant specialist departments. The logistics concept and a project plan can also be drafted in parallel to the above activities.

Only the detailed technical planning then allows for a detailed cost planning. This requires development, procurement, production, quality and logistics costs as well as any other costs attributable to the project to be recorded. Ideally, the cost planning can be based on a process costing which ascribes both variable as well as fixed costs to the relevant project (Plinke and Rese 2006, p. 134 et seq.).

3.3 Conclusion

Once all the preparatory work for the detailed planning has been performed, both the technical as well as the production planning are fundamentally in place. However, the project team assigned to prepare the proposal will then consolidate all the preparatory work prior to the final preparation of the proposal. The actual proposal documents are then prepared and reviewed by the relevant specialist departments. The Engineering Department then finalizes the technical proposal with all the necessary specifications, customer duties of cooperation, technical drawings, a detailed schedule, etc. The Sales and Legal Department draft the commercial offer, which includes the commercial conditions, the financing conditions (cf. chapter "Order Financing and Financial Engineering"), the offer price (cf. chapter "Pricing and Revenue Planning in the Project Business") and the relevant legal conditions (cf. chapter "Contract Management"). In this phase, Controlling is responsible for reviewing the cost coverage.

The final result is a complete proposal which, once it is accepted by the customer, becomes the legal basis for what is often a lengthy cooperation between the supplier and the customer. For this reason, the final process step should involve the final review of the proposal by all the involved specialist departments as well as approval by the relevant individuals responsible, before the proposal is transmitted to the customer and the customer negotiation phase commences.

3.4 Critical Assessment

The example proposal preparation process presented here distinguishes between three phases and is specifically tailored to the preparation of major technical plants. It must therefore be assumed that companies that offer other services also have other processes for the quick preparation of high quality proposals. In particular, the study on behalf of The Association of German Engineers showed that, in many companies, proposal preparation is an established and constantly changing process (Schmidt 2008, p. 5). The process is frequently established and optimized in the form of process instructions as part of a company's quality management system.

However, we considered it important to illustrate this kind of process by way of an example in order to better classify the following chapters with their special issues in the marketing process of major plants and projects.

Exercises

1. How does the inquiry evaluation and selection become embedded in the marketing process?
2. How do the strategic and operational perspectives differ in relation to inquiry evaluation and selection?

3. Name and describe the two most important variables in operational inquiry evaluation! Which criteria need to be considered?
4. Which advantages and disadvantages are associated with the checklist method for inquiry evaluation?
5. Which types of criteria should a checklist for inquiry evaluation contain and why?
6. To what extent do the profile comparison and additive scoring models expand on the ideas of the checklist method?
7. How do AHP models differ from pure scoring models?
8. Name the reasons why many inquiry evaluation models are not used in practice!
9. Identify the challenges faced when preparing a proposal! What process steps are involved?

Literature

Abell, D. F. (1980). *Defining the business—the starting point of strategic planning*. Englewood Cliffs, NJ: Prentice Hall.

Ahmad, I., & Minkarah, I. A. (1988). Questionnaire survey on bidding in construction. *Journal of Management in Engineering, 4*(3), 227–243.

Albers, S., & Krafft, M. (2000). Regeln zur Bestimmung des fast-optimalen Angebotsaufwands. *Zeitschrift für Betriebswirschaft, 70*(10), 1083–1107.

Backhaus, K. (1980). *Auftragsplanung im industriellen Anlagengeschäft*. Stuttgart: Poeschel.

Backhaus, K., & Dringenberg, H. (1984). Anfragenselektion. In K. Backhaus (Ed.), *Planung im industriellen Anlagengeschäft* (pp. 53–92). Düsseldorf: VDI-Verlag.

Backhaus, K., & Meyer, M. (1986). Ansätze zur Beurteilung von Länderrisiken. *Zeitschrift für betriebswirtschaftliche Forschung, 38*(20/86), 39–59.

Backhaus, K., & Voeth, M. (2010). *Industriegütermarketing* (9th ed.). München: Vahlen.

Barrmeyer, M. C. (1982). *Die Angebotsplanung bei Submission*. Dissertation, Münster.

Bonoma, T. V., Zaltman, G., & Johnston, W. J. (1977). *Industrial buying behavior*. Cambridge: Marketing Science Institute.

Deutscher Corporate Governance–Kodex. (2012). www.corporate-governance-code.de/ger/kodex/4.html

Dozzi, S. P., AbouRizk, S. M., & Schroeder, S. L. (1996). Utility-theory model for bid markup decisions. *Journal of Construction Engineering and Management, 122*(2), 119–124.

Eisenführ, F., & Weber, M. (2010). *Rationales Entscheiden* (5th ed.). Berlin: Springer.

Feuerbaum, E. (1979). Controlling in einem projektorientierten Unternehmen. In D. Solaro, H. D. Bürgel, E. Feuerbaum, J. Funk, W. F. Gerke, H. R. Kunkowsky, et al. (Eds.), *Projektcontrolling* (pp. 1–47). Stuttgart: Poeschel.

Fischer, W., & Minolla, W. (1981). *Rationalisierung der technischen Angebotsbearbeitung*. Berlin: Beuth-Verlag.

Gerke, W. F. (1979). Manuelle und EDV-gestützte Projektplanungs- und Kontrollverfahren in einem Ingenieu-runternehmen des Industrieanlagenbaus. In D. Solaro, H. D. Bürgel, E. Feuerbaum, J. Funk, W. F. Gerke, H. R. Kunkowsky, et al. (Eds.), *Projektcontrolling* (pp. 81–118). Stuttgart: Poeschel.

Heger, G. (1988). *Anfragenbewertung im industriellen Anlagengeschäft*. Berlin: Duncker & Humblot.

Heger, G. (1998). Anfragenbewertung. In M. Kleinaltenkamp & W. Plinke (Eds.), *Auftrags- und Projektmanagement* (pp. 69–115). Berlin: Duncker & Humblot.

Homburg, C., & Krohmer, H. (2009). *Marketingmanagement* (3rd ed.). Wiesbaden: Gabler.

Jungermann, H. (1976). *Rationale Entscheidungen*. Bern: Huber.
Jungermann, H., Pfister, H. R., & Fischer, K. (2005). *Die Psychologie der Entscheidung* (2nd ed.). München: Spektrum.
Kambartel, K. H. (1973). *Systematische Angebotsplanung in Unternehmen der Auftragsfertigung*. Dissertation, Mainz.
Kleinaltenkamp, M., & Plinke, W. (1998). *Auftrags- und Projektmanagement*. Berlin: Springer.
Kleinaltenkamp, M., & Saab, S. (2009). *Technischer Vertrieb—Eine Praxisorientierte Einführung in das Business-to-Business-Marketing*. Berlin: Springer.
Körsmeier, R. (1996). *Kundennahe, rechnerunterstützte Angebotserstellung im Vertriebsaußendiesnt für komplexe Investitionsgüter* (Vol. 89, Fortschrittsberichte VDI, Vol. 16). Düsseldorf: VDI Verlag.
Krause, F.-L., Kind, C., & Müller, C. (2005). Prozessoptimierung in der Angebotserstellung. *Wt Werkstattstechnik online, 95*(1/2), 7–10.
Kuhlmann, E. (2001). *Industrielles Vertriebsmanagement*. München: Vahlen.
Naert, P. (1978). Some cost-benefit considerations in marketing model building. In E. Topritzhofer (Ed.), *Marketing* (pp. 447–464). Wiesbaden: Gabler.
Naert, P., & Leeflang, P. (1978). *Building implementable marketing models*. Leiden: Nijhoet seq.
Parkinson, S. T., & Baker, M. J. (1986). *Organizational buying behavior—purchasing and marketing management implications*. Houndmills: Macmillan.
Plinke, W., & Rese, M. (2006). *Industrielle Kostenrechnung* (7th ed.). Berlin: Springer.
Porter, M. E. (1999). *Wettbewerbsstrategie (Competitive Strategy): Methoden zur Analyse von Branchen und Konkurrenten* (10th ed.). Frankfurt: Campus.
Saaty, T. L. (2006). The analytic network process. In T. L. Saaty & L. G. Vargas (Eds.), *Decision making with the analytic network process* (pp. 1–26). New York: Springer.
Schmidt, H. (2008). *Studie zum Angebotsmanagement*. Düsseldorf: VDI Verlag.
Steppan, G. (1990). Know-how-Datenbanken mit einer integrierten Zeichnungsverwaltung im Angebotswesen. In VDI-Gesellschaft (Ed.), *Erfolgreich im Vertrieb—Innovative Informationssysteme zur Angebotserstellung* (pp. 43–64). Düsseldorf: VDI.
Strebel, H. (1975). *Forschungsplanung mit Scoring-Modellen*. Baden-Baden: Nomos.
Webster, F. E., & Wind, Y. (1972). *Organizational buying behavior*. Englewood-Cliffs, NJ: Prentice Hall.

Pricing and Revenue Planning in the Project Business

Wulff Plinke and Matthias Claßen

1 Principles

Large projects such as industrial plants, tunnel constructions, airports and urban large-scale constructions are one-time acts. They are unique in their technical and commercial configuration and are therefore individually planned and implemented specific to the task, make use of long implementation periods and exhibit a corresponding sales volume. Accordingly, the form of the counter performance also exhibits substantial peculiarities which allow the project business to appear fundamentally different from the product business and the system business and require a particular methodology and analysis.

In the industrial plant business the remuneration for the supplier's service is identified as **revenue**. In terms of content this is equivalent to the price. One process that is directed at finding an offering price decision is identified as **revenue planning** and the bidding price to be found as **planned revenue**.

Finding a price decision is a complex and time consuming process. Price decisions in the industrial plant business are always one-time decisions because of the project structure. Each plant is different and each price must be found individually. The interests of the supplier and customer are nearly completely contrary with regard to the pricing. While the supplier's perceptions are directed toward asserting his goals of cost coverage and profit, i.e., his subjective planned revenue or his lowest price limit, the customer's perceptions by contrast are to not exceed certain subjective maximum amounts (upper price limits) derived from budgeting and investment planning. The determination of a price is a **search**

W. Plinke
European School of Management and Technology, Berlin, Germany
e-mail: wulff.plinke@esmt.org

M. Claßen (✉)
School of Business and Economics, Freie Universität Berlin, Berlin, Germany
e-mail: matthias.classen@fu-berlin.de

M. Kleinaltenkamp et al. (eds.), *Business Project Management and Marketing*,
Springer Texts in Business and Economics, DOI 10.1007/978-3-662-48507-1_3

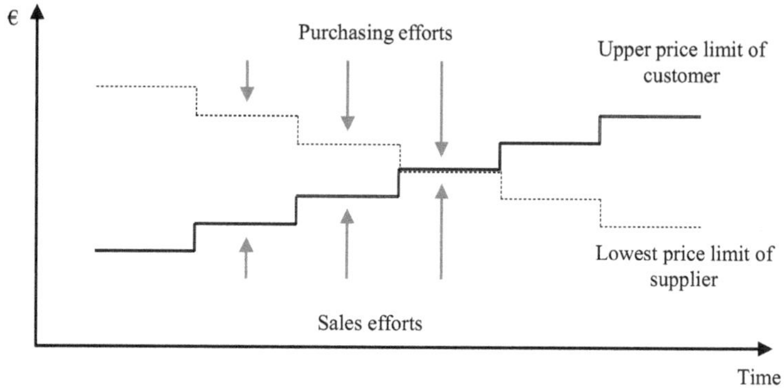

Fig. 1 Development of the customer's upper price limit and the supplier's lowest price limit as the result of acquisition efforts

process for both sides of an exchange in which the supplier's and the customer's perceptions are gradually brought closer to each other. Figure 1 clarifies the process. It is evident that an agreement is only possible if the subjective upper price limit of the customer lies above the subjective lowest price limit of the supplier.

The industrial plant business takes place in individual transactions which constitute projects. Projects in the industrial plant business are of a long-term nature. Periods which extend from several months to a number of years lie from the first contact between the supplier and the customer until the final conclusion of the business transaction. The average duration for large-scale plants lies between 2½ and 4½ years (Backhaus and Voeth 2010, p. 330; Engelhardt and Günter 1981, p. 35; cf. also Spiegel-Verlag 1972, p. 29). The period between the first project-related contact with the customer and the final closing down of a project is identified as **project episode** (Kirsch 1978, p. 70 et seqq.; Kirsch et al. 1977, p. 54 et seqq.).

The project episode allows itself to be broken down into **phases** according to the type of each ensuing activity which are clearly separated from each other by certain events or decisions (Engelhardt 1977, p. 26; Backhaus and Voeth 2010, p. 329 et seqq.; Plinke 1985, p. 7 et seqq.). Six consecutive project phases are distinguishable in an ideal-typical way: Pre-inquiry phase, inquiry phase, offer phase, negotiation phase, delivery phase and warranty phase.

The project episode constitutes a **mutual problem solving process** of the companies involved, in which conflicts are dealt with under cooperating common goals as well as divergent goals (Gemünden 1980, p. 26; Gemünden 1981, p. 19 et seq.; Herbst 2007, p. 31). The phases prior to the conclusion of the contract allow themselves to be interpreted as a search process in which all those involved try to find a problem solution which can be considered as satisfactory for them.

During the project episode—simultaneously and consecutively—an abundance of influencing variables affect the results of the project so that at the beginning it cannot be overlooked if revenue will be generated all at the end of the project episode and if yes what amount it will have. The supplying company must nevertheless have perceptions about the value dimension of a project from the beginning and this means that from the beginning of the project episode **planned revenue** is required as the standard for management and control of the project:

- Planned revenue is the benchmark for a "non-binding" estimate of the project volume in terms of value which the prospective customer often desires for his investment planning in the early stage of the project,
- Planned revenue is required for the submission of a bid,
- Planned revenue constitutes the information basis of the supplier's dispositions in the negotiation process with the customer.

A contradiction appears to lie between the impossibility of anticipating the revenue which is ultimately achieved by a project in the project's early stage and the requirement of already ascertaining planned revenue as management and control information at the beginning of the project episode. This contradiction, however, allows itself to be resolved via revenue planning appropriate for the project's stage of development. The price decision in the industrial plant business is resolved in phase-based revenue planning where the planned revenue is adjusted to the changing level of information from phase to phase, i.e., is updated.

Other issues come about in the individual phases for the planned revenue in each case. Table 1 compiles these issues. The structuring of the project episode into clearly distinct phases results from the felt uncertainty of the companies involved concerning the quantitative, qualitative and chronological characteristics of the service as well as about the costs to be expected for the service on the one hand and the uncertainty about the appropriateness of the amount and the chronological provision of the counter-performance on the other hand (cf. also Sandstede 2010, p. 28 et seqq.).

Planned revenue of an entirely different quality and an entirely different function comes about in the course of the project conditioned by the phase structure of the project. The submission of an estimated value to the customer during the **inquiry phase** for the project volume is by and large unbinding and primarily indicates the magnitude of the project. The inquiry phase is characterized by the fact that the supplier requires large amounts of data which are difficult to obtain particularly for complex facilities. In addition, the facility is mostly only vaguely specified by the supplier. The precise technical designs are normally unknown to the supplier (Backhaus and Voeth 2010, p. 357). During the **offer phase** an offer is presented to the customer which contains the revenue desired by the supplier. This value is binding to the extent that as a rule it can no longer be exceeded without the changing of the underlying product service offerings. The value should also not be set too high. Otherwise, the supplier could quickly be in an inferior position to competing suppliers with his demands in terms of price. The planned revenue from the offer phase constitutes that amount which the supplier deems adequate and attainable with regard to his goal as well as to his assessment of the market and company situation. We call this amount the **offering price**. The offering price is

Table 1 Phase structure and characteristics relevant for the planned revenue of a project (Plinke 1985, p. 9)

Project phase	Activities	Event or decision at the end of the phase	Characteristics relevant for planned revenue
Pre-inquiry phase	General acquisition	Entering of an inquiry	–
Inquiry phase	Review of the inquiry/ negotiations via the creation of a preliminary study	Approval of the inquiry for the creation of an offer/ entering of a bid	Submission of an estimated value for the investment volume to be expected
Offer phase			
Single offer	Creation of a technical proposed solution/cost estimation/scheduling	Submission of the offer to the customers	Binding stipulation on the maximum asking price with respect to the customer
Partner-oriented offer	Like a single offer; in addition negotiations about the form of cooperation	Submission of the offer to the supplier community	Early stipulation on the revenue demand with respect to the offer partners
Partner-oriented negotiations	Negotiations with offer partners concerning performance and revenue portion	Cooperative submission of the offer to the customers	Binding stipulation on the maximum asking price
Negotiation phase			
Single offer	Negotiations with customers concerning performance and revenue	Conclusion of contract	Binding stipulation on contract revenue or on the method for determining revenue
Cooperative offer	Like a single offer; additionally negotiations with offer partners concerning adjustment of performance and revenue portion	Conclusion of contract	Binding stipulation on contract revenue or on the method for determining revenue
Delivery phase	Project planning, manufacture, assembly/ pre-calculation, concurrent calculation	Declaration of acceptance by the customers	Revenue realized within the meaning of commercial law and recoverable claim
Warranty phase and financial transaction	Warranties, financing service, post-calculation	Expiration of warranty period/ final payment	Monetary realized revenue without risk reservations

the result of the pre-inquiry phase, inquiry phase and offer phase which we summarize with reference to the tasks for the planned revenue for the **offer phase in a broader sense**.

In the case of the cooperative offer (e.g. consortium) (cf. chapter "Project Cooperation") a partner-oriented offer and negotiation phase is additionally included in the offer phase which can be looked upon as the intermediate step for

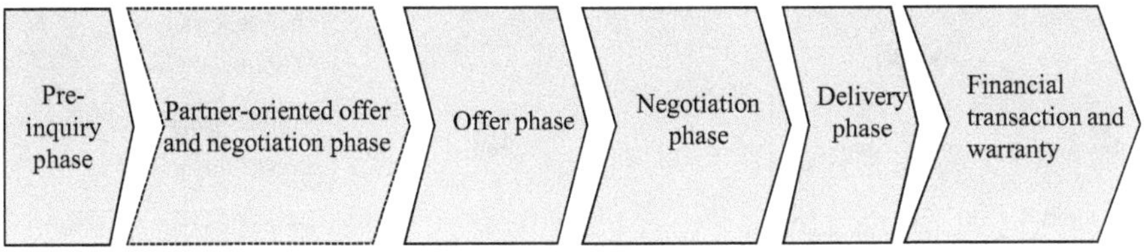

Fig. 2 Phase structure of the industrial plant business

the determination of the offering price (Günter 1979, p. 169; Backhaus and Voeth 2010, p. 328; 351 et seq.). The offer price is the input for the **negotiation phase** in which it is attempted to determine the possible market price via negotiations between suppliers and customers concerning performance and counter performance. The offer price constitutes one of the substantial benchmarks during the negotiation phase for the process of the coordination of the supplier's perceptions with the opportunities of the market. If an agreement results then the result is the **contract price (contract revenue).** It is—on condition of the fulfillment of contract by the suppliers—legally secured.

Questions of planned revenue and revenue control still exist even after the conclusion of a contract which will not be further pursued in this chapter (cf. Plinke 1985, p. 147 et seqq.; Gaismayer 2011, p. 110 et seq. in addition). The problem of price planning—the finding of an appropriate price—is solved with the conclusion of a contract or with the termination of negotiations. Figure 2 summarizes the phase sequence of the industrial plant business.

In addition to the chronological structure, the planned revenue in the industrial plant business possesses a material structure. This results from the fact that the complex hardware-software bundle "system" is normally not satisfied as a lump sum in a single sum but rather according to materially segmented partial services. We can therefore differentiate a whole range of **revenue types** for industrial plant businesses in the majority of cases. Revenue types are the positive and negative components of the total revenue from the industrial plant business (Laßmann 1979, p. 137; Kolb 1978, p. 39). Figure 3 shows an overview of the most important revenue types in the industrial plant business.

We differentiate two categories, namely revenue types which result from deliveries and services and correction variables. They describe the content of the price planning in detail. Price planning has the task of determining the one amount of revenue for a project which fulfills the company goals considering the given and expected environmental conditions. The **planned price** is thus a variable which the supplying company deems reasonable and achievable. The indicator for the **appropriateness** of the planned price is an offer price calculated according to "normal" coverage requirements and viewed as required. **Attainability** expresses itself in the perceived upper limit of the pricing policy leeway.

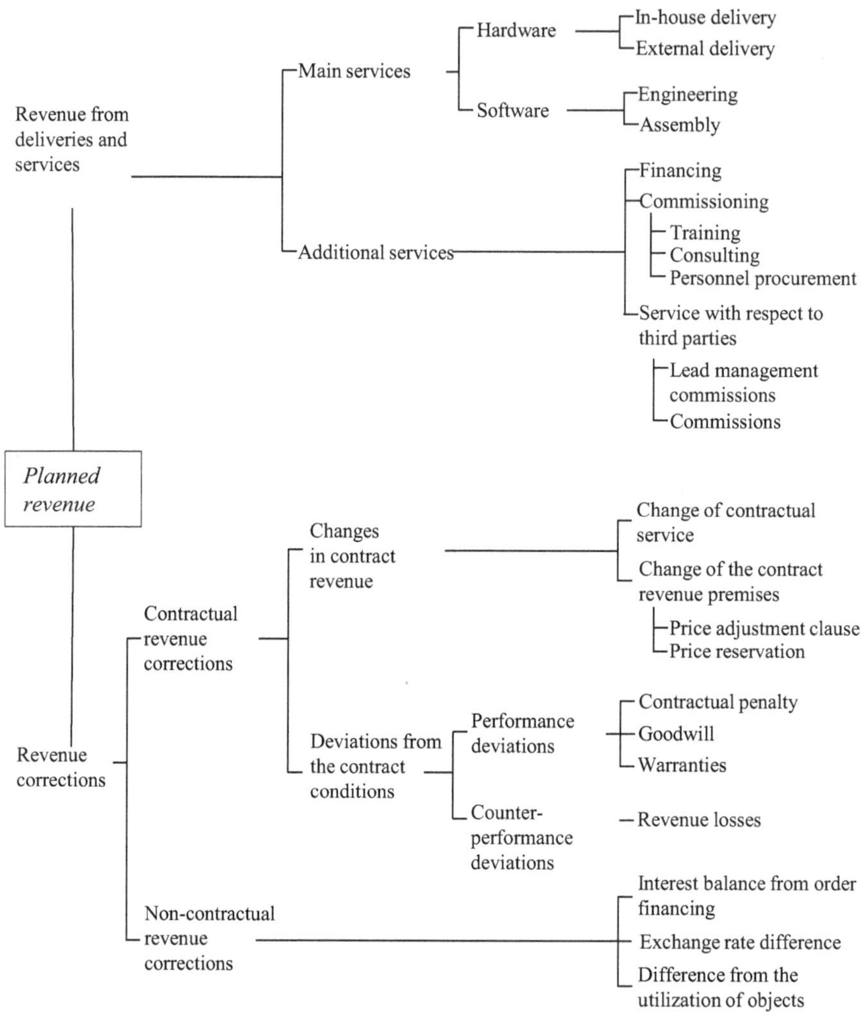

Fig. 3 Revenue types in the industrial plant business

2 Decision About the Price Level

2.1 Calculation of the Order Price

2.1.1 Problem

Practically nothing else remains for the supplier than to determine the offer price based on the calculated **costs** due to the absence of or uncertainty of market data in the offer phase. The price planning methods in the offer phase are thus the **calculation methods**.

The demand results from the supplier's company goal that all revenue together shall be as high as all costs together in the long run. From this demand it can again be deduced that the revenue of an individual project must render a contribution, which is to be "somehow" defined, to the total cost coverage. The total costs of a specific project can now be divided into two categorically different complexes:

- costs which are directly caused by the project—they are the **project direct costs**. Project direct costs are only incurred if the project is implemented at all, i.e., these are the costs which are added to the company total costs by the project.
- costs, which are incurred regardless of the existence of the project within the company, these are the **project indirect costs**. They are not affected in their amount by the project itself.

If in the long run all of the company's revenues must cover all of the company's costs, it is evident that the individual project must not only cover the project direct costs with its revenue but rather must furthermore generate an amount for the coverage of the project indirect costs. This "contribution margin" from the individual project summarizes all other projects with the contribution margins and shall ensure the complete cost coverage of the company as well as ensure profit. The planned price thus has the task to ensure the coverage of the project direct costs as well as a partial coverage of the project indirect costs.

The **coverage requirement for direct costs** results from three dimensions of the project direct costs—the **quantity structure**, the **assessment structure** and the **time structure**. The quantity structure constitutes the commodity amounts entering the project (hardware and software including services), the assessment structure constitutes the commodity prices, which are multiplied with the commodity amounts, and the time structure ultimately indicates the time of the costs incurred which plays an important role for the lasting value of the projects. Figure 4 constitutes the influencing variable of the coverage requirement for direct costs.

The **coverage requirement for overhead** is determined on the one hand by the amount of the project overhead overall, i.e. by the amount of the total coverage volume and on the other hand by the planned portion of the project on the total coverage volume. Figure 5 summarizes the influencing variables of the coverage requirement for the overhead.

It catches one's eye that the number of influencing variables of the total coverage requirement is very high. The number is still substantially larger in a specific planning case since more detailed categorizations—primarily in the materials and manufacturing sector—are necessary. However, the costs of the know-how drainage are difficult to quantify and to consider as the case may be (Yang and Mattfeld 2007). Such costs can arise if this concerns an international project and it is agreed upon due to a *local content* contractual condition that a part of the value creation shall take place locally—abroad.

The supplier only possesses highly incomplete information about most of the influencing variables during the offer phase. Procurement of information is time-consuming and costly. A substantial planning risk results from this. Since the

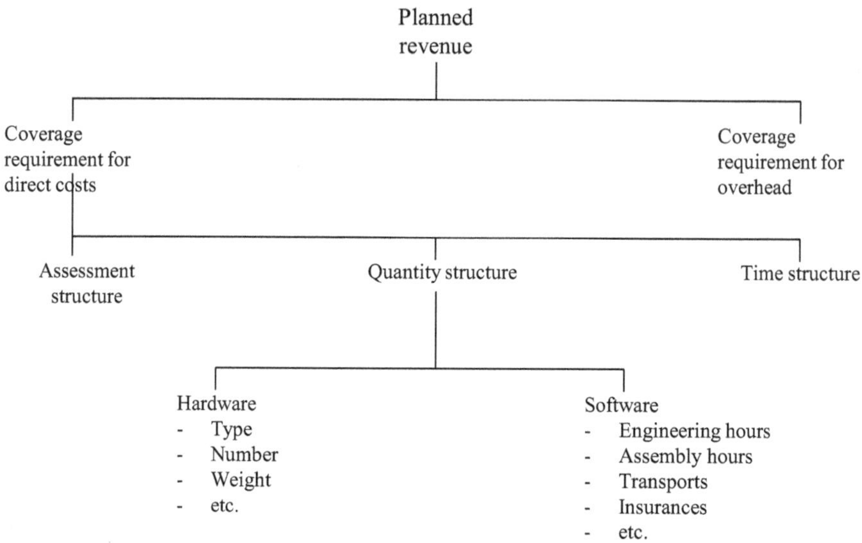

Fig. 4 Influencing variable of the planned revenue: coverage requirement for direct costs

supplier is normally bound to his offer after the submission of a tender, he can no longer exceed his asking price. Miscalculations of the coverage requirement occasionally lead to substantial losses (Opitz et al. 1971, p. 16).

Deviations occurred in up to 90 % of the cases in the study by Opitz et al., which exceed a reasonable amount by far particularly considering the high absolute sales volume of the projects. Other empirical studies result in comparable results (Wellensiek 2007, p. 10; Eversheim et al. 1977, p. 18 et seqq.; Feuerbaum 1979, p. 5). In individual cases of larger projects, relatively minor deviations can lead to absolutely devastating consequences: "In the case of a large-scale order errors in the precalculation of the purchase values to the tune of 4–5 % would exceed the reporting company's share capital" (Feuerbaum and Witte 1977, p. 156).

In light of such **planning risks** an extremely thorough and comprehensive planning behavior and analysis of possible risks must actually be the consequence. Numerous models and guidelines were developed to identify risks in the project itself and in the project environment. Belonging to this are among other things risks in the areas of construction, procurement, production planning, manufacture and assembly, logistics and overhead, however, also socio-economic and political risks (Yosha 2012; Rimpau 2011; Bhattacharyya and Dey 2007; Floricel and Miller 2001; Dey et al. 1994). Such a thorough planning and risk assessment is, however, only possible to a very limited extent because the submission of offers only leads to actual orders to a lesser extent. Quotas of less than 5 % to less than 10 % are mentioned in empirical studies (Oo et al. 2012, p. 31; Krause et al. 2005, p. 10; Feuerbaum 1979, p. 12; Eversheim et al. 1977, p. 8; Opitz et al. 1971, p. 8). Upon the simultaneous absolute increase of the number of offers—attributable to the worldwide competition of system suppliers—an additional cost factor lies in the

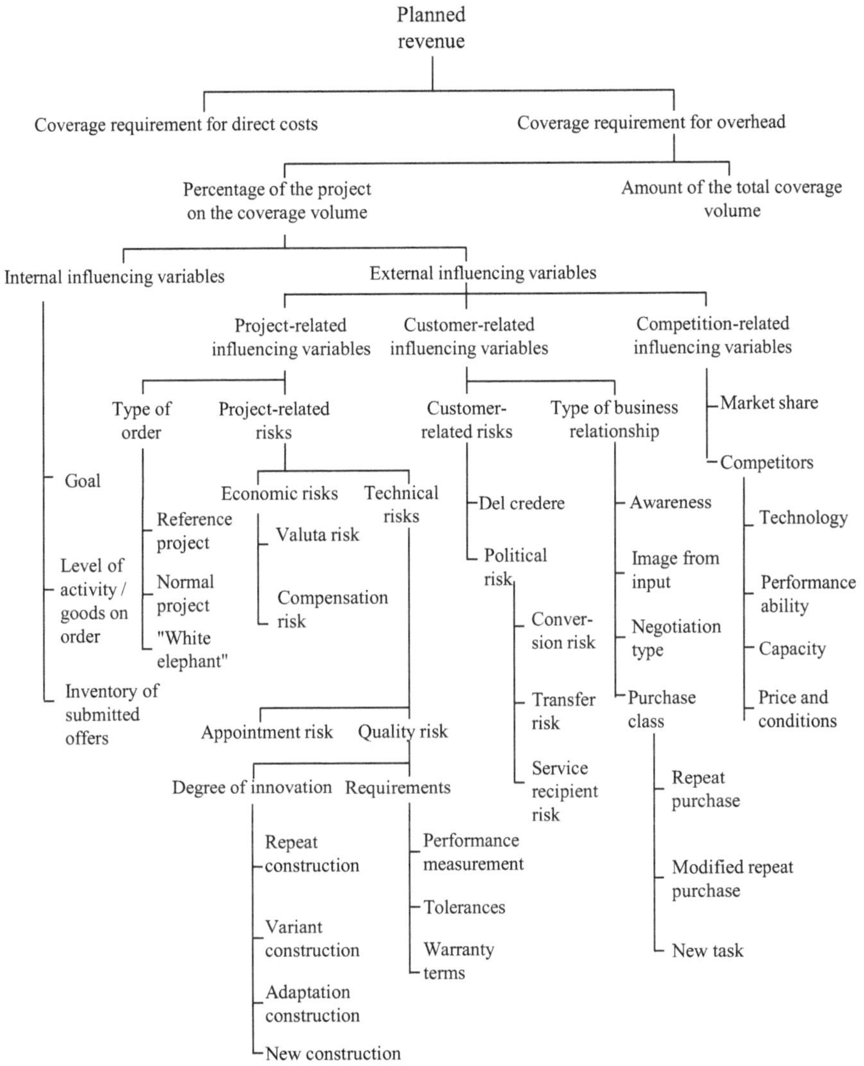

Fig. 5 Coverage requirement influencing variables for overhead

low order conversion rate since the offers are not re-compensated and may constitute up to 25 % of the total project expenditure (Weiber and Kleinaltenkamp 2012, p. 250).

The determination of the offer price thus presents itself as an extremely complex problem of **information processing** which is characterized by

- a wide range of heterogeneous influencing variables, which are predominantly unknown

- high planning costs, associated with limited order attainment probability and
- high risks of mis-planning in the case of the order placement.

The economic problem of price planning during the offer phase is to determine a planned price which fulfills the company goal during this phase under these circumstances. This means a planned price must be formed that is so high that it covers the project direct costs with sufficiently high probability and furthermore renders a contribution viewed as acceptable for the coverage of the project indirect costs and contribution to the business performance. At the same time, it may not be so high that the offer is withdrawn from the inquiring customers from the outset. The question is thus reflected in three tasks:

1. Rational methods of price planning must be developed which enable a reliable estimate of the coverage requirement for direct costs.
2. Reliable criteria must be developed for the determination of the coverage requirement for overhead.
3. Criteria must be developed for upper price limits.

2.1.2 Cost Estimate (Kilo Cost Methods)

The kilo cost method is a procedure for the pre-calculation of the manufacturing costs of similar products, which is based on the basic assumption that the weight of the product (and thus the material cost percentage) is the sweeping **cost influencing factor**, more precisely: a functional relationship exists between the manufacturing costs of the product and its weight. Such a relationship can also be produced for various other cost influencing factors outside of weight, e.g. "meter roll train" for cold rolling mill, tons per day output at cement factories or megawatts at power plants. We will exemplarily present the product weight here as a cost influencing factor.

The kilo costs are an average value which results from experience with processed orders:

Kilo cost methods

$$k_{Hj} = \frac{k_H^* \cdot x_j}{x^*}$$

Whereby

k_{Hj} = Manufacturing costs for product j (pre-calculation)
x_j = Quantity of the material consumption for product j (in kg)
k^*_{Hj} = average manufacturing costs of the previous products (actual costs)
x^* = average material weight of the previous products

If the kilo cost method is applied without thinking substantial miscalculations can occur in this way. We want to demonstrate the computational difficulty of cost estimation in a fictitious example in which the kilo costs are determined based on five manufacturing cost values from the past (Plinke and Rese 2006, p. 181 et seqq.). Three data sets are placed next to each other for the clarification of the problem which

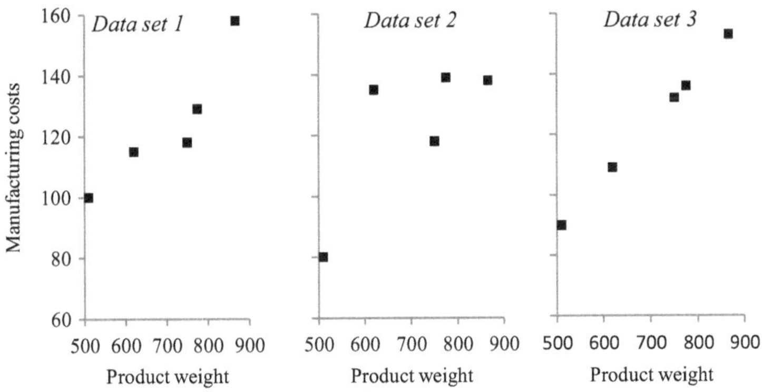

Fig. 6 Correlation of manufacturing costs and product weight

Table 2 Example for kilo cost method

	Data set 1		Data set 2		Data set 3	
Product	Manufacturing costs	kg	Manufacturing costs	kg	Manufacturing costs	kg
1	100.–	510	80.–	510	90.–	510
2	115.–	620	135.–	620	109.–	620
3	118.–	750	118.–	750	132.–	750
4	129.–	775	139.–	775	136.–	775
5	158.–	866	138.–	866	153.–	866
Total	620.–	3521	620.–	3521	620.–	3521
k_H/kg	0.176		0.176		0.176	

each have identical kg values, however, have deviating manufacturing costs information. However, all three data sets result in an identical kilo cost value: 0.176 €/kg. What is a reliable value and what isn't?

A plot of the three data sets gives a prima facie answer to this question (cf. Fig. 6; Table 2). Obviously the frequency of the correlations between the three data sets is pronounced differently: While the third data set nearly lies in a straight line the second spreads extremely and the first data set moderately.

The reliability of the kilo cost rate as the calculation basis decisively depends on how tight the correlation between the manufacturing costs and the weight of the product was in the past. The kilo cost method cannot make any statement about this; therefore further deliberations are necessary.

The **simple linear regression analysis** is the method for the examination of the connection between the manufacturing costs and the weight of a product. It is a mathematical-statistical technique for the estimation of a linear function based on empirical values from the examined variables.

In the case of the kilo cost method the dependent variable of the amount of the manufacturing costs is the independent variable of the product weight. A general relationship is sought from the type

$$y = a + b \cdot x$$

meaning:

$$\text{manufacturing costs}_j = a + b \cdot \text{weight}_j$$

The manufacturing costs of the product j is interpreted as the linear function of its weight. The weight is known for the pre-calculation of the manufacturing costs. The amount of the manufacturing costs y_j results from both parameters *a* and *b* of the cost function.

The determination of these parameters takes place based on the **least squares method** (cf. also Backhaus et al. 2011, p. 67). It leads to the following definitions for the parameters *a* and *b*.

Definition 1 Regression equation

$$b = \frac{n\left(\sum_{i=1}^{n} x_i \cdot y_i\right) - \left(\sum_{i=1}^{n} x_i\right) \cdot \left(\sum_{i=1}^{n} y_i\right)}{n\left(\sum_{i=1}^{n} x_i 2\right) - \left(\sum_{i=1}^{n} x_i\right)^2} \qquad a = \overline{y} - b \cdot \overline{x}$$

Whereby

a = constant term
b = regression coefficient
n = number of observations
x_i = weight of the product i
y_i = manufacturing costs of the product i
$\overline{x}, \overline{y}$ = averages

The determination of the cost function is shown in data set 1 by way of example. For that to happen, the data must be initially processed. The values can now be directly used in the definition (cf. Table 3). The complete cost function is:

$$\text{manufacturing costs}_j = 24.816774 + 0.1408453 * \text{weight}_j$$

The administrative and sales overhead costs are added as a percentage to the manufacturing costs calculated in such a way.

The core issue from now on is how reliable a cost estimate is which is based on the basis of such a kilo cost function. The parameter, which states something about the reliability of the estimate, is the **coefficient of determination**.

Table 3 Determination of the regression equation: preparation of the data from the observations

Observation value i	Manufacturing costs y	kg x	$x \cdot y$	x^2
1	100.–	510	51,000	260,100
2	115.–	620	73,300	384,400
3	118.–	750	88,500	562,500
4	129.–	775	99,975	600,625
5	158.–	866	136,828	749,956
Total	620.–	3521	447,603	2,557,581
Average value	124.–	704		

$b = \frac{5*447{,}603 - 3{,}521*620}{5*2{,}557{,}581 - 3{,}521^2} = 0.1408453$

$a = 124 - 0.1408453 * 704.20 = 24.816774$

Definition 2 Coefficient of determination of the costs function

$$r^2 = 1 - \frac{\sum_{i=1}^{n} (y_i - \hat{y}_i)^2}{\sum_{i=1}^{n} (y_i - \bar{y})^2}$$

Whereby

r^2 = coefficient of determination ($0 < r^2 < 1$)
y_i = observation value manufacturing costs
$\hat{y}_i$ = estimated value of manufacturing costs base on x_i
$\bar{y}$ = average value of y

The data must be processed again for the use of this definition on sample data set 1 (cf. Table 4).

The parameters materially mean that 82.7 % of a variation of the manufacturing costs can be traced back to a variation in the material weight—a result, which indicates a limited accuracy of the estimate for the kilo costs method.

The kilo cost method should only be used if a careful test of the cost function has been conducted. The necessary scope of empirical cost records is $n \geq 30$ complete data sets. Caution is moreover required for severely volatile material prices (Fig. 7). In this case, useful tenders can only be submitted subject to a material index.

2.1.3 Material Costs Method

The material costs method is a method for the pre-calculation of manufacturing costs of **similar products**, which originates from the relationship

$$\text{Material costs} : \text{Labor costs} : \text{Production overhead} = \text{const.}$$

Table 4 Determination of the coefficient of determination of the cost function from the observations

i	y_i	$\hat{y}_i$	$y_i - \hat{y}_i$	$(y_i - \hat{y}_i)^2$	$y_i - \bar{y}$	$(y_i - \bar{y})^2$
1	100	96.65	3.35	11.24	−24.00	576.00
2	115	112.14	2.86	8.17	−9.00	81.00
3	118	130.45	−12.45	155.02	−6.00	36.00
4	129	133.97	−4.97	24.70	5.00	25.00
5	158	146.79	11.21	125.69	34.00	1156.00
Total				324.84		1874.00
Average value	124					

The following arises from this $r^2 = 1 - \frac{324.84}{1,874.00} = 0.82665$

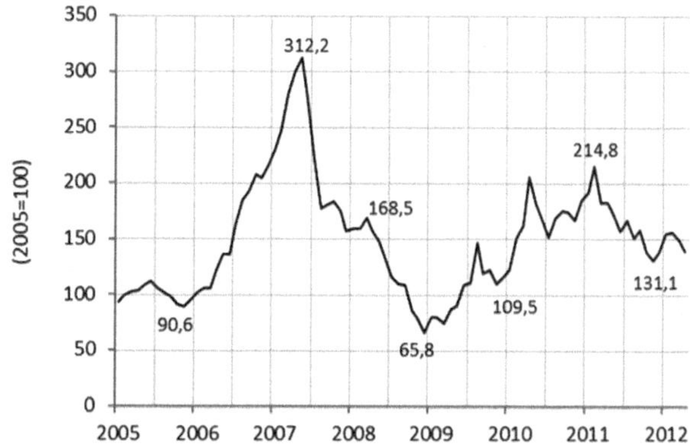

Fig. 7 Producer price index for nickel products (Statistisches Bundesamt 2012)

If one knows this cost relationship from a number of processed orders the total manufacturing costs can be estimated solely based on the material costs (or just as well based on the estimated labor costs). The cost estimate is made based on the following formula:

Definition 3 Material costs method

$$k_H = \frac{k_m}{m}$$

Whereby:

k_H = manufacturing costs of the product
k_m = estimated material costs of the product
m = material cost percentage $(0 < m < 1)$

The administrative and sales overhead costs are again added as a percentage to the manufacturing costs calculated in such a way.

The assumption of a constant cost structure across products is just as problematic as the kilo cost method, i.e. it is fraught with estimate uncertainties if the correlation

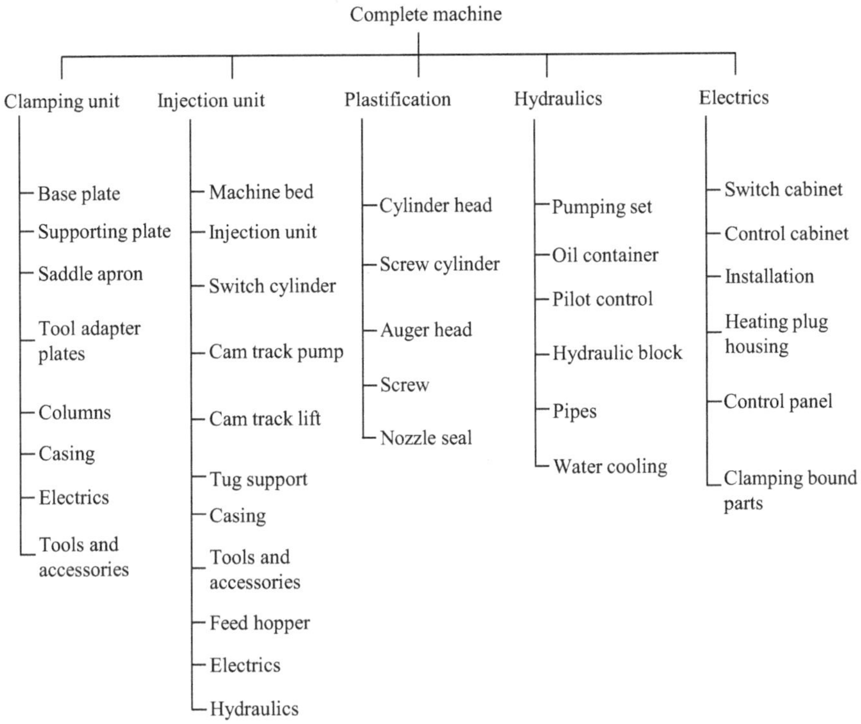

Fig. 8 Classification tree for a plastic injection molding machine (Eversheim et al. 1977, p. 33)

is not tested empirically. The kilo cost method can be methodically referenced for this purpose.

2.1.4 Calculation of Influencing Variables (Calculation with Cost Functions)

The pre-calculation with a number of cost influencing variables assumes that there is usually a limited amount of cost influencing variables which determine the amount of manufacturing costs of **comparable** products or components.

Since the **components** are no longer comparable at all in the case of high technical complexity the heterogeneous components are initially differentiated into **modules**. Figure 8 shows an example.

At the module level relatively homogeneous elements can be more easily found which are examined for their cost influencing variables. Thus an analysis of the **possible** cost influencing variables is performed per module (e.g. weight, dimensions, performance indexes, machining processes etc.) and these are again based on empirical records (cf. Table 5).

It becomes clear that this approach is merely an extension of the kilo cost method which has been presented above. The difference is

Table 5 Data collection sheet for the determination of costs functions

Observation	Module j Manufacturing costs	Weight	Volume	Performance index	...	...	... →
1							
2							
3							
4							
5							
6							
Σ							

- that the end product (the components) is not analyzed for its cost influencing variable but rather the modules are and
- that one independent variable (cost influencing variable), namely the weight, is not taken into consideration but rather a number of cost influencing variables are taken into consideration.

In order to develop a cost function for a module, as many as possible potential cost influencing factors must initially be included in the examination. The **multiple regression analysis** then creates clarification about which variable actually has a significant influence on the amount of the manufacturing costs (cf. also Backhaus et al. 2011, p. 69).

Figure 9 schematically shows the calculation procedure with costs functions.

The costs function of a module then has the form:

$$\text{Manufacturing costs module } j = a + b_1x_1 + b_2x_2 + \ldots + b_ix_i + \ldots + b_nx_n$$

Whereby

a = constant term

b_i = Regression coefficient of the cost influencing variable i

x_i = cost influencing variable i

If a cost function is given for each module, only the name of the required modules as well as their dimensions are needed for the pre-calculation in order to be able to estimate the manufacturing costs.

The administrative and sales overhead costs are again added as a percentage to the manufacturing costs calculated in such a way.

The **limitations** of the method shall be emphasized once again.

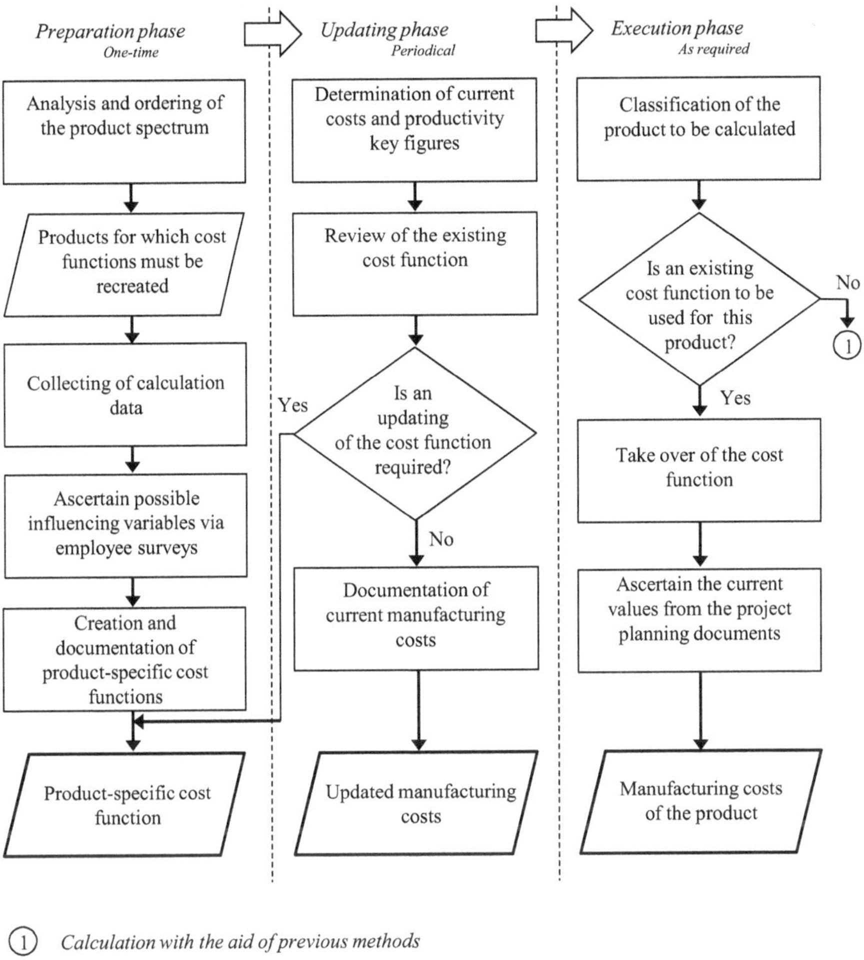

Fig. 9 Determination of a multivariate cost function (Eversheim et al. 1977, p. 73)

1. The analysis must refer to similar products. In addition to this, it is usually necessary to undertake a systematic product classification so that relatively similar modules can be isolated.
2. Knowledge about cost influencing variables must be given.
3. Comprehensive empirical records must be given concerning the manufacturing costs and the characteristics of the cost influencing variables.
4. The correlation between manufacturing costs and cost influencing variables must be linear.
5. The method does not make any statements about the calculation of administrative and sales costs.

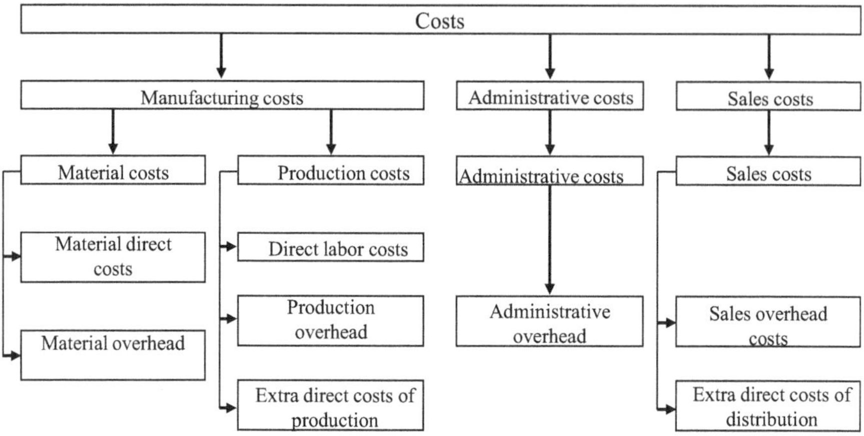

Fig. 10 Structure of costs for differentiating surcharge calculations

2.1.5 Detail Calculation

The detail calculation either proceeds from existing post-calculations of similar products and matches the individual calculation positions with the modified offer situation or it performs a complete recalculation. The scope of the calculation efforts is extremely high in the latter case. Planning the quantity structure of the product's direct costs is what is most difficult here since the construction still is not fixed for good in the offer phase.

The detail calculation constitutes a differentiating **allocated production overhead calculation** (cf. also Plinke and Rese 2006, p. 122 et seq.; Plötner et al. 2010, p. 130 et seq.). The fundamental principle of the allocated production overhead calculation is the division of the primary total costs of the company into direct costs and overhead costs and here into project direct costs and project indirect costs. The differentiating allocated production overhead calculation attributes the direct costs to each project directly without exception wherein no cost accounting problem is inserted but rather a cost finding problem is inserted at best (documentation of the amount and the chronological accrual of direct costs). The core issue of the allocated production overhead calculation is the allocation of overhead to projects. This is made via a **surcharge** on the direct costs. The surcharge shall be measured in such a way that it reasonably represents the use of company resources by the project as far as possible.

The differentiating surcharge calculation does not allocate the overhead in one flat-rate cost rate to the project but rather divides the overhead according to its development areas and forms one or a number of cost rates per development area. **Cost center accounting (cost distribution sheet)** supplies the numerical data for the formation of cost rates. One cost rate is formed per final cost center of the cost distribution sheet, i.e. each final cost center individually allocates its overhead to the cost unit. The surcharge calculation uses a calculation procedure which is differentiated according to company functional areas; the basic structure of this procedure is displayed in Fig. 10.

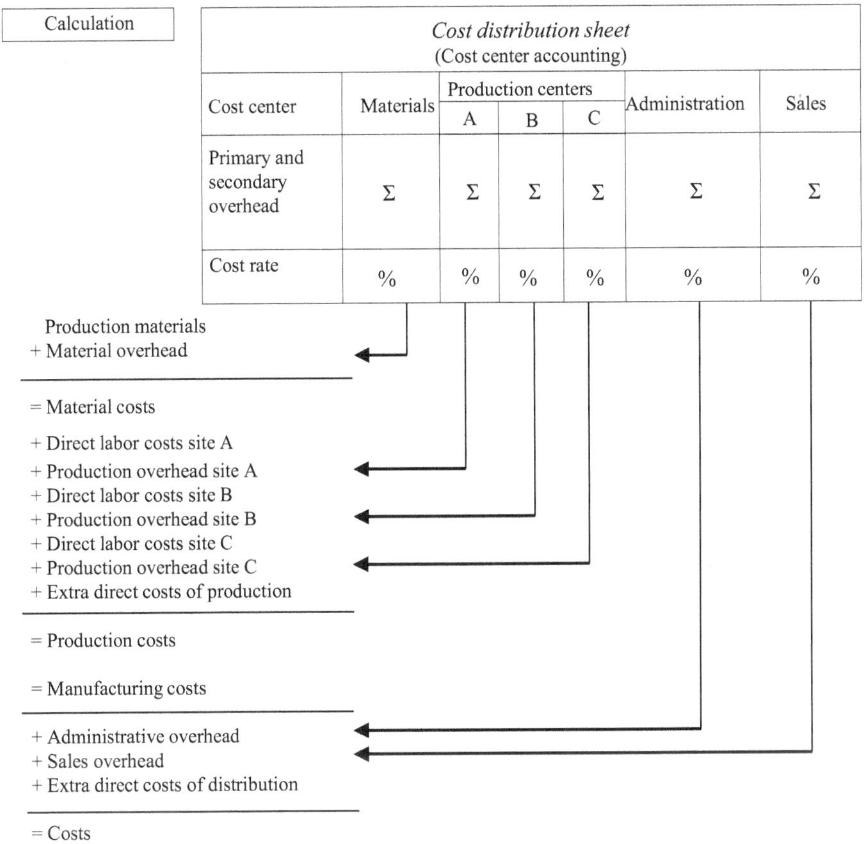

Fig. 11 Correlation of cost accounting and calculation (Plinke and Rese 2006, p. 125)

The cost rates are formed per final cost center in accordance with the same principle: The surcharge basis constitutes the basis for allocation for the overhead. The more is given from the surcharge basis (e.g. direct costs) for the project the higher the proportional inclusion of overhead. Figure 11 shows the correlation between the cost distribution sheet and the surcharge calculation. A practically relevant outline of a detail calculation shows Table 6.

2.1.6 Comparison of Calculation Methods

The individual calculation methods promise variably specific and reliable results. The reliability of calculation results is furthermore linked to the intensity of the calculation efforts. Figure 12 schematically presents the tendential correlation.

2.2 Upper Price Limit

2.2.1 From Calculation Result to the Offer Price

The planned price, which results from the calculation, is created based on standardized procedures—possibly even broadly computer generated. Hence it

Table 6 Example for a differentiating surcharge calculation

Line No.	Calculation items	Calculation basis	Calculation structure	Order No. Date Pre-calculation	Post-calculation	Deviations	Remarks
A	b	c	d	e	f	g	h
1	Raw materials						
2	Small parts (indirect production materials)						
3	Finished parts						
4	Purchased larger objects						
5	External processing						
6	Material overhead (MGK)						
7	./. Waste material credits (scrap)						
8	Material costs	(1–7)					
9	Direct labor costs, mechanical processing						
10	Production overhead (FGK), mechanical processing						
11	(a) Costs of plant and machinery						
12	(b) Remaining overhead						
13	Direct labor costs, manual labor						
14	Production overhead (FGK), manual labor						
15	Miscellaneous processing						
16	Production costs	(9–16)					
17	Models, devices and special tools						
18	Calculation Production risks (rejects + rework)						
19	Extra costs of production	(18 + 19)					
20	Manufacturing costs A	(8 + 17 + 20)					

21	Research, development and construction costs						
22	External installations						
23	Manufacturing costs B	(21–23)					
24	Administrative overhead (VwGK)						
25	Sales overhead costs (VtGK)						
26	Costs A	(24–26)					
27	Commissions and licenses						
28	Freight, transport and packaging						
29	Miscellaneous						
30	Extra costs for distribution	(28–30)					
31	Distribution risk costs						
32	Costs B	(27 + 31 + 32)	100 %				
33	Profit/loss						
34	Retail price (net)/revenue						

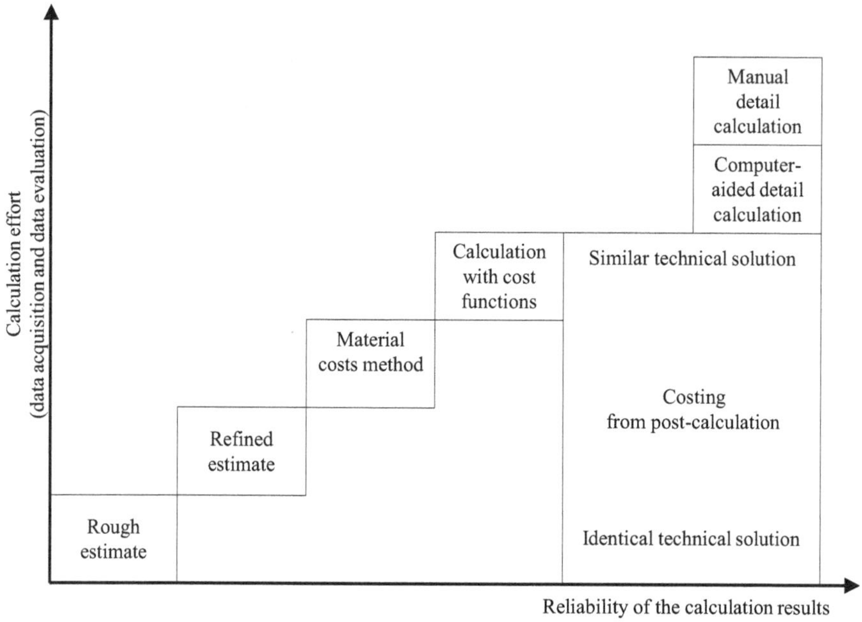

Fig. 12 Correlation between the calculation effort and the reliability of the calculation results (Verein Deutscher Ingenieure 1983, p. 221)

can only be a first approach to an offer price since it is necessary to at least carefully slip the existing information and estimates about the market condition into the offer. The core problem of an offer pricing in the industrial plant business consists in "coming closer" to external conditions from internal circumstances. Therefore the value derived from the calculation must be adjusted to the (subjectively estimated) **conditions of the market**.

This primarily takes place during the negotiation phase. However, an analysis of the market situation and its consideration in the determination of the asking price is also already necessary during the offer phase for projects which include negotiations namely for a number of reasons:

1. The inclusion of cost increases in the offer price is absolutely necessary in the case of a longer-term commitment to the offer or for long and often multi-year processing periods (e.g. **fixed-price surcharge or price adjustment clause**)
2. The **profit margin** is often applied in an initial calculation—in view of the missing possibility of market assessment—with a standard percentage. However, great upward and downward flexibility exists for this component of the offer price depending on how the market situation is assessed. However, an overly generous assessment of the profit margin with regard to the expected necessary negotiation concessions can also turn out to be dangerous. On the one hand it can happen that the supplying company is not invited at all to the

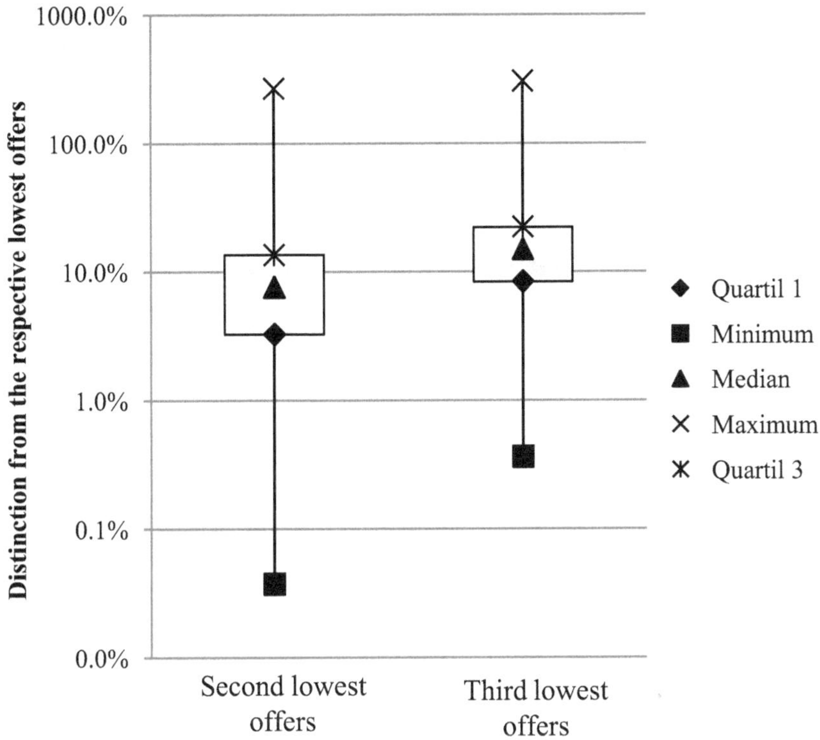

Fig. 13 Deviations between the asking prices of several suppliers

negotiations at first due to the amount of the offering price. An evaluation of construction projects in rail transport (n = 200 submissions in the year 2011 and 2012) shows that average deviations of over 50 % occur between the suppliers' asking prices. In every tenth construction project even deviations of over 100 % occur, the absolute amount of the construction project occasionally lying in a range of 106 €. Opitz et al. also arrived at similar results for construction projects in the energy industry (1971, p. 16 et seq.). Figure 13 shows the allocation of the submitted offers compared to the lowest offer. On the other hand, the supplier cannot automatically assume that concessions by the customer during the negotiation process are always evaluated positively. The supplier can easily stumble into a light which leaves him appearing as dubious if he includes negotiating margins which are too high in his offers asking price. The offer price must assume a magnitude in conformity with the market even upon a prospect for negotiations. What must be considered as "in conformity with the market" in an individual case is also connected to the respective customer and his cultural environment.

3. A **methodically** correct determination of the profit margin can arise from an analysis of the customer's upper price limit alone—in the event of given

opportunities for information. We will return to this in the following section concerning the economic analysis of the customer benefit and concerning competitive bidding.

4. A negative profit margin—a lower deviation of the calculation results—can also be established from sales policy viewpoints. This is to be addressed in the following section about lowest price limits.

2.2.2 The Economic Analysis of the Customer's Benefit

The customer's **upper price limit** lies at that price level which makes it economically equal for the customer,

- to switch to another supplier of a comparable product service offering or
- to absolutely refrain from the planned investment and take other capital appropriations in sight.

The upper price limit is thus governed by the customer's benefit perceptions or profitability expectations. The central starting point for an influence from the supplier's point of view must thus be to influence the customer's benefit perceptions or profitability expectations in accordance with the wishes of the supplier. This initially posits a clear perception of the supplier about what the customer intends to specifically do with the plant, i.e. which quantities he will produce, which intensities he intends to run and which chronological workload the plant will have. The plant's utilization concept can be ascertained via technical discussions.

It must be figured out in a second step which operating expenses the customer will presumably have in his utilization concept. In the first section of this chapter we emphasized that it is the customer's total financial burdens which he relates to the expected use of the plant in order to substantiate his decision for the awarding of the contract. Therefore a path to an estimate of the customer's upper price limit can be found in that respect for the customer to comprehend the customer's investment appraisal as objectively as possible or (provided that the customer permits it) to implement it together with the customer.

From the customer's view, the **net present value** of an investment is defined as

$$C_0 = -A_0 + \sum_{t=1}^{n} (E_t - A_t) \cdot (1 + q)^{-t},$$

In words: The net present value C_0 at the time 0 (date of contract) is equal to the difference of discounted periodic deposit surpluses $(E_t - A_t)$ across all periods t (from 1 to n) of the plant's usage time and the initial payout A_0, which stands for the purchase price (the payment series in a real case can be represented in a more differentiated way and this does not change anything in principle). The required rate of interest q expresses the investor's right to interest from the investment and is derived from alternative investment opportunities.

If one initially assumes that the supplier does not have any competitors—the customer thus only decides if he will or not at all conduct the investment with this supplier—then the customer's upper price limit is reached in cases where the net present value is zero, i.e. the discounted periodic deposit surpluses offset the cost price. The investment then earns interest exactly in the amount of the required rate of interest q. If the **supplier** can realistically estimate this interest rate as well as the periodic positive and negative cash flows, he can also estimate the upper price limit, thus the price for which the customer estimates an alternative investment for the interest rate q (q = percent/100) as equally worthy of choice.

$$0 = -A_0 + \sum_{t=1}^{n} (E_t - A_t) \cdot (1+q)^{-t}$$

$$P_{max} = \sum_{t=1}^{n} (E_t - A_t) \cdot (1+q)^{-t}$$

If the competitor situation amongst the suppliers comes into consideration the theoretical upper price limit is determined by the distance to the respective strongest competitor. P^S is the price of the supplier considered and P^C is that of the competitor. E^S and A^S are the periodic cash flows of the considered supplier's plant and E^C and A^C are accordingly the cash flows of the competitor's plant. The advantageousness of the considered supplier's plant is defined as follows with respect to that of the competitor:

$$C_0^S - C_0^C = -(P^S - P^C) + \sum_{t=1}^{n} \left[(E_t^S - E_t^C) - (A_t^S - A_t^C) \right] \cdot (1+q)^{-t}$$

By setting the **net present value** equal to zero and by resolving the equation according to the P^S, you will achieve the price for which the customer considers both competitors as economically equal.

$$0 = P^C - P^S + \sum_{t=1}^{n} \left[(E_t^S - A_t^S) - (E_t^C - A_t^C) \right] \cdot (1+q)^{-t}$$

$$P_{max}^S = P^C + \sum_{t=1}^{n} (EÜ_t^S - EÜ_t^S) \cdot (1+q)^{-t}$$

In words: The considered supplier can make himself stand out from the considered competitor by the difference of the total of the discounted deposit surpluses **(superiority premium EÜ)** in the price.

A series of deposit payments are frequently not ascertainable for an investment. In these cases a comparison of the payout burdens offers itself across the economic life (Oxenfeldt 1966, 1977, 1979; Backhaus and Voeth 2010, p. 365):

$$C_O^C - C_O^S = (P_O^C - P_O^S) + \sum_{t=1}^{n} (A_t^C - A_t^S) \cdot (1+q)^{-t}$$

$$P_{\max}^S = P_O^C + \sum_{t=1}^{n} (A_t^C - A_t^S) \cdot (1+q)^{-t}$$

In words: The supplier can make himself stand out from the competitor in price by the total of the present value of the operating expense advantages.

This computational analysis initially clarifies the principle alone. In a real case substantial information problems will emerge (competitor prices, operating expenses, deposit series, etc.). However, one should still be aware that the upper price limit exists **in principle** and that the supplier should try to draw near it in pricing policy and should seek to change it with other means than pricing policy in order to assert itself in the competition.

2.2.3 Competitive Bidding

The supplier's uncertainty about the customer's order allocation behavior (i.e. his preferences) as well as the competitors' behavior has a paramount influence on the decision in certain price planning situations. Such situations are given, for example in **bids**. The point here for the supplying company is to underbid the competing suppliers in terms of price within the scope of competitive bidding. The company which submits the most economical offer to the customer shall be awarded the contract (Homburg 2012, p. 735). Such a bidding process thus depicts the mirror image of an auction so that one also speaks of *reverse auction* (Alznauer and Krafft 2004, p. 1059). The supplier usually does not know the competitors' offers and may only speak one "last word" for his offer before the customer makes an awarding decision.

A conceptual structuring of such an offer or negotiation situation is not easy. Above all, reliable and practical methods of price planning for this purpose are still not at hand. However, it is helpful to systematically dissect the decision making situation into its components in order to extract the benefit for the price decisions in difficult "*show-down*" situations. We will use the model by **Edelman** for this purpose (Edelman 1965). This model attempts to simulate the optimum price decision of a supplier in a bid in which only one competitor (the "most dangerous") is included in the analysis. If the "most dangerous" and the majority of other competitors are unknown in reality an "average" competitive bidder can be included in the analysis (Alznauer and Krafft 2004, p. 1066 et seq.).

The model starts from four estimated values (**point estimates**). The starting point is the customer's allocation behavior. From his point of view there is a distance to the competitive price which would mean that the competitor (3) will receive the order with certainty and also such a distance which would mean that the order is retained with certainty (4). The model's data input is thus the upper and lower **marginal price**. The model furthermore requires a statement about the likelihood of an order in the event of price equality, that is the **customer preference** (1) and a statement about how the likelihood of an order changes upward and

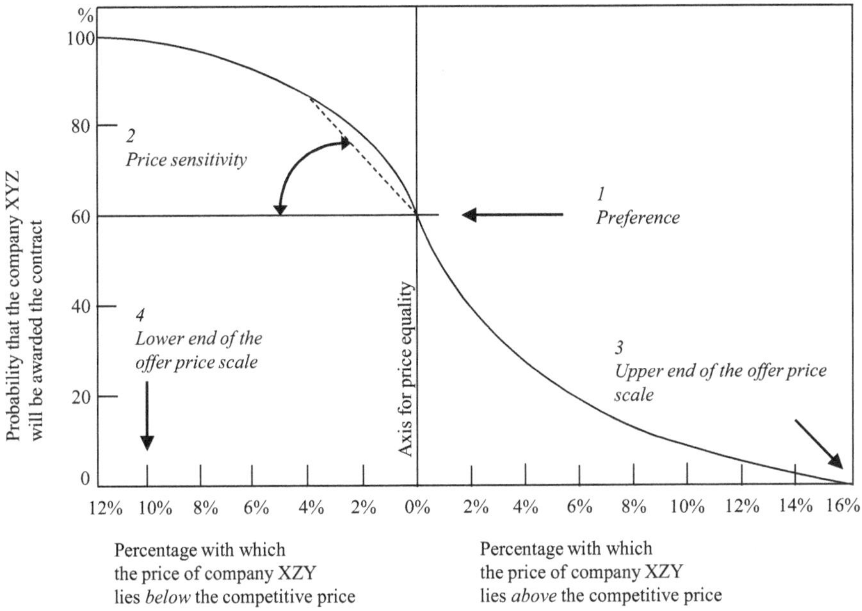

Fig. 14 Price surcharge function (Edelman 1965, p. 105)

downward for a minor deviation of the price equality, that is the **price sensitivity** (2). Based on this data input, the model can estimate a **price surcharge function**. Figure 14 shows this function and the four estimate points.

An additional data input is an estimate about the possible spectrum of the competitive price with subjective probabilities of occurrences. The estimates may be undertaken even more precisely the better the supplier knows his market environment, the customer and the competitor. Above all, information about the cost situation and the business policy of the company competing for the order must attract attention. In so doing, experiences about the behavior of competitors from earlier tenders offer themselves to slip into the estimations. The customer's personal preferences and the relative geographical position of the supplier's location must also be taken into consideration (Kuß 1977, p. 68).

Based on this data input about the competitor situation, the model can now initially specify the probability of a bid acceptance for each conceivable combination of own price/competitive price. The probability of a bid acceptance p* is then given by the sum of all paired probabilities of a bid acceptance for this price for a certain own price. In the majority of tenders, however, a customer will not make a decision for one supplier completely alone based on the asking price. He will rather also consider other criteria into his decision such as delivery reliability and delivery times so that the probability of bid acceptance for one supplier is not automatically equal to zero if its asking price lies above that of the competition. The example in Table 7. clarifies this.

Table 7 Determination of the probability of a bid acceptance (example) (Backhaus and Voeth 2010, p. 367)

	Competitor prices											
Own prices	5500	5630	5760	5890	6020	6150	6280	6410	6540	6670	6800	p*
5360	1	1	1	1	1	1	1	1	1	1	1	1
5550	0.49	0.92	1	1	1	1	1	1	1	1	1	0.9555
5730	0.12	0.36	0.73	1	1	1	1	1	1	1	1	0.8329
5910	0	0.06	0.24	0.55	0.94	1	1	1	1	1	1	0.6255
6100	0	0	0	0.16	0.43	0.81	1	1	1	1	1	0.4167
6280	0	0	0	0	0.11	0.31	0.6	0.96	1	1	1	0.2595
6460	0	0	0	0	0	0.05	0.2	0.48	0.87	1	1	0.1635
6650	0	0	0	0	0	0	0	0.15	0.37	0.68	0.98	0.0894
6830	0	0	0	0	0	0	0	0	0.1	0.27	0.54	0.0347
7020	0	0	0	0	0	0	0	0	0	0.05	0.18	0.0079
7200	0	0	0	0	0	0	0	0	0	0	0	0
	0.07	0.11	0.13	0.21	0.13	0.12	0.05	0.05	0.05	0.05	0.03	

Probability of occurrence of the competitive prices

Table 8 Determination of the expected value of the contribution margin

Own price (in K€)	Project direct costs (in K€)	Contribution margin (in K€)	Probability of a bid acceptance (p*)	Expected value of the contribution margin (in K€)
5360	5550	−190.00	1.0000	−190.00
5550	5550	0.00	0.9555	0.00
5730	5550	180.00	0.8329	149.92
5910	5550	360.00	0.6255	225.18
6100	**5550**	**550.00**	**0.4167**	**229.19**
6280	5550	730.00	0.2595	189.44
6460	5550	910.00	0.1635	148.79
6650	5550	1100.00	0.0894	98.34
6830	5550	1280.00	0.0347	44.42
7020	5550	1470.00	0.0079	11.61
7200	5550	1650.00	0.0000	0.00

For one's own price K€ 6100 results as the probability of a bid acceptance p*:

$$\begin{aligned}&(0.00*0.07 + 0.00*0.11 + 0.00*0.13 + 0.16*0.21\\&+0.43*0.13 + 0.18*0.12 + 1.00*0.05\\&+1.00*0.05 + 1.00*0.05 + 1.00*0.05\\&+1.00*0.03) = 0.4167\end{aligned}$$

The computational probability of a bid acceptance can be determined in this way for all of one's own prices.

If one now deducts the project direct costs from one's own possible prices then the contribution margin can be obtained in this way. In the continuation of the example from Table 7 the following coupling results from the contribution margin and the probability of a bid acceptance for the assumed project direct costs of K€ 5550 (cf. Table 8):

It is apparent that the expected value of the contribution margin initially increases with the increasing price and then—due to the disproportionately decreasing likelihood of an order—decreases again. Thus there is a computational optimum offer price at K€ 6100.

Figure 15 again graphically shows the correlation between the price, contribution margin, likelihood of an order and the expected contribution margin.

The model by **Edelman** has a few restrictive premises which limit its use:

- Only one competitor is considered. In reality a competitor situation mostly cannot be simplified in this way.
- It is subject to risk neutrality, i.e. a contribution margin of 100 with a probability of 0.1 is assessed in the same way as a contribution margin of 10 with the probability 1.0.
- The project is viewed isolated without linkages to other projects.

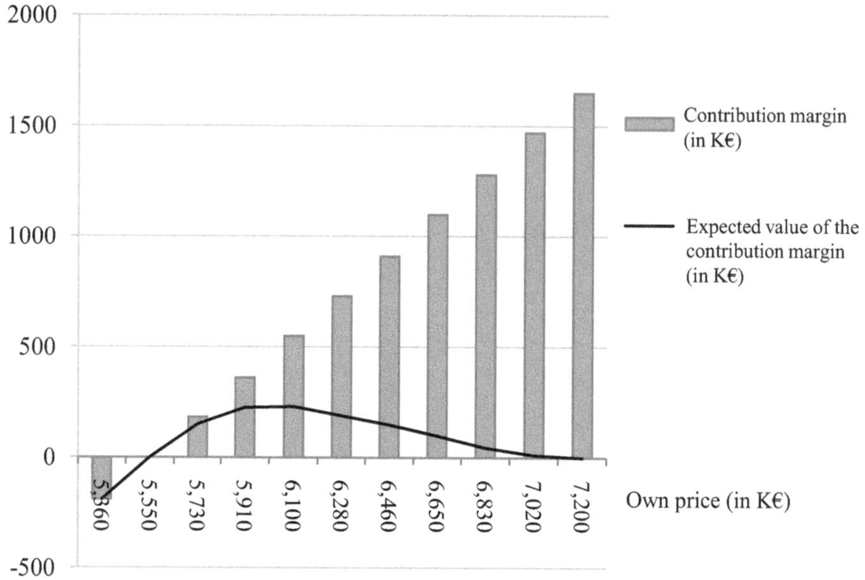

Fig. 15 Contribution margin and expected value of the contribution margin as a function of one's own price

- Knowledge which is not always given in practice is assumed about competitor activities and exact estimations of the probabilities of occurrences of competitor offers.

Further models have been developed (Backhaus 1980 with bibliographical references). The actual value of models like those presented here lies less in the direct application but rather in the conceptual structuring of the decision situation thus in a heuristic contribution to the overcoming of the extreme complexity.

2.3 Lowest Price Limit

If the price pressure is so strong that conventional, cost-oriented methods of the pricing of an offer do not lead to a marketable price then various possibilities present themselves to the supplier to absorb the pricing pressure (Günter 1979, p. 179; Plinke 1985).

The first starting point offers negotiations about the technical construction of the plant. The goal consists in binding the buyer's given benefit perceptions with a scaled-down construction of the plant so that a cost-covering price is enabled.

The pricing pressure can furthermore be passed on to the upstream supplier by the supplier in turn exerting intensified pressure on the purchase prices. Even this approach can lead to a modified planned price which can prevent or reduce an impending undercoverage of costs.

Only if all these starting points cannot eliminate the impending deficits do the most painful possibilities come into consideration: the lower deviation of the offer price via concessions which constitute a real waiver of coverage.

If the cost accounting, upon which the pricing of an offer is based, is correct and precise and if the premises of the cost accounting are correct, the negative order result arising in this way is a real company loss. One only voluntarily accepts these in an offer situation if it promises a benefit. Benefits which do not spring from this business must consequently be derived from other businesses: **money-losing businesses are always a trade off between "certain losses today against hope for tomorrow."** The following reasons come into consideration for such a business:

- Additional order in the future from this customer: The supplier invests in the business relationship with his customer via the cost coverage waiver by granting the customer benefits today which shall bring about beneficial effects for the supplier in the future.
- **Market entry:** The supplier invests in a new market via the cost coverage waiver or a prestigious reference project from which he expects benefits for himself in the future.
- **Technology entrance:** The supplier invests in the acceptance of a new technology via the cost coverage waiver from which he expects benefits for himself in the future.

In all these cases the expectation of follow-up business exists, i.e. a **revenue network** between a number of projects possibly exists which influences the planning. In addition to this (desired) revenue network reasons of the defense of the existence of the company can be mentioned:

- Securing of the job: The supplier views it as more favorable to accept below-capacity employment associated with a cost coverage waiver than to reduce capacities and if necessary to build up again later. He thereby defends his existence.
- The supplier views it as more favorable to accept below-capacity employment associated with a cost coverage waiver than to not receive an order at all and thus increase the **danger of the market exit.** He thereby also defends his existence.
- The supplier views it as more favorable to accept below-capacity employment associated with a cost coverage waiver than to enable the **market entry of competitors**. He thereby defends his competitive position.

To offer services from the reasons mentioned below the cost coverage limit will indeed lead to a very high likelihood within the scope of competitive bidding models to receive an order but in reality can lead to exactly the opposite. It can thus be that the supplier will indeed not receive the order for a very low offer because the customer suspects that the supplier will attempt to obtain higher revenue in later renegotiations. This would consequently lead to disputes between the contractual partners and thus almost inevitably lead to increased project costs or project delays so that the customer would prefer a competing supplier in spite of higher prices (Ioanno et al. 2010, p. 936).

As would seem natural in situations of cost coverage waiver the supplier looks into the calculation which is the computational and content-related basis of the offer price. If the supplying company is strongly interested in the order, however, cannot implement a full cost-covering price the question emerges for which **positions** in the calculation can coverage be waived "if need be". The fundamental principle means: If costs have been responsibly acquired and must be covered. If the costs ascribed to the project based on an overarching coverage plan are not covered in this project they must be **additionally** covered by other chronologically subsequent projects. In other words: Each coverage waiver for the costs of a project leads to the increase of the costs of future projects.

Two perspectives must be differentiated for the analysis of the calculation with respect to possible cuts in the cost positions:

- The **economic** perspective of the urgency of coverage of the individual cost types,
- The **company related** perspective of the urgency of coverage of individual cost types.

2.3.1 Economic Perspective

Not all cost types are of the same urgency of coverage **in the short term**. The **project direct costs** are of another short term urgency of coverage than the **project indirect costs** because the project direct costs are caused by the project, however, the project indirect costs are not. Costs which arise due to the implementation of the project are also referred to as relevant costs. If the order had not been accepted these costs also would not have arisen (Plinke and Rese 2006, p. 38; Plötner et al. 2010, p. 24 et seq.). Thus it is obvious to see the relevant costs or project direct costs with an absolute urgency of coverage. To this extent in the literature it is spoken of an "**absolute lowest price limit**" which lies with the project direct costs (thus constitutes a **cost-economical** lowest price limit).

However, such a formulation is suitable to facilitate misunderstandings, if not to produce them: The "absolute lowest price limit" presumes the economic profit objective and assumes a **short-term decision without effects on the subsequent decisions**. This means the lowest price limit decision takes place in one world, which doesn't exist: In the real world cost and revenue linkages always exist for previous or subsequent projects which must be included in the decision making. There are therefore no rules at all for the lowest price limit from an **economic sales** point of view. Every waiver of coverage must be seen as an **investment** in terms of economic sales which shall secure future sales opportunities. In the extreme case the lowest price can be zero or even be negative from this point of view. However it must be considered that depending on the type of project or type of plant the revenue linkages are more differently pronounced since a customer usually only requests one or fewer plants within a certain period. The further the customer's purchase decisions are set apart from each other the more the bonds will fail due to the technological advance or organizational changes (Rese and Herter 2004, p. 975; Plinke and Rese 2000, p. 709).

If one directs one's view on the protection of the company's solvency, a **fiscal** lowest price limit can be found in addition for the **payments-out** induced by the project in the short term.

2.3.2 Company-Related Perspective

The company-related perspective of the coverage urgency of individual cost types is directed at possible "reserves" in the calculation. Thus it can, for example result in a substantial cognitive distance concerning the content of the calculation due to the division of labor between accounting, project planning and sales, in other words: Those who "produce" the calculation have other premises and expectations in the meaning than those who "utilize" the cost information (i.e. take as a basis for price decisions).

Figures 16 and 17 show the various perceptions of the urgency of coverage for common types of costs for business people and technicians in the industrial plant business. Therefore the case occasionally occurs that "fat is put on" deliberately in the creation of the calculation in order to counteract the expected price concessions of the supplier. The latter again suspect or know that or believe to know it and subsequently adjust their behavior accordingly by subtracting out the "fat" again. The manufacturers and users of the calculation mutually counteract their tasks in this way. The consequence in such situations is that suppliers develop a disastrous attitude toward the urgency of coverage of certain types of costs which can condense in price negotiations in too large of a concession.

We can summarize: starting points for the justification of coverage waivers in difficult negotiation situations lie

- in the project indirect costs,
- in the first long-term payments-out associated with portions of costs,
- in the investment character of a coverage waiver and
- in suspected calculation reserves.

The first two viewpoints result in the short-term perspectives which do not apply in the industrial plant business with its long-term structure. Thus they cannot be called upon in the industrial plant business for the justification of coverage waivers.

The last viewpoint leads to an odd way of behaving because no one in the company ultimately still retains the overview of what the calculation actually includes materially, i.e. how great the coverage pressure really is.

The only economically acceptable way to justify coverage waivers lies in the fact that certain company goals are taken as a basis for the price decision. These can be directed towards maintaining or creating potentialities and positions. In the case

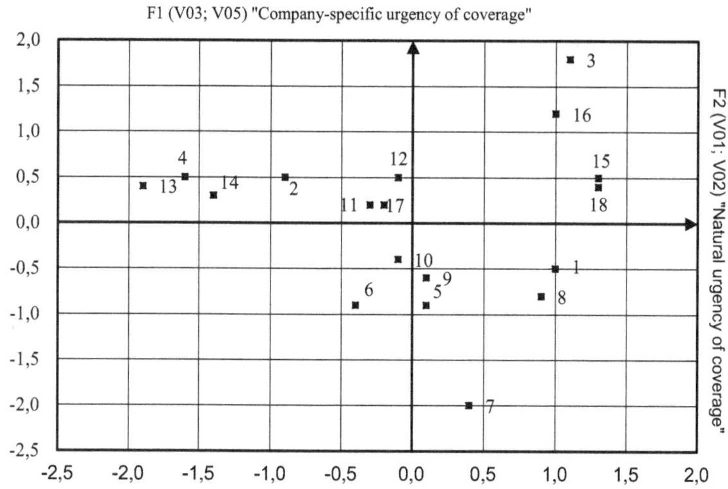

1 Materials
2 Material costs
3 Direct labor costs
4 Production overhead
5 Extra costs of production
6 R&D
7 Engineering
8 Finance costs
9 Currency risks
10 Technical risks
11 Risks from liability
12 Warranties
13 Administrative overhead
14 Sales overhead
15 Freight
16 Commissions
17 Fixed-price surcharge
18 Distribution extra costs

Fig. 16 Perceived urgency of coverage of typical costs types by marketing experts in the industrial plant business (technicians)

of such a justification a coverage waiver must be considered **costs** of the affected measure.

An interpreting of the individual calculation positions with respect to coverage waivers must be avoided in this case. The principle of the greatest possible objectivity and closeness to reality applies for the calculation and that excludes a shortening of individual positions.

The perspective of the coverage waiver as "**the costs of a certain company measure**" also creates the clear necessity of a corresponding explicit justification and furthermore the chance of an efficient long-term coverage control.

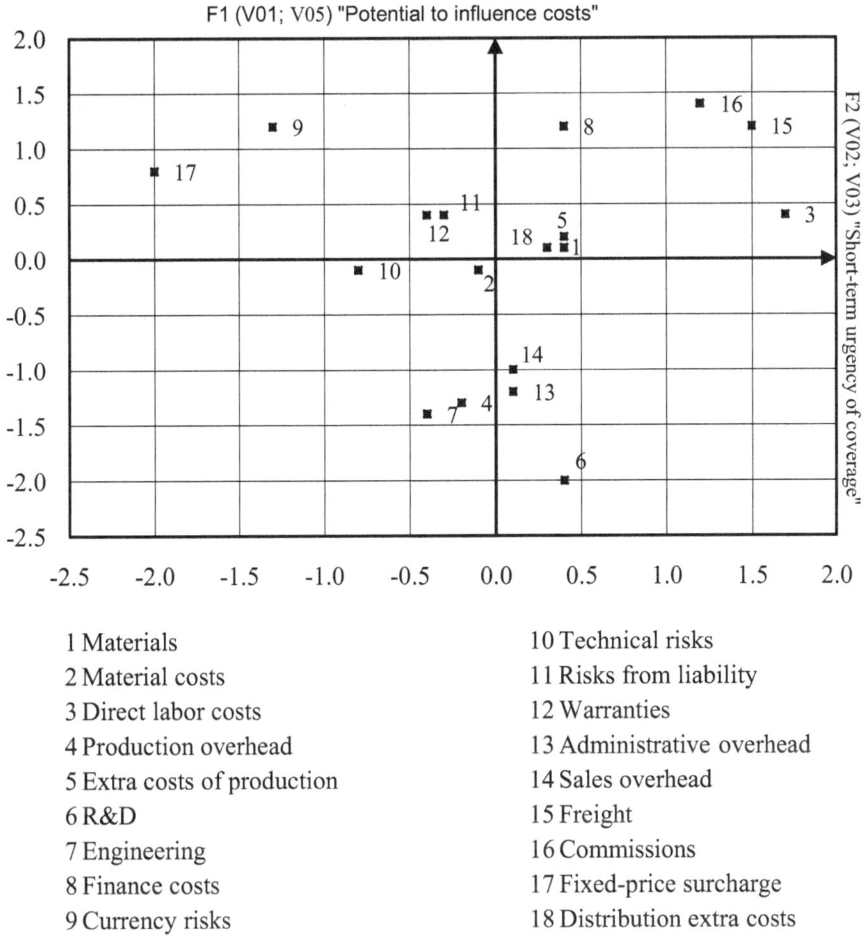

Fig. 17 Perceived urgency of coverage of typical costs types by marketing experts in the industrial plant business (business people)

3 Decision About Calculation Risks

3.1 Problem

A very large number of risks arise in the industrial plant business. The Chapter, however, only deals with the risk resulting from the long-term nature of the project episode and the complexity of the calculation. It is the risk that the cost will turn out different ex post—namely higher—than determined in the offer. The supplier has various options to protect himself against this risk.

One possible approach for the supplying company to cope with the complexity of the planning problem is the adaptation of the **bid form** to the accuracy of the calculation. The reduction of the "commitment" is intended with the differentiation of the offer form which is associated with the offer. It is not always appropriate to assign the plan to a binding **fixed offer**. Rather there are frequent cases in which planned prices are sufficient which are merely roughly estimated. The conditions, under which such an approach appears justified, are

- the inquiring customer is apparently (still) not interested in an order placement at all,
- the supplier is—in general or at this time—not interested in an order but believes in having to provide an offer from fundamental sales policy viewpoints or that the planning period available for the submission of a tender is too short to be able to submit a binding offer.

Two types of offers result from this which contain a substantially reduced risk. In case 1 the supplier creates an **estimated offer** or **provisional offer** on which he is not bound or is bound only in certain spectra to its remuneration amount and appointment details (Kambartel 1973, p. 47 et seq.; Grabowski and Kambartel 1978, p. 38 et seqq.; Weiber and Kleinaltenkamp 2012, p. 264).

In case 2 a **pro forma offer** is submitted which either declared as unbinding or contains such generously measured compensation claims and appointment details that the risk remains manageable. Estimated and provisional offers can by absolutely performed due to the decreased binding nature of the offer with the aid of the kilo cost and material cost methods if corresponding estimate reserves are included.

The actual problem of price planning during the offer phase, however, occurs with **fixed offers**. The supplier's commitment is high, his level of information is low and therefore the uncertainty about the coverage requirement is high. The obvious approach which could reduce the uncertainty would be a detailed project planning prior to the offer submission which constitutes the foundation of a reliable bill explosion and direct cost calculation. The expenditure of time and the costs of these methods are, however, not justified in light of a likelihood of an order of < 1 and because the submission of a tender usually not being recompensed so that other methods of the limiting of the calculation risk must be sought (cf. also Girmscheid 2010, p. 25). These are the fixed-price surcharge, the price reservation and the price adjustment clause.

3.2 Fixed-Price Surcharge

The **fixed price surcharge** shall balance inflationary price developments between the day of calculation and the day of settlement of the project. A lump sum is estimated and the calculated costs are added. The fixed-price surcharge is thus a real cost component and not negotiation reserves. In principle, the fixed-price surcharge is only the computational balance for an incorrect evaluation of the individual positions in the calculation (which is mostly based on current values and not on future values).

3.3 Price Reservation

A fixed price can, however, only be economically reasonable for the supplier if the technical and economic risks are manageable and not to large. In the case of often extreme value volumes from large plants a supplier would possibly realize losses on a single project which endangers his existence if he enters unpredictable risks. One thinks of, for example, the construction of large mountain tunnels, subways, military equipment etc. The **price reservation** in such situations is the contractually agreed upon form of a cost reimbursement price, i.e. the supplier only specifies an initial price which is, however, modified depending on the actual development of costs. The supplier covers calculation risks in the **quantity structure and in the assessment structure** of costs in this manner. The price reservation thus constitutes a method of a contractually anchored **flexible transfer of costs** or cost increases on the customer. This is actually a very welcome instrument for the suppliers (VDMA 1971). The customer will, however, only approve a large procurement risk of this kind if no other supplier is prepared to name a fixed price for the project.

3.4 Price Adjustment Clause

A very large time span partially lies between the conclusion of a contract and the individual service provision in which the cost structure or other framework conditions of the supplier can be permanently changed by general inflation, labor cost increases, raw material price fluctuations or similar. In order to be able to account for such a development and the change in the basis of transaction since the conclusion of contract a **price adjustment clause** is often incorporated into contracts with such long time spans. A proportionality of costs and price development is sought with the price adjustment clause in order to guarantee an equality of performance and counter performance across the entire time span between the conclusion of a contract and the service provision. The price adjustment clause thus constitutes a method of a contractually anchored flexible takeover of price changes by the customer. In contrast to the price reservation it is primarily used to avert uncertainties for commodity prices resulting from the long-term nature of a project. This does not concern the quantity structure for this instrument, but rather solely concerns the **assessment structure** of the costs.

The price adjustment clause has the effect that the price changes for certain commodity types have an effect in a weighting scheme agreed upon beforehand by the supplier and customer. The weighting scheme determines the project revenue and is based on a mathematical formula. It is commonly referred to as price escalation formula.

3.4.1 Configuration of the Price Adjustment Clause

The configuration of a price escalation formula shall be presented in detail in the following with the aid of maintenance contracts from a well-known manufacturer of gas turbines in power plants. The service components of such contracts are mainly spare parts and their assembly and disassembly as well as inspections and repairs of plant sections.

The relevant cost elements of such a contract, which frequently runs across 10 years, are material prices and wages which are contractually agreed upon in the price adjustment clause between the supplier and the power plant operator.

Price escalation formulas in long-term contracts are mostly individually negotiated with each customer depending on the contractually agreed upon scope of services. The weighting of the **main cost factors**, wage and materials as well as the weighting of the fixed proportion, if agreed in a contract, are of special importance in the process. The fixed proportion constitutes the non-adjustable price component. The determination of the deadlines, thus the length of the exact period, across which the prices run, is also of importance and must be determined before the conclusion of the contract.

A typical price escalation formula, as it is used in the gas turbine business but also in other branches, looks like the following:

$$P_1 = P_0(a + m^*(M_1/M_0) + 1^*(L_1/L_0))$$

P_1 is the price to be paid at the time of the service provision. $\mathbf{P_0}$ is the strike price at the time of the conclusion of the contract. M_1/M_0 constitutes the development of a certain index M (material). $\mathbf{M_0}$ constitutes the value of the index at the time of the submission of a tender and $\mathbf{M_1}$ the value of the same index at the time of the service provision. However, a deviating time, for example a fixed deadline can be agreed upon (Gaßmann 2009, p. 18). With the index L and its values $\mathbf{L_0}$ and $\mathbf{L_1}$, which constitute the development of a certain index for wages, it behaves similarly. The factors m, 1 and a result in sum 1. The factor **m** or **l** in the formula prior to the respective index ratio specifies the weighting of the respective index. A factor without index, as in example **a**, mirrors the agreed upon fixed proportion. This proportion of the revenue is not dependent on the market developments and must be paid by the customer without escalation adjustment for the service provision. The fixed proportion in the price escalation formula is not influenced by any index and is thus not adjustable. The inclusion of a fixed proportion in the price escalation formula is based on the idea that a certain percentage of costs of the service to be rendered remains fixed over the entire project period. For example, these could be plants which are already completely written off and thus no longer depict any annual costs in an accounting sense. However since an allegedly fixed costs are subject to price changes across long periods, as they apply for long-term contracts, a real fixed proportion cannot be spoken of in principle. The replacement costs for durable goods, as e.g. production plants are, must also namely be added to the services to be created and must be adjusted in terms of price on an escalation scale. If fixed proportions are agreed upon in the maintenance contract, this means a supplier's concession to the customers for usually increasing main cost factors. The supplier does not invoice all actually incurred cost increases for the customer here. In the event of reverse index development the supplier would not pass on all lowering of costs to the customer. In addition to the traditional form of a price escalation formula depicted above enhancements of the formula also exist for example in the logistics supplier business. These can take into consideration even more indexes, rendered advanced or partial payments as well as flexible ratios of cost components which were necessary due to operational streamlining or technical advances (Witte 2005, p. 31; Backhaus 1979a, p. 44), so-called ratio agreements.

It is necessary during the selection of the index to find such cost factors which are not manipulable and to weigh them in such a way that they are used in the price escalation formula and depict the actual price changes as accurately as possible. Neutrality and independence must be paid attention to in addition during the ascertainment of the index value. The indexes upon which the supplier and the customer agree should therefore be ascertained and published by independent third party institutions (e.g. statistical office, chambers of industry and commerce) so that they can be equally examined by both contracting parties.

Indexes for materials are usually used during the determination of the cost factor materials which mirror the cost development for the material which is mainly required for the service provision. In our example, an index for certain steels or iron products would be suitable for the supplier of gas turbines since a majority of the spare parts are made of steel. However, components from other materials (e.g. nickel alloys and ceramics) are used for maintenance as spare parts so that the actual change in cost can by necessity no longer be depicted by a single material index. Therefore, an index is often used which depicts the price changes for a finished product or a certain product group of which various materials are required for their production. Therefore the so-called turbine index is used in maintenance contracts which contains the price development of related machines. The data from the index development is prepared monthly by the Federal Bureau of Statistics in Wiesbaden, Germany.

If to a great extent the price of a service is dependent on the development of the labor costs, a wage index will be inserted into the price escalation formula as the main cost factor. The wage index shall mirror the development of the wage level.

Since no in-house data can be used due to the influence of the index by the suppliers and for the protection of company secrets an index has to be found which cannot be directly controlled by the supplier. The selected index should therefore depict the developments of wages of an entire industry rather than of a single firm. In the example described, the index is mostly used for the base wage of a skilled worker in the metal and electric industry along with the statutory surcharges according to the tariff for the corresponding tariff zone in Germany. Thus it is possible to preserve neutrality with respect to cost control and to represent the supplier's labor costs in the plant as precisely as possible where a large part of the maintenance personnel is employed. The development of the index is confirmed by the Nuremberg Chamber of Industry and Commerce.

If a substantial portion of the service is rendered abroad by foreign professionals it appears appropriate to integrate a local (foreign) labor cost index into the price escalation formula in addition which, however, can fail in the availability or trustworthiness of the data. An additional problem with the foreign labor cost index lies in the fact that upon the conclusion of a contract it is often still not exactly certain which service shall be provided by domestic or foreign personnel (Backhaus 1979b, p. 6).

During the weighting of factors it must be noted that not only the current allocations of costs but also future developments must be anticipated, in particular new technologies. Since economies of scale or technological advances are often achieved across long project durations which would lower the initial material costs compared to the labor costs. Reversed developments are also conceivable such as for the gas turbine maintenance contracts described by way of example. There more turbine and plant parts could potentially be repaired across the project duration due to improved procedures and no longer had to be replaced by new parts. In so doing it would be offered to consider such cost shifting of material and wage costs and to weigh more heavily the wage costs for the repair services than at the moment of the conclusion of the contract.

3.4.2 Particularities and Contractual Solutions

Not only economic and technical aspects may indeed be taken into consideration during the contractual configuration of a price adjustment clause. Such clauses must also withstand a legal test. In Germany, contracts, which possess a price escalation formula for the determination of the price to be paid, are liable to the so-called **Price Clause Act** (Preisklausel G). This law says in its current version of September 2007 that basically the amount of money debt may not be determined directly and automatically by the price or the value of other goods or services which are not comparable to the agreed upon goods or services (§ 1 Par. 1). The background of the law is that an unlimited use would automatically benefit effective escalation clauses for a monetary value loss, as it happened in the 1920s, and would promote inflation (Reul 2007, p. 445).

Two essential exceptions to the law are formed by the so-called **Suspense clauses** (§ 1 Par. 2 No. 2) and **Cost element clauses** (§ 1 Par. 2 No. 3). A suspense clause sets the change of the amount owed in a relationship to other goods and services if these other goods and services are similar or comparable in essence (Reul 2007, p. 447). In the price escalation formula presented above in the maintenance contracts, the dependency of a part of the price from the turbine index forms a suspense clause. A part of the price for the gas turbine components is measured here with the aid of the development in terms of price of related products, other so-called internal combustion engines.

If the owed amount is made dependent on the development in terms of price for goods or services which have a direct influence on the supplier's costs, one speaks of a cost element clause (§ 1 Par. 2 No. 3). During the use of a cost element clause in a contract it must be considered that in the event of the rise in cost of a cost element this rise in cost is not completely transferred to the total price. A price increase may only take place in the scope in which the cost element has a percentage in the total costs. This means if, for example the wage index increases the price increase resulting from this may only take place in so far as the wage costs also actually determine the total costs of the service to be rendered. This requires a precise as possible factor weighting.

Furthermore the possibility basically exists in the project business or in long-term (supply) contracts to establish a so-called *Ceiling* in a contractual clause in order to protect oneself against too severe price changes. The *Ceiling* constitutes a limitation of the prices ascertained upward by the price escalation formula. The supplier solely bears the risks for cost increases which extend beyond the agreed upon value. The supplier can, however, likewise insist on clauses which prevent revenue erosion to a certain extent in the case of negative index development.

Experience has shown that customers will press for capital goods markets at a fixed price conclusion. The pricing policy starting points also constitute the escalation clause if and when they can be offered parallel to a fixed price offer as alternatives. A broader use of the price adjustment clause as an instrument of the assumption of planning risks by the customer usually only appears in practice when project periods are more than 2 years.

Exercises

1. What is a planned revenue? In which context are planned revenues spoken of?
2. Which relation does the order price bear to the planned revenue?
3. Which order price calculation methods in the industrial plant business do you know? How are these methods distinguished?
4. How do you calculate the quality of a kilo cost estimate?
5. Which relation do the customer benefit and the upper price limit bear to each other?
6. How can an upper price limit be ascertained within the scope of planned revenue?
7. How is the process of competitive bidding characterized? Describe a process for the systematic determination of prices for competitive bidding situations.
8. To what extent is the activity level important for the determination of lowest price limits?
9. Which dangers arise for pricing policy due to misunderstandings of the calculation?
10. Where does the so-called lowest price limit lie in terms of economic sales?
11. To what extent is a price adjustment clause suitable as an instrument for the reduction of calculation risks? Which aspects must be taken into consideration for the configuration of such a clause?

Literature

Alznauer, T., & Krafft, M. (2004). Submissionen. In K. Backhaus & M. Voeth (Eds.), *Handbuch Industriegütermarketing. Strategien—Instrumente—Anwendungen* (pp. 1057–1078). Wiesbaden: Gabler.

Backhaus, K. (1979a). Preisgleitklauseln als risikopolitisches Instrument bei langfristigen Fertigungs- und Absatzprozessen. *Schmalenbachs Zeitschrift für betriebswirtschaftliche Forschung, 31*, 3–10.

Backhaus, K. (1979b). Preisgleitklauseln aus beschaffungsorientierter Sicht. *Beschaffung aktuell, 12*, 41–44.

Backhaus, K. (1980). *Auftragsplanung im industriellen Anlagengeschäft*. Stuttgart: Poeschel.

Backhaus, K., Erichson, B., Plinke, W., & Weiber, R. (2011). *Multivariate Analysemethoden. Eine anwendungsorientierte Einführung* (13th ed.). Berlin: Springer.

Backhaus, K., & Voeth, M. (2010). *Industriegütermarketing* (9th ed.). München: Vahlen.

Bhattacharyya, S. C., & Dey, P. K. (2007). Managing risk in a large rural electrification programme in India. *Impact Assessment and Project Appraisal, 25*(March), 15–26.

Dey, P. K., Tabucanon, M. T., & Ogunlana, S. (1994). Risk management planning for project control through risk analysis: A petroleum pipeline-laying project. *International Journal of Project Management, 12*(1), 23–33.

Edelman, F. (1965). Art and science of competitive bidding. *Harvard Business Review, 43*(1), 53–56.

Engelhardt, W. H. (1977). Grundlagen des Anlagen-Marketing. In W. H. Engelhardt & G. Laßmann (Eds.), Anlagen Marketing. *Sonderheft 7 der Zeitschrift für betriebswirtschaftliche Forschung* 9–37.

Engelhardt, W. H., & Günter, B. (1981). *Investitionsgütermarketing*. Stuttgart: Kohlhammer.

Eversheim, W., Fischer, W., & Minolla, W. (1977). *Angebotskalkulation mit Kostenfunktionen in der Einzel- und Kleinserienfertigung*. Berlin: Beuth.

Feuerbaum, E. (1979). Controlling in einem projektorientierten Unternehmen. In D. Solaro, H. D. Bürgel, E. Feuerbaum, J. Funk, W. F. Gerke, H. R. Kunkowsky, et al. (Eds.), *Projektcontrolling* (pp. 1–47). Stuttgart: Poeschel.

Feuerbaum, E., & Witte, K. (1977). Steuerung der Auftragsabwicklung im Großanlagenbau durch Bildschirm-Dialogverkehr. *IBM-Nachrichten, 27*, 153–160.

Floricel, S., & Miller, R. (2001). Strategizing for anticipated risks and turbulence in large-scale engineering projects. *International Journal of Project Management, 19*, 445–455.

Gaismayer, J. (2011). *Verminderung von Hold-up-Risiken in Nachverhandlungssituationen. Eine empirische Analyse aus der Perspektive von Logistik-Dienstleistern am Beispiel des Kontraktlogistik-Geschäfts*. Wiesbaden: Springer Gabler.

Gaßmann, J. (2009). *Bilanzielle Abbildung von Preisanpassungsklauseln. Im Rahmen von Unterneh-menszusammenschlüssen nach IFRS 3 (rev. 2008)*. Hamburg: Kovac.

Gemünden, H. G. (1980). Effiziente Interaktionsstrategien im Investitionsgütermarketing. *Marketing—Zeitschrift für Forschung und Praxis, 2*(1), 21–32.

Gemünden, H. G. (1981). *Innovationsmarketing. Interaktionsbeziehungen zwischen Hersteller und Verwender inno-vativer Investitionsgüter*. Tübingen: Mohr.

Girmscheid, G. (2010). *Angebots- und Ausführungsmanagement—Leitfaden für Bauunternehmen. Erfolgsorien-tierte Unternehmensführung vom Angebot bis zur Ausführung* (2nd ed.). Berlin: Springer.

Grabowski, H., & Kambartel, K. H. (1978). *Rationelle Angebotsbearbeitung im Unternehmen mit Auftragsfertigung*. Essen: Girardet.

Günter, B. (1979). *Das Marketing von Großanlagen. Strategieprobleme des Systems Selling*. Berlin: Duncker & Humblot.

Herbst, U. (2007). *Präferenzmessung in industriellen Verhandlungen*. Wiesbaden: Gabler.

Homburg, C. (2012). *Marketingmanagement. Strategie—Instrumente—Umsetzung—Unternehmensführung* (4th ed.). Wiesbaden: Gabler.

Verein Deutscher Ingenieure. (Ed.) (1983). *Angebotserstellung in der Investitionsgüterindustrie*. Düsseldorf: VDI.
Ioanno, P. G., Asce, M., & Awwad, R. E. (2010). Below-average bidding method. *Journal of Construction Engineering and Management, 136*, 936–947.
Kambartel, K. H. (1973). *Systematische Angebotsplanung in Unternehmen der Auftragsfertigung*. Dissertation, Aachen.
Kirsch, W. (1978). *Die Handhabung von Entscheidungsproblemen*. München: Kirsch.
Kirsch, W., Lutschewitz, H., & Kutschker, M. (1977). *Ansätze und Entwicklungstendenzen im Investitionsgütermarketing*. München: Schäffer-Poeschel.
Kolb, J. (1978). *Industrielle Erlösrechnung. Grundlagen und Anwendung*. Wiesbaden: Gabler.
Krause, F.-L., Kind, C., & Müller, C. (2005). Prozessoptimierung in der Angebotserstellung. *Wt Werkstattstechnik online, 95*(1/2), 7–10.
Kuß, A. (1977). Competitive-Bidding-Modelle. *Zeitschrift für betriebswirschaftliche Forschung, 29*(4), 63–70.
Laßmann, G. (1979). Erlösrechnung und Erlösanalyse bei Großserien- und Sortenfertigung. *Schmalenbachs Zeitschrift für betriebswirtschaftliche Forschung, 31*(135–142), 153–162.
Oo, B. L., Lo, H.-P., & Lim, B. T.-H. (2012). The effect of bidding success in construction bidding. *Engineering, Construction and Architectural Management, 19*(1), 25–39.
Opitz, H., Brankamp, K., & Kambartel, K. H. (1971). *Systematisierung der Angebotsplanung im Rahmen des integrierten Informationsflusses der Unternehmen*. Opladen: Westdeutscher Verlag.
Oxenfeldt, A. R. (1966). *Executive action in marketing*. Belmont, CA: Wadsworth.
Oxenfeldt, A. R. (1977). The computation of costs for price decisions. *Industrial Marketing Management, 6*(2), 83–90.
Oxenfeldt, A. R. (1979). The differential method of pricing. *European Journal of Marketing, 13* (4), 199–212.
Plinke, W. (1985). *Erlösplanung im industriellen Anlagengeschäft*. Wiesbaden: Gabler.
Plinke, W., & Rese, M. (2000). Analyse der Erfolgsquellen. In M. Kleinaltenkamp & W. Plinke (Eds.), *Technischer Vertrieb—Grundlagen des Business-to-Business Marketing* (2nd ed., pp. 691–760). Berlin: Springer.
Plinke, W., & Rese, M. (2006). *Industrielle Kostenrechnung* (7th ed.). Berlin: Springer.
Plötner, O., Sieben, B., & Kummer, T.-F. (2010). *Kosten- und Erlösrechnung. Anschaulich, kompakt, praxisnah* (2nd ed.). Berlin: Springer.
Rese, M., & Herter, V. (2004). Preise und Kosten—Preisbeurteilung im Industriegüterbereich. In K. Backhaus & M. Voeth (Eds.), *Handbuch Industriegütermarketing. Strategien—Instrumente—Anwendungen* (pp. 969–988). Wiesbaden: Gabler.
Reul, A. (2007). Aufhebung der Genehmigungspflicht bei Wertsicherungsklauseln—Das neue Preisklauselgesetz (PreisklauselG). *Mitteilungen des Bayerischen Notarvereins, der Notarkasse und der Landesnotarkammer Bayern (MittBayNot) 6/2007*.
Rimpau, C. (2011). *Wissensbasierte Risikobewertung in der Angebotskalkulation für hochgradig individualisierte Produkte*. Munich: Utz.
Sandstede, C. (2010). *Verhandlungen unter Unsicherheit auf Industriegütermärkten*. Wiesbaden: Gabler.
Spiegel-Verlag. (1972). *Entscheidungsprozesse und Informationsverhalten in der Industrie*. Hamburg: Spiegel-Verlag.
Statistisches Bundesamt. (2012). Erzeugerpreisindizes gewerblicher Produkte: Deutschland, Monate, Güterverzeichnis (GP2009 2-5-Steller Hierarchie).
VDMA. (1971). *Preisvorbehaltsklauseln in rechtlicher Sicht* (Vol. Sonderveröffentlichung Nr. 2/71). Frankfurt a.M.: Abteilung Recht und Wettbewerbsordnung des VDMA.
Weiber, R., & Kleinaltenkamp, M. (2012). *Business- und Dienstleistungsmarketing*. Stuttgart: Kohlhammer.

Wellensiek, M. (2007). Präzision bereits in der Planung—Featurebasiertes Kostenmanagement in frühen Phasen der Produktgestaltung. *Tools—Informationen der Aachener Produktionstechniker, 14*(1), 10–11.
Witte, H. (2005). Die Bedeutung der Preisgleitklausel für Verträge mit Zulieferern in der Logistikkette. *Europa Regionum, 8*, 25–36.
Yang, J., & Mattfeld, D. C. (2007). Entscheidungsunterstützung für die Ressourcenallokation im internationalen Großanlagenbau. In H.-O. Günther, D. C. Mattfeld, & L. Suh (Eds.), *Management logistischer Netzwerke. Entscheidungsunterstützung, Informationssysteme und OR-Tools* (pp. 137–155). Heidelberg: Physica.
Yosha, R. (2012). Make it not go wrong. Risk management can keep projects from fulfilling Murphy's Law. *Industrial Engineer, 44*(6), 36–42.

Order Financing and Financial Engineering

Klaus Backhaus, Philipp Hupka, and Nico Wiegand

1 Order Financing as a Marketing Tool

As a rule, the execution of major industrial projects and infrastructure works not only poses a series of technical challenges for companies, it also frequently poses considerable financial difficulties for their principals. The reasons for these difficulties can be found in the characteristics of the projects and their principals. On the one hand, major installations require major capital investment long before the first surpluses can be generated. Major projects can reach a scale of up to 500 million euros (cf. VDMA [German Machinery and Plant Manufacturers' Association] 2011b). Due to the long construction phases of up to 10 years, the resulting financial burden can be serious. A concept for bridging the funding gap is therefore often crucial to the concluding of the order. On the other hand, the buyers are often public institutions in financially weak, developing or newly industrializing countries. About a third of the orders received by German plant manufacturers originate from developing and newly industrializing countries (VDMA 2010, p. 7). The provision of funds for the (partial) advance financing of the costs of the project by the buyer is therefore an exception to the rule. It is not an infrequent occurrence for the principal to find it impossible even to secure loans to cover the order price. As such, it is no wonder that in the vast majority of tenders the supplier is asked to submit a detailed financing concept. This enables the customer to spread the adverse impact that the capital expenditure has on its liquidity over a longer period, and to generate at least part of the repayment tranches out of the cash flows produced by the plant (cf. Hombach et al. 1987, p. 3). However, a problem from the supplier's viewpoint is the fact that the relatively small number of projects and their high monetary value as well as the lengthy tendering processes leads to

K. Backhaus (✉) • P. Hupka • N. Wiegand
Marketing Center Münster, Westfälische Wilhelms-Universität Münster, Münster, Germany
e-mail: Klaus.Backhaus@uni-muenster.de; philipp.hupka@uni-muenster.de;
nico.wiegand@uni-muenster.de

M. Kleinaltenkamp et al. (eds.), *Business Project Management and Marketing*,
Springer Texts in Business and Economics, DOI 10.1007/978-3-662-48507-1_4

considerable transparency as regards the financing conditions, which increases their convergence. The structuring of the financing concept consequently becomes a creative challenge and a marketing tool in its own right.

Order financing always becomes necessary if payment overhangs arise due to the different timing and/or amounts of incoming and outgoing payments (cf. Backhaus and Molter 1989, p. 50). Measures for funding these overhangs are the subject of **order financing in the literal sense of the term**. In the export field in particular these measures include not merely the mere procuring of borrowed capital by specialist banks, but also the arranging of credit insurances without which the provision of sufficient capital frequently cannot be ensured. Since major project business is highly international in nature—foreign business accounted for almost 80 % of German plant manufacturers' turnover in 2010 (cf. VDMA 2011a)—in the field of plant financing we generally talk about export-oriented financing concepts.

Order financing activities in the broader sense also include the servicing and handling of the transactions that are connected with the financing. Among these are the selection of the banks for notifying and confirming letters of credit (LCs) and the obtaining of insurances for transferring any risks (cf. Hombach et al. 1987).

As has already become clear, this means that order financing differs considerably from corporate financing. The latter includes all the measures for determining how liquid assets are to be used for refinancing the entire company. International order financing has a different focus: it concentrates on financing a clearly defined project. As such, the term **financial engineering** in the context of order financing must be differentiated from its interpretation as a pure capital market concept. There, financial engineering is understood to mean the structuring of securities to create bespoke financial products (Perridon et al. 2009, p. 24). The financing of major projects includes the capital market option, but it also refers to a combination of further alternatives for planning and devising financing concepts for specific problems which ensure the provision of liquidity during the service provision phase. In practice the combining of various financing options into a single overall package frequently involves fulfilling a series of conditions, which predetermine a specific structure for the bid in advance. Principals may for instance demand special methods of financing, maximum interest rates, or payment terms which extend far into the future—of up to 50 years. In addition, legal provisions in the country to which funds are to be sent, such as the mandatory inclusion of domestic suppliers or credits in the local currency, may influence the options available to the suppliers.

2 Components of Order Financing

2.1 Financial Components

The exact coinciding of inward and outward payments in the construction phase of major international projects represents a theoretical borderline case. Instead, the supplier, which is generally a consortium of various companies, has to ensure that adequate liquid assets are available to provide advance financing for the

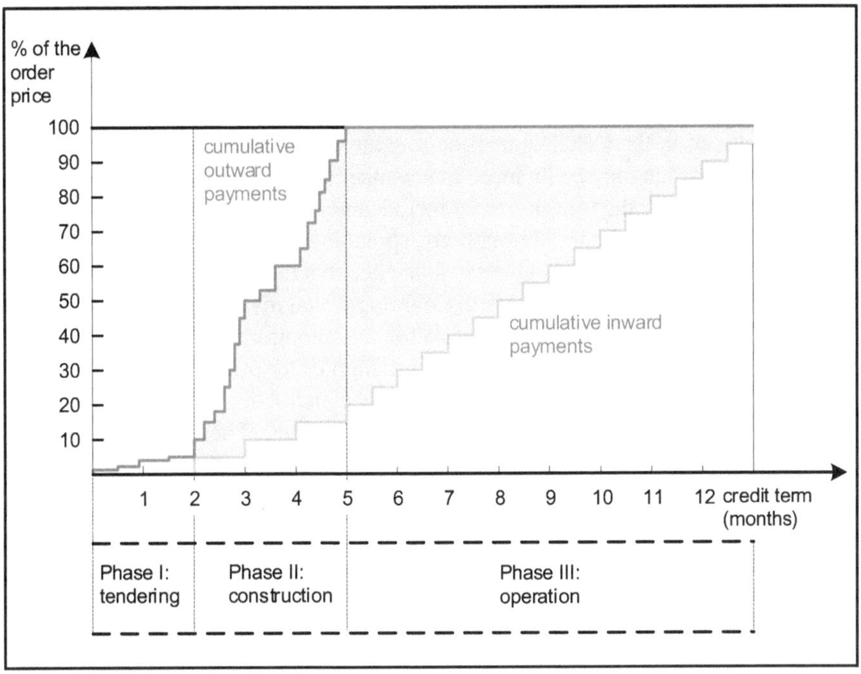

Fig. 1 Illustrative order financing payment profile (based on Backhaus and Molter 1989)

construction. However, that does not mean that the principal does not have to fulfill any financial obligations before the project is completed. In its guidelines on the granting of export credits (the so-called OECD consensus) the OECD specifies that the buyer must pay at least 15 % of the total order price before the beginning of the repayment phase in the form of a down and interim payment (cf. OECD 2011, Chap. II. 10). Repayments of the remaining 85 % of the order price must then be made in equal installments. The stated aim of these rules is to give the financing of exports a binding institutional framework so as to facilitate comparison of financing conditions in competitive tenders, and to base the awarding decision on the determinants of quality and price. Figure 1 shows an example of inward and outward payments in both project phases (construction phase and operational phase) in line with the OECD minimum requirements.

Before an inquiry or tender becomes an order, as well as making efforts to acquire the business the supplier may also already have deposited a tender guarantee and carried out the planning and/or preparation services. Since these **bid costs** are however not included within the order price, they are paid by the supplier alone.

The project's **material and labor costs** are key elements of the order price that has to be financed. It is not only necessary to calculate as precisely as possible in advance the cost of these items throughout the construction phase—and possibly beyond it, any future developments must also be forecast and catered for as necessary. This means that changes in price levels in relation to procurement may drive up construction costs, and consequently also the financing requirements. The parties involved in the project must also cater for the possibility of technological developments and/or a change in customer needs making modifications necessary which may influence both the order price and the length of the construction phase.

Also included in the OECD guidelines are any **profit margins** for the supplier, up to 100 % of which may be financed in advance (cf. OECD 2011, Chap. II. 10). It is normal practice for the margins to be included within the credit, or the insurance taken out in relation to them. Alternatively, spreading the profit over the repayment period may be conceivable, or paying it all at once together with the final repayment installment. However, in these cases discounting of the inward payments would be necessary, which would represent a risk for the supplier that would be hard to calculate given the long repayment phase and high order price.

In addition to the operative costs during the construction phase and the profit shares, **costs are incurred for financing** the project. These have immediate financial implications and they may make up 30 % or more of the overall price of the plant (cf. Feuerbaum 1979). The financing costs include interest payments on the borrowed capital, as well as costs for using hedging instruments for covering risks relating to the financing of exports (Export Credit Cover, ECC). Without these systemic instruments many major projects would fail already at the financing stage. The variety of risks and their relevance as part of order financing are addressed in the following sections.

2.2 Export Finance Risks and the Provision of Cover for Them

The peculiarities of the international industrial plant business that were mentioned at the outset lead to the providers of services being exposed to a multitude of significant risks. Although these risks primarily result from the international nature of the export business and may therefore also be found in sectors other than major plant engineering and construction, the financial loss potential is much higher here (cf. Feuerbaum 1979, p. 23; Funk 1986, p. 17). In addition, the low number of orders placed prevents the natural balancing of risks through the law of large numbers. Figure 2 shows an overview of typical risks of the plant engineering and construction business from the supplier's viewpoint—risks which may be of economic and/or political origin.

Manufacturing and payment default risks are significant due to the customer-specific nature of the services provided. If a buyer is unable, or not allowed, to accept delivery of the plant, the supplier is literally left virtually empty-handed (apart from the portions of the order price that have already been paid prior to completion). The proceeds of any fire sale or resale of the plant are generally significantly lower than the contract price that was negotiated (cf. Häberle 2002a, p. 4). The reasons for the customer's failure to take delivery or its inability to pay may be economic in nature (insolvency), or—something which can also not be excluded depending on the countries to which the exports were intended to be sent—political tensions between the countries which result in trade restrictions. The

	Economic	Political
Manufacturing risk	Customer goes bankrupt prior to completion	Import ban, war, embargo
Payment risk	Customer bankruptcy, composition with creditors	Prohibition of payments, moratorium
Exchange rate risk	Exchange rate of the contract currency falls in relation to the national currency	
Interest risk	Interest rates rise, and increases cannot be passed on	
Costs risks	Prices of supplies increase, wage increases	

Fig. 2 Economic and political risks in the international plant engineering and construction business (Hombach et al. 1987, p. 18)

manufacturing risk commences when the construction works begin, and it ceases once they end. When the completed plant is handed over the supplier usually becomes entitled to payment of the contract price less the advance payments made (cf. Backhaus and Molter 1989[5]). The acquiring of this entitlement to payment (receivable) also marks the point in time when the payment default risk originates, a risk which only ceases once the final installment has been paid. In practice, suppliers can use export credit insurances or banking hedging instruments such as letters of credit and payment guarantees to cover both risks (cf. Häberle 2002a, p. 286).

Since pricing and the calculation of the financing requirements take place prior to the actual provision of the services, trends in the costs of raw materials and labor have to be estimated in order to calculate the order price. The long construction periods make reliable forecasts difficult. If inadequate contractual consideration is given to possible price trends relating to the factors of production, an uncovered **risk of cost increases** arises for the supplier (cf. Backhaus 1979, p. 3). What's more, depending on how the financing conditions are structured, the financing of the order may lead to unexpected costs for the supplier if the interest or the exchange rates alter to its detriment **(interest and exchange rate risk)**. This group of risks is only partly covered by export credit insurances. Since payment guarantees are not used in this area, the risks must above all be mitigated by means of appropriate contract clauses or derivative financial instruments (cf. Hombach et al. 1987, p. 21).

Insurances covering the manufacturing and payment default risks are regularly needed in order to obtain borrowed capital for financing a major project (cf. Sauer 1997, p. 429). That is why it is **export credit insurances** in particular which are used in international plant engineering and construction, and which cover the lion's share of the inherent risks. They compensate the exporter in the event of a payment default or delayed payment on the part of the buyer. There are many financial products available to German exporting companies, each of which is adapted to the particular requirements of various export projects. For an overview of the products available in the Federal Republic of Germany, please go to: www.agaportal.de. The aim of these instruments is to support exporters so that as many projects as possible are carried out due to facilitated access to capital. Unlike private sector companies, state insurance agencies also offer cover for political risks, which is why the majority of coverage instruments are provided by public bodies. The range of causes of manufacturing and payment default risks covered is wide, and it typically includes (cf. Bödeker 1992, p. 372; Matschke and Olbrich 2000, pp. 65–66):

- inability to pay due to insolvency, composition with creditors or unsuccessful enforcement of payment,
- unconditional non-payment and late payment,
- official measures, war, uprisings or revolutions,
- the impossibility of converting or transferring foreign means of payment,
- the impossibility of performing the contract for political reasons,
- destruction or confiscation.

The order price is always insured, less the down payments already made. As a rule, any interest that is incurred is therefore not included in the sum insured. The cover for the manufacturing risk relates to the supplier's own production costs that have been incurred at the time when the insured loss occurs. By contrast, the payment default cover relates to the period following the completion and handover of the plant, and the subject matter of this insurance is consequently the receivable that has been paid to the principal. Specific aspects must also be taken into account, depending on the nature and structure of the credit insurance.

The conditions applying to insurance products mainly differ according to the relevant credit term and amount, the country risk of the country to which the exports are to be sent, and the debtor's creditworthiness (cf. Euler Hermes 2011a, p. 3). In each case a deductible of 5 % of the sum insured is payable by the insured. This residual risk is consequently borne by the supplier. The costs of credit insurance typically comprise charges and processing fees. The latter are solely dependent on the order price that is to be covered, whereas charges are additionally adjusted according to the risk factors that have been described above (cf. Euler Hermes 2011b, p. 2). Classification into country categories plays a key role in this regard for estimating the country-specific risks. Differing charges have to be paid depending on which of seven risk groups (1 = lowest risk, to 7 = highest risk) applies (cf. Euler Hermes 2011b, p. 3). The eighth country category, 0, comprises OECD high-income countries as well as the countries in the eurozone, and is given special treatment in relation to the calculating of charges. A similar classification procedure is used when reviewing the creditworthiness of individual buyers.

As well as export credit insurance instruments, there are also banking hedging products which protect the exporter against payment defaults or the buyer's failure to accept delivery. These include the **payment guarantee** and the **documentary**

	Coverage instruments
Manufacturing risk	- HERMES cover - Irrevocable, confirmed letter of credit - Down payment
Payment default risk	- HERMES cover - Irrevocable, confirmed letter of credit - Payment guarantee issued by a bank - Forfaiting
Exchange rate risk	- Foreign currency option transaction, forward exchange transaction - Foreign currency credits - Forfaiting - Internal compensation of foreign currency receivables with payables - Exchange rate escalation clause
Interest rate change risk	- Interest swap transaction - Passed on to sub-suppliers

Fig. 3 The covering of risks in the long-term exporting field (Hombach et al. 1987, p. 21)

letter of credit. The latter can be used as a payment processing tool and is characterized by the fact that the importer's bank takes its place and acts as the borrower vis à vis the exporter. All the claims for payment must then be settled by the bank after presentation of the appropriate documents substantiating the payment claim (cf. Blomeyer and Kuttner 1992, pp. 60–61). If a second bank which is based in the exporter's country confirms the letter of credit, thereby giving its own promise to pay to the supplier, this mitigates the political risks associated with the purchasing country as well as the economic risks relating to the buyer.

Payment guarantees fulfill a similar function to letters of credit, but are structured differently. Like the letter of credit, they are abstract, i.e. they are independent of the underlying transaction. However, a payment guarantee is not a processing instrument, but a pure hedging instrument. Whereas the documentary letter of credit ensures that performance and counterperformance are carried out equally correctly for both parties, the guarantee is a unilateral cover protecting the supplier against the buyer's payment default or late payment. Here too, political risks can be avoided if the guarantor is based in the exporter's country, or if a bank which is based there gives a counter-guarantee to the importer's bank.

In addition to the typical covering of the manufacturing and payment default risk there are also instruments available for dealing with the other risks that can be covered in the export field. These include products for hedging against interest rate increases and exchange rate fluctuations, such as derivatives which are traded in the capital market (e.g. caps, floors, swaps), or instruments offered by export credit insurers (e.g. interest make-ups, pure cover guarantees, currency guarantees; cf. Ex-Im 2011). The precondition for the necessity of such hedging measures is flexible and volatile underlyings (in this case interest or exchange rates). Figure 3 shows in summary form the typical risks in the international major plant field, and the options for covering them.

3 Parties Involved in the Financing of Major Projects

3.1 Principals and Supplier Consortia

Over the last two decades the market situation with regard to customers and competition in the major international installations market has changed considerably. This is largely due to the meteoric economic rise of the **BRIC states** (Brazil, Russia, India and China), but above all China, which has now become the most important purchasing country for German plant manufacturers (cf. VDMA 2010, p. 8). Over 30 % of the total orders received by German plant manufacturers in 2010 originated from the four BRIC states (cf. here and below VDMA 2011b). Twenty years ago it was less than 10 %. The fastest rate of order volume growth by far is in China, with an increase of 83 % compared to the previous year. Only about a quarter of all exports of major items of plant are to buyers in industrialized countries—mainly the United States (cf. VDMA 2010, p. 6). The share going to newly industrializing countries and developing countries is correspondingly high.

However, the effects of this structural shift in the global balance of economic power can also be seen among suppliers. The number of companies with global operations in the major plant engineering and construction field is constantly increasing (cf. here and below VDMA 2011c). Rapidly growing supply contrasts with only slowly growing demand, which noticeably exacerbates the worldwide competitive situation. It is not least these trends which enable principals to make exacting demands of potential bidders right from the tendering phase. Due to the strength of the customers' position, one also comes across the term **buyer's market** in this connection (cf. Petersen 2004, p. 172).

Due to the complexity of customer requests, special customer preferences, the high degree of specialization involved in the provision of services, and limited access to financing facilities, suppliers often have to put together **consortia of companies** for undertaking major projects. These supplier consortia may include companies from various sectors and/or the same sector (cf. here and below Backhaus and Voeth 2014, p. 406). Frequently it is not only domestic but also foreign, companies that are brought together in a consortium (cf. Häberle 2002a, p. 686). In particular for the very common instances where the submission of a detailed financing concept is specified in the tender specifications as a precondition for the awarding of the contract, banding together in a supplier consortium is absolutely essential (cf. Fieten 1985; König 1982; Siepert 1987). This is due to the following reasons (cf. Siepert 1987):

- Since the financing and insurance of individual customers or countries is only possible to a very limited extent for reasons of risk spreading, the supplier

consortium frequently becomes a **precondition** for a major project being able to be implemented.
- The spreading of the financing and insurance contributions across several members of a consortium or several sub-suppliers, often from different countries, can provide the supplier consortium with **access to more favorable conditions**, which increases the attractiveness of the order financing arrangements for the customer, and consequently the likelihood of the supplier's bid being accepted.
- Due to their differing assessments of the risks, and/or their differing willingness to assume risks, the support of various national export credit insurers may bring about "matching", so that even relatively long fixed-term financing arrangements can be put in place.
- International supplier consortia enable especially favorable **exchange rate trends** to be exploited and the **export subsidies** offered by the respective countries to be used.

Even when various companies come together to form international supplier consortia, the individual project partner nevertheless remains responsible for providing its own share of the financing.

3.2 Financial Intermediaries

The risk structures of international order financing frequently lead to consortia also being formed by the credit institutions involved (cf. Backhaus and Voeth 2014, p. 407). This is not surprising in the light of the large financial sums that have to be financed. Three groups of financial intermediaries may be involved in financing major projects: **private commercial banks** (e.g. Deutsche Bank), **public commercial banks** (e.g. WestLB), and **specialist institutions** (e.g. in Germany KfW IPEX-Bank or AKA-Bank). The banks have various roles in the provision of order finance, including

- as a direct provider of credit (e.g. in connection with supplier or buyer credits),
- as an intermediary between the supplier's foreign bank and the buyer (e.g. in connection with buyer credits), or between the supplier and specialist institutions,
- as a guarantor of the cover of various buyer and supplier risks (e.g. in connection with letters of credit or guarantees).

In Germany it is the commercial banks as a whole which play the most significant role in the provision of export finance. Above all, they act as providers of medium- and longer-term loans, or as intermediaries between the exporter and the specialist institution, and they may be involved in the provision of credit by the latter (cf. Büter 2007, p. 311).

In addition, leading German credit institutions which are particularly involved in the financing of major plant exports have come together under the umbrella of **AKA-Bank (Ausfuhr-Kreditgesellschaft mbH)**. The consortium provides numerous products, both in the field of conventional order financing (e.g. buyer credit or factoring) and for structured financing (e.g. project financing), and in other fields too (e.g. advice and administration services). Various credit lines (limits) are available for the differing purposes for which credit may be provided. AKA-Bank is consequently the equivalent under private law of KfW IPEX-Bank, which is under federal and regional government ownership.

3.3 Export Credit Insurances

In virtually all the export-oriented industrialized countries credit insurance institutions have developed which act as intermediaries between companies and the state for the promotion of exports (so-called Export Credit Agencies or ECAs). These ECAs may operate both as public institutions acting directly on the respective state's instructions, or as private companies acting on behalf of the state (cf. OECD 2011; Stephens 1999). They typically provide instruments for covering risks in order to facilitate the provision of credit for export purposes by the banks. However, depending on the structure of their business model, ECAs may also act directly as providers of credit.

In Germany, Euler Hermes Kreditversicherungs-AG and PricewaterhouseCoopers AG WPG provide so-called **export guarantees** on behalf of the federal government, as well as other insurance products. Since Euler Hermes is the leading German credit insurer with a market share of almost 40 % (cf. Atevis 2011) and it is the federal government's leading appointed representative, in practice these products are also called **"Hermes covers"**.

In the international field Berner Union (BU) is the largest association of export credit insurers (cf. here and below von Bernstorff 2007, pp. 106–107). Its members have set themselves the goal of ensuring adherence to international standards, above all the OECD guidelines, and of supporting the development of new, properly functioning ECAs. In order to achieve these goals the BU has among other things drawn up a "General Understanding" based on the OECD consensus which takes up certain points in the OECD rules and specifies them in greater detail.

4 Financing Instruments

A multitude of financing options has developed for covering the liquidity requirements relating to major international projects. As well as the "classic" forms of finance provision, loans and forfaiting, further options have been developed for providing infrastructure projects with the necessary capital (cf. Metschies 1995, pp. 111–112). This development is attributable in particular to the fact that the conventional order financing instruments are reaching their limits more and more frequently when it comes to financing really large plant or infrastructure projects. The conventional and other financing options are shown below.

4.1 Conventional Order Financing

4.1.1 Supplier Credit

The term 'supplier credit' is frequently misinterpreted since in the field of international exports it precisely does not relate to the provision by the supplier of a payment term for the buyer. If the supplier provides the buyer with a "credit" in the form of a payment condition, this is called a **supply contract credit** (cf. von Bernstorff 2007, pp. 104–105). This involves the customer paying off the export receivable in stages according to the agreed payment schedule once delivery has been taken of the exported goods.

However, in order to refinance the payment term that has been agreed, the supplier uses a **supplier credit** from his export bank if it cannot itself muster the financial resources to finance upfront the costs which arise. The supplier credit is accordingly always based on an export supply contract which specifies a payment obligation on the part of the customer (cf. von Bernstorff 2007, p. 109 [**11**]). The repaying of the credit provided is linked on a regular basis to the receipts of the repayment installments from the buyer. The supplier's export bank checks in advance the creditworthiness both of the exporter with which it is in a direct credit relationship and of the importer on whose payments it is effectively reliant. In order to reduce the manufacturing and payment default risk, it also demands certain forms of security (Hermes cover, payment guarantee issued by the importer's bank, assignment of the export account receivable, rights of lien). In practice, the credit securities are limited in the majority of cases to the Hermes cover and to forms of assignment of receivables by the exporter (cf. von Bernstorff 2007, p. 109 [**11**]). Whilst the transfer of the export receivables can be undertaken without being disclosed, the assignment of the export security to the bank must be notified to the importer (cf. Büter 2007, p. 310 [**15**]). From the perspective of the export bank both instruments have to be used simultaneously in order to

- reduce the risk of payment default by the buyer (Hermes cover), and
- to cover the risk of payment default by the supplier (assignment of receivable).

Figure 4 shows the structure of a supplier credit in conjunction with Hermes cover in a simplified manner.

In some cases this basic structure is expanded by the inclusion of additional participants. A specialist institution (AKA or in exceptional cases KfW-IPEX Bank) may therefore be used to provide credit, which involves the export bank undertaking the (partial) refinancing of the supplier credit in this set-up (cf. Voigt and Müller 1996, p. 139). Depending on how the credit relationship is structured, other configurations are conceivable in which specialist institutions may play differing roles.

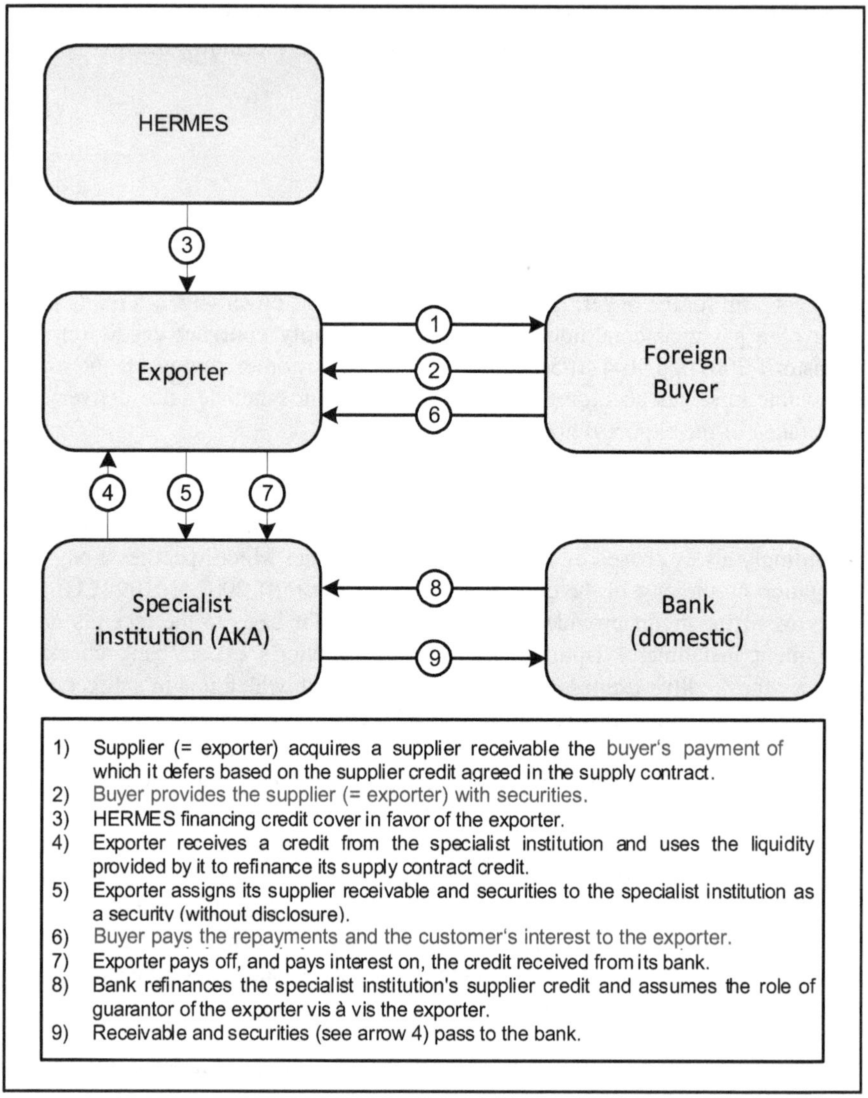

Fig. 4 Basic structure of a supplier credit in conjunction with Hermes cover (Häberle 2002a, p. 703)

In comparison with the early days of German export promotion, the practical significance of the supplier credit has diminished in overall terms (cf. Büter 2007, p. 310). Indeed, supplier credits are now only used by KfW-IPEX Bank in justified exceptional cases. The buyer credit has developed into the main instrument of conventional order financing (KfW-IPEX 2011, p. 8), and this will be examined in more detail below.

4.1.2 Buyer Credit

A buyer credit involves the export bank concluding a **direct credit agreement** with the importer (conventional buyer credit) or with the importer's main bank (bank-to-bank credit) (cf. Matschke and Olbrich 2000, p. 97). In order for a buyer credit to be provided it is not the foreign purchaser or buyer but the exporter which has to submit an application to its export bank (cf. Häberle 2002a, p. 709). However, apart from making the application, the exporter is not involved in the financing and consequently it also does not burden its balance sheet with additional risks (cf. Häberle 2002a, p. 694).

In contrast to the supplier credit, the buyer credit was originally used purely for financing the importer's obligation towards the exporter **following the completion of the plant/installation**, in other words for financing the supply contract credit. In these cases it was necessary from the supplier's point of view to provide a different form of advance financing of the costs which arise during the construction phase (e.g. by using a supplier credit). It is now increasingly agreed that the buyer credit should be paid out on a **pro rata** basis in line with progress towards completion, and the buyer credit is consequently a form of financing which is closely tied to service provision, and a more comprehensive alternative to the supplier credit (cf. Becker 2000, p. 68).

In the case of the buyer credit, the credit amount may be paid out in various ways. It is possible to transfer the capital **directly to the customer**, and this is often undertaken via its import bank (cf. Häberle 2002a, p. 693). The customer uses the liquidity to repay the supply contract credit, so that the exporter's account receivable is extinguished. However, from the customer's point of view it is merely the creditors which have changed, so that the amount to be repaid and the interest no longer has to be paid to the supplier under the supply contract credit, but is instead payable to the supplier's commercial bank under the buyer credit.

In the case of a **bank-to-bank credit** the customer's import bank handles the customer's payment obligation independently, in other words without forwarding the funds to the customer. It is also possible to avoid entirely sending the funds via the country to which the plant is to be exported, and the buyer credit can be directly paid out to the exporter. Figure 5 shows the aforementioned form of buyer credit where payments are made to the exporter.

It becomes clear that the transfer of securities is also a prerequisite for the provision of a buyer credit in order to protect the export bank from payment default. As a rule, the commercial bank providing the credit demands that the borrower (buyer or importer) provides cover for the repayment in the form of a payment guarantee issued by the import bank or the respective state (cf. Häberle 2002a, p. 711). Furthermore, financing credit cover provided by Hermes or another ECA is regularly used (cf. AKA Bank 2011). Only in exceptional cases (e.g. excellent creditworthiness of the buyer, guarantee provided by an especially credit-worthy import bank, low political risk etc.) can financing without, or with only partial, Hermes cover be considered (cf. Häberle 2002a, p. 711).

In addition, further duties have to be fulfilled by the exporter. The supplier's commercial bank frequently demands the provision of a so-called **export**

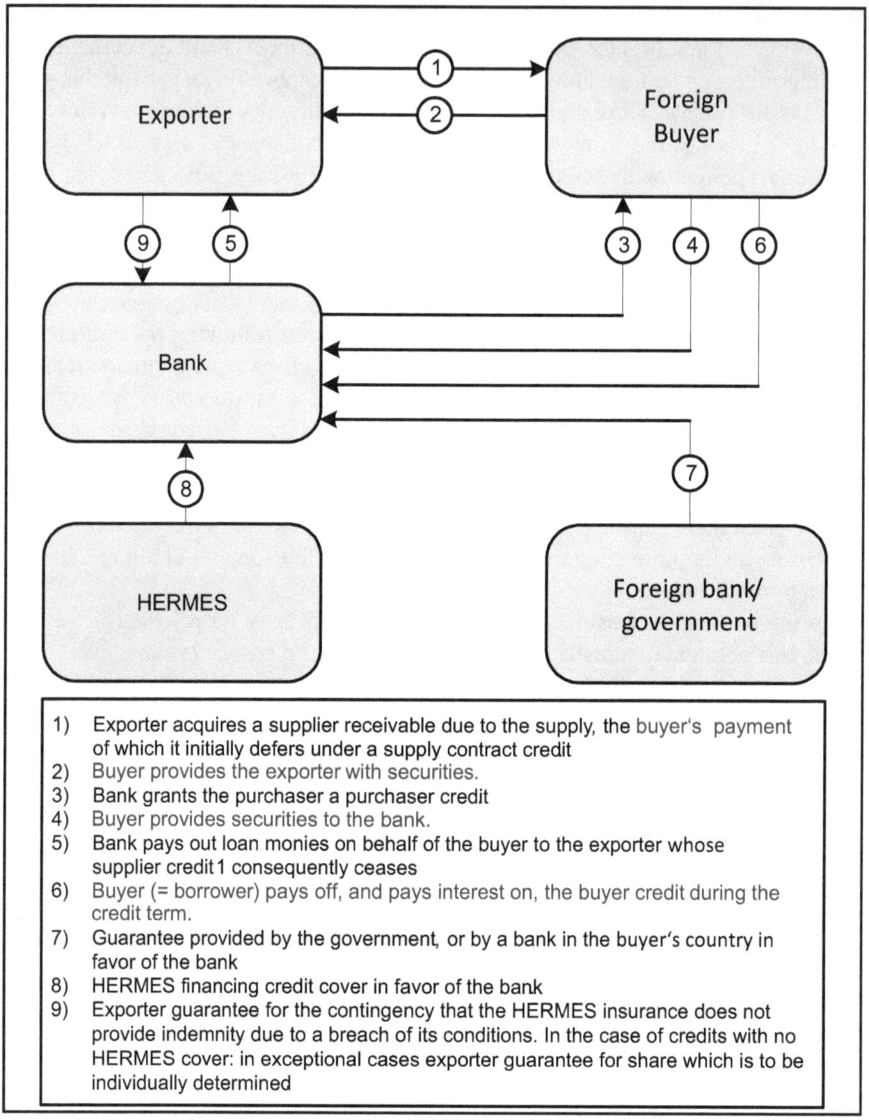

Fig. 5 Basic structure of a buyer credit in conjunction with Hermes cover (Voigt and Müller 1996, p. 191)

guarantee which contains specific duties relating to the provision of information and certain contingencies, and which may include an obligation to pay the charges for the Hermes cover (cf. AKA 2011; Häberle 2002a, p. 712). It also sets out provisions for the payment by the exporter of the interest differential which arises if the bid interest rate specified in the supply contract credit is lower than the interest rate allowed by the credit institution under the buyer credit (cf. Backhaus and Voeth 2014, p. 408).

4.1.3 Forfaiting

Forfaiting means the **sale without recourse of the export account receivable** of the supplier (seller) to a buyer of receivables, the so-called forfaiter (cf. Matschke and Olbrich 2000, p. 100). The buyers are usually banks or specialized forfaiting companies (cf. Bannier 2005, p. 1). As in the case of a buyer credit, the basis of the sale of the receivable by the exporter is the provision of a payment term to the importer, i.e. the existence of a supply contract credit. The term forfaiting is derived from the French "à forfait" ("lock, stock and barrel" in English), i.e. the receivable is sold together with **all of its inherent opportunities and risks** (cf. Büter 2007, p. 323). The assigning of the receivable is therefore explicitly accompanied by the waiving of any recourse against the seller of the receivable. The exporter is only liable for the legal existence of the receivable. Figure 6 shows the parties involved and their roles in a forfaiting transaction.

Unlike **export factoring**, forfaiting involves the sale of individual high-value receivables (cf. Büter 2007, p. 324). This means that they generally relate to major industrial projects, and not consumer goods or service transactions as is usual in the case of factoring. Moreover, in line with the characteristics of international plant business, the cover for transaction-specific risks is more comprehensive in the case of forfaiting, and it includes political and exchange rate risks in addition to the customer's payment default caused by business reasons (cf. Büter 2007, p. 324).

From the exporter's point of view the sale of its export receivable produces a series of advantages (cf. Matschke and Olbrich 2000, pp. 103 and 104):

- Transfer of all the risks associated with the receivable to the forfaiter
- Alleviation of the balance sheet
- Increase in liquidity margins
- Release from the duties involving financial outlays in relation to the administration and collection of receivables
- ECA cover not necessary
- Reduction of interest charges due to possible repayment of existing credit lines
- Simple processing of the sale of the receivable

Despite all the advantages, in practice it turns out that the sale of the receivable cannot be carried out, or can only be carried out by accepting certain restrictions. On the one hand, due to the comprehensive transfer of all the liability risks, forfaiting involves considerable **costs** for the supplier. These are dependent on a large number of influencing factors and include in particular an interest rebate (discounting of the future repayments to be made by the importer), a risk premium, the costs of processing the receivable, and any commitment fee (cf. Voigt and Müller 1996, p. 194 and following). Also, certain preconditions must be fulfilled in order to be able to use forfaiting as a financing and coverage instrument:

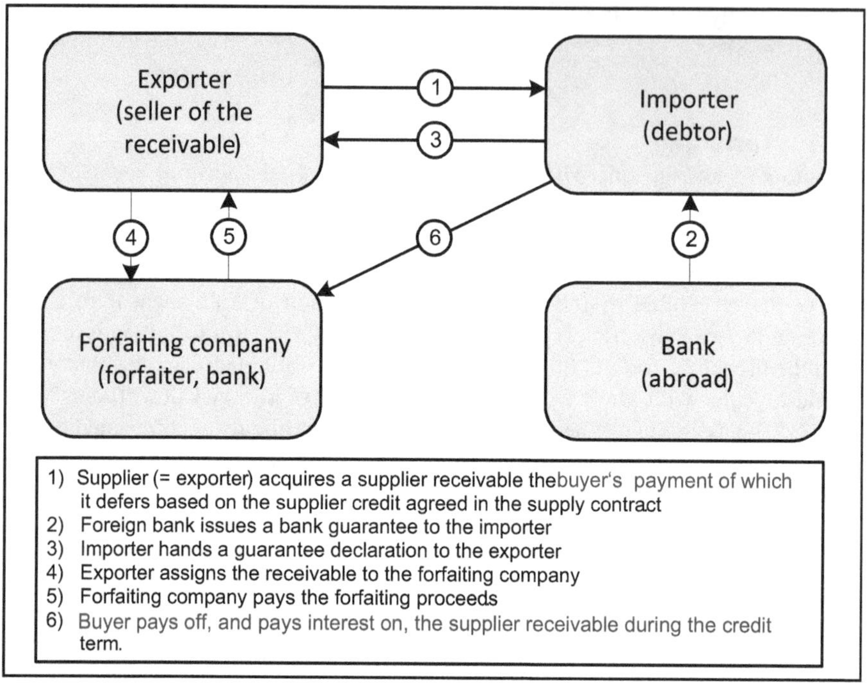

Fig. 6 Basic structure of forfaiting (Häberle 2002a, p. 774)

- Forfaiting relates to the purchase of medium- or long-term receivables. Typically accepted residual terms range from 6 months to 5 years (cf. Putnoki 2000, p. 143) and are dependent on the assessment of the customer and country risks. Forfaiting is not possible if creditworthiness is poor.
- The export receivable must generally be secured by the importer's bank, e.g. through the provision of a payment guarantee (cf. Häberle 2002b, p. 311).
- Due to the high value of the receivable and the risks associated with this, it is often not possible to transfer the whole receivable to a forfaiter. It must instead be possible to make partial transfers.
- Since the forfaiter cannot issue hedging instruments in all valid currencies and utilize refinancing options with matching maturity periods, the receivable must be issued in a freely tradable currency (as a rule the currencies of the principal industrialized countries) (cf. Häberle 2002b, p. 304 et seq.).

Due to these obstacles which are insuperable in some cases, many exporters are frequently left with no option but to have recourse to the tried and tested instruments of supplier credit and/or buyer credit. In addition, over time financial engineering has produced other forms of financing which provide new possibilities for spreading risk and can be used in the export field.

4.2 Further Financing Options

4.2.1 Mixed and Co-financing

A further financing option is provided by mixed and co-financing. Both financing models are a combination of development aid finance and commercial development credits provided through the financial collaboration (FC) between the **Federal Ministry of Economic Cooperation and Development** (BMZ) and KFW Development Bank (cf. Backhaus and Voeth 2014, p. 421). In the context of public development aid these forms of financing are part of the bilateral development aid which is directly provided to a developing country, in contrast to multilateral development aid funds which are provided to international development aid organizations (cf. Backhaus and Siepert 1987, pp. 261 and 262). The FC is based on the development policy idea of supporting measures which are of lasting importance for the development of partner countries (cf. here and below BMZ 2012). The current focus here is in particular on investment projects for education and health systems, and for water supply and waste water/sewerage systems, the energy sector, climate protection, and agriculture. In Germany the funds are pledged in a standard credit agreement and allocated by KFW Development Bank so that the private commercial banking sector does not have any access to public development aid funds (cf. Klöpper 1990, p. 103). The conditions for the allocation of funds are separately reviewed and determined for each investment project by the BMZ in cooperation with the Federal Ministry of Finance, the Federal Foreign Office, and the Federal Ministry for Economic Affairs and Energy.

An **export guarantee** issued by Hermes-Kreditversicherungs-AG plays an important role within mixed financing as the precondition for the awarding of the export credit by KFW Development Bank. Due to the guarantee being restricted to German supplies and services, the Hermes insurance system, and consequently also mixed financing, are to be regarded as a means of promoting exports by German companies (cf. here and below Backhaus and Voeth 2014, p. 422). The BMZ awarding guidelines support the Hermes cover being formally linked to numerous clear indicators of the intent to promote exports. This intent is put into practice in the tendering of services which takes place exclusively in the German market. This means that German companies are very involved in the selection process for development projects. Such projects are only reviewed once the contract has been awarded to a German company.

Mixed financing is not an exclusively German phenomenon, it is actually used by a large number of nations. This entails the danger of a subsidy competition between various industrialized countries aiming to secure orders for their own exporters. In order to counter this danger, the **OECD consensus** has since 1987 incorporated a so-called **"gentleman's agreement"** which is intended to ensure the proper allocating of officially supported export credits (cf. OECD 2011, p. 5). Export credits linked to supplies are accordingly now only to be provided for countries, sectors or projects which cannot demonstrate any other means of access to capital markets.

Developments over recent years show that the consensus rules are being accepted. Mixed financing is consequently becoming less and less important, and it is being replaced by co-financing (cf. here and below BMZ 2012). In co-financing the funds provided are secured by a guaranty which is shown within a separate overall guaranty limit in the federal budget. The consequence of this is that companies are not tied to the supplies and services of German companies. The increasing importance of this financing instrument is made clear by the amount of the funds provided by KfW Development Bank. Whereas in 2006 the total amount of support was barely 2.4 billion euros, 4 years later—despite the financial crisis—pledges constituting a 4.5 billion euros facility were made (cf. KfW 2011, p. 53).

4.2.2 Export Leasing

In general terms, export leasing is one of the financing instruments with a medium- or long-term refinancing timeframe. Synonyms for this term are often found in the literature on the subject, such as cross-border leasing, or international leasing. All the terms are based on the idea that a lessor concludes a contract with a buyer or lessee that is not based in the same country for the provision of consumer durables and capital goods in return for the payment of lease installments for a specific period (cf. Häberle 2002a, pp. 739–740). A **classification of variants of export leasing** can be undertaken based on the type of leased property, the nature of the relationship between the lessor and the lessee, the place where the lessor has its head office, or also the nature of the obligations in the lease contract. Figure 7 provides an overview of the classification of export leasing contracts, whilst Fig. 8 shows the basic structure of export leasing financing arrangements.

If the focus is on the type of leased goods, then it is possible to distinguish between the leasing of movable property, immovable property, specialist goods, and general goods (cf. here and below Matschke and Olbrich 2000, p. 112). Movable property leasing means the leasing of movable consumer durables. By contrast, the term 'immovable property leasing' is used "if the leased goods which form the basis of the export transaction are immovable consumer goods". These are often so-called turnkey projects which are handed over to the lessee by foreign suppliers in a ready-to-operate condition. In 2011 movable property leasing accounted for 21.4 % of total German investment in equipment, whereas immovable property leasing represented a smaller share of overall construction industry investment at just 2.4 % (cf. Ifo Institut 2011, p. 6). The difference between the leasing of general goods and specialist goods can be attributed to the specifying of a product for the lessee. Whilst standardized products may be included in the general goods leasing category, the leasing of products which are tailored to the lessee's specific needs is designated as specialist goods leasing.

However, if instead of differentiating according to the type of leased property one differentiates according to the relationship of the foreign lessee to the domestic producer of the leased goods, a distinction can be made between direct and indirect export leasing. If the exporter of the product is also the lessor, one generally refers to this as direct export leasing (cf. Voigt and Müller 1996, p. 188). If a leasing company handles the contractual arrangements between the lessor and the lessee,

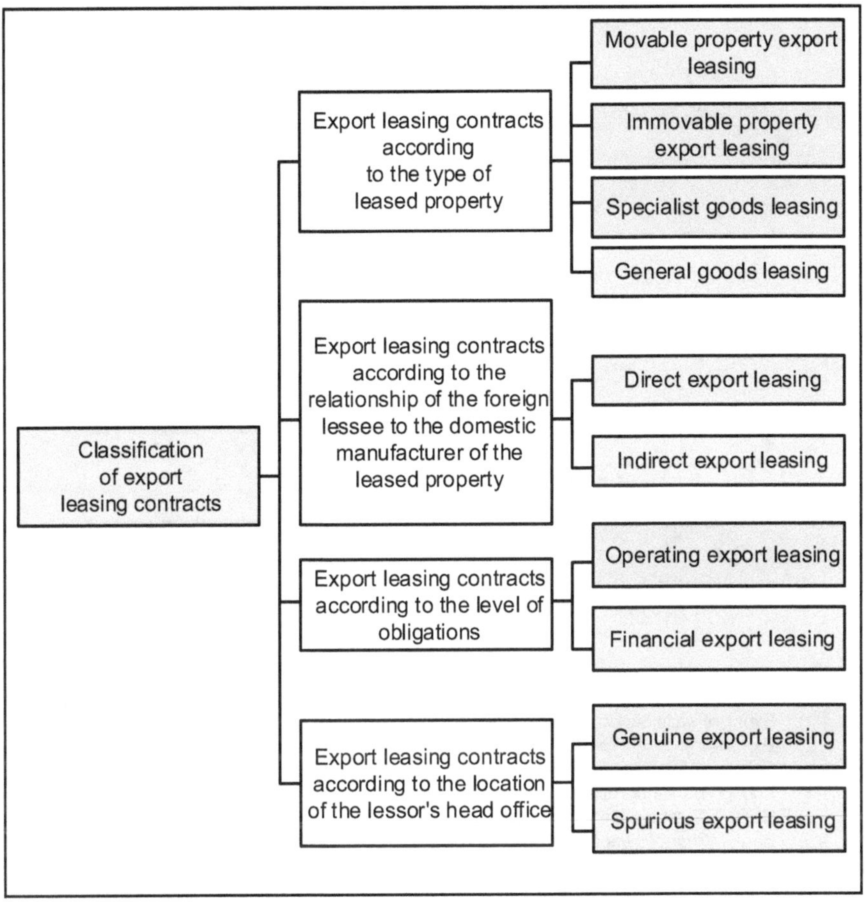

Fig. 7 Classification of export leasing contracts (Matschke and Olbrich 2000, p. 112)

and if the leasing company is refinanced by a bank, this is referred to as indirect leasing.

Operating export leasing and financial export leasing are distinguished from each other based on the level of obligations arising from the export leasing contracts (cf. here and below Matschke and Olbrich 2000, p. 114 **[39]**). Operating export leasing is based on a type of rental agreement which either party can withdraw from either immediately or subject to observing short notice periods. This entails some risks for the lessor:

- Bad investments which lead to the breaking off of the contractual relationship must be liquidated in order avoid losses as far as is possible.
- The risk of the accidental destruction of the leased property is borne by the lessor.

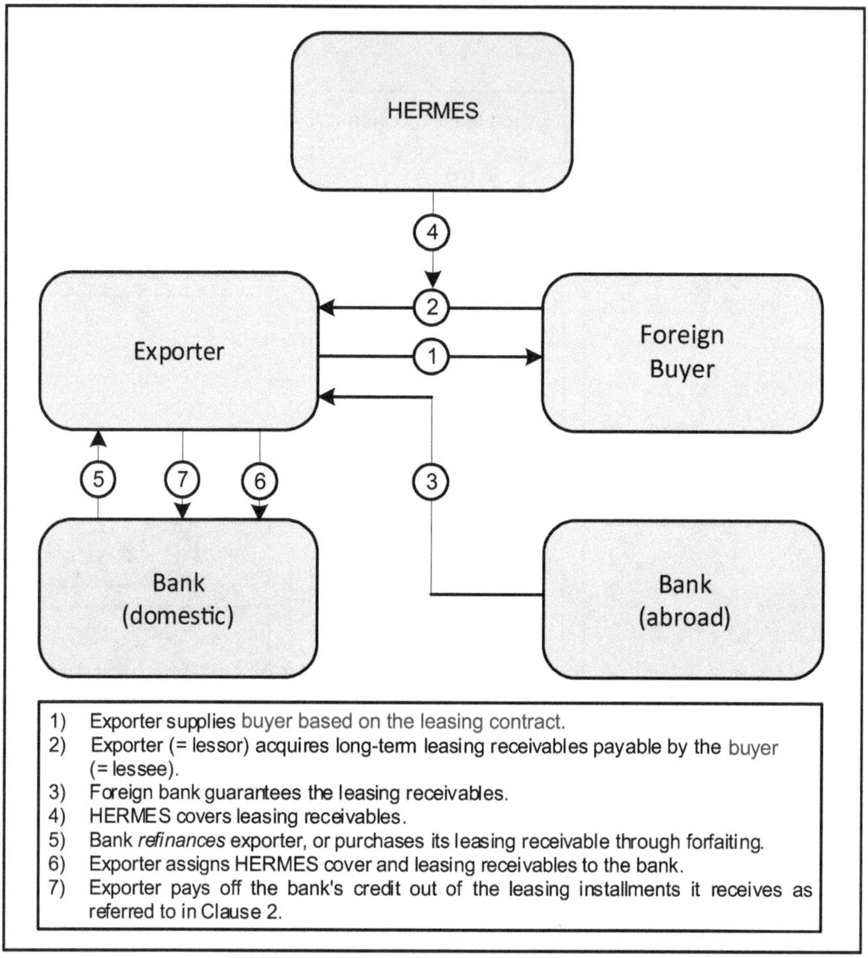

Fig. 8 Structure of export leasing financing arrangements (Voigt and Müller 1996, p. 191)

- The costs of maintaining the leased property (e.g. for service and repair) have to be borne by the lessor.

This type of export leasing is therefore only suitable for **standard goods** of no, or limited, individuality. Standardization also leads to maintenance costs being minimized.

However, the level of obligations imposed by the export leasing contracts may also relate to the benefits in kind provided by the leased property. In this type of leasing **(financial export leasing)** a basic rental period is agreed which is based on the anticipated period during which the leased goods will be used. This therefore rules out the possibility of early cancellation, which means that the lessee bears the

		1	2	3	4	5	6
		Exporter	Buyer	Leasing firm in home country 3)	Leasing firm abroad 3)	Bank in home country 3)	Bank abroad 3)
1	Exporter		leased to ⇧	sold to ⇧	sold to ⇧	sold to ⇧	(sold to) ⇧
2	Buyer	leased from ⇧		leased from ⇧	leased from ⇧	(leased from) ⇧	(leased from) ⇧
3	Leasing firm in home country 3)	purchased from ⇧	leased to ⇧		leased to ⇧	is financed by ⇧	is financed by ⇧
4	Leasing firm abroad 3)	purchased from ⇧	leased to ⇧	leased from ⇧		(leased)/ is financed by ⇧	is financed by ⇧
5	Bank in home country 3)	purchased from/ finances⇧	(leased to) ⇧	finances 1) ⇧	finances/ (leased to) ⇧		finances 1) ⇧
6	Bank abroad 3)	(purchased from) ⇧	(leased to) ⇧	finances 1) ⇧	finances 1) ⇧	finances 1) ⇧	

1) Financing arrangements: credits or forfaiting relating to a single transaction
2) Abroad = buyer's country
3) Home country = exporter's country.

Entries in brackets: non-typical relationships
Marked fields: component of a spurious export leasing arrangement

Fig. 9 True and spurious export leasing financing arrangements (Voigt and Müller 1996, p. 190)

risks referred to above. This form of export leasing is used in particular in the case of **non-standardized goods** in order to protect the lessor.

Genuine export leasing only exists when the lessee and the lessor do not have their registered head office in the same country. Otherwise the term used is spurious export leasing (cf. Fig. 9). The forms which spurious export leasing takes depend on the basic variants of export financing that have already been mentioned above: supplier credit, buyer credit, and forfaiting. An overview of true and spurious leasing based on how the relationships between the parties involved are configured clarifies the mechanisms used for export financing.

Various aspects have a bearing on the decision to use an export leasing solution and the specific structure that it will take (cf. Voigt and Müller 1996, pp. 189–190):

- the tax treatment of lessee and lessor compared to the purchasing of a capital good,

- tax incentives for leasing transactions undertaken with lessors in the ordering country compared to leasing transactions where the lessor is outside the ordering country,
- interest rate differentials between the countries which may lead to more favorable refinancing conditions being obtained from a foreign bank compared to a domestic bank,
- differences in the taxation of interest between the ordering country, the exporting country and other states,
- the existence and structuring of bilateral double taxation agreements,
- political risks in the various countries,
- technical know-how of the leasing parties.

The large number of factors to be taken into account shows the complexity of the situation in which the decisions are to be made. This financing instrument has not been used particularly frequently up to now, at least not in Germany. Only in the case of leased goods such as major installations etc. can specialized providers of financial services be found in the market which offer appropriate leasing solutions (cf. Voigt and Müller 1996, p. 193).

4.2.3 Compensation

If due to **a lack of clarity concerning future political developments** normal export financing instruments and risk covers cannot be considered, or their use is made more difficult, compensation agreements are frequently considered for the processing of exports instead of financial credits (cf. Sauer 1997, pp. 436–437). **Compensation transactions** in the context of industrial goods marketing are defined as transactions in which "specific economic entities intentionally engage in the reciprocal exchanging of real goods (in other words material goods and/or services), irrespective of whether or not payments are also made" (Schuster 1979, p. 15). Cowdell et al. (2000) basically cite two factors which have led to the development of compensation transactions:

- **Lack of financial strength** in the form of foreign exchange assets does not allow some countries to raise the financial consideration that needs to be provided in exchange for imports. Compensation transactions are consequently the only available means left to them for participating in global trade.
- Developing countries use the option of compensation transactions in order to **encourage** their own **export sector** by linking exports to import transactions.

Compensation transactions should be differentiated as between full and partial compensation transactions, and between own and third party compensation. (cf. here and below Kutschker and Schmid 2008, pp. 35–36). **Full compensation** always occurs if it is exclusively real goods and services which are exchanged. If part of the service is offset by money, this is known as **partial compensation**. It is possible to make a distinction between **own and third party compensation** according to whether the exporter of the service uses the goods deriving from the compensation transaction exclusively for its own purposes, or whether the compensation goods are provided to third parties (e.g. intermediaries or end consumers).

In practice, various versions of compensation transactions have developed. Two categories of compensation transactions should be distinguished in this regard. Firstly, there are the so-called **barter transactions**, which include the classic barter, the closed-end barter and the clearing account barter. These transactions are handled within a single contract and are always full compensation transactions. Then there are **parallel transactions**, which are frequently found in practice. These include counter-purchase and offset transactions as well as buyback and cooperation agreements (Cowdell et al. 2000, pp. 232–233; Büter 2007, p. 87 and following; Kutschker and Schmid 2008, pp. 36–37). In the case of parallel transactions, two separate contracts are concluded between the importer and the exporter in respect of performance and counterperformance.

The **classic barter** (often also called "pure barter") means an exclusive exchange transaction involving real goods or services between the exporter and the importer (cf. here and below Büter 2007, p. 87). This is why classic barter transactions are always full compensation transactions. The pure exchanging of real goods or services does not harbor any exchange rate risks, which is advantageous in the case of long contract terms and uncertain exchange rate trends. However, the risk of imperfect evaluation of value and counter-value is associated with the exchanging of real goods and services. This results from the fundamental problem that the reciprocally provided services cannot be objectively equated to each other.

This is the problem which the form of transaction called **close-end barter** seeks to address. In this type of exchange of goods and/or services the exporter initially receives the consideration that is to be provided, which is then checked and used, or re-sold in a sales market. This enables an objective evaluation based on market prices to be obtained, which minimizes the risk for the exporter of an uncertain valuation of the consideration that is to be provided.

Clearing account barters are a special form of barter transactions in which a bilateral trade agreement is concluded between the parties. This contract is valued in so-called clearing account units which serve as a line of credit at the central banks of the countries of the contracting parties and are managed in a clearing account (cf. Huszagh and Barksdale 1986, p. 23). The exchanging of goods and services is settled via this clearing account (cf. with respect to the details of this Hennert 1990, p. 244).

The barter transactions referred to here are to be viewed as **basic types of compensation transactions** where no financial consideration is provided. In practice there are often variations of these types of transaction. If, for example, more than two parties are involved in the compensation transaction, these barter transactions are also called switching transactions (cf. Kutschker and Schmid 2008, p. 37).

In addition to pure exchange transactions, parallel transactions are also often found. These are characterized in particular by the fact that performance and counterperformance are agreed in two separate contracts. Furthermore, they are partial compensation transactions.

Countertrade transactions are by definition linked transactions which are agreed in two separate contracts. However, the contracts are linked by a memorandum (sometimes also called a framework agreement). Performance and counterperformance are separately invoiced and processed (cf. Büter 2007, p. 87). "Parallel trades" and "junctim trades" are distinguished from each other according to the chronological sequence of the transactions. Whereas in the case of a "parallel trade" the core service is as a rule provided initially before the exchange goods are supplied, in the case of a "junctim trade" the opposite should be assumed. In a conventional countertrade transaction, the products or services which are to be provided as counterperformance are not connected with the supplier's products/services, and they are therefore sold. The **offset** transaction represents a special instance of a countertrade transaction in this context, since the counterperformance can usually be incorporated into the supplier's production processes (cf. Huszagh and Barksdale 1986, p. 23).

Buyback transactions are often found in the plant engineering and construction business. This so-called buyback compensation involves the exporter receiving consideration consisting of a predetermined percentage of the goods produced in the production plant that has been supplied (cf. Büter 2007, p. 88). If the countervalue of the goods equals the original value of the plant, this can be termed a full compensation transaction (cf. Kutschker and Schmid 2008, p. 37).

The **cooperation agreement** is a special form in which three separate exchanges of goods or services between the supplier, the buyer of the core service and the buyer of the compensation transaction are carried out (cf. Huszagh and Barksdale 1986, p. 23). This three-way relationship may be structured in the form of barter transactions or parallel transactions.

In the relevant literature there are numerous estimates of the global significance of compensation transactions. These estimates range from 5 % to 20 % of global trade (cf. Büter 2007, p. 86). It is not however possible to make authoritative statements.

4.2.4 Project Finance

Project finance is an option for financing major industrial projects which has fallen somewhat out of favor as a result of the financial and economic crisis. This is a **specifically structured financing option,** and not just a generic term relating to the financing of projects in general. Having originated in its modern form in the United States for the financing of oil production, the technique of project finance quickly expanded into other fields (cf. Matschke and Olbrich 2000, p. 105; Tytko 1999, p. 4). Due to its inherent flexibility it can meet the specific requirements of a large number of different projects. Its fields of use are corresponding broad. They range from state infrastructure projects and the securing of energy and water supplies to the private sector manufacture of industrial goods (cf. Yescombe 2002, p. 6).

The basic idea behind project finance is the servicing of debt from the **cash flows** generated by the project (cf. Backhaus and Uekermann 1990; Bötcher and Blattner 2006). Consequently, the reviewing of the creditworthiness of potential investors does not, as is usual in the case of the conventional order financing instruments, relate to the project principal, but to the profitability of the project itself. The opportunity that this provides for **spreading risk** across several investors of equity and borrowed capital enables major projects to be carried out despite a lack of financial strength or willingness on the part of the customer to take risks ("Good projects with poor debtors").

Although the form taken by various project finance structure may vary greatly, most projects have some basic features in common. Central to project finance is the project company, which is founded as a **"Special Purpose Entity"** (SPE) by the parties involved in the project specifically for the purpose of administering the project. As a legally autonomous entity it is detached from its equity investors, the so-called **"sponsors"**, and as a rule it is designed so as to avoid the need for it to feature in the annual financial statements or to be consolidated in the group annual financial statements (cf. Wolf et al. 2011, p. 88). In the light of this, the term **"off-balance sheet financing"** is used. The project company accordingly operates as an instrument used by the sponsors to implement their project concept (cf. Bötcher and Blattner 2006, p. 28). The equity investors' risk that is mitigated in this way is either fully or partially transferred to the parties involved in the project finance. These are primarily the **investors of borrowed capital**, above all the commercial banks which generally provide between 70 % and 90 % of the total financing requirements (Esty 2004, p. 55). In the case of **non-recourse financing**—something which is rare in practice—the sponsors (at least once a certain amount of progress has been made in the operation of the project) are released from any liability over and above their equity investment. However, if the project does not generate any cash flow, or generates too little, an option for partially limiting the risk from the perspective of the investors of borrowed capital is the organizing of a **"limited-recourse" financing structure**. However, in both cases it is essential for there to be a thorough process for identifying and evaluating the risks which are inherent in the project (cf. Decker 2008, pp. 33–34). Figure 10 provides a simplified comparison of the provision of capital funding through conventional corporate credit and through project finance.

Despite the possibility of holding equity investors (partly) liable, the servicing of debt is largely dependent on the success of the project company. Due to the low proportion of equity capital and the enormous financing requirements, in the structure shown above the financial risk remains comparatively high (cf. Backhaus and Köhl 2001, pp. 1717 and 1718). There is therefore a need to spread any risks associated with the project among further participants (cf. Tytko 2003, p. 17). This is done through numerous individual contracts which are concluded with parties involved in the project and which specify certain entitlements, and can consequently be used as credit guarantees (cf. Wertschulte 2005, p. 39 and following). The plethora of companies involved and the need to firmly define the assumption of any risks can mean that the contract wording which is produced is extremely comprehensive. The following is a simplified outline of the resulting key contractual relationships:

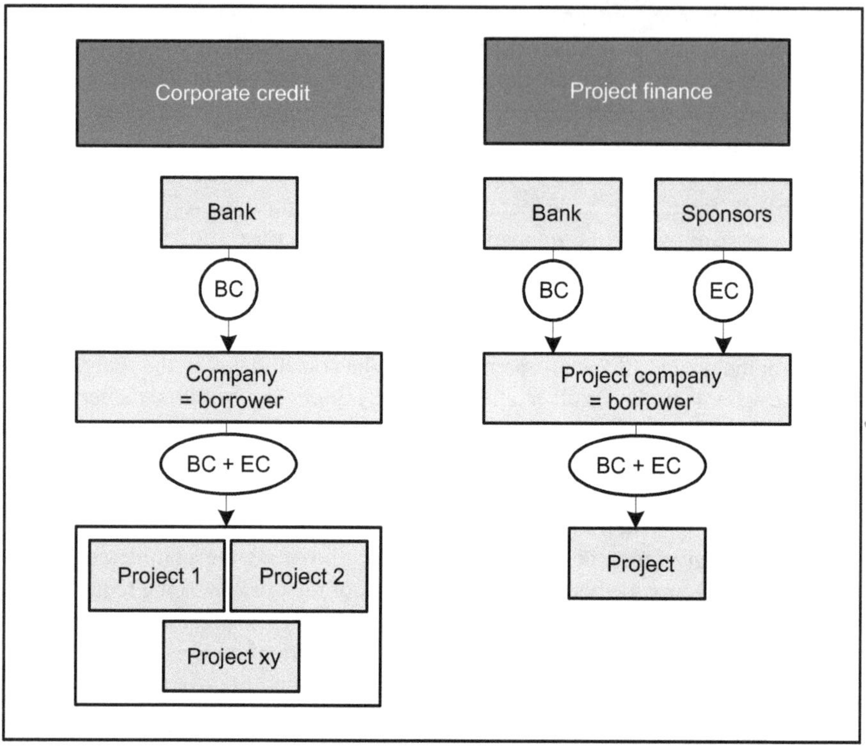

Fig. 10 Allocation of equity and borrowed capital through corporate credit and through project finance (Uekermann 1993, p. 4)

- The assumption of risk in the initiation and drafting phase is specified in the "construction contract". The contract is concluded between the project company and the companies involved in the construction of the plant/installation (the contractors). In addition to fundamental matters such as the costs that arise and the completion deadline, its subject matter comprises all the technical and financial details which are connected with the construction of the installation.
- Under the supply contract the project company undertakes to supply the service which has been produced (e.g. power generated in a power station) to a private sector buyer (e.g. a factory operator) or to public authorities. In the former case the relevant supply agreement is called an "off-take contract" (cf. here and below Yescombe 2002, pp. 69–70). The project company ensures that the buyer (offtaker) is supplied with its products once the plant has been completed. From the SPE's perspective this means that uncertain future cash flows are firmly specified (to a certain extent). If a service is commissioned by public authorities, the project company guarantees, generally through a "concession agreement", that it will be provided properly. This agreement is a contract which grants the project company the right to provide certain services on behalf of the

public sector. A typical example of such a project is the operation of the truck toll system on German express highways.
- The operational management and maintenance contract specifies the rights and duties of the operator of the system, which does not also have to be a sponsor of the project. If the provision of the services requires special technical expertise that cannot be provided by the sponsors, it makes sense to use an operating company (cf. Wolf et al. 2011, p. 92).
- Long-term supply contracts are usual as a means of ensuring the availability of the necessary upstream products and raw materials, and as a way of countering dependence on fluctuating market prices.

Depending on the structure of the project finance, additional participants can be contractually involved. Normal practice is for insurances to be used to cover further risks, for external advisers and experts to be used in the planning and implementation phase, and for trustees to be used for administering the funds (cf. Wolf et al. 2011, p. 95). State institutions also play a not inconsequential role, particularly in international projects. As already described, they can grant concessions in their direct role as project management organizations. Furthermore, the implementation of major projects almost exclusively requires state approvals. These range from technical construction regulations relating to environmental conditions to approvals for financing and foreign currency transactions (cf. Wolf et al. 2011, p. 93). And not least, the political and economic framework conditions must be created in order for investments to be possible in the first place.

As seen from the above example, the various tasks of the parties involved in the project can rarely be clearly delineated. Rather, some participants are usually involved in the financing structure in a variety of roles. For instance, the project sponsor can simultaneously be the general contractor, and consequently have the chief responsibility for the construction of the plant. Equally, it is conceivable for the buyer of the service that is to be produced to provide borrowed capital for financing purposes. Many combinations are theoretically possible. Figure 11 provides a highly simplified summary of the various roles of the parties involved in the project and their contractual relationships.

It is becoming clear that project finance is characterized by a complex structure which is held together by comprehensive contracts. The setting up of such a structure is a protracted process which is often accompanied by tough negotiations. Furthermore, the risks are many and varied and are difficult to assess in advance given the very lengthy repayment timeframe. Nevertheless, between 1994 and the crisis year, 2009, the sector notched up average annual growth rates of almost 17 % in terms of the amount of capital invested (cf. Moody's 2010, p. 4). In many cases project finance is the only option available for actually implementing a project. This is due to a series of favorable features which form the basis of its **special suitability for handling major industrial projects**. From the equity investors' viewpoint it provides the following advantages among others (cf. Böttcher and Bötcher and Blattner 2006, p. 28 and following; Yescombe 2002, p. 14 and following):

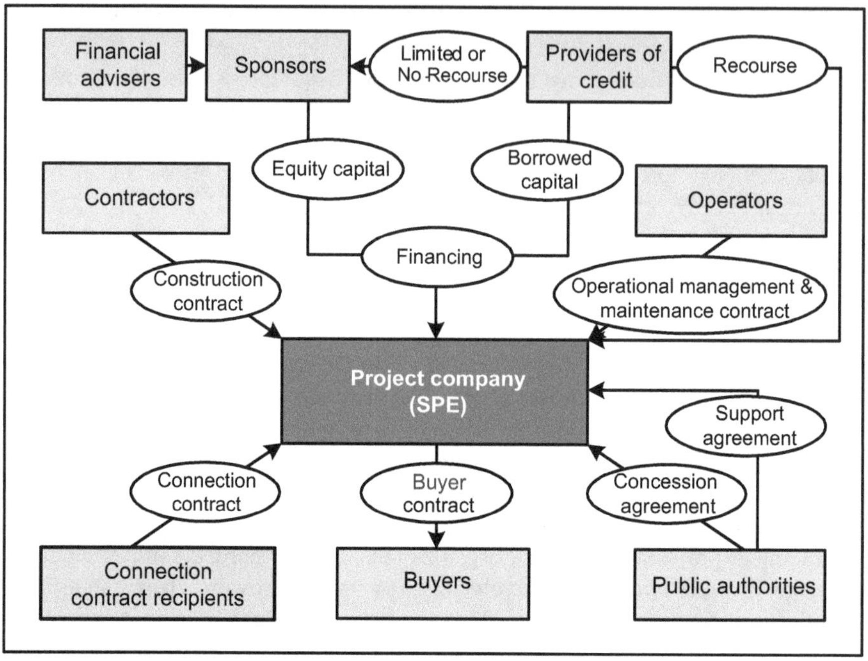

Fig. 11 Basic structure of project finance (Yescombe 2002, p. 8)

- The **liability** of the project sponsors is normally limited. In the case of limited recourse financing, recourse generally ceases once the plant is completed. As from this point in time the project is liable via its cash flows.
- The **low proportion of equity capital** (usually under 30 % of the project costs) makes a high level of investment return possible. Investors benefit from the **leverage effect**.
- The involvement of a large number of parties in the project breaks down the complex risk structure of a major project into **individual risks** which can be separately regulated through bilateral contractual relationships.
- The possibility of **off-balance sheet financing** keeps a company's activities within project finance structures off its balance sheet. Borrowed capital obtained by the SPE accordingly does not appear in the books of the project management organizations, which can be advantageous as regards obtaining further funds in the capital markets. In addition, the structuring of a legally autonomous project company facilitates the acquiring of large amounts of **borrowed capital**, and makes it easier to involve further **equity investors**. This enables even relatively financially weak companies to implement project concepts which would otherwise not get off the ground due to the significant investments required.

Furthermore, other stakeholders too benefit from the special structures of project finance. Since the planned projects are often infrastructure projects for the benefit of the public, the state has a very direct interest in their success. The possibility of obtaining large volumes of capital and the collaboration with other sponsors from the private sector (Public Private Partnerships) result in infrastructure investments being made which would otherwise not be possible on account of budget restrictions. In this case, public authorities can also make use of the employees' expertise, which is indispensable for the planning and implementation of long-term major projects. Finally, the allocation of risks between the parties involved in the project can help to reduce the burden on the public purse resulting from subsequent increases in project costs. The reductions in project costs due to the high level of use of borrowed capital indirectly benefit the buyers. In the case of structures with a greater proportion of borrowed capital, lower surpluses are necessary in order to satisfy the same expectations on the part of the sponsors regarding equity capital interest (cf. Yescombe 2002, p. 17). Other things being equal, the unit costs of the products and services that are provided therefore fall.

As initially explained, a large proportion of industrial plant engineering and construction takes place in newly industrializing and developing countries. Given the advantages of project finance structures, their success in these countries in particular is perfectly understandable. For instance, in the first half of 2011 India was able to obtain almost a third of global investment undertaken in this form, with the amount of its share being US$50.3 billion (cf. Dealogic 2011). Although the market has largely been stagnating since the global financial and economic crisis, a major recession has been averted thanks above all to the dynamic emerging economies of Asia.

However, new major projects entailing large amounts of investment are also imminent here in Germany. In order to make provision for the constantly increasing energy requirements of the European national economies, projects such as Desertec and Transgreen are targeting clean energy from the desert regions of Africa. The intention is for large-scale solar panel installations to generate electricity in an environmentally efficient manner which will then be transported to the industrialized countries of Europe. The development of the plant and grid requires capital investments worth hundreds of billions of euros, which cannot be provided by individual project sponsors (cf. Wolf et al. 2011, p. 83). Variations of project finance which are suitable for equipping the projects with the equity and borrowed capital will therefore continue to play an important role in future.

Exercises

1. Explain the degree to which the structuring of a financing concept for major projects can be regarded as a marketing instrument.
2. What causes of manufacturing and payment default risks are generally covered by export insurances?
3. Explain what a supplier credit is. What role does the Hermes cover play in this?
4. Explain what a buyer credit is. Which contracting parties bear which risks in this regard?

5. What is meant by operating export leasing? What opportunities and risks result for the lessor?
6. What aspects should be taken into account when making the decision regarding export leasing?
7. What advantages does the exporter derive from the forfaiting of its receivables?
8. What is meant by compensation transactions?
9. What forms of compensation transactions are there, and what reasons can be advanced for such a financing solution?

Literature

AKA Bank. (2011). *Grundzüge des ECA-gedeckten Bestellerkredites*. Retrieved June 20, 2012 from https://www.akabank.de/deutsch/produkte/besteller/grundzuege.html

Atevis. (2011). *Kreditversicherung—Branchenkennzahlen 2010 Deutschland und weltweit*. Retrieved June 20, 2012 from www.atevis.com/service/news/artikelanzeige/article/c0fe58f0c3.html?tx_ttnews[backPid]=290&cHash=bf64009b06

Backhaus, K. (1979). Preisgleitklauseln als risikopolitisches Instrument bei langfristigen Fertigungs- und Absatzprozessen. *Zeitschrift für betriebswirtschaftliche Forschung—Kontaktstudium, 31*(1), 3–11.

Backhaus, K., & Köhl, T. (2001). Projektfinanzierung. In W. Gerke & M. Steiner (Eds.), *Handwörterbuch des Bank- und Finanzwesens* (pp. 1715–1735). Stuttgart: Schäffer-Poeschel.

Backhaus, K., & Molter, W. (1989). Auftragsfinanzierung, internationale. In K. Macharzina & M. K. Welge (Eds.), *Handwörterbuch Export und Internationale Unternehmung* (pp. 49–67). Stuttgart: Schäffer-Poeschel.

Backhaus, K., & Siepert, H.-M. (1987). *Auftragsfinanzierung im industriellen Anlagengeschäft*. Stuttgart: Schäffer-Poeschel.

Backhaus, K., & Uekermann, H. (1990). Projektfinanzierung—Eine Methode zur Finanzierung von Großprojekten. *Wirtschaftswissenschaftliches Studium, 19*(3), 106–112.

Backhaus, K., & Voeth, M. (2014). *Industriegütermarketing* (10th ed.). Munich: Vahlen.

Bannier, C. (2005). *Die schuldrechtlichen und wechselrechtlichen Haftungsprobleme bei der Forfaitierung von Exportforderungen*. Berlin: Tenea Verlag.

Becker, P. S. (2000). *Absatzfinanzierung im Anlagengeschäft—eine Analyse aus netzwerktheoretischer Perspektive*. Berlin: Verlag für Wissenschaft und Forschung.

Blomeyer, K., & Kuttner, K. (1992). *Exportfinanzierung: Nachschlagewerk für die Praxis* (3rd ed.). Wiesbaden: Gabler Verlag.

Bödeker, V. (1992). *Staatliche Exportkreditversicherungssysteme: ihre Rechtsgrundlagen, Vertragsbedingungen und Funktionsweisen in Deutschland, Frankreich, Großbritannien, den USA und Japan*. Berlin: de Gruyter.

Bötcher, J., & Blattner, P. (2006). *Projektfinanzierung*. Munich: Oldenbourg Wissenschaftsverlag.

Bundesministerium für wirtschaftliche Zusammenarbeit und Entwicklung (BMZ). (2012). *Finanzielle Zusammenarbeit*. Retrieved June 20, 2012 from http://www.bmz.de/de/was_wir_machen/wege/bilaterale_ez/zwischenstaatliche_ez/finanz_zuzusammenarbe/index.html

Büter, C. (2007). *Außenhandel—Grundlagen globaler und innergemeinschaftlicher Handelsbeziehungen*. Heidelberg: Springer.

Cowdell, P., Hyde, D., & Watson, A. (2000). *Finance of international trade* (7th ed.). Canterbury: Financial World.

Dealogic. (2011). Dealogic half-year 2011 league tables. *Project Finance Magazine* (3rd ed.). Retrieved June 20, 2012 from http://www.projectfinancemagazine.com/Article/2877824/Type-League-Tables/Dealogic-half-year-2011-League-Tables-Analysis.html

Decker, C. (2008). *Internationale Projektfinanzierung, Konzeption und Prüfung*. Dissertation, Universität Bremen.
Esty, B. C. (2004). *Modern project finance: A casebook*. New Jersey: Wiley.
Euler Hermes. (2011a). *Finanzkreditdeckung*. Retrieved June 20, 2012 from www.agaportal.de/pdf/produktinfo/pi_finanzkredit.pdf
Euler Hermes. (2011b). *Hermesdeckungen Spezial. Entgeltberechnung*. Retrieved June 20, 2012 from http://www.agaportal.de/pdf/hds/hds_entgelt.pdf
Ex-Im. (2011). *Competitiveness report 2010*. Retrieved June 20, 2012 from http://www.exim.gov/about/reports/compet/documents/2010_Competitiveness_Report.pdf
Feuerbaum, E. (1979). Risk Management in der Investitionsgüter-Industrie. In W. Goetzke & G. Sieben (Eds.), *Risk Management—Strategien zur Risikobeherrschung, Gebra-Schriften* (5th ed.). Gebera: Köln.
Fieten, R. (1985). Financial Engineering. Komponente des industriellen Großanlagengeschäfts. In K. Macharzina (Ed.), *Finanz- und bankwirtschaftliche Probleme bei internationaler Unternehmenstätigkeit* (pp. 163–194). Stuttgart: Poeschel.
Funk, J. (1986). *Langfristiges Anlagengeschäft—Risiko-Management und Controlling*. Düsseldorf: Verlagsgruppe Handelsblatt.
Häberle, S. G. (2002a). *Handbuch der Außenhandelsfinanzierung* (3rd ed.). Munich: Oldenbourg.
Häberle, S. G. (2002b). *Einführung in die Exportfinanzierung* (2nd ed.). Munich: Oldenbourg.
Hennert, J.-F. (1990). Some empirical dimensions of countertrade. *Journal of International Business Studies, 21*(2), 243–270.
Hombach, H., Kockelkorn, G., & Molter, W. (1987). Einführung in die Auftragsfinanzierung. In K. Backhaus & H. M. Siepert (Eds.), *Auftragsfinanzierung im industriellen Anlagengeschäft* (pp. 3–21). Stuttgart: Schäffer-Poeschel.
Huszagh, S. M., & Barksdale, H. C. (1986). International barter and countertrade: An exploratory study. *Journal of the Academy of Marketing Science, 14*(1), 21–24.
Ifo Institut. (2011). *Leasing zurück auf der Überholspur 12 % Wachstum bei Mobilien 2011—gedämpfte Erwartungen für 2012*. Retrieved June 20, 2012 from http://downloads.leasingverband.de/fileadmin/internet/downloads/2012-01-03_ifo_sonderdruck.pdf
KfW. (2011). *Jahresbericht über die Zusammenarbeit mit Entwicklungsländern 2010*. Retrieved June 20, 2012 from http://www.kfw-entwicklungsbank.de/ebank/DE_Home/I/Download_Center/PDF-Dokumente_Jahresberichte_-KfW_Entwicklungsbank/2010_Jahresbericht_D.pdf
KfW-IPEX. (2011). Volle Kraft voraus. Daten, Fakten, Hintergründe. Themendienst für die Pressestelle. *KfW Bankengruppe* (pp. 8–9).
Klöpper, M. (1990). *Mischfinanzierung und Kofinanzierung als Instrumente der Auftragsfinanzierung im industriellen Anlagegeschäft: Eine Analyse aus der Sicht des deutschen Anlagenexporteurs*. Munich: Florentz.
König, N. (1982). Ausgeprägte Multinationalität im Anlagenbau. *Die Bank, 4*, 165–171.
Kutschker, M., & Schmid, S. (2008). *Internationales management* (6th ed.). Munich: Oldenbourg.
Matschke, M. J., & Olbrich, M. (2000). *Internationale und Außenhandelsfinanzierung*. Munich: Oldenbourg.
Metschies, U. (1995). Rausholen was geht. *Wirtschaftswoche, 49*(51), 110–112.
Moody's. (2010). *Default and recovery rates for project finance bank loans, 1983-2008*. New York: Moody's.
OECD. (2011). *Arrangement on officially supported export credits*. Retrieved June 20, 2012 from www.oecd.org/officialdocuments/displaydocumentpdf/?cote=tad/pg%282011%2913&doclanguage=en
Perridon, L., Steiner, M., & Rathgeber, A. (2009). *Finanzwirtschaft der Unternehmung* (15th ed.). Munich: Vahlen.
Petersen, J. (2004). *Local-Content-Auflagen—betriebswirtschaftliche Relevanz und Handhabung am Beispiel des internationalen Großanlagenbaus*. Wiesbaden: Deutscher Universitätsverlag.
Putnoki, H. (2000). *Grundlagen der Außenhandelsfinanzierung*. Munich: Oldenbourg.

Sauer, D.-H. (1997). Formen der Finanzierung von Exportgeschäften. In K. Macharzina & M.-J. Oesterle (Eds.), *Handbuch internationales Management* (pp. 421–437). Wiesbaden: Gabler.

Schuster, F. (1979). *Gegen- und Kompensationsgeschäfte als Marketing-Instrument im Investitionsgüterbereich*. Berlin: Duncker & Humblot.

Siepert, H. M. (1987). Multinationale Anbietergemeinschaften in der Exportfinanzierung. In K. Backhaus & H. M. Siepert (Eds.), *Auftragsfinanzierung im industriellen Anlagengeschäft* (pp. 145–162). Stuttgart: Schäffer-Poeschel.

Stephens, M. (1999). *The changing role of export credit agencies*. Washington, DC: International Monetary Fund.

Tytko, D. (1999). *Grundlagen der Projektfinanzierung*. Stuttgart: Schäffer Poeschel.

Tytko, D. (2003). Grundlagen der Projektfinanzierung. In K. Backhaus & H. Wertschulte (Eds.), *Projektfinanzierung—Wirtschaftliche und rechtliche Aspekte einer Finanzierungsmethode für Großprojekte*. Stuttgart: Schäffer-Poeschel.

Uekermann, H. (1993). *Risikopolitik bei Projektfinanzierungen: Maßnahmen und ihre Ausgestaltung*. Wiesbaden: Deutscher Universitätsverlag.

VDMA. (2010). *Kennzahlen des Großanlagenbaus 2009*. Retrieved June 20, 2012 from www.vdma.org/wps/wcm/connect/874fb5004dd2159dbde8fdd1f693e3d9/Kennzahlen+Gro%C3%9Fanlagenbau+2009.pdf?MOD=AJPERES&CACHEID=874fb5004dd2159dbde8fdd1f693e3d9

VDMA. (2011a). *Kennzahlen des Großanlagenbaus 2010*. Retrieved June 20, 2012 from http://www.google.de/url?sa=t&rct=j&q=vdma%20kennzahlen%20des%20gro%C3%9Fanlagenbaus&source=web&cd=4&ved=0CFEQFjAD&url=http%3A%2F%2Fwww.chemietechnik.de%2Fmedia%2Ffile%2F9705&ei=ZdjZT93kO83jtQaKsuHICA&usg=AFQjCNGM-dN5gHMKm8waa98lR6w6BDxQug&cad=rja

VDMA. (2011b). *Auslandsgeschäft: BRIC-Staaten mit wachsender Bedeutung*. Retrieved June 20, 2012 from www.vdma.org/wps/portal/Home/de/Branchen/G/AGAB/Wirtschaft_und_Politik/Konjunktur/AGAB_A_20110315_Dt_Auslandsgeschaeft_Lagebericht_2011_de?WCM_GLOBAL_CONTEXT=/wps/wcm/connect/vdma/Home/de/Branchen/G/AGAB/Wirtschaft_und_Politik/Konjunktur/AGAB_A_20110315_Dt_Auslandsgeschaeft_Lagebericht_2011_de

VDMA. (2011c). *Großanlagenbau im Fokus: der jährliche Lagebericht*. Retrieved June 20, 2012 from www.vdma.org/wps/portal/Home/de/Branchen/G/AGAB/Wirtschaft_und_Politik/Konjunktur/AGAB_A_20111125_Dt_Lagebericht_2011_Grossanlagenbau_im_Fokus_de?WCM_GLOBAL_CONTEXT=/wps/wcm/connect/vdma/Home/de/Branchen/G/AGAB/Wirtschaft_und_Politik/Konjunktur/AGAB_A_20111125_Dt_Lagebericht_2011_Grossanlagenbau_im_Fokus_de

Voigt, H., & Müller, D. (1996). *Handbuch der Exportfinanzierung* (4th ed.). Frankfurt am Main: Knapp Fritz GmbH.

von Bernstorff, C. G. (2007). *Die Exportfinanzierung*. Köln: Bundesanzeiger.

Wertschulte, H. (2005). *Kreditrisikomessung bei Projektfinanzierung durch Risikosimulation*. Wiesbaden: Deutscher Universitätsverlag.

Wolf, B., Hill, M., & Pfaue, M. (2011). *Strukturierte Finanzierungen* (2nd ed.). Stuttgart: Schäffer-Poeschel.

Yescombe, E. R. (2002). *Principles of project finance*. San Diego, CA: Academic.

Contract Management

Georg Berkel

1 Introduction

Proper contract management is an important precondition for the success of plant engineering and construction and project business. This chapter conveys the principles of successful contract management. Its basic **content, aims and methods of contract management** are shown.

The subject matter of the article overlaps with the content of the "Negotiation Management" and "Project Management" chapters. The focal point of this chapter is a physical object, namely the contract. "*Negotiation management*" is mainly concerned with the process of negotiation. This process plays an important role in contract management particularly, since the contract is of course the result of negotiation. The *"project management"* chapter on the other hand presupposes that a contract has been concluded. Project management is not infrequently about the issue of how a contract is to be performed. During the execution of the contract the enforcing and defending of additional demands, or *claims*, play an important role. This in turn also forms part of contract management. Since this volume approaches the same topics from three different angles, repetitions cannot be entirely excluded. This also means however that the reader can expect an especially comprehensive and thorough consideration of plant and project business.

1.1 An Illustration

> It is the largest industrial order ever to be awarded in Germany. In 2011 Deutsche Bahn ordered up to 300 high speed trains from Siemens. (. . .) The state railway operator is paying about 6 billion euros for 220 trains. The mega-order may be increased to ten billion euros

G. Berkel (✉)
Negotiation Consulting, Freising, Germany
e-mail: berkel@negotiationconsulting.com

M. Kleinaltenkamp et al. (eds.), *Business Project Management and Marketing*, Springer Texts in Business and Economics, DOI 10.1007/978-3-662-48507-1_5

> (...). Deutsche Bahn boss Rüdiger Grube, a veteran of the industrial sector who left Daimler's executive board in 2009 to take over the top job at the state-owned company, secured considerably better cover for the deal than had been usual in the case of previous major orders placed by the railway operator. The contracts with Deutsche Bahn run to 8,000 pages, and they contain quite a few bitter pills for the Siemens managers to swallow. (Jungbluth 2012)

This short extract from a newspaper article illustrates the important role of the **customer contract in order and project management,** and specifically in the capital goods business. The following points that can be deduced from the article are characteristic of this role:

- The supplier's business model is geared towards securing the order. This is done by signing a **highly complex contract.**
- When signing the contract, the supplier had to swallow quite a few "bitter pills". At the time when the **bid was submitted** the supplier had hoped to secure better conditions.
- However, during the course of the **negotiations** it decided to make concessions in order to win the order. The conditions of the original bid were therefore gradually amended. This was how the supplier and the customer jointly produced the contract which was then signed.

At this point we can also note that there seem to be two main things at stake in the contract. Firstly, the parties are vying for an appropriate allocation of the risk. Each side seeks to cover itself at the other's expense. Secondly, what is at stake is fixing the size of the order and maximizing the benefits for both parties. An option may even be agreed for extending the scope of the contract later on.

- Deciding on the benchmark data for the contract is a **management task.** Even if the article only explicitly mentions the customer's CEO, it can be inferred from this that the highest level of management must have been involved on the supplier's side too.
- When the article was published the contract had only just been signed. At this point none of the parties involved can know whether or not the **execution** of the project will be successful.
- Even if the article does not address this, one can assume that both companies will carry out a detailed **analysis** of whether or not the project was a success at the latest when the execution of the project is completed.

At the time when the contract is concluded the supplier and the customer are in the same situation as the reader of the newspaper article. They know that the order has been placed, but whether or not the order will actually turn out to be a success will only become apparent later on. Good contract management should enable a reasonable forecast of the success of the project to be made. Above all however, it provides some resources which are crucial for success. What precisely does this mean? This is what we want to consider in more detail below.

1.2 The Four Phases of Contract Management

Like its German equivalent (Vertragsmanagement) in German-speaking countries, the term "**contract management**" (or "*claim management*") does not have a consistent meaning. Rather, the term may cover very different activities and forms of organization in different companies. This article is based on the widest conceivable understanding of the term.

We want to approach the term by considering the **timeline** of the tasks involved in contract management. To do this, we can take our bearings from the main events in the course of the project. We can distinguish four phases which are separated from each other by these events. In each of these four phases there are specific requirements relating to the work that has to be undertaken on the contract. These requirements which are typical of specific phases enable us to outline what "contract management" actually is. The example cited above of the supplying of trains to Deutsche Bahn by Siemens can also be used by us here as an illustration.

I. At the start of the project, the supplier has to decide whether it actually wants to submit a bid (the so-called ***bid decision***). In the example given, this decision should have been easy for Siemens to make, given the importance of Deutsche Bahn as a customer. The decision to submit a bid ushers in the first phase, which is when the bid is actually put together. As we can see from the article, this was probably an extraordinarily complex task for Siemens: the majority of the 8000 pages probably consisted of product specifications which already had to be drawn whilst the bid was being drawn up.
II. Once the bid has been completed, it is submitted to the customer (**bid submission**). If the bid arouses the customer's interest, the negotiation phase begins. In this phase the expectations of both sides are clarified and an attempt is made to reconcile them. In view of the massive size of the order, the negotiations between Deutsche Bahn and Siemens must have been complicated and protracted. If the negotiations are successful, they lead to the contract being concluded. As we know, in the example given the supplier had to make some concessions. In the end however, the 8000-page 'concoction' was signed.

Since the article was written at the time when the contract was concluded, it naturally cannot say anything about the last two phases:

III. The **concluding of the contract** marks the start of its implementation. The parties must now deliver to each other what has been promised and settle any disagreements that may arise.
IV. Once the project has ended (**end of the contract**), each party should carry out an analysis from which lessons can be learned for future projects.
V. Once the ***lessons learned*** have been drawn up, the contract management of the project is ended, and the foundations for the next project are also laid.

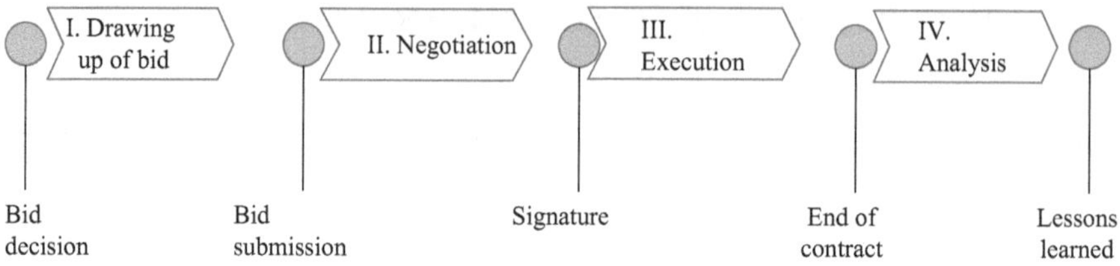

Fig. 1 The four phases of contract management

We can derive the following definition from what has been said so far:

Definition ***"Contract management"*** can be defined as the performance of the contract-related tasks which arise in the four phases of project execution. In the last two phases it is also known as "claim management".

This is clearly shown in the diagram Fig. 1.

1.3 Focus of the Chapter

In this section we concentrate on contract management in the context of order and project management, specifically in the plant engineering and construction business and for large service projects. It is therefore principally concerned with the **customer contract** on which these transactions are based. We restrict ourselves in this regard to private sector contracts. As the name already suggests, these contracts are subject to the rules of private law. These are contracts entered into by one company with another company, or with public authorities if they are operating on the basis of private law. By contrast, contracts which are under the overall control of public authorities are subject to public law. Public law has some peculiarities (such as tendering and budgeting laws), and it deprives the parties of many aspects of the freedom to draft contracts as they choose. It is not possible to examine these peculiarities here.

In line with the main focus of this volume, we consider contract management predominantly from the **viewpoint of the supplier**. However, what has been said also applies to the customer, even if the other way round.

Customer contracts, whether relating to plant engineering and construction business or to services projects, are so-called "**exchange contracts**" which are called like this because each party provides performance in exchange for the counterperformance provided by the other party. The contract of sale, which comprises the services of "goods" in exchange for "money", may be regarded as a typical example. Contracts of exchange must be differentiated from unilateral contracts (e.g. donations) and company statutes (e.g. articles of incorporation of a limited liability company).

1.4 Structure of the Chapter

In line with our definition of contract management, we intend to examine the four phases of contract management in detail in this chapter. We will consider the questions "**what**", "**when**" and "**how**": first, we will examine the event which marks the start of each phase, then we will highlight the contract management tasks in that phase. And lastly, we will explain which processes should be used for completing these tasks.

First of all though, we wish to clarify one point. In Sect. 1.2 we had identified five events which characterize the course of the project: bid decision, bid submission, concluding of the contract, end of the contract, and lessons learned. These events are dependent on each other and therefore always occur in the order shown. This is not necessarily so in the case of the four phases of contract management. It is actually perfectly possible for the phases to overlap. For instance, when the bid is being put together the supplier may seek to clarify with the customer what its main expectations are. These discussions may well come to take the form of a negotiation. Likewise, lessons for other projects are often not only drawn once the project has been fully completed, but also while the contract is being carried out. The four phases of contract management are therefore not actually as distinct from each other in reality as is suggested in our model. However, the "**apportioning**" of contract management into four phases makes it simpler and easier to present. The intention of this chapter is to provide a concept that is easy to grasp and understand. The idea is to make this complex topic as accessible as possible for the reader. If the phase model leads to over-simplification, this is pointed out at the relevant point. We should therefore have "covered all the bases" by the end of the article. We hope this will not strain the reader's patience.

2 Phase I: Putting Together of the Bid

As we have seen, the putting together of the bid starts with decision to make an offer to the customer to conclude a contract ("**bid decision**"). But what actually is an "offer" to conclude a contract? A legally valid offer is quite simply a complete contract which the other party simply needs to sign in order for it to become effective.

Definition **Offer** = A binding offer is the proposal made by the supplier to the customer to conclude a specific contract. The customer must be able to accept it simply by saying "yes" and appending his signature, without this leaving any points which have to be clarified/resolved. The bid therefore consists of a complete contract.

In this section we are therefore going to examine the elements which make up a customer contract in the capital goods and plant engineering and construction field. As we do this, it will become clear that the putting together of a bid in such a complex field of business is something which can only be done as part of a structured and interdisciplinary process. We will therefore also direct our attention to the **process of putting a bid together**.

2.1 The "Bid Decision"

Not every potential project which the supplier finds out about is actually pursued by it. Putting a bid together involves considerable expense and manpower, whereas the company's resources are limited. Management must therefore often decide in advance how the resources can best be used. This entails weighing up the **effort and expense involved** against the **prospects of success**. Decisive factors are the probability of the project going ahead and the likelihood of winning the order.

The **probability of the project going ahead** indicates how likely it is that the project will be implemented by the respective customer. The potential customer often has to beat its competitors first in order to be able to implement the project. This may for instance apply in the case of a group of investors which is seeking a license from the government of a country for the construction and operation of a power station. Only if this group itself wins the tendering process does it have any orders to place. The probability of the project going ahead therefore means the likelihood of the potential *customer* winning out against its competitors.

On the other hand, the **likelihood of winning the order** indicates the potential *supplier's* prospects of winning out against its competitors.

Both probabilities are influenced by a host of commercial and technical factors, for example the efficiency of the technology used and the expected time needed to carry out the project. The two probabilities are not infrequently linked to each other. For instance, it is usual in relation to the construction of power stations for various groups of bidders to compete for the same government license. Each group of bidders consists of investors and potential subcontractors. The state will then evaluate each bid in its entirety and award the order to one group.

Therefore the "bid/no bid" decision basically involves analytical considerations relating to the market and the competition. It may also be the case that considerations relating to the customer contract are already incorporated into the decision-making process at this stage. This applies above all in the case of **high-risk contractual arrangements**. Such an arrangement may for instance exist if the customer has such great market power that it can pass virtually all the project risks to its suppliers. This is quite common in the case of state-sector customers in newly industrializing countries for example. As we will see later, every bid is however based on a specific risk profile. If the customer expects significantly more risks to be assumed but is not prepared to increase the contract price accordingly, the business may very well have to be avoided.

Examples of other contractual considerations which may lead to a "no bid decision" are doubtful legal certainty in the project country, or the need to create an **open consortium**. In an open consortium several suppliers come together in order to put forward a joint bid. They hope that this will enable them to conclude a contract that none of them would have been able to carry out on its own. In the plant engineering and construction business it often happens that various suppliers jointly promise to erect the structure. This involves each member of the consortium undertaking a precisely specified share of the works. If the construction of the facility is beyond the capabilities of a single supplier, the supplier may alternatively act as the **general contractor**. As such, it is then the only party to have a direct contract with the customer, to whom it gives an undertaking to construct the whole plant. The general contractor simultaneously obtains pledges from the subcontractors that they will carry out the works which it cannot undertake itself. This arrangement may be a so-called "silent" (or "closed") consortium since the cooperation of several companies is not visible to the customer, unlike in the case of the open consortium.

The open consortium has one major advantage compared to a bid by a single general contractor. The general contractor purchases the services of the other suppliers and when selling them on to the customer it has to apply its usual mark-ups to them in order to achieve the required profitability in the project. However, this can make the overall price unattractive for the customer. The suppliers do not have this problem in the case of the open consortium—they each carry out a part of the project and are remunerated for doing so; the overall price for the customer is nothing more than the sum total of the prices for the individual parts.

This advantage of the open consortium is however gained at some cost, since the consortium members promise the customer that they will be jointly and severally liable for the performance of the contract. **Joint and several liability** means that the customer may demand the performance of the *whole* contract from *any* one member of the consortium. This then becomes a problem if one of the members of the consortium does not perform its share of the contract (e.g. due to insolvency). The other members of the consortium then have to do so in its place and at their own expense and risk. An open consortium therefore leads to the supplier also being responsible for something which it cannot itself influence (or can only influence to a limited degree). This risk should already be borne in mind when making the "bid/no bid decision". If the supplier cannot carry out the project competitively as a general contractor but has little confidence in the abilities of the potential consortium members, it may make sense not to draw up a bid for the project at all.

The practice in many companies is to use a **two-stage bidding process**. Initially the customer is frequently provided with a non-binding "standard" bid together with a rough price. If it agrees with the key benchmark data, (the price in particular of course), a detailed and binding bid is drawn up. Due to the often considerable effort and expense involved in drawing up a binding bid, initially only preprinted documents are used for the bid. This procedure makes economic sense. As we will see in the section relating to the process of putting a bid together (cf. Sect. 2.4), the use of standard documents entails a legal risk which one should be aware of.

Fig. 2 The structure of the contract

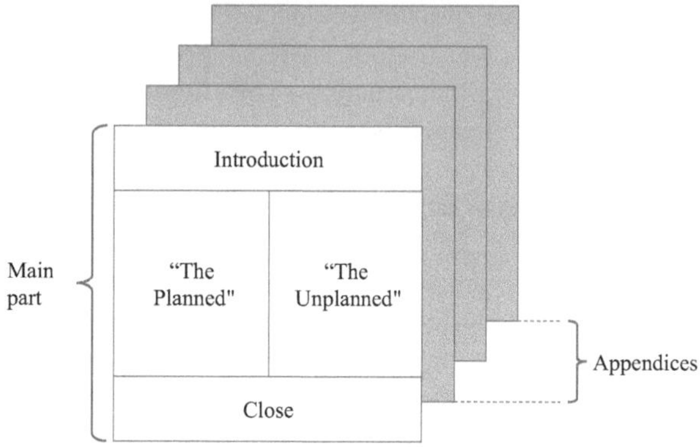

2.2 Overview of the Structure of the Contract

As we have seen, a legally binding bid is effectively a complete contract which only needs to be signed by the other party. So what does a complete contract consist of?

A contract between supplier and customer is basically made up as follows. It generally consists of a main part and appendices. Naturally enough, the main part begins with the title, followed by the designation of the parties concluding the contract. This is frequently followed by a preamble which acts more or less as an introduction to the contract. For the sake of simplicity we will call all this the "*Introduction*" This is followed by the actual core of the contract, in other words the provisions relating to the **rights and duties of the contracting parties**. Firstly there is a description here of the obligations on account of which the parties actually wish to conclude the contract (e.g. construction of a production plant in exchange for the payment of the contract price). We simply refer to this part as "*The Planned*". Then there follow the provisions for the eventuality of something **unforeseen** happening (referred to here as "*The Unplanned*"). The main part of the contract is rounded off by the final legal provisions, which we simply call the "*Close*" herein. Particularly in the case of the complex exchange contracts relating to the capital goods business, the main part is followed by extensive technical appendices. These specify and flesh out the rights and duties that have been recorded in the main part. Figure 2 shows in diagrammatic form the structure of a(n) (exchange) contract.

Occasionally, especially in international business, there are contracts that have a much more complicated structure than the one shown in our diagram. This is the case particularly if the rights and duties don't arise from a single document (the main contract), but are distributed across various appendices. What we have in mind here is in particular general terms and conditions which are linked to the main document. Usually such a structure is requested by the customer, combined with a call for its purchasing conditions to be made the basis of the bid. Where at all possible, the supplier should avoid going down this road. It is extraordinarily difficult to understand the exact rights and obligations of the parties when they are so dispersed among various documents. If it is possible to do so, it often turns out that the confusing structure was deliberately chosen in order to disguise an unreasonable allocation of risk.

The following can be said about the **scope** of the constituent parts of the contract: The appendices are almost invariably more comprehensive than the main part. Even in the case of highly complex power station contracts, the main part usually only runs to 100 or 200 pages. However, there is a difference in this respect between contracts which are governed by continental European *civil law* systems (e.g. in Germany, Switzerland and Austria), and those governed by "Anglo-Saxon" "*common law*" (e.g. in the USA or Great Britain). Civil law contracts generally seek to have highly abstract provisions and their aim is to be able to infer from a written principal how it is to be applied to an individual case without having to settle the specific individual case. Things are different in the case of common law contracts. A greater level of detail therefore has to be provided for them. However, under both types of legal system the overwhelming bulk of the contract consists of the various appendices. The reason for this is simply that the entire technical description of the project has to be contained in the appendices.

What precisely do the individual constituent parts of the contract contain? This is what we want to consider next.

2.3 The Constituent Parts of the Contract in Detail

We can differentiate between the "Introduction" (the title, the designation of the contracting parties, and the preamble), the "Planned", the "Unplanned", the "Close", and the appendices.

2.3.1 Title and Designation of the Contracting Parties

The **title** should actually specify the type of contract in a clear and accurate manner. As we will see in Sect. 2.3.3 (The Planned), it is often difficult, even for lawyers, to determine what the strictly correct type of contract for a specific project contract is. Even if this does prove to be possible, not very much is actually gained, since how a contract is interpreted in the event of a dispute primarily depends on the content of its provisions—not the designation given to it. A pragmatic contract manager will therefore choose a descriptive and graphic title. Instead of having to undertake protracted legal deliberations about the academically correct title to give to the contract, one can therefore simply call it "Contract relating to ... (*project name*)".

After the title, the **contracting parties** are listed. In the B2B market that concerns us here these are exclusively companies. The individuals who act on behalf of the companies which are concluding the contract must be distinguished from those companies. The contract is of course negotiated and signed by people who have been authorized to do so by the contracting parties. The question of whether or not the individuals who are undertaking the actions are actually authorized to do so is not addressed in the contract itself. It is determined instead by the corresponding powers that have been given to the individuals who are undertaking the actions (e.g. power of attorney or general commercial power of representation). However, particularly in Romanic countries it may be that the naming of the parties is also followed by naming of each person representing them (e.g. “Contract concluded between XY AG, represented by Mr. Müller B.Sc. (Eng.), and ABC GmbH, represented by Dr. Meier”).

At first glance, the naming of the contracting parties seems to be a pure technicality. However, in practice it is not uncommon for it to be unclear precisely which company will actually sign the contract at the end of the negotiations. This may for instance be the case if various affiliated companies are involved in the project. Particularly in international business it is usual for the bid to be put together by **several group companies**. This often involves the parent company and the local subsidiary company cooperating on putting the bid together. The company which then submits the final bid (and subsequently signs the contract) not infrequently depends on tax considerations, which may still change in the course of the negotiations.

In turn, it is frequently the case that a **project company** is founded specifically for the project, with its name and ownership structure often only being finally determined towards the end of the negotiations. Even though it is of course not necessary to already know the name of this project company when putting the bid together, it is however necessary to be sure of the identity of the parties. If the contract is “only” concluded by a project company which has been specifically established for this purpose, its financial resources are generally limited. This may influence the assessment of the customer’s creditworthiness, and make an adjustment of the payment schedule necessary. Corresponding considerations naturally apply with respect to the supplier. If the bid is put together by a group subsidiary, the customer will often expect corporate or payment guarantees to be provided. The supposed “formality” of naming the contracting parties therefore already plays an important role when the bid is being put together.

2.3.2 Preamble

The preamble gives the parties an opportunity to describe the **genesis and objectives** of the contract. The contents of the preamble are not therefore usually controversial. It may however be that the discussion of the wording gives rise to differing expectations, for instance regarding the allocation of roles between the parties involved in the project. The preamble can therefore be used to ensure that all the parties are proceeding from the same basic assumptions. Once the contract has been concluded, the preamble serves above all to help future readers (for instance the project manager or an arbitrator) to get a feel for the document. The preamble which it writes when drawing the bid up therefore gives the supplier the opportunity to suggest the general ‘line of travel’ of the contract and how it should subsequently be interpreted.

2.3.3 The Planned

In a contract the business partners specify above all what services they are promising each other. Because the fulfilling of this promise is the actual aim of the contract, the duties which relate to it are also called **"primary duties"**. For instance, in a contract of sale one undertakes to supply goods, and in a rental contract to grant the other party the use of an item of property. The counterperformance in these cases is generally a monetary payment by the person or entity that receives the property. The examples given are archetypal forms of contract which are commonly found. In Germany they are regulated by the Civil Code (BGB), which was enacted as long ago as 1900.

A common feature of the commercial world nowadays is **mixed purpose contracts**, i.e. contracts which combine various types of primary duties. An example of a mixed purpose contract is the **EPC (Engineering, Procurement and Construction) contract**, which is widespread in the capital goods market. Examples of the typical subject matter of an EPC contract are the construction of a production plant or power station. In this case the supplier not only draws up the design plans, it also procures the necessary materials and carries out the construction works. Often the supplier even commits itself in the EPC contract to do "everything necessary" to ensure that the works are able to be handed over at the promised point in time as a finished **turnkey project**. Due to its complex and multifaceted nature, such a contract cannot be clearly categorized according to the BGB (Huck 2006, p. 41). However, it is clear that a turnkey contract basis entails the risk for the supplier of having to carry out works which are not explicitly referred to in the contract in any way. Indeed, as a rule this is precisely why the customer wishes to have such a contract. What matters to it is that it gets the plant that it wants at the previously agreed price. It does usually not want to assume the risk of the works which have been costed by the supplier not actually being adequate for this purpose. We will examine the subject of "risk allocation" in more detail later. At this point it should be sufficient to stress that in the first part of the contract the parties should describe as precisely as possible what it is that they are promising to the other side: Who does what, and when and how?

Definition **"The Planned"** = the parties' promises of what they will do for the other party, and when and how they will do it (primary duties).

Unlike the customer, the supplier is interested in specifying its primary duties as conclusively as possible. In any case the parties should describe the primary duties as precisely as possible and specify them in the contract appendices. Although it is often said that the best contract is one which the parties never read again, such an expectation is unrealistic, particularly in the case of complex services and industrial goods. The parties need the **utmost clarity** in this area in order to be able to draw up a realistic project costing. Such clarity can however only be achieved as from the negotiation phase—through the exchanging of information with the other side. The exchanging of information is only possible based on the bid.

Another point: as a rule contracts are not performed by the same people as those who negotiated them. Instead, in many companies there is an organizational separation of the marketing and project execution functions. This means that when in doubt the people performing the contract only do and demand what they can see in the contract document. Besides, only an obligation that has been incorporated into the contract is actually legally effective and enforceable.[1]

The primary aim of putting a bid together is therefore to provide a detailed, clear and conclusive description of what is planned.

2.3.4 The Unplanned

When putting the bid together (and later on, during the negotiations), the supplier naturally focuses on the primary duties. However, it must also consider what would happen if things do not go as planned. For if the primary duties that have been assumed are not fulfilled as promised, this will naturally lead to subsequent claims. For example, in the case of delayed supply, the supplier may become liable to provide compensation. Conversely, in the event of a delay in paying the purchase price, the customer generally undertakes to pay late payment interest. Such duties are called **"secondary duties"** because they only arise from an infringement of a primary duty**.** If both sides fulfill the contract as agreed, then they do not incur any secondary duties. However, it is precisely the complex business transactions which interest us here which are not as a rule carried out precisely as originally planned.

Whilst the secondary duties relate to infringements of the contract due to a party's actions or omissions, "unplanned" obligations may of course arise even without the assistance of the parties. This primarily relates to **unforeseen events**, such as force majeure, unexpected shortages of raw materials, unfavorable weather conditions, accidents, or changed general economic circumstances. These are only some of the difficulties that a project manager often has to contend with. What is common to everything "unplanned" is that they may lead to time delays, additional costs and financial losses for the contracting parties.

Definition **"The Unplanned"** = the agreement between the parties as to what they want to do if infringements of primary duties or other unforeseen events should occur.

This part of the contract therefore mainly deals with **how risks are handled.** Many risks can be minimized or mitigated, for instance by creating accounting contingencies or taking out insurances. But they cannot as a rule be completely eliminated. The parties therefore have no alternative but to agree on who should bear the corresponding risk. The way in which this is done is only decided in the negotiation phase. We will therefore examine it in more detail in Sect. 3 (Phase II: negotiations). However, we already wish to show at this point the subjects which should always be addressed in the exchange contract under the heading of "The Unplanned".

---

[1] As shown above by the example of the EPC contract, this applies both to explicit duties and also to those which are only implicit. However this statement does not of course apply to duties which already oblige the parties by law. The supplier of a power station is therefore of course already legally obliged to adhere to the locally applicable environmental and occupational health and safety rules and regulations.

One preliminary comment about this: when putting the bid together the supplier should not forget that the customer usually does not merely sign the contract that is submitted, but actually wants to negotiate it. And this negotiation will hardly lead to an improvement in the supplier's position. This is significant in two respects. Firstly, the supplier's initial bid normally represents its **"best case"**. Although negotiations often take unexpected turns, no customer will demand in the negotiations that it should take on more risks than the supplier has allocated to it in the bid. So the supplier must already have incorporated into the bid whatever it hopes to achieve during the negotiation phase.

At the same time, it must also leave itself some **room for negotiation**, for negotiations are normally only successful if one is able to make concessions to the other side. This must also be taken into consideration already when drafting the bid. At the same time, the risk profile offered to the customer must not of course be so extreme that the latter does not even want to engage in negotiations. The specifying of "The Unplanned" in the bid therefore involves treading a fine line between the expectations of the supplier and those of the customer.

The precise rights and duties that can and have to be specified in relation to unplanned contingencies naturally depend on the system of law to which the contract will be subject. The parties are basically free to choose the**applicable law** as they wish. This means that a German plant manufacturer and its Chinese customer may, for instance, agree on German, Chinese or even Swiss law. We will examine the subject in more detail in the next section, which deals with the final provisions (cf. Sect. 2.3.5).

Here is therefore a brief sketch of four important topics in the "Unplanned" category which should be addressed in any event:

Quality Defects

In the bid the supplier must set out what it wishes to do if a defect arises in relation to the goods that have been supplied. If the contract does not comment on this, the provisions of the system of law which is applicable to the contract apply. The legal quality defect provisions vary greatly between different countries. Contracting parties from different countries often therefore have a differing understanding of this overall subject area. It is therefore advisable for the supplier to propose a **definition** of what a "quality defect" actually means. It may for instance choose to take the same approach as the provisions under German law, where a quality defect is defined as a deviation of the goods supplied from the contractually agreed specification (cf. Sect. 434 of the BGB). The specification of the goods then usually exceeds the limits of the main contract itself and is specified in the detailed technical appendices.

The bid should also specify the timeframe over which the goods are guaranteed to be free of defects. The supplier should also establish what exactly it proposes to do if a defect does arise. This may, for instance, mean repairs or additional deliveries. In both instances the question then arises of the length of time for which the now repaired or re-delivered property is guaranteed. It is also important to establish whether the supplier or the customer is allowed to choose between various defect rectification measures.

Delayed Delivery

The supplier should also state its position with regard to delayed delivery on its part. It will generally try to limit its liability for the customer's losses to a specific sum. It is advisable to specify a as **"liquidated damages"** a specific sum per delay period (*e.g. 100 euros per day*). Delays to the project may cause enormous economic losses for the customer. If the supplier offers liquidated damages, it must prepare itself for contentious discussions in the negotiation phase. On the one hand the figure offered may be so unattractive that the customer is not interested in it in the first place. On the other hand, it is often economically impossible for the supplier to assume this risk in its entirety. A sense of proportion is therefore required when drawing up the bid. For this, the level, frequency and upper limit of the liquidated damages can be varied. The question of which delays if any the supplier is to be responsible for must also be addressed here. In addition, the bid should include a proposal regarding the action to be taken in a "*worst case*" scenario—in other words if due to excessive delay the customer loses its economic interest in the project.

Late Payment

At issue in the case of late payment is the question of what happens if the customer does not fulfill its primary duty to pay the contract price on time. The benchmark for determining the late payment interest is the supplier's **financing costs** and the **normal commercial interest rate**. The usual arrangement in practice is for late payment interest of X percent above a commonly used reference interest rate (*e.g. EURIBOR + 3 %*) to be incurred.

Damages

One of the most important questions which the supplier must answer when putting the bid together is how it will deal with losses which it itself causes. On the one hand it is an evident requirement of **fairness** that one is responsible for losses which one has caused. On the other hand, due to the high level of risk involved, strict adherence to this requirement would often lead to the business **not being economically attractive** for the supplier. This relates both to damage to the customer's property and to consequential financial losses (e.g. due to loss of profit or injury caused to the customer's employees). The supplier's liability may arise both from its breach of contract and from statutory provisions (e.g. product liability laws) (Cummins et al. 2011, p. 80). The financial expenditure may be enormous in these cases since the customer's economic survival may be threatened in an extreme case. The supplier demanding a limitation of liability for losses it has caused therefore constitutes a major problem. As the customer sees it, this is tantamount to trying to wriggle out of any responsibility in advance. In this case, the supplier is asking for nothing less than "**carte blanche**" to do as it pleases. Alternatively, it must quantify all the risks which are expected to be associated with the contract in accordance with proper accounting principles. However, what is involved here is indemnifying losses which simply cannot be quantified in advance. That is why, unlike in the case of liquidated damages, any a priori limiting of the amount of compensation is difficult. For example, the damaging of the customer's production facility may lead to it being liable to pay compensation to its own customers. However, at the time when the bid is being drawn up the supplier usually does not know with whom the customer has concluded purchase contracts. Still less will the customer inform it of the precise contents of those contracts. It is therefore impossible for the supplier to know how great the customer's losses would turn out to be. So here too it must try to determine in advance the provisions which would make economic sense for it whilst also being acceptable to the customer.

2.3.5 Close

The provisions relating to what is planned and what is unplanned are followed by the contract's final provisions (the "Close"). These are primarily formalities which ensure the effectiveness and legal operability of the contract independently of the specific project. They include, for instance, the so-called written form requirement which stipulates that changes to the contract are only effective if they are recorded in writing. Frequently found are also clauses stating that the contract as such remains valid even if individual provisions of the contract are invalid; such provisions are called severability clauses (or salvatorius clauses from the Latin "salvare" = to rescue) because they "rescue" the overall contract even if a court should rule that individual parts of the contract are ineffective. Lastly, the final provisions also include clauses dealing with the assignment of specific rights and duties by the contracting parties; often such provisions are only permitted with the prior agreement of the other party. However, the final provisions also include two subject areas that are crucial to the success of the project: the provisions relating to the choice of law and those relating to the resolution of disputes.

Choice of Law

Choice of law means the parties' decision as to which system of law is to apply to the contract. As we have established, the parties are basically free to agree on the **applicable law**. If two German companies conclude a contract for the construction of a facility in Germany, they will normally make the contract subject to German law: since it is applicable to them in any event, no explicit provision to this effect has to be made. The situation is different in the international business sphere. If the other contracting party is a foreign company, the question arises as to which system of law the contract and its execution are to be evaluated under.

If the contract says nothing about this, this question is decided according to the respective **"international private law" (IPL)** of the countries concerned. In contrast to what is often assumed, IPL is not a separate legal system in its own right, instead it (only) decides which national law is to be applied to the contract. By contrast, as a treaty under international law the United Nations Convention on Contracts for the International Sale of Goods, (CISG) of 11th April 1980 is an autonomous source of law which can take the place of national sale of goods legislation. However, the CISG is not generally suitable for order and project management contracts since it exclusively governs the sale of movable property. Since 2009 this is being determined in all the member states of the European Union according to the same regulation (EC Regulation on the law applicable to contractual obligations no. 593/2008, also known as "Rome I"). However, in the context of professional contract management it is essential to clarify this point fully and explicitly in advance. As is generally known, the legal systems of different countries differ greatly. The decision regarding which system of law the contract is to be subject to sets the framework in which the provisions relating to what is planned and what is unplanned can be written. Only if the contract lawyer knows which legal system he is dealing with can he draft the contract in the first place. It is therefore essential for the applicable law to have been clearly specified when the bid was being drawn up.

The **customer's** anticipated **reaction** should also be considered in this regard. In the case of a foreign customer with little experience of German law, it may be advisable for the German supplier to offer from the outset to use the law of a third country (e.g. Switzerland). This means that neither side has "home advantage", as both sides are on unfamiliar terrain when negotiating the contract. It is then fundamentally important for the supplier to draw up the contract with the help of lawyers who are familiar with the system of law that is involved. Lastly, it must be borne in mind that an international project contract must always also take at least some account of the law of the customer's country, for even if the parties agree on a foreign system of law, this does not invalidate the mandatory legal provisions that apply in the customer's country. For example, if a German builder of power stations undertakes to construct a facility in Asia, it must naturally abide by the local environmental or health and safety regulations. It is therefore essential to also consult a lawyer from the customer's country about the drawing up of the bid.

Dispute Resolution Mechanism

Closely connected with the applicable law is the question of how to deal with a **dispute relating to the parties' rights and duties**. Here too, the parties are basically free to choose the dispute resolution mechanism which suits them. This is by no means just a "formality". Even if the bid is put together carefully and the contract negotiations are detailed, it must be assumed that differences of opinion or conflicts will arise between the parties in the course of the performance of the contract. We will examine in more detail what constitutes a conflict and the principles according to which it can be resolved in the next section which relates to the execution phase of contract management (see Sect. 4.5). With regard to the putting together of the bid, it should be sufficient here to provide a brief overview of what the dispute resolution mechanism in the contract should look like.

It is advisable to have a **three-stage dispute resolution mechanism** (Greger and von Münchhausen 2010, pp. 239 and 240):

I. Negotiation between the parties (initially at the employee level, and if unsuccessful at a higher management level)

II. Involvement of a neutral third party (mediation, evaluation)
III. Ruling by a court or an arbitration tribunal

The following applies with regard to involving a neutral third party: at the time when the bid is drawn up or when the contract is concluded it is difficult to foresee the exact type of conflicts which may arise or to make an a priori decision to use a specific procedure (e.g. mediation or conciliation) (Greger and von Münchhausen 2010, p. 240). The dispute resolution clause is therefore intended to provide a **flexible mechanism** which leaves the parties free to choose the best option in each specific case. As an example of this, see the 2001 Alternative Dispute Resolution rules of the International Chamber of Commerce (ICC), Art. 5, according to which the neutral third party is initially selected which then jointly comes to an agreement with the parties regarding the best procedure to be used.

2.3.6 Appendices

The contract described at the start of this work which was concluded between Deutsche Bahn AG and Siemens AG for the purchase of ICE trains is enormous in scope, running to 8000 pages. By far the **largest part of the contract** consists of appendices. This may be viewed as being typical of contracts for the capital goods sector. It makes no difference what the appendices are called. The terms "annex", "enclosure", "attachment" and "exhibit" are all equally common. All that matters is that the terms chosen are used consistently and uniformly throughout the contract.

The annexes do not contain any provisions of their own. Rather, they are needed in order to specify the provisions that have been incorporated in the main contract regarding rights and duties. Their intended purpose is therefore above all the **"sifting out" of data** which would encumber the contract wording, or even make it unreadable (Langenfeld 2010, p. 27). For example, the builder of a power station may give its assurance in the main contract that the plant will be capable of providing a specific minimum level of power. The main contract itself would then include the supplier's primary duty to construct a power station with a level of efficiency X. As a rule, the factors used to calculate the level of efficiency, and how they are to be measured, is only specified in the annexes. Two things are therefore important when putting the bid together: firstly, the supplier must ensure that it provides all the information in the annexes that is required for an understanding of the rights and duties which are set out in the main contract. Secondly, it must ensure that this information is also fully and correctly linked to the main contract. This is the only way of guaranteeing that the customer is properly able to understand the provisions in their entirety.

2.3.7 Summary

As we have seen, the bid is primarily concerned with provisions about what is planned and what is not planned, but nevertheless taken into account. At the same time however, the bid must also contain an introduction and final provisions, so in effect it is nothing other than a complete contract. Hence the bid represents the

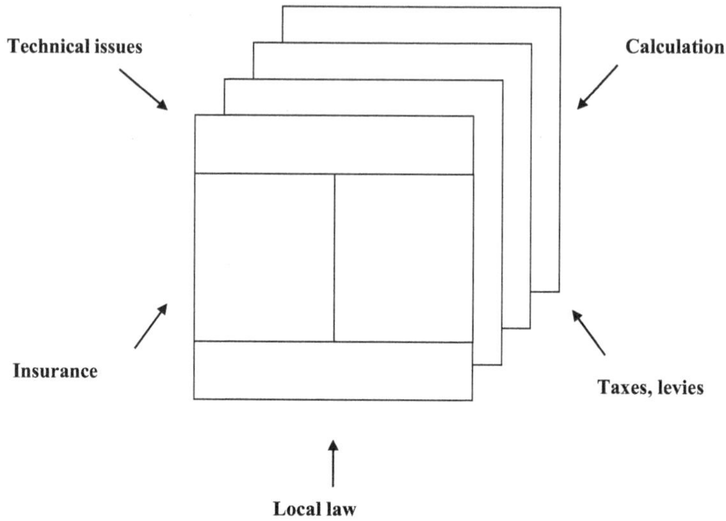

Fig. 3 The bid as the implementation of the project strategy

bringing together of all the relevant technical, commercial and legal aspects of the project strategy. Figure 3 is intended to illustrate this.

2.4 The Process of Drawing Up the Bid

How must the process of drawing up the bid be structured in order to arouse the customer's interest whilst also leaving the supplier scope for negotiation? This question must now be answered taking account of all the relevant aspects of the product strategy. This requires **interdisciplinary collaboration** between all the parties involved in the supplier's organization.

Otherwise there is a risk of the drafters of the main contract and of the enclosures respectively not feeling responsible for the other part. That could lead to both parts being developed, and being negotiated, independently of each other. **Discrepancies** might arise between the two constituent parts of the contract. This must naturally be avoided. In particular, the main contract must not, for instance, refer to the wrong enclosure. It is even more important that the main contract does not refer to enclosures which don't even exist. Equally, there must not be any enclosures which are not referred to at all in the main contract. This danger exists above all if brochures or product information are enclosed with the bid without having been linked to the contract beforehand. At best, such discrepancies "merely" lead to doubts as to the supplier's professionalism; at worst, they may form the basis of legal duties which the supplier had never intended. Such errors can only be avoided if all the parties involved are familiar with all the constituent parts of the contract, and if they closely coordinate their work.

Like any other form of **teamwork**, the putting together of the bid requires a clear assignment of responsibilities and separation of tasks. Also indispensable is the designating of a person in overall charge who coordinates the work in the team. In many companies this overall responsibility lies with the Sales department member of staff who is responsible for the customer. As a specialist in relation to the product that is offered, this person usually has a technical background. The following explanatory comments are intended to provide pointers as to what needs to be looked out for when collaborating on the putting together of a bid:

A lawyer should of course draft the main contract. Ideally, the supplier will have its own **contract lawyers** (i.e. legally qualified **contract managers**) who act not just as specialists on legal issues relating to the putting together and negotiating of the bid, but who above all also understand the supplier's business model. There is one major advantage of this compared to using external legal experts such as attorneys. From what has been said so far, it is clear that the drafting and negotiating of the bid is equivalent to implementing the supplier's business model. The people who are entrusted with this process must therefore develop a detailed understanding of the supplier's strengths and weaknesses in order for the business to be made an economic success. This requires in-depth insights into the supplier's internal data, decision-making processes, and calculations. Many suppliers prefer to restrict the provision of such knowledge to their own employees only. Similar considerations apply, even if to a lesser extent, regarding the consulting of local lawyers which is necessary for business transacted abroad. As mentioned, the law of the customer's country is often declared to be the applicable law for the contract; even if this is not the case, the mandatory legal rules of the customer's country must be observed. Ideally therefore, the supplier should have a subsidiary company in the customer's country on whose support it can count. If this is not the case, then consulting an outside lawyer as a local expert does not as a rule present any problem. This is because the in-house lawyer who is familiar with the business model can direct the outside lawyer's attention to the individual issues which are relevant (e.g. local requirements regarding the form of the contract and environmental protection legislation), without all the internal matters having to be disclosed.

From the description of the primary services onwards, the contract manager must collaborate closely with his technical colleague, who is often an engineer. Only if what is feasible, and intended to be achieved, from a technical standpoint is understood can it be properly legally worded. The necessity of collaboration continues with the handling of the unplanned: it is essential to have a common understanding of what can go wrong from a technical point of view—and of what is technically possible in terms of solving problems which do occur.

It goes without saying that the costs, risks and expected profits that are connected with all these issues must be commercially assessed and approved. Consolidated in the pricing are all the factors which are incorporated into the putting together of the bid. The team must naturally therefore include a **commercial specialist** too, who influences the entire bidding process.

These three "faculties" (the technical, the commercial and the legal expert) must therefore collaborate particularly closely. For example, the legal expert must explain the main part of the contract to his colleagues. This involves him referring to the links with the appendices and explaining the degree to which the content of the appendices has a bearing on the contract. Then, the engineer who is charged with drafting the product specification must, for instance, be clear about what the legal consequences of not achieving the specification would be (e.g. rejection of the product, liability for quality defects). In turn, the commercial expert must clarify (and/or explain) what the economic consequences of not achieving the specification would be (e.g. repayment of the purchase price or rectification costs).

For his part, the legal expert must also of course understand where he needs an appendix for incorporating the required data into the contract. He can then link existing technical and commercial documents with the main contract.

The need for support to be provided by further experts, in particular **tax, export, or insurance experts**, underlies the entire contract. These people can usually be consulted in order to clarify specific individual issues. However, the overall picture of the bid must be conveyed to them in order for them to be able to provide expert advice.

The interdisciplinary bid team will work more effectively together the more staff are willing and able to look beyond the limits of their own specific area. The best possible bringing together in the bid of all the relevant, technical, commercial and legal aspects of the business is only possible if all those involved cultivate an understanding of their counterparts' aspects and therefore keep the **"bigger picture"** in view.

Lastly, a further comment—about the use of **specimen** or**standard contracts**. The complex process of putting a bid together can be greatly simplified if the supplier uses specimen contract wordings for the purpose. Once the feat of interdisciplinary collaboration that has been described has been successfully accomplished, it naturally seems to make sense to use the contract which has been devised in this way as the basis for the submission of further bids also. Specimen contracts which then only have to be adapted to the specific features of each respective project are kept on hand for this purpose in many companies. Care should however be taken when using such specimen contracts. In many jurisdictions particularly exacting requirements are applied to contracts that have been drawn up in advance by one party as standard wordings. This is because the relevant legislation frequently assumes that specimen contracts indicate that the party using them is in a disproportionately powerful position. This is because specimen contracts are usually worded very heavily in this party's favor. If such contracts are then actually used, the legislation in many countries assumes that the other side, which is supposedly weaker, is particularly worthy of protection. This is because it could be coerced into agreeing to the preformulated standard conditions against its will. In this case the clauses which favor the drafter of the standard contract are then subject to particularly rigorous checking of their validity. For instance, in Germany such contracts often have to be gaged against the **law relating to "standard terms of business"**. This can lead to clauses which are particularly favorable to their user being declared invalid when they are reviewed by a court. Statue law, more unfavorable for the user, would then apply instead, which would naturally have implications for the profitability of the project.

It is therefore essential to ensure that any specimen wordings are adequately customized when putting the bid together. Likewise, the impression should be avoided that one is presenting the customer with one's "standard conditions". However, this is already required from a marketing point of view since it is precisely customers in project and plant engineering and construction business who naturally expect not be given "standard bids" but a "special bid" which is tailored to their needs.

2.5 Summary

We have seen that a contract must be drafted in the phase when the bid is put together. We have also looked at the constituent parts of the contract and the processes which are necessary for drawing it up. We now wish to see what happens if the customer is interested in the bid.

3 Phase II: Negotiation

What do we have to know about the negotiation phase from the viewpoint of contract management? For a comprehensive and detailed presentation of negotiation management in plant engineering and construction and project business, reference can be made to the article written by Geiger (see chapter **"Negotiation Management"**). We can therefore restrict ourselves to the following key points:

We initially want to examine when the negotiation phase actually begins. It usually, but not always, begins when the bid is submitted (Sect. 3.1).

The submitting of the bid basically marks the starting point of not one but two negotiations, which run in parallel. On the one hand of course, the negotiations between the supplier and the customer regarding the customer contract take place (**external negotiations**). On the other hand, negotiations also takes place between the negotiating team and its management (**internal negotiations**). Both on the supplier's and the customer's side, the external negotiating team can only act in accordance with its negotiating remit. The progress of the external negotiations therefore makes it necessary for the teams to continually confer with their own respective organizations about how the other side's demands should be handled. In line with the main focus of this section, we will approach both negotiations from the viewpoint of the supplier. However, what is stated here applies correspondingly to the customer's side.

In the external negotiations (cf. Sect. 3.2) the two main constituent parts of the contract are handled differently: the agreeing of "what is planned" tends to require "win-win" negotiations (cf. Sect. 3.2.1), whereas the unplanned contingencies elaborated in "win-lose" negotiations (cf. Sect. 3.2.2). The fact there is nevertheless a need to take a nuanced view of this principle is explained in Sect. 3.2.3.

The internal negotiation (cf. Sect. 3.3) mainly consists of two processes. In order to decide how to handle the customer's demands in the external negotiations, they must be continually evaluated and quantified. In Sect. 3.3.1 the process of risk quantification is therefore briefly described. This forms the basis of the second internal process, the approval procedure, in which management can decide on the content of the local team's negotiating remit. We will look at this process in more detail in Sect. 3.3.2.

3.1 Submitting the Bid

If the customer shows interest, the negotiation phase begins with the submission of the bid by the supplier. As has been seen, this consists of a full contract together with a **covering letter**. The letter states both that the bid is binding, and the length of time for which it remains so. In addition, the letter does of course provide the opportunity to refer to the special advantages of the bid, and to lay the ground for the start of negotiations.

Two tools are frequently used in connection with the submitting of the bid—the **Memorandum of Understanding**" and the "**Letter of Intent**". They are both in a sense "auxiliary contracts" which are intended to make the stage-by-stage performance of the actual customer contract possible. Such step-by-step performance is usual especially in the case of major projects. If two companies get into discussions with each other in order to sound out the possibilities of working together, the outcome is of course uncertain. The reason for them talking to each other is precisely to find out whether or not it may be in their mutual interests to conclude a contract. However, the factors which have a bearing on the decision usually lie only partly within the control of the companies themselves. This is, for instance, the case in relation to the question of whether the supplier has the necessary technical expertise, or whether the customer does actually want to carry out the project at all.

However, many other factors affecting the decision **are outside the parties' control** and can only be clarified in the course of the negotiations. For example, the customer generally negotiates the financing of the project in parallel to its negotiating of the exchange contract. These two negotiations influence each other. For instance, the choice of a specific technology or a specific supplier often influences the possibilities of obtaining third party finance. At the same time, investors or the providers of credit often demand certain protection mechanisms in the exchange contract. In order to secure their "return on investment" or the repayment of the credit provided, a minimum output capacity is often specified for the facility. The rights of recourse which the provider of credit has in the event of the customer's insolvency are another example.

In order to clarify such issues, the companies involved must of course expend resources and exchange information with each other. Then, gradually over the course of the clarification process more and more **benchmark data relating to possible collaboration** emerges. In a situation like this the parties often sign declarations of intent. In international trade these are usually called a

"Memorandum of Understanding" (MoU) or "Letter of Intent" (LoI). The former is a declaration of intent that is signed by both sides, whilst the latter actually represents a unilateral declaration by one party only. However, as a rule this distinction is only of a theoretical (legal) nature, and in practice both terms are usually used without differentiation.

In both cases the purpose of the declaration of intent is to record the benchmark data which is starting to take shape, to describe the further process of clarification, and to agree on the allocation of the costs that are incurred. The declaration of intent is also often used as a way of concluding non-disclosure agreements. This is advisable if, for instance, the potential customer is interested in detailed technical information or component tests. The supplier may only be prepared to disclose the corresponding data if the recipient treats it as confidential. Such issues can be clarified in a legally binding manner in a MoU or a LoI without either party already having to commit itself to concluding the exchange contract.

In the case of the step-by-step methods of concluding contracts that have been described, the task of contract management is to flesh out what the parties want and to clearly differentiate between what is legally binding and what is intended but not binding.

3.2 External Negotiations

The external negotiations with the customer mainly focus on the two main constituent parts of the contract. In this regard the negotiating of what is planned differs from what is unplanned. As already indicated, the former may be characterized as a "win-win"—negotiation, whereas the latter tends to be a "win-lose" negotiation. We wish to clarify the reasons for this in this section. We can use Fig. 4 as a basis for doing so.

What exactly is meant by the terms "win-win" and "win-lose"? The interpretation of both terms provided by Bühring-Uhle et al. (2009) may be helpful: value creation for "win-win", and the claiming of value for "win-lose" (Bühring-Uhle et al. 2009, p. 54). **Value-claiming negotiations (win-lose)** are those in which a limited resource or a risk is shared between two parties in such a way that any gains for one side entail losses for the other—and vice versa. In figurative terms, such a "zero-sum game" involves "dividing up" a cake of a limited size at the other party's expense (*"slicing the pie"*).

By contrast, **value-creating negotiations (win-win)** aim to make the cake bigger (*"enlarging the pie"*). The aim in this case is a negotiating outcome which puts both parties in a better position. How this can be achieved is what we want to examine next.

3.2.1 The Planned and "Win-Win"

Under the heading of "what is planned" we had summarized those aspects of the project which actually matter to the parties. From the customer's **point of view this is above all a precise description of the scope of supply** and services. From the

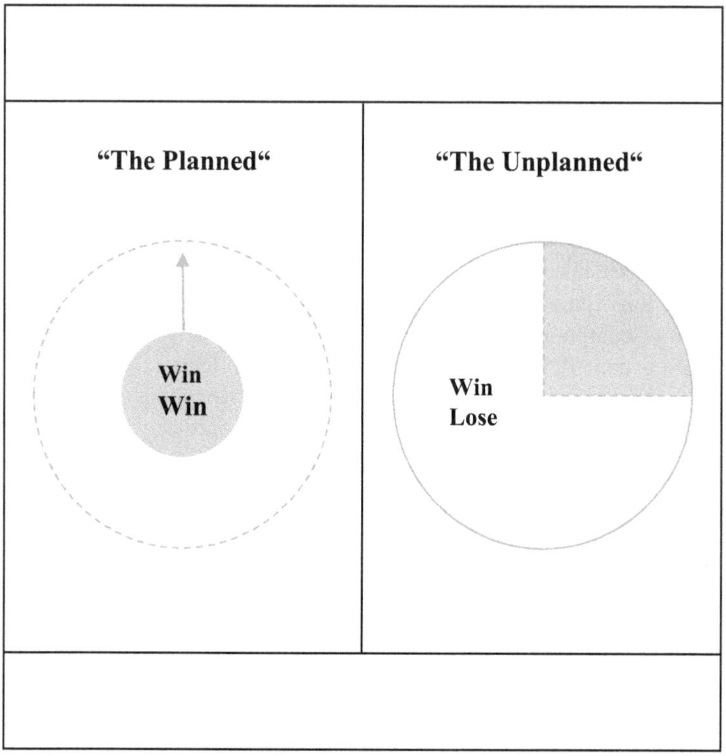

Fig. 4 The contract in the negotiations with the customer

supplier's point of view what matters is the price to be paid for this. Once the parties begin to confer regarding these two aspects, they start a joint search for the **optimal combination of performance and counterperformance**. The optimal combination is found when the package can no longer be altered any further without making the result worse for one of the two sides. In practice the achieving of this ideal (and virtually pareto-optimal) combination is of course very difficult. But even an approximation to it is rightly understood to be a "win-win solution", and the negotiations aiming to achieve it can be characterized as "value-creating". This approximation can be achieved in three ways, which we want to examine briefly below.

The value-creating negotiations hinge on the parties' **interests**. This means the underlying needs, motives and wishes which form the basis of one side's demands. A party's interests differ from the **positions** which a party adopts: a position is a specific demand. Positions are often irreconcilable, or have to lead to compromise. The nature of compromise is that neither side can get its position accepted in full. By contrast, value-creating negotiation looks behind the position—and by doing so attempts to do justice to both sides' interests.

In contrast to what is frequently assumed, value-creating negotiation does not, for instance, center on the search for common ground between the parties. Quite the contrary: in order to put together an ideal package of performance and counterperformance the parties must above all come to appreciate their ***differences***. This is because it is precisely if the parties' preferences and/or expectations differ that they can be combined together for their mutual benefit.

First, let us look at an example of **differing preferences**: the supplier of a facility is an industrial enterprise with international operations which benefits from favorable financing costs due to its size. The customer is a company which is founded by investors specifically for the project (a so-called "*Special Purpose Company*"). The financial resources of such a Special Purpose Company are of course limited. In the discussions, two important subjects of negotiation are firmed up: the time of payment and the security of payment. In our example it may be the case that the supplier is particularly concerned about the customer's ability to pay and therefore insists on a payment guarantee e.g. in the form of a bank guarantee. On the other hand, a deferral of the payment schedule may not be so crucial to the supplier due to its low financing costs. It would therefore be more important for the supplier to receive a payment guarantee than to achieve an ideal payment schedule.

From the customer's point of view the situation may be the exact opposite: what particularly matters to it is making payments as late as possible, since its high financing costs significantly erode the profit which it is aiming to make. The costs which it incurs in order to obtain a bank guarantee may be significantly lower in comparison. It would therefore be more important for it in relative terms to agree extended payment terms than to save the expense of obtaining a bank guarantee.

In this situation a **trade-off** is possible: the parties agree on considerably extended payment terms for the customer, subject to a bank guarantee having previously been issued for the supplier's benefit. The solution which is found in this way is not ideal for either side—but it is better for both sides than the position that they started from. In particular, it is better than a compromise between the original positions (limited payment guarantee and only moderately extended payment terms).

The basis of this solution is formed by the differing preferences of the parties. When these are identified they can be combined in a trade-off in a way which creates value.

A "win-win solution" can also be found if the parties have **differing future expectations**. In relation to a solar power plan for example, the customer and the supplier may have differing opinions regarding the anticipated feed-in tariffs: the supplier expects there to be future increases in the public subsidies paid to the customer. The customer does not share this view. No trade-off is possible in this situation. The only sensible option for the customer is to base the discussion about price solely on its own income forecasts. Nonetheless, there is still the potential in this case to achieve an agreement which creates value. The supplier can attempt to get the customer to agree to a *conditional* contract clause (a so-called "*contingent contract*"): They jointly agree the purchase price (based on the customer's expectations). If the customer's income were to increase subsequently (contrary to its expectations), the purchase price would increase in line with it. In this case, the potential for creating value therefore lies in one side promising the other side something which is of no value to itself, but does nonetheless have a value for the other side.

The third option for creating value lies in seeking **complementary interests**. For example, both the customer and the supplier of a production plant can use it as an important reference model for future business. It may therefore be in both sides' interests to jointly undertake and pay for the certification of the facility.

To summarize: a value-creating win-win solution can be found in three ways:

- The parties having differing preferences
- The parties having differing expectations
- The parties having complementary interests

As was made clear by the examples used to illustrate these three points, the finding of win-win solutions depends on the parties' willingness to communicate openly with each other. Only if both sides exchange information about their interests, preferences and expectations can they jointly find solutions which create value.

For this to be done, contract management has to cope with **conflicts** which are inherent to value creation. This phase of the negotiations is critically dependent on the free exchanging of information and the creative search for joint solutions. Negotiators typically want to avoid tying themselves to specific details before a consensus is within their reach and the process can be concluded (Lewicki et al. 2003, p. 92). Commitments to precisely defined terms, yet alone written agreements, are often felt to be disruptive to the process, and consequently avoided. This naturally conflicts with the legal requirement for a contractual agreement to be clearly worded with nothing left unresolved (Langenfeld 2010, pp. 26 and 27). The structuring of the negotiations which create value is therefore always a **balancing act.** The more experience the parties involved have, the better at it will they become. However, it is always advisable to direct the value-creating negotiations to specific provisions which are laid down in writing at the earliest possible stage. The reason for this is simple: in what tends to be superficial discussions about principles and demands there is often only an illusion of agreement. Only once the attempt is made to put the joint understanding into words do the parties notice that they were not actually thinking along the same lines at all. It is only through striving together to find the right wording that agreement is actually reached. Teamwork is recommended in this regard too, instead of separating the two steps in time and space (supposed initial agreement reached by the negotiators followed by the respective contract lawyers/managers tying up the loose ends): Both sides' negotiators should arrange for their contract lawyers to attend the discussions in order to provide direct support for them.

3.2.2 The Unplanned and "Win-Lose"

As we have seen, under the heading of "The Unplanned" the contract mainly deals with the allocation of risks. Normally no party will state its willingness to assume all the conceivable contractual risks. The parties must therefore negotiate about who is to assume which risk. The allocating of risks is a classic **risk distribution negotiation**: what is to one side's disadvantage is to the other's advantage—and vice versa. Each side can therefore only get its way at the other side's expense. This means that when negotiating about "The Unplanned" the supplier basically wants the opposite of what the customer wants: e.g. a short (instead of a long) defects liability period, no liability (instead of full liability) for financial losses, and a high (instead of a low) interest rate.

The party's **sphere of responsibility** into which the risk concerned falls can be an indicator of how it should be allocated. However, as a rule it is the parties' economic constraints which are crucial. For instance, the supplier is often not able to assume liability for all the losses caused by it at a price which is acceptable to the customer. If it were to assume this responsibility it would have to factor substantial provisions into its pricing. The price which this would produce would frequently exceed the customer's budget. Therefore it is the case in project and plant engineering and construction business in particular that the parties will agree on various exclusions and limitations of liability. As the owner or operator of the facility, the customer is then frequently able to insure the remaining risks. Something similar applies in respect of the customer's frequent demand for the supplier to be responsible for any unexpected changes to the project without any alteration in the price. However, the customer often only has a limited amount of money to invest, and it has no possibility of making any appreciable additional payments subsequently.

In the negotiations about "unplanned contingencies", the demands made by one side are frequently at odds with the other side's **subjective views of what is fair**. In addition, lawyers are above all heavily involved in this part of the negotiations, and are therefore occasionally regarded as "professional pessimists", or "stumbling blocks to the concluding of contracts" by the other 'faculties'. It is therefore especially important in this regard that the whole negotiating team displays unity. The positions taken by the supplier's lawyer only offer a prospect of success if they have technical and commercial backing. Effective **teamwork** is therefore crucial to the supplier's success in this part of the negotiations also.

3.2.3 The "Negotiator's Dilemma" and the Parties' Room for Negotiation

In relation to "The Unplanned" the negotiation team therefore demands something **completely** different from what the team needs to do in respect of what is planned. Whereas the negotiating of what is planned was mainly about **value-creating cooperation**, the negotiating of what is unplanned is primarily about **getting one's own position accepted**. The two aspects of the negotiations therefore pursue conflicting goals and require contrasting negotiating tactics. This is the crux of what is called **the negotiator's dilemma.** The best results are achieved by negotiating teams who are good at handling this dilemma. For details of the negotiating tactics and the handling of the negotiator's dilemma, see chapter "Negotiation Management".

However, the principle that has just been set out must be considered in a nuanced manner in order to take account of the realities of the exchange contract. The negotiating of what is planned also requires the distribution of value. At the same time, the negotiating of unplanned contingencies also has the potential to create value:

The distribution of value also plays a major role in the negotiating of what is planned, since—in figurative terms—the parties also have to share out even an enlarged cake among themselves. If the parties have agreed one of the three options for a win-win solution, they nevertheless have to negotiate the way in which value will be distributed. This is also shown by a look at the examples cited above:

Value can be created by the supplier and the customer agreeing on a deferment of the payment schedule in exchange for a bank guarantee. This does not however state how long the deferment should be, or how extensive the bank guarantee should be. The answering of these questions is in turn associated with costs and risks for both sides. They can only be answered in a way which allocates value, i.e. at the expense of the other side.

Of course, this also applies to our example relating to diverging expectations. Even if the customer does not anticipate getting increased subsidies, this does not of course mean that it would be prepared to hand over 100 % of them to the supplier. The specifying of the precise proportion is again necessarily subject to the "win-lose" rationale.

And the same ultimately applies in relation to the existence of complementary interests. Even if the parties agree in principle to carry out certification procedures jointly, this still does not answer the question of how the costs which arise are to be apportioned. In this case too, the parties have no option but to distribute value amongst them.

Conversely, the negotiating of "The Unplanned" also provides opportunities to create value. The parties regularly assess risk probabilities differently. They are equally likely to have differing preferences with regard to the assumption of the various risks. This is also confirmed by a look at the examples we provided above: the supplier may for instance attach greater importance to the level of the arrears interest rate than to the length of the defects liability period. Conversely, the customer may have exactly the opposite preference. In the middle of the value-allocating negotiations there are therefore usually also opportunities for trade-offs which create value.

In summary, we can therefore state that in the customer negotiations each party wants to structure the contract for its own benefit. The dilemma that they face in doing so is that value creation and value distribution conflict with each other whilst also being inextricably linked. Their room for negotiation is set by the potential benefits for them. The supplier will typically submit an initial bid which is primarily designed for its benefit. The customer will respond with counterclaims that are at the other end of the spectrum. In the course of the negotiations both sides must then resolve the negotiator's dilemma for mutual benefit. In this process the negotiating

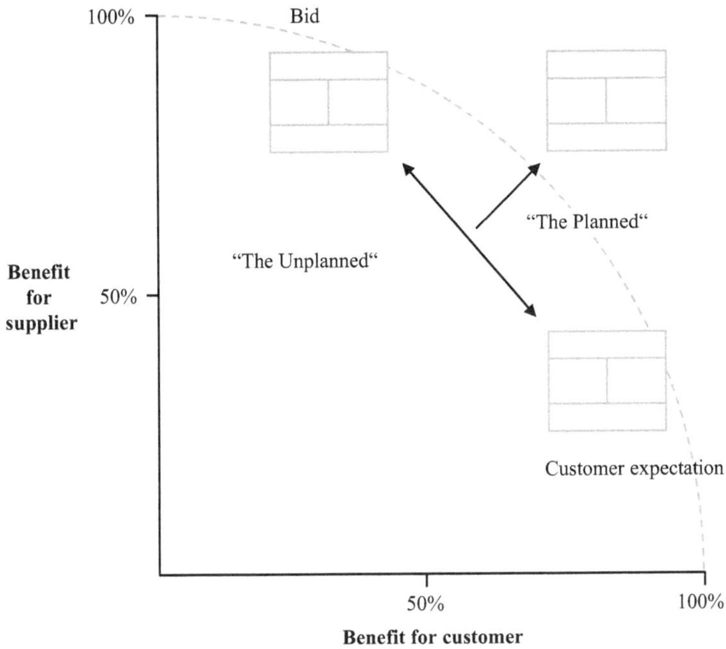

Fig. 5 The room for negotiation

of what is planned tends to lead to the joint creation of value, whereas the negotiating of "The Unplanned" tends to result in the apportioning of value to the benefit of one side only. The customer contract which results from the negotiations is therefore the outcome of a complex process. Figure 5 illustrates this in diagrammatic form.

What has been said also includes **conclusions that can be drawn for the drawing up of a bid**: when undertaking this the supplier should assume risks in such a way that they are in line with the cost-based provisions. Depending on its market power and the anticipated course of the negotiations, it should also leave room for concessions. For example, the supplier may accept average costs of 1 % of the purchase price for a 1-year defects liability period. If it assumes that the customer will not agree to the period that is offered and will demand at least a 2-year defects liability period, it must prepare for this eventuality already when putting the bid together. It either incorporates the 2 % provision—which it would need assuming a constant probability of defects over 2 years—directly into the price. Or alternatively, it must proceed based on the certainty that it raise the price during the negotiations. If it thinks there is not much prospect of either option being possible, it must already assume when it is putting the bid together that the project will not generate the expected profitability.

Finally, a few comments about the **make-up of the team** and the proper structuring of the negotiation process: in the case of complex capital goods transactions, it is usually teams which are tasked with carrying out the negotiations both by the supplier and the customer. Each side's team mainly consists of two groups of people:

- The actual **negotiating team** which engages in direct discussions with the other side. This includes in any event the project manager, who in the case of German industrial companies often has a technical background. He should be directly supported by a contract lawyer/manager. The latter must put the results of the negotiations into words, in other words he must write and update the draft contract during the meetings.
- The negotiating team relies on the assistance of **specialists** who can be consulted on technical, business or legal issues. The negotiating team is generally unable to assess 'then and there' the implications of any changes or additional requirements which the customer wants to have included, and it needs to confer with its company's in-house specialists. For example, the detailed planning of many capital goods is a highly complex task involving entire departments at the supplier's premises. The on-site negotiating team will have to refer to their specialist colleagues for the clarification of specific customer requests. This may also apply to the accountants who undertake detailed calculations of costs and prices. It is often also essential to involve experts in relation to the subjects of import and export regulations, taxes and levies, and the local legal system and jurisdiction.

As regards the structuring of the negotiating process, two further facets of it should be examined: the linking of the main contract and the appendices, and the subdivision of the negotiating teams into sub-groups. As we have seen, (cf. Sect. 2.4), a key challenge during the bid drafting phase is linking the main contract and the appendices together correctly. This **linking of the main contract and the appendices** must also of course be maintained during the negotiations. This can be laborious and time-consuming since the supplier's and customer's teams are often divided into sub-groups in the case of complex transactions. These teams then negotiate in parallel to each other regarding technical, commercial, or legal details. A major challenge for the project manager and his team is therefore maintaining an overview of the individual partial negotiations.

In addition, if the **negotiating team is divided into sub-groups** it is not uncommon for there to be a loyalty problem: it may happen that in the individual specialist negotiations loyalties switch from allegiance to the organization to allegiance to the specialist subject. This is because the value-creating negotiation of what is planned is mainly concerned with what is technically feasible and commercially desirable. By contrast, value-claiming negotiations are concerned with anticipating and apportioning risks. Engineers and business experts are therefore usually heavily involved in value-creating negotiations, whereas it is lawyers who are mainly involved in value-claiming negotiations. This means that the view may take hold among the former that agreement would be reached if only the lawyers didn't unnecessarily complicate matters. This naturally leads to the danger of an intercompany alliance being formed which influences the negotiations to the supplier's detriment. It is not uncommon for experienced customer teams to actively foster precisely such conflicts of loyalty in order to then exploit them for their own advantage. The manager who is responsible for the negotiating team must avert this danger. Scheduling regular consultation sessions has been shown to be one of the best ways of doing this.

3.3 The Internal Process

On both sides there is an internal process which runs in parallel to the external negotiations. As a rule, the on-site negotiating team is not authorized to take decisions on all the aspects of the transaction on its own. Rather, it acts according to the remit which it has been given by its own management. If and insofar as the other side's demands go beyond this remit, the team has to ask for it to be correspondingly extended. This may take place through a **structured internal approval process** as outlined in Sect. 3.3.2. This process is generally based on the **quantifying** of the risks concerned. Therefore we now want to examine how this can be done.

3.3.1 Risk Quantification

As we have seen, the negotiating of the exchange contract involves the interplay of the expected benefits and expected costs. As a rule, the expected benefit of an agreement for the supplier is the adjustment of the contract price. As a monetary benefit, it is already quantified and can therefore be directly incorporated into the internal approval process. This also applies to agreements the implementing of which would entail direct costs.

Dealing with **risks** is more difficult. When putting the bid together, the supplier must link the costing of the purchase price and the expected profit to a specific contractual risk profile. In the negotiations it then finds itself confronted with the customer's demands, which will usually result in it facing additional risks. In line with the nature of the exchange contract, the customer's demands for an increased assumption of risk usually relate to subjects within the field of "The Unplanned". Figure 6 illustrates these interrelationships.

In order for decisions regarding the assuming of such risks to be able to be made properly, they have to be quantified. For instance, in relation to the examples cited above in connection with the description of "The Unplanned", the supplier would have to answer the following questions: How would the customer's demand for a longer defects liability period affect the profitability of the contract? What financial consequences would a restructuring of the payment schedule or a reduction of the arrears interest rate have?

However, risk quantification is not only crucial to the value-distributing negotiations. One can also only get involved in value-creating trade-off if one quantifies the various options and consequently makes them comparable.

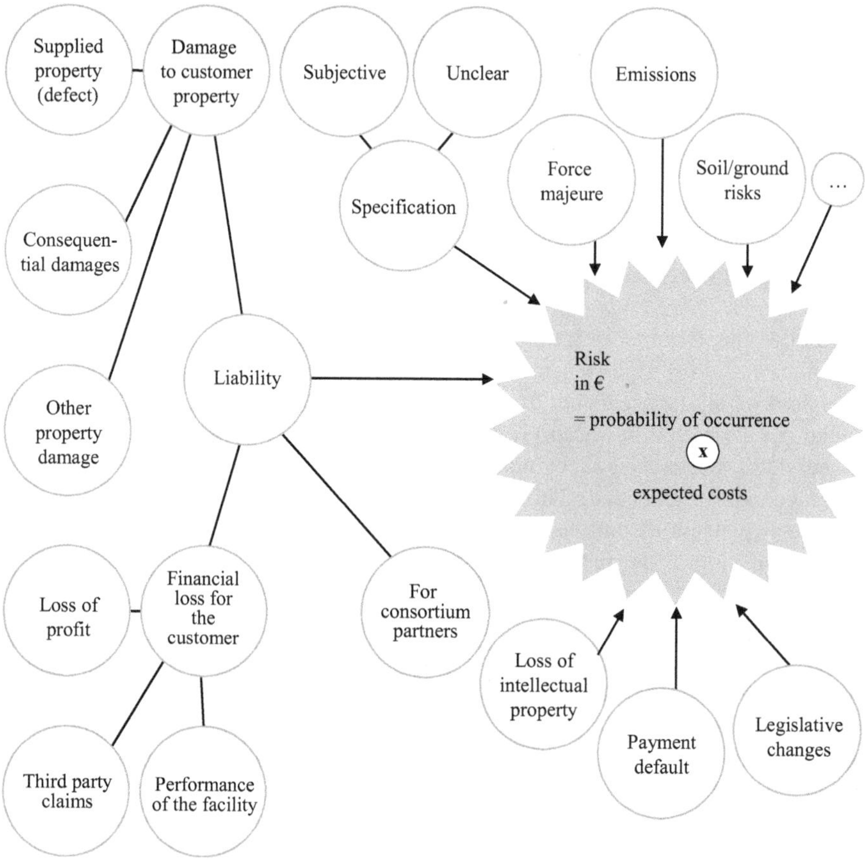

Fig. 6 Risks in the exchange contract

The **risk quantification process** comprises the following steps:

I. Identifying of the risk
II. How great is the probability of the risk occurring (in percent)?
III. How high are the expected costs if the risk does occur (in euros)?
IV. Does multiplying (II) by (III) produce a significant risk that has to be recorded in accordance with proper accounting principles?

If it does:

V. Is it possible to minimize the risk, or even exclude it, during negotiations?

If the costs and benefits of the relevant customer demands have been quantified, the negotiating team can present them to their own management for a decision to be made.

3.3.2 Internal Approval

The internal approval process for the handling of customer demands is an important element in the supplier's implementation strategy. For it is only through negotiation that the practical viability of the strategy becomes clear. Can the business model as 'idealized' in the bid be implemented in the market? In line with the dynamics of the bidding process, the negotiating team must brace itself for a deterioration of the risk profile once the bid has been submitted. The decision regarding how to deal with the main customer demands is a **decision regarding the expected profitability** of the chosen business model. That is why it is a key management responsibility in many companies. We intend to outline briefly here how such a process can be organized.

The management levels which have business responsibility for the project must make decisions regarding its benchmark data. If several management levels are involved (e.g.: managers at local, regional, and global level), the process should be tiered. In line with the **principle of subsidiarity** each level can make decisions regarding the risks which lie within its own area of business responsibility. The locally responsible management should decide about risks which have little impact on profitability. This could, for example, apply to the responsibility for obtaining local construction permits. The decision as to whether the local organization has the necessary resources and staff for this should be made at this level. By contrast, risks which potentially have company-wide implications (e.g. the assumption of unlimited liability or putting the bid together as part of an open consortium) must properly be decided at the level which has global responsibility. The negotiating team will compile all the relevant information and documents to help prepare for these decisions. Starting at the first management level, decisions are taken in successive meetings regarding the respective relevant risks, and the higher-level risks are escalated to the next level. This means that all the levels involved maintain the overview of the project that they need in order to exercise their business responsibility.

The ways in which the supplier can respond to demands for it to assume additional risks are shown in Fig. 7.

The internal approval process may turn out to be both a disadvantage and an advantage in the external negotiations. In terms of negotiation tactics it may be possible to get the other side to agree to concessions by referring to one's own ("bureaucratic and laborious") approval requirements. On the other hand, the other side may feel under pressure to bypass the on-site negotiating team and to establish contact directly with the management to which the team reports.

The result is that the negotiating of an exchange contract is an **iterative process** between the customer and its own management. Figure 8 shows the process in diagrammatic form.

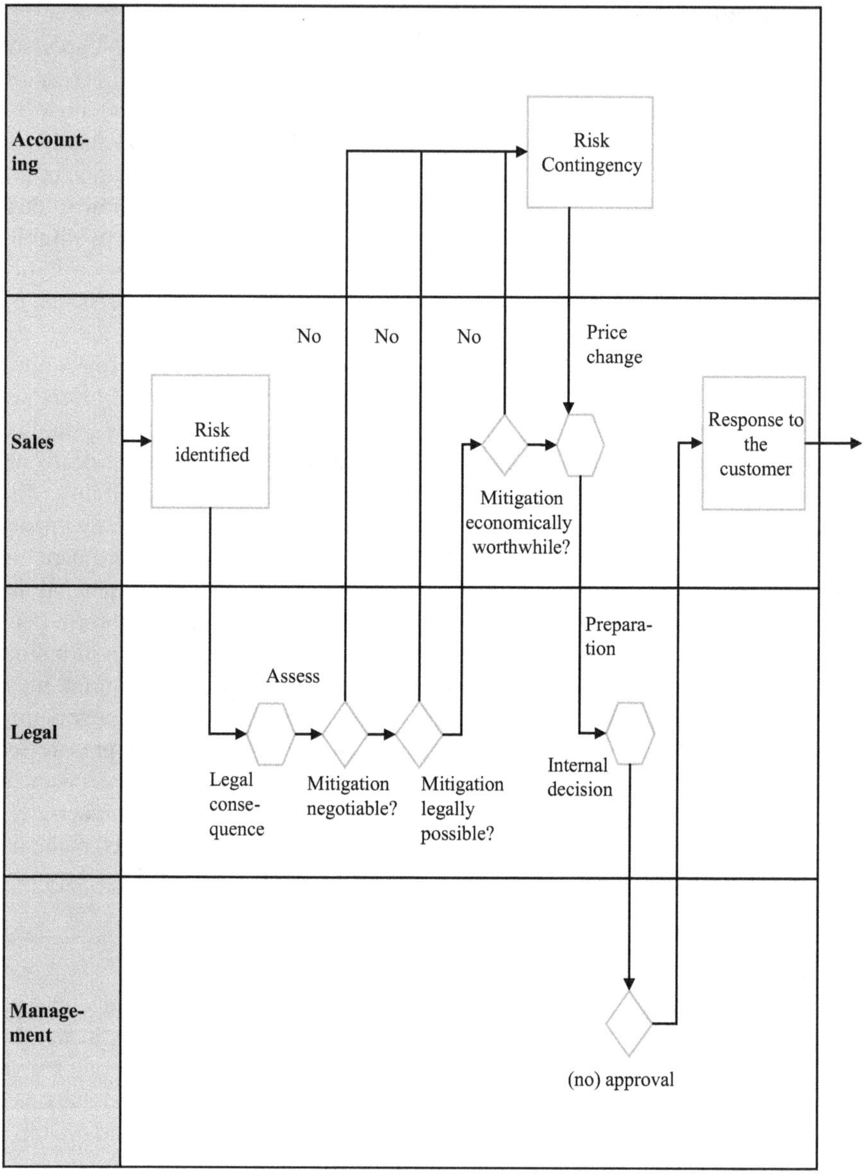

Fig. 7 Handling risks in the customer negotiations

3.4 Summary

As we have seen, the negotiating of the contract of exchange in plant engineering and construction and project business requires both an internal and external process. Particularly in the case of external customer negotiations, it revolves around the

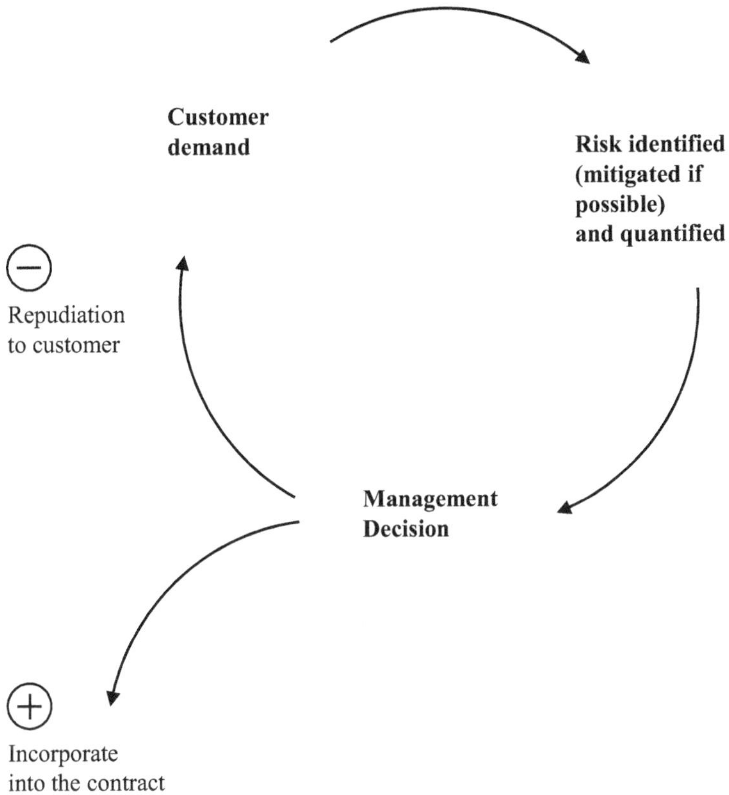

Fig. 8 The negotiation as an iterative process between customer and own management

"negotiator's dilemma", i.e. achieving the right balance between value creation and value allocation. The correct handling of risks is especially important in this regard. We now want to examine the responsibilities of contract management that result from the successful concluding of the contract.

4 Phase III: Execution

The execution phase begins with the effective concluding of the contract. It is subdivided into two sub-phases—the actual performance of the contract and the defects liability period which follows it.

In the latter phase what matters above all is that the obligations which have been assumed are actually fulfilled. This entails maintaining, or if possible even increasing, the profitability of the project. This is done by making one's own additional demands and fending off those made by the customer. In this phase, contract management is therefore concerned above all with issues relating to the making and pushing through of such additional demands. We will examine this more closely under the headings of "claim management" and "conflict resolution".

4.1 The Coming into Force of the Contract

In Sect. 4.1.1 it is shown that the coming into force of the contract fundamentally depends on the **parties' intentions**. However, Sect. 4.1.2 makes it clear that its coming into force may also be linked to **conditions** that are independent of the parties' intentions.

4.1.1 The Coming into Being of the Contract

We first want to examine how an exchange contract effectively comes into being, and then to briefly consider the problem of "battles of forms".

A contract comes into being through an **offer being made by one party and itsacceptance by the other party**. This principle applies both in German law (where it results from the rationale of Sects. 145 et. seqq. of the BGB despite there being no explicit reference to it), and in common law. It must be differentiated from a mere "invitation to bargain" ("invitatio ad offerendum") given to the other side, i.e. an invitation to make an offer. Shop window displays or goods in a supermarket constitute such an invitation. According to both German law and common law the actual offer to conclude a contract is only made by the customer at the checkout, and only accepted by the seller when it states the invoice amount. This fundamental principle is also an enduring one in international legal transactions, even in the internet era, although over the years courts have of course investigated how numerous scenarios are to be categorized within this classification system.

In every case acceptance must match the offer. If on the other hand the response to the offer includes altered terms, this does not generally constitute acceptance. For example, if you respond to an auto dealer's offer to buy a car for 5000 euros by saying that you will buy it for 4500 euros, your declaration does not constitute acceptance. No contract has therefore so far come into being. Both under common law and German law your statement will instead be understood as a rejection of the offer, and also the **making of acounter-offer**.

How relevant are these considerations to contract management in the order and project management context? As we have already seen, a valid offer is one that can be accepted simply by saying yes. A valid acceptance is accordingly one which fully accepts the offer without making any changes to its conditions. Therefore the norm is for real acceptance to take place only right at the end of the negotiation phase. Up until that point the offer has been revised in the customer's favor several times in the course of the discussions, so the latter is eventually able to agree the offer without any further reservations.

At this point we also wish to examine briefly the **concluding of contracts without any negotiation at all**. It is by no means unknown for the parties to only discuss the commercial key data of the contract (price, quantity, delivery period/

time, payment terms), but not the other conditions (in other words the provisions regarding "The Unplanned" in particular). In this case the question arises as to whether a valid contract has actually been concluded—since the parties have after all not (yet) agreed on important key details of their collaboration. A critical factor in terms of the validity of the contract is therefore whether the parties begin the performance of the contract (e.g. by paying the contract price or by delivering the promised goods) without further discussion of the unresolved points. If they do, the courts assume the contract to be effective, for if the unresolved points were evidently not so important to the parties as to make them delay performance, then—according to case law—they cannot have been very concerned to clarify these points. In other words, the parties wanted the contract without considering it necessary to explicitly agree on all the details. Such a contract has then validly come into being. Such a scenario always arises, for example, if the parties refer to their respective **standard terms of business** without going into the contradictions between them and resolving them through negotiation (Cummins et al. 2011, p. 197). For instance, it is not uncommon for a supplier to make an offer based on its "standard terms of business", and for the customer to accept it based on its own "standard purchasing conditions". If the parties now proceed to the performance of the contract, it is highly likely that a valid contract is in place. Even if there may be agreement about "what is planned", now the major problem is that the other provisions are unclear. For what kind of contract terms now apply? The seller's standard terms of business? Or the buyer's standard purchasing conditions? Experience generally indicates that either of these documents may specify the precise opposite of the other. The question of how to handle such a situation of **clashes between different terms of business or *"The Battle of the Forms"*** is answered differently in different legal systems. Sometimes the "theory of the final word" is followed according to which the conditions that are to apply are the last ones to be stated by either of the two sides. However, this line of reasoning is frequently rejected as being arbitrary and random. In Germany for instance, a different approach is taken. An investigation is carried out to ascertain the extent to which the terms of business do actually contradict each other. Where they do, neither the buyer's nor the seller's provisions apply, but general statute law.

As a rule, this poses problems for the supplier in particular. This becomes clear when we look again at the statements made about "The Unplanned": due to reasons of economic necessity, the supplier is not generally able to assume unlimited risks. It must therefore in particular limit its liability, and completely exclude liability for certain losses (see Sect. 2.3.4). Even if such a limitation of one's own responsibility is legally possible, it is at odds with legal principles. The general position taken by the law in all legal systems naturally assumes that one must actually be held liable for the losses which one causes. For the supplier this means that it is unable to achieve the limitation of liability which it seeks by deliberately not mentioning the subject and instead relying on its standard terms of business. The position is reversed for the customer. It may be in its interests not to broach the subject. In this constellation the parties would end up in the statutory legal position—and in this case this is generally more favorable to the customer than to the supplier.

We therefore find that this again confirms what has already been emphasized in connection with the drawing up of the bid: in order to ensure maximum clarity it is strongly recommended that all the contractual issues are "put on the table" and individually negotiated.

4.1.2 Conditions Precedent

Even if the parties have jointly agreed to conclude the contract, it may the case that not all the preconditions for the project have yet been fulfilled. For instance, in the case of major projects the financing arrangements may not have been fully clarified at the time when the contract is signed. Or it is not yet clear that the customer itself will be awarded the order for the project by its own customer. In such cases the parties may declare the fulfilling of the outstanding **preconditions to be "conditions precedent"**. Only once these preconditions have been fulfilled does the contract with all its rights and duties become legally effective. When drafting the conditions precedent, contract management must take care to ensure that they are actually restricted to factors that are not fully under the parties' control. Otherwise, by establishing supposed conditions precedent one party may actually just be giving itself a loophole to allow it to withdraw from the contract later on without suffering any adverse consequences. This is not usually acceptable to the other party. In exchange for making its own commitment, each party expects a corresponding commitment from the other side. If the other party subsequently wishes to back out of the project, compensation will at least be expected for one's own effort and expense. If one of the parties is still not intent on reaching agreement, this should be clearly raised as an issue, and the contract should not actually be signed for the time being. Alternatively, one can also resolve the problem by providing an appropriate right of cancellation with compensation for the effort and expense incurred.

If the contract is then signed and any conditions precedent have been fulfilled, the actual performance of the contract begins.

4.2 Performance of the Contract and Defects Liability

Once the contract is in force, the parties are obliged to fulfill the promises made in the contract. As shown, this primarily means that **what is planned** must be now carried out. Naturally enough, the main burden in this regard is on the supplier's shoulders. The customer usually makes a down payment (often simultaneously and in return for the handing over of a guarantee), and it gives the supplier access to the site where the project is to be carried out. In other respects it is above all the supplier which now has to take action. It will receive the agreed contract price in line with its step-by-step performance of the contract.

Two phases of the execution of the contract can be distinguished. Firstly and primarily, the period from when the contract takes effect until the actual completion of the contract. As a rule, the contract has been completed once the customer takes formal acceptance of the project. **Formal acceptance** by the customer takes place when the supplier has fully delivered the facility as agreed. The facility then passes into the customer's ownership, the final installment of the contract price becomes payable, and the defects liability period starts to run. The customer now takes over the project at the same time as the supplier withdraws from it. It is difficult to generalize about precisely how this transition is organized without reference to a specific project. The supplier may still have to undertake minor rectification works or instruct the customer in the use of the project. For its part, the customer now begins to derive the economic benefits of the project. It is of course possible for it to still be working with the supplier company on the basis of other contracts. For example, if the owner of a power station is a financial investor which does not itself have the know-how needed to operate a power station, it is usual for it to conclude two contracts with the same company: one contract for the construction of the power station and one contract relating to its subsequent operation. Even if a single company builds the power station and then operates it on behalf of the customer, it still does via two different contracts. What has been said here then applies equally, but independently, to both contracts. As a rule therefore, formal acceptance marks the point in time at which the parties have fulfilled their final primary duties; occasionally the customer's final payment does not fall due until the end of the defects liability period. Although it may be a complicated matter to categorize along strict legal lines the duties which exist at the time of formal acceptance, this is not something which has to concern us here. It is more important above all to provide a pragmatic assessment of the question of when the supplier has essentially provided the services which it is contracted to provide.

This is when the final phase of the project begins. It lasts until the contract has been finally ended. This occurs at the end of the **defects liability period**. During this period the parties essentially do not have anything further to undertake in relation to "what is planned". However, the supplier must take action if a defect arises.

4.3 Objectives of Claim Management

In organizational terms for the supplier, the project is often handed over from the sales team to the project management function at the time when the contract comes into force. The second type of contract management now also starts—**claim management** (cf. also chapter "Project Management"). Up to now, no generally accepted definition of this term has emerged. The definitions provided by Huck (2006, p. 41) are appropriate when they state that "claims" are demands, rights to alter legal relationships, or objections which are rooted in circumstances relating to the contract and which relate to the contract in terms of their timing or their financial or factual aspects. Accordingly, one may regard "claim management" as meaning the sum of all the measures used to pursue contractual claims against the other contracting party, or to defend such claims made by it.

Claim management has **three** main **objectives.** Now what matters is to secure the expected revenue, and if possible to actually increase it. The securing of the revenue is achieved firstly through carrying out what is planned, and secondly through mounting a defense against the customer's additional demands. The revenue may be increased through the supplier for its part submitting additional demands to the customer.

The three objectives of claim management:

I. The securing of the revenue through adhering to what is contractually agreed
II. The securing of the revenue through mounting a defense against unplanned customer's demands
III. The increasing of revenue through the making of additional demands

We now wish to examine these three objectives in more detail:

I. **The securing of the revenue "through adhering to what is contractually agreed"** may perhaps sound trivial, but is by no means so. In practice it may actually be frightening to realize how little notice the project manager takes of the contract. For instance, it is not uncommon for only excerpts of the contract to be read. Then of course one's lack of knowledge means that it is not even possible to adhere to the formal requirements or the process steps which have been negotiated with the customer in painstaking detail. In the most extreme case, the project manager works with the annexes of the contract on a daily basis without "daring" to read the main legal part of it. Even assuming that, as referred to above, the contract has been clearly and unambiguously written and its wording is self-explanatory, it is of course essential to have a certain understanding of the legal language used in contracts—and of the nomenclature too. In addition, it is unfortunately often the case that the final version of the contract is not sufficiently clear for an outside third party. As a compromise solution—which is generally found when working under time pressure, and perhaps even across cultural and linguistic boundaries—the final contract almost invariably contains discrepancies or even contradictions which can only be explained by reference to the history of the negotiations.

   What all this means for claim management is that the clear-cut handover of the project to project management is especially important. Claim management must support the project manager with advice afterwards too, in order to clear up any queries relating to comprehension and interpretation which arise during the period when the project is being carried out. This then enables strategies to be jointly found and put into words regarding lines of reasoning to be used for dealing with any gaps or inconsistencies.

II. This also touches on the second point—the **securing of revenue through mounting a defense against unplanned customer demands.** A rigorous analysis of what has been contractually agreed is often enough to enable a supposed customer claim to be rejected. When dealing with unclear points in the contract, the good line of reasoning that has already been mentioned can be of help. Many cases also involve disputes about whether specific services have been provided on time as promised. One of the main tasks of the claims management function is therefore the documenting of the steps which it itself has taken in the performance of the contract.

III. The documenting of what has occurred also plays a key role in the **increasing of revenue through the making of additional demands**. A claim is only worth anything if it could be enforced against the other side's wishes, for if a claim which has been made would be dismissed out of hand by an arbitration tribunal or a court, why should the business partner agree to it? However, in order for a claim to be legally enforceable it must be capable of being proved. For the supplier this means above all that it must document any additional costs on which it can base its additional demands.

Even more than is the case with the handling of the customer's additional demands, the making of one's own additional demands to the customer **is not primarily a legal matter.** Contract management can indeed highlight what is legally possible based on the contract. However, whether this makes business sense, and the degree to which it does so, must be decided taking account of customer loyalty and one's market image. This weighing up of the securing and/or increasing of revenue on the one hand and the sustainable development of the business on the other hand must be undertaken by management. Consequently, many organizations utilize a "Limits of Authority" procedure over the course of project management in order to ensure that the company's overall interests are also safeguarded while the contract is being performed. However, this is also basically a question of corporate culture. Companies in the English-speaking world often have a highly efficient claim management function whose contribution to the company's net operating results is planned in advance. For other companies, having a satisfied customer and having the project run as smoothly as possible is more valuable than the potential additional earnings. Just like contract management during the first two phases of contract management, claim management therefore also necessitates a holistic strategy.

But how can claims be handled which are the subject of dispute between the parties to the contract? If one contracting party makes a claim which is repudiated by the other party, this is virtually a textbook example of a conflict. Claim management is therefore not only one of the two types of contract management, it is also a form of conflict management.

4.4 Claim Management as Conflict Management

Following Berkel (2011, p. 54), we can distinguish four different types of conflict: conflicts about values, conflicts about facts, relationship conflicts, and internal conflicts. This applies not only to conflicts within an organization, but also in the case of conflicts between organizations. The **various types of conflict** are depicted in Fig. 9.

Since any dispute about claims always revolves around the existence of legal rights, this a classic case of the **"conflictabout facts".** The parties argue about

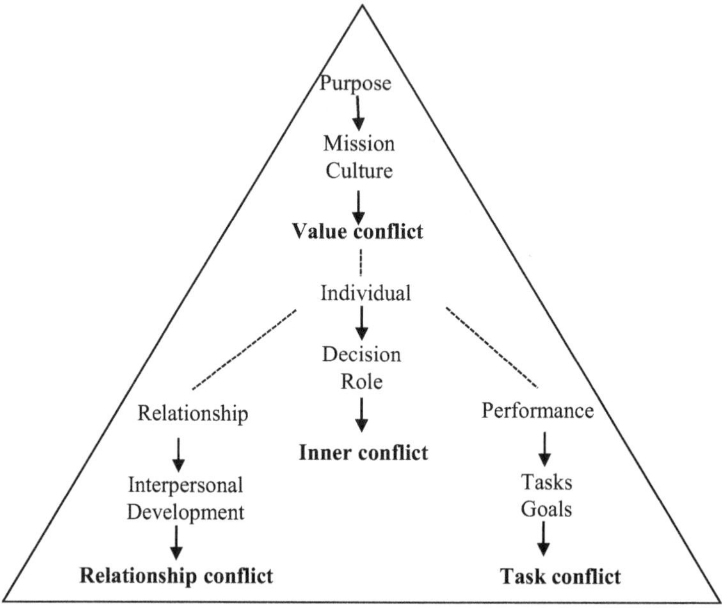

Fig. 9 Types of conflict (Berkel 2011, p. 54)

whether or not a specific service is to be provided. Conflict research has provided some answers regarding how conflicts about facts (disputed claims) can be handled. We will examine them in the next section.

4.5 Conflict Resolution

We have already briefly alluded to the various options for contractual conflict resolution under the heading of conflict resolution mechanisms (negotiation, involvement of a third party, and decision by a third party) in Sect. 2.3.5. Ury et al. (1993) made what has now become the conventional differentiation of available **options for conflictresolution**: a conflict can be resolved based on power, the law, or interests. "Power" means the ability to assert one's own views, even against the other side's wishes. "The law" means the ability to secure victory in legal proceedings. The term "interests" has exactly the same meaning as set out in the chapter on value creation (Sect. 3.2.1). Interests are the underlying issues at stake in the demands made by one party. These three options can be represented as shown in Fig. 10.

The graphical representation of the three terms should not however mislead us into viewing them as being strictly dichotomous or even conflicting. **The types of conflict resolution mechanism sometimes overlap:** this means that one party's legal right is in many cases a perfect expression of its interests. Indeed, it is precisely the job of legislators and the courts to formulate and develop law in the

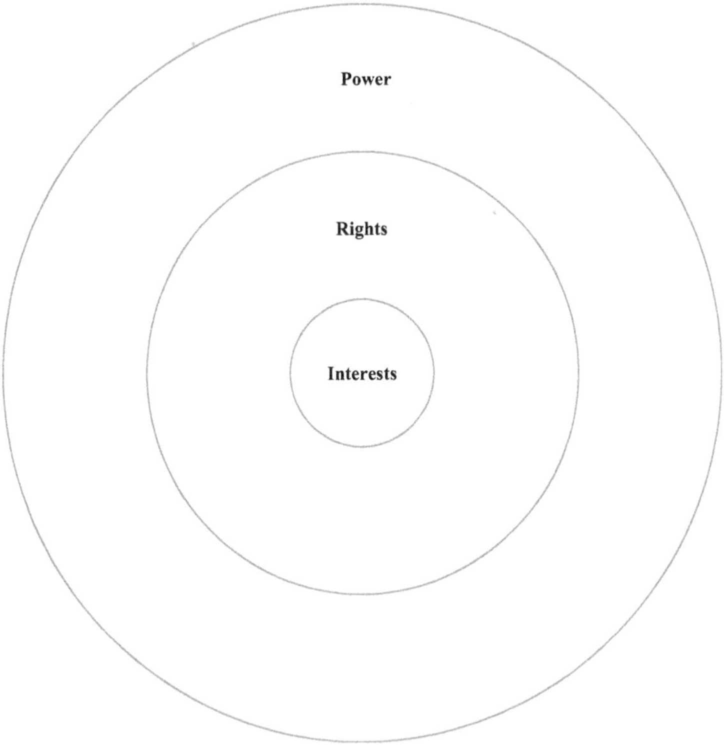

Fig. 10 The three options for resolving conflicts (Ury et al. 1993, p. 9)

interests of the parties involved in legal transactions. Similarly, as shown in this work, it is the job and aim of contract management to develop the parties' rights based on their interests.

Ury et al. (1993) nonetheless chose a representation in the form of concentric circles in order to illustrate the interactions of the three types of conflict resolution. On the one hand, the parties negotiate **"in the shadow of the law"** (Mnookin and Kornhauser 1979): Someone who has been disadvantaged due to a breach of contract by the other side will only agree in the negotiations to a solution which puts him in at least as good a position as he would expect to be in if he took legal proceedings (Eidenmüller 2001, p. 2). On the other hand, even the law cannot operate with complete disregard for power. Even the best court ruling would be of no use to the supplier if it could enforce it against its main customer only at the price of then having to abandon the transaction.

The following are therefore the main **conflictresolution mechanisms** available to the parties:

- Negotiation
  In negotiations the parties attempt to resolve the conflict themselves by means of an amicable agreement. A staggered procedure has proved to be effective in this regard, which involves the parties' higher levels of management becoming involved if more junior staff are unable to reach agreement. If the negotiations fail, a third party will generally be consulted in order to broker an agreement or make a decision. Both sides must therefore judge the potential outcome of any negotiations by comparing it to what they could probably have expected from these other proceedings.
- Mediation
  In the case of meditation a neutral third party assists the parties with their negotiations. It does so by managing the process and if necessary putting forward its own proposals for a solution, but without itself having any authority to make decisions. Therefore mediation likewise only enables the conflict to be resolved by means of an amicable agreement between the parties.
- Adjudication
  Adjudication is a procedure for the out-of-court conflict resolution of construction disputes which offers the major advantage of being quickly carried out. An impartial third party—the adjudicator—manages the proceedings, and if no amicable agreement is reached it concludes them by issuing a ruling which is provisionally binding on the parties. The ruling becomes definitively binding if the parties agree this to be the case, or if they do not file an objection within a specified period; otherwise the parties can have the ruling reviewed by a court of law (cf. Greger and von Münchhausen 2010, p. 179 et seqq.):
- Arbitration
  In arbitration proceedings the parties have to abide by the arbitrator's ruling in the same way as they would have to abide by the judge's ruling in court proceedings. This procedure is recommended in particular if neutral court proceedings in accordance with the rule of law cannot always be guaranteed in the project country. Since the parties are free to select the arbitrators, it also possible to select third parties who are especially knowledgeable about the subject matter. Lastly, arbitration proceedings also have the advantage of being "private", in other words they can be held in camera.
- Court proceedings
  The parties are of course also free to have their dispute settled in a public court.

In a nutshell, one could say that the focus of conflict resolution in these five procedures shifts from the parties' **"interests"** towards their **"legal rights"**. Whereas the former are the predominant consideration in negotiations, an arbitration or court ruling is based on the latter. The procedures that are available for resolving conflicts can be shown in simplified form in Fig. 11.

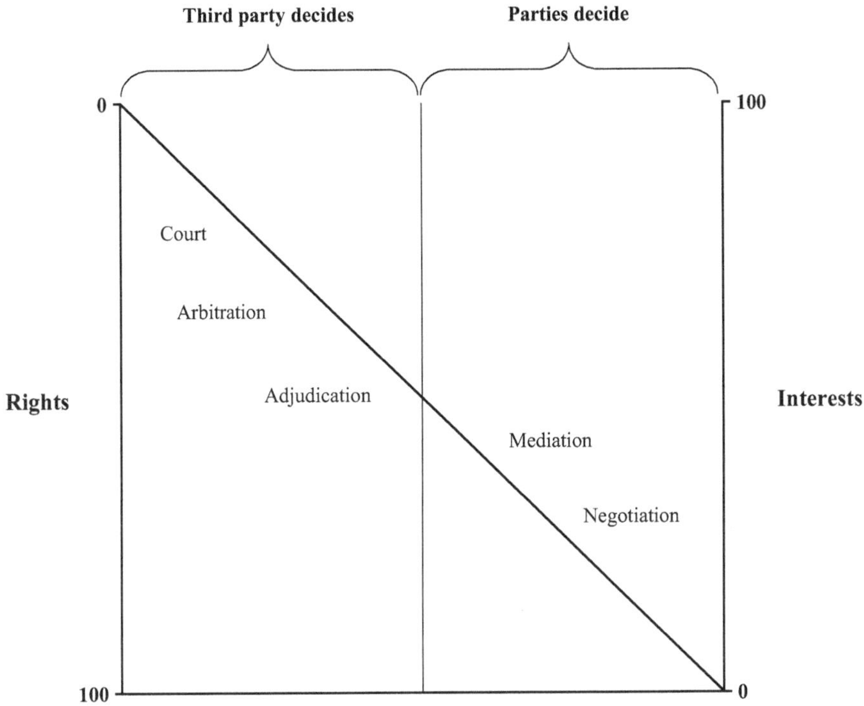

Fig. 11 Conflict resolution procedures as a function of legal rights and of interests

An important aspect of the selection of the suitable procedure or proceedings is the weighing up of costs and benefits, and the time involved. A (process) risk analysis can be used to determine whether it is worthwhile to take the matter to arbitration or before a court. This involves considering the likelihood of actually being able to prove an alleged entitlement and get it upheld by the court (cf. for instance Hagel 2011). This step is therefore similar to the quantification of contractual risks described above.

4.6 Summary

We have seen that the third phase of contract management is dominated by the handling of claims. Contract management in the form of claim management aims to secure and improve the net operating profit. It has the instruments of conflict management at its disposal for this purpose. The choice between these instruments should be made based on a weighing up of their costs and benefits. Finally, we want to consider what the task of contract management is once the project has been completed.

5 Phase IV: Analysis

As we have seen, the contractual relationship finally ends only when the defects liability period has expired. As a rule this is also when the parties' contractual liability ceases. The parties have then not only carried out what was planned, there are also no longer any unplanned duties that may arise.

At the start of this chapter we looked at a newspaper article about the supplying of high speed trains. Since it was written at the time when the contact was signed, it was not able to say anything about the actual success (or failure) of the project. We have now reached the end of our consideration of the execution of projects. Perhaps in a few years' time another article will be published which will **take stock with the benefit of hindsight** following the delivery and bringing into operation of the trains. Once the project has ended, both Siemens and Deutsche Bahn will have drawn some lessons from it regarding what they would do in the same way and what they would do differently in future deals. Such an ex-post analysis is recommended for all the parties involved in project business. The reason for this is obvious. On the journey from the "bid decision" to the ending of the contract the parties have weighed up a whole series of considerations and made decisions accordingly. Only in retrospect is it possible to see whether or not these were correct. This enables the parties to draw important lessons for future projects. To do this, it now seems sensible to think through the **phases of contract management again—in reverse order**. Starting with the analysis of the actual situation at the end of the project, conclusions can be drawn regarding the success of the bidding and execution phase. At the end of the analysis recommendations are then in place for drawing up future bids. The following checklist may be of assistance:

Checklist

I. Performance of the contract:
   a. Was the desired outcome of the project achieved?
   b. Was claim management successful in terms of securing and improving profitability?
   c. Was the cost/benefit analysis used when selecting the conflict resolution mechanisms appropriate?
   d. Were the conditions precedent that were stipulated reasonable and adequate?
   e. How can the performance of future contracts be made (even) more successful?

II. Contract negotiation:
   a. Was the desired objective of the negotiations achieved?
   b. Were the risks that were subject to negotiation appropriately quantified?
   c. Were all the relevant risks appropriately described in the internal approval process?
   d. Were the right decisions made with regard to the quantifying of risks and internal approval?

   e. Was the negotiating of what was planned successful? Was the mutual win-win potential of the business fully exploited?
   f. Was the negotiating of "The Unplanned" successful? Were the win-lose negotiations effectively conducted for our own benefit?
   g. How can future negotiations be conducted (even) more successfully?
III. Putting together of the bid:
   a. Was the correct bid/no bid decision made?
   b. Were all the important constituent parts of the contract appropriately incorporated into the bid?
   c. Was the right balance struck between establishing our own position and anticipating the customer's wishes?
   d. How can future bids be put together (even) more successfully?

This checklist does of course merely provide some pointers. It should be adapted according to the specific characteristics of the respective project business.

6 Conclusion

In this chapter it has been shown that efficient contract management is crucial to the success of order and project management. It also described the chronological sequence of the project and identified the four phases of contract management: the drawing up of the bid, negotiation, execution, and analysis. The challenges posed for contract management in each phase were outlined, and strategies were proposed for coping with them. Only if the contractual, technical and commercial aspects of the project business are handled in an interdisciplinary and holistic manner can the supplier's business model be successfully put into practice.

Exercises

1. What arguments are there for and against consulting external lawyers during the process of drawing up the bid?
2. Give reasons why open communication is necessary in the negotiation phase in order to bring about win-win solutions.
3. Explain how it is that opportunities to create value also exist in supposed win-lose situations.
4. Describe how the negotiating of what is planned tends to lead to the creation of value for both sides, whereas the negotiating of "The Unplanned" tends to have a value-distributing effect.
5. What is meant by the negotiator's dilemma?
6. Describe the hazard posed by the loyalty problem which can arise due to the splitting up of the negotiating team into sub-groups. How can this danger be averted?

7. Explain what is meant by the "battle of the forms" in connection with the coming into being of a contract.
8. What is laid down in the conditions precedent? What in particular must be given due attention in this regard?
9. Under what circumstances in claim management does it make sense to refrain from taking court proceedings that are likely to be successful?
10. What are the basic procedures for resolving conflicts that are available to the parties to the contract? According to what criteria should they be selected?
11. State what the main tasks and aims of claim management are.

Literature

Berkel, K. (2011). *Konflikttraining. Konflikte verstehen, analysieren, bewältigen.* Hamburg: Windmühle-Verlag.

Bühring-Uhle, C., Eidenmüller, H., Nelle, A. (2009). *Verhandlungsmanagement. Analyse, Werkzeuge, Strategie.* München: C.H. Beck.

Cummins, T., David, M., Kawamoto, K. (2011). *Contract and commercial management—the operational guide.* Zaltbommel: Van Haren Publishing.

Eidenmüller, H. (2001). *Vertrags- und Verfahrensrecht in der Wirtschaftsmediation.* Köln: Otto Schmidt.

Greger, R., & von Münchhausen, C. F. (2010). *Verhandlungs- und Konfliktmanagement für Anwälte.* München: C.H. Beck.

Hagel, U. (2011). Der Unternehmensjurist als Risikomanager. *SchiedsVZ*, pp. 65–74.

Huck, W. (2006). Prozess- und Ergebnisorientierung durch Claim-Management. Eine Condition sine qua non im Anlagengeschäft? *Projektmanagement Aktuell, 1*, 40–46.

Jungbluth, R. (2012 March 29). Sonne, Wind und Verluste. *Die Zeit.*

Langenfeld, G. (2010). *Grundlagen der Vertragsgestaltung.* München: C.H. Beck.

Lewicki, R., Saunders, D., Barry, B. (2003). *Negotiation.* New York: McGraw-Hill.

Mnookin, R. H., & Kornhauser, L. (1979). Bargaining in the shadow of the law. The case of divorce. *The Yale Law Journal, 88*(5), 950–997.

Ury, W., Bret, J., Goldberg, S. (1993). *Getting disputes resolved. Designing systems to cut the costs of conflict.* Cambridge, MA: Jossey-Bass.

Negotiation Management

Ingmar Geiger

Every time that the top German government bodies end an extended visit to an economically important partner country of the Federal Republic of Germany, the media reports on large-scale business transactions that the accompanying delegation from the national industry has concluded with companies or other organizations in the host country. Frequently, this type of high profile trip is primarily used by the companies involved to publicize what a large number of managers in the supplier company and the customer organization have prepared and agreed upon in a number of negotiation rounds.

However, the details of what takes place until this kind of high profile conclusion can be reached remain sealed to even the most attentive observer of the discussion. The internal assessments of potential projects by the supplier, the income structure, and extensive preparatory activities in the financial and legal area have been covered by other chapters in this book.

This chapter deals with the question of which factors have an influence on the structure and outcome of specific negotiations regarding this kind of project and how a supplier involved in the project business can use the findings for their marketing.

This first requires the specification of what characterizes a negotiation in the industrial plant and project business and which areas of interaction between the supplier and potential customers we want to and can consider as belonging to the negotiation with respect to time, personnel, organization and content. This occurs in Sect. 1. A specific academic perspective can then be taken regarding the specified subject under investigation, which is linked to appropriate modeling (Sect. 2). The introduced terminology can then be used to present the numerous influencing factors on a negotiation and its outcomes and to discuss the relevant effects. Section 3 presents this core part of the chapter. Section 4 provides specific

I. Geiger (✉)
School of Business and Economics, Freie Universität Berlin, Berlin, Germany
e-mail: ingmar.geiger@fu-berlin.de

M. Kleinaltenkamp et al. (eds.), *Business Project Management and Marketing*, Springer Texts in Business and Economics, DOI 10.1007/978-3-662-48507-1_6

information on how a future negotiation situation may be structured successfully for a supplier, as it covers the preparations for a negotiation. The conclusion (Sect. 5) wraps up the chapter.

1 Examination of Negotiations in the Industrial Plant and Project Business

1.1 Characteristics and Definition of a Negotiation Situation

People are constantly negotiating: Spouses negotiate over the distribution of the tasks in the family, teenagers negotiate with their parents about the time they have to return home at night, friends negotiate about the restaurant they want to go to for dinner, unions and employers' associations negotiate collective conditions for employees in a certain sector and region, politicians negotiate about legislation, countries negotiate about trade barriers or even war and peace, and companies negotiate about business transactions, corporate purchases or the salaries of management personnel. Despite the sometimes completely different backgrounds, every negotiation that takes place is fundamentally the same. They are characterized by the following **features**:

- A negotiation requires **at least two parties**. Negotiations always involve interpersonal or inter-group processes (Lewicki et al. 2010, p. 6; Rubin and Brown 1975, p. 6).
- In a negotiation, the decisions reached by the parties are **interdependent**. In a negotiation, no party can reach a mutually binding decision, which displays comparable costs or income with regard to a genuine negotiation result, without the consent of the other party (Lax and Sebenius 1986, p. 7; Rubin and Brown 1975, p. 7).
- In principle, there are three situations in which parties negotiate with each other: (a) in order to allocate limited resources, such as land, an inheritance or time, (b) in order to create something new, which the negotiating parties would not be able to do independently, and (c) in order to resolve a problem or a conflict between them (Lewicki et al. 2010, p. 2). What is common to all of these generic situations is that the parties are attempting to **improve** their **situation** in relation to the status quo by negotiating with each other (Kutschker 1972, p. 237).
- Negotiations are necessary if parties are pursuing different interests with regard to the object of the negotiation, i.e. there is a **conflict of interest** (Lewicki et al. 2010, p. 6; Pruitt and Carnevale 1993, p. 2). If both parties wanted exactly the same thing, this would only involve a coordination of the joint interests. This is not a negotiation.
- Interdependent decision-making in negotiations takes place in that parties identify **demands** and **offers** and are confronted by the same from the counterpart. Even if the parties involved initially fight for their starting positions and do not

budge, they ultimately give way and make agreement possible by way of mutual **concessions**, i.e. a process of give and take (Lewicki et al. 2010, p. 7 et seq.).

- Negotiations are held in order to improve the position of the relevant party as a result of the negotiation result, than would have been the case without the agreement. A negotiation therefore involves **mutual influence attempts** and **strategic actions**. Strategic actions refer to the fact that both parties include the likely actions of the other party into their own considerations. In doing so, the parties attempt to induce the other party to give more than they would voluntarily be prepared to give (Geiger 2007, p. 17).

In summary, a negotiation can be defined as follows (Geiger 2007, p. 17):

> A negotiation is an interaction between at least two parties who are attempting to reach a mutually acceptable decision by balancing opposing interests as part of a joint decision-making process by exchanging offers and information, from which they expect greater benefits compared to the relevant alternatives.

1.2 Temporal Definition of Negotiations in the Marketing Process

However, the formal definition is not sufficient to adequately define a "negotiation" for the industrial plant and project business. In particular, for negotiations that are embedded into one, more or less continuous, flow of interaction between two parties, in our case at least between the supplier company and the customer organization, the time at which a negotiation starts and when it ends is important. The literature has established various phase models in order to deal with this problem. An overview is provided in Fig. 1.

While Backhaus and Günter (1976, p. 257 et seq.) and Koch (1987, p. 56 et seq.) distinguish between a preliminary inquiry and proposal preparation phase, Utikal (2001, p. 42 et seq.) combines these into one initiation phase. However, this classification is not appropriate from a negotiation theoretical perspective. In accordance with the definition of negotiation used here and, particularly, due to the factors influencing a negotiation identified below (see also Sect. 3.4.2), the supplier's proposal preparation already forms part of the negotiation and should therefore be considered as part of the negotiation phase, as argued by Geiger (2007, p. 18 et seq.).

According to this phase classification, a transaction begins with the **preliminary inquiry and initiation phase**. Supplier activities in this phase include establishing contact, customer consultation and the definition of the customer's problem or the customer's requirements. The inquiry evaluation (see Chap. 2) by the potential supplier generally starts in this phase. The customer focuses its efforts on determining its requirements, consisting of the problem identification and a review of the fundamental realization options. The preliminary inquiry and initiation phase on the customer side often concludes with a formal open or structured request for proposal

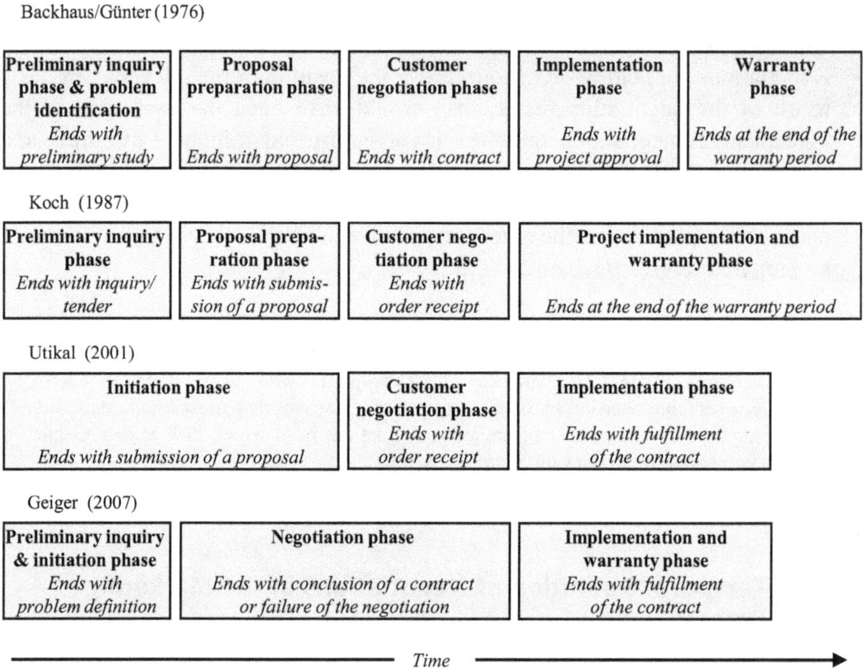

Fig. 1 Phase models for the temporal definition of the negotiation (Geiger 2007, p. 18)

(RFP). The interactions during the preliminary inquiry and initiation phase are generally limited to the exchange of information. It must also be noted that both the supplier company and the customer organization interact with several potential business partners in this phase in the knowledge that they will only actually conclude a negotiation and a transaction with one or less partners.

The start of the **negotiation phase** is frequently heralded by a **RFP** or an official **inquiry** by the principal. If the potential contractor fundamentally considers the RFP or inquiry to be attractive, they develop a specific proposal that includes technical as well as economical and legal aspects. In some cases, this may already involve an extensive interaction between the companies involved, depending on the complexity and the amount of customization of the required solution and the scope of the potential order. After the supplier company has submitted the proposal, it is evaluated by the customer organization. If the result of this evaluation is positive, this is followed by specific, intense contractual negotiations, whose positive conclusion is also formally recorded to the extent possible, at least in the industrial plant and project business (see Chap. 5). This concludes the negotiation phase. The negotiation phase also ends if the negotiation parties are not able to reach an agreement, but no transaction takes place.

If an agreement is reached in the negotiation phase, the agreed performance is provided in the **implementation** and **warranty phase**, during which varying

Table 1 Activities in the transaction process phases (Geiger 2007, p. 20)

Supplier activities	Intercompany interactions	Customer activities
Preliminary inquiry and initiation phase		
Customer acquisition Establishment of contact Consulting/preliminary study Recording of customer problems	**Exchange of information to define the customer problem**	**Identification of requirements** Problem identification Review of fundamental realization options
Negotiation phase		
Inquiry selection **Proposal preparation** Conception of an appropriate overall package to resolve the problem (technical design, services accompanying the product) Commercial and legal proposal preparation Delivery schedule	**Formulation of the inquiry** **Clarification of queries for proposal preparation** **Contractual negotiation** **Agreement or disagreement** on technical offering features and the scope of the overall package Order modalities (economic and legal conditions)	**Preparation of inquiries** **Supplier preselection** Proposal evaluation Proposal comparison
Implementation and warranty phase		
Order processing **Technical and commercial specification and implementation of the solution** **Delivery, installation and assembly** **After-sales support**	Information exchange to coordinate the supplier and customer activities as part of the service creation Delivery/assembly Qualification/approval Processing of warranty claims Possible renegotiations	**Supporting the supplier's service creation** **Use of the plant**

degrees of duties of cooperation may be assigned to the principal. This may include the provision of the necessary infrastructure (construction of roads, rail connections or a port) or the execution of approval processes, especially for major technical plants. This requires permanent coordination between the parties, which is frequently based on the concluded contract. Genuine renegotiations may become necessary if unforeseen events occur. The following considerations are also applicable for any renegotiations, although they are not the explicit focus of the deliberations. An overview of the supplier and customer activities in the various phases is displayed in Table 1.

1.3 Organizational Characteristics

Another specification relating to "negotiation" in the context of the industrial plant and project business lies in the description of the parties involved (Geiger 2007, p. 22 et seq.). In his earlier research on the subject of negotiations in the capital

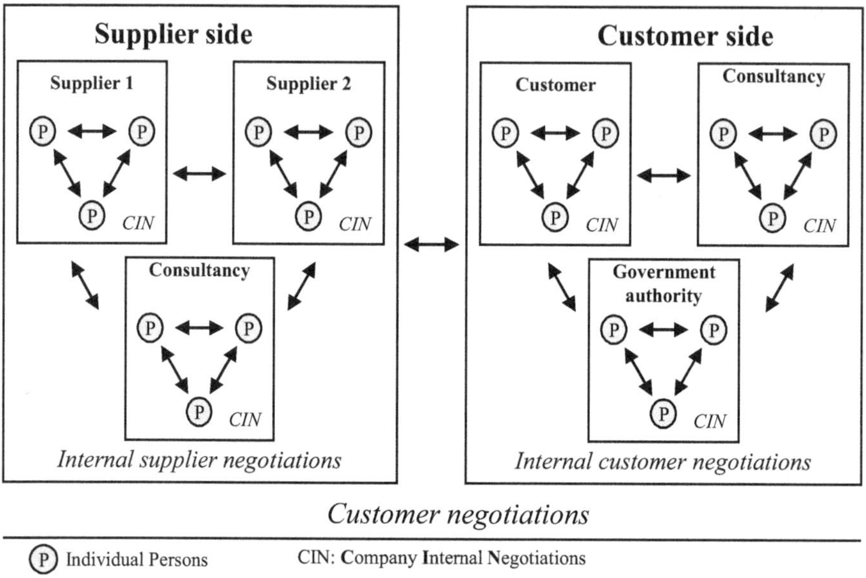

Fig. 2 Negotiation hierarchy for negotiations in the industrial plant business (Geiger 2007, p. 23)

goods sector, Koch (1987) stated that a genuine negotiation network particularly exists for the marketing of industrial plants. This means that various individuals as well as departments and **third parties** are involved in the central customer negotiations between supplier companies and customer organization on both sides, at least indirectly. This kind of negotiation hierarchy is displayed in Fig. 2.

In particular, for major industrial projects, consulting companies (such as for engineering services), financial service providers (banks, credit insurance companies, project finance institutions) and public authorities may be involved in the negotiations on both the supplier and the customer side (Backhaus and Voeth 2010, p. 351 et seq.; Engelhardt and Günter 1981, p. 109 et seq.). It is frequently also the case that a proposal is not just received from a single supplier company alone, but rather that a **supplier consortium** is involved in major projects, so that a considerable need for negotiation exists between the individual consortium companies themselves (see Chap. 8). Negotiations also take place within the individual organizations on both the supplier and the customer side based on the differing interests of the individual departments and managers. This type of interaction has already been extensively investigated, at least descriptively, in studies on the **Buying** and **Selling Center** (e.g. Hutt et al. 1985; Johnston and Bonoma 1981; Venkatesh et al. 1995).

Even though both internal negotiations as well as those between the individual parties involved on both the customer and the supplier side can be important, no further attention is paid to these in the following. However, as is the case for renegotiations in the implementation and warranty phase, the concepts described hereafter can also be applied to these kinds of negotiations. However, their inclusion in the considerations would unnecessarily complicate the analysis of negotiation in the industrial plant and project business, which is the focus of this investigation. As a result, when the supplier (or the supplier company) and the customer (or customer organization) are mentioned in the following, this refers to the groups of people in two entities, whose knowledge and authorities place them in a position to conclude a transaction. For the time being, it is unimportant whether a dyadic personal negotiation or a dyadic multiorganizational negotiation is referred to for the fundamental concepts and models. Deviations from this assumption may occur when considering individual influencing factors on negotiations where explicit constellations are considered.

1.4 Content Characteristics

In addition to their temporal and organizational complexity, negotiations in the industrial plant and project business are also characterized by a medium to high complexity of content. In contrast to other sectors of business-to-business marketing, such as the product business, in which negotiations primarily relate to prices and delivery conditions, the degree of technological, commercial, and legal freedom in the negotiation of the establishment of a major industrial plant or the implementation of a long-term service project are considerably greater.

Besides the price as the service charge, which often plays a dominant and conflicting role (Kutschker and Kirsch 1978, p. 53), a negotiation also frequently covers the following issues (Geiger 2007, p. 24):

- Technological design of the core offering
- Scope and type of additional services
- Purchaser's duties of cooperation
- Delivery quantity, deadlines, packaging and logistics
- Scope of liability, improvements, and warranties
- Financing and payment conditions

Koch (1987, p. 86) classifies the content of negotiations in business-to-business marketing with a focus on the degree of technological freedom of the core offering. He distinguished between three situations:

- In **"solution given" negotiations** the principal technological offering is defined. Only the purchase price and delivery, service and financing conditions are negotiation issues.
- In contrast, **"solution ready-made" negotiations** include those in which the technological design of the core offering to resolve the customer's problem is largely determined in the negotiation.
- **"Solution modified" negotiations** are in between the two extremes and are also the negotiations that apply most frequently in real life situations. The core offering is adapted to the customer's requirements by various available

components and technologies in the underlying transactions. These negotiations focus on both the price as well as the structure of the core offering, supplemented by accompanying contractual issues.

While this classification can provide important information with regard to the intensity of the preparation for the negotiation (e.g. type and number of individuals involved, information gathering on alternatives), the following consideration of negotiations will abstract from this classification. The structural mechanisms of a negotiation are deeper than specific negotiation content, as we will see in the following sections.

2 Investigation of Negotiations in Research

2.1 Research Perspectives and Contributions

While the skill of negotiation management has been passed on from generation to generation for thousands of years, the academic study of the topic is a relatively recent phenomenon. Despite the range of findings now available, the titles of many standard works still allude to the long tradition of the art of negotiation (Howard Raiffa: "*The art and science of negotiation*"; Leigh Thompson: "*The mind and heart of the negotiator*").

The first systematic investigation of negotiation situations took place in the 1940s and 1950s in **game theory** (Luce and Raiffa 1957; Nash 1950, 1953; Schelling 1960; von Neumann and Morgenstern 1944). Based on so-called games, namely extremely simplified interdependent decision-making situations, these researchers attempted to predict the behavior of individuals based on the assumption of complete rationality and one-dimensional utility maximization. The derivation of mathematically optimal solutions to these games was then tested on "real people"—and failed to a large extent. Many of the participants in these game theoretical experiments did not focus on pure utility maximization; rather they were subject to certain cognitive limits as well as other precepts of real human actions, e.g. fairness considerations. The inability of a tenet based purely on game theory to explain real-life negotiation behavior also resulted in the **negotiation analytical approach** introduced by Raiffa, which attempted to combine game and decision-making theory with findings from behavioral science for the analysis of negotiation situations (Raiffa 1982; Raiffa et al. 2002).

Building on the initial game theoretical approaches, researchers from other disciplines developed an interest in the investigation of negotiations. In **sociology**, this resulted in a much cited, seminal work of "*A Behavioral Theory of Labor Negotiations*" (Walton and Mckersie 1965). It was based on game theoretical, economic, psychological, and sociological works and made extensive observations on distributive as well as integrative negotiation situations. Subsequent sociological studies also dealt with the topic of negotiating power (Bacharach and Lawler 1976, 1981a).

However, **social psychologists** have had the greatest impact on the field since the 1960s, by further developing the simple games of the game theorists and selecting another research focus (Fouraker and Siegel 1963; Kelley 1966; Pruitt and Drews 1969). Instead of the game theoretical approach to predicting human behavior under certain assumptions and structural parameters (e.g. time restrictions, information asymmetries; Rubinstein 1985) based on normative considerations, their approach is more descriptive and explicative: it attempts to describe human behavior in negotiation situations and explain this based on cognitive, motivational, and emotional processes at an individual level as well as based on interaction processes. Somewhat later, **communication researchers** also contributed to this **behavioral science research approach** in the broadest sense (Donohue 1981). With the introduction of new communication media, many **management information system specialists** have also addressed the issue of negotiations since the mid-1990s using behavioral science as well as technology-based approaches (Kersten 2001; Vetschera et al. 2006).

Besides the research approaches mentioned above, which can generally be considered to be applied basic research; since the start of the 1980s, a large number of more practical, heuristic writings in the **management literature** have been established, which deal with the phenomenon of negotiations from an advisor perspective. The most famous example of this might be the book "*Getting to yes*" whose principles are based on the extensive practical experiences of the authors (Fisher et al. 1992).

Marketing research has previously rather bypassed the topic of negotiations, despite their importance especially in the business-to-business sector. Most of the works that have been published follow a behavioral science paradigm (Geiger 2007; Graham 1986; Wilken et al. 2010), which is also able to incorporate structural considerations. In contrast to the partially closed concepts of some economic theories, behavioral science contributions to negotiation research need to be thought of more as a collection of modules, whose value and explanatory power depends on the situation being considered.

2.2 The Problem Structure in Negotiations

In spite of the various research approaches, there is agreement about at least one fundamental distinction of negotiation situations on which every negotiations that occurs in practice is based: distributive and integrative negotiation situations.

2.2.1 Distributive Negotiation Situations

In a **distributive negotiation**, suppliers and customers only negotiate about one object, frequently the price, with regard to which their preferences are precisely opposed. In this case, the supplier wants to achieve a high price, while the customer wants to achieve the lowest possible price. Distributive negotiations can be modeled in Raiffa's (1982) negotiation zone model, which is displayed in Fig. 3.

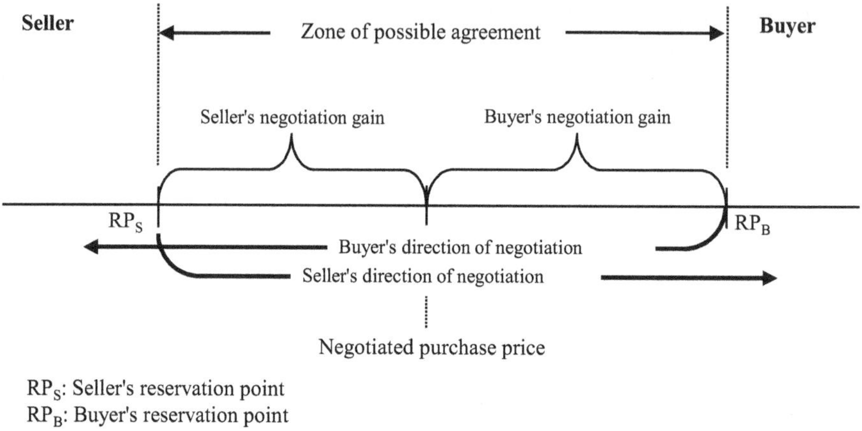

Fig. 3 Raiffa's negotiation zone model (1982) (Geiger 2007, p. 32)

According to the negotiation zone model, the benefit of a possible deal by one party depends on the extent to which this deal can provide a higher (monetary) gain for the party than its best alternative. A party's best alternative is referred to as the **BATNA** (Best Alternative To a Negotiated Agreement) in negotiation research and its calculated value determines the **reservation point** (Raiffa 1982, p. 45). If, in a sales negotiation, the buyer's reservation point is at a higher price than that of the seller, a positive **zone of possible agreement (ZOPA)** exists: By agreeing to a price between the two reservation points, the negotiating parties place themselves in a better position compared to their respective best alternatives and achieve a so-called **negotiation gain**. However, if no positive ZOPA exists, i.e. the reservation points of both parties do not overlap, it would be better for both parties not to reach an agreement. Each of the parties' best alternatives would be the better solution for them both. These considerations indicate that the determination of the best alternatives and their calculated value are extremely important, if the negotiating parties want to behave rationally with regard to a potential completion of a negotiation. It must be noted that the BATNA may be uncertain and that not only monetary values are included when determining the reservation point.

If the ZOPA is positive in this type of negotiation, meaning that it is fundamentally sensible for both parties to reach an agreement, the parties only need to divide the bargaining zone between them. This also refers back to the derivation of the term distributive negotiation. It is clear that this is a zero-sum game: What one party gains during the negotiation is necessarily lost by the other.

2.2.2 Integrative Negotiation Situations

The overwhelming majority of negotiations in the industrial plant and project business are not distributive negotiations. Rather, several issues are negotiated rather than just the price. For several negotiation issues, the negotiation partners generally do not have precisely symmetrically opposing priorities and preferences.

Rather, the parties assign varying levels of importance to the various issues. If this is the case, provided there is a positive ZOPA, there are some deals that place both parties in a better position than alternative deals. The **bargaining range** is variable and can be enhanced. As this involves the (partial) integration of the interest of the negotiating parties, the term **integrative negotiations** is used.

How can negotiating parties now identify whether their interest can be combined to form a bigger "bargaining pie". In principle, the **differences between the parties** with regard to the following points can be used:

- Relative importance of the individual negotiation issues, e.g. regarding the purchase price and maintenance costs
- Future expectations regarding the occurrence of certain events, e.g. on the price development of supplier parts that are only required in later project phases
- Risk sensitivity, e.g. on insuring against strikes or Force Majeure events
- Resources and skills regarding the service to be provided, e.g. activities to implement the project that are much cheaper for the buyer to implement than for the contractor
- Time preferences, e.g. on the time of invoicing

Furthermore, the negotiation pie can be enlarged if the parties identify issues in which their interests align (Thompson and Hrebec 1996, p. 403 et seq.). It may sometimes also be possible to generate greater benefits for both parties by including third parties (Lax and Sebenius 1986, p. 114 et seq.).

How more integrative contracts can be concluded, if differences exist between the parties, is illustrated in Fig. 4. This relates to the benefit point diagram and the associated contract space of the negotiation simulation by Pruitt and Lewis (1975), which was most frequently used in behavioral science research. In the contract space, every point represents a possible distribution of resources between the parties. It becomes clear that some contracts place the two parties in a better position than others.

For example, assuming a solution in which the parties meet precisely in the middle for all negotiation issues (level E), both would receive a gain of 4000 points. However, this type of deal does not consider the fact that the delivery date is much more important for the buyer (B) than for the seller (S), but that the opposite applies for financing. Whereas, if the parties manage to identify these different priorities, they can achieve a deal that provides for level A for delivery time and level I for financing, which would place both in a better position and achieve a benefit of 5200 points. In general, if there is no other possible contract that would place at least one party in a better position, without causing the other party's position to deteriorate, the negotiated solution is said to be **pareto-efficient**. The contract space in Fig. 4 includes all these types of solution at the top right boundary, the so-called efficient boundary.

The simple example displayed in Fig. 4 only contains the option of enlarging the bargaining range by exploiting differences regarding the importance of various issues between the parties. In negotiations, this can take place by **logrolling**: S

Issue	Delivery time		Discount		Financing	
Level	Gain S	Gain B	Gain S	Gain B	Gain S	Gain B
A	0	4000	0	2400	0	1600
B	200	3500	300	2100	500	1400
C	400	3000	600	1800	1000	1200
D	600	2500	900	1500	1500	1000
E	800	2000	1200	1200	2000	800
F	1000	1500	1500	900	2500	600
G	1200	1000	1800	600	3000	400
H	1400	500	2100	300	3500	200
I	1600	0	2400	0	4000	0

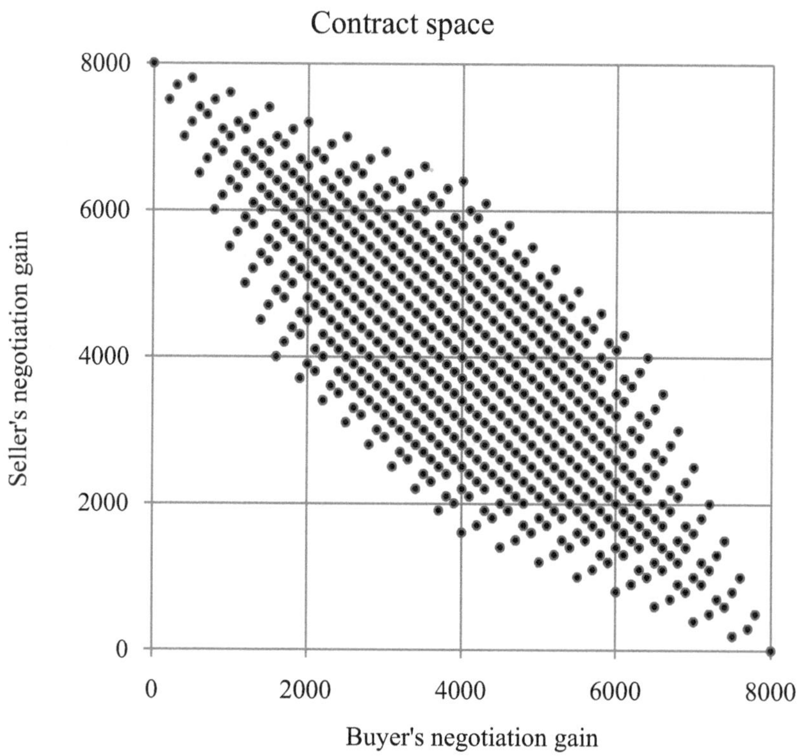

Fig. 4 Contract space in an integrative negotiation (Geiger 2007, p. 36)

could offer B a concession regarding delivery time and request B to provide a concession on the issue of financing in return. This means that both move away from their maximum requirement, but each receive a larger subjective piece of the pie. Logrolling, in the broadest sense, can be used for all items for which differences exist between the parties.

As a result, another option for generating and increasing the **integrative potential** is to increase the differences between the parties. For example, this may include splitting an individual, comprehensive negotiation issue into several small issues (Thompson 2005, p. 80 et seq.). It may also be appropriate to include additional issues in the negotiation, which have nothing to do with the actual transaction, but which increase the room for negotiation, so-called ***side deals*** (Thompson 2005, p. 71 et seq.).

Different future expectations also allow for **contingency clauses**, which define what the negotiating parties have to do to fulfill their contract if certain events occur. However, in order to be used as a meaningful instrument, contingency clauses should have certain characteristics (avoidance of conflicts of interest, enforceability, clarity and measurability of the contingency criteria; Thompson 2005, p. 85 et seq.).

When considering integrative negotiation situations, it must not be forgotten that every possible enlargement of the bargaining range is also linked to a specific distribution. The enlargement of the bargaining range generally requires a more detailed exchange of information, which, in the case of imbalance, may also mean that the bargaining pie is distributed in a one-sided manner, to the detriment of the party that has disclosed more information. As a result, integrative negotiations involve a mixture of conflicting and problem-solving elements, which negotiation research refers to as a *mixed motive* situation, which becomes a *Negotiator's Dilemma* for the relevant party (Lax and Sebenius 1986, p. 29 et seq.). How this situation can be dealt with is also covered by Sect. 3.4.1.

2.3 Non-economic Aspects of a Negotiation Situation

As important as the economic modeling is for a clear understanding of a negotiation situation, the fact that a negotiation is fundamentally an activity performed by individuals must not be forgotten. While the research in the past 50 years in relation to outcomes of a negotiation has primarily focused on economic variables, more recent studies (Curhan et al. 2006) show that the non-economic results, such as the **satisfaction with the negotiation** of the parties involved, the **perceived quality of the relationship** with the negotiating partner or **fairness** of an agreement are extremely relevant for the implementation of a negotiated agreement as well as for future rounds of negotiations. In the context of salary negotiations when starting a job, Curhan et al. (2009) were even able to show that the subjective evaluation of the salary negotiation were better able to predict the subsequent job satisfaction and period of employment with the employer than economic components of the contract such as the salary, bonus, etc.

Although negotiations in the industrial plant and project business generally involve considerably fewer individuals than are involved in implementing the contract, the subjective components of the evaluation of a negotiation must not be forgotten. Whether difficulties that arise during the implementation of the project

Table 2 Subjective value of a negotiation (Curhan et al. 2006, p. 501)

Subjective value in relation to...	Aspects
... the instrumental result	• Satisfaction with one's own result, i.e. the extent to which this contributes to the achievement of your objectives • Satisfaction with the balance between your gains and the counterpart's gains • Feeling of having lost/won • Perception of the extent to which the result achieved aligns with certain principles (fairness, legal principles, industry standards, ...)
... the self	• Feeling of having saved or lost face • Self-perception of competence as a negotiator • Feelings of having negotiated according to your own rules and principles • Impact of the negotiation on the negotiator's self-perception
... the negotiation process	• Feelings of the extent to which the counterpart responded to your concerns • Fairness of the process • Perception of how easy or difficult it was to reach an agreement • Extent to which the counterpart considered your wishes and requirements
... the relationship with the counterpart	• Overall impression of the counterpart • Satisfaction with the relationship with the counterpart • Trustworthiness of the counterpart • Perception of whether the negotiation forms a good basis for a future relationship with the counterpart

are approached with good will by representatives on both sides, also depends on how they personally perceived the original negotiations.

What exactly do non-economic aspects or the subjective evaluation of a negotiation refer to? This question was investigated by Curhan et al. (2006), who compiled four evolutionary studies which showed that the aspects displayed in Table 2 affect the subjective value of a negotiation across the various negotiation situations.

The consideration of the subjective evaluation of a negotiation is relevant for its future importance as well as a second reason: a party frequently lacks the reference point based on which a certain economic negotiation result can be evaluated as "good" or "bad". For example, it is often not completely clear whether the counterpart would have accepted a considerably higher price or significantly greater concessions on other points, which would have increased the party's own economic outcome. Instead, the evaluation of a deal is often linked to the satisfaction with the same. However, on closer inspection, this is extremely problematic, if this does not take place together with an assessment of what the satisfaction is actually based on. This is covered in more detail in the following.

According to the *expectancy disconfirmation paradigm* (Oliver et al. 1994), which has been shown to explain the development of satisfaction in various

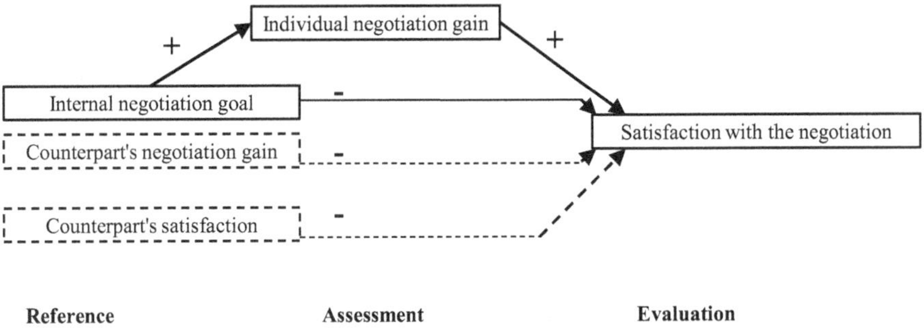

Fig. 5 Development of negotiation satisfaction

contexts, satisfaction with something (e.g. a negotiation, a product, an organization) always arises by comparing internal expectations with the assessment of the object of reference. If the assessment of the object of reference (in negotiations: the negotiated gain) meets or exceeds internal expectations (negotiation goals), this results in satisfaction, while dissatisfaction is recorded if expectations are not met. These fundamental relationships also apply in the context of a negotiation. However, negotiations also involve additional variables and relationships, which complicate the understanding of the development of satisfaction, as illustrated in Fig. 5.

For a start, this includes the importance of the **negotiation goals**, which represents the internal expectations in the development of satisfaction. Negotiators that set higher goals also negotiate more relentlessly, attempt to identify more options for efficient contracts and achieve higher individual gains, on average, than those with lower objectives. However, several empirical studies have shown (Geiger 2007, p. 212 et seq., 2014) that, in comparable situations, negotiators with a much higher individual gain were significantly less satisfied than those with a lower gain, so perception and reality have been reversed in their case. This is due to the effect of the negotiation goal on the negotiated gain and the development of satisfaction: on the one hand, as a benchmark, it has a direct negative effect on satisfaction, while on the other hand, it has an indirect positive influence through the individual gain. If the direct negative influence on satisfaction is greater than the indirect positive influence, negotiated gain and satisfaction systematically fall apart.

A second mechanism in the development of negotiation satisfaction lies in the fact that, in addition to their internal objectives, negotiators sometimes also (unknowingly) include additional reference points to evaluate their own result of the negotiation. These may include the satisfaction or the negotiated gain of the counterpart (Geiger 2014), if these figures are available. The development of satisfaction is then also subject to a social comparison (Thompson et al. 1995, p. 469). If the perceived satisfaction or the presumed negotiation gain of the counterpart is high, this initiates a process of counterfactual thinking (Galinsky et al. 2002, p. 272): The high satisfaction (or high gain) of the counterpart leads the negotiator to conclude that he or she could have "got more out of" the negotiation and has a negative effect on their internally perceived satisfaction, once again completely independent from his or her actual negotiation gain.

As these deliberations show, satisfaction with the result is only a more or less reliable factor for evaluating a deal, if the partially contradictory influences outlined here are considered in relation to the development of satisfaction.

3 Influencing Factors in Negotiations

After presenting how the various academic disciplines deal with the topic of negotiation and the fundamental structure negotiations are based upon, the question arises which factors have an influence on the course and outcomes of a negotiation.

As a preliminary remark, it is difficult to make deterministic if-then statements on the progress and outcome of negotiations based on the parameters presented subsequently. First of all, this is due to the fact that every negotiation displays a combination of different boundary conditions, sometimes with reinforcing and sometimes with rescinding effects. Secondly, negotiations are also characterized by unforeseeable events due to their interactive character, so that the negotiation dynamic makes a significant independent contribution to a certain result of a negotiation. Despite these limitations, it is appropriate to summarize the key influencing factors in a coherent model. This was performed by Neale and Northcraft (1991) for the case of two-party negotiations. Their model is displayed in Fig. 6 and is briefly outlined below.

In their model, Neale and Northcraft distinguish between static context factors and dynamic influences, which only evolve during the negotiation. To obtain a better understanding of and to better analyze a negotiation, both context factors as well as the dynamic influences need to be taken into account. However, as the outcome of a negotiation is ultimately always based on the specific interaction, it is almost impossible to apply general rules that would predict a certain result. Negotiations may be explained from various research perspectives to a certain extent, but they also remain subject to the skill of the negotiator and the specific interaction of the relevant circumstances to some extent. This must be taken into account for the presentation of the following influencing factors and their (average) effects on the progress and result of a negotiation.

3.1 Structural Context

3.1.1 BATNA and the Power-Dependency Relationship

As already implied under Sect. 2.2.1, possibly the greatest single influence on a negotiation lies outside of the negotiation itself; namely the BATNA, the best alternative. If negotiators want to behave rationally, the BATNA defines the "ultima ratio", i.e. the point which defines whether a deal under certain conditions is ultimately beneficial or not for the relevant party. The BATNAs of both negotiating parties determine the mutual power-dependency relationship (Emerson

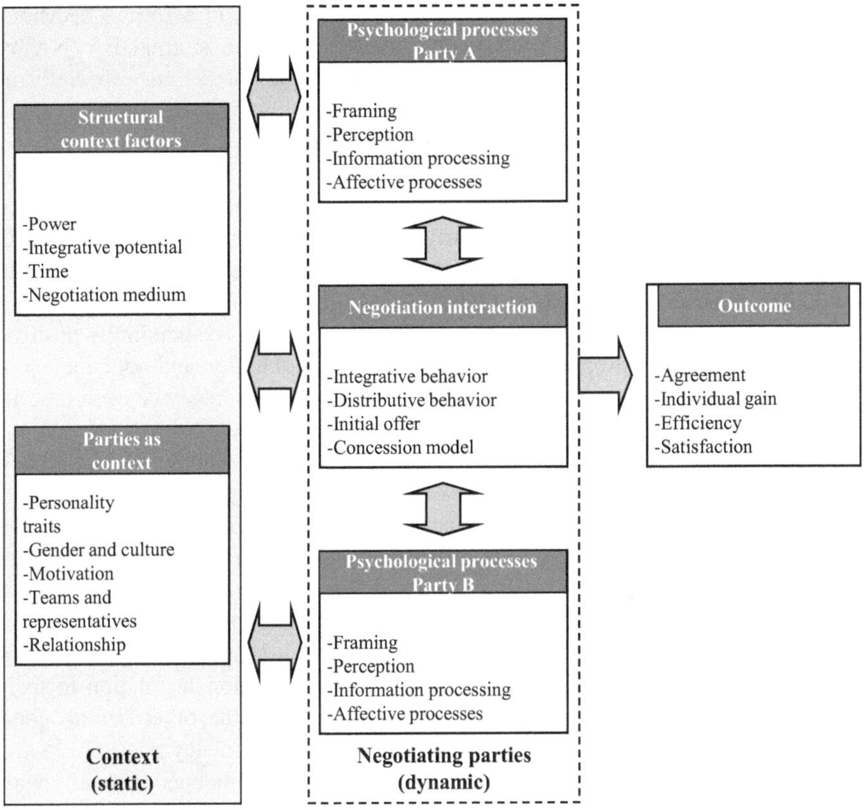

Fig. 6 Two-party negotiation model (based on Neale and Northcraft 1991, p. 177)

1962; Geiger 2007, p. 80 et seq.). If a supplier company operating in the project business has a good BATNA in a specific negotiation, such as in the form of full order books or another incoming order that utilizes capacity, it is less dependent on the outcome of the negotiation and the associated order. If it had a poor BATNA it would much more rely on a positive negotiation outcome to achieve its own economic objectives. The same argument naturally applies for the customer organization, whereby their alternatives frequently relate to the economic-technical performance of the competing suppliers.

Due to the central importance of the BATNA for a negotiation, a negotiating party must ask themselves how to best determine their BATNA. While the "inventors" of the BATNA abbreviation consider it to be a secure alternative option if a negotiation fails (Fisher et al. 1992, p. 109), Raiffa (1982, p. 37 et seq.) and Lax and Sebenius (1986, p. 50 et seq.) suggest that all possible alternative solutions to achieve the internal objectives need to be considered to determine the BATNA. This may also include uncertain options, which should then be considered with a certain probability of occurrence. In this case, the reservation point, i.e. the mathematical value of the BATNA, can be calculated using a formal decision-making model. In any case, it is sensible to strengthen the internal BATNA by exploring and potentially improving alternative courses of action, especially in negotiations that will be held over a longer period of time.

At this point, it must be noted that a party's own BATNA should in no way be confused with other possible decision-making guidelines as part of a rational negotiation, such as the company's or division's fundamental profitability requirements. For example, if the party's BATNA is comparatively poor, this may mean that a negotiated result below the company's profitability requirements could be a more positive outcome than allowing the transaction to fall through. By contrast, in the event of a very good order situation and a correspondingly positive BATNA, it may be appropriate to withdraw from a negotiation and not conclude a business transaction, even though the profitability requirements have been met. In this case the opportunity costs would be too high.

The BATNA is not just of central importance due to its quality as a fallback option, but also as a determining factor of the relative strength in a negotiation and the associated option of pushing for concessions by the counterparty. This requires the BATNAs of both parties to be considered. If both parties have good BATNAs, they are only reliant on each other to a limited extent; excessive concessions from either party cannot be expected. Rather, both parties must be interested in making the bargaining pie as large as possible (see Sect. 2.2.2) in order to arrive at a negotiated result that places both parties in a better position in relation to their BATNAs. If only one party has a good BATNA, while the other has no good alternatives, both negotiate in an asymmetrical power-dependency relationship and it is highly likely that the more powerful party, i.e. the more independent party with the better BATNA, could demand and receive substantial concessions. However, this requires that they are informed over the counterparty's BATNA situation. If both parties have poor BATNAs, they are highly dependent on each other and the negotiated result. In this situation, the availability of information on the position of the counterparty plays the most important role: A balanced situation for a specific negotiation, as is the case if both parties have good BATNAs, only arises if the mutual perception of the respective opposing party's BATNA is correct. However, if, despite a poor own BATNA, a party is able to give the impression of independence and strength to the counterparty and simultaneously intimate that the party is aware of the poor position of the other party, this information asymmetry has an effect that is similar to a genuine power-dependency asymmetry (Perdue 1992, p. 46). This means that, apart from determining a party's own BATNA, acquiring information relating to the counterparty's BATNA is also extremely important (Morton et al. 2011), especially if the internal alternatives could be better than what is available to the counterparty.

The positive effect of a good BATNA for one party on the individual gain of the stronger party has been clearly demonstrated in the empirical research (Geiger 2007, p. 192; Kim 1997, p. 276; Mannix and Neale 1993, p. 124; McAlister et al. 1986, p. 234). This effect is reinforced by the stronger party's awareness of the asymmetrical power-dependency relationship (Pinkley 1995, p. 408) and an individualistic approach by the same (Giebels et al. 1998, p. 15). The positive effects of a position of strength on the success of the individual negotiation are also reflected in a higher negotiation satisfaction (Dwyer and Walker 1981, p. 121 et seq.; Lawler and Yoon 1993, p. 476). In contrast, the findings on the effect of a power-dependency relationship asymmetry on the efficiency of a negotiation are unclear (Geiger 2007, p. 98 et seq.). With regard to the course of a negotiation, negotiators with a good BATNA set themselves higher goals, submit higher initial offers, offer fewer concessions and have a higher tendency towards competitive negotiation behavior (Geiger 2007, p. 100 et seq.). In contrast, the impact of a power-dependency asymmetry on problem-solving behavior has not been conclusively clarified.

3.1.2 Negotiation Issues and Integrative Potential

Negotiations in the industrial plant and project business are characterized by their comparably high degree of freedom in relation to finding a solution for the customer organization and its implementation. In this respect we have covered "solution ready-made" negotiations (Sect. 1.4), which are both an opportunity and a challenge. The opportunity exists in that a good understanding of the mutual interests allows the various negotiation issues to be regulated so that the largest possible bargaining pie is created. The challenge is that the type and number of the issues to be negotiated increase the complexity of the negotiation and may result in existing integrative potential remaining unused. An increase in complexity frequently also leads to a rise in dissatisfaction amongst the business partners (Naquin 2003, p. 105).

A distinction may be made between the following types of negotiation issues, whereby the subjective assessment by each negotiating party is decisive for their classification:

- **Purely distributive issues** are of relatively equal importance for both parties compared to all other issues and in relation to which both parties have opposing preferences. In the example of Fig. 4, this would refer to the "Discount" item.
- **Compatible issues** are issues for which both parties have the same preferences, i.e. both parties prefer the same regulation. For example, when negotiating an industrial plant contract, this may be the maintenance regulation, for which both parties want the maintenance to be performed by the contractor, although this may be for different reasons.
- **Differentially valued issues or logrolling issues** are any issues for which the parties have different preferences, but for which further differences also exist, such as with regard to their relative importance in the overall contract, the associated risk tolerance or assessments of the future as well as the associated skills and resources available to the parties.

The latter two types of negotiation issues can be used to enlarge the bargaining pie, whereby the primary key to an efficient result, i.e. a true win-win situation, is a good knowledge of internal priorities and preferences as well as the most accurate possible assessment of the counterparty's preference structure. A meta study shows that even compatible negotiation issues are frequently not identified (Thompson and Hrebec 1996, p. 400). The parties instead agree on a partial solution that both parties believe represents a compromise, even though both parties would have preferred a different solution. With regard to logrolling issues, Moran and Ritov (2007) show that not just the knowledge of the counterparty's fundamental priority structure, but also of minor differences in preferences improve the efficiency of an agreement. Van Boven and Thompson (2003) demonstrate that the win-win potentials are best exploited if both parties have a similar (correct) mental model of the priority and preference structure of both parties in the negotiation. However, a party frequently does not have a clear idea of the relevant counterparty's preference structure prior to the actual negotiation, so the relevant information has to be acquired during the negotiation itself. If a party is able to achieve this for a certain issue, this will have a positive effect on the relevant issue (Young et al. 2012). However, only very inexperienced counterparties provide one-sided information, as this demonstrably leads to a poorer result for the party providing the information (Murnighan et al. 1999). The exchange of information regarding priorities as a type of integrative negotiation is looked at in greater detail in Sect. 3.4.1.

The types of negotiation issue are assigned greater relevance as a framework parameter of the negotiation if a party decides to develop a formal negotiation model. This idea, based on Raiffa's (1982) analysis of a negotiation has been included in the *Negotiation Support Systems* (NSS) of business information specialists in the past few years (Vetschera 2006). These NSS can help a party ensure that no efficiency potentials remain unused by modeling the problem structure of a negotiation (see Sect. 2.2) and also to ensure that their own slice of the bargaining pie is as large as possible.

3.1.3 Time: Final Deadlines and Time-Related Costs

Negotiations take time. As important agreements are generally negotiated and concluded by busy and highly paid managers, the factor of time was assigned a certain importance at an early stage in negotiation research and associated investigations were performed. Conceptually, a distinction must be made between at least two types of time influences on a negotiation: final deadlines and time-related costs.

Final deadlines arise if negotiations need to be concluded by a certain point in time before they are deemed to have failed. Final deadlines are very similar to situations in which one or both parties assume that the negotiation must conclude within a certain, defined time window, because, for example, the relevant delegation will then depart from the location in which the negotiation is being held. From a negotiation analysis perspective, final deadlines apply for both parties, even though they are sometimes forgotten in the actual negotiation.

Empirical research shows that final deadlines increase the perceived importance of agreement for the negotiating parties. They also reduce the perceived room for agreement and give negotiators a reason to make concessions (Pruitt and Drews 1969, p. 57). They also limit the objectives of negotiators, reduce the level of demands and the tendency to bluff. Concessions are made more frequently and are larger in size (Smith et al. 1982, p. 882). The extent to which final deadlines help to make a deal more likely, as suggested by the meta analysis by Stuhlmacher et al. (1998), depends on certain framework parameters. A negative effect was demonstrated for individualistic negotiators and those who are accountable to a constituency, which includes more aggressive negotiating behavior, less exchange of information and lower negotiation efficiency (Carnevale and Lawler 1986, p. 655; Mosterd and Rutte 2000, p. 239). The effect seems positive if these framework conditions are not present, i.e. final deadlines increase the probability of agreement. Besides an altered, i.e. greater and faster, concession behavior, final deadlines also seem to contribute to a change in information processing by negotiators: Negative information is weighted more heavily, risk aversion rises, information is processed more quickly overall and combined differently than without time pressure (Stuhlmacher and Champagne 2000, p. 471 et seq.). Perdue (1992) also reported that the generation of time pressure by imposing final deadlines was the second most often used means of applying pressure by purchasing managers in order to obtain additional concessions from sellers (p. 48). However, Moore (2004) rightly points out that this kind of strategy can only be considered successful if the relevant counterparty is subject to an egocentric bias and does not recognize that the final deadline not only applies for themselves and their concession behavior, but that it also applies equally for the counterparty (p. 121 et seq.).

Time-related costs, i.e. the costs that arise if the conclusion of a negotiation is delayed, have a different impact. They frequently affect the negotiating parties in different ways. For collective negotiations, this may relate to costs that arise as a result of additional strike days on the employer side. For negotiations in the industrial plant and project business this may relate to delayed future cash flows from the plant for the principal, if the delays in the negotiations lead to further delays, such as for approvals, during construction or commissioning. Considered from an analytical perspective, increased costs of delays for a party represent a genuine disadvantage, as they constantly have to weigh up whether quick concessions are more cost-effective than increased time-related costs of delays.

3.1.4 Negotiation Medium

An aspect that has received greater attention, especially in the past 15 years, is the issue of the **negotiation medium**. In principle, negotiations can take place face-to-face, via video conference, telephone, email or other forms of electronic text-based communication, such as designated Internet chats. Studies by Ambrose et al. (2008) and Cano et al. (2005) show that several media are frequently used during a negotiation process. As different media can impact on the negotiation process and the result of a negotiation in different forms, this issue requires further discussion, especially given the introduction of more recent communication technologies (mobile phone, email, SMS, Skype, etc.) which has significantly changed our media usage behavior.

In this line of research, *Media Richness Theory* (Daft and Lengel 1984, 1986) in connection with the *Task/Media-Fit Hypothesis* (McGrath and Hollingshead 1993) initially attempted to predict the influence of media on the progress and outcomes of a negotiation. The *media richness* of a medium depends on how many channels this medium provides for transmitting information, how easy it is to provide feedback and how personalized it is. According to this theory, *face-to-face* has the highest *media richness*, while email, for example, only displays a low *media richness*. According to the *Task/Media-Fit Hypothesis*, particularly rich media are best suited to implementing complicated communicative tasks such as negotiations. This hypothesis was supported in several empirical investigations (Naquin and Paulson 2003; Purdy et al. 2000) in which, on average, rich media led to higher joint gains, higher individual gains and increased satisfaction. In contrast, other studies came to an opposite conclusion (Citera et al. 2005; Croson 1999; Geiger 2014) or did not find any difference with regard to the negotiated result (Galin et al. 2007, p. 794). Hence, the extent to which a general media influence in negotiations can be assumed is unclear.

The overall only partially convincing predictions of *Media Richness Theory* and the *Task/Media-Fit Hypothesis* are due to the fact that they do not precisely specify what exactly a good task performance is (Dennis et al. 2008, p. 577). As a result, Dennis et al. (2008) propose assessing communication media based on how well they enable the two tasks of **transmitting facts (*conveyance*)** and **establishing a mutual, uniform understanding** of the problem discussed and its solution (***convergence***). In order to describe how well various media are suited to these two communication tasks they investigate different media characteristics, which then determine the *media synchronicity*. They implicitly draw on the considerations by Clark and Brennan (1991), who, in a very similar approach, show how different media characteristics need to be considered in order to establish *grounding*, i.e. the same understanding about the content of a communication between two different parties. Tables 3 and 4 provide an overview of the discussed, relevant media characteristics and the extent to which these are displayed by individual media used in negotiations.

Dennis et al. (2008) also argue that media with a low *media synchronicity*, such as email, are better suited for the transmission of facts (*conveyance*) in a communication situation than high synchronicity media. The recipient then has the time to process the new information and reconcile it with his or her state of knowledge. For example, in the industrial plant and project business, detailed plans or solution outlines are important information for the negotiation process that should be transmitted using this kind of media. In contrast, high *media synchronicity* media are better suited at developing a common understanding of a problem and its (negotiation) solution (*convergence*), as rapid detail clarifications (questions and feedback) allow information to become fundamentally established.

With regard to *face-to-face* negotiations, additional importance may be ascribed to the **negotiation location**. It is doubtlessly true that some of the legends of uncomfortable chairs, room temperatures and lighting for the visiting party stem from real situations and may have established a "visitor disadvantage" in many

Table 3 Media characteristics based on *Grounding in Communication* (Clark and Brennan 1991, p. 141)

Media characteristics	Face-to-Face	Video conference	Telephone	Email
Co-presence: A and B are located in the same physical environment	Yes	No	No	No
Visibility: A and B can see each other	Yes	Yes	No	No
Audibility: A and B can talk to each other	Yes	Yes	Yes	No
Co-temporality: B receives something at the same time that it is sent by A	Yes	Yes	Yes	No
Simultaneity: A and B can send and receive at the same time	Yes	Yes	Yes	No
Sequentiality: The communication by A and B cannot be interrupted by third parties	Yes	Yes	Yes	No
Reviewability: B can review the messages sent by A	No	No	No	Yes
Revisability: A can revise their messages to B	No	No	No	Yes

Table 4 Media characteristics based on *Media Synchronicity Theory* (Dennis et al. 2008, p. 581 et seq.)

Media characteristics	Face-to-Face	Video conference	Telephone	Email
Symbol sets: Number of ways in which the medium enables communication to be encoded, i.e. the number of channels and language diversity	Large	Medium	Small	Medium, by attachments
Transmission velocity, at which the message can be sent to the desired recipient(s)	High	High	High	High
Reprocessability: Extent to which the medium allows the message to be reviewed or edited	Not possible	Possible if recorded	Possible if recorded	Possible
Rehearseability: Extent to which the medium allows the sender to practice or perfect a message before sending	Not possible	Not possible	Not possible	Possible
Parallelism: Number of possible parallel transmissions of a message	Limited to attendees	Strict technical restrictions	Medium	Very large
Total: *Media Synchronicity*	Very high	High	Medium–high	Low–medium

negotiations. However, a series of current empirical studies show that a "home ground advantage" exists in distributive negotiations, which is reflected in higher individual negotiated gains and can also be explained by the higher self-confidence of the hosting party (Brown and Baer 2011, p. 197 et seq.).

3.2 Personal Context

The fact that negotiations between organizations and their outcomes are predominantly characterized by certain individuals and personalities is obvious at first glance. However, much less obvious is the issue of which personality variables have a stable influence on negotiations or the extent to which their possible influence is displaced by situational factors (Lewicki et al. 2010, p. 420). The following section considers previously investigated general personality traits and individual differences as well as gender, culture and motivation (which is more unstable over time). The composition of negotiation teams and the use of negotiators is naturally also important, especially in negotiations in an interorganizational context. Finally, the issue of past history and the relationship between the negotiating parties must be related back to the personal context.

3.2.1 Personality Traits

Personality traits are measurable, stable tendencies of an individual to think, feel and act in a certain manner. As a result, they are particularly suited to predicting human behavior, even though there is a debate in psychology in relation to what extent of the behavior is due to personality traits and situational factors (Funder 2001, p. 199). Current approaches for investigating the influence of personality traits on behavior are the global consideration of personality based on the "Big Five" personality traits as well as the consideration of individual personality traits, such as social value orientation or Machiavellianism.

The ***Big Five*** include the following personality traits (Barrick and Mount 1991, p. 3 et seq.), each with their independent attributes:

- Extraversion (vs. Introversion)—gregarious, confident, forthcoming, active
- Neuroticism (vs. emotional stability)—anxious, uncertain, apprehensive, awkward
- Agreeableness—flexible, cooperative, friendly, cheerful, courteous, tolerant
- Conscientiousness—responsible, organized, foresighted, goal-oriented
- Openness to experience—curious, original, imaginative, open

The empirical findings on the influence of the Big Five on negotiation behavior and the outcomes of a negotiation are significantly weaker compared to other contexts (e.g. with regard to performance at the workplace). In one of the first large-scale studies, Barry and Friedman (1998) were able to show that extraversion and agreeableness have a negative influence on individual gains in distributive negotiations, which they partially ascribed to the susceptibility of the respective individuals to cognitive anchors due to extreme offers by the counterparty (also see Sect. 3.4.2). Agreeable people also tended to grant larger concessions (DeRue et al. 2009, p. 1040). However, the anchor effect was not identified in integrative negotiations. An expected influence of conscientiousness, extraversion and agreeableness on the negotiation efficiency could also not be demonstrated, while the cognitive abilities of the negotiator (which are not included as personality traits) displayed a positive influence on negotiation efficiency. A more recent study by Dimotakis et al. (2012) was able to replicate and expand on the findings relating to the negative impact of agreeableness on individual gain in distributive negotiations. However, these authors also found a positive correlation between agreeableness and negotiation efficiency in integrative negotiations and declared that their results were linked to a higher state of arousal if the extent of agreeableness (low, high) matched the negotiation situation (distributive, integrative).

With regard to integrative negotiations, the effects of **social value orientation** on a negotiation was identified as relatively stable. Negotiators with a pro-social value orientation prefer an outcome that suits all parties, while pro-self negotiators do not care about the other party and are only interested in their outcome (Van Kleef and De Dreu 2002, p. 60). Various empirical studies have shown that pro-social negotiators show more trust, integrative negotiation behavior, make more concession and are more satisfied with their results than pro-self negotiators (De Dreu and Boles 1998; De Dreu and Van Lange 1995; Olekalns et al. 1996).

Another repeatedly investigated personality trait in negotiation research is the **Machiavellianism** of an individual. People with a high degree of Machiavellianism are only interested in their objectives and are not afraid of using manipulation to achieve this objective (Brooks and Rose 2004, p. 126). They have a strategic, opportunistic and, in some cases, unethical approach and also tend to tolerate this type of behavior from others (Lewicki et al. 2010, p. 428). Machiavellianism leads to a distributive behavior in negotiations, but not necessarily to a higher individual gain, as shown by the study by Dion and Banting (1988, p. 45).

3.2.2 Gender

The influence of **gender** on negotiations has long been an object of debate in research, with no end in sight. Most researchers agree that men and women experience negotiations differently (Stuhlmacher et al. 2007, p. 329). In the majority of studies, men achieved a higher average individual gain than women (Curhan et al. 2008; Neu et al. 1988; Stuhlmacher and Walters 1999). It has also been repeatedly shown that the negotiation behaviors of men and women differ; women negotiate more cooperatively and men more distributively (Kimmel et al. 1980; Walters et al. 1998). However, in negotiations in which men and women negotiate with each other the reason for the disadvantage for women may also lie in the fact that the male counterpart introduces higher demands due to the gender of their negotiating partner, than would be the case for a male counterpart (Kray and Thompson 2005; Stuhlmacher et al. 2007, p. 330).

An important background to this finding is provided by the **social role theory** (cf. to this section Stuhlmacher et al. 2007, p. 331 et seq.). According to this theory, people develop an expectation of their own behavior and the behavior of other people in certain roles. These expectations may be either of a descriptive or normative nature, i.e. the relevant behavior could be either described as well as prescribed. In addition, an individual can always fill several social roles in a certain situation, such as an expert, manager, negotiator and man. The social roles are linked to certain typical role attributes that describe how individuals behave, or should behave, in the respective role. In most societies men and women have different social roles and it is expected that they fulfill their respective social roles. For example, with regard to communication, the social role of the woman is characterized by the attributes of "friendly", "warm", "supportive" and "selfless", while the role of men tends to include traits such as assertiveness, self-confidence and dominance.

The extent to which gender roles apply depends on the relevant situation. Some authors argue that negotiations fundamentally represent a masculine situation (Kray and Thompson 2005) in which primarily male attributes and behavior lead to success, although feminine and neutral behavior are naturally also required (Stuhlmacher et al. 2007, p. 332). This theoretical explanation is supported by a range of empirical findings, whereby both gender as well as the stereotype associated with gender develop predictive power for a negotiation. Kray and coauthors were able to show that the activation of relevant male stereotypes improved the negotiation performance of men, while the activation of relevant female stereotypes (expressiveness, good listening ability) did the same for women (Kray et al. 2001, 2002). However, if women were made aware of the male stereotype, this led to reactance and their negotiation performance improved significantly (Kray et al. 2001, p. 955). The clearly differentiated impact of gender stereotypes in negotiations is displayed by a study by Curhan and Overbeck (2008) which shows that more powerful negotiators behave precisely the opposite to the gender-specific stereotype, if they want to impress the counterparty.

3.2.3 Culture

The aspect of negotiations that is probably responsible for the greatest number of empirical studies is the **culture** of the negotiator. According to the GLOBE project (*Global Leadership and Organizational Behavior Effectiveness*), culture can be defined as "shared motives, values, identities, and interpretations or meanings of significant events that result from common experiences of members of collectives that are transmitted across generations" (House and Javidan 2004, p. 15) This definition already points to the complexity of the concept of "culture", on which the vast number of conceptualizations and measurement approaches of culture are based.

Three approaches have been established in negotiation research for making culture more tangible through operationalization and measurement and for deriving hypotheses on the impact of certain cultural personality traits on negotiations. Perhaps the most frequently quoted works are those of Geert Hofstede, who, in his book "*Culture's Consequences*", filtered out four independent bipolar dimensions to characterize the most important traits of a national culture. His work is based on survey data from employees in the IBM group in 66 countries (collected between 1967 and 1973) (Hofstede 1984):

- Power distance: Expectation of members of a group that power is distributed unequally in this group.
- Uncertainty avoidance: Intolerance towards uncertainty and ambiguity.

- Individualism vs. Collectivism: Extent to which individuals are integrated into groups.
- Masculinity vs. Femininity: Assertiveness and competitiveness versus modesty and caring.

He subsequently supplemented these dimensions with long-term orientation (Neun 2011, p. 28). In addition to his endeavors to split the culture concept into five dimensions, another reason for the proliferation of this approach may be that Hofstede published values for individual culture dimensions for a total of 40 countries (McSweeney 2002, p. 91). Subsequently, researchers could refer to these values by using them for individuals from the relevant country. The dimensions of "Individualism vs. collectivism", "Power distance" and "Long-term orientation" are frequently used as a predicator for negotiation behavior and outcomes, whereby the empirical results of these negotiation studies are only consistent to a certain extent.

Then again, Hofstede's approach has also been strongly criticized for both theoretical as well as methodological reasons (McSweeney 2002). Criticism includes the now advanced age of his comparative values and the exclusive reference to members from a single global organization (IBM), which is also a bearer of (corporate) cultural values.

The GLOBE project represents a much cleaner development in terms of both content and method (House and Javidan 2004). It initially attempted to develop a measuring instrument for culture in 62 societies and then used this measuring instrument among managers to investigate these cultures in greater detail. Table 5 shows the individual cultural dimensions that were identified as part of the GLOBE project as well as the characteristics for Germany and China. The similarity of the GLOBE dimensions to Hofstede is clearly visible, although they enable a differentiated image of the concept of culture to be established.

Another approach for recording the influence of culture on negotiations is defined by Hall (1976), who regards the cultural context of communication (cf. Fig. 7). In many Western cultures, communication norms provide for direct communication, in which the message to be transmitted is clearly contained in the words that are used and on the surface of the message (Adair and Brett 2005, p. 37). This is considered to be low context communication. By contrast, communication in many East Asian countries is indirect and based on the context, which is why it is referred to as high context communication. The subtle message transmitted in correspondence often lies between the words used and can only be deciphered by the individual receiving the message with knowledge of the context. Consequently, a kind of translation ability is required to correctly understand the communication. People from a *low context* culture do not tend to have this ability (Adair et al. 2007, p. 1064) and are frequently at a disadvantage when negotiating with negotiators from *high context* cultures, as the latter also tend to understand low-context communication (Adair and Brett 2005, p. 38).

Table 5 Cultural dimensions of the GLOBE study and example values for Germany and China (Neun et al. 2012, p. 26)

Cultural value	Description	Germany	China
Assertiveness	The degree to which individuals are assertive, confrontational, and aggressive in their relationships with others	3.23	5.52
Uncertainty avoidance	The extent to which a society, organization, or group relies on social norms, rules, and procedures to alleviate the unpredictability of future events	3.70	5.34
Gender egalitarianism	The degree to which a collective minimizes gender inequality	5.02	3.73
Performance orientation	The degree to which a collective encourages and rewards group members for performance improvement and excellence	6.26	5.72
Future orientation	The extent in which individuals engage in future-oriented behaviors such as delaying gratifications, planning, and investing in the future	5.21	4.70
Collectivism I—Institutional	The degree to which organizational and societal institutional practices encourage and reward the collective distribution of resources and collective action	4.97	4.52
Collectivism II—In-group	The degree to which individuals express pride, loyalty, and cohesiveness in their organizations or families	5.42	5.12
Power distance	The degree to which members of a collective expect power to be distributed equally (R)	2.70	3.01
Humane orientation	The degree to which a collective encourages and rewards individuals for being fair, altruistic, generous, caring, and kind to others	5.60	5.34

Comments: The characteristics of the various cultural dimensions lie between 1 and 7 and represent actual values (not target values). A higher value for power distance means a high power distance, despite the reverse definition of the dimension

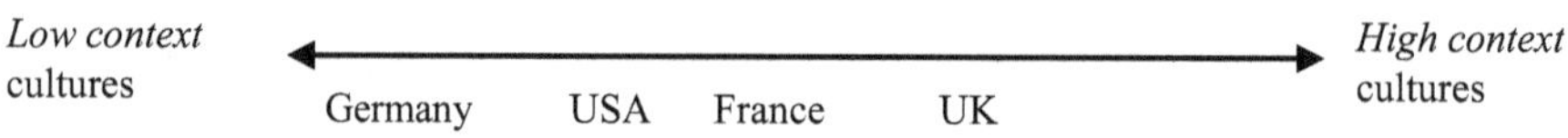

Fig. 7 Classification of cultures by High and Low Context (based on Campbell et al. 1988, p. 54)

Besides these three theoretical approaches to recording culture and predicting its impact on negotiations, many empirical studies also use characterizations of typical country-specific behaviors in advice books (Campbell et al. 1988; Salacuse 1999).

A distinction between two types of studies can be made with regard to culture and negotiations: comparative-intracultural and intercultural studies. Some studies also combine both types (Adair et al. 2001; Kamins et al. 1998; Neun 2011).

Important findings from the comparative-intracultural studies relate to cultural differences in the negotiation process and the associated results. For example, Adair et al. (2007) showed that early offers in US negotiations (*low context* culture with direct communication) led to an anchor effect (see Sect. 3.4.1), which impaired the negotiation efficiency, while Japanese negotiators (*high context* culture with indirect communication) used these for the implicit exchange of information and thus increased negotiation efficiency. In their study, Adler et al. (1992) found that US and Chinese negotiators differed in the frequency of interruptions and questions, but that both reached more efficient results with a problem-solving approach to negotiations. Arunachalam et al. (1998) identified the reason for the greater negotiation efficiency in negotiations amongst Hong Kong Chinese compared to US negotiators: The former come from a collectivist culture, while the latter come from an individualistic culture. The study by Graham et al. (1988) showed that US negotiators achieved a higher negotiation efficiency when they focused on problem-solving, while competitive tactics were more likely to succeed for Chinese negotiators in this respect. The list of individual empirical findings could be continued; however, we do not intend to do so. Instead, it must be noted that negotiations differ, on average, in different cultures, while it should not be forgotten that a country's culture is only one of many influences and that individual members of a culture may differ significantly (Neun 2011, p. 29).

With regard to intercultural negotiations, many authors assume that they generally lead to less efficient outcomes then intracultural negotiations (Adair 2003; Adair et al. 2001; Brett and Okumura 1998). They base this assertion on potential adaptation problems that occur in intercultural negotiations. Only once these adaptation issues have been overcome can intercultural negotiations lead to similarly efficient outcomes as intracultural negotiations. Neun et al. (2012) were able to show that in German-Chinese negotiations with a German seller, this adaptation was performed by the German, whereby this is due to both the importance of the seller's role for the Chinese as well as the reasons for acculturation, i.e. cultural adaptation. Imai and Gelfand (2010) make the cultural intelligence of the negotiator responsible for a successful adaptation and efficient outcomes of a negotiation, which they define as the ability of a person to adapt to new cultural circumstances (p. 84). Furthermore, a high degree of collectivism in relation to the negotiator and particularly the seller seems to lead to more efficient outcomes of negotiations in intercultural negotiations, which can be explained by better exchange of information, more frequent package offers and less distributive behavior of the seller (Cai et al. 2000, p. 608).

3.2.4 Motivation

While personality traits, gender and culture represent permanent personal features, **motivation** is a more short-term, but frequently very important, personal influence factor. Motivation refers to the targeted and medium-term stable driving force that drives human perception and behavior (De Dreu 2004, p. 114). It is fueled by the perceived difference between a Status Quo and an objective to be achieved.

In an overview of the importance of motivation in negotiations, De Dreu (2004) distinguished between the following relevant types of motivation (p. 114):

- Social motivation: Need to achieve a certain distribution of resources between the individual and the other party.

- Epistemic motivation: Need to achieve a multi-faceted and true understanding of the world.
- Impression motivation: Need to generate and maintain a certain image of oneself and the other party.

Greatest attention is paid to social motives in negotiations, whereby a rough distinction can be made between a pro-social, cooperative motivation from a pro-self, egoistic motivation (Beersma and De Dreu 1999; Giebels et al. 2000). Both the one's own result as well as that of the negotiating partner is important to a negotiator with a pro-social motivation, while an egoistically motivated negotiator is only interested in his or her own gain. Various studies have shown that the respective motivation is reflected in the course and outcome of the negotiation. Pro-self negotiations are characterized by a lower level of trust in the negotiating partner as well as more distributive behavior and ultimately less negotiating efficiency than cooperatively motivated negotiators (Beersma and De Dreu 1999; De Dreu and Van Lange 1995; Olekalns and Smith 2003). They are also less satisfied than pro-social negotiators (Gillespie et al. 2000) and are more likely to lead the negotiation to an impasse with regard to subaspects of the negotiation (Trötschel et al. 2011). Furthermore, pro-socials are more likely to adapt their behavior to the counterparty's behavior than is the case for pro-selfs (Weingart et al. 2007).

While almost no research is available for epistemic motivation in relation to negotiation behavior and outcomes, impression motivation plays a role if negotiators want to consciously influence the perception of the counterparty with regard to themselves. This may be the case if a negotiator attempts to give him- or herself the image of a "tough character", or if a certain strategy such as "Good Cop/Bad Cop" is implemented in a negotiation team (Brodt and Marla 2000). For example, the constant review of an individual's own behavior (self-monitoring) led to increased integrative behavior in the study by Ohbuchi and Fukushima (1997).

3.2.5 Roles as a Negotiator: Agents, Constituencies, and Negotiation Teams

Besides the influencing factors in a personal context, which are inherent in the negotiator as an individual, determinants in a personal context, which are inherent in the role of the negotiator, have also gained a certain amount of attention. By way of example, at this point, we focus on (a) agents who negotiate on behalf of and for the account of a constituency, and (b) negotiation teams, in which the personalities and roles of the individual negotiators in a team interact.

An negotiation **agent** refers to a negotiator who is not negotiating for one's own account, but rather for a constituency. Strictly speaking, most negotiators in the industrial plant and project business are agents, negotiating on behalf of and for the account of the company by which they are employed, unless the company owner negotiates him or herself. According to principal-agent theory, the agent is directly accountable to the principal, i.e. the constituency. If the perception of being held accountable is particularly pronounced, then negotiators in the industrial plant and project business can also be considered agents. This accountability then means that agents place great value on a positive evaluation by their principal (Neale and Northcraft 1991, p. 158), which is generally the case if a high individual gain is achieved. This frequently leads to competitive negotiation by the agents, which reduces the probability of agreement, but which may increase individual gain in the event that a deal is reached (Bazerman et al. 1992, p. 62 et seq.). The higher commitment to their position, which is generated by high accountability, means that agents are at risk of overlooking alternative options (Neale and Northcraft 1991, p. 158). This reasoning particularly applies if the accountability relates to the negotiated result. In contrast, Fassina (2004) argues that these problems do not occur if a principal, i.e. the manager responsible for the negotiation team's division, does not enforce accountability for the final negotiated result, but rather for the approach and the behavior of their agents (p. 438 et seq.). Similarly, O'Connor (1997) was able to show that the limiting effects of accountability on agent negotiators do not arise if teams are assigned as agents, as accountability is then distributed across several individuals and none of the negotiation team is subject to excessive personal pressure.

Most negotiations in the industrial plant and project business take place in **negotiation teams**, i.e. several individuals are seated at the negotiating table and participate in the negotiation for both the supplier and the contractor. The various individuals in a team bring different skills and expertise (e.g. technical, commercial, legal) and, despite a common overarching interest in a positive business transaction, may have difference preferences and priorities. Different individuals in a team may also take on different tactical negotiating roles, such as the chief negotiator, the listener, the devil's advocate, the expert, the strategist, etc. (Thompson 2005, p. 231). In addition, all members of a team also add their specific personality traits (see Sect. 3.2) so that the negotiation situation between teams is exponentially more complex than between two solo negotiators (Brodt and Thompson 2001, p. 209).

However, some relatively stable empirical findings have still emerged. For example, Thompson et al. (1996, p. 72 et seq.) report that the use of a team improved the negotiation efficiency in relation to negotiations between solo negotiators, which is explained by the higher exchange of information and a better perception with regard to the interests of the counterparty. When a team interacted with an individual negotiator, the team was also able to achieve a higher individual gain (Polzer 1996, p. 690). However, in order to exploit the positive effects of a negotiation team on negotiation efficiency and the internal negotiated gain, it seems important that the team members contribute different knowledge (Peterson and Thompson 1997, p. 374 et seq.) and that there is positive cooperation in the team (Keenan and Carnevale 1989). Higher team cohesion is also important in this respect (Backhaus et al. 2008, p. 384). If these requirements are met, teams tend to negotiate more cooperatively. Furthermore, the mirror imaged staffing of negotiation teams (*Matching*) with regard to various features (professional background, nationality, gender) is conducive to the positive course and outcome of a negotiation, as shown by the Buying Center literature (Geiger and Kleinaltenkamp 2011,

p. 290 et seq.). A strengthening of the in-group—out-group differences between the negotiating parties with increasingly competitive negotiation behavior and negative effects on negotiation efficiency takes place if the collaboration within the team is already conflictive (Halevy 2008, p. 1694; Keenan and Carnevale 1989, p. 990). Naquin and Kurtzberg (2009) make an interesting contribution to the perception of the counterparty. They show that the trustworthiness of the opposing team always depends on the least trustworthy team member and not the average trustworthiness of the individual team members.

3.2.6 Past History and Relationship Between the Negotiating Parties

A final influencing factor of the personal context in negotiations is the **past history** and **relationship** between the parties. It is easy to see that negotiations between parties that have not previously interacted with each other will progress differently than if they are already familiar with the other party. Both cases arise in the industrial plant and project business, whereas many other interactions on the capital goods markets, such as in the supplier business, almost exclusively include a past history or a relationship of some kind.

With regard to negotiations between organizations, Geiger (2007) argues that a past history or relationship between the parties is primarily reflected in a higher level of mutual knowledge, trust and commitment (p. 64 et seq.). Commitment also integrates future prospects, namely the expectation of executing future transaction following the current negotiation with the counterparty (Patton and Balakrishnan 2010). According to Greenhalgh and Chapman (1998), a strong relationship between two negotiating parties also involves features such as openness, common interests, empathy, respect and a few additional attributes, which are primarily applicable for personal relationships (p. 483).

Despite the dominance of negotiations with a past history in practice, i.e. some type of relationship between the parties, surprisingly little research has dealt with the influence of past history and relationships (Gelfand et al. 2006, p. 428). This lack can partially be ascribed to the research economy and the limited access to time series data. The studies available paint a fundamentally positive picture of the impact of a past history or relationship (with positive connotations) on the course and outcome of a negotiation. In their study, O'Connor et al. (2005) show that the presence of a positive past history (i.e. a successful conclusion rather than the failure of the first negotiation) led to a higher probability of agreement and higher negotiation efficiency in a subsequent negotiation (p. 357 et seq.). In an industrial business relationship simulation, Geiger (2007, p. 213) was able to demonstrate that this reduced the competitive behavior of the negotiating partners, increased the integrative behavior and ultimately led to higher rates of agreement and higher negotiation efficiency. However, the studies by Fry et al. (1983) and O'Connor and Arnold (2011) show that a positive past history and relationship does not automatically lead to better economic outcomes of negotiations: For example, if the endeavor to maintain or extend the relationship is too great, this may deter the parties from pushing through conflictive phases of a negotiation, which would be necessary to achieve more efficient results.

3.3 Psychological Processes of the Negotiating Parties

The previous sections have already introduced us to several influencing factors on negotiations that are inherent in the negotiators themselves. However, without exception, this has related to factors that are set at the start of a negotiation, some of which are even fully determined, such as gender or the cultural background of a negotiator. In contrast, the following section focuses on dynamic factors in relation to the negotiator, i.e. psychological processes that take place in the minds and bodies of negotiators during the negotiation. These include conscious and unconscious perception and information processing processes that determine the experience and actions in the negotiation interaction. At its core, this relates to the fact that negotiators attempt to ascribe meaning to their experiences and actions and, in doing so, are confronted with various challenges. As we will see, negotiators do not "function" as "rational machines", rather they are constantly deceived by their own senses, as we already saw when discussing the development of negotiation satisfaction.

3.3.1 Framing: The Different Glasses (Frames) Worn by a Negotiator

Negotiations are socially embedded, communicative situations with a considerable scope for interpretation, which every negotiator experiences and interprets based on his or her internal personal expectations and experience. Bateson (1972) and Goffman (1974) describe the mechanism of attributing meaning in this kind of situation as ***Framing***. A frame helps the negotiator to pay particular attention to certain things in the negotiation, to interpret information in a certain way, and to assign a certain form to a negotiation as well as change this form. Frames help us to perceive and understand a person, an event, or a process in a certain light and to separate this from the complex, random world around it. They also determine how we record, process, and interpret general information and special elements of the communication process (pattern of messages, linguistic and socially constructed meanings) and how we behave ourselves (Putnam and Holmer 1992, p. 129). For example, the concept of a frame can help us understand why two people in the same social situation perceive and interpret this situation differently (Lewicki et al. 2010, p. 142). Frames are particularly important in negotiations, as the conflicting interest of the parties often do not come to light, but may be partially concealed, which allows for a significant scope of interpretation that every negotiator fills with their own experience. The way negotiators define and interpret certain negotiation issues provides a clear indication of which points they find important, which objectives they are pursuing, which information they are after, and which information they ignore, as well as how they negotiate for their own cause (Lewicki et al. 2010, p. 142). It is important to note that negotiators always use frames, or that they are always wearing certain glasses through which they perceive the negotiation and participate themselves.

As these frames have a great influence on the perception and information processing processes described in the following sections (Pinkley and Northcraft 1994, p. 194), an awareness of the possible frames is a first step towards understanding the process of *framing* and controlling it to a certain extent. Various authors propose various categories of frames, which are outlined below.

A categorization, which is predominantly based on unpublished works by Gray and co-authors (Lewicki et al. 2010, p. 143 et seq.; Putnam and Holmer 1992, p. 135 et seq.), distinguishes between the following frames based on the linguistic analysis of transcripts of negotiations:

- The **substantive frame** focuses on what the conflict or the negotiation is actually about.
- The **outcome frame** focuses on a single or a few specific desirable results that a party targets in a negotiation. Negotiators with a pronounced outcome frame run the risk of becoming inflexible due to the strict focus on outcomes as well as not considering the counterparty and negotiating in a distributive manner.
- The **aspiration frame** attempts to perceive the negotiation as an open interaction that aims to satisfy the wide-ranging own interests and needs. This type of frame often integrates the position and interests of the counterparty and is a good prerequisite for reaching efficient, integrative agreements.
- The **process frame** attempts to ensure that the parties follow a specific course of a negotiation that is considered to be adequate. The path that the actual content of the negotiation takes is secondary for negotiators with a strong process frame.
- The **identity frame** aims to maintain the negotiator's identity, i.e. how a negotiator sees him- or herself and would like to be seen, and potentially strengthen this identity during the negotiation. For example, the great importance assigned to saving face for negotiators from the Far East (Neun 2011, p. 34 et seq.) can be explained by the identity frame.
- The **characterization frame** decides on how the counterparty is perceived and treated. It is frequently influenced by the status of the counterparty, their reputation or behavior at the start of a negotiation.
- The **loss-gain frame** determines whether a negotiator is likely to view the potential outcome of a negotiation as a loss or a gain. This particularly plays an important role for the impact of cognitive reference points.

For this categorization it is important to note that negotiators may be wearing multiple frames during a negotiation, for which the importance may change during the course of the negotiation. For example, a strict process frame may lead to the development of a relationship of trust between the two parties, while together with a strong aspiration frame, this may result in the most efficient possible agreement. The various focuses of the individual frames makes it clear that these can lead to different courses of a negotiation. This may result in particular conflict constellations if the two parties are wearing different frames. For example, a strong outcome frame by one party and a loss frame by the other, may lead, despite integrative potential, to a spiral of competitive behavior so that the negotiation ultimately fails.

Another empirically derived categorization of frames in conflicts and related negotiations is given by Pinkley (1990). Three dimensions of conflicts were

Task: The negotiator is focused on resolving a specific task.	↔	**Relationship:** The negotiator's most important concern is the maintenance/restoration of a good relationship with the counterparty.
Intellectual: The negotiation is considered to be an intellectual activity, for which certain actions are expedient.	↔	**Emotional:** The negotiation is considered to be an activity in which emotional balance plays an important role.
Compromise: The negotiation is considered to be a situation in which both parties reach a balancing compromise.	↔	**Win:** The negotiation is considered as a victory and defeat situation in which only one party can win.

Fig. 8 Three dimensions of frames in conflicts (based on Pinkley 1990)

identified based on the description of various conflicts and the assessment of their similarities. These are displayed in Fig. 8. A follow-up study investigated the influence of these frames on a specific negotiation in the context of a business relationship (Pinkley and Northcraft 1994). It was found that the frames of negotiators in a dyad converge during a negotiation. The authors were also able to show that negotiators with an intellectual frame were more satisfied with the negotiation, regardless of the outcome of the negotiation, than those with an emotional frame. With regard to individual gains and negotiation efficiency, the task frame came out to be superior to the relationship frame, while the compromise frame was superior to the win frame (p. 200).

A final approach to frames in this section is provided by Ury et al. (1988), who distinguish between three categories of how negotiators can approach a negotiation:

- **Interest-driven**: This perspective corresponds to the aspiration frame described above. Interest-driven negotiators attempt to satisfy their internal needs and interests in the negotiation and separate these from their positions. For them, positions are proposals for satisfying their interests, but which can be easily rearranged if better proposals are provided.
- **Rights-driven**: Many negotiators perceive a negotiation from a frame of what is right and fair. For them, it is extremely important that fair solutions are identified and that agreements correspond to a certain principle of fairness or certain recognized (legal) rules and (social) norms.
- **Power-driven**: Power-driven negotiators see the negotiation as a test of strength. They ask themselves, who can force the other to concede, who will win and who will lose. For these negotiators, the structure of the respective positions of power (Geiger 2007, p. 85 et seq.) is a key element of preparing for a negotiation.

It is easy to see that the course of a negotiation is extremely dependent on which approach a negotiator selects and how their approach develops during the

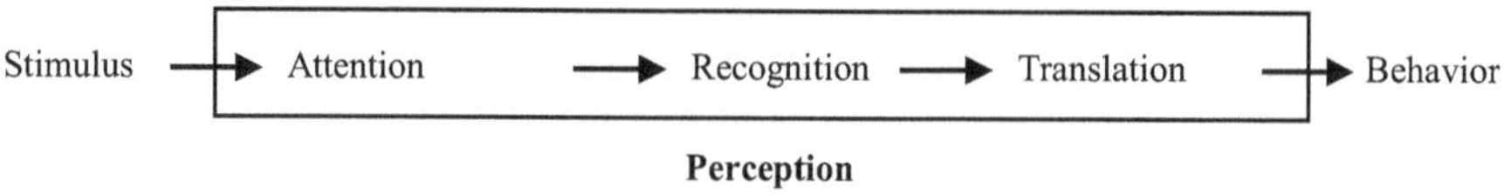

Fig. 9 The perception process (based on Lewicki et al. 2010, p. 139)

negotiation. This applies regardless of which categorization of frames the reader leans towards. In any case, this section has hopefully made it clear that frames, as glasses worn by negotiators, have a considerable impact on their perception and information processing.

3.3.2 Perception: The Window to Subjective Reality

The first fundamental psychological process that a negotiator uses to establish a connection with their social environment and the negotiation situation is their **perception**. An important objective of perception in negotiations is the correct reception and interpretation of what the other party says and attempts to transmit. The extent to which this is achieved depends on many factors, including the frames that a negotiator (consciously or unconsciously) uses, their prior knowledge and experience, personality variables (intelligence, empathy), the role (for example, in team negotiations a person may be assigned just to listen and so has a more comprehensive and sharper perception than the chief negotiator in the same team), their mental and physical condition or the external conditions of the negotiation (temperature, noise, local environment, etc.).

Perception itself is a complex physiological and psychological process, which includes the detection, selection and interpretation of sensory stimuli to create meaning for the individuals (Lewicki et al. 2010, p. 139). The interpretation and attribution of meaning in relation to the stimuli received is almost exclusively relative, i.e. relates to a certain reference value (exception: people with perfect pitch are able to state the pitch of a sound without a benchmark). Whether a negotiator is perceived as more aggressive or conciliatory depends on factors such as their reputation or past history (Hilty and Carnevale 1993).

Given that a negotiator's environment is generally extremely complex and that it contains a vast number of stimuli, perception from an individual's perspective always involves a reduction of the number of stimuli that can be incorporated. As a result, perception is always selective perception, a type of subjective window to the negotiator's reality. As shown in Fig. 9, the perception process includes the steps of attention, recognition and translation.

The need to address perception, as a specific psychological process in connection with negotiation, is especially necessary due to the fact that perceptual biases regularly and systematically occur in negotiations, and the view of reality through the subjective window does not always show the true reality. Perceptual biases cannot always be selectively distinguished from cognitive biases, which we look at in greater detail in the next section and which deal more with information processing.

An important perceptual bias that occurs in negotiations relates to the formation of judgments (frequently about the counterparty) based on little information. Lewicki et al. (2010, p. 140 et seq.) distinguish between stereotyping and the halo effect. When **stereotyping**, the negotiator judges their counterparty based on a single piece of information, which signals their affiliation with a certain social group (e.g. young and female). The perceptual bias then occurs if, in addition to the obvious information, additional stereotypical attributes of the social group are then transferred to the counterparty (e.g. young women are generally not engineers). In the ***halo*** **effects**, additional, unverified features are assigned to a counterparty based on initial information. For example, a smiling person is also perceived to be more honest than a person who looks grim, even though there is no correlation between honesty and smiling (Lewicki et al. 2010, p. 140). Halo effects may be positive or negative, so that individual, particularly prominent positive attributes result in the entire individual being viewed in a more positive light, while individual negative attributes have the opposite effect. Stereotyping and halo effects are particularly likely in negotiations (compared to other social situations), as negotiators are frequently required to quickly obtain an overview of their counterparty and so can only include a limited number of stimuli. The generalization of the available information then leads to the described perceptual biases, which can then be reinforced by the selective perception, following the first impressions, to confirm the initial image (Bazerman 2002, p. 34).

Another type of supplementation of missing information to complete a perception is defined as **projection**. Projection occurs if negotiators assume that their perception of a situation is the same as the counterparty's perception. Projection is problematic in a negotiation situation if it relates to the structure of the negotiation issues: The assumption that issues that are particularly important for one side, must also be important for the counterparty, results in a **zero-sum perception**, which rules out the possibility of differences of preferences and priorities (Thompson and Hastie 1990, p. 102 et seq.). If negotiating parties are subject to this kind of misperception, the likelihood of concluding efficient contracts is limited. A watered-down form of zero-sum perception if the **illusion of transparency** (Van Boven et al. 2003): In this case, the negotiator is aware that the parties have different priorities, but significantly overestimates the counterparty's knowledge of their internal preference structure, even if they have transmitted information of their preference structure during the negotiation.

3.3.3 Information Processing and Cognitive Biases

Negotiations are at least characterized by the fact that the information available to resolve the negotiated problem is distributed asymmetrically between, and often also within the parties. Information (offers, arguments, background facts, etc.) are exchanged during a negotiation, which partially eliminates the information asymmetries. For individual negotiators, this means that they are in a constant process of information acquisition (perception) and **information processing**. Information processing is primarily distinguished from information acquisition by the fact that it ends in a decision and action (Lewicki et al. 2010, p. 150).

As the human brain is not only confronted with countless stimuli, and so is subject to selective perception, but also receives a very high amount of information that requires further processing, many information processing methods include mental shortcuts, so-called heuristics. These often need only a very small amount of information in order to make a decision, which, in most cases, is a good decision (Cialdini 1993, p. 3 et seq.). However, these heuristics do not always lead to accurate judgments and decisions and result in cognitive biases in many cases relevant in negotiations. A psychologically skilled negotiator can easily turn the knowledge of cognitive biases and the underlying mechanisms into a tool in order to influence a negotiation in their favor, or even massively manipulate their counterparty psychologically (Lewicki et al. 2010, p. 240 et seq.; Thompson 2005, p. 163 et seq.). The details of how the latter can occur and how to protect against it, is impressively described by Cialdini (1993) in his book "*Influence—The Psychology of Persuasion*".

The following section focuses on the most important of these methods of processing information, the potential cognitive biases as well as their impact on the course of a negotiation and the outcome of a negotiation.

Cognitive Reference Points

In negotiations, as situations subject to uncertainty and incomplete information, negotiators use various **cognitive reference points** to measure the course of the negotiation and certain offers and solution options for the negotiated conflict. This allows them to assess the extent to which they will continue to negotiate, reach an agreement or withdraw from a negotiation. The effect of cognitive reference points can be most clearly illustrated in a purely distributive price negotiation from a seller's perspective, as shown in Fig. 10. Various information is used as cognitive reference points to which the seller links their agreement to make a sale: their reservation point (see Sect. 2.2.1), potentially available information on a (fair) market price and their target point (Blount et al. 1996, p. 2). As the value of these reference points may differ significantly, the seller's success in a negotiation is significantly dependent on which reference point they use to assess the arguments and offers put forward by their counterparty. This is decisive, as the assessment of a proposal put forward by the counterparty always takes place relative to a reference point, never in a vacuum. However, the human brain evaluates positive and negative deviations from a reference point differently—negative deviations are recorded as a loss and positive deviations as a gain with regard to the reference point. In addition, losses receive greater attention than gains; psychologists refer to losses as having a greater salience. This means that humans expend greater effort on minimizing potential losses than on maximizing potential gains (Kahneman and Tversky 1979). Psychologists refer to this as *loss framing* and *gain framing*. In negotiations, this means that negotiators, who are attempting to minimize a (perceived) loss, make more aggressive offers or demands, make fewer concessions and accept the failure of the negotiation more often than negotiators who believe that they are maximizing a perceived gain (De Dreu et al. 1994, p. 91).

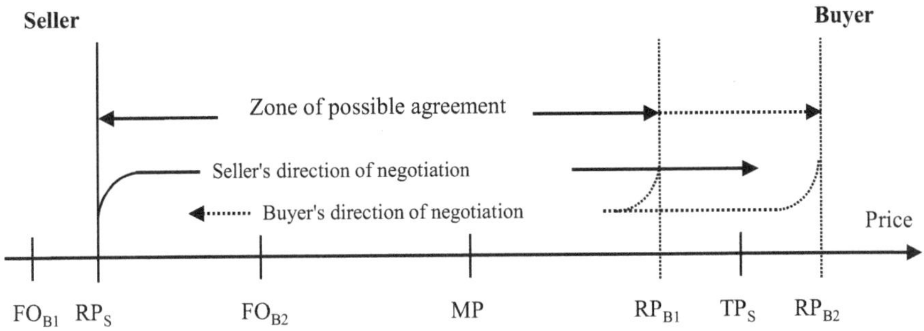

RP_S: Seller's reservation point
MP: (Notional) market price
TP_S: Seller's target point
FO_{B1}: Buyer's ambitious first offer
FO_{B2}: Buyer's less ambitious first offer
RP_{B1}: Buyer's lower possible reservation point (estimated from the seller's perspective)
RP_{B2}: Buyer's higher possible reservation point (estimated from the seller's perspective)

Fig. 10 Cognitive reference points in the bargaining zone model of a purely distributive price negotiation

Whether a negotiator is more likely to minimize a perceived loss or maximize a perceived gain depends greatly (a) on the type of reference point and (b) on the position of the relevant reference point. In principle, looking at one's own reservation point (RP_S) as a lower limit is more likely to lead to gain framing and maximizes the probability of an agreement, but it also tends to concede the possibility of achieving a higher individual gain. However, if the seller predominantly aligns to their target point (TP_S), this increases the probability of a higher individual gain.

In negotiations, it may also be the case that the individual reference points are subject to a certain amount of uncertainty. An uncertain reference point is highly likely to lead to loss framing compared to a secure reference point. The corresponding consequences in relation to the reservation point were displayed by Wilken et al. (2010): Sellers with **variable cost information**, who used the logical, secure reservation point in an individual sales negotiation, achieved lower negotiated profits than those with **full cost information**, who formed an uncertain estimate of the reservation point and an overall higher reference point (p. 80).

This study also shows that, besides the type of reference point, the level also plays an important role: The higher the reference point, the more likely it is that a party will negotiate with loss framing and try harder to avoid a potential loss. This particularly applies for target points that a negotiating party can easily influence themselves. As long as the target points remain realistic, i.e. do not lie far outside the zone of possible agreement, it is sensible for a negotiating party to aspire to high (specific) objectives. This not only tends to lead to higher negotiated gains in distributive negotiations (Huber and Neale 1986, p. 358), but also helps to enlarge the bargaining pie in integrative negotiations (Pruitt and Lewis 1975, p. 626). Huber and Neale (1986) also identified that it is better for a negotiator to have a specific negotiation objective, than to simply "do their best" without any specific objective.

In addition to the previously discussed cognitive reference points, which all relate to information available to a party prior to a negotiation and their own behavior based on this information, reference points that only occur during a negotiation also play a role in relation to the course of a negotiation. Perhaps the most important cognitive reference point during a negotiation is the counterparty's **first offer**. This is frequently the first information that can be used to derive where the counterparty's reservation point is located and the size of the ZOPA and the potential individual gain. However, this judgment regarding the size of the ZOPA from the initial counteroffer information is problematic, as the human brain takes shortcuts. Instead of combining all the possible information about the counterparty's reservation point, it uses the counterparty's first offer as a so-called cognitive anchor (Galinsky and Mussweiler 2001). An adjustment now takes place in relation to this anchor in order to estimate the relevant value. While human cognition often correctly identifies the direction of the adjustment (up or down from the cognitive anchor), the extent of the adjustment is often insufficient, even amongst experts in their area of specialization (Mussweiler et al. 2000). The estimate of the counterparty's reservation point depends largely on the level of the cognitive anchor, i.e. the counterparty's initial offer. This is illustrated in Fig. 10 by the two possible initial offers by the buyer, FO_{B1} and FO_{B2}, which, as a result of the **anchor effect** give the seller the impression of a lower or higher buyer reservation point, (RP_{B1}, RP_{B2}). This kind of anchor effect can be circumvented if a negotiator considers other available information, such as the counterparty's BATNA or their own negotiation objective, in order to weaken the salience of the anchor (Galinsky and Mussweiler 2001, p. 666).

Besides the previously addressed *loss/gain framing* due to cognitive reference points and the anchor effect based on first offers, additional cognitive biases also frequently occur in negotiations (Tversky and Kahneman 1974). A brief overview of these biases is provided below.

Information Availability

The importance of the salience of information has already been covered in the previous section. In principle, the human brain tends to include particularly salient, i.e. prominent, information in its judgment (Bazerman 2002, p. 14 et seq.). This may lead to cognitive biases and incorrect decisions in negotiations, if unimportant information is easily available and particularly salient, e.g. due to a particularly vivid or multi-sensory presentation by the counterparty, and important information for a decision is simultaneously less accessible or less salient. The higher weighting of the salient, easily accessible, but unimportant information may lead to incorrect decisions.

Winner's Curse

Winner's Curse refers to the evaluation of a negotiation by a negotiator, after the negotiation has concluded much more quickly than they expected. Frequently, the negotiation only consists of an initial offer by the relevant negotiator being immediately accepted by the counterparty. Because the negotiator has not anticipated the counterparty's immediate consent, it leads them to ask themselves whether they could have received a better deal with another offer, or whether something is wrong with the item for negotiation, especially in a sales situation. In principle, the apparent gain (acceptance of their initial offer by the counterparty) has transformed into a curse, as they could obviously have gained more. This subjective assessment of the negotiation, referred to as the *winner's curse*, is at least partially based on counter-factual thinking by the negotiator. Instead of admitting to themselves that they were obviously not sufficiently informed of the counterparty's position or the value of the item for negotiation and that they have made an error with their initial offer, they interpret the negotiation in light of a "what would have happened, if I had submitted a higher offer?" with a correspondingly unsatisfactory response (Galinsky et al. 2002).

Overconfidence Bias

Another phenomenon of cognitive biases is the **overconfidence bias** in one's own judgment and one's own abilities. According to Lewicki et al. (2010), overconfidence in one's own abilities in negotiations may lead to the advocation of one's own position and proposals with more conviction, which helps to achieve a benefit. On the other hand, it regularly results in counterparty proposals and assessments being dismissed as less accurate and less valuable, which restricts the scope of the negotiation.

Endowment Effect

The **endowment effect** may also be problematic, as, in this case, a good that is owned by an individual is assessed as being more valuable by the same individual than the same good that is not owned by the individual (Kahneman et al. 1990, p. 1326). For a sales team, the endowment effect may become problematic, if the goods to be sold are assessed as being much more valuable than the value assigned to the goods by the potential customer. Furthermore, in negotiations, the endowment effect also relates to offers. Regardless of the content of the offer, negotiators prefer their own offers to those of the counterparty (Curhan et al. 2004, p. 149).

As these examples have shown, even negotiators that want to behave rationally are subject to certain cognitive limitations. These are virtually impossible to exclude entirely, but even just awareness of these limitations provides the option of allowing the cognitive biases to flow into one's own behavior and, for example, constantly reviewing available information in a negotiation for their relevance and potential undesirable effects.

3.3.4 Affective Processes in Negotiations

While perception and information processing effects in negotiations have already been extensively studied for three decades, **affective processes**, the last psychological process considered in this section, are a field of investigation that has only received greater attention in the past few years. Affective processes in negotiations relate to actions that are triggered by a negotiator's **emotions** or **moods** (Barry and Oliver 1996, p. 128). Emotions are short-term, intuitive reactions by a human, caused by a certain event or reference object, which can be very strong, but also subside relatively quickly (Barry 2008, p. 98). In contrast, moods are less intense, last longer and can rarely be traced back to a single reason. In this section we use affect as a general term for emotions and moods. It may differ in its intensity and its valence (positive/negative). Positive affective processes include happiness, curiosity, empathy or wonder, while fury, anger, disappointment, sadness, or fear are among the negative affects (Druckman and Olekalns 2008, p. 4).

The first, and for a long time the only, empirical study on the impact of positive affect on an integrative negotiation showed that this reduced competitive behavior and had a positive effect on the efficiency of a negotiation (Carnevale and Isen 1986, p. 7). The latter effect was replicated in follow-up studies (Allred et al 1997, p. 183; Anderson and Thompson 2004, p. 130; Carnevale 2008, p. 58): According to this, negotiators in a positive mood achieve integrative outcomes more easily than negotiators in a negative mood, whereby the relative distribution of the enlarged bargaining pie does not shift in favor of the positively minded negotiator. Positive affect or happiness also have a positive influence on the tendency to negotiate together again in the future and to expand the relationship (Allred et al. 1997, p. 183; Pietroni et al. 2009, p. 86), even if the positive emotion is applied strategically, i.e. the primary reason for arousing the impression of a positive emotion (Kopelman et al. 2006, p. 88). In addition, positively minded negotiators enjoy more trust (Anderson and Thompson 2004, p. 130) and, in certain circumstances, they can expect higher concessions from their negotiation partners than neutral or negatively minded negotiators (Kopelman and Rosette 2008, p. 95; Steinel et al. 2008, p. 366).

Besides positive affect, e.g. happiness, the impact of anger has also received increased attention in the past few years. For example, Van Kleef et al. were able to show that anger in a negotiator persuades their negotiation partner to concede more (Sinaceur et al. 2011, p. 1023; Van Kleef et al. 2004, p. 62) and to place fewer initial demands in any potential future negotiations (Van Kleef and De Dreu 2010, p. 755). The fact that negotiators faced with an angry counterparty tend to concede more is due to the fact that the anger displayed by the counterparty evokes fear and is regarded as a threat, while the longer-term impacts are based on the perception of the angry negotiator as a particularly hard negotiator. Interestingly, another negative, but less aggressively perceived emotion has a very similar effect on the counterparty: Studies by Van Kleef and Van Lange (2008) and Van Kleef et al. (2006) show that a counterparty is more likely to concede if a negotiator shows disappointment instead of no emotion.

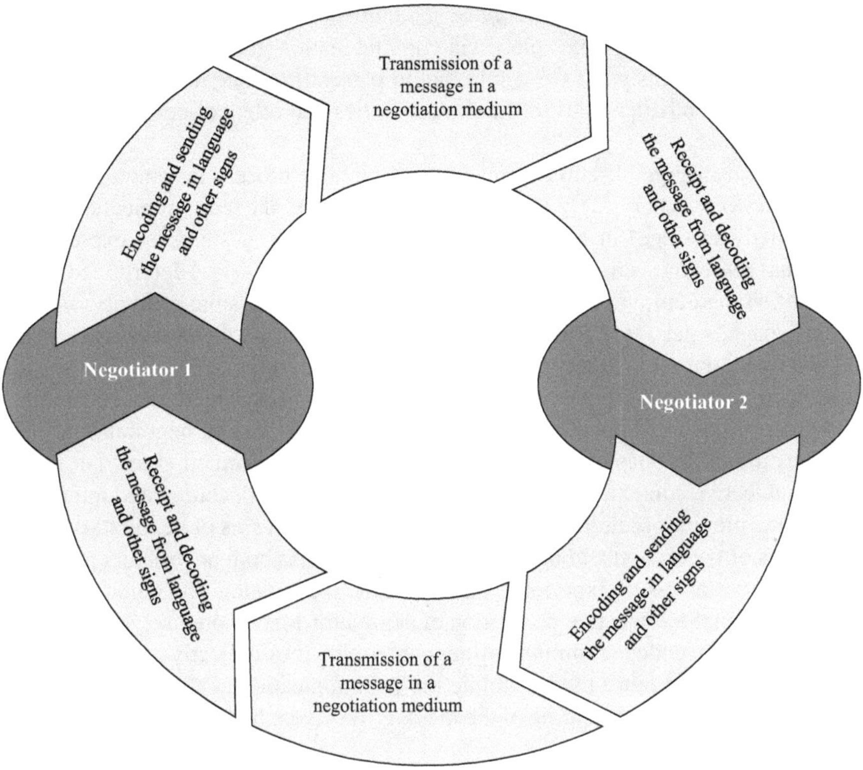

Fig. 11 Communication in negotiations (based on Lewicki et al. 2010, p. 174)

However, besides the influences of affect on negotiations that have been covered above, a couple of boundary conditions also need to be taken into account. If the negotiators in a dyad are in different moods, in the event of a power divide between the negotiating parties, only the mood of the more powerful negotiator has an impact on the negotiation (Anderson and Thompson 2004, p. 130; Overbeck et al. 2010, p. 134). The cultural background of negotiators also helps to determine the extent to which emotions impact the course of the negotiation (e.g. the tendency of the counterparty to make concession or to exchange information). This was more likely to be the case for East Asian negotiators than negotiators from the Western hemisphere (Kopelman and Rosette 2008, p. 73; Liu 2009, p. 162).

3.4 Communication and Negotiation Interaction

Regardless of the context and the parties, their disposition and psychological processes, a negotiation always represents a form of interpersonal **interaction**: At its core, a negotiation is **communication** (Putnam and Roloff 1992, p. 3). This also means that the factors mentioned above can influence the outcome of a negotiation, but that this necessarily takes place via communication in the negotiation (Geiger 2007, p. 106). At this point we would like to present a simple model of communication in order to better analyze the characteristics and effect of communication in negotiations.

As shown in Fig. 11, communication is a circular process in which negotiator 1 first encodes (encrypts) and sends the content of the communication to be transmitted (message) in language and other signs, e.g. gestures or expressions. As we have already seen, the scope of the available symbol sets is determined by the negotiation medium; not every medium provides all the possible symbols (writing, audio, image, smell, etc.). The transmission of the message then takes place in the relevant negotiation medium, at which point changes to the message may already start to occur; for example, signs can get lost in background noises or other transmission errors. In the next step, the message arrives at negotiator 2, who receives it and decodes and interprets (decrypts) the transmitted signs, i.e. places it in a subjective context. We have already gotten to know decoding and interpretation, in the previous section about the psychological processes of negotiators, under the names of perception and information processing. As both negotiators generally have different levels of experience and available information, the communication content sent in the subjective perception of negotiator 1 never precisely aligns to the received and decoded communication content in the subjective perception of negotiator 2. If the latter then continue the communication as the sender, they do so in light of their understanding of the message received. In doing so, they continue the cycle of communication.

The circular and dynamic process of communication and the subjectivity of the communication media means that an analysis of the negotiation communication is virtually impossible based on a deterministic understanding ("if A, then B"). Instead, attempts are made to gain insights regarding the development of the negotiation process and ultimately the influence on the outcome of the negotiation based on the occurrence of certain **communication elements**, including certain types of message content, as well as sequences and phases of these elements. A frequently practiced approach includes recording the negotiation communication (by video, tape recorder or as text, e.g. for email negotiations) and to put it in writing, then subjecting the data material to a content analysis (Weingart et al. 2004). This involves the abstract description of certain communication content and their classification to theoretically defined communication categories (types of negotiation behavior), which can then be quantitatively investigated. The connection of the communication elements identified in this manner and various outcome measures, primarily the efficiency of a negotiation, allows for an analysis of what behavior is likely to benefit efficiency and which is likely to have a negative impact. Although, in some cases, the individual categories of communication elements differ considerably, research in the past thirty years has shown that most elements fall into one of two larger categories: Integrative or cooperative negotiation behavior and distributive or competitive negotiation behavior (Geiger 2007, p. 120 et seq.; Weingart et al. 2007, p. 1000).

The extent to which the individual behaviors interact in certain sequences or phases has not previously received a great amount of attention (Adair and Brett 2005; Koeszegi et al. 2011); an established knowledge base is lacking. However, significantly more attention has been paid to a certain sub-area of negotiation communication, namely the offer and counteroffers in a negotiation. The following section will now take a closer look at these findings.

3.4.1 Integrative and Distributive Negotiation Behavior

The starting point for the fundamental investigations of negotiation behavior was the observation that one and the same negotiation task led to completely different outcomes in different negotiations, especially with regard to negotiation efficiency. As a result, the outcome of a negotiation was taken as the starting point for examining the negotiation process, which attempted to find and understand the differences between negotiations with an efficient outcome, an inefficient agreement or even the failure of a negotiation (Olekalns and Smith 2000; Weingart et al. 1990). Although the individual behaviors, their definition and effect may differ slightly depending on the study, there is general agreement on the overarching categories of negotiation behavior. While integrative or cooperative behavior is appropriate for enlarging the bargaining pie, distributive or competitive behavior aims at enlarging the party's own share of the bargaining pie, but regularly leads to the conclusion of agreements that are inefficient as a whole.

Integrative Negotiation Behavior

Two fundamental options, which partially overlap, can be considered in order to increase the integrative potential of a negotiation: Either both negotiating parties have to develop a somewhat consistent, explicit awareness of the mutual interests, priorities, skills and resources in the negotiation in order to draft an agreement that both parties would prefer compared to other possible agreements (Pruitt and Lewis 1975, p. 632). However, this requires a great deal of mutual trust as the basis for this kind of explicit information exchange, in which neither party believes that they will be cheated by the other party. The second option is a trial-and-error process, in which the parties successively submit mutual offers and change these until both are convinced that they cannot position themselves any better (Kelley 1966, p. 70). This behavior can also be viewed as implicit information exchange (Adair et al. 2007, p. 1056 et seq.).

Empirically, both the increased exchange of information on priorities, skills and resources, as well as the use of package offers (offers that relate to more than one negotiation issue), on which the trial-and-error process are based, have proven themselves to benefit the efficiency of an agreement (Olekalns and Smith 2000, p. 541; Pruitt and Lewis 1975, p. 630; Weingart et al. 1990, p. 25). With regard to the **priority information exchange** Geiger (2007, p. 133 et seq.) writes: "If a negotiation is a multi-issue negotiation, its integrative potential is based on differences with respect to (a) preferences and priorities regarding individual issues and their temporal effect, (b) the available resources, (c) the risk tendencies and (d) the future expectations of the parties. In order to uncover this integrative potential, the parties must develop an awareness of the priorities of the other party. The simplest approach in this respect is the direct exchange of information about priorities and needs (*priority information exchange*). Negotiation partners can only conclude integrative contracts, which are not concluded accidentally, based on an awareness of the preferences and priorities of the other party. Active information exchange about priorities is extremely important in order to achieve efficient agreements, as humans tend to overestimate their counterparty's level of information. However, the provision of this kind of information by one side may also result in the more communicative party being exploited by the other party."

The positive impact of **package offers** on negotiation efficiency is based on both their use in trial-and-error processes and the fact that only package offers allow the negotiating parties to offer a concession on one issue that is of no importance for the respective party, while requesting a concession from the counterparty on a more important issue, all in one go. If there is a difference of priorities between the parties, these mutually beneficial trade-offs allow efficiency gains to be realized. For example, a supplier could expand their offering in relation to the construction of an industrial plant by including training for the operating personnel (which presumably does not cost much, but is of great benefit for the customer) while simultaneously requesting a larger advance payment, if they (but not the customer) have to deal with liquidity bottlenecks. In this case, this kind of trade-off, training against earlier advance payment, would be beneficial for both parties in the negotiation compared to the status quo.

Moreover, based on empirical findings, **process management** can be assigned to integrative negotiation behavior (Olekalns and Smith 2003, p. 110; Pruitt and Lewis 1975, p. 626). This refers to a kind of meta-communication in which the negotiating parties agree on certain rules that they want to follow in the negotiation. For example, they may agree to submit package offers instead of single issue offers, not conclude any subsets of issues before the overall package is agreed upon. They may also offer delayed reciprocity, i.e. make a specific concession at time t_0 for a concession by the counterparty, still to be determined, at time t_1. Process management can help to break free from the vicious cycle of competitive behavior and establish a joint basis if there is great uncertainty regarding the object of negotiation, or to lead a negotiation out of an apparently hopeless situation (Geiger 2007, p. 137 et seq.).

Distributive Negotiation Behavior

Negotiations in general, and in the industrial plant and project business in particular, serve to satisfy or assert the interests of the negotiating parties. In addition to resolving a specific problem, parties are particularly interested in the benefits that they can generate from a specific agreement. As a result, the largest part of a negotiation is normally taken up by distributing the bargaining pie, as shown by field studies by Ramsay (2004) and Zachariassen (2008). This behavior can be subsumed under the term **distributive negotiation behavior**. However, interestingly, the positive impact of distributive behavior on the user's individual gain could only be demonstrated in special cases (Geiger 2007, p. 122). By contrast, its fundamentally negative influence on negotiation efficiency is relatively undisputed empirically. A main reason for this influence lies in the reciprocity of distributive behavior: In the vast majority of cases, a distributive message by one party (e.g. a threat) is followed by a distributive message by the counterparty (e.g. a rebuff). However, these spirals of distributive behavior require great cognitive capacity by both negotiating parties and leave less space for creative, interest-based solutions.

Possibly the most common distributive behavior is the **information exchange about positions**. This category contains any kind of discussion that supports the positions of a negotiating party and gives them a reason to insist on their own offer instead of making concessions. It includes self-serving facts relating to the context and fairness standards as well as assigning blame (Geiger 2007, p. 121). In principle, this kind of information appeals to the counterparty's reason with regard to conceding their own demands. They are perceived as rational arguments and contain the least risk that the negotiation will get out of hand due to showdowns, injured pride, personal attacks or the like. This type of information exchange about positions can also be characterized as friendly persuasion attempts.

Considerably less friendly is the use of threats, warnings, bluffs and commitments that negotiators may use to gain concessions from the counterparty. A **threat** consists of the two elements of demanding that a certain action be taken, and the announcement of taking action, which hurts the counterparty, if the demand is not fulfilled (Schelling 1960, p. 123). The consequence of carrying out a threat, if the threatened party has not met the demand, is generally more serious for both parties overall, than if the threat were not expressed, or the threatened party had given in to the demand made by the threatening party. A threat therefore significantly constrains the room for maneuver of both parties and determines the next steps: If the threatened party meets the demands made by the threatening party, the threatening party was able to force the counterparty to yield. However, if the threatened party refuses to meet the demand, the threatening party must carry out their announced punishment. If they do not, the threat is subsequently deemed to be a **bluff**, a threat without substance. A **warning** differs from a threat in that the counterparty only vaguely indicates the consequence of non-fulfillment of the demand. The effectiveness of this unfriendly leverage depends on how the counterparty assesses the capacity for punishment and the probability of its implementation by the threatening party (Bacharach and Lawler 1981b, p. 116). The credibility of this kind of leverage depends greatly on a **commitment** as defined by Schelling. This is an action, which the threatening party takes and which restricts the party's own scope for decision-making in the sense that the implementation of the punishment is better for them than to withdraw the threat, if the threatened party has not met the original demand (Geiger 2007, p. 127). Interestingly, the empirical research has shown that these kinds of unfriendly competitive tactics are only successful for the user under certain conditions (Shapiro and Bies 1994; Sinaceur and Neale 2005; Sinaceur et al. 2011), but that they regularly lead to a reduction of the bargaining pie.

The effect of affective **negative reactions**, such as insults, allegations, ridicule or other personal attacks on the counterparty at the negotiating table can be just as unfriendly. This frequently relates to defense measures, which can quickly lead to a spiral of aggressive and competitive behavior. Rebuffs or ignorance of the counterparty's arguments have a similar effect. This also involves the risk of escalation in order to obtain a slight benefit in a fight for positions that does not benefit either side *in summa*.

Besides the negative consequences of excessively distributive behavior on negotiation efficiency, it also leads to lower satisfaction with the negotiation amongst the parties involved (Geiger 2007, p. 213; Hüffmeier et al. 2014).

3.4.2 First Offers and Concession Patterns

Offers and counteroffers represent special elements of the communication process, as, in contrast to arguments for a certain position, they always represent a specific potential solution for the negotiated conflict of interest. They are instrumental for the successful conclusion of a negotiation. Given that, apart from in special cases (e.g. the *Winner's Curse*, see Sect. 3.3.3), parties always make several offers and use these to reach an agreement, both the first offer as well as the concession pattern have received increased attention in research. A negotiation and especially the manner in which the parties converge their offers is frequently compared to a dance (Adair and Brett 2005; Raiffa 1982, p. 47) in which they try and find out what outcome would be acceptable for the relevant counterparty. The following section now focuses on first offers and the subsequent concession behavior.

First Offer

The great importance of the **first offer** is due to the previously discussed cognitive bias that is based on the anchoring effect: A high initial offer by one party may lead to the other party changing their assessment of the ZOPA and adapting their counteroffer to this new assessment. The subsequent consequence of mutual concessions then leads to an increased individual gain for the party that submitted the high first offer (Galinsky and Mussweiler 2001, p. 661). However, this only works if the counterparty is not aware of the anchoring effect and does not focus on other reference points. The anchoring effect of the first offer also seems to disappear in repeated negotiations between the same parties and even reverse (Cotter and Henley 2008, p. 37). Further studies found that the anchoring effect of a high first offer is limited

- for negotiators who view the outcome of certain events that they are affected by, more in their behavior than in external factors (Shalvi et al. 2010, p. 239),
- if the initial offer is too extreme and this results in no agreement being reached (Schweinsberg et al. 2012, p. 228), or
- if the level of the initial offer has been supported by arguments and good counterarguments are simultaneously provided: The latter results in the counter-offer being more extreme than if the initial offer has not been supported by arguments (Maaravi et al. 2011, p. 249).

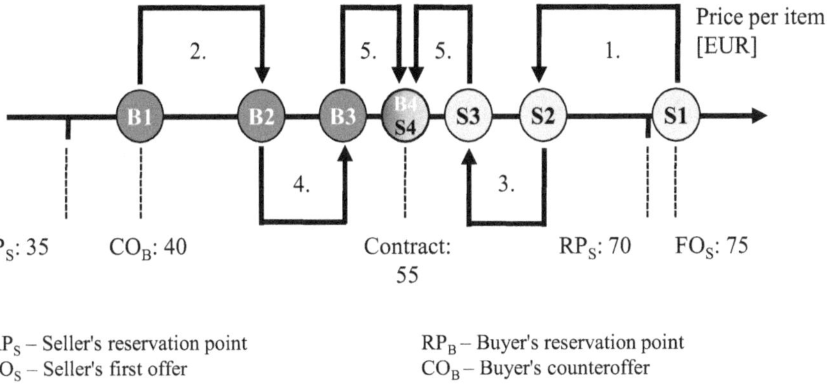

Fig. 12 Concession pattern for a purely distributive purchase negotiation

Concession Behavior

Concession behavior refers to the sequence of various offers by both negotiating parties. Although there are generally no formal rules for the series of offers, certain norms have been established in negotiating practice that are implemented in practically every negotiation. **Reciprocity** is the first norm: A party does not normally submit two offers or concessions in a row, but waits until they have received a counteroffer before submitting a new offer (Lewicki et al. 2010, p. 52 et seq.; Thompson 2005, p. 51). Interestingly, this norm of reciprocity is true independent of culture (Cialdini 1993, p. 19). If this is breached, it can be assumed that it is due to important reasons, such as the fact that a negotiating party cannot make any further concessions, but would be more likely to withdraw from the negotiation. A possible concession model for a sales negotiation is displayed in Fig. 12, in which the circles represent the respective offers by the buyer (B) and the seller (S).

A second norm regarding concession behavior says that once a concession has been offered, it cannot be withdrawn—negotiators need to thoroughly consider how many concessions to make in a new offer and which potential future concessions they wish to retain. In addition, the size of the concession by a negotiating party also depends on the perceived stubbornness of the counterparty, the respect given to the counterparty and their external appearance (Pietroni et al. 2008, p. 44 et seq.).

The effect of a party's own concessions on the counterparty was investigated by Kwon and Weingart (2004) and Hilty and Carnevale (1993). These showed that gradual concessions led to higher partner satisfaction and higher perceived procedural fairness than immediate or significantly delayed concessions (Kwon and Weingart 2004, p. 269). The study by Hilty and Carnevale (1993) demonstrated a cognitive bias in relation to the size of two successive concessions by a party, which is based on the contrast effect: A negotiator who first made a small concession and then a large concession is perceived as significantly more cooperative than one who first made a large concession and then a small one, even though both concessions together were precisely the same in both cases. The probability of agreement was also considerably higher in the first case (p. 454 et seq.).

4 Preparation for a Negotiation

Due to the importance of individual orders for a firm's overall success, for companies and their managers who operate in the industrial plant and project business, it is extremely important that they are aware of the influences on and in negotiations that lead to the desired orders. However, awareness of these influences is only really helpful if they can be used for their own actions in the lead up to a negotiation process. In contrast to the neutral perspectives taken when providing descriptions and explanations in this chapter, we will now change our perspective and place ourselves in the position of a party about to take part in an important negotiation. What measures can they take to influence the upcoming negotiation in the desired direction as effectively as possible?

According to Thompson (2005, p. 13), an appropriate **preparation** for an important negotiation should account for 80 % of time and expense, while activities during the negotiation phase take up about 20 %. Raiffa (1982, p. 120 et seq.) also considers the ability to prepare and plan as the most important of 34 criteria of successful negotiation; ahead of knowledge of the negotiation issues, clear reasoning, including under pressure, or rhetorical abilities. So, what is adequate preparation? A meaningful classification distinguishes preparation items relating to the party's own side, the counterparty and the negotiation situation. In the following sections we refer to the considerations by Raiffa (1982), Thompson (2005, Chap. 2) and Lewicki et al. (2010, Chap. 4) in summary form, based on diagnostic questions, in order to raise awareness of the most important points of preparing for a negotiation. Please note that preparing for a negotiation is not a linear process; rather, those responsible for preparing and planning for a negotiation constantly have to jump between the various preparation points, as they are often related.

4.1 One's Own Side

With regard to one's own side, the following preparation points play an important role:

One's Own Preference Structure

Prior to a negotiation, a company generally has one or more vague expectations of what needs to be clarified in the negotiation. Successful preparation includes the specification of these vague expectations by identifying precise responses to the following questions. Negotiators can only make rational decisions during a negotiation based on a previously agreed priorities and preference structure.

- *What issues need to be negotiated?* This question relates to the individual items that we want to include in the negotiation. For example, these may include the scope of the offering, the type and amount of customer integration, the purchase price, warranties, risk distribution, provisions for future eventualities, etc. The issues that we would prefer not to negotiate must also be clarified. The question of how certain negotiation topics are related must also be addressed. Finally, confirmation of whether many issues need to meet minimum standards from our perspective should also be provided.

- *What solution options exist for the individual negotiation topics and how important are they for us?* Once we have clarified the possible negotiation issues, there is still the issue of which specific solution options exist; so, for example, the following questions need to be answered: What is a realistic corridor for the purchase price? Why? What are the different types of services that could be offered? What forms could customer integration take? What options are available to us regarding the warranty? The more detail that is provided when describing and assessing the individual options for each issue, the more likely it is that they can be offered in the negotiation in a targeted manner and included as a bargaining chip.
- *How important are the individual issues for us and what trade-offs are possible?* Not all negotiation topics are of equal importance for us and not all issues will be resolved entirely in our favor in the negotiation. As a result, it is important to think about which points are particularly important in order to agree to a possible contract and where we can make concessions.
- *What risk are we prepared to take and how do we estimate the probability of occurrence of certain future events?* Some issues for negotiation involve a greater or lesser risk, such as with regard to implementation by a contract partner and/or unforeseeable environmental influences (price changes of components, political and legal changes, etc.). If there are differences in the risk tendencies and future expectations between the parties, these can subsequently be used for trade-offs.

Responding to these questions should establish a formal negotiation model which, when implemented for information purposes, allows for the rapid comparison of various contractual options that are subsequently discussed (Kersten and Lai 2007). In the negotiation, these rapid comparisons enables various model contracts to be identified and helps the negotiation team to act rationally in their own decisions.

In addition to the substantial negotiation topics, we also need to clarify our expectations in relation to the **negotiation process** and what kind of **relationship** we want to develop with the counterparty (Lewicki et al. 2010, p. 124). Relevant questions may include: To what extent do we want to consider the counterparty's interests? Do we want to act opportunistically if there is an opportunity to do so, or always maintain certain ethical standards? Are we looking for a partnership with the counterparty or do we consider the other party to be a one-off business partner? When answering these questions, we should also consider that our own approach to the process and the counterparty will affect the course of the negotiation and the substantial results. For example, an opportunistic approach to the process and no real interest in further business with the counterparty are not positive prerequisites in order to reach efficient results in a complex multi-topic negotiation.

Alternatives and Objectives

A second important step, following the discussion and recording of our own preference structure, our **alternatives** and **objectives** must be clarified in order to get a feel for the ZOPA. Only once we are aware of the alternatives that are available to us if the negotiations fail can we reach a rational decision on the acceptance or rejection of a final counterparty offer in an extremely negative case. Also, in a positive case, our internal discussions and negotiation strategies will have the best impact if we have clear expectations of our objectives, i.e. a result that is achievable in the (unlikely, but possible) optimal case. This means that the following questions need to be answered:

- *What are our alternatives (BATNA)? What is our reservation point?* As we have already seen in Sect. 3.3.1, our alternatives to the conclusion of a contract, our BATNA, are the most important reference point in the negotiation: once the counterparty's final offer has been submitted, our decision on an acceptance or rejection of the negotiation should only be based upon how good our alternative courses of action are to this offer. As a result, it is extremely important to collect and assess all the possible alternative courses of action. This may range from the rejection of an order and the non-incurrence of variable costs in our most unfavorable case, through to a contract that is ready to be signed with another partner, but which would utilize all our capacities. If our alternatives involve uncertainties, formal, analytical decision-making instruments can also be used to determine the reservation point (Lax and Sebenius 1986, p. 50 et seq.), in which the expected result and cost values are evaluated based on their probability of occurrence. When using a formal negotiation model to determine preferences, it is useful to estimate a numerical reservation point and include this in the model.
- *What objectives do we want to achieve?* Due to the importance of cognitive reference points for our perception and information processing and the associated actions, the formulation of clear and ambitious objectives are highly advisable. If there are different personnel involved in the negotiation preparations and the actual negotiation itself, it may be useful to communicate these objectives to the subsequent negotiation manager and potentially measure their performance based on these values. The counterparty's situation must also be considered when developing these objectives—if the counterparty is highly dependent on us, our objectives can be considerably more ambitious than if there is a considerable amount of competition to secure the order.
- *What cognitive reference points could influence us?* Besides the reservation point and our negotiation objectives, other cognitive reference points may also emerge in a negotiation, such as previous negotiation results, reference projects, certain market prices or indices. Due to their impact on our perception and information processing capacity, we need to check their potential influence on the negotiation and establish possible lines of argument in order to prevent their potentially negative impact.

Anticipation and Preparation for the Negotiation Process

The clarification of our preference structure and the identification of upper and lower limits for the best and worst case represent the most important steps of the defensive planning: we are prepared for the negotiation in relation to ourselves. However, we now need to be able to implement the formulated interests and positions in the negotiation, so the last step of preparation for our side relates to the planning of the negotiation process, to the extent that this is possible. To do so, we pose the following questions:

- *What initial offer do we want to submit?* In order to use the opportunity to set a cognitive anchor in our favor for an insufficiently prepared counterparty, we must prepare an ambitious, but serious initial offer. This should not contain any ranges for numerical items for negotiation, but rather include clear values (e.g. for the price or the completion), as ranges always provide scope for interpretation. Furthermore, an initial offer should not include any anticipated concessions—these can always be made during the negotiation.
- *To which offers do we ascribe a roughly equivalent value?* The counterparty will naturally not accept our first offer (at least if we have prepared well); rather both parties will converge during the negotiation. As we may not be completely informed of the counterparty's interests and priorities before a negotiation, it is advisable to prepare different offers, each with the same value for us, in order to exploit the integrative scope of the negotiation without adding any value to the negotiation ourselves. This may occur by submitting our roughly equivalent offers either jointly or soon after one another and assessing the counterparty's reactions. The offer that is most attractive to the counterparty is then the most efficient and can be used as an additional starting point.
- *What arguments help our interests and positions?* Negotiations over a major order are generally conducted in a relatively rational manner. As a result, to a certain extent, we can assume that our own arguments will be believed and respected by the counterparty. In mutual encounters, well-prepared lines of argument may ensure that the counterparty makes concessions more quickly, or that we can insist on a currently negotiated offer for longer, without the negotiation drifting into a spiral of competitive behavior. As every negotiation represents a competition for distribution of the bargaining pie, well-prepared and executed arguments are more helpful than threats or rejections due to a lack of preparation.
- *What parameters in the negotiation situation will help us? Who should be at the table on our side? What other precautions are necessary?* In addition to the above considerations that relate to the content of a negotiation, it is also useful to influence the framework parameters in our favor to the extent that this is possible. An important issue in this regard is the composition of the negotiation team. For example, which experts are required and to what extent are language, intercultural, or specific interpersonal competencies required? Other considerations include whether the composition and size of our negotiation team can be matched to the counterparty's delegation. A clear distribution of roles and tasks is also helpful.

4.2 The Opposing Party

> If you know the enemy and know yourself, you need not fear the result of a hundred battles.
> Sun Tzu.

This quote by the ancient Chinese war strategist shows that preparing for a negotiation without acquiring and evaluating information about the counterparty and anticipating their interests, positions and the individuals involved means that the preparation is incomplete. Before assessing the counterparty's interest and preference structure and their alternatives, we first need to clarify who the counterparty actually is.

The Identity of the Counterparty

A negotiation in the industrial plant and project business does not take place in a vacuum. Various interested parties come to the negotiating table, potentially even a public interest. A common illustration compares this kind of negotiation situation to a football game. Certain parameters are set: the quality of the pitch, the spectators, the lineups, the kick-off time, etc. But, the result of the negotiation primarily depends on how the teams, i.e. the negotiating delegations, perform in 90 min and how the game develops.

This illustration leads to a series of questions that are covered below.

- *Who is the other party?* This question relates to the counterparty's line-up, represented by the letter B in Fig. 13. Ideally, we should know who will be negotiating for the counterparty, as only this knowledge will allow us to ensure that we have an optimal line-up. Important information about the counterparty's line-up also includes the number of team members, their hierarchical position, their technical and cultural background, their expertise, their gender, their age and experience, their reputation and their role in the team. As we saw when discussing personality traits, it can be very useful to match the counterparty's team in our own line-up, i.e. consciously establish similarities, such as with respect to technical and cultural background, age, hierarchical position between team members of both teams, in order to increase mutual understanding.
- *Are there any influencers who are not present at the negotiating table?* Although a football game is basically a game between the two parties on the pitch, there are also parties who attempt to have a specific external influence (C), primarily the coaching staff, who provides tactical and strategic instructions and also has substitutes available. As a result, it is important to anticipate who might not be at the table for the counterparty, but will still attempt to exert influence during and between the rounds of negotiation. This may include indirectly involved executive or supervisory boards or, in the case of contracting authorities, parties that are indirectly affected, such as higher authorities or government politicians. How far the decision-making powers of the opposing negotiating delegation extend also needs to be clarified, i.e. whether a contract needs to be ratified by other committees. In this case, it may be advisable to hold background discussions

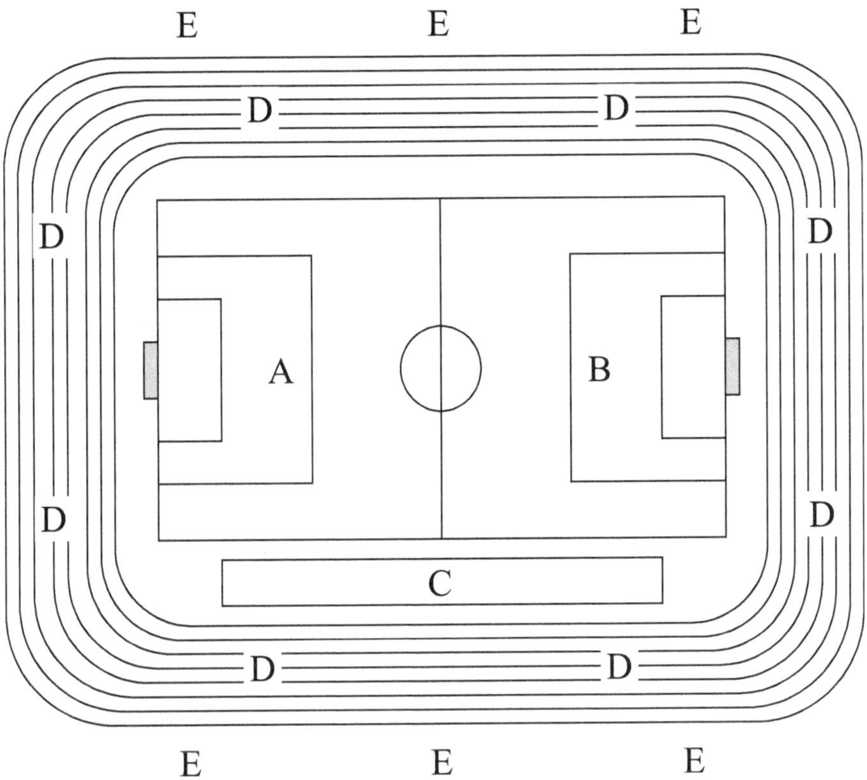

A: Own team: Participants on own side directly involved in the negotiation
B: Opposition: Participants on the opposition side directly involved in the negotiation
C: Trainers and dugout: Indirect involvement in the negotiation
D: Public and fans: Interested observers
E: Environment outside the stadium (weather, other games): Relevant negotiating environment

Fig. 13 The negotiation as a football game: negotiation participants (based on Lewicki et al. 2010, p. 128)

with these indirect influencers in addition to the direct negotiations. In addition, indirect influencers may also be much further removed, such as the public at a football game (D). This may include participants in an even broader sphere, who hold an interest in the outcome of the negotiation and may attempt to exert their influence indirectly: residents and citizens, unions, political parties, shareholder associations, etc. As is the case in a football match, their influence is not direct, but it may have a specific, indirect impact.

- *Is the other party monolithic? What diverging interests does the counterparty have and how can these be exploited?* These questions aim to identify the extent to which the interests of the counterparty's individual team members diverge and how this circumstance can be used for our benefit. For example, in football, the central defender, who received a yellow card in the tournament's semi-final and would miss the final if he received a second yellow, has a slightly different starting position than his colleagues without any cards, which the opposing coach can identify and potentially exploit. In negotiations it may also be the case that some of the counterparty's team members would associate more without one of our proposals in certain points, such as with regard to certain technical solutions. Potential allies in the opposing camp on certain issues must be identified so that diverging interests in the counterparty can be exploited for our benefit.

The Counterparty's Perspective of the Substantial Issues in a Negotiation
However, being aware of the counterparty's various participants is only helpful to the extent to which we have also mentally slipped into the role of the opposition with regard to the substantial issues of the negotiation. A distinction must therefore be made between three sets of questions:

- *What fundamental interests is the counterparty pursuing? What issues are particularly important for the counterparty?* The first step towards understanding the counterparty is to identify the interests that they are trying to satisfy by implementing the project. This involves the anticipation of various motives for the negotiation and the implementation of the project. For example, whether the counterparty considers the project to be a "normal" investment, places great importance on a technology transfer, or primarily considers the project to be an opportunity to access public subsidies, may make a huge difference to the negotiation. Certain resource bottlenecks, such as costs of delay or statutory provisions, which help to shape the counterparty's interests, may also play an important role. Once the counterparty's fundamental interest situation has been identified, it is advisable to transfer this to an anticipated priorities and preference structure in relation to the negotiation issues. Of particular importance in terms of maximizing the bargaining pie is to identify points that are especially important to the other party but not quite as important to ourselves: this may allow for mutually beneficial trade-offs to take place at a later time. It is also important to identify potential issues in which both parties share the same interest and clarify these accordingly. It can by no means be taken for granted that negotiating parties will identify these compatible interests in a negotiation (Thompson and Hrebec 1996).
- *What is the counterparty's alternative?* Anticipating the counterparty's possible alternatives is essential to formulate our own objectives and prepare our own negotiating position. If the counterparty has a good alternative to concluding a contract with us, it may mean that we have little scope for negotiation, while poor alternatives indicate a greater scope for negotiation in our favor. A poor alternative for the counterparty can be helpful as a cognitive references point during the negotiation.
- *What positions will the other party take?* The last question discussed in this section relates to the positions likely to be taken by the counterparty and their line of argument. We have already covered the effectiveness of arguments in the

previous section. If we are able to more or less anticipate which arguments and positions the counterparty will use to support its negotiation strategy, we can adjust our strategy and neutralize the counterparty's arguments.

4.3 The Negotiation Situation

As shown by the illustration of the negotiation participants in Fig. 13, environmental factors of a negotiation may also have important influences on the course of the negotiation. We must therefore ensure that we are adequately prepared of these factors. This involves responding to the following questions, which may impact on the preparation in relation to ourselves or the counterparty:

- *Is this a one-off, repetitive or regular negotiation?* Even if projects are characterized by a clear start and end (acceptance), the extent to which the negotiations contain repeat elements must still be covered. You may be faced with the negotiator in another project or another function once again in the future. This means that the temporal relevance of a current negotiation situation must be considered, especially with regard to the trust between two parties, their relationship and your own reputation.
- *Does past history play a role?* A very similar questions, but relating to the past, covers the past history between the parties and the participants at the negotiating table. The negotiation will certainly have a different course, if there are old scores to settle between certain negotiators or if a certain relationship of trust exists.
- *Do economies of scope with other negotiations/transactions exist?* When determining internal interests and the associated preference structure, it is important to anticipate the economies of scope of a negotiation and the potentially associated transaction on negotiations with other parties. For example, the positive reference impact of a plant that ensures profitability for the constructor, could also have a positive long-term spill-over. On the other hand, concessions that are made to a counterparty in a negotiation could also be demanded by future business partners, such as in relation to warranty periods. As a result, both the direct effects of certain negotiation options, as well as indirect spill-over effects must be considered in the preparation.
- *Do the negotiation outcomes need to be ratified?* This question (in the language identified in Fig. 13) defines the relationship of the participants at the negotiating table (teams A, B) and the indirect participants (C, i.e. substitutes and dugout). In large projects, contracts are sometimes concluded which need to be ratified by certain corporate committees to become legally valid. If this is the case, and if preference differences exist between a party's negotiators and those with decision-making authority, this must be included in the negotiation preparation and execution.
- *Are there time limits or costs of delays?* This question also targets the framework parameters that influence the preference structure of both parties. For example, if

a party has to worry about costs of delays, their alternatives will continue to deteriorate over the course of the negotiation. As a result, the power-dependency relationship may shift over the course of the negotiation, so that it may either be sensible for our side to ensure that no time is lost, or to protract the negotiations, in order to gain an advantage.

- *Is a formal contract concluded or is the agreement informal?* With regard to the conclusion of a negotiation, it is important to obtain clarity over which parts of the contract need to be confirmed in writing and whether exclusively verbal parts of the agreement exist. Establishing clarity over this matter, potentially via meta-communication (process management) can ensure that an agreement is reached much more quickly. For example, verbal agreements may be necessary due to cultural conventions.
- *Where will the negotiations take place?* Many advice books speculate on the role played by the place of a negotiation. A home-ground advantage is generally assumed, so that a neutral location for negotiations is deliberately agreed in many negotiation situations.
- *Will the negotiations take place in the public eye?* The question of whether the negotiations will take place in the public eye may be extremely important. This generally limits the flexibility of the negotiating parties, as the public can be used as leverage and publicized positions have an effect similar to a commitment: it is difficult for a party to withdraw from a public position without losing face. As a result, it may be useful to maintain communication channels of which the public is not aware in order to establish a certain degree of flexibility.
- *Is a negotiation legal?* In particular, negotiations relating to projects with public authorities have strict boundaries, such as with regard to the selection of a supplier and renegotiation opportunities. These boundaries must be taken into account when preparing for the extremely formal negotiation process. In these cases, a formal offer frequently needs to be adapted to a bidding process which only includes some traits of a negotiation. Submitting an ambitious initial offer in this case would result in the certain loss of the order—a better idea would be to formulate an offer based on *Competitive Bidding* models (Kuß 1977, see also Chap. 3).
- *Is there any chance of involving third parties?* This question may point to various options in the industrial plant and project business. It may be possible to enlarge the scope of the negotiation by including another partner. For example, this needs to be taken into account if the negotiations are being conducted by a consortium on the supplier side and, during the negotiations, it turns out that a contract could only be awarded with the inclusion of another consortium partner. The questions of a third party may also be relevant in the case of extremely protracted or large projects to identify the extent to which provisions need to be made for future disputes during implementation or for any potentially necessary additional or subsequent negotiations. In this case it is advisable to stipulate the mandatory involvement of a mediator or court of arbitration.

5 Concluding Remarks

Negotiations are extremely important in many respects in the industrial plant and project business. First of all, they create the basis for the establishment of a transaction, i.e. they decide whether a supplier will or will not be considered for a project and the resulting economic benefits that they stand to gain. For the purchaser, it also defines the extent to which, and how creatively, their problem can be resolved and their interests satisfied by the project. Secondly, the agreements reached in negotiations frequently form the basis for decades of cooperation between the parties, which is necessary in order to implement the project.

In this chapter we have attempted to show how a negotiation situation is fundamentally structured, the relevant influencing factors and how these factors can impact on the success or failure of a negotiation. We have considered both static-structural as well as dynamic categories of influencing factors. Certainly, many observations, with regard to the outcome achieved as well as certain courses of negotiation, can be explained ex post. However, it should also be clear that, due to their dynamic character, negotiations are extremely difficult to forecast and that systematic analyses and preparation (the science of negotiation and the mind of the negotiator) as well as the personal, subjective side (the art of negotiation and the heart of the negotiator) play an important role.

Nevertheless, knowledge of the influencing factors and effects described in this chapter together with the advice and suggestions for preparing for a negotiation for members of a negotiation team should provide valuable information on how you can more successfully prepare for and conduct your next negotiation.

Exercises

1. What characterizes a negotiation situation?
2. What organizational constellations for negotiations in the industrial plant and project business are you aware of? What characterizes these constellations?
3. What characterizes negotiations in the industrial plant and project business?
4. Explain Raiffa's (1982) zone of possible agreement model!
5. What sources of integrative potential in negotiations are you aware of?
6. What distinguishes the subjective value of a negotiation according to Curhan et al. (2006)?
7. Explain the process behind the formation of satisfaction with a negotiation!
8. What does the BATNA refer to and what impact does it have on a negotiation?
9. How important is the factor of time in negotiations?
10. What influence does the negotiator's personal context have on a negotiation?
11. Describe the process of *Framing* in negotiations and discuss which frames are used!
12. Explain why a high initial offer can have the effect of a cognitive anchor and shift the outcome of the negotiation in favor of the party who submits the initial offer!

13. What characterizes integrative and distributive negotiating behavior?
14. What points should a conscientious preparation for a negotiation include?

Literature

Adair, W. L. (2003). Integrative sequences and negotiation outcome in same- and mixed-culture negotiations. *International Journal of Conflict Management, 14*(3/4), 273–296.

Adair, W. L., & Brett, J. M. (2005). The negotiation dance: Time, culture, and behavioral sequences in negotiation. *Organization Science, 16*(1), 33–51.

Adair, W. L., Okumura, T., & Brett, J. M. (2001). Negotiation behavior when cultures collide: The United States and Japan. *Journal of Applied Psychology, 86*(3), 371–385.

Adair, W. L., Weingart, L., & Brett, J. (2007). The timing and function of offers in U.S. and Japanese negotiations. *Journal of Applied Psychology, 92*(4), 1056–1068.

Adler, N. J., Brahm, R., & Graham, J. L. (1992). Strategy implementation: A comparison of face-to-face negotiations in the People's Republic of China and the United States. *Strategic Management Journal, 13*(6), 449–466.

Allred, K. G., Mallozi, J. S., Matsui, F., & Raia, C. P. (1997). The influence of anger and compassion on negotiation performance. *Organizational Behavior and Human Decision Processes, 70*(3), 175–187.

Ambrose, E., Marshall, D., Fynes, B., & Lynch, D. (2008). Communication media selection in buyer-supplier relationships. *International Journal of Operations and Production Management, 28*(4), 360–379.

Anderson, C., & Thompson, L. L. (2004). Affect from top down: How powerful individuals' positive affect shapes negotiations. *Organizational Behavior and Human Decision Processes, 95*(2), 125–139.

Arunachalam, V., Wall, J. A., & Chan, C. (1998). Hong Kong versus U.S. negotiations: Effects of culture, alternatives, outcome scales, and mediation. *Journal of Applied Social Psychology, 28* (14), 1219–1244.

Bacharach, S. B., & Lawler, E. J. (1976). The perception of power. *Social Forces, 55*, 123–134.

Bacharach, S. B., & Lawler, E. J. (1981a). *Bargaining: Power, tactics, and outcomes.* San Francisco: Jossey-Bass.

Bacharach, S. B., & Lawler, E. J. (1981b). Power and tactics in bargaining. *Industrial and Labor Relations Review, 34*(2), 219–233.

Backhaus, K., & Günter, B. (1976). A phase-differentiated interaction approach to industrial marketing decisions. *Industrial Marketing Management, 5*, 255–270.

Backhaus, K., van Doorn, J., & Wilken, R. (2008). The impact of team characteristics on the course and outcome of intergroup price negotiations. *Journal of Business-to-Business Marketing, 15*(4), 365–396.

Backhaus, K., & Voeth, M. (2010). *Industriegütermarketing* (9th ed.). Munich: Vahlen.

Barrick, M. R., & Mount, M. K. (1991). The big five personality dimensions and job performance: A meta-analysis. *Personnel Psychology, 44*(1), 1–26.

Barry, B. (2008). Negotiator affect: The State of the art (and the science). *Group Decision and Negotiation, 17*(1), 97–105.

Barry, B., & Friedman, R. A. (1998). Bargainer characteristics in distributive and integrative negotiation. *Journal of Personality and Social Psychology, 74*(2), 345–359.

Barry, B., & Oliver, R. L. (1996). Affect in dyadic negotiation: A model and propositions. *Organizational Behavior and Human Decision Processes, 67*(2), 127–143.

Bateson, G. (1972). *Steps to an ecology of mind.* New York: Ballantine Books.

Bazerman, M. H. (2002). *Judgment in managerial decision making* (5th ed.). New York: Wiley.

Bazerman, M. H., Neale, M. A., Valley, K. L., Zajac, E. J., & Kim, Y. M. (1992). The effect of agents and mediators on negotiation outcomes. *Organizational Behavior and Human Decision Processes, 53*(1), 55–73.

Beersma, B., & De Dreu, C. K. W. (1999). Negotiation processes and outcomes in prosocially and egoistically motivated groups. *International Journal of Conflict Management, 10*(4), 385–402.

Blount, S., Thomas-Hunt, M. C., & Neale, M. A. (1996). The price is right – or is it? A reference point model of two-party price negotiations. *Organizational Behavior and Human Decision Processes, 68*(1), 1–12.

Brett, J. M., & Okumura, T. (1998). Inter- and intracultural negotiation: U.S. and Japanese negotiators. *Academy of Management Journal, 41*(5), 495–510.

Brodt, S. E., & Marla, T. (2000). Working together but in opposition: An examination of the "good-cop/badcop" negotiation team tactic. *Organizational Behavior and Human Decision Processes, 81*(2), 155–177.

Brodt, S., & Thompson, L. (2001). Negotiating teams: A levels of analysis approach. *Group Dynamics: Theory, Research, and Practice, 5*(3), 208–219.

Brooks, B. W., & Rose, R. L. (2004). A contextual model of negotiation orientation. *Industrial Marketing Management, 33*(2), 125.

Brown, G., & Baer, M. (2011). Location in negotiation: Is there a home field advantage? *Organizational Behavior and Human Decision Processes, 114*(2), 190–200.

Cai, A., Wilson, R., & Drake, E. (2000). Culture in the context of intercultural negotiation. *Human Communication Research, 26*(4), 591–617.

Campbell, N. C. G., Graham, J. L., Jolibert, A., & Meissner, H. G. (1988). Marketing negotiations in France, Germany, the United Kingdom, and the United States. *Journal of Marketing, 52*(2), 49–62.

Cano, C. R., Boles, J. S., & Bean, C. J. (2005). Communication media preferences in business-to-business transactions: An examination of the purchase process. *Journal of Personal Selling and Sales Management, 25*(3), 283–294.

Carnevale, P. (2008). Positive affect and decision frame in negotiation. *Group Decision and Negotiation, 17*(1), 51–63.

Carnevale, P. J. D., & Isen, A. M. (1986). The influence of positive affect and visual access on the discovery of integrative solutions in bilateral negotiation. *Organizational Behavior and Human Decision Processes, 37*(1), 1–13.

Carnevale, P. J. D., & Lawler, E. J. (1986). Time pressure and the development of integrative agreements in bilateral negotiations. *Journal of Conflict Resolution, 30*(4), 636–659.

Cialdini, R. (1993). *Influence – The psychology of persuasion* (2nd ed.). New York: Quill William Morrow.

Citera, M., Beauregard, R., & Mitsuya, T. (2005). An experimental study of credibility in E-negotiations. *Psychology and Marketing, 22*(2), 163–179.

Clark, H. H., & Brennan, S. E. (1991). Grounding in communication. In L. B. Resnick, J. M. Levin, & S. D. Teasley (Eds.), *Perspectives on socially shared cognition* (pp. 127–149). Washington, DC: American Psychological Association.

Cotter, M. J., & Henley, J. A. (2008). First-offer disadvantage in zero-sum game negotiation outcomes. *Journal of Business-to-Business Marketing, 15*(1), 25–44.

Croson, R. T. A. (1999). Look at me when you say that: An electronic negotiation simulation. *Simulation and Gaming, 30*(1), 23–37.

Curhan, J. R., Elfenbein, H. A., & Kilduff, G. J. (2009). Getting off on the right foot: Subjective value versus economic value in predicting longitudinal job outcomes from job offer negotiations. *Journal of Applied Psychology, 94*(2), 524–534.

Curhan, J. R., Neale, M. A., Ross, L., & Rosencranz-Engelmann, J. (2008). Relational accommodation in negotiation: Effects of egalitarianism and gender on economic efficiency and relational capital. *Organizational Behavior and Human Decision Processes, 107*(2), 192–205.

Curhan, J. R., Neale, M. A., & Ross, L. (2004). Dynamic valuation: Preference changes in the context of face-to-face negotiation. *Journal of Experimental Social Psychology, 40*(2), 142–151.

Curhan, J. R., & Overbeck, J. R. (2008). Making a positive impression in a negotiation: Gender differences in response to impression motivation. *Negotiation and Conflict Management Research, 1*(2), 179–193.

Curhan, J. R., Xu, H., & Elfenbein, H. A. (2006). What do people value when they negotiate? Mapping the domain of subjective value in negotiation. *Journal of Personality and Social Psychology, 91*(3), 493–512.

Daft, R. L., & Lengel, R. H. (1984). Information richness: A new approach to managerial behavior and organization design. *Research in Organizational Behavior, 6*, 191–233.

Daft, R. L., & Lengel, R. H. (1986). Organization information requirements, media richness, and structural design. *Management Science, 32*(5), 554–571.

De Dreu, C. K. W. (2004). Motivation in negotiation: A social psychological analysis. In M. J. Gelfand & J. M. Brett (Eds.), *The handbook of negotiation and culture* (pp. 114–138). Stanford, CA: Stanford University Press.

De Dreu, C. K. W., & Boles, T. L. (1998). Share and share alike or winner take all? The influence of social value orientation upon choice and recall of negotiation heuristics. *Organizational Behavior and Human Decision Processes, 76*(3), 253–276.

De Dreu, C. K. W., Carnevale, P. J. D., Emans, B. J. M., & Van de Vliert, E. (1994). Effects of gain-loss frames in negotiation: Loss aversion, mismatching, and frame adoption. *Organizational Behavior and Human Decision Processes, 60*(1), 90–107.

De Dreu, C. W., & Van Lange, P. A. M. (1995). Impact of social value orientation on negotiator cognition and behavior. *Personality and Social Psychology Bulletin, 21*(11), 1178–1188.

Dennis, A. R., Fuller, R. M., & Valacich, J. S. (2008). Media, tasks, and communication processes: A theory of media synchronicity. *MIS Quarterly, 32*(3), 575–600.

DeRue, D. S., Conlon, D. E., Moon, H., & Willaby, H. W. (2009). When is straightforwardness a liability in negotiations? The role of integrative potential and structural power. *Journal of Applied Psychology, 94*(4), 1032–1047.

Dimotakis, N., Conlon, D. E., & Ilies, R. (2012). The mind and heart (literally) of the negotiator: Personality and contextual determinants of experiential reactions and economic outcomes in negotiation. *Journal of Applied Psychology, 97*(1), 183–193.

Dion, P. A., & Banting, P. M. (1988). Industrial supplier-buyer negotiations. *Industrial Marketing Management, 17*(1), 43–47.

Donohue, W. A. (1981). Analyzing negotiation tactics: Development of a negotiation interact system. *Human Communication Research, 7*(3), 273–287.

Druckman, D., & Olekalns, M. (2008). Emotions in negotiation. *Group Decision and Negotiation, 17*(1), 1–11.

Dwyer, F. R., & Walker, O. C. (1981). Bargaining in an asymmetric power structure. *Journal of Marketing, 45*(1), 104–115.

Emerson, R. M. (1962). Power-dependence relations. *American Sociological Review, 27*(1), 31–40.

Engelhardt, W. H., & Günter, B. (1981). *Investitionsgütermarketing*. Stuttgart: Kohlhammer.

Fassina, N. E. (2004). Constraining a principal's choice: Outcome versus behavior contingent agency contracts in representative negotiations. *Negotiation Journal, 20*(3), 435–459.

Fisher, R., Ury, W., & Patton, B. (1992). *Getting to yes – Negotiating agreement without giving* (2nd ed.). London: Random House.

Fouraker, L. E., & Siegel, S. (1963). *Bargaining behavior*. New York: McGraw-Hill.

Fry, W. R., Firestone, I. J., & Williams, D. L. (1983). Negotiation process and outcome of stranger dyads and dating couples: Do lovers lose? *Basic and Applied Psychology, 4*(1), 1–16.

Funder, D. C. (2001). Personality. *Annual Review of Psychology, 52*(1), 197–221.

Galin, A., Gross, M., & Gosalker, G. (2007). E-negotiation versus face-to-face negotiation: What has changed – if anything? *Computers in Human Behavior, 23*(1), 787–797.

Galinsky, A. D., & Mussweiler, T. (2001). First offers as anchors: The role of perspective-taking and negotiator focus. *Journal of Personality and Social Psychology, 81*(4), 657–669.
Galinsky, A. D., Seiden, V. L., Kim, P. H., & Medvec, V. H. (2002). The dissatisfaction of having your first offer accepted: The role of counterfactual thinking in negotiations. *Personality and Social Psychology Bulletin, 28*(2), 271–283.
Geiger, I. (2007). *Industrielle Verhandlungen - Empirische Untersuchung von Verhandlungsmacht und -interaktion in Einzeltransaktion und Geschäftsbeziehung*. Wiesbaden: DUV.
Geiger, I. (2014). Media effects on the formation of negotiator satisfaction: The example of face-to-face and text based electronically mediated negotiations. *Group Decision and Negotiation, 23*(4), 735–763.
Geiger, I., & Kleinaltenkamp, M. (2011). Interne Umsetzung des Geschäftsbeziehungsmanagements. In M. Kleinaltenkamp, W. Plinke, I. Geiger, F. Jacob, & A. Söllner (Eds.), *Geschäftsbeziehungsmanagement* (pp. 255–258). Wiesbaden: Gabler.
Gelfand, M. J., Major, V. S., Raver, J. L., Nishii, L. H., & O'Brien, K. (2006). Negotiating relationally: The dynamics of the relational self in negotiations. *Academy of Management Review, 31*(2), 427–451.
Giebels, E., De Dreu, C. W., & Van de Vliert, E. (1998). The alternative negotiator as the invisible third at the table: The impact of potency information. *International Journal of Conflict Management, 9*(1), 5–21.
Giebels, E., De Dreu, C. W., & Van de Vliert, E. (2000). Interdependence in negotiation: Effects of exit options and social motive on distributive and integrative negotiation. *European Journal of Social Psychology, 30*(2), 255–272.
Gillespie, J. J., Brett, J. M., & Weingart, L. R. (2000). Interdependence, social motives, and outcome satisfaction in multiparty negotiation. *European Journal of Social Psychology, 30*(6), 779–797.
Goffman, E. (1974). *Frame analysis*. New York: Harper & Row.
Graham, J. L. (1986). The problem-solving approach to negotiations in industrial marketing. *Journal of Business Research, 14*(6), 549–566.
Graham, J. L., Kim, D. K., Lin, C.-Y., & Robinson, M. (1988). Buyer-seller negotiations around the Pacific Rim: Differences in fundamental exchange processes. *Journal of Consumer Research, 15*(1), 48–54.
Greenhalgh, L., & Chapman, D. I. (1998). Negotiator relationships: Construct measurement, and demonstration of their impact on the process and outcomes of negotiation. *Group Decision and Negotiation, 7*(6), 465–489.
Halevy, N. (2008). Team negotiation: Social, epistemic, economic, and psychological consequences of subgroup conflict. *Personality and Social Psychology Bulletin, 34*(12), 1687–1702.
Hall, E. T. (1976). *Beyond culture*. New York: Random House.
Hilty, J. A., & Carnevale, P. J. D. (1993). Black-hat/white-hat strategy in bilateral negotiation. *Organizational Behavior and Human Decision Processes, 55*(3), 444–469.
Hofstede, G. (1984). *Culture's consequences* (2nd ed.). Newbury Park, CA: Sage.
House, R., & Javidan, M. (2004). Overview of GLOBE. In R. House, P. Hanges, M. Javidan, P. Dorfman, & V. Gupta (Eds.), *Culture, leadership, and organizations – The GLOBE study of 62 societies* (pp. 9–28). Thousand Oaks, CA: Sage.
Huber, V. L., & Neale, M. A. (1986). Effects of cognitive heuristics and goals on negotiator performance and subsequent goal setting. *Organizational Behavior and Human Decision Processes, 38*(3), 342–365.
Hüffmeier, J., Freund, A., Zerres, A., Backhaus, K., & Hertel, G. (2014). Being tough or being nice? A meta-analysis on the impact of hard- and softline strategies in distributive negotiations. *Journal of Management* 40(3), 866–892.
Hutt, M. D., Johnston, W. J., & Ronchetto, J. (1985). Selling centers and buying centers: Formulating strategic exchange patterns. *Journal of Personal Selling and Sales Management, 5*(1), 33–40.

Imai, L., & Gelfand, M. J. (2010). The culturally intelligent negotiator: The impact of cultural intelligence (CQ) on negotiation sequences and outcomes. *Organizational Behavior and Human Decision Processes, 112*(2), 83–98.

Johnston, W. J., & Bonoma, T. V. (1981). The buying center: Structure and interaction patterns. *Journal of Marketing, 45*, 143–156.

Kahneman, D., Knetsch, J. L., & Thaler, R. H. (1990). Experimental tests of the endowment effect and the coase theorem. *Journal of Political Economy, 98*(6), 1352.

Kahneman, D., & Tversky, A. (1979). Prospect theory: An analysis of decision under risk. *Econometrica, 47*(2), 263–291.

Kamins, M. A., Johnston, W. J., & Graham, J. L. (1998). A multi-method examination of buyer-seller interactions among Japanese and American businesspeople. *Journal of International Marketing, 6*(1), 8–32.

Keenan, P. A., & Carnevale, P. J. D. (1989). Positive effects of within-group cooperation on between-group negotiation. *Journal of Applied Social Psychology, 19*(12), 977–992.

Kelley, H. H. (1966). A classroom study of dilemmas in interpersonal negotiation. In K. Archibald (Ed.), *Strategic interaction and conflict*. Berkeley, CA: Institute of International Studies, University of California.

Kersten, G. E. (2001). Modeling distributive and integrative negotiations. Review and revised characterization. *Group Decision and Negotiation, 10*(2), 493–514.

Kersten, G. E., & Lai, H. (2007). Negotiation support and E-negotiation systems: An overview. *Group Decision and Negotiation, 16*(6), 553–586.

Kim, P. H. (1997). Strategic timing in group negotiations: The implication of forced entry and forced exit for negotiators with unequal power. *Organizational Behavior and Human Decision Processes, 71*(3), 263–286.

Kimmel, M. J., Pruitt, D. G., Magenau, J. M., Konar-Goldband, E., & Carnevale, P. J. (1980). Effects of trust, aspiration and gender on negotiation tactics. *Journal of Personality and Social Psychology, 38*(1), 9–22.

Koch, F.-K. (1987). *Verhandlungen bei der Vermarktung von Investitionsgütern*. Dissertation, Darmstadt.

Koeszegi, S., Pesendorfer, E.-M., & Vetschera, R. (2011). Data-driven phase analysis of E-negotiations: An exemplary study of synchronous and asynchronous negotiations. *Group Decision and Negotiation, 20*(4), 385–410.

Kopelman, S., & Rosette, A. S. (2008). Cultural variation in response to strategic emotions in negotiations. *Group Decision and Negotiation, 17*(1), 65–77.

Kopelman, S., Rosette, A. S., & Thompson, L. (2006). The three faces of eve: Strategic displays of positive, negative, and neutral emotions in negotiations. *Organizational Behavior and Human Decision Processes, 99*(1), 81–101.

Kray, L. J., Galinsky, A. D., & Thompson, L. (2002). Reversing the gender gap in negotiations: An exploration of stereotype regeneration. *Organizational Behavior and Human Decision Processes, 87*(2), 386–410.

Kray, L. J., & Thompson, L. (2005). Gender stereotypes and negotiation performance: An examination of theory and research. *Research in Organizational Behavior, 26*, 103–182.

Kray, L. J., Thompson, L., & Galinsky, A. D. (2001). Battle of sexes: Gender stereotype confirmation and reactance in negotiations. *Journal of Personality and Social Psychology, 80*(6), 942–958.

Kuß, A. (1977). Competitive-Bidding-Modelle. *Zeitschrift für betriebswirschaftliche Forschung, 29*, 63–70.

Kutschker, M. (1972). *Verhandlungen als Elemente eines verhaltenswissenschaftlichen Bezugsrahmens des Investitionsgütermarketing*. Dissertation, Mannheim.

Kutschker, M., & Kirsch, W. (1978). *Verhandlungen in Multiorganisationalen Entscheidungsprozessen*. Munich: University.

Kwon, S., & Weingart, L. R. (2004). Unilateral concessions from the other party: Concession behavior, attributions, and negotiation judgments. *Journal of Applied Psychology, 89*(2), 263–278.

Lawler, E. J., & Yoon, J. (1993). Power and the emergence of commitment behavior in negotiated exchange. *American Sociological Review, 58*(4), 465–481.

Lax, D. A., & Sebenius, J. K. (1986). *The manager as negotiator*. New York: Free Press.

Lewicki, R. J., Barry, B., & Saunders, D. M. (2010). *Negotiation* (6th ed.). New York: McGraw-Hill.

Liu, M. (2009). The intrapersonal and interpersonal effects of anger on negotiation strategies: A cross-cultural investigation. *Human Communication Research, 35*, 148–169.

Luce, R. D., & Raiffa, H. (1957). *Games and decisions*. New York: Wiley.

Maaravi, Y., Ganzach, Y., & Pazy, A. (2011). Negotiation as a form of persuasion: Arguments in first offers. *Journal of Personality and Social Psychology, 101*(2), 245–255.

Mannix, E. A., & Neale, M. A. (1993). Power imbalance and the pattern of exchange in dyadic negotiation. *Group Decision and Negotiation, 2*(2), 119–133.

McAlister, L., Bazerman, M. H., & Fader, P. (1986). Power and goal setting in channel negotiations. *Journal of Marketing Research, 23*(3), 228–236.

McGrath, J. E., & Hollingshead, A. B. (1993). Putting the 'group' back in group support systems: Some theoretical issues about dynamics in groups with technological enhancements. In L. M. Jessup & J. S. Valacich (Eds.), *Group support systems: New perspectives* (pp. 78–96). New York: MacMillan.

McSweeney, B. (2002). Hofstede's model of national cultural differences and their consequences: A triumph of faith – a failure of analysis. *Human Relations, 55*(1), 89–118.

Moore, D. A. (2004). The unexpected benefits of final deadlines in negotiation. *Journal of Experimental Social Psychology, 40*, 121–127.

Moran, S., & Ritov, I. (2007). Experience in integrative negotiations: What needs to be learned? *Journal of Experimental Social Psychology, 43*(1), 77–90.

Morton, F. S., Silva-Risso, J., & Zettelmeyer, F. (2011). What matters in a price negotiation: Evidence from the U.S. auto retailing industry. *Quantitative Marketing and Economics, 9*, 365–402.

Mosterd, I., & Rutte, C. G. (2000). Effects of time pressure and accountability to constituents on negotiation. *International Journal of Conflict Management, 11*(3), 227–247.

Murnighan, J. K., Babcock, L., Thompson, L., & Pillutla, M. (1999). The information dilemma in negotiations: Effects of experience, incentives, and integrative potential. *International Journal of Conflict Management, 10*(4), 313–339.

Mussweiler, T., Strack, F., & Pfeiffer, T. (2000). Overcoming the inevitable anchoring effect: Considering the opposite compensates for selective accessibility. *Personality and Social Psychology Bulletin, 26*(9), 1142–1150.

Naquin, C. E. (2003). The agony of opportunity in negotiation: Number of negotiable issues, counterfactual thinking, and feelings of satisfaction. *Organizational Behavior and Human Decision Processes, 91*(1), 97–107.

Naquin, C. E., & Kurtzberg, T. R. (2009). Team negotiation and perceptions of trustworthiness: The whole versus the sum of the parts. *Group Dynamics: Theory, Research, and Practice, 13* (2), 133–150.

Naquin, C. E., & Paulson, G. D. (2003). Online bargaining and interpersonal trust. *Journal of Applied Psychology, 88*(1), 113–120.

Nash, J. F. (1950). The bargaining problem. *Econometrica, 18*, 155–162.

Nash, J. F. (1953). Two-person cooperative games. *Econometrica, 21*, 128–140.

Neale, M. A., & Northcraft, G. B. (1991). Behavioral negotiation theory: A framework for conceptualizing dyadic bargaining. *Research in Organizational Behavior, 13*, 147–190.

Neu, J., Graham, J. L., & Gilly, M. C. (1988). The influence of gender on behaviors and outcomes in a retail buyer-seller negotiation simulation. *Journal of Retailing, 64*(4), 427–452.

Neun, H. (2011). *Verhandlungen im internationalen Vertrieb*. Hamburg: Verlag Dr. Kovac.

Neun, H., Geiger, I., Lügger, K., & Backhaus, K. (2012). Group and individual level cultural influences in intra- and intercultural negotiation between German and Chinese negotiators. In *Proceedings of the 25th IACM Annual Conference.*

O'Connor, K. M. (1997). Groups and solos in context: The effects of accountability on team negotiation. *Organizational Behavior and Human Decision Processes, 72*(3), 384–407.

O'Connor, K. M., & Arnold, J. A. (2011). Sabotaging the deal: The way relational concerns undermine negotiators. *Journal of Experimental Social Psychology, 47*(6), 1167–1172.

O'Connor, K. M., Arnold, J. A., & Burris, E. R. (2005). Negotiators' bargaining histories and their effects on future negotiation performance. *Journal of Applied Psychology, 90*(2), 350–362.

Ohbuchi, K.-I., & Fukushima, O. (1997). Personality and interpersonal conflict: Aggressiveness, self-monitoring, and situational variables. *International Journal of Conflict Management, 8*(2), 99–113.

Olekalns, M., & Smith, P. L. (2000). Understanding optimal outcomes. *Human Communication Research, 24*(4), 528–556.

Olekalns, M., & Smith, P. L. (2003). Testing the relationship among negotiators' motivational orientations, strategy choices, and outcomes. *Journal of Experimental Social Psychology, 39* (2), 101–117.

Olekalns, M., Smith, P. L., & Kibby, R. (1996). Social value orientation and negotiator outcomes. *European Journal of Social Psychology, 26*, 299–313.

Oliver, R. L., Balakrishnan, P. V. S., & Barry, B. (1994). Outcome satisfaction in negotiation: A test of expectancy disconfirmation. *Organizational Behavior and Human Decision Processes, 60*(2), 252–275.

Overbeck, J. R., Neale, M. A., & Govan, C. L. (2010). I feel, therefore you act: Intrapersonal and interpersonal effects of emotion on negotiation as a function of social power. *Organizational Behavior and Human Decision Processes, 112*(2), 126–139.

Patton, C., & Balakrishnan, P. V. (2010). The impact of expectation of future negotiation interaction on bargaining processes and outcomes. *Journal of Business Research, 63*(8), 809–816.

Perdue, B. (1992). Ten aggressive bargaining tactics of industrial buyers. *Journal of Business and Industrial Marketing, 7*(2), 45–52.

Peterson, E., & Thompson, L. (1997). Negotiation teamwork: The impact of information distribution and accountability on performance depends on the relationship among team members. *Organizational Behavior and Human Decision Processes, 72*(3), 364–383.

Pietroni, D., Van Kleef, G., Rubaltelli, E., & Rumiati, R. (2009). When happiness pays in negotiation. *Mind and Society, 8*(1), 77–92.

Pietroni, D., Van Kleef, G. A., & De Dreu, C. K. W. (2008). Response modes in negotiation. *Group Decision and Negotiation, 17*(1), 31–49.

Pinkley, R. L. (1990). Dimensions of conflict frame: Disputant interpretations of conflict. *Journal of Applied Psychology, 75*(2), 117–126.

Pinkley, R. L. (1995). Impact of knowledge regarding alternatives to settlement in dyadic negotiation: Whose knowledge counts? *Journal of Applied Psychology, 80*(3), 403–417.

Pinkley, R. L., & Northcraft, G. B. (1994). Conflict frames of reference: Implications for dispute processes and outcomes. *Academy of Management Journal, 37*(1), 193–205.

Polzer, J. T. (1996). Intergroup negotiations: The effects of negotiating teams. *Journal of Conflict Resolution, 40*(4), 678–698.

Pruitt, D. G., & Carnevale, P. J. D. (1993). *Negotiation in social conflict.* Buckingham: Open University Press.

Pruitt, D. G., & Drews, J. L. (1969). The effect of time pressure, time elapsed, and the opponent's concession rate on behavior in negotiation. *Journal of Experimental Social Psychology, 5*(1), 43–60.

Pruitt, D. G., & Lewis, S. A. (1975). Development of integrative solutions in bilateral negotiations. *Journal of Personality and Social Psychology, 31*(4), 621–633.

Purdy, J. M., Nye, P., & Balakrishnan, P. V. (2000). The impact of communication media on negotiation outcomes. *International Journal of Conflict Management, 11*(2), 162–187.
Putnam, L. L., & Holmer, M. (1992). Framing, reframing and issue development. In L. L. Putnam & M. E. Roloff (Eds.), *Communication and negotiation* (pp. 128–155). Newbury Park, CA: Sage.
Putnam, L. L., & Roloff, M. E. (1992). Communication perspectives on negotiation. In L. L. Putnam & M. E. Roloff (Eds.), *Communication and negotiation* (pp. 1–17). Newbury Park, CA: Sage.
Raiffa, H. (1982). *The art and science of negotiation*. Cambridge, MA: Harvard University Press.
Raiffa, H., Richardson, J., & Metcalfe, D. (2002). *Negotiation analysis – The science and art of collaborative decision making*. Cambridge, MA: Belknap Press of Harvard University Press.
Ramsay, J. (2004). Serendipity and the realpolitik of negotiations in supply chains. *Supply Chain Management: An International Journal, 9*(3), 219–229.
Rubin, J. Z., & Brown, B. R. (1975). *The social psychology of bargaining and negotiation*. New York: Academic.
Rubinstein, A. (1985). A bargaining model with incomplete information about time preferences. *Econometrica, 53*, 1150–1172.
Salacuse, J. W. (1999). Intercultural negotiation in international business. *Group Decision and Negotiation, 8*, 217–236.
Schelling, T. C. (1960). *The strategy of conflict*. New York: Oxford University Press.
Schweinsberg, M., Ku, G., Wang, C. S., & Pillutla, M. M. (2012). Starting high and ending with nothing: The role of anchors and power in negotiations. *Journal of Experimental Social Psychology, 48*(1), 226–231.
Shalvi, S., Moran, S., & Ritov, I. (2010). Overcoming initial anchors: The effect of negotiators' dispositional control beliefs. *Negotiation and Conflict Management Research, 3*(3), 232–248.
Shapiro, D. L., & Bies, R. L. (1994). Threats, bluffs and disclaimers in negotiations. *Organizational Behavior and Human Decision Processes, 60*(1), 14–35.
Sinaceur, M., & Neale, M. A. (2005). Not all threats are created equal: How implicitness and timing affect the effectiveness of threats in negotiations. *Group Decision and Negotiation, 14* (1), 63–85.
Sinaceur, M., Van Kleef, G. A., Neale, M. A., Adam, H., & Haag, C. (2011). Hot or cold: Is communicating anger or threats more effective in negotiation? *Journal of Applied Psychology, 96*(5), 1018–1032.
Smith, D. L., Pruitt, D. G., & Carnevale, P. J. (1982). Matching and mismatching: The effect of own limit, other's toughness, and time pressure on concession rate in negotiation. *Journal of Personality and Social Psychology, 42*, 876–883.
Steinel, W., Van Kleef, G. A., & Harinck, F. (2008). Are you talking to me?! Separating the people from the problem when expressing emotions in negotiation. *Journal of Experimental Social Psychology, 44*, 362–369.
Stuhlmacher, A. F., & Champagne, M. V. (2000). The impact of time pressure and information on negotiation process and decisions. *Group Decision and Negotiation, 9*(6), 471–491.
Stuhlmacher, A., Citera, M., & Willis, T. (2007). Gender differences in virtual negotiation: Theory and research. *Sex Roles, 57*(5), 329–339.
Stuhlmacher, A. F., Gillespie, T. L., & Champagne, M. V. (1998). The impact of time pressure in negotiation: A meta analysis. *International Journal of Conflict Management, 9*(1), 97–116.
Stuhlmacher, A. F., & Walters, A. E. (1999). Gender differences in negotiation outcomes: A meta-analysis. *Personnel Psychology, 52*(3), 653–677.
Thompson, L. (2005). *The mind and heart of the negotiator* (3rd ed.). Upper Saddle River, NJ: Pearson.
Thompson, L., & Hastie, R. (1990). Social perception in negotiation. *Organizational Behavior and Human Decision Processes, 47*(1), 98–123.
Thompson, L., & Hrebec, D. (1996). Lose–lose agreements in interdependent decision making. *Psychological Bulletin, 120*(3), 396–409.

Thompson, L., Peterson, E., & Brodt, S. E. (1996). Team negotiation: An examination of integrative and distributive bargaining. *Journal of Personality and Social Psychology, 70*(1), 66–78.

Thompson, L., Valley, K. L., & Kramer, R. M. (1995). The bittersweet feeling of success: An examination of social perception in negotiation. *Journal of Experimental Social Psychology, 31*(6), 467–492.

Trötschel, R., Hüffmeier, J., Loschelder, D. D., Schwartz, K., & Gollwitzer, P. M. (2011). Perspective taking as a means to overcome motivational barriers in negotiations: When putting oneself into the opponent's shoes helps to walk toward agreements. *Journal of Personality and Social Psychology, 101*(4), 771–790.

Tversky, A., & Kahneman, D. (1974). Judgment under uncertainty: Heuristics and biases. *Science, 185*(4157), 1124–1131.

Ury, W. L., Brett, J. M., & Goldberg, S. B. (1988). *Getting disputes resolved.* San Francisco: Jossey-Bass.

Utikal, H. (2001). *Die Organisation industrieller Geschäftsbeziehungen.* Wiesbaden: Gabler.

Van Boven, L., Gilovich, T., & Medvec, V. H. (2003). The illusion of transparency in negotiations. *Negotiation Journal, 19*(2), 117–131.

Van Boven, L., & Thompson, L. (2003). A look into the mind of the negotiator: Mental models in negotiation. *Group Processes and Intergroup Relations, 6*(4), 387–404.

Van Kleef, G. A., & De Dreu, C. K. W. (2002). Social value orientation and impression formation: A test of two competing hypotheses about information search in negotiation. *International Journal of Conflict Management, 13*(1), 59–77.

Van Kleef, G. A., & De Dreu, C. K. W. (2010). Longer-term consequences of anger expression in negotiation: Retaliation or spillover? *Journal of Experimental Social Psychology, 46*(5), 753–760.

Van Kleef, G. A., De Dreu, C. K. W., & Manstead, A. S. R. (2004). The interpersonal effects of anger and happiness in negotiations. *Journal of Personality and Social Psychology, 86*(1), 57–76.

Van Kleef, G. A., De Dreu, C. K. W., & Manstead, A. S. R. (2006). Supplication and appeasement in conflict and negotiation: The interpersonal effects of disappointment, worry, guilt, and regret. *Journal of Personality and Social Psychology, 91*(1), 124–142.

Van Kleef, G. A., & Van Lange, P. A. M. (2008). What other's disappointment may do to selfish people: Emotion and social value orientation in a negotiation context. *Personality and Social Psychology Bulletin, 34*(8), 1084–1095.

Venkatesh, R., Kohli, A. K., & Zaltman, G. (1995). Influence strategies in buying centers. *Journal of Marketing, 59*, 71–82.

Vetschera, R. (2006). Preference structures of negotiators and negotiation outcomes. *Group Decision and Negotiation, 15*(2), 111–125.

Vetschera, R., Kersten, G., & Koeszegi, S. (2006). User assessment of internet-based negotiation support systems: An exploratory study. *Journal of Organizational Computing and Electronic Commerce, 16*(2), 123–148.

von Neumann, J., & Morgenstern, O. (1944). *Theory of games and economic behavior.* Princeton: Princeton University Press.

Walters, A. E., Stuhlmacher, A. F., & Meyer, L. L. (1998). Gender and negotiator competitiveness: A meta-analysis. *Organizational Behavior and Human Decision Processes, 76*(1), 1–29.

Walton, R. E., & McKersie, R. B. (1965). *A behavioral theory of labor negotiations.* New York: McGraw-Hill.

Weingart, L. R., Brett, J. M., Olekalns, M., & Smith, P. L. (2007). Conflicting social motives in negotiating groups. *Journal of Personality and Social Psychology, 93*(6), 994–1010.

Weingart, L. R., Olekalns, M., & Smith, P. L. (2004). Quantitative coding of negotiation processes. *International Negotiation, 9*(Special Issue on Research Methods in Negotiation and Social Conflict), 441–455.

Weingart, L. R., Thompson, L. L., Bazerman, M. H., & Carroll, J. S. (1990). Tactical behavior and negotiation outcomes. *International Journal of Conflict Management, 1*(1), 7–31.

Wilken, R., Cornelißen, M., Backhaus, K., & Schmitz, C. (2010). Steering sales reps through cost information: An investigation into the black box of cognitive references and negotiation behavior. *International Journal of Research in Marketing, 27*(1), 69–82.
Young, M. J., Bauman, C. W., Chen, N., & Bastardi, A. (2012). The pursuit of missing information in negotiation. *Organizational Behavior and Human Decision Processes, 117*(1), 88–95.
Zachariassen, F. (2008). Negotiation strategies in supply chain management. *International Journal of Physical Distribution and Logistics Management, 38*(10), 764–781.

Project Management

Wolfgang Rabl

1 Intro: It Can't Be Done Without Project Management

Today project management is a fundamental management competency. In practically every company no matter what sector of the economy it is in, in NPOs, in public administration, and even in the private sphere, work is carried out in projects. The role of project manager is perceived to be a job description in its own right. Corresponding career development models and career paths leading to project management are established features of many companies. There are many reasons for these developments, which are also above all based on the increasingly complex—and especially increasingly dynamic—environment in organizations, on today's radically shorter product life cycles, and on the trend to increasingly offer customers bespoke solutions as well as standard ones. Working in projects in relation to the drawing up of bids and **order processing** is a crucial factor for success which still poses particular organizational and personnel challenges for many companies today.

In line with these challenges, more and more companies see the necessity of creating professional framework conditions for handling projects in order to safeguard their competitiveness, and ideally even a competitive advantage, and to increase their flexibility, particularly in organizational terms.

This chapter provides an overview of project management definitions, processes, organizational structures, methods and techniques, focusing on **customer projects** and professional order management.

The great relevance of project management is also attested to by the project management standards that have been established globally:

W. Rabl (✉)
next level holding GmbH, Vienna, Austria
e-mail: wolfgang.rabl@nextlevelconsulting.eu

M. Kleinaltenkamp et al. (eds.), *Business Project Management and Marketing*,
Springer Texts in Business and Economics, DOI 10.1007/978-3-662-48507-1_7

Table 1 Definitions of the term project management

DIN 69901-1	. . .the totality of management tasks, organization, techniques and resources used for initiating, defining, planning, directing and completing projects (German Institute for Standardization 2009a, b)
PMI	. . .the application of knowledge, skills, tools and methods to project processes in order to fulfill the requirements of the project (Project Management Institute 2010)
IPMA	The planning, organization, oversight and monitoring of all aspects of a project, and the management and leadership of all the persons involved in order to ensure the achievement of the project objectives in accordance with the targets set in relation to timing, costs, outputs, and quality standards (IPMA 2006, p. 120)
PRINCE2	Is the planning, delegating, monitoring and control of all aspects, and the motivation of those involved, to achieve the project objectives within the expected performance targets for time, cost, quality, scope, benefits and risks (OGC 2009, S. 4)

- PMI®—Project Management Institute: American standard with about 378,749 members worldwide
- IPMA®—International Project Management Association: European standard with about 53,462 members worldwide
- PRINCE2®—Projects in Controlled Environments: British Standard with about 200,000 PRINCE2 practitioners worldwide.

There is of course also a DIN standard relating to project management. Table 1 provides an overview of the definitions of the term project management according to these standards.

2 Not Every Order Is a Project

If one thinks that the term "project" means the same thing to everyone, one will be quickly disabused. It is evident that the term project is used in an inflationary manner in companies. It is apparent in many cases that virtually every assigned task is termed a project. A person is then put in charge of it (the "project manager", and that's about it. It almost seems as though the appointing of a "project manager" is a kind of motivation to "saddle" someone with the respective task that has to be done, and what's more, to signal: "We take a professional approach to the handling of our tasks". And the question: "How many projects do you currently have running in the company"? elicits the reply: "A whole load, we don't know exactly how many."

This applies very specifically to companies which handle external projects, in other words **customer projects**. In the first—typical—case one is then faced with the fact that customer orders are generally described as "projects", regardless of their size and complexity. The end result of this is that even the very smallest tasks—which take only a few hours of work and are completed within a couple of days—are "projects" for the employees concerned.

A very striking practical example of this is a company's "project" to change the header of the company's letter paper for the printers (new telephone number)!

The difficulties then start when one attempts to apply project management methods. Even though this is theoretically possible even for the smallest tasks, it seldom makes sense. When the employees concerned are faced with the power of project management methods, widespread skepticism and a lack of understanding for the subject of project management takes hold among them.

However, project management is not intended to be applied indiscriminately to each and every customer order. This is because if the task is not sufficiently complex or large, the result is simply increased bureaucracy which does not enhance the quality of execution in any way.

The second case—which is also typical—is no less interesting. In various sectors, like a lot of industrial plant manufacturing companies for example, it has become established practice to designate a scheme which is still in the sales phase as a "project". "Project" as used in this case is obviously a synonym for something which is imminent.

However, once the contract has been concluded with the customer, the term "project" disappears and is replaced by "order". This is remarkable in the sense that far less use of project management generally needs to be made in the sales phase than later on when a project is being executed. And although this is not questioned by any sales manager or any project execution manager, this use of terminology proves to be stubbornly persistent.

A possible way of resolving this in both cases is the implementation of clear and measurable criteria relating to what merits the status of a project. This also generally enables a "project-worthiness analysis" to be quickly introduced in the company, as well as—in theory at least—greater clarity and a targeted application of project management.

The far greater challenge is at the cultural level. Often—despite project-worthiness criteria—the old terminology is remarkably persistent. This can continue for months, and sometimes even years, which again proves that it is neither possible nor desirable to reduce project management to a methodological, structural level. The introduction of professional project management is therefore a "cultural change", which will only be successful if work is done on the corporate culture as well as the structure with the help of a properly thought-through change processes.

A project is a difference which makes a difference (Gareis 1991, p. 20). Table 2 shows a series of **project definitions** according to cited international standards:

Based on the general theoretical **project definitions**, the following have proved to be useful ways of bringing precision to the definition of projects, and also to the handling customer orders, in practice.

Projects are **temporary assignments** with **special characteristics** (e.g. involving risk, unique, socially and technically complex, dynamic, etc.). They are distinguished by their high level of complexity from line activities which are carried out within the defined core business processes and line organization structures. The consequence of this viewpoint is that it is necessary to differentiate between those orders which are defined as a project and those which are not. One tool for doing this is a project-worthiness analysis (Sect. 7.2). This

Table 2 Definitions of the term project

DIN 69901	A scheme which is mainly characterized by the uniqueness of its overall conditions, e.g. the objectives set for it and its timing, financial, personnel and other constraints, a project-specific form of organization (German Institute for Standardization 2009a, b)
PMI	A project is a time-limited scheme for creating a unique product, or a service, or a result (Project Management Institute 2010)
IPMA	An assignment with a limited timeframe and budget for providing a series of clearly defined results (deliverables), which serve to achieve the project objectives in compliance with specific quality standards and requirements (IPMA 2006, p. 13)
PRINCE2	Is a temporary organization that is created for the purpose of delivering one more business products according to an agreed Business Case (OGC 2009, S. 3)

results in the use of specific **project management methods** and the implementation of appropriate organizational structures.

Projects can be viewed as **social systems**. The consequence of adopting this standpoint is to link projects to three fundamental criteria of system theory. Firstly: Every social system defines itself through a "within/without" demarcation, i.e. what does and does not form part of the social system. Secondly: Every social system has internal structures a key feature of which is that they make self-organization processes possible. This consequently identities the main characteristic of the current project management approach. Projects which are perceived as social systems are self-referential. This means that the organizational structure and the processes within projects, as well as the project roles and the communications structures in projects, are absolutely critical to their success. This organizational theory approach to project management will be discussed in detail at several points in this chapter. Thirdly: Social systems are existentially dependent on their relationships to other social systems. These relationships, which are also called the social context, must be identified and managed. The management of the **project context** in a social, factual and time dimension determines the success or failure of projects.

Projects are **temporary organizations**. In line with this organizational theory approach, the most important thing is to set up temporary information—and especially temporary decision-making –structures. Projects consequently become one option for the organizational structuring of a company (Gareis 1991). A series of key questions about the organizational structure of projects arise from this approach, above all in relation to **order processing**. An appropriate level of maturity is necessitated in particular by the interplay between the permanent line organization and the **temporary project organization**.

The following is an anonymized practical example of the **definition of a project** in a company undertaking **customer projects** in the IT and telecommunications sector:

Table 3 Example of project definition

Criterion	Scheme/ measure	Project	Program
Organizational units involved	At least 2	At least 3	At least 5
Duration	At least 1 month	At least 3 months	At least 16 months
Internal resource expenditure (person days)	>20 PDs	>50 PDs	>500 PDs
External expenditure	>EUR 5000	>EUR 20,000	>EUR 100,000

Example of Project Definition (cf. Table 3)
Strategic measures, projects and programs are described as schemes and they are tasks of a unique nature—uniqueness in terms of the conditions of their execution:

- There is no process description that can be directly applied to the carrying out of tasks.
- The objectives of the task (type and quality of the results, completion deadlines, limits on resources expended) are definable.
- The task can be clearly differentiated from other schemes and standard tasks.

3 Project Management with a Difference

Without an integrated approach no excellence in project management (Gregory Balestrero, CEO PMI®, 2006).

In order to permanently guarantee professional project management in companies, an integrated view of project portfolio management and of specific structural elements of line operations is necessary. Therefore, in **project-oriented companies** the three levels—project management, project portfolio management, and project framework organization/PM governance—form the subject of implementation, optimization and continuous improvement (cf. Fig. 1).

Following this approach enables the architecture of a ***project-oriented company*** to be described as follows based on the elements of the organizational structure and on workflow organization/processes (cf. Fig. 2).

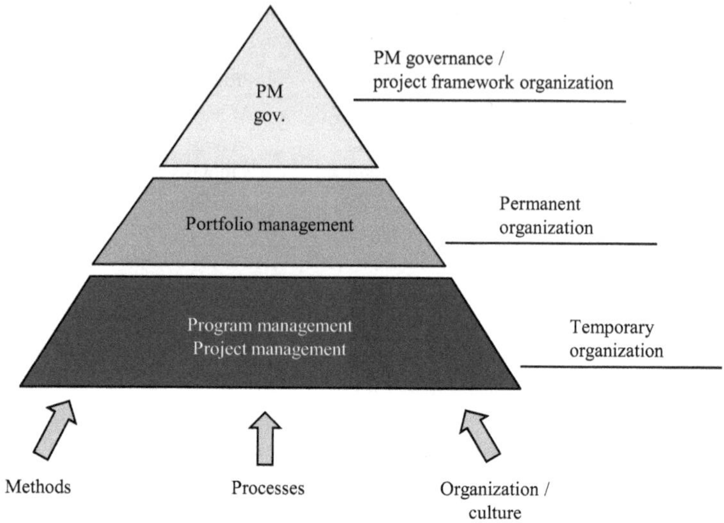

Fig. 1 The three levels of the project-oriented company

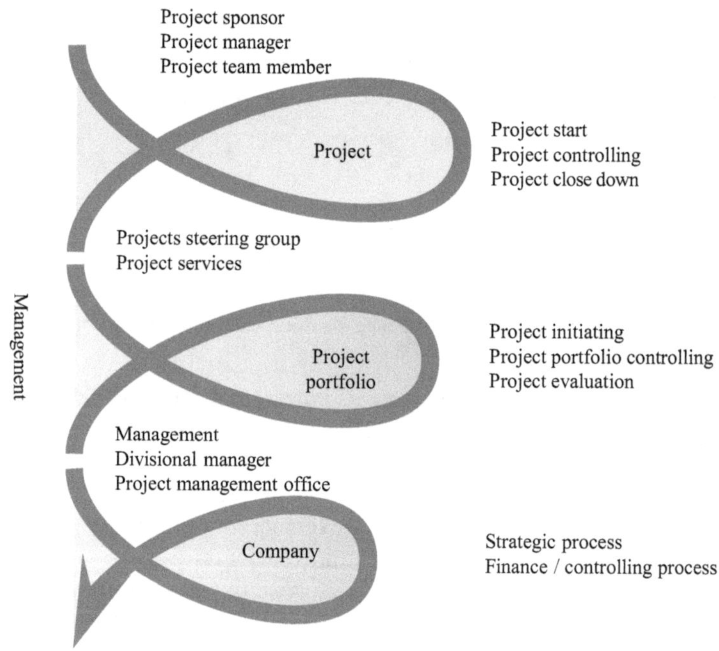

Fig. 2 The project-oriented organization

From the project perspective, we talk of the following organizational structure, i.e. processes, in the project management context: project start process, project controlling process, and project close-down process. We will provide a detailed description of these processes in order processing projects later on.

From the project portfolio perspective, the following workflows/processes must be defined: project initiating process, project portfolio controlling process, project prioritizing process, and the project evaluation process. Within the project initiating process it must be specified how projects progress from being a proposal to being an order. The key criteria for making decisions in this regard are their strategic relevance and the management of resource constraints. It is also in this process that the project owner, and if applicable the project manager, are specified. The project portfolio controlling process principally manages the overall optimization of the project portfolio based on the assumption that there are financial and personnel resource constraints. This involves increasing or reducing the relative priorities of projects at regular intervals, putting them on hold, or aborting them. In the project evaluation process the achievement of objectives, the business case and/or the benefit derived from the project are evaluated 6–12 months after its completion.

Relevant processes from the line operations perspective are the strategy process and the finance/controlling (FI/CO) processes. In this respect it is in particular the linking of these processes with the project portfolio processes which is relevant. From the strategy process are derived the framework conditions for the project portfolio in terms of strategic relevance and conformity to strategy. Derived from the FI/CO process is the budgeting process in particular which determines the budgeting rules and the budgetary controlling of the project portfolio, and also the overall management of personnel resources which is the cornerstone of the management of resource constraints in the project portfolio.

Like the organization of workflow, the organizational structure must also be defined on three levels. This is done by having appropriate roles. At the project level the roles to be implemented are: project owner, project manager, and project team member. Crucial to the success of the role of project manager are:

- The "highlander" principle: "There can only be one."
- The positioning of the role of project manager as temporary managing director/CEO.
- The defining of managerial and decision-making authority.

The project owner is most effective if he is appropriately empowered, just like the project manager. In English the role is also described as project owner, the person who 'owns' the project. In operational projects the project owner is the "final decision-maker" in the project-related decision space. As a rule therefore there is also no need for project steering committees or the like within projects.

The challenge in terms of the role of project team member is generally having dual reporting responsibilities, within both the line and the project organizations. An appropriate defining of roles which specifies the allocation of competencies between the project manager and the line manager ensures that he will be able to act effectively. Example of a matrix organization: What, when, and up to what level does the project manager make decisions. Who, how, and how well does the line manager make decisions.

At the project portfolio level, the following roles must be established: projects steering group and project services. The projects steering group, also called the project portfolio board, is made up of members of the company's two most senior levels of management. This permanent role is responsible for the processes of project portfolio management, and it meets regularly every 4–6 weeks. One of the main ground rules in this connection is that this steering body does not intervene at the level of individual projects. Project services, sometimes also called project controller or project portfolio controller, is responsible for the continual refining of the project portfolio and the corresponding preparing of decision-making proposal documents for the projects steering group. At the same time, project services provides quality assurance and plausibility checks in the preparation of individual projects.

The final body which must be represented at the line operations level is the project management office (PMO). The PMO is responsible for PM governance in the company and is primarily responsible for the organizational and workflow structures at the project and project portfolio levels. In addition, a series of further service and support-oriented tasks are generally undertaken in the PMO. Examples of these are the drawing up of skills enhancement measures for project management personnel, the provision of support for the PM Community, the administration of PM tools, the coaching of project managers, and knowledge management in relation to project management.

Key Message: Criteria for the Success of the Project-Oriented Organization

- Principle of people holding multiple roles
- Commitment from top management
- Projects as temporary organizational structures make the organization of the company more flexible
- Working in temporary information and decision-making structures is seen as a competitive advantage

4 Criteria for the Success of Project Management Processes

The process-oriented approach in project management opens up the planning, control and monitoring of the individual project management processes at the meta level. Processes are defined by means of a start and end event, a process

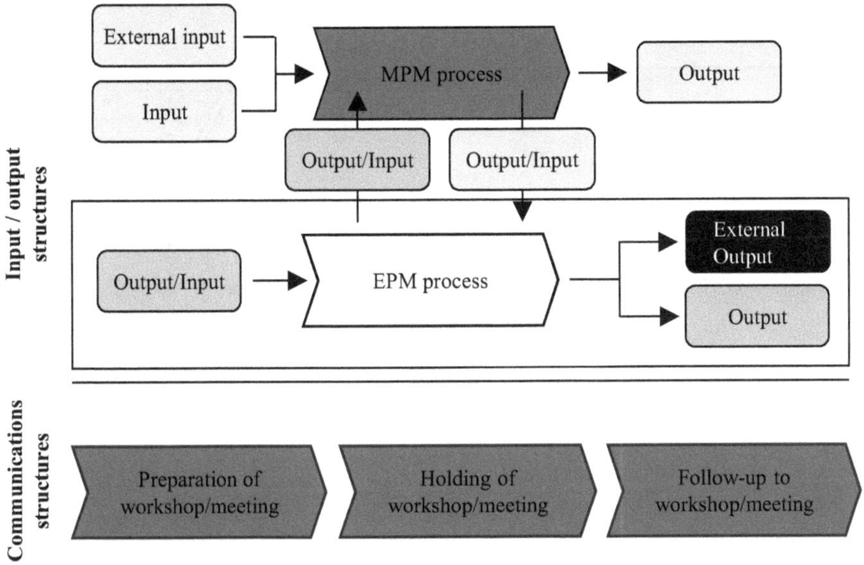

Fig. 3 Integrated project management—process description

sequence consisting of individual work steps, and standardized inputs and outputs/deliverables. In addition, communications processes can be specified and resources, tools and standard templates provided.

In the project-oriented approach it is above all necessary to pay attention to the interaction between the project (IPM) and the project portfolio (MPM) in relation to the processes. The fundamental structure of a process within individual project management and multiple project management is outlined in Fig. 3.

It is possible to speak of a **project-oriented company** if the organization of structures and workflows is depicted in a standardized way in an organizational manual, if factors which are critical to success are defined, and if responsibility for project management standards is established in the form of a project management office (cf. P3M3 maturity Model according to: OGC 2010a, PRINCE2® according to OGC 2010b). As well as the individual project management and project portfolio management roles, the processes in particular are described in detail and embedded through appropriate linking of the three levels: project, project portfolio, and line operations.

The following anonymized example from the IT and telecommunications sector illustrates a correspondingly standardized project management model (cf. Fig. 4).

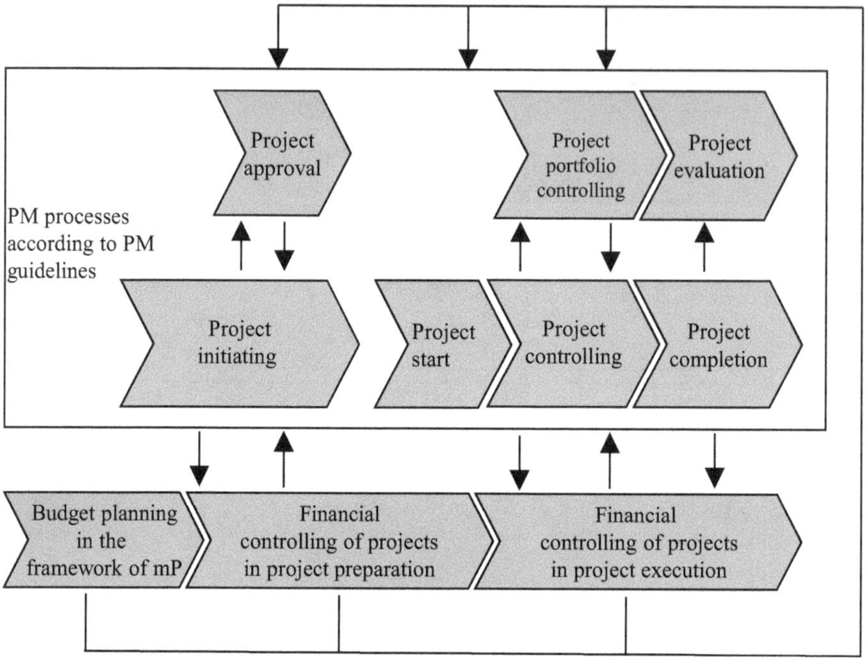

Fig. 4 The integrated project management process (customer example)

5 Launching and Planning Customer Projects

Who can launch a project and how? How is the decision in favor of or against implementation made, and also the decision regarding the mode of working/the organizational form? How is the project owner and the project manager selected? These questions, as well as a series of further ones, arise before the start of a project.

In order to take appropriate account of the importance of the drawing up of projects, the first phase of projects can be subdivided into an initiation phase and a launch phase. Figure 5 shows an overview of a possible rough delineation of these initial process steps in the context of the individual project management process.

5.1 Project Initiation Process

In the initiation process (cf. Fig. 5) the framework conditions for a project are clarified. The aim is a project approval based on adequate rough planning. The project has to be delineated in order to be able to carry out rough planning appropriately.

It is delineated by defining "What is an objective and what is not an objective of the project?" (Sect. 7.5). This facilitates planning, since only what is delineated can actually be planned.

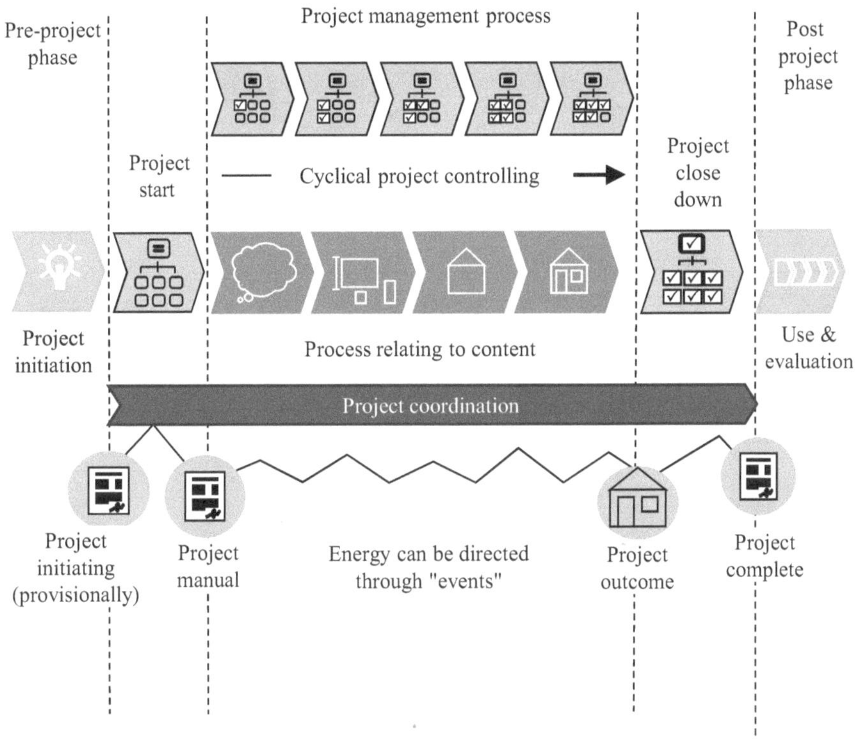

Fig. 5 Project management process

As well as the delineating of projects, a contextual analysis of projects should also be carried out at this point (Sects. 7.6 and 7.7) according to the motto "the project does not exist in isolation".

The first two process steps represent two decision nodes. The process step which consists of evaluating the idea/assignment, or the bid/order in this context, leads to the decision as to whether or not the idea/assignment or the bid is to be taken forward/the order is to be carried out.

This results in a clear distinction between internal projects and external, so-called **customer projects**, since the decision as to whether or not to carry out an order is purely hypothetical. It is nevertheless advisable to carry out this evaluation step even in the case of a customer order, precisely in order to prepare the framework conditions appropriately.

In the second step this strategic, subject-specific and business decision is followed by the question of project-worthiness. In this step it is decided whether the bid/order is to be carried out in a **temporary project organization** or in the permanent line organization.

The individual steps are explained in detail below based on the overall overview of the initiation process.

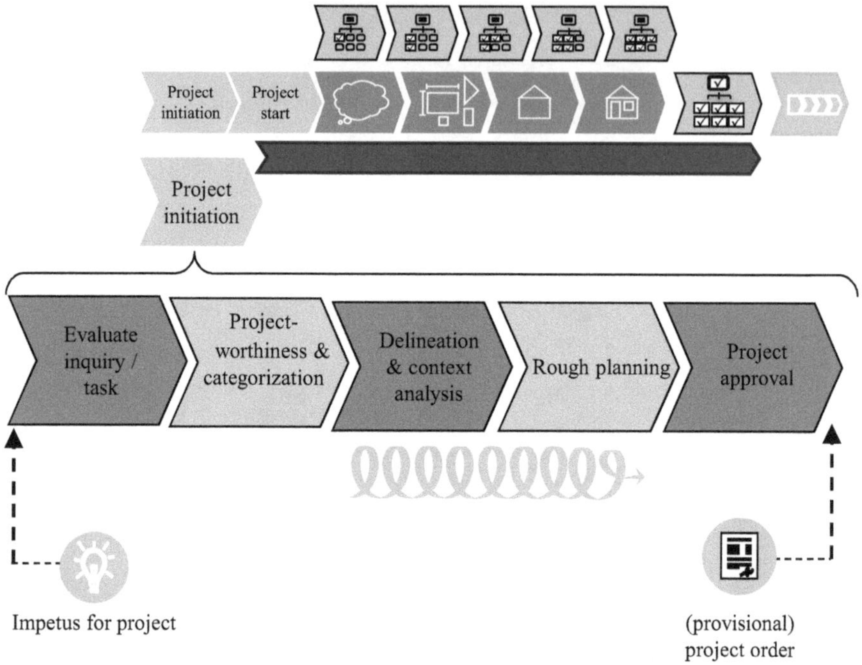

Fig. 6 Project initiation process

Key Message

- Each individual step is obligatory for project approval.
- The relative prominence of the individual steps differs according to the type of project.
- As well as skipping the initial sub-process consisting of evaluating the idea/ assignment, there may be other defined areas of the initiation process which are skipped.

In the evaluation of the idea, the decision regarding the implementation of a scheme is taken.

Three criteria are relevant to the step of evaluating the bid/order (cf. Fig. 6):

- Conformity to strategy
- Technical feasibility
- Profitability

The issue of conformity to strategy mainly concerns on the one hand the question of the extent to which the bid/order accords with the corporate strategy, and on the other hand the issue of optimizing the overall order portfolio. It is the second issue in particular which involves consideration of resource constraints. These may be both financial resources and the budget as well as personnel resources.

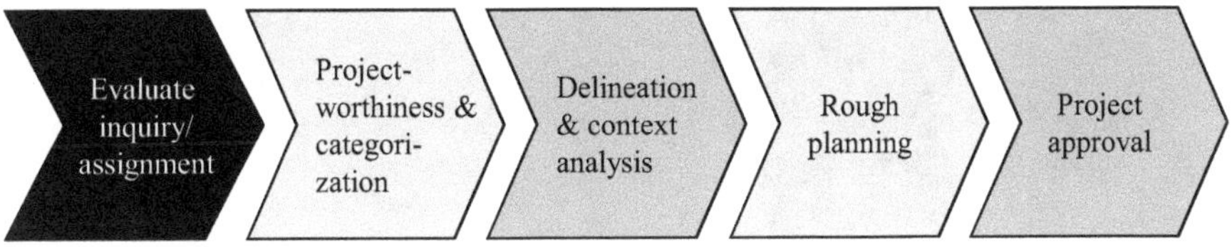

Fig. 7 Sub-process: evaluating the inquiry/order

Technical feasibility is governed by the achievability of the objectives and results of the bid/order, and of the solutions offered by it. As a rule, feasibility studies are carried out in this regard. In practice, an analysis of technical feasibility in external bid/**customer projects** has proved to be a key input for risk management, and one which may subsequently become a critical factor in the success of the execution of the project.

The criterion of profitability is a critical success factor in the context of bids and orders. In addition to comparing costs/benefits over the entire life cycle (business case), the analysis of uncertainties and the devising and comparison of alternatives are important work steps which are necessary for showing profitability.

In order to arrive at a final evaluation of the bid/order, holistic consideration of the three target variables (outputs, deadlines and resources) is required since they are interdependent. The relevant decision-makers must also specify which of the three target variables are to be prioritized within the project.

The result of this sub-process is the formal decision to submit the bid/undertake the order. The detailed results are of course useful for the subsequent work steps in the initiation process, and in particular for rough planning.

The analysis of project-worthiness and the categorization of projects are an input for **project definition** and for the decision regarding the option of organizational form to be used when carrying out the project.

The analysis of project-worthiness and project categorization is an established tool in most companies. Key criteria for this analysis are (cf. Fig. 7):

- Organizational units involved
- Duration (throughput period)
- Internal resource expenditure (person days)
- External expenditure (CAPEX, OPEX)

It is above all the number of organizational units involved which is an indicator of project-worthiness since organizational complexity is a major decision-making criterion for a project organization.

The throughput period is relevant in this regard since project management requires an appropriate (extra) expenditure of resources, and it is only worthwhile for throughput periods of 3 months or more.

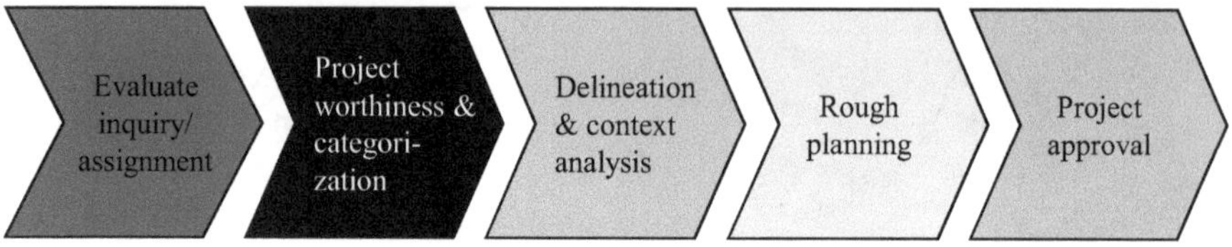

Fig. 8 Process step: analysis of project-worthiness and categorization

The following organizational forms can be set up in the context of project categorization:

- Scheme/measure
- Project
- Program

These different organizational forms firstly enable the line organization to be distinguished from the **temporary organization,** and secondly they determine the degree of organizational complexity in the structuring of temporary information and decision-making structures.

The following example from the IT/telecommunications sector shows the use of the project-worthiness analysis and of project categorization in practice (cf. Fig. 8).

Based on the project-worthiness analysis and project categorization, the project owner and the project manager are generally named, and the first (core) team members may also be nominated.

Typical challenges facing the project manager as from this process step in the initiation phase are a series of issues, including: The subject has so far only been vaguely described. The expectations that relevant stakeholders have of the project manager? Who is to be involved in clarifying the project objectives? etc.

The outcome of this sub-process is the decision to handle a bid/order either via a **temporary organization** as a project, or as a program. In addition, the nature and scope of organizational structures in projects can be specified, and the use of project management methods and tools can also be agreed.

Key Message

The project-worthiness analysis and project categorization must be specifically defined in every company. In practice it is necessary to define appropriate criteria and standards for the project-worthiness analysis and project categorization taking account of the level of organizational maturity with respect to project management within the company and the type and complexity of projects involved. The delineation and context analysis process step is the first major step towards drawing up the project order (cf. Fig. 9).

Delineation and context analysis is one of the most important **project management methods** (Sect. 7.5).

Project delineation determines what are the aim and contents of the project, and what are not its aims and contents. This defining of what is "within" and "without" is based on the systemic approach and the approach which perceives projects as social systems.

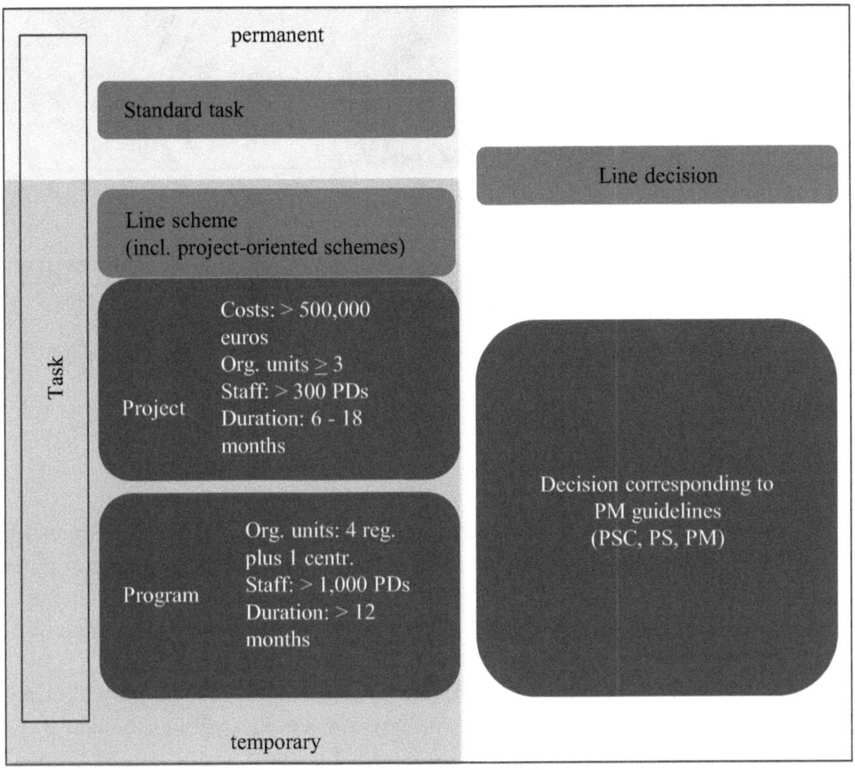

Fig. 9 Project-worthiness analysis (customer example)

In practice, inadequate **project delineation** can often be observed. Projects are delineated too restrictively. The necessary complexity is not designed in, or alternatively projects are not delineated tightly enough. The project boundaries are then unclear or "woolly".

One factor in the success of the delineation of projects is firstly producing a common viewpoint ("construct") within the project team. Secondly, it is necessary to manage the delineation in iterations via the initiation process, the launch process, and the project controlling process.

Key Message
A common viewpoint within the project team which is shared by the project owner is a prerequisite for a successful project. The "big project picture" is a criterion of success.

The analysis of the context includes the description of the framework conditions in which the project is to be carried out. Key framework conditions are:

- The pre-project phase
- Other projects running in parallel
- Relevant social systems

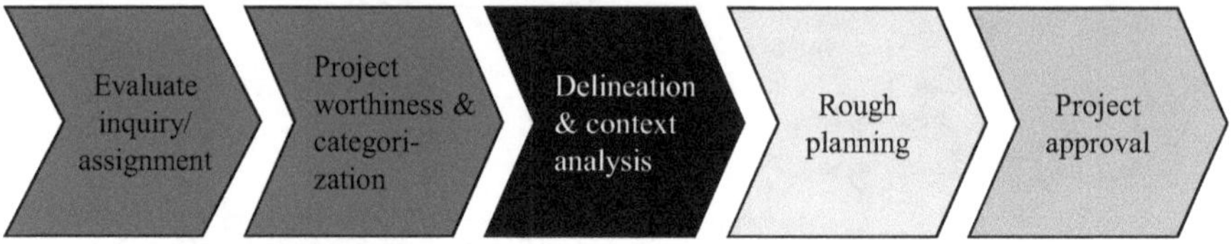

Fig. 10 Delineation and context analysis process step

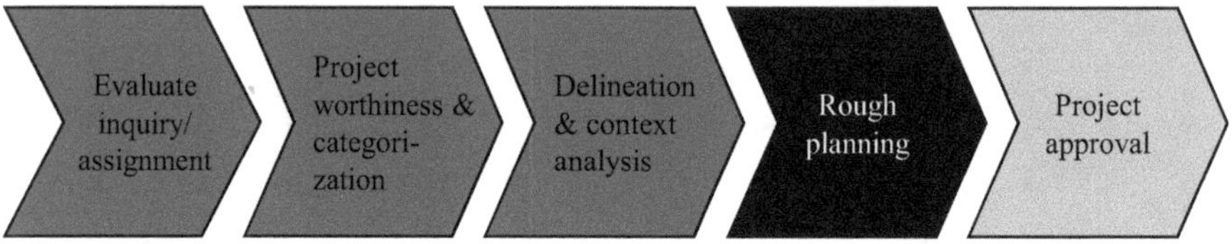

Fig. 11 Rough planning process step

The "story" of how the project came into being is of relevance to the planning and organization of the project. Typical issues are: What has happened prior to the launch of the project? What decisions have already been made? What documents have already been drawn up? Who has supported the carrying out of the project, and who has hampered it?

Projects which are running in parallel have an influence on the project. There may be synergies between the projects, or they may conflict with each other if, for example, several projects compete for constrained resources.

Relevant systems are internal and external environments which have an influence on the project. Examples of internal environments are organizational units, management, the works council. Examples of external environments may be customers, suppliers, and authorities. The active management of the relevant context is a factor in the success of the execution of the project.

Key Message
The delineation of projects reduces complexity, and the consideration and management of context builds up complexity within projects.

The outcome of this sub-process is an initial draft version of the **project order** as well as the basic input for the planning and organization of the project.

Rough planning is the final step in the project initiation process and rounds out the draft version of the **project order** (cf. Fig. 10).

The areas to be focused on in rough planning are the outputs, deadlines, resources and costs. This "magical" triangle is the common thread running through the planning of a project (cf. Fig. 11).

Various **project management methods** can be used for the planning of outputs, deadlines, and resources/costs. The selection of methods is dependent on the nature and complexity of the project (Sect. 7.2). The precondition for rough planning in projects is that none of the three areas to be focused on is neglected, and that at least the following methods of rough planning are available:

- Output planning: Project structure plan
- Time scheduling: Milestone schedule
- Resources/costs plan: Phase plan for resources and costs

Key Message

The methods of rough planning are essential for the quality of the **project order**.

The primary thing which the project structure plan must contain is a complete description of the outputs to be provided within a phase or property-based structure. The project structure plan is drawn up within the project team, if it has already been established, or otherwise within a team of experts. This is intended to ensure a common understanding, but above all an acceptance, of the contents of the project and the rough course of the project.

The milestone scheduling is based on the components of the project structure plan, and it depicts a rough time schedule framework for the project. This planning step is also carried out in the project/expert team. The common step of defining milestones involves on the one hand reviewing the quality of the project structure plan and/or consolidating the common understanding, and on the other hand it enables a common view to be taken of time-critical events in the project.

The minimum approach to resource and costs planning is phase-oriented rough planning based on the project structure plan. This involves assigning types of resources and costs at the initial level of subdivision (phases/objects) of the project structure plan. A low level of detail is consciously accepted in order to be able to determine the initial orders of magnitude of the resources and costs involved in the project without entailing undue workload. The aim of doing so is to draw up this rough plan with an accuracy of $\pm 15\ \%$ as regards the approved resource and costs targets.

The outcome of the rough planning is the drawing up of a (provisional) **project order** which can be submitted for project approval.

Project approval is a gate in which the project start process is commissioned (cf. Fig. 12).

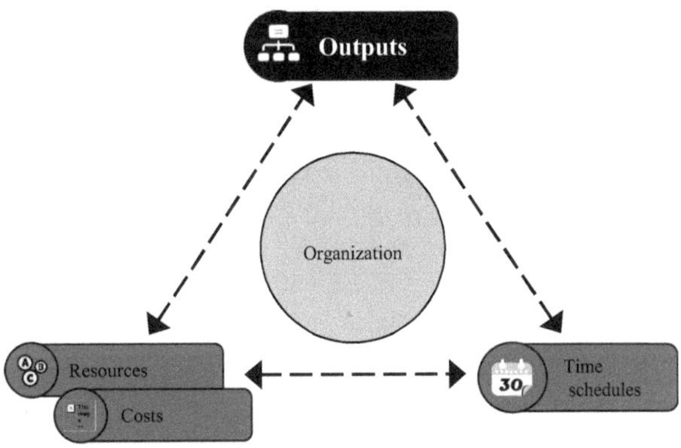

Fig. 12 The "magical" PM triangle

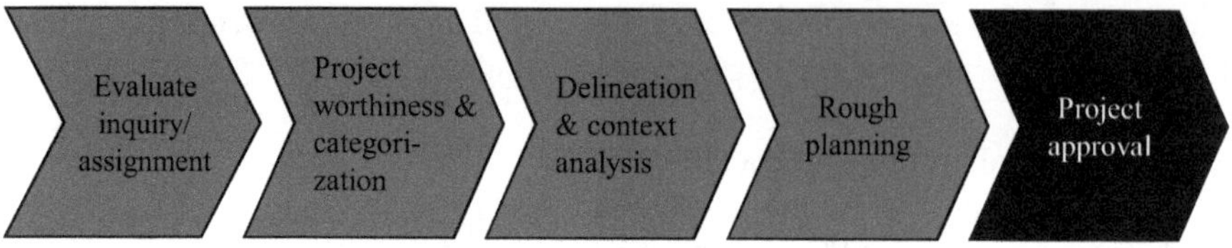

Fig. 13 Project approval process step

The objectives of this process step are to reflect on the current planning status, and to make a decision regarding different options for project execution. In addition, the profitability calculation is verified. This means that project approval is also a key quality assurance step in the setting up of projects.

The decision-making bodies involved in project approval are the project owner at the level of individual project management on the one hand, and the projects steering group at the project portfolio management level on the other hand.

In a constitutive project owner meeting the **delineation of the project** and the rough planning of the project based on the **project order** are discussed between the project owner and the project manager, and a common viewpoint is established. The project owner formally takes acceptance of the **project order** and prepares the **project order** for project approval by the projects steering group.

In the project approval, the projects steering group reviews the focus and impact on the corporate strategy based on the current project portfolio. In addition, a review is undertaken of the resources which are needed, in particular the availability of the constrained resources that are required. These may be both financial resources and the budget as well as personnel capacities.

Key Message

The quality of the project initiation process determines the quality of the detailed planning and the structuring carried out during the project start process.

The outcome of the review is the formal order to undertake the project start process. A summary of the illustrative initiation process is shown in Fig. 13.

5.2 Project Start Process

The formal launch of a project occurs when approval to carry out the project is given by the projects steering group.

The following key challenges arise in this process step: How does the project manager create workable structures within the project organization with clear assignments of roles as quickly as possible? How does the project manager transfer the know-how from the pre-project phase to the project team and produce a common view of the subsequent action to be taken?

In addition, it is necessary to determine which elements of the planning are to be worked on further, and in what level of detail. In order to underpin the operative setting up of the project organizational structures and the production of detailed output, deadline, resource and cost plans, the communications structures to be used

	Review and evaluate idea	Project-worthiness & categorization	Delineation & context analysis	Rough planning	Project approval
Activities:	» Rough description of idea » Review technical feasibility » Review conformity to strategy » Draw up business case	» Review project-worthiness » Categorize project complexity » Appoint PS & PM	» Devise 6 steps (and variants as applicable) » Undertake environment analysis » Initial risk assessment	» Verify 6 steps & environment analysis » Initial draft of output, deadline, resource and cost plans	» Agree draft project order and project manual with PS » Verification of the business case
Roles involved:	» Accounter, Sales » Line department » Controlling	» PS » PMO » PSC	» PS & PM » Any designated PTMs	» PM » Designated PTMs » Experts	» PS » PM
Communication method:	» Individual planning » One-to-one discussions	» Individual planning » One-to-one discussions	» One-to-one discussions » **Initial PS meeting**	» **Planning WS**	» **PS meeting**
Results	» Implementation decision	» Project category » Initial project roles	» Initial draft of project order » **Proposal re. planning process**	» Enhanced project order » Initial draft of project manual	» (provisional) approval of project order

Fig. 14 Example of initiation process

with the project team and the project owner must be determined and corresponding workshops/meetings carried out, in particular the project start workshop and the first regular project owner meeting.

The detailed steps in the project start process can be depicted as shown in Fig. 14.

In order to establish a project organization, a series of organizational elements must be set up and implemented:

- Production of an organizational chart
- Definition of project roles

- Drawing up of a communications plan
- Agreeing of ground rules
- Clarifying of the organizational incorporation of the project into the line organization

In this regard it must be borne in mind that a project organization dos not arise 'to order', rather it has to be actively structured. In any event, it is necessary to involve all the relevant people with know-how in the form of a participative organization. When doing so, account must be taken of internal and external organizational units which are directly linked to the project.

An organizational chart means the organizational structure which defines the temporary information and decision-making structures in projects (Sect. 7.18).

The key challenge which this poses is ensuring acceptance of the interdisciplinary structures which often also span various hierarchical levels.

The defining of project roles involves in particular the specifying of the tasks, competencies and responsibilities of the members of the project organization (Sect. 8). Since project roles are temporary, it can be assumed that the respective role holders also have a permanent role, or other temporary roles, at the same time. In this case, one talks of a multiple role holder principle, which requires managers and experts to have a sound understanding of project management.

Operational effectiveness is ensured by means of an appropriate project communications plan. The precondition for appropriate project communications structures is distinguishing between the process-directing communications structure and the content-related communications structure (e.g. project controlling meeting vs. regularly scheduled project meetings).

Project ground rules enable a common view of expected individual behavior to be established as well as of internal and external interactions, and of agreed sanctions mechanisms if the ground rules are not adhered to.

The organizational incorporation measures govern the delimitation of responsibilities and managerial authorities between the line and project organization. What is crucial at this point is not the organizational strength of the project organization but the transparency and common acceptance of the formal structural boundaries.

The project culture which develops as part of the process of building a project organization is a factor which is absolutely critical to success. The project culture enables a project identity to be established. This process can be supported through active interventions made in connection with the launch of the project. Examples of this are the creation of a project name, and of logos or slogans in projects. The establishing of "rituals" in the course of the project, for example the carrying out of a "lightning update" at the start of every session or meeting, or the creation of time and space for informal interaction (social events, project café, . . .) are some of the elements comprising the active shaping of the project culture.

All the organizational measures are ultimately intended to ensure that the team can function well. The particular challenge in this regard in projects is to arrange and carry out this process of team development as efficiently as possible.

Guidance for targeted team activities in this phase of the project is set out in the known and established team development process (cf. Fig. 15).

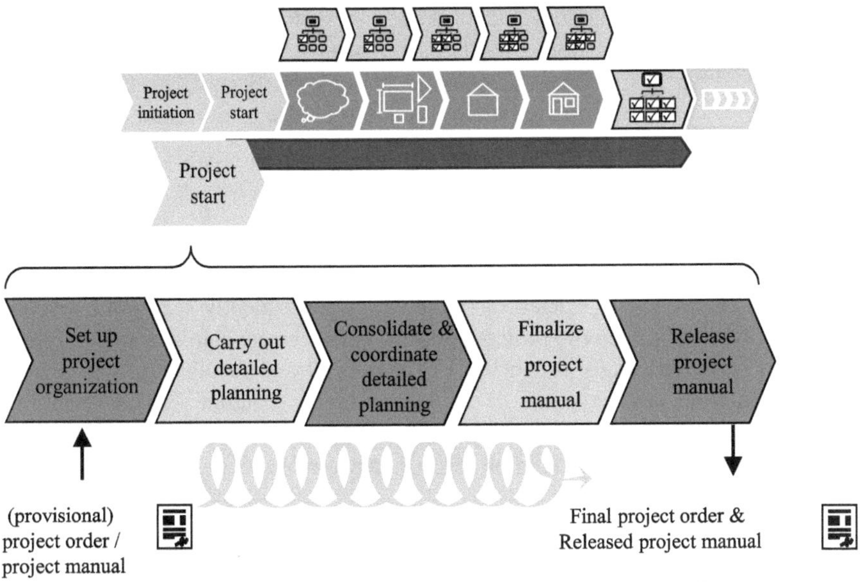

Fig. 15 Project start process

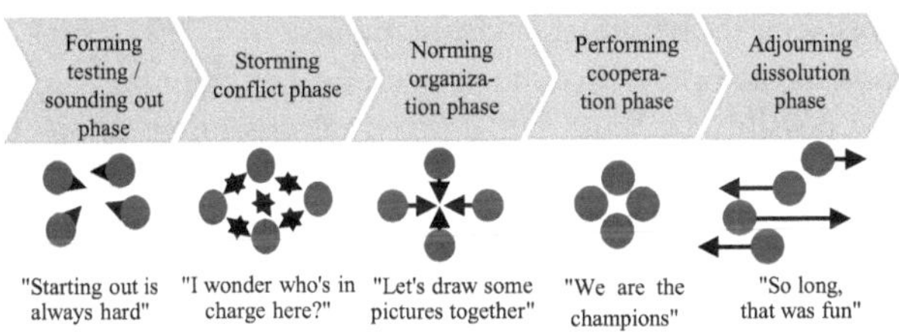

Fig. 16 Team development process

Further project planning methods and techniques are used in the detailed planning process step (cf. Fig. 16).

Key elements of the detailed planning are the allocation of the actual tasks and the work package specification.

An activity distribution chart can be used as a method of allocating the content of tasks (Sect. 7.10). This involves allocating specific responsibilities for work packages according to the people who are responsible for carrying them out and the people who will assist them. The activity distribution chart subsequently also forms the basis of the detailed resource planning.

The work specification is a detailed planning step within the project structure plan. It sets out what the aims, work steps and results of each work package are (Sect. 7.9). Above all, the work package specification forms the basis of the reviewing of progress made with the project.

The detailed planning also includes all the methods used for the in-depth planning of deadlines, resources, and costs. Examples of detailed time schedules are the linked bar chart or the milestone trend analysis (Sect. 7.12). Detail can be achieved in resource and costs planning through the use of time-related plans and graphical presentation options (e.g. histograms).

Key Message

The level of detail of the project planning must match the level of detail used in the project controlling processes.

In practice, the level of detail of the planning is frequently seen not be in line with the data available in the project controlling processes. If it is only possible to achieve a correspondingly rough level of structural and factual detail in project controlling, it makes no sense to undertake highly detailed project planning. Therefore as part of project planning attention should already be paid to the level of detail which is possible in relation to the data available for the project controlling processes.

The next process step involves consolidating and coordinating the detailed planning (cf. Fig. 17).

The aim of this process step is to ensure that a common view of project planning is held by the team. It makes sense to undertake preparatory work in individual or bilateral planning loops. Final coordination of the project planning is carried out in a follow-up workshop to the project start workshop.

Depending on the complexity of the project, further planning loops and planning workshops may possibly be required. In external **customer projects** a need also generally arises for the separation of internal and external coordination cycles since in **customer projects** the customer is intended to be part of the project organization on the one hand, but not all the detailed plans are agreed with the customer (e.g. project costs, project calculations).

The next step is finalizing the project manual (PM) (cf. Fig. 18). The core document within the project manual is the **project order**, which is a formal project document. The project manual contains all the project plans and the project organization and communications structures, and any additional project management tools, such as the project risk analysis, which may be necessary. The project manual gives all the people who are involved in the project ready access to all the information. It ensures the integration of all the project management tools that are used. In the event of changes in personnel, the project history is able to be tracked.

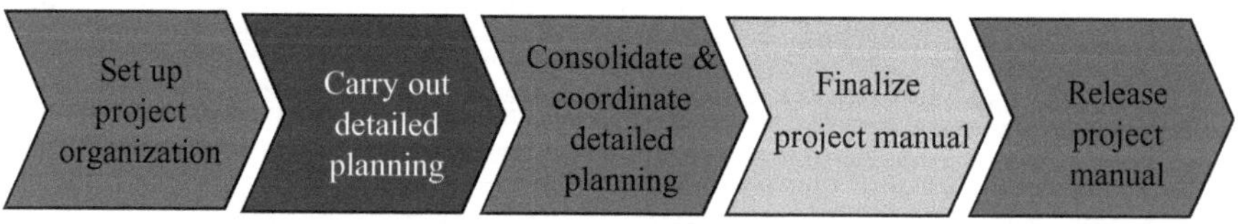

Fig. 17 Process step: "execution of detailed planning"

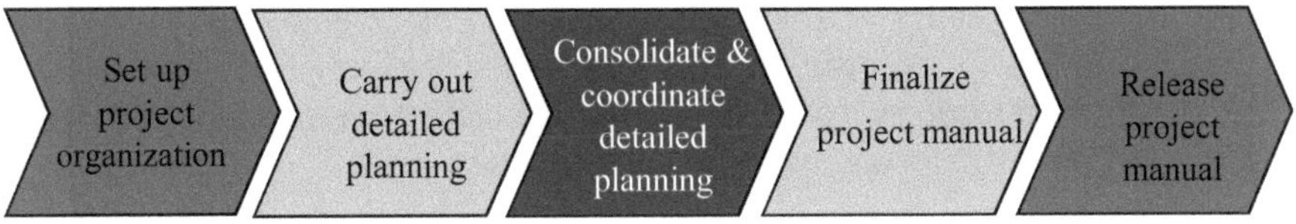

Fig. 18 Process step "consolidating and coordinating detailed planning"

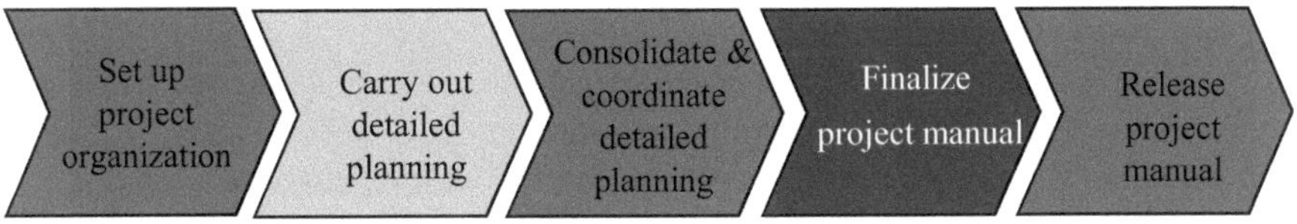

Fig. 19 Process step "finalizing the project manual"

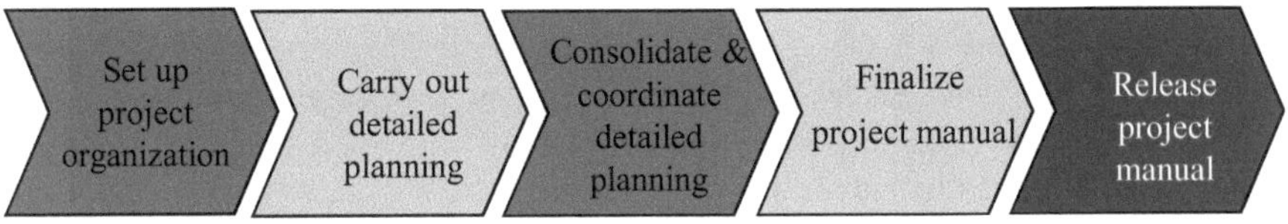

Fig. 20 Process step "approving the project manual"

And not least, the project manual supports organizational learning in the project and in **project-oriented companies** (Sect. 9; Example of next project project manual).

The last step in the project start process is the approval of the project manual by the project owner (cf. Fig. 19).

The precondition for this is that the project manager and the project owner have a common view of the planned course of the project. In this step, the **project order** is formally signed by the project manager and the project owner at a project owner meeting.

This formal action means that the project plans are saved as the project baseline. This gives the project a reference point for subsequent project controlling.

A summarized example of the project start process is shown in Fig. 20.

5.3 Contract Management as a Process that Is Relevant to the Project Initiation and Project Start Process

Project contracts are not specifically regulated by law and they require particularly thorough structuring of the contract, in particular in the case of customer projects. The contractually specified target state can often not be conclusively defined at the time when the contract is concluded within projects.

The necessary setting of goals sometimes takes place gradually, typically at different 'firming-up' or iteration levels during the course of the project. This requires close interaction between the contracting parties, which must be managed through contractual rules and organizational structures.

Key Message
Professional project management is the basis of the successful processing of contracts, but without a sound contract even the best project management does not ensure successful processing of projects.

Holistic consideration of both the drawing up and processing of contracts and the setting up and managing of projects is required. It therefore makes sense to synchronize contract management with the **project management process**.

Customer projects are based on an external/legal contract which cannot be easily amended. The bid phase is frequently separated from project execution in organizational terms, i.e. different people are involved in each case. This leads to there being a risk of a gap in communications at the time when the contract is concluded ("Chinese whispers" or "telephone" effect). In some cases the organizational units involved (Sales and Processing) even have contrary interests.

The project must be suffused with a minimum level of planning in order to enable a valid bid to be submitted. The components of contract management and project management operate in some cases on the basis of redundant information (e.g. customer specifications or specification of services).

A simple measure for dealing with this context appropriately is involving the department concerned right from the drawing up of the bid. If it is a complex **customer project** involving subcontractors, one option is to also involve the key supplier in drawing up the bid, and if necessary in the drafting of the contract. Then it is generally advisable to set the submission of the bid up as a project.

A typical contract management process which ensures integration with the project start process can be set up as shown in Fig. 21.

Realistic contract conditions are important in order not to jeopardize the assignment or project from the very outset. In practice the following ground rules have proved to be useful:

- Description of the requirements to be as detailed as possible.
- A good level of performance comes at a price.
- The supplier's concerns should be taken seriously.
- Take heed of one's own duties to cooperate.
- Critical questioning of whether fixed prices and fixed delivery deadlines are realistic (e.g. in the case of standard services)—a contract with fixed prices and deadlines is often pushed through by the principal before the level of planning precision that is necessary for this can be achieved.
- Since evidence of losses is generally difficult to provide, sanctions which have a noticeable effect must be specified in case of poor performance or non-performance.

	Set up project organization	Carry out detailed planning	Consolidate & coordinate detailed planning	Finalize project manual	Release project manual
Activities:	» Present and validate results obtained to date » Clarify roles, communication, and ground rules	» Draw up WP specification » Estimate detailed deadlines, resources and costs	» Complete bar chart, plan for use of staff and costs plan, risk analysis etc. » Set up project marketing	» Combine all the plans in the project manual and send to all PTMs » Hold last internal round of consultation	» Final presentation of plans to PS/PSC for release » Agree roles and communications structures
Roles involved:	» PM » PTM, PE » if applic. PS	» PM » PTM	» PM » PTM	» PM » Project assistant » PTM	» PS / PSC » PM
Communication method:	» **Kick-off** » **Launch WS**	» Individual plans » One-to-one discussions » Launch WS	» Individual planning » One-to-one discussions » **Follow-up WS**	» Email » One-to-one discussions	» **PS meeting** » **PSC meeting**
Results	» Operationally effective project organization » In line with big picture	» Detailed WP	» Validated and enhanced plans	» Validated and enhanced plans	» Released project manual version 1.0

Fig. 21 Overview of project start process

- The agreeing of interim steps and/or partial services, and the linking of them to the payment dates make better monitoring and management of resources by the supplier possible.

In addition to contract management, claim management is also (cf. also Sect. 4.3 in Chap. 5) a process which is crucial to the success of **customer projects**.

	Acquisition	Drawing up of bid	Contract negotiation	Project handover	Contract analysis & detailed planning
Activities:	» Evaluate customer expectations » Check tech. & comm. achievability » Plan bid process	» Detailed planning of the bid project if applicable » Draw up contractual, comm., content part of bid » Risk assessment » Obtain approval	» Hand bid to customer » Incorporate feedback » Appoint negotiating team » Negotiate contract » Conclude contract	» Appoint project manager and team » Brief project organization » Approve actions of bid team	» Analysis of contract re. parties' duties » Identification of risks/outstand-ing points » Planning of the project
Roles involved:	» Sales	» Sales » Line department	» Sales » Line department	» Sales » Line department » PM	» PM » PTM
Results	» Rough BC » Initial risk assessment » Customer require-ments » Bid planning	» Bid documenta-tion » BC & project plans » Negotiation strategy	» Adjusted bid » Contract doc.	» Project organization set up » Project order » Bid team disbanded	» Implementa-tion planning » Risk analysis » Claim / CR strategy

Fig. 22 Overview of contract management process

5.4 The "Next Level Planning Navigator"

Just like a project, the planning process can also be delineated, planned, set up and managed. From the time when he is appointed, the project manager is responsible for process management. In particular, he has the task of creating transparency in terms of the project-specific planning process. This involves deciding which planning steps should be carried out at the initiation stage, and which during the project start. In addition, various communications structures can be used. In any event, the corresponding process steps and use of project management methods must always be defined according to the actual situation.

The details of what the initiation process and the project start process look like mainly depends on whether there is an official commissioning process for projects

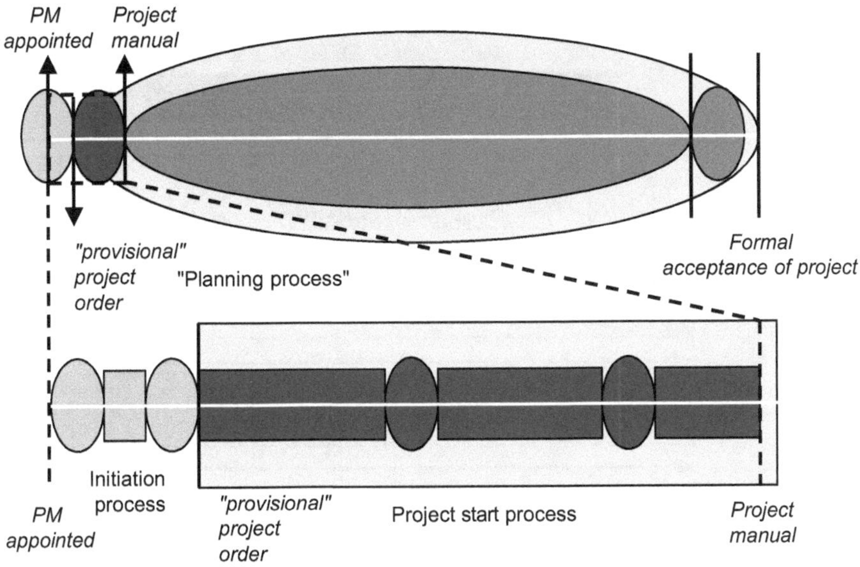

Fig. 23 "Next level planning navigator"

in the company. The "next level planning navigator" can be used to provide structured support for the project manager in his organizing of these processes (cf. Fig. 22).

The "next level planning navigator" helps to match the process levels in the planning process, and it makes it possible to consider a **customer project** from various perspectives. A key challenge is integrating these various points of view, since the levels can shift in relation to each other (cf. Fig. 23).

The delineating of the contents of customer orders determines the subsequent processes. Projects therefore segment processes, i.e. projects are a possible operational/organizational form for implementing a single process step, or several or all of them. The complexity of the project varies depending on how its content is delineated. The nature and scope of project complexity in turn influence the planning process.

The "next level planning navigator" is subdivided into the following levels:

- Generic project management process
- Definition and allocation of the planning and communications process
- Specifying of the contents of the project phases
- Definition and allocation of the deliverables and project management methods

Figure 24 shows a highly complex customer project:

At levels 2 and 3, the "stabilizers" can be used by the project manager in consultation with the project owner according to the requirements made of the

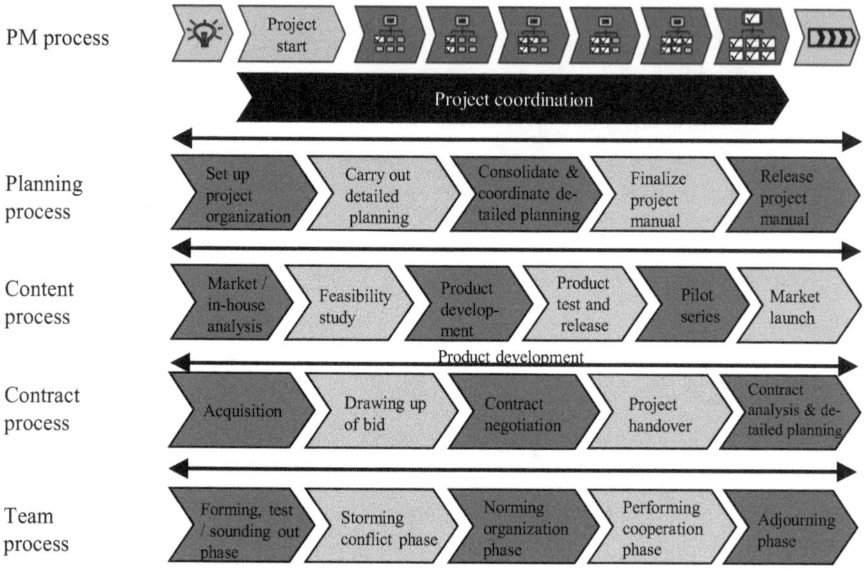

Fig. 24 Process levels in order processing projects

project management process. The relevant deliverables and methods at level 4 are then allocated correspondingly.

This process management tool allows a uniform and transparent procedure to be adopted for organizing the entire planning process in line with the situation.

6 Managing and Concluding Customer Projects

The managing of projects includes the project coordination and project controlling processes.

6.1 Project Coordination Process

The continual quality assurance of the (interim) results of work packages and continual communication within the project organization occur in the project coordination process. In addition, continuous organizing of the relationships with relevant environments is carried out as part of project coordination. A central task within project coordination is the planning of the procurement and use of project resources.

Project coordination is a continuous task extending from project initiating to the formal acceptance of the project and is the responsibility of the project manager.

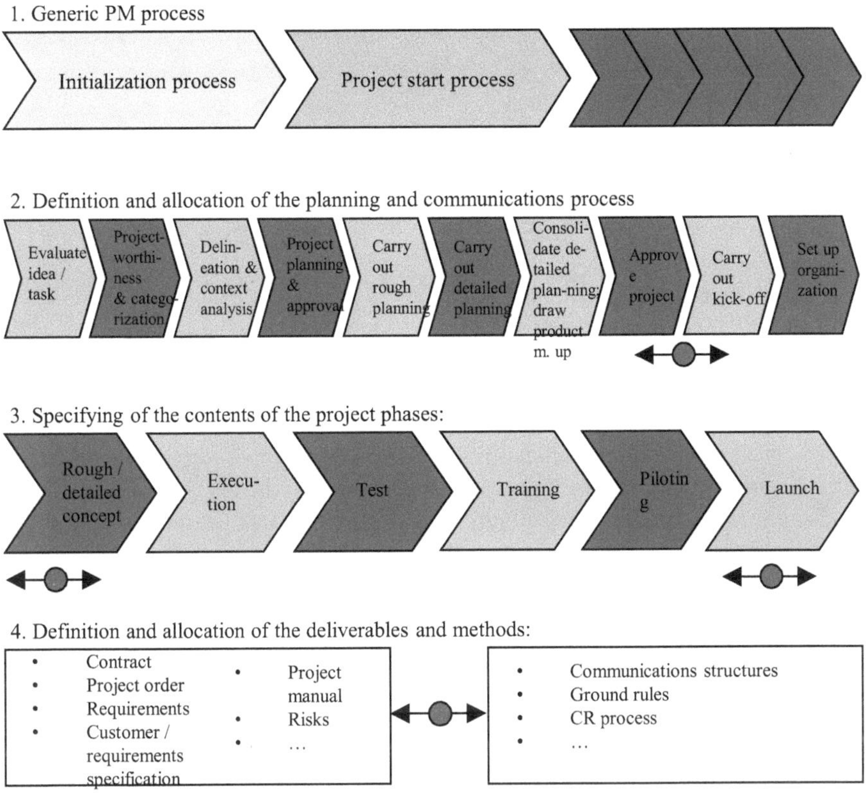

Fig. 25 "Next level planning navigator" (example)

6.2 Project Controlling Process

Project controlling involves the cyclical consideration of the project based on a comparison of actual values to planned values, on a deviation analysis, and on re-planning of the project as a result of this.

Project controlling is a **project management process** which is described in a structured and standardized manner in a company's project management standards. A major factor in its success is the making available of necessary resources as part of the re-planning process step in the individual project controlling cycles (cf. Fig. 25).

The project controlling process can be viewed as a social construct. Controlling is carried out in the project team and is consequently not only the project manager's responsibility. Both hard and soft factors are relevant to project controlling. When considering soft factors, the term "social project controlling" is also used in this context.

Hard factors are:

- Outputs
- Deadlines
- Resources, costs
- Risks

Soft factors are:

- Project organization and communication
- Context of social environments
- Relationships within the project team
- Project culture

The basic course of project controlling involves as a first step the recording of the status of the ongoing work packages by the person who is responsible for work packages. In the "project controlling" work step these actual values are compared with the target values and a deviation analysis is drawn up as a result.

The crucial step is the carrying out of re-planning based on the deviations in terms of outputs, deadlines, resources and costs. The re-planning in the form of an updated plan is summarized in a progress report.

The progress report is approved by the project owner at the project owner meeting in each project controlling cycle.

The last work step consists in communicating the project progress and the project owner's decisions to the project team, and if applicable to the relevant project stakeholders.

In addition, each project controlling cycle is archived in order to have a corresponding project history available. Figure 26 shows this key process within project controlling in graphical form.

The project planning methods form the basis of project controlling.

In principle, all the methods used in planning are to be used in controlling. The following provides a summary list of the methods which are required as a minimum.

- Objectives: Objectives plan
- Context: Project environment analysis, relationship to other projects
- Outputs: Project structure plan, work packages specification
- Deadlines: Milestone schedule, bar chart schedule
- Resources and costs: Resources and costs plan
- Organization and communication: Organizational chart, communications structures, description of roles, ground rules

Practical experience shows that the rigorous and professional use of these basic project management methods is generally perfectly adequate for managing projects successfully.

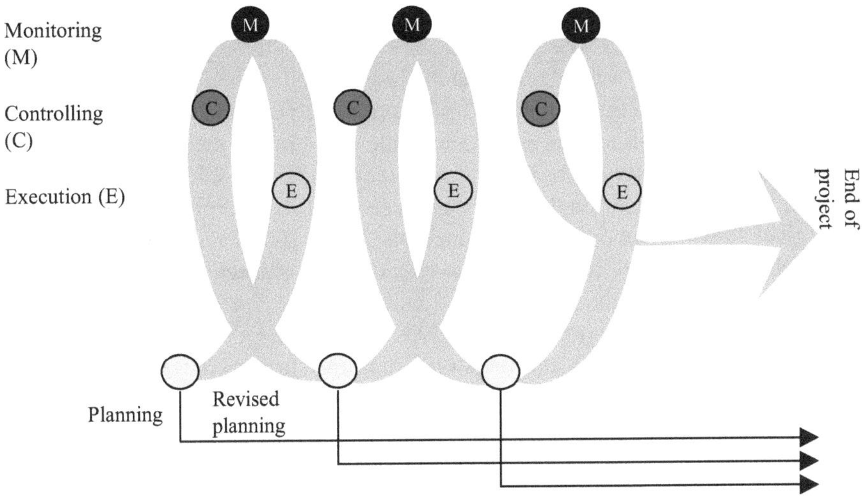

Fig. 26 Project controlling process

Social Project Controlling
The work in interdisciplinary teams spanning different hierarchies requires appropriate management expertise on the part of the project manager. Differing perspectives, diverging goals, and also conflicts and resistance are a fact of life within project teams, due to them being a temporary organizational form.

Added to this is the complexity of the influence exerted by various stakeholders who are in any event crucial to the success of the project, and even to its very existence. This context merits being explicitly addressed with a structured, social form of project controlling.

Key Message
As a rule, projects fail not due to issues or problems which are technical in nature or which relate to content, but due to the social relationships within and between the relevant internal and external environments.

Social conflicts take priority! Based on this hypothesis, structures which allow reflection and feedback in the team are required. Examples of tools for this are the "lightning update" and the "mood barometer".

In the "lightning update" the project team members and the project manager reflect on the following three questions: How are things going? How was it? What is outstanding?

The question: How are things going? is not in this case a question asked by way of politeness, but an opportunity for each person who is involved in the project to personally bring up with the others the events which have taken place, whether they are positive or negative. This prevents hidden conflicts about content-related issues which are not relevant to the joint work being acted out in it, and in particular in the controlling cycles. This consequently ensures functional effectiveness.

The question: How was it? relates to the last controlling period, the work results and the work process. Supplementary questions which can be asked are: What has gone well? What hasn't gone well? Above all, these questions also form a structured feedback opportunity for the project manager who can reflect on the management of the project based on the feedback received from his project team members. This gives him the opportunity to reduce his "blind spots" (cf. Luft and Ingham 1955), and above all to intervene in the course of the project either directly or by making adjustments to the process management.

The question: What is outstanding? gives the team members the opportunity to articulate their expectations and fears regarding the further course of the project. The consequences of this may be further work packages or agreements, or also ground rules for cooperation.

The "mood barometer" provides a simple snapshot of the team member's personal—usually emotional—attitude to the status of the project.

It is advisable in this regard to bring the mood barometer into line with the project controlling cycles, and consequently to get an appropriate picture of how the project team's mood changes.

What is crucial in this regard is the joint reflection undertaken by the project team and the project manager, based on their current overall mood, relating to issues such as the team's operational effectiveness, feedback on the course of the project, and the raising of issues which are not clear etc.

The overall mood which is depicted over the course of the project (cf. Fig. 27) is also an opportunity to identify trends, and it can be used as an early warning system in relation to team performance.

As well as these two tools used for the social controlling of projects, countless other methods and tools exist for this purpose.

What is crucial is not how they operate, but the fact that enough time and space is devoted to social project controlling in the cyclical project controlling meetings.

The results of the analysis and reflection, and of the feedback process as a whole, must be jointly recoded in agreements and measures. Not doing this is a cardinal

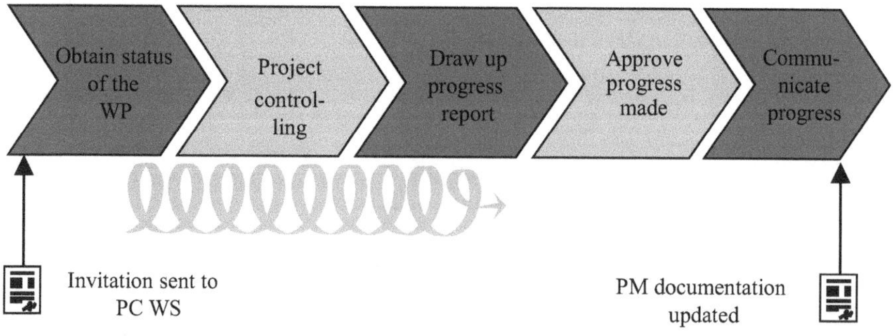

Fig. 27 Key process within project controlling

error since the failure to draw the necessary conclusions from feedback and reflection usually leads to the people involved becoming demotivated, and to a massive reduction in their willingness to "buy into" the processes of "social project controlling".

The conclusions drawn may be the adapting of role definitions or of communications structures. The project ground rules can be expanded on a cyclical basic. However, more sizable interventions in the field of social project controlling are also possible, such as changing team members, or alternatively the assembling of new teams.

The fundamental results of these controlling measures are incorporated into the project progress report.

6.3 Relevant Controlling Processes in Customer Projects

In practice, the processing of **customer projects** always involves changes being initiated by the customer in relation to objectives, outputs, deadlines, resources and costs. The term 'change requests' is used in this connection, and these do of course have to be appropriately processed in the project controlling cycles.

Change requests are generally additional orders based on an amendment of the contract, and are therefore initiated by the principal (customer) in most cases. If they are processed in a properly professional and structured way, these additional orders represent additional business for the contractor, and as such they improve the contribution margin in **customer projects**—sometimes significantly.

The primary objective for the project manager is to reach mutual agreement with the customer, i.e. the external principal, regarding additional/amending requirements and the corresponding additional expenditure in the project.

It must been ensured that change requests are supplemented in the form of contract amendments—before the project manager and his core project team provide the project outputs.

The result of the change request process is a change order, or variation order. These lead to initial measures and the subsequent course of action being jointly discussed, and also agreed within the core project team, and to the project owner's sign-of being obtained for them.

Figure 28 shows a standard change request process.

Structured and professional use of change requests secures the long-term success of the project.

6.4 The Project Close-Down Process

The project close-down process is to be understood as a process which has as its aim the formal completion of the project. The wrap-up process primarily involves the structured transition of the process organization into the line organization.

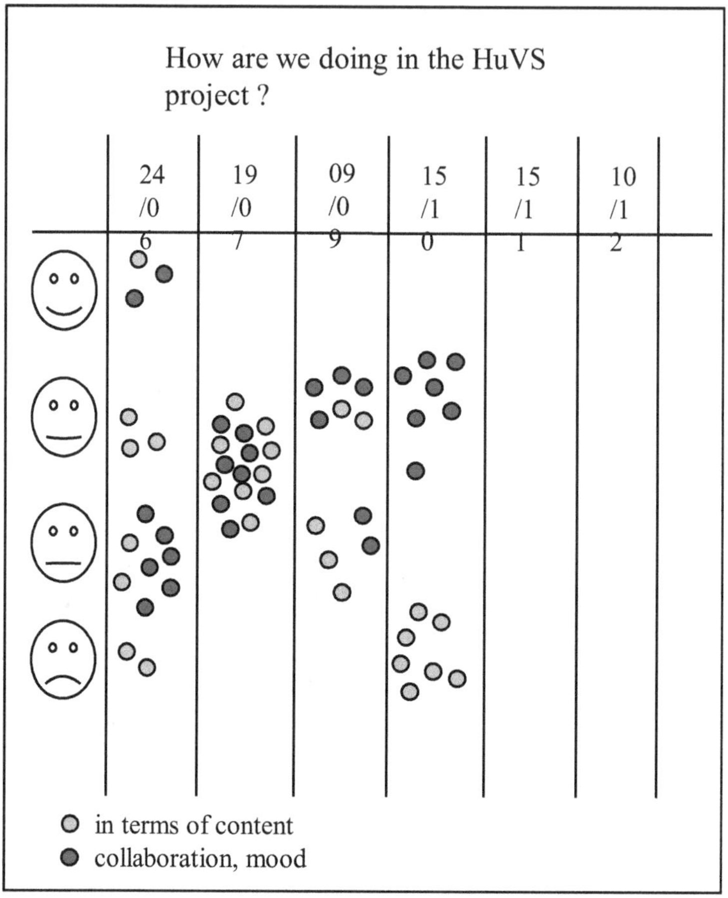

Fig. 28 Example of a picture of overall mood

This phase is critical to the success of the completion of the project since in practice the responsibilities within the line organization are not defined and agreed, or not adequately so, during the dissolution of the **temporary project organization**. The result of this is that projects become a "never ending story" because people who were responsible in the project organization which was previously in place are still viewed as being the people responsible even after the completion of the project, and are still turned to as such. Moreover, the transfer of know-how to the permanent organization and to other projects is a relevant subject matter for ensuring organizational learning in **project-oriented companies**.

For the project organization, and the core project team in particular, the project close-down process involves a structured freeing up of resources and energies. This step is important since tendencies to wind things up can often be observed when projects are approaching completion, but without unclear process areas having been defined, and consequently without any common view of the duties, responsibilities, and competencies of the individuals who are involved in the project.

Another key element is the internal and external communication of the completion of the project and the project results. Internally the primary task, apart from the transparency of the activities of the project close-down process, is to undertake an evaluation of the project results. The focus of the external communication activities is the active dissolution of relationships between the project and the relevant project stakeholders (social environments). The relationships with various environments can be dissolved at different points in time.

Finally, activities, measures and agreements for the post-project phase are jointly decided on by the project team and the project manager together with the project owner. This process step is of course closely connected with the transferring of the project organization into the line organization.

Key Message
The quality of the project close down can be measured at the end of the project close-down process, and by the results of it.

The efficient and effective organizing of the project close-down process is a final criterion of the project's success. However, practical experience shows that this **project management process** requires a particularly high level of energy from all the people involved.

The project close-down process must be explicitly planned. Its timing requires appropriate project management expertise:

- Agreeing of the timing: The project close-down process generally starts before all the tasks relating to the project's content have been completed.
- Sensitivity to decreasing energy levels: For example, avoiding having project meetings attended by stand-ins.
- Deciding on the formal acceptance of the project: it must be ensured that the usefulness of the **temporary organization** is not forgotten, whilst simultaneously ensuring that the project organization is transferred into the line organization in a timely manner.
- Formal acceptance before all objectives fully achieved: Taking account of claims, which can be handled by the line organization in the post-project phase.

Compared to other **project management processes**, little has been written about the completion of projects, and there is consequently little theoretical work on the subject. However, above all in the IPMA, PMI® and PRINCE 2® international standards, the need for professionalization, and therefore ultimately standardization, is becoming increasingly clear.

Figure 29 recaps the main steps in the project close-down process.

A first step in drawing up the final project report is the final defining of the **delineation of the project**. This also provides the basis for an evaluation of the achievement of the project objectives.

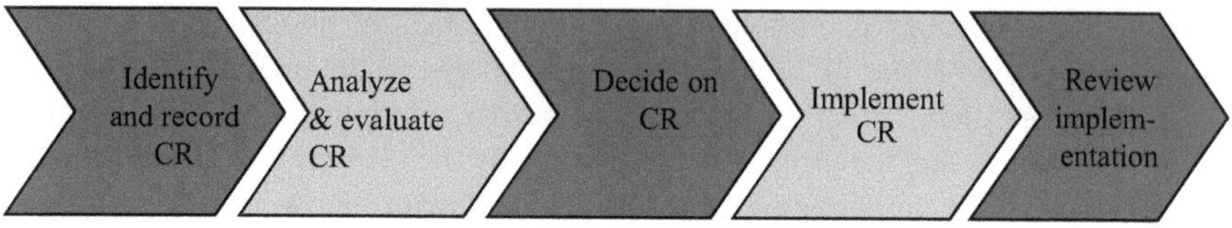

Activities:	• Identify change • Submit CR application • If applicable, initial assessment by applicant • Send application	• Classify CR • Record CR in change control list • Analysis of implications for proj. • Evaluate CR	• Decide on CR: approve, amend, reject, defer • Inform applicant & PM	• Update project plan • Communicate changes • Implement changes	• Controlling of progress with outputs • Close and invoice CR
Roles involved:	• Applicant	• PM • Person resp. for WP	• PS / PSC • Change control board	• PM • Person resp. for WP	• PM • Person resp. for WP
Method of communication:	• CR form • One-to-one discussions	• Individual planning • One-to-one discussions • Controlling WS	• PS / PSC meeting	• One-to-one discussions • Written information	• Controlling WS
Results	• Change request	• Evaluated CR • Updated change control list	• Change order • Updated change control list	• Updated project manual	• Updated change control list

Fig. 29 Standard change request process

A further step is the documenting of the actual course of the project: how did the project actually go in practice? Based on the evaluation of objectives and the actual course of the project, an assessment of the success of the project can be made by the project team as a whole together with the project owner.

The balancing of different viewpoints is important in this regard, since in practice differing views are always held on this subject due to the involvement of people from a number of disciplines, and sometimes these differences are large.

An important aspect is the internal and external marketing of the project results. In accordance with the principle "Do good and talk about it", the final project report can be used as a basis for both for internal and external communication.

The project documentation and securing of knowledge work step entails the completion of the project manual, which involves in particular the "as is" presentation of outputs, deadlines, resources and costs. This final documentation is among other things a means of securing the knowledge gained in the project.

Based on this, the transfer of know-how can take place within the organization. This comprises firstly the lessons learned within the project team, and secondly recommendations of actions to be taken by the company, and/or for other ongoing and future projects.

The handing over of residual activities work step means both the planning of tasks for the post-project phase and the dissolution of the **temporary project organization**. This involves carrying out the following activities:

- Evaluating the project manager and the project team
- Handover of activities, responsibility and competencies to the line organization
- Planning the use of resources, and
- Informing relevant project environments of the dissolution of the project organization

Formal acceptance of the project is provided by the project owner in consultation with the project manager at a final project owner meeting. The approved final project report is handed to the projects steering group (project portfolio management) and the corresponding line managers.

The project manager then formally ends the project at a project close down workshop. It is also a good idea in any event to hold one last joint social event for the project team and the project owner.

6.5 Organizational Learning in Projects

In practice it is evident that projects represent the form of organization which is the least able to learn. In permanent organizational structures such as departments or divisions for example, organizational learning can be organized much more easily because it can also be standardized.

Projects run once only, and what one sees in practice is that individuals with know-how relating to the project are "scattered to the four winds", or return to the line organization as quickly as possible, or are already busy with the next project.

Key Message
Structured organizational learning in projects can significantly improve efficiency and effectiveness of project work in **project-oriented companies**.

One does not just learn from successes, but above all from the many "wrinkles", conflicts and barriers, and from failed measures etc. This does however necessitate addressing the *lessons learned* in projects in a structured way. Tools for organizational learning are firstly the documents that have already been mentioned, such as the final project report or the final project presentation.

However, analogous methods can also be used, such as holding a project 'open day' event. This involves preparing the results for a general target audience (management, experts, other project managers and project teams), both in terms of their content and symbolically in the form of artefacts relating to the project work.

The use of this method is appropriate above all if several projects which have been completed or are in the process of being completed can be jointly presented at an "open day" event. This does not involve giving a presentation in the conventional sense, rather "artists" present their "works of art" which are marveled at and

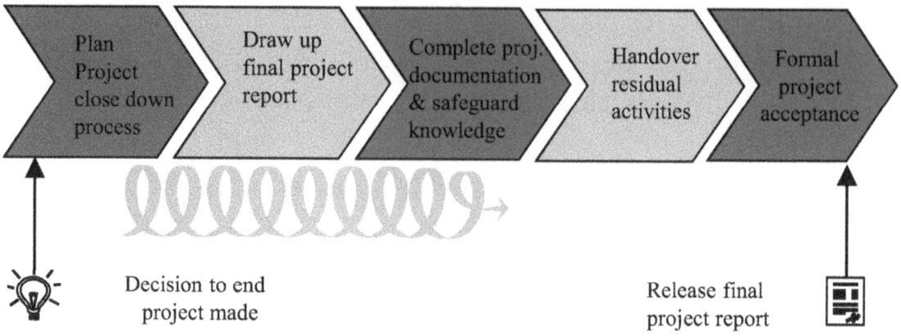

Fig. 30 Project close-down process

interpreted and discussed by the guests. Experience in practice shows that this setting enables lasting learning to be achieved because the event itself at least is memorable.

In highly developed **project-oriented companies** knowledge bases are also used. A proven technique in this respect is to set up the basic clustering of the knowledge base in line with the **project management processes**, i.e. launch, controlling, and wrap-up. The individual learning points within these specific processes are documented by the project manager in a structured way which also shows the respective contact persons, findings and results, and any project plans that refer to them.

As a matter of principle, it is advisable to file the completed projects at least in a project archive.

Finally, some further methods of working and issues relating to the completion of the project are presented which are helpful for organizational learning in particular (cf. Fig. 30).

- My view of the results of the project in relation to individual project objectives is. . .
- What worked particularly well was. . .?
- What worked particularly poorly was. . .?
- How do I feel overall about the completion of the project?

7 Use of Project Management Methods

In the following chapter the most important methods and tools are described in detail and supplemented with practical examples.

The methods and tools are the basic know-how, the tools of the trade for the project manager. Another crucial requirement for the effective and efficient use of the **project management methods** is for the project owner and the core project team to have a fundamental understanding of the **project management methods**.

In practice, the methods and techniques of project management are a key component of skills enhancement measures for specific target groups.

The following method headings are described:

- Review of conformity to strategy
- Review of project-worthiness
- Project name
- Project logo
- Project order
- Project environment analysis
- Analysis of relationships with other projects
- Project structure plan
- Work package specifications
- Project activity distribution chart (responsibility matrix)
- Milestone schedule
- Milestone trend analysis
- Project bar chart (Gantt diagram)
- Plan for use of project personnel (project resources plan)
- Project costs plan
- Business case
- Claim management
- Organizational chart
- Allocation of competencies between the project and line operations
- Relational descriptions of project roles
- Project communications structures
- Project-specific ground rules
- Risk analysis of the course of the project
- Earned Value Analysis (EVA)

7.1 Review of Conformity to Strategy

The "project initiating" multiple project management process step involves reviewing the project objectives contained in a project proposal in relation to their conformity to the strategy of the multiple project management area of reference. The outcome of the review of conformity to strategy is a statement of the level of conformity to strategy which is part of the basis of decision-making in relation to project approval.

Preparatory area- or department-specific requirements must be established for the use of a review of conformity to strategy. For this, the strategy of the business unit must be described, which may, for instance, be derived from the corporate strategy or result from the business unit's product portfolio.

Furthermore, area-specific scaling must be established. Depending on the area of use, various levels of detail may be useful in the scaling (e.g. project objectives correspond to corporate strategy: 100 %; project objectives do not correspond to corporate strategy: 0 %; or establishing of defined intermediate levels).

In the end, an area-specific assessment procedure must be drawn up in order to assign the project objectives to the corporate strategy.

7.2 Review of Project-Worthiness

A project is a scheme which is of such complexity in terms of content and its organization that it demands the use of employees from several organizational units (interdisciplinary make-up of the project team). The minimizing of the objective-attainment risks (outcome risk, deadline risk, costs risk and quality risk) requires the use of special tools, and it justifies the additional workload involved in planning, budgeting for, monitoring, and managing the completion of tasks, as well as the formation of a temporary project organizational unit.

The evaluation of project-worthiness is carried out by project services during the project initiating process. Defined characteristics are used to differentiate between standard tasks, schemes, projects and programs.

7.3 Project Name

Employees from various corporate and/or departmental cultures are involved in interdepartmental or inter-company projects. If no specific project culture is defined in the project team, these various cultures clash, and conflicts may arise. The specifying of a project name can provide a sense of identity and contribute to the creation of a project culture. A memorable and distinctive project name contributes to the identification of the project and to improved external communication (e.g. "prof pm reloaded" similar to the film "Matrix Reloaded").

7.4 Project Logo

The provision of information and communication are a key factor in the success of projects. Also, in **project-oriented companies** several projects are carried out simultaneously and in parallel. Like the project name, a unique, distinctive project logo contributes to the identification of the project, to the recognition of project-related information, and to improved external communication. In addition, a project-specific logo helps to establish a feeling of "togetherness" within the project team, and it fosters team development processes as well as a project culture.

7.5 Project Order

The **project order** is a written agreement between the project owner and the project manager regarding important framework conditions for the project. The **project order** (cf. Fig. 31) is the formal commission for the launching of a project and consequently it is the trigger for the project start process. Through it the project manager assumes responsibility for achieving the agreed objectives with the agreed outputs within the agreed time schedules and the specified budget. In return, the

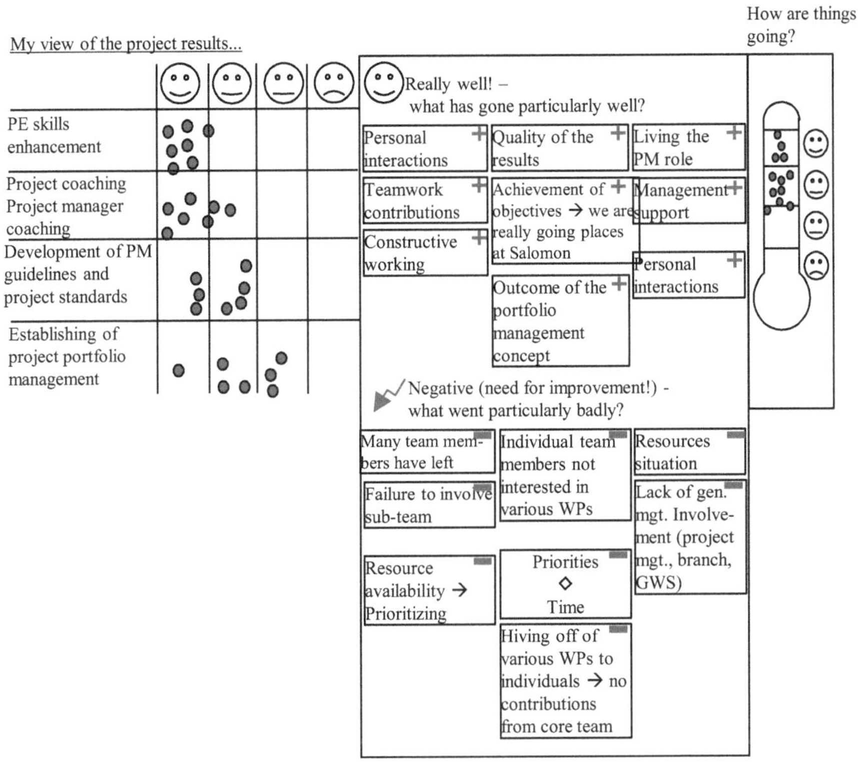

Fig. 31 Examples of methods of working and issues relating to the completion of the project

project owner promises to provide the project manager with the agreed resources and the agreed budget. Their signatures underline the reciprocal agreement.

Adjustments and additions may be made however in the course of the detailed planning, so that a distinction can be made between the provisional and the final **project order**. If in the course of the project the framework conditions alter to such an extent that the main factors (those relating to timing or of a factual or social nature) change, this necessitates the updating of the project order and the associated concluding of a fresh agreement between the project owner and the project manager.

The **project order** is drawn up based on the **delineation of the project** and the analysis of the project context, and it must have at least the following contents:

- Project name
- Start date/time; end event/time and date
- What are and are not project objectives
- Content of the project (project phases)
- Project resources and costs
- Project owner, project manager, core project team

7.6 Project Environment Analysis

The project environment analysis is based on the analysis of the project's social context. It is a tool for managing the social relationships within a project, and it examines the project's relationships with the relevant environments. Relevant environments means all the people or institutions which may have an influence (positive and/or negative) on the project (cf. Fig. 32).

The project environment analysis firstly involves collecting, listing and grouping all the relevant environments within the project team. They are then represented in a project environment diagram. If all the relevant environments have been recorded in a structured form of presentation, the project environments can be analyzed in terms of their relationships to the project (reciprocal expectations, potentials, and conflicts).

Based on this, it is possible to develop strategies and measures for organizing relationships in a project environment table. Moreover, continual "social controlling" can be supported throughout the project period.

7.7 Analysis of Relationships with Other Projects

A project is frequently connected with other projects which are being carried out or are planned. The so-called factual context analysis involves analyzing the connections with other projects and the corporate strategy from the perspective of the project, and organizing them in the form of measures.

Such relationships may produce synergies or lead to conflicts. This analysis facilitates the organizing of the transfer of information and the organizing of consultations. As in the case of the project environment analysis, either a diagram (cf. Fig. 33) or a project table (cf. Fig. 34) can be used as the actual tool.

7.8 Project Structure Plan

The project structure plan (PSP) is a structured representation of the outputs that are to be provided in a project. The outputs can be subdivided into phases (2nd level process-oriented) and work packages (3rd and following levels process- and object-oriented).

The work packages should be able to be planned and monitored, i.e. the throughput period for any work package should not be longer than the sequence of the project controlling cycles. In addition, they need to be clearly assigned by the person who is responsible for work packages.

The PSP is the key planning and controlling tool as well as the key communication tool for the project owner, project manager, project team and relevant project environments, and it forms the integrative basis for all the following planning tools (time schedule, personnel resources plan, costs plan, activity distribution chart, work packages specification). The PSP is drawn up within the core project team

Get detail data

next project

project assignment

ITSys

start event:	start date*:
kick-off meeting started	02.07.2014

end event:	end date*:
it system approved	27.03.2015

objectives:

1 the it system meets the technical and legal requirements
2 users are able to use the it system (practically and technically)
3 cost reduction of the supported process by 100,000 € until the end of 2012

non-objectives:

1 complete exchange of the existing it system
2 realisation of interfaces to the it system abroad the enterprise borders (to suppliers and customers)

critical factors for success and main risks:

main tasks*:

description	date
PROJECT MANAGEMENT	27.03.15
ANALYSIS AND DECISION	24.08.14
DETAIL PLANNING	03.10.14
IMPLEMENTATION	16.01.15
TEST AND TRAINING	13.03.15
LAUNCH	20.03.15

resources / costs*:

cost types	efforts (md)	costs (€)
personnel	517,0	258.500,0
personnel ext.	12,0	12.000,0
third-party costs		12.000,0
other costs		27.700,0
Maier	technology	

project owner*:		project manager*:	
Hans Gruber	headquarter	Günther Maier	TECH

pm team*:

- Maria Gates	IT	- Josef Balmer	TECH
- Susanne Dell	IT	- Sophie Huber	IT
- Lutz Bene	TECH	- Alexander Peschke	IT
- Martin Sprenger	HR	- Ludwig Rostoff	EXT
- Herbert Doku	TECH		

Hans Gruber, (project owner) Günther Maier, (project manager)

Fig. 32 Next project example of a project order

Refresh

project stakeholder analysis

ITSys

next project

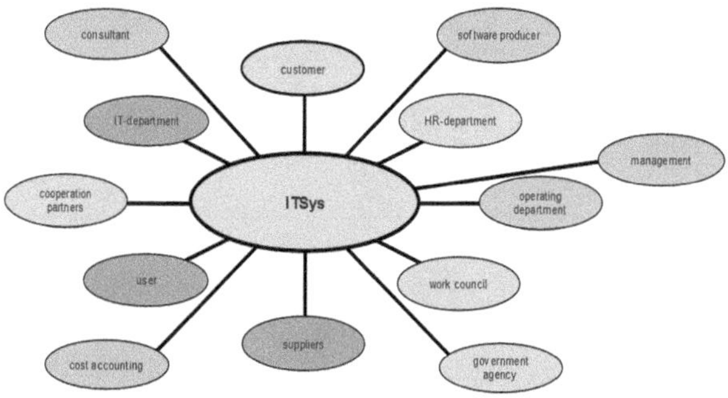

stakeholder/projects	evaluation	relation	measures	responsibility	date
customer	neutral	Basically positive if there are no more wrong productions, perhaps also rearrangements of different forms	Maintain the possible same terminology, in case of rearrangements inform customers as early as possible	Maier	constantly
suppliers	critical	There are probably rearrangements necessary, some suppliers have old electronic interfaces	A contact person of the main supplier is integrated in the project	Maier	constantly
cooperation partners	neutral	Cooperation partners are probably not concerned	none planned	Maier	01.01.15
operating department	supporting	Are the main stakeholders, management and employees interested in change	Use motivation (no concrete measures planned at the moment)	-	-
IT-department	critical	Still a lot of insecurity concerning solution (qualification need), IT department is mostly overloaded	Clear separation of concept and realization, when required integration of a consultant, detailled resource planning with nlc phb xl	Maier	15.07.14
HR-department	neutral	Involved in project, no shortage of resources expected	none planned	-	-
user	critical	Only some users have a negative position to the project. If the users don't accept the system it will fail.	Very early integration by interviews in the analysis, invitation of a user's representative, training of the users already with the beta version to get usability feedback	Sprenger	constantly
work council	neutral	Basically against changes in the enterprise, sensitive data and additional efforts might cause a problem.	Should get current information, keep a positive contact	Sprenger	constantly
software producer	supporting	Basically positive, there is a risk that the quality does not meet the promised expectations	Use interest, take not necessarily the economical provider (trust base must exist)	Gates	during SW analysis
consultant	supporting	Bring in his know how on implementing and customizing an IT system	Integration in the delicate phases of the concept and implementing, because the IT department experience is missing	Gates	on demand
cost accounting	supporting	Interested in rearrangement, has problems with wrong information from the operating department	Include in analysis	Sprenger	during SW analysis
government agency	neutral	IT rearrangements should have no official relevance	In doubt clear with legal department (no concrete measures planned)	-	-
management	supporting	Is interested in a solution	In case of shortages escalate up to managment	Maier	on demand

Fig. 33 Next project project environment analysis

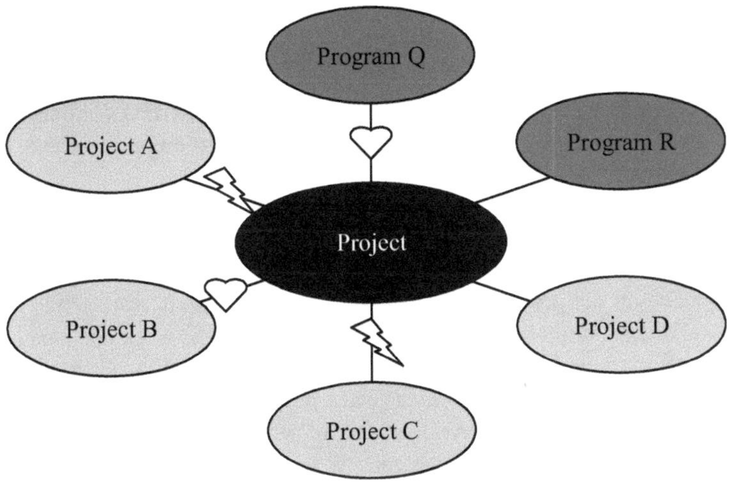

Fig. 34 Factual context analysis

Project / Program	Relationship (potential / conflicts)	Measures	Responsi-bility	Dead-line
Project X	• Market analysis may be useful • Competes for same resources	• Obtaining of the results • Agreeing of availability		

Fig. 35 Factual context analysis table

(interdisciplinary approach) with the aid of creative techniques (post-its), and it should be presented with the help of IT systems.

The starting point for drawing up the PSP is the delineation of the project from a timing and factual perspective. If the project is sufficiently complex, the drawing up of a PSP requires the presentation of a results plan which subdivides the overall entity into corresponding areas to be focused on (partial results/deliverables).

Firstly, the 6–8 phases of the project are defined. In this regard, the process-oriented presentation of the phases is a critical factor in achieving structures which can be continuously planned and controlled. In line with the phases, corresponding work packages are defined in a top-down manner which comprise the verb (activity) and noun (object). Each work package and each phase must be provided with a PSP code so that each work package can be clearly assigned.

Based on the PSP, the detailed work package specifications and the workflow plans and time schedules can then be drawn up, the manpower requirements estimated, the project costs planned, and risk planning and quality assurance can also be carried out and the project can be documented. Figure 35 shows the next project project structure plan as an example.

7.9 Work Package Specifications

The work package specification is based on the project structure plan (PSP) and provides a detailed description of work packages (objectives, tasks, inputs/outputs). This method provides a high level of guidance, in particular for extensive and complicated work packages.

The work package specification provides a detailed description and delineation of the content and results of a work package (WP) from a quantitative and qualitative perspective in order to ensure that all the people who are involved in the project (above all the project manager and the person who is responsible for work packages) have a common understanding of what a specific work package is. Work package specifications may also contain further information, such as resource outlays, duration, or criteria for measuring progress with outputs, as shown in Fig. 36. A specification is not required for all work packages, but only for those the nature and scope of which is unclear.

Work package specifications are drawn up by the person who is responsible for work packages and are agreed in the project team. As well as the increased precision of planning which they allow, work package specifications are also a valuable supplementary tool for the controlling of outputs.

7.10 Project Activity Distribution Chart (Responsibility Matrix)

Due to their complexity, projects require cooperation between several people, and often even cooperation between several organizational units. The activity distribution chart (cf. Fig. 37) is used for the detailed planning of the allocation of tasks, as the basis of objectives agreements, and for conflict management. The starting point for the activity distribution chart is the project structure plan (PSP), and also the project organization and the project environment analysis.

An activity distribution chart is arranged in the form of a 2-dimensional matrix. The work packages are listed in the rows, and the project roles are listed in the columns (project owner, project manager, project team members). The roles which are to be undertaken are shown in the intersection cells of the matrix (V = responsibility, i.e. person responsible for work package; M = cooperation; I = receives or provides information, and E = decision).

7.11 Milestone Schedule

A milestone is a key event in the course of the project, e.g. the project start, the putting together of a work package, the issuing of an approval, or the end of the project.

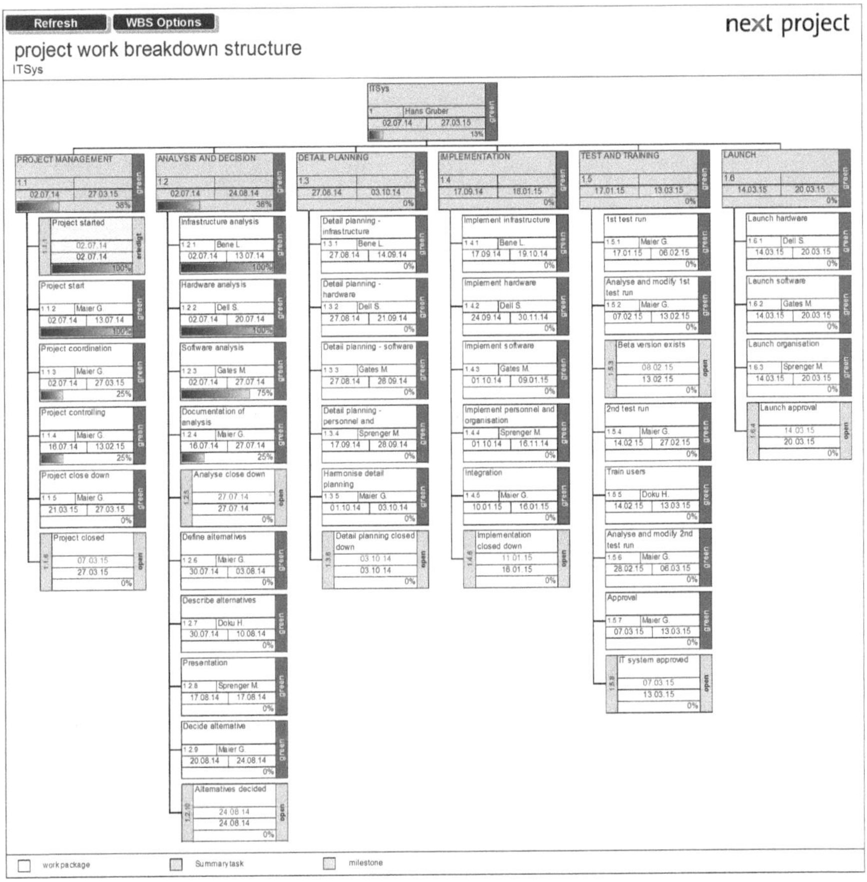

Fig. 36 Next project project structure plan

The milestone schedule provides the rough time scheduling of the whole project by listing the timing of key, critical project events. In addition, during controlling the milestone schedule provides an overview of the current status of the project, and it is therefore a suitable tool for communicating with the project owner.

The basis for the milestone schedule (cf. Fig. 38) is the project structure plan (PSP). Initially, time-critical events within the project are defined and listed. Then, dates are assigned to the milestones (base/current/actual), which are expressed in terms of events and comprise a verb and a noun.

Seven to nine milestones should be defined per project, and the project start and end are obligatory milestones. A milestone should be formulated for each phase/controlling cycle. The milestone dates can form the basis for milestone trend analysis.

workpackage specifications — **next project**

ITSys

wbs code	1.1.2	work package	Project start		
progress	100%	responsibility	Maier G.		
status	green	start	02.07.14	end	13.07.14
milestone		resources	14.0	costs	8.750,00

WP content

» Prepare project start
» Planning and execution of project start workshop
» Definition of project boundaries and project context, carrying out of project context analysis
» Prepare detailed project plans (scope, schedule, resources, costs, risks)
» Establishment of project organisation, building of teams, distribution of responsibilities
» Adjustment of boundaries and plan details with the project owner
» Documentation of project planning and project handbook

WP results

» Project objectives, project plans, project organisation, risk management plan
» Project handbook

WP progress measuring

Fig. 37 Next project work package specifications

7.12 Milestone Trend Analysis

The milestone trend analysis is used for the monitoring of time scheduling. It is mainly an information and visualization tool, but not a tool for researching causes. Preconditions for the use of milestone trend analysis are a realistic time schedule and an open work atmosphere. Since the estimating of adherence to milestone dates can only be carried out subjectively, it is important to create an atmosphere in which it is possible to admit to mistakes.

Figure 39 shows how in the case of milestone trend analysis the originally scheduled milestone dates are entered in a right-angled triangle along the vertical axis, and the reporting time points are entered at the same scale along the horizontal axis (depending on the project period these vary between every 2 weeks and every quarter).

The response of the person who is responsible for a milestone to the question: "When will your milestone be reached" provides both the reporting date/time and the coordinates of the milestone. If dates are repeatedly postponed, the line rises. If the schedule is adhered to, the line is horizontal. If the line falls, deadlines are reached earlier than planned.

next project

RACI - matrix

ITSys

no.	wbs code	description	responsib.	Gruber H.[1]	Maier G.[2]	Müller M.	Herz G.	Gates M.[3]	Dell S.[3]	Bene L.[3]	Sprenger M.[3]	Doku H.[3]	Balmer J.[3]	Huber S.[3]	Peschke A.[3]	Rostoff L.[3]
			project role													
1	**1**	**ITSys**	**Hans Gruber**													
2	**1.1**	**PROJECT MANAGEMENT**														
3	*1.1.1*	*Project started*														
4	1.1.2	Project start	Maier G.	A	R			C	C	C	C	C				
5	1.1.3	Project coordination	Maier G.		R											
6	1.1.4	Project controlling	Maier G.	A	R			C	C	C	C	C				
7	1.1.5	Project close down	Maier G.	A	R			C	C	C	C	C				
8	*1.1.6*	*Project closed*														
9	**1.2**	**ANALYSIS AND DECISION**														
10	1.2.1	Infrastructure analysis	Bene L.							R	C		C			
11	1.2.2	Hardware analysis	Dell S.						R					C		
12	1.2.3	Software analysis	Gates M.					R							C	
13	1.2.4	Documentation of analysis	Maier G.		R			C	C	C	C	C				
14	*1.2.5*	*Analyse close down*														
15	1.2.6	Define alternatives	Maier G.		R			C	C	C	C					
16	1.2.7	Describe alternatives	Doku H.									R				
17	1.2.8	Presentation	Sprenger M.		C			C	C	C	R	C				
18	1.2.9	Decide alternative	Maier G.	A	R											
19	*1.2.10*	*Alternatives decided*														
20	**1.3**	**DETAIL PLANNING**														
21	1.3.1	Detail planning - infrastructure	Bene L.							R	C		C			
22	1.3.2	Detail planning - hardware	Dell S.						R					C		
23	1.3.3	Detail planning - software	Gates M.					R							C	
24	1.3.4	Detail planning - personnel and organisation	Sprenger M.								R					C
25	1.3.5	Harmonise detail planning	Maier G.	A	R			C	C	C	C	C				
26	*1.3.6*	*Detail planning closed down*														
27	**1.4**	**IMPLEMENTATION**														
28	1.4.1	Implement infrastructure	Bene L.							R			C			
29	1.4.2	Implement hardware	Dell S.						R					C		
30	1.4.3	Implement software	Gates M.					R							C	
31	1.4.4	Implement personnel and organisation	Sprenger M.								R					C
32	1.4.5	Integration	Maier G.		R			C	C	C	C	C				
33	*1.4.6*	*Implementation closed down*														
34	**1.5**	**TEST AND TRAINING**														
35	1.5.1	1st test run	Maier G.		R			C	C	C	C		C	C	C	C
36	1.5.2	Analyse and modify 1st test run	Maier G.		R			C	C	C	C					
37	*1.5.3*	*Beta version exists*														
38	1.5.4	2nd test run	Maier G.		R			C	C	C	C		C	C	C	C
39	1.5.5	Train users	Doku H.					C	C	C	C	R				
40	1.5.6	Analyse and modify 2nd test run	Maier G.		R			C	C	C	C					
41	1.5.7	Approval	Maier G.	A	R											
42	*1.5.8*	*IT system approved*														
43	**1.6**	**LAUNCH**														
44	1.6.1	Launch hardware	Dell S.	I	C				R					C		
45	1.6.2	Launch software	Gates M.	I	C			R							C	
46	1.6.3	Launch organisation	Sprenger M.	I	C						R					C
47	*1.6.4*	*Launch approval*														
END																

(R)esponsible, (C)onsulted, (A)ccountable, (I)nformed

[1] project owner, [2] project manager, [3] PM Team

Fig. 38 Next project activity distribution chart

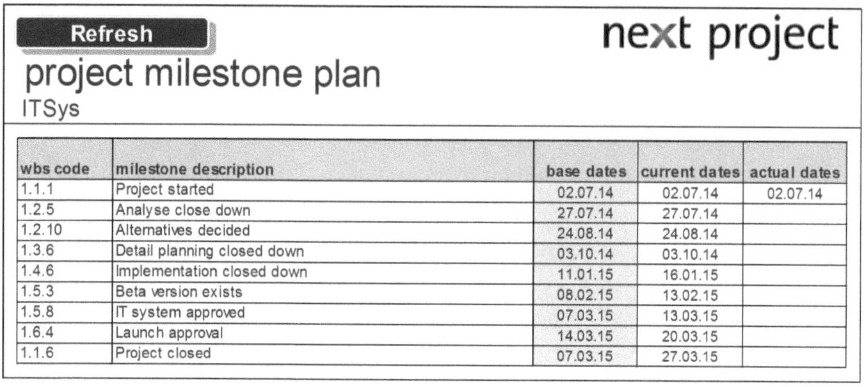

Refresh

next project

project milestone plan

ITSys

wbs code	milestone description	base dates	current dates	actual dates
1.1.1	Project started	02.07.14	02.07.14	02.07.14
1.2.5	Analyse close down	27.07.14	27.07.14	
1.2.10	Alternatives decided	24.08.14	24.08.14	
1.3.6	Detail planning closed down	03.10.14	03.10.14	
1.4.6	Implementation closed down	11.01.15	16.01.15	
1.5.3	Beta version exists	08.02.15	13.02.15	
1.5.8	IT system approved	07.03.15	13.03.15	
1.6.4	Launch approval	14.03.15	20.03.15	
1.1.6	Project closed	07.03.15	27.03.15	

Fig. 39 Next project project milestone schedule

7.13 Project Bar Chart (Gantt diagram)

Bar charts are suitable for the diagrammatic representation of simple project workflow structures. They illustrate the timing and logical dependencies of the work packages and the associated project phases.

The project structure plan (PSP) serves as the basis for the project bar chart. Depending on their complexity, the work package deadlines or phases are shown in the form of time bars, and milestones can also be incorporated into the bar chart. If due to the complexity of the project it is necessary to illustrate the logical sequence, further detail can be provided in the form of linked bar charts.

As in the case of the milestone schedule, a distinction is also made in the controlling activities related to the project bar chart between the deadline, the basis plan and the current plan (cf. Fig. 40).

7.14 Plan for Use of Project Personnel (Project Resources Plan)

The plan for use of project personnel is based on the output planning, and it quantifies the resource requirements (manpower requirements) for each work package or phase of the overall project. It provides an overview of staff availability in conjunction with the time schedule so that resource constraints can be identified.

In the plan for use of project personnel all the project's human resources are planned according to empirically ascertained values, and based on the project structure plan. The manpower requirements (in person days) for the project are shown in a table format in (cf. Fig. 41). The detailed planning of the use of manpower can be carried out both at the work package and the phase levels, and the level of detail of the planning should match that of the controlling for reasons of comparability.

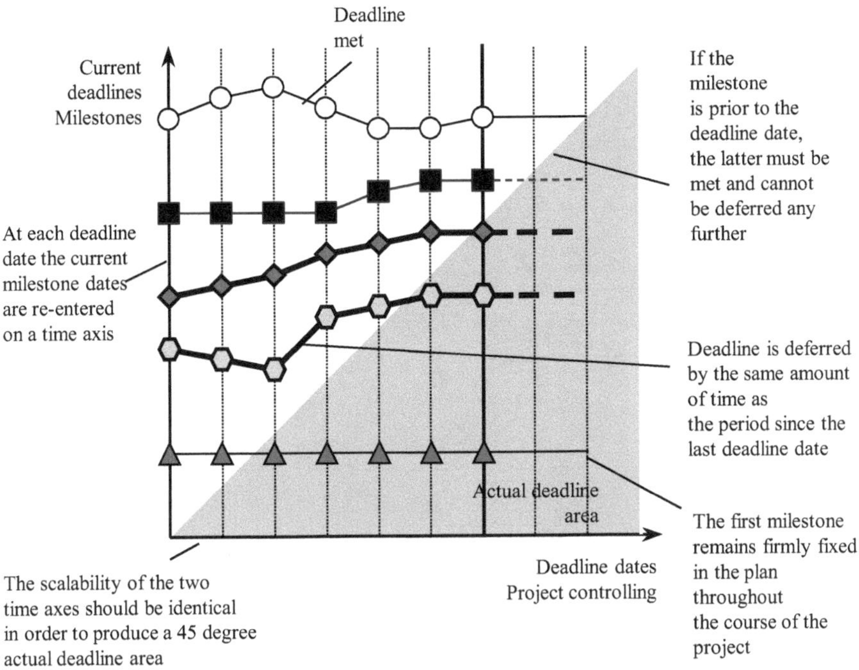

Fig. 40 Milestone trend analysis

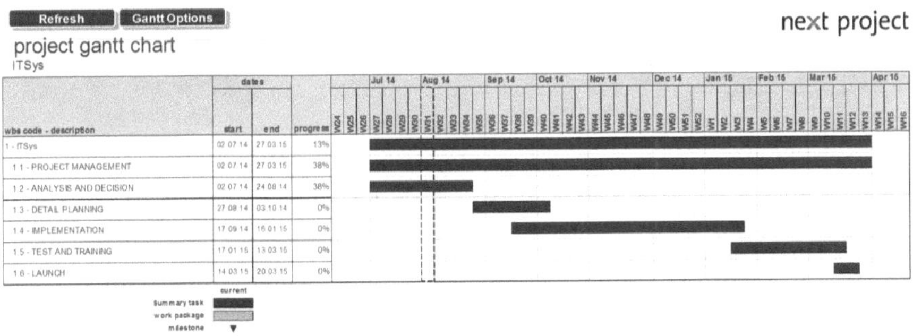

Fig. 41 Next project project bar chart

The plan for use of project personnel consequently facilitates not only the use of staff and cost control, it is also used for ascertaining the success of the project and for monitoring the project's profitability.

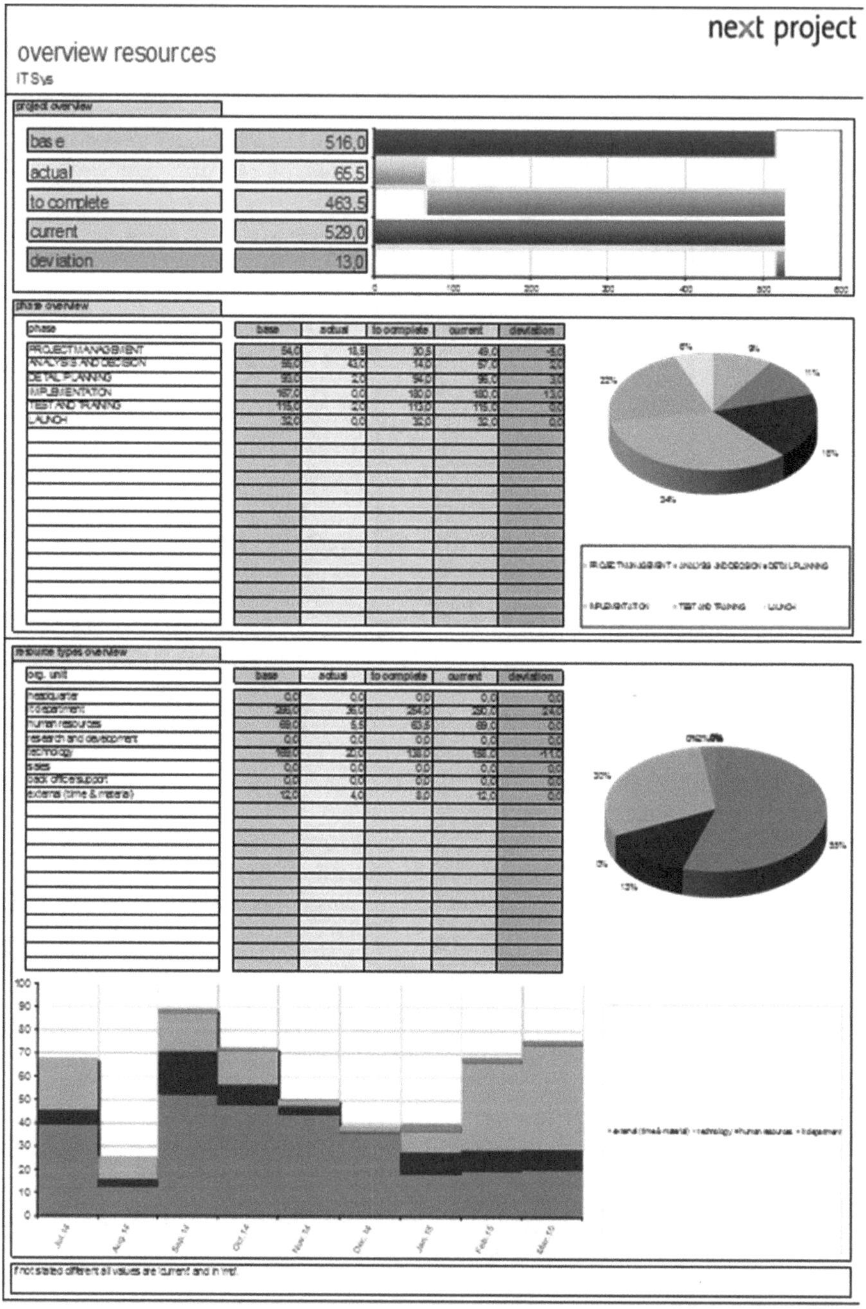

Fig. 42 Next project overview of resources

7.15 Project Costs Plan

The project's costs plans are drawn up based on the output plans and the types of costs that will be incurred in the project, and they provide information about the planned costs (budget) of the project and help to identify resource constraints (cf. Fig. 42).

The basis of the cost planning (cf.) is the project structure plan (PSP). Firstly, the cost categories (personnel, materials etc.) are defined. The detailed costs planning can be carried out both at the work package and the phase levels, and the level of detail of the planning should match that of the controlling for reasons of comparability. Then, a specification of inputs is drawn up for each cost category and phase/work package, and the overall costs are determined. When doing this, care must be taken to ensure that only the costs which can clearly be allocated to the project between the start and end of the project are included.

The project cost plan consequently facilitates not only cost control, it is also used for ascertaining the success of the project and for monitoring the project's profitability.

7.16 Business Case

The business case involves a comparison of two or more alternatives which are of sufficient complexity and entail sufficient risks to warrant the effort of carrying out a detailed analysis and evaluation. The method involves the analysis of the actual and target state, and the development of potential solution options, including implementation planning for the meaningful assessment of benefits, costs and risks.

The business case is used to reveal the profitability of a project, and it concerns itself with the scheme regardless of its project-worthiness or **project delineation**. An assessment requires detailed planning of alternative versions using appropriate assumptions. Project costs are therefore one or more of the relevant payment flows for the business case. The project budget is not necessarily identical to the business case, but it frequently forms a part of it (cf. Fig. 43).

The business case starts out by showing the actual situation, and it then sets out a desired target state and describes alternative approaches that can be taken to achieve it as well as detailed plans. This is followed by the (financial) evaluation using the methods of conventional investment analysis (cf. Fig. 44). Finally, the decision is formulated and implemented.

7.17 Claim Management

According to DIN 69901-5 issued by the German Institute for Standardization (2009a, b), claim or claims management is the "monitoring and evaluation of deviations and/or changes and their economic consequences for the purpose of ascertaining and asserting claims". In project business, claim management is one of the tools that is available both to the principal and the contractor. Its aim is to clarify, with both parties' agreement, the commercial consequences of events which

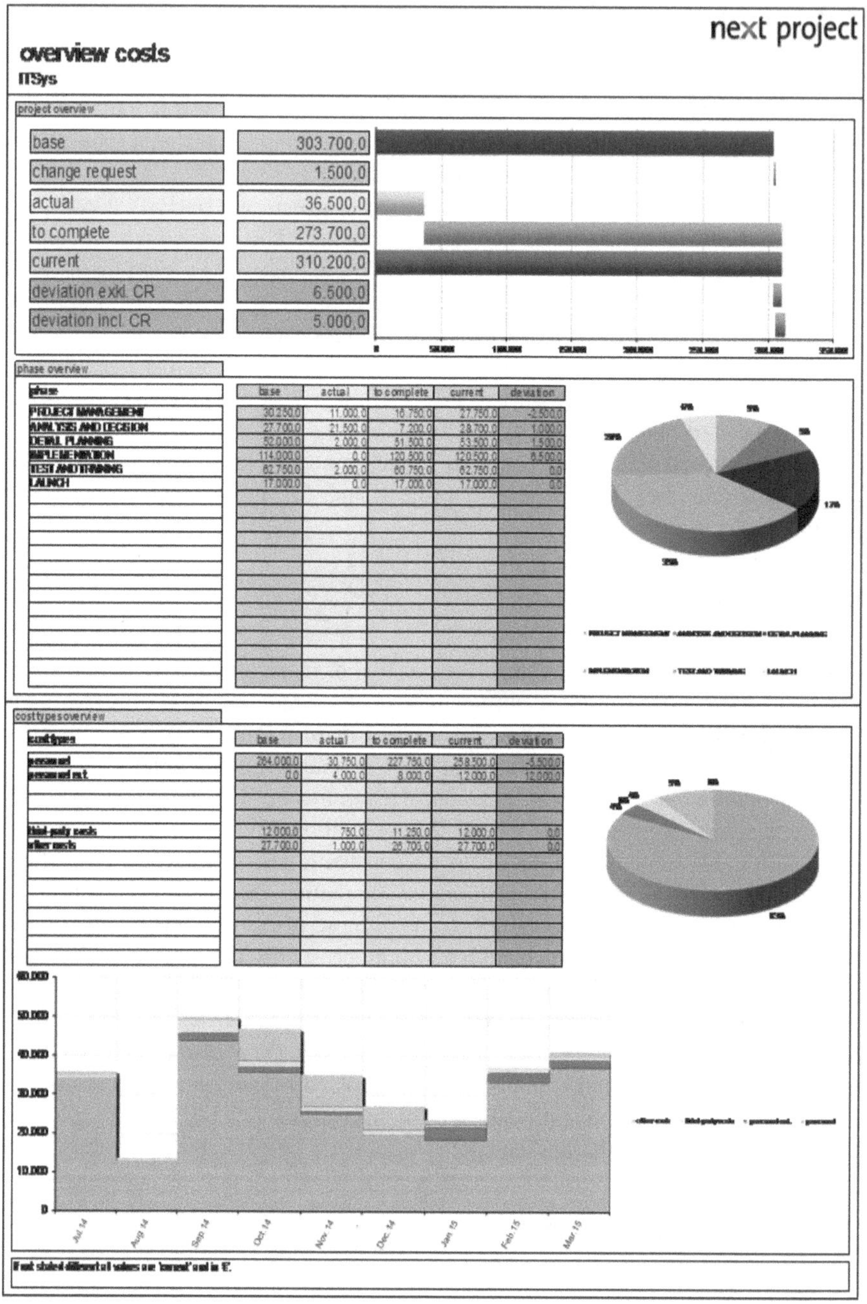

Fig. 43 Next project overview of costs

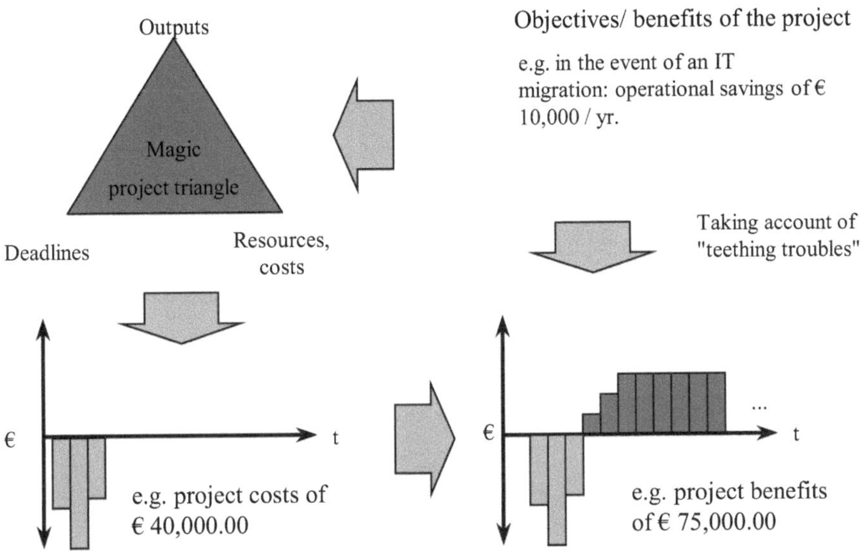

Fig. 44 Example of the connection between a business case and a project

occur during the course of the project but which were not foreseeable at the time when the contract was concluded. Claim management consequently comprises all the tasks involved in averting claims, making provision for claims, dealing with claims, and also establishing claims.

In practical terms this means preventing claims from arising, keeping the additional costs involved in carrying out the project low, enforcing (justifiable) claims against another contracting party, mounting a defense against (unjustifiable) claims made by another contracting party, and avoiding expensive legal disputes. Claims may relate to quantitative and/or qualitative deviations or changes in performance/outputs, or consist of time delays and/or additional costs.

7.18 Organizational Chart

The organizational chart presents the project's organizational structure and consequently clarifies who works on the project and in what role. It provides an overview of the **temporary organization** of the project. At the same time, it acts as a communication tool and provides the basis for the definition of responsibilities within the project organization. It shows details of the structuring of the project organization into project roles, the relationship of the people who have roles in the project to each other, and the functional composition of the project team.

Presentation in a "network form" is recommended rather than a hierarchical form of presentation (cf. Fig. 45). This focuses much less on the hierarchy than on the cooperation between the role holders and/or on their communication structures within the project. Project roles can also be carried out by people from outside the department or company as part of an integrated project organization.

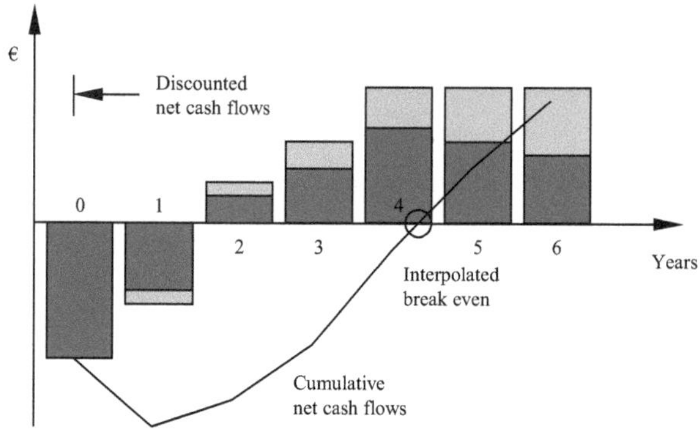

Fig. 45 Example of a business case in practice

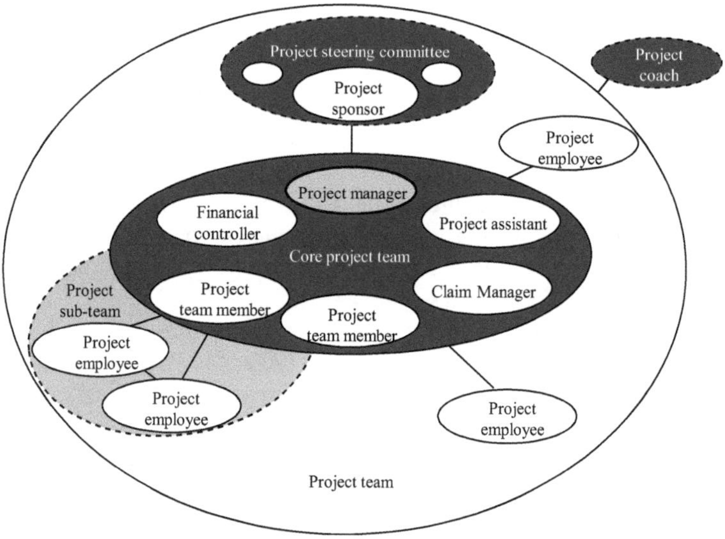

Fig. 46 Example of a project organization

7.19 Allocation of Competencies Between the Project and Line Operations

With regard to the organizational integration of projects, three types of project organization can be distinguished:

Influence Project Organization
The project staff remain in their specialist departments (cf. Fig. 46); the management of resources is carried out by department managers. Disadvantages of this are extended decision-making procedures, time-consuming escalation, and the members of the project team not fully identifying with the project. The project

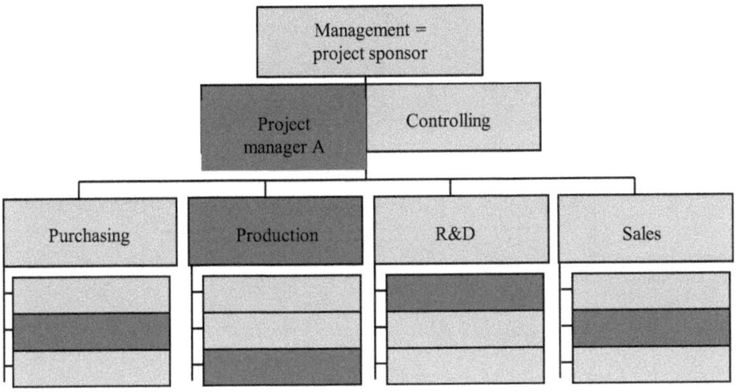

Fig. 47 Example of influence project organization

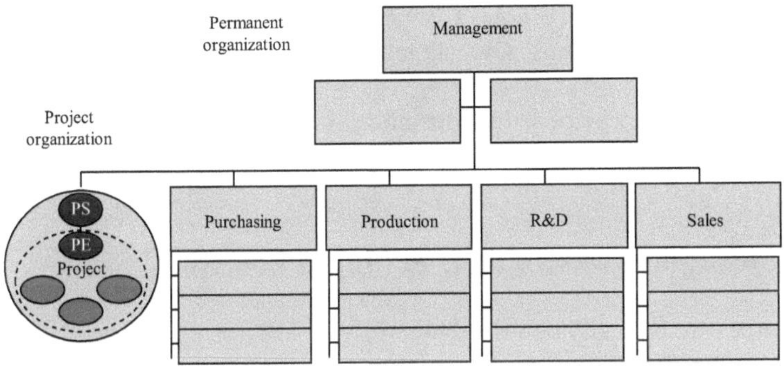

Fig. 48 Example of a pure project organization

manager does not have the authority to issue instructions; line activities frequently take priority over the project.

Pure Project Organization

A separate project organization exists alongside the permanent organization (cf. Fig. 47). The project staff concentrate fully on the project, and decisions are taken speedily. Problems may nevertheless arise in relation to the provision of staff and the coordination of resources; the project staff lose their links to the permanent organization.

Matrix Project Organization

The project organization is temporarily interwoven with the line organization, and the project team members remain assigned to their respective departments (cf. Fig. 48). This leads to a flexible, planned use of staff between the line

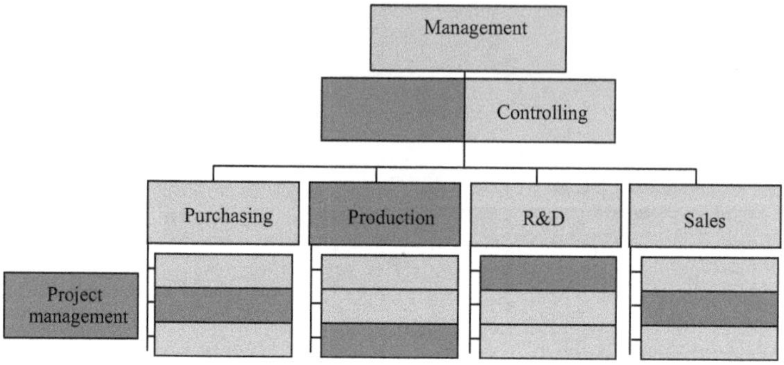

Fig. 49 Example of matrix project organization

organization and the project. Due to the dual reporting responsibilities of the project team members, the matrix project organization is however very demanding in resource management terms. Overall responsibility for the project lies with the project manager.

A recommended way of settling the allocation of competencies is to answer six questions which are shown in Fig. 49.

7.20 Relational Descriptions of Project Roles

Project roles are basically described in terms of tasks (responsibilities) and competencies (authorities). The tasks which are assigned and the responsibilities which result from them should go hand in hand with the transfer of competencies.

A relational (reciprocal) defining of roles gives the people who are involved in the project the opportunity to agree with each other what their respective expectations and competencies are. These agreements provide guidance on how to act in the relationships between the role holders, and therefore help to prevent conflicts about roles.

For this, it is firstly necessary for the project manager to define the expectations which the project owner might have of him, and the competencies which he in turn expects the project owner to give him. He then puts into words what he himself is looking for from the project owner and the tasks which he sees as falling within the latter's area. In a discussion with the project owner the project manager coordinates and agrees the formulated expectations and authorities with the project owner (cf. Fig. 50).

A similar procedure can take place between the project manager and the project team. If they are provided, the standard role descriptions in the company project management guidelines can be used as a basis for discussion. This makes it easier to allocate tasks and to ensure the provision of competencies.

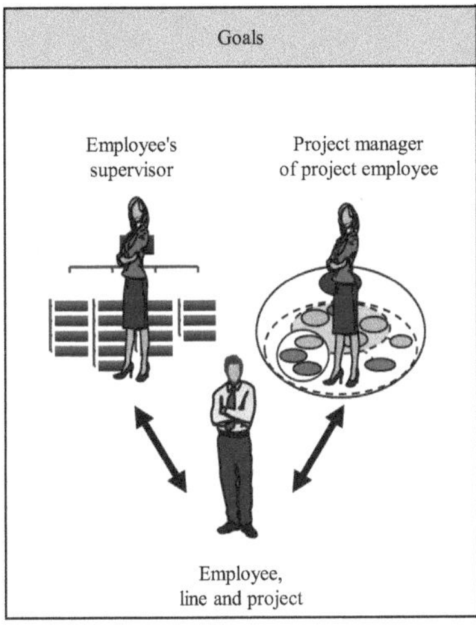

Create clarity regarding managerial authorities		
	in terms of content	in terms of personnel
What?	Work package, contents	Tasks, competencies
When?	WP deadlines, time limits	Holidays, time off in lieu
How?	Methods, procedures	Skills provision, equipment
How well?	Quality	Performance assessment
How much?	Resources, costs	Salary, bonuses
Who?	Person resp. for WP	Selection of PTM/PE

Fig. 50 Competency matrix for project and line roles

7.21 Project Communications Structures

Project communications structures govern the project's periodic communication requirements (cf. Figs. 51 and 52). They facilitate the provision of information and decision-making, and the structuring of environmental relationships. Examples of possible forms of communication are one-to one discussions, meetings, workshops, and presentations. Communications structures should be planned on a cyclical basis and decided on within the project team.

Project meetings are a key management tool, and they enable, for example, the exchanging of information, coordination of results, decision-making, and/or the agreeing of objectives. The communicating of differing types of information requires different types of meeting of various length to be held at various frequencies with different people attending them. It is important to distinguish between meetings about content (e.g. sub-team meetings to discuss detailed problems and agree technical concepts and solutions, etc.) and periodic project management meetings, such as controlling meetings and project owner meetings, in which project management subject matter (objectives, outputs, deadlines, resources and costs as well as the organization and context) are the main focus.

If project communication problems arise in the course of the project, the cause may lie in the communications structures that have been defined. Examples of possible ways of amending them are changes to their frequency or content, holding additional meetings or cutting out some meetings, or making changes in terms of the people who attend them.

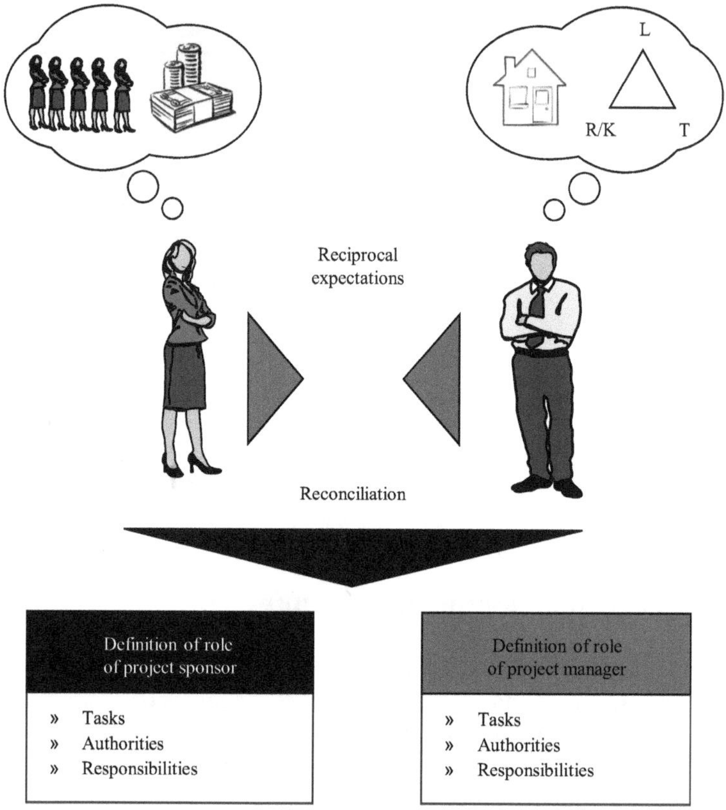

Fig. 51 Relational defining of roles

7.22 Project-Specific Ground Rules

Project-specific ground rules provide guidance for cooperation within the project team. Particularly in the case of complex projects, ground rules may foster the establishing of an appropriate project culture.

It is the project manager's job to establish a common culture defined by values, standards, communication and ground rules etc., and to reflect it in the project controlling activities, and/or to initiate appropriate management measures. Ground rules should be jointly devised within the project team. In order to underline their binding nature, ground rules can also be documented in the project manual, as shown in Fig. 53.

7.23 Risk Analysis of the Course of the Project

Risk analysis is the systematic identification of potential loss events/deviations from target and their implications. Risks associated with the course of the project are identified and assessed using the criteria of adherence to deadlines and budget

Project communication
prof pm reloaded

Description	Content	Participants	Deadlines
Project sponsor meeting	• Project status • Decision-making for subsequent course of action • Release of project progress report	Project sponsor, sub-team leader if required	
Project controlling meeting	• Project status • Controlling of work packages, deadlines, resources and costs • Controlling of environmental relationships • Social project controlling • Decision preparation for PS meeting	Project manager, project employee project coach	

Fig. 52 Example of a communications plan from technical project manual D dated 4.04

project communication
ITSys
next project

description	content	participants	frequency	location
project owner-Meeting	- Discussion project status, deviations in the project - Decision-making on the basis of the PC-meeting - Release production protocol	project owner, project manager, possibly Subteam owner	monthly	seminar room XY
Project controlling-Meeting	- Controlling scope, appointments, resources and costs - Controlling of the environmental relations - Social project controlling - Discussion of problems - Prepare dessions for PO meeting - Planning next steps	project manager, project team, project coach	monthly	
Jour fixe	- Operative coordination of the project involved parties - Discussion of problems - Planning next steps	project manager, project team	monthly	
Subteam-Meeting	- Coordination Subteams - Discussion of problems - Planning next steps	subteam	on demand	

Fig. 53 Next project project communication

and attainment of actual goals, as shown in Fig. 54. The fundamental task is to identify risk factors and their negative impact on the progress of the project.

The first stage of risk analysis is to identify risks by assessing the following criteria: meeting deadlines (D), attainment of actual objectives (O), adherence to budget (B). The risk evaluation which follows this determines the probability of their occurrence and the possible implications for the progress of the project. This

No stand-ins 	• We do not send any stand-ins to our meetings • We arrange the timing of meetings well in advance and stick to it (e.g. agreed breaks) • If a member does not attend a meeting, the meeting team is quorate even in his absence (the persons attending are able to make decisions) • Meetings with fewer than half the scheduled number of attendees are called off
No smoking, no phones 	• The meetings are non-smoking • Break times are jointly agreed in advance • Mobiles must be switched off during meetings • If a person attending has to be able to be contacted, this is agreed before the meeting and the mobile is switched to silent mode (the conversation must be held outside the meeting room)
Agenda and minutes 	• We have an agenda prepared for each meeting, and we designate a chairperson and someone who is responsible for taking the minutes • The agenda is circulated to all attendees at least 2-3 days in advance • The minutes should be circulated to all attendees within 3 days of the meeting • If objections are raised to the minutes, they are notified to the PM within 3 days
Commu-nication 	• Emails are the primary method of communication that we use • Where possible, results are circulated via email • Documents which are circulated to other people (outside the project team) are sent via the project manager • The project manager is the primary external point of contact for the project
We are the project team 	• We try to achieve the defined objectives as a project team, and each of us feels responsible for the results of the entire project • We "market" the project jointly (the individual team members stand full square behind the project) • We resolve conflicts within the team, escalating them if necessary to the project manager or project sponsor (conflicts within the team are not raised via the line organization) • We communicate openly in the team; "sensitive" information must be defined as such and is not disclosed outside the team
Traffic light status 	• We notify green status if the project managed by the project team is progressing as planned • Time schedule and cost deviations of under 5% never require escalation • We notify yellow status once there are relevant deviations or if measures have to be specified outside the project organization • We notify red status if there are major deviations

Fig. 54 Example of project-specific ground rules

evaluation is based on intuition, experience, and consideration of comparable risks. Risk classes make it possible to decide which bodies risks are to be handled in, whether risk prevention measures are to be specified, and whether specific risk prevention measures must also be implemented immediately. The risks may, for instance, be presented in the form of a matrix.

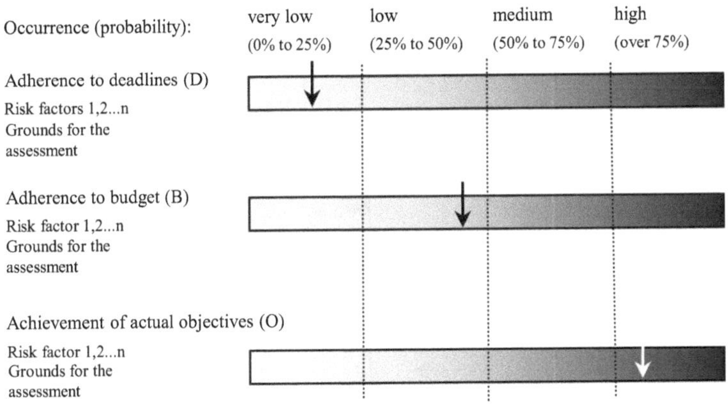

Fig. 55 Example of the risk analysis of the course of the project

7.24 Earned Value Analysis (EVA)

Earned value analysis is used to assess the progress of projects, and it does so by describing the current situation in relation to deadlines and costs by means of performance indicators. Key values in this regard are planned costs, actual costs, and earned value (cf. Fig. 55). The tracking of performance indicators makes trend analysis possible.

The project structure plan is used as the basis for determining the earned value. Above all, earned value analyses provide useful information in the case of cost-driven projects with clear calculation procedures (techniques) and in the case of projects with relatively stable outputs (fixed price bids).

The original base calculation (costs base plan) is used during the execution of the project as a benchmark against which the actual progress of the project (in other words the partial results of the project) is measured. Progress is determined by the amount of time needed for it, and the costs that are required for it. Earned value analysis only tends to be worthwhile if appropriate IT support is available.

7.25 Best Practice in Terms of the Use of Project Management Methods

In the case of organizations which are sufficiently project-oriented, rules are provided regarding the use of project management methods. These rules are binding on the project manager and are appropriately monitored and reviewed by the project management office, which will if necessary consistently demand adherence to them.

Figure 56 shows a best practice approach for customer order projects (throughput period 4–10 months and involving more than two organizational units).

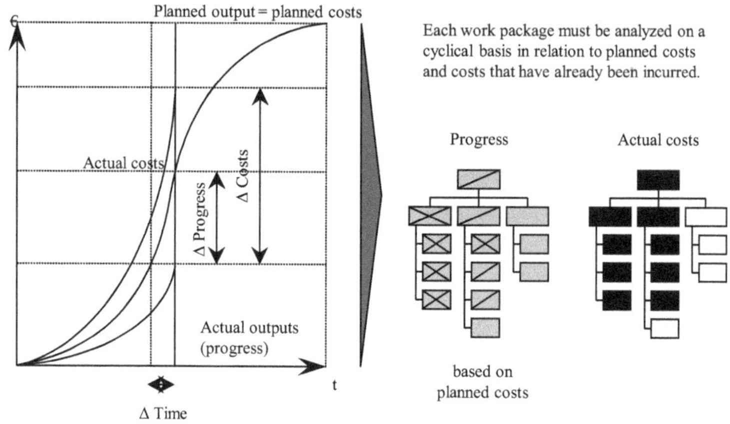

Fig. 56 Earned value analysis

8 Project Organization/Project Roles

In this section the most important project roles are described based on the best practice approach of next level consulting. The description of roles is structured as follows: organizational position; tasks; responsibility; authorities.

The tasks involved in the individual project roles are described in relation to the **project management processes**. In practice, the project roles may be adapted for specific companies based on these standard descriptions. It is also usual for there to be supplementary specific project roles depending on the sector which the company is in and the type of project. In the context of customer order projects, the roles of Claim Manager and Project Controller are described in addition to the standard project roles.

8.1 Project Owner

Organizational Position

- Is part of the project organization.
- Is appointed by the projects steering group and reports to it.
- Has the financial resources at his disposal, or procures them, as well as the personnel resources (if available) in conjunction with the project steering committee.
- Is the spokesman of the project steering committee (if one has been set up).
- The project owner is the project manager's technical manager.

Tasks

In Relation to Project Initiating

- Clarifying and firming up the project proposal
- Specifying project end date
- Provision of project resources
- Provision of initial draft outlining project objectives and areas which are not project objectives
- Provision of initial draft outlining the benefits of the project
- Contributing to the project environment analysis/to the **project context**
- Following its approval by the projects steering group, issuing the project order to the project manager (who is likewise selected by the projects steering group) as well as to the core project team (provided by the responsible line managers)
- Clarifying the content and scope of the project start process with the project manager (constitutive project owner meeting relating to the project start process)

In Relation to Project Start

- Holding a constitutive project owner meeting
- Approval of the project plans and project organization
- Approval of the project communications structures (incl. project steering committee if applicable)
- Ensuring adherence to project management standards

In Relation to Project Controlling

- Holding of project owner meetings according to the defined project controlling cycles (generally every 4–6 weeks)
- Ensuring the continuous availability of the project resources (submits applications to the projects steering group)
- If necessary, act in escalation role
- Approval of the (revised) plans for the project

In Relation to the Wrap-up of the Project

- Take part in the project close down workshop
- Take formal acceptance of the project result
- Feedback to/from project manager and core project team
- Drawing up of an interim assessment for the project manager
- Ensuring the transfer of know-how
- Ensuring that agreements are reached regarding the post-project phase, and in particular the transferring of the project (results, benefits, organizational responsibility) to the line organization

Responsibilities

- Responsible to the projects steering group for objectives, resources (staff, finance), project result and project benefits
- Safeguarding of the company's interests in relation to the project (strategic conformity as specified by the projects steering group)
- Commissioning and providing support for the project manager and core project team (in particular ensuring the availability of resources)
- Technical management and interim assessment of the project manager
- Arranging the timely involvement of the controlling function
- Provision of the project owner-specific communications structures

Authorities

- Allocating the assignment to the project manager and the core project team
- Technical management of the project manager
- Authority over defined project budget (sign-off authorization)
- Changing of the project objectives, deadlines and resources in conjunction with the projects steering group
- Specifying when there is a crisis in the project, and use of the associated escalation measures
- Aborting the project in conjunction with the projects steering group and controlling
- Carrying out project close down
- Approval of the project manager's actions in the final project report
- Commissioning of project audit and coaching

8.2 Project Manager

Organizational Position

- Is a member of the core project team
- Reports to the project owner and project services
- Technical management of the project team members and the sub-team leaders
- Represents the project externally

Tasks

In Relation to Project Initiating

- Assisting the project owner with the clarifying and firming up of the project proposal
- Arranging the timely involvement of the controlling function

- Assisting the project owner with drawing up initial draft version of the benefits of the project
- Production of project structure plan, and of workflow and resource plans
- Clarifying the resources required with the project owner
- Production of the project environment analysis and the project risk analysis with the support of project services
- Clarifying the content and scope of the project start process with the project owner (briefing meeting relating to the project start process)

In Relation to Project Start
- Working out the detail of the project plans and project organization together with the project team members
- Setting up an appropriate project organization, in particular communications and decision-making structures
- Measures to develop a project culture
- Planning of measures for risk management, crisis prevention, and crisis preparedness within the core project team
- Analysis of the project environmental relationships, and using this to produce initial measures for structuring relevant relationships
- Holding of a project start workshop and constitutive project owner meeting
- Documenting the project plans and project organization in the project manual (cf. Sect. 9 example of next project project manual)
- Establishing of project controlling process

In Relation to Project Controlling
- Ascertaining project status in relation to outputs, deadlines, resources and the context in the core project team
- Agreeing and/or undertaking management measures within the core project team, and adapting all the project plans and project organization
- Drawing up of project progress reports
- Monitoring the work assignments that have been allocated, and releasing work results
- Active management of project context relationships

In Relation to the Completion of the Project
- Releasing the work results for sign-off by the project owner
- Transfer of know-how to the permanent organization in consultation with the core project team and representatives of the permanent organization
- Holding of a project close down workshop with the project owner and project team
- Handover of wrap-up documentation to project services in order to safeguard knowledge

Responsibilities

- Upholding the interests of the project
- Ensuring the achievement of the project objectives
- Responsibility for defined project outputs, deadlines and resources
- Ensuring the operational effectiveness of the project team

Authorities

- Convening of project owner meetings and project controlling meetings
- Technical management of the project team members and the sub-team leaders
- Full responsibility for use of budgeted project resources (staff, finance)
- Purchasing decisions within the project budget (in accordance with sign-off rules)
- Release of work results
- Carrying out of employee assessments for project team members who have been assigned to the project for over 50 % of their hours of work for a period of more than 6 months

8.3 Core Project Team Member

Organizational Position

- Is a member of the project organization
- Reports to the project manager
- May be a sub-team leader

Tasks

In Relation to Project Initiating

- Assists with project structure plans, deadline plans, and resource requirements planning
- Clarifies the project budget requirements overview with the project manager
- Assists with the project environment analysis, the project benefits analysis and the project risk analysis
- Assists with the drawing up of the project proposal

In Relation to Project Start

- Actively assists with the project start process
- Agreeing of work packages with the project manager
- Helps draw up details of the project plans

- Assists with the planning of measures for risk management, crisis prevention, and crisis preparedness
- Assists with the structuring of project context relationships
- Takes part in the project start workshop (core team)

In Relation to Project Controlling

- Actively assists with the project controlling process
- Helps ascertain the project status based on autonomous progressing of work packages as regards outputs, deadlines, and resources
- Agreeing and undertaking management measures on a work package basis
- Assists with the structuring of project context relationships
- Takes part in project controlling meetings

In Relation to the Wrap-up of the Project

- Actively assists with the project close-down process
- Assists with the transfer of know-how to the permanent organization and to other projects
- Takes part in the project close down workshop

Responsibilities

- Upholding the interests of the project
- Helping to ensure the achievement of the project objectives
- Responsibility for defined quality, deadlines and resources for assigned work packages
- Using expertise to complete work packages autonomously
- Assisting with the management of the project

Authorities

- Decisions relating to quality, deadlines and use of resources for completing work packages according to specification
- Leading of sub-teams

8.4 Project Team Members

Organizational Position

- Is a member of the project organization
- Reports to the project manager and/or sub-team leader

Tasks

In Relation to Project Initiating

- Assists with project structure plans, deadline plans, and resource requirements planning
- Assists with the project environment analysis and the project risk analysis

In Relation to Project Start

- Assists with the project start process
- Agreeing of work packages with the sub-team leader (optional)
- Helps draw up details of the project plans
- Assists with the planning of measures for risk management, crisis prevention, and crisis preparedness
- Assists with the structuring of project context relationships

In Relation to Project Controlling

- Assists with the project controlling process
- Helps ascertain the project status based on progressing of work packages as regards outputs, deadlines, and resources
- Assists with the structuring of project context relationships
- Takes part in sub-team meetings (optional)

In Relation to the Wrap-up of the Project

- Assists with the project close-down process
- Takes part in the project close down workshop

Responsibilities

- Upholding the interests of the project
- Helping to achieve the project objectives
- Using expertise to complete work packages autonomously
- Assisting with the management of the project

Authorities

- None

8.5 Project Coach (Optional)

Organizational Position

- Advisory, outside the project organization
- Reporting structures according to commissioning by coaching commissioner

Tasks

- Coaching relating to project management processes (commissioning, launch, controlling, crisis, wrap-up)
- Building up the project management know-how of the project manager, and the core project team
- Sparring with project owner (optional)
- Assisting with the drawing up of the project management documentation (if required)
- Drawing up of the position and observations papers relating to project management
- Conducting interviews with project environments
- Viewing all the documents relating to the project

Tasks Do not Include

- Taking over of project functions and tasks (e.g. project management or assistance tasks)

Responsibilities

- Providing assurance that he will respect the confidentiality of the information arising from the coached system
- Contribution of know-how to the structuring of the project management processes

Authorities

- None

8.6 Claim Manager (Optional)

Organizational Position

- Is a member of the core project team
- Reports to the project manager and the accounter

Tasks

- Comparisons with tasks of core project team member
- Prevention of claims
- Reviews of/research into the contract

- Claim preparedness
  - Helping the project manager to define the claim competencies
  - Helping the project manager to define the specific communications channels
  - Compiling and maintenance of claim documentation
  - Assistance with the setting up of an early warning system
  - Setting up and maintenance/updating of a claim-tracking list
- Setting up claims
  - Assistance with the identification of claims
  - Development of the claim strategy
  - Claim preparation, documentation, and checking of possible counter-claims
  - Assisting the project manager with the reporting of claims
- Defense of claims
  - Putting together of counter-statements and counter-claims
  - Assisting the project manager with the notification of counter-statements
- Claim negotiations
  - Assisting with claim negotiations

Responsibilities

- Shared responsibility for the economic success of the project
- Responsibility for the transparency of the contract and outputs
- Contribution of contractual expertise and provision of legal support (in particular in connection with purchasing processes and contract negotiations)
- He is the internal project adviser for all decision-makers with regard to contractual and legal issues

Authorities

- None

9 Excursus: Example of Project Manual for IT Systems Customer Project

The project manual is the key information and communications tools in projects. It includes the **project order**, the delineation and context analysis of the project, the project organization, and all the planning and controlling tools used in the project.

1	Review of conformity to strategy	optional
2	Review of project-worthiness	optional
3	Project name	mandatory
4	Project logo	optional
5	Project order	mandatory
6	Project environment analysis	mandatory
7	Analysis of relationships with other projects	optional
8	Project structure plan	mandatory
9	Work package specifications	optional
10	Project activity distribution chart	optional
11	Milestone schedule	mandatory
12	Milestone trend analysis	optional
13	Project bar chart	optional
14	Plan for use of project personnel	mandatory
15	Project costs plan	mandatory
16	Business case	optional
17	Contracts / claims	optional
18	Project organigram	mandatory
19	Allocation of competences between the project and line operations	optional
20	Relational descriptions of project roles	optional
21	Project communications structures	mandatory
22	Project-specific ground rules	optional
23	Risk analysis	optional
24	Earned Value Analysis	optional

Fig. 57 Best practice approach for customer order projects

Responsibility for the drawing up and continuous updating of the project manual lies with the project manager. He receives assistance with these tasks from a project office or project assistant, above all in the case of larger projects.

A project manual is shown in this section using the "next project" PM tool of the next level consulting company (cf. Figs. 57 and 58).

At next project, the methods and tools that are to be used can be determined according to the project category (cf. Figs. 59 and 60). This ensures consistent documentation of the projects in the project manual.

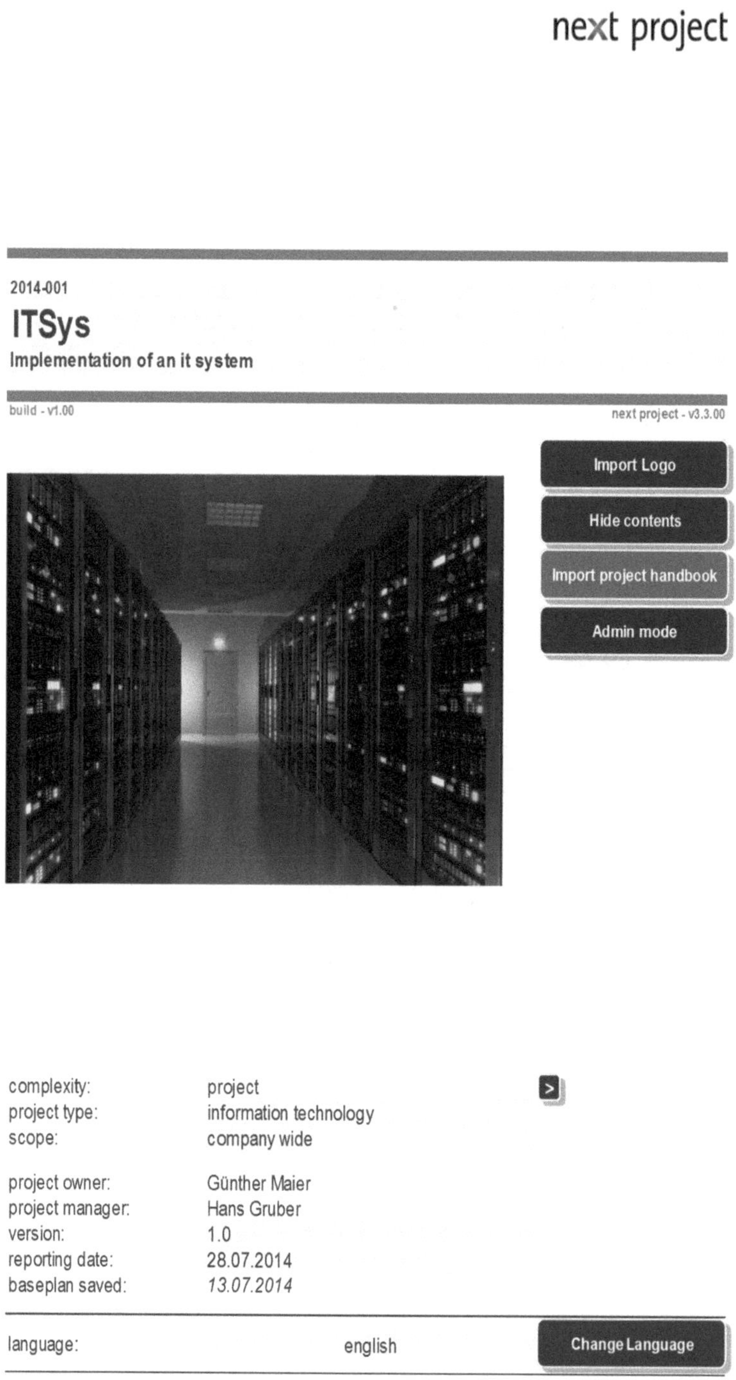

Fig. 58 Next project cover sheet

content
ITSys

next project

	methods	programme	project	small project	sheet selection	print selection
1	cover	M	M	M	x	x
2	content	M	M	M	x	x
3	list of changes				x	x
4	project assignment	M	M	M	x	x
5	project organisation	M	M		x	x
6	contact information				x	x
7	time context				x	x
8	project stakeholder analysis	M	M		x	x
9	project detail data	M	M	M	x	x
10	RACI - matrix	M	M		x	x
11	project work breakdown structure	M	M	M	x	x
12	workpackage specifications				x	x
13	project milestone plan	M	M	M	x	x
14	project gantt chart	M	M	M	x	x
15	overview resources	M	M		x	x
16	detailed resources	M	M		x	x
17	overview costs	M	M		x	x
18	detailed costs	M	M		x	x
19	project communication	M	M		x	x
20	project ground rules and documentation				x	x
21	project risk				x	x
22	change request	M	M	M	x	x
23	status report	M	M	M	x	x
24	project close down report				x	x
25	to do list				x	x

M - Mandatory

select all | select programme | select project | select small project | show / hide contents | print selection | save selection as PDF

Fig. 59 Next project project categories and use of PM tools

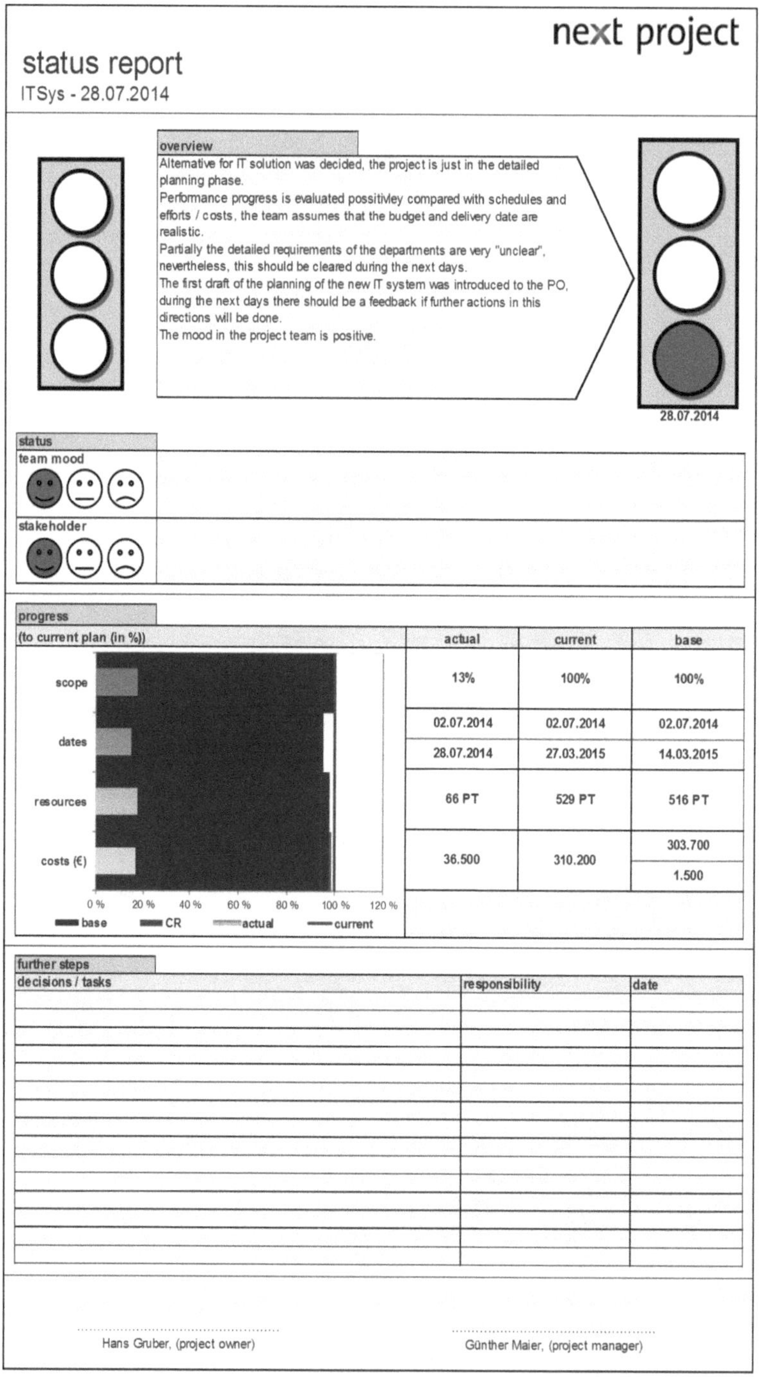

next project

status report
ITSys - 28.07.2014

overview

Alternative for IT solution was decided, the project is just in the detailed planning phase.
Performance progress is evaluated possitivley compared with schedules and efforts / costs, the team assumes that the budget and delivery date are realistic.
Partially the detailed requirements of the departments are very "unclear", nevertheless, this should be cleared during the next days.
The first draft of the planning of the new IT system was introduced to the PO, during the next days there should be a feedback if further actions in this directions will be done.
The mood in the project team is positive.

28.07.2014

status
team mood
stakeholder

progress

(to current plan (in %))	actual	current	base
scope	13%	100%	100%
dates	02.07.2014	02.07.2014	02.07.2014
	28.07.2014	27.03.2015	14.03.2015
resources	66 PT	529 PT	516 PT
costs (€)	36.500	310.200	303.700
			1.500

further steps

decisions / tasks	responsibility	date

Hans Gruber, (project owner)

Günther Maier, (project manager)

Fig. 60 Next project progress report

Exercises

1. What features are used to describe a project?
2. State and describe the most important roles of the project team members at the respective project levels.
3. What criteria should be used to decide whether an order is to be handled as a project with a temporary organization?
4. Explain the extent to which detailed project planning and project controlling are connected.
5. Describe the hard and soft factors in project controlling. In what context are they used?
6. What do you understand the term "social project management" to mean? What tasks does it include?
7. What type of project meeting would you propose in the context of communications structures in the case of a customer project? What matters should not be discussed in project meetings?
8. Which project management methods do you consider to be especially important in the case of internal projects? And which methods for customer projects?
9. State and describe the methods which are suitable for promoting organizational learning through projects.

Literature

Deutsches Institut für Normung e. V. (2009a). *DIN 69901–1 Projektmanagement – Projektmanagementsysteme – Teil 1: Grundlagen.*

Deutsches Institut für Normung e. V. (2009b). *DIN 69901–5 Projektmanagement – Projektmanagementsysteme – Teil 5: Begriffe.*

Gareis, R. (1991). *Projektmanagement im Maschinen- und Anlagenbau.* Wien: Manz.

International Project Management Association (IPMA). (2006). *ICB – IPMA-Kompetenzrichtlinie Version 3.0.* Nijkerk: Eigenverlag.

Luft, J., & Ingham, H. (1955). The Johari window: A graphic model of interpersonal awareness. In *Proceedings of the Western Training Laboratory in Group Development.* Los Angeles.

Office of Government Commerce (OGC). (2009). *Managing successful projects with PRINCE2.* London: TSO.

Office of Government Commerce (OGC). (2010a). *Portfolio, programme and project management maturity model (P3M3®). Introduction and Guide to P3M3®.* Accessed October 4, 2012, from http://www.p3m3officialsite.com/nmsruntime/saveasdialog.aspx?lID=456&sID=210

Office of Government Commerce (OGC). (2010b). *PRINCE2® maturity model (P2MM).* Accessed October 4, 2012, from http://www.p3m3officialsite.com/nmsruntime/saveasdialog.aspx?lID=462&sID=210

Project Management Institute. (2010). *A Guide to the Project Management Body of Knowledge (PMBOK Guide).* ISBN13: 9781935589679

Project Cooperation

Bernd Günter

1 Cooperation in Business-to-Business Marketing: A Path to Competitive Advantages

At the end of September 2012, the "Handelsblatt" was entitled: "Cooperation instead of conflict—why cooperation works much better than competition and conflict in modern capitalism" (Handelsblatt 2012). This kind of title clearly shows the significance that cooperation and alliances, networks and other forms of cooperation have gained and their importance for success in markets.

In many cases, sales of technical products and services and/or products and services intended for companies cannot take place based on standardized catalog offers for which the scope of services and standard prices is defined in advance. Rather, in large parts of business-to-business marketing, customized, order- and project-based, individual proposal planning and order processing is required. This creates specific requirements on the strategic positioning of companies and the tactical marketing planning, especially if this relates to individual products and/or products manufactured on behalf of a customer, or even complex service bundles consisting of systems, modules, products and services, such as in the industrial plant business or in the construction industry and infrastructure planning. In these cases, the scope of services and remuneration must first be defined within customer negotiations and the proposal preparation. Frequently, this process is initially used to define *who* the customer's contract partner shall be on the supply side and *who* will fulfill the required subtasks. The sale of many complex capital goods and services is planned and transacted in cooperation with complementary suppliers. Furthermore, situations occur in business-to-business marketing and in technical selling, which lead to a vertical cooperation between suppliers and customers

B. Günter (✉)
Faculty of Business Administration and Economics, Heinrich-Heine-Universität Düsseldorf, Düsseldorf, Germany
e-mail: guenter@uni-duesseldorf.de

M. Kleinaltenkamp et al. (eds.), *Business Project Management and Marketing*, Springer Texts in Business and Economics, DOI 10.1007/978-3-662-48507-1_8

motivated by marketing considerations. This section primarily covers the planning of cooperative marketing in these types of areas, sectors and market situations. The specific focus is on project-based cooperation between complementary suppliers in the market. The following company and market situation is used as an example.

Example 1
When selling an integrated power plant, manufacturers from the electrical engineering, control engineering, boiler construction, turbine construction (special purpose machine construction) and civil engineering sectors, etc., work together, potentially with planning companies and consultancies on the supplier side, as well as installation companies and other service providers. By expanding the circle of those involved in an offer, cooperation partners can also include financing banks, potential agents/sponsors as contact brokers and information service providers as well as customer consultants and financiers.

But it is not just the suggested constellations that require a temporary, project-based collaboration. "Projects" are isolatable, independent, temporary plans with a specific objective, but often initially unstructured (Bea et al. 2011). The term "project-based cooperation" then also includes activities such as:

- The joint development of products by several supplier companies.
- The joint development of products and assemblies by suppliers and users, e.g. as part of simultaneous engineering or with key customers based on the Lead User concept (Weiber and Jacob 2000).
- Cooperation when developing a special market.
- The joint organization of events, fairs and exhibitions, performance demonstrations, commercial events, etc.

These cases are also included under the term "project-based cooperation", which need to be designed, implemented and controlled in business-to-business marketing and in technical selling.

An inter-company cooperation in sales management is always beneficial from marketing perspectives, from a participating supplier's point of view, if it helps to establish, strengthen, develop and permanently expand competitive advantages. This also includes the case in which a company seeks to cooperate with a stronger company in the respective field in order to address internal competitive disadvantages. Competitive advantages acquired by the affiliation of companies (such as a syndicate or supplier coalition) are directly related to the individual positioning, the reputation and the perceived competitive advantages by customers of each of the companies involved. There is generally a correlation between the isolated market position of the individual cooperation partners and their performance as one of a group of companies cooperating in a project (or beyond a single project).

2 Forms of Horizontal and Vertical Cooperation

In principle, market-related cooperation can be classified into horizontal and vertical cooperation, depending on the type of parties involved and the value creation levels in which they operate (Günter 1992; Zentes et al. 2005).

Vertical cooperation exists when companies from different value creation levels along the supply chain within a sector cooperate, i.e. companies in the supplier level (s) with companies in the purchaser level(s), whereby this may relate to downstream processors, downstream users or downstream sellers (dealers, distributors).

When marketing technical products, the service planning and definition of the service providers (suppliers) frequently take place in coordination with the principal, the customer ("*downstream cooperation*"). In this case, the customer's specifications must be taken into consideration or negotiated. Joint developments with customers are becoming increasingly common. Studies in business-to-business marketing have shown that the "*in-supplier*" has an advantage in these kinds of negotiations. This is the supplier who already maintains supply relationships with this customer, rather than other competitors ("*out-supplier*").

In addition, the customer occasionally provides goods, services, or property rights that are required for the success of the overall delivery. The integration of these project elements also requires a cooperation or coordination between the customer and the supplier(s).

Another form of cooperative business relationships may be required for a supplier upstream: with subcontractors (suppliers). In this case developing an offer for the customer must also include the integration of deliveries ("*upstream cooperation*").

Besides the two forms of *vertical* cooperation mentioned above for sales planning and implementation, *horizontal* cooperation is also possible and often necessary on the supplier level. This refers to the cooperation with

(a) Suppliers, which provide *supplementary* deliveries and services ("*horizontal-complementary cooperation*")
(b) Suppliers, which provide *similar* services ("*horizontal-competitive cooperation*")

Cooperation between suppliers in group (b) is necessary if the customer divides a homogeneous overall order across several suppliers, e.g. in order to reduce procurement risk, or if an individual supplier is not able to manage the entire order capacity alone. Competition regulations problems must always be reviewed for this kind of cooperation, but are only likely to arise in the latter case, if at all.

Table 1 provides an overview of the important forms of horizontal and vertical cooperation in business-to-business marketing. It already includes the difference

Table 1 Forms of vertical and horizontal cooperation (**examples**, based on Günter 1992, p. 800)

	Horizontal cooperation		Vertical cooperation	
	With competitors	With complementary suppliers	With companies at supplier level(s)	With companies at purchaser level(s)
Project-based cooperation	• Syndicates • Industrial consortia • Underwriting consortia • Sales promotion campaigns, e.g. fair cooperation	• Industrial consortia (plant engineering) • Sales promotion campaigns	• General contractors with subcontractors • R&D cooperation • Simultaneous engineering	• R&D cooperation • Development cooperation • Lead user concepts
Cross-project cooperation	• Joint ventures (type A) • Export associations • Purchasing associations • Joint advertising, sector advertising • Strategic alliances (type A)	• Joint ventures (type B) • Export associations • Logistics systems • Strategic alliances (type B) • Distribution cooperations	• Just-in-time systems • Subcontracting/ contract manufacturing • Framework contracts	• Just-in-time systems • Distribution cooperations • Multi-stage marketing • Framework contracts

between project-based and cross-project cooperation, which will be explained below.

What are the main reasons for the affiliation of independent companies in one of these forms of cooperation?

Two considerations play a particularly important role as influence factors for horizontal and vertical cooperation in business-to-business marketing. Firstly, joint offers, i.e. system transactions (system selling, "package offers", major projects, turnkey transactions) generally require the cooperation of suppliers with complementary goods and services. This is particularly the case for horizontal-complementary cooperation in the industrial plant business and in business with system technologies (Backhaus and Voeth 2010; Backhaus et al. 1994; Engelhardt and Günter 1981). Horizontal cooperation between competitors has also become a key topic in recent years for a second reason. The combination of resources is required in order to become and remain competitive in international markets in the light of rapid technological progress. This is also at the heart of the discussion regarding strategic alliances, which are often formed between competitors to combine resources to pursue (potentially global) strategic objectives. Other objectives of horizontal forms of cooperation are shown in Table 2.

A key reason for vertical cooperation between manufacturers and downstream processors or assemblers is the intended acceleration of development projects and product innovations. This aspect is currently particularly important for cooperation between suppliers and their purchasers, such as cooperation in the form of

Table 2 Typical objectives of horizontal marketing cooperation

1. Capacity expansion, exploitation of economies of scale
2. Program extension, economies of scope
3. Access to unique selling points, know-how, etc., acquisition/strengthening of competence
4. Market access, market development (esp. national markets with governmental access barriers, or the like)
5. Risk reduction (e.g. in connection with the distribution of project deliveries)
6. Strengthening the market position on markets

simultaneous engineering. In this case, the particularly intense coordination of development planning—an important variable in the level of loyalty—is expected to save time and prevent errors and changes (Chelsom 1989). Ultimately, the joint development and management of an end consumer market is an incentive for vertical cooperation for the primary stages, which market capital goods in the broadest sense and which is extremely important in the face of the derived demand for raw and input materials, semi-finished products and components/parts in these areas.

3 Project-Based and Cross-Project Cooperation

Inter-company cooperation may initially relate to a single project defined by collaboration partners. In this case, the cooperation ends on conclusion (execution, delivery) of the project. The intensity of the cooperation, the form of the relationships, the involvement of departments and employees may vary during the course of the project.

The term "supplier association" or *supplier coalition* is used to describe the cooperation of suppliers in a horizontal cooperation, as well as a supplier network with subcontractors, for an individual project (Günter 1977). This kind of cooperation may take different structural, organizational and contractual forms. These kinds of coalitions are covered in Sect. 5.

In some cases of cooperation decisions there is the option to continue an initial cooperation beyond a single project. This cross-project cooperation involves various benefits for the partners. For example clear interfaces, positive experiences of a smooth cooperation, cost aspects, image factors and other reasons may prompt repeat cooperation. In this case the project-based marketing is transformed to relationship marketing (Bruhn 2012).

The following section focuses on cooperation based on a single project and the associated marketing decisions.

4 Marketing-Based Features of Project Cooperations

4.1 Customer Orientation Through Cooperation

Suppliers may cooperate for a variety of reasons and motives. From a marketing perspective, these kinds of decisions are embedded in terms of the intended position in achieving potential competitive advantages (comparative competitive advantages). This immediately raises the question of the market and customer orientation of cooperation strategies.

Vertical project cooperation between suppliers and customers represents an element of customer acquisition and customer loyalty from the perspective of the participating suppliers. Similar to vertical diversification or downstream integration and the path to downstream processing, this cooperation aims to influence the purchaser level and generate commitment (Söllner 1993, p. 134) in favor of the supplier. In this case, cross-level considerations can play a significant role. For example, this is the case if the supplier targets the downstream stages of their direct customer in terms of multi-stage marketing and targets the development of downstream markets together with this customer, e.g. downstream processing or OEM companies and end users (Günter 1997, p. 215 et seqq.).

Horizontal cooperation between suppliers in technical selling enable the creation and bundling of competitive advantages on sales markets based on a joint appearance. Customer analysis plays a key role in this respect. The analysis of performance requirements and the buying network (Bristor 1987; Klöter 1997 p. 44 et seqq.) must be used to review which competitive advantages perceived by the customer (customer benefits; Günter 2007) the supplier being considered has and which benefits potential cooperation partners can add in a cooperation. This also shows that, in addition to performance elements and conditions, soft factors, such as the reputation of a cooperation partner perceived by customers, are important for partner selection and the cooperation process (Günter 1992, p. 804; Helm et al. 1996).

4.2 The Cooperation Process

The course of cooperation decisions in marketing complex capital goods and services can typically be represented in a process model (VDI 1991).

Project cooperation deals with complex, often imprecisely outlined order volumes and structures in the early stages, for which even the type of cooperation and the group of participants is still to be defined. The diverse, partly technical, partly commercial and legal tasks as part of the project cooperation can expediently be broken down according to the progress of the project for further analysis, i.e.—such as in mechanical and plant engineering—following the acquisition and processing of orders.

Table 3 provides an overview of the individual phases of project management in cases in which several suppliers are working together in order to prepare a joint

Table 3 Course and decision-making levels of a cooperation process

Step	Activity	Outcome
1	Reviewing the tender/inquiry	Project requirements
2	Competition analysis	Competition situations
3	Definition of the internal objectives	Necessity of cooperation
4	Definition of the company's position in the cooperation	Deliveries and services to be acquired from partner(s) (cf. make-or-buy)
5	Specification of the parameters influencing the form of cooperation	Basis for the weighting
6	Review and weighting of the parameters, summarised evaluation	Decision on the form of cooperation
7	Compilation of the partners to be considered and their key features	Preselection of possible partners and decision on establishing contact
8	Contact with potential partners and clarification of fundamental questions	Partner selection
9	Drafting and negotiation of the cooperation contract	Conclusion of the cooperation contract

proposal for a plant and successfully process an order. The *industrial plant business* (Systems Selling; Günter 1979) sector and business type is a good example to use when discussing the typical content of decisions and problems of project cooperation. The following section looks more closely at the individual sub-decisions in the project management phases.

Table 3 shows that one of the first steps is to check whether a potential project to be managed in cooperation should even be approached and whether the customer and the project content requires a specific form of cooperation and/or specific partners. This takes place within the scope of the inquiry evaluation and project analysis (cf. Chap. 2).

Preliminary decisions for a project cooperation arise based on customer specifications and based on the way in which an inquiry reaches a supplier under consideration. Preferences by the individuals responsible for reaching the purchase decision on the customer side may require supplier cooperation with suppliers of certain products or from certain countries. In these cases, the supplier only has a limited opportunity to convince the customer of different proposal constellations.

In many cases the information about a project or customer inquiries for capital goods are not received by a supplier directly. Rather, inquiries for sub-plants or for components (i.e. individual benefits in kind or services) are also brought to the attention of suppliers and cooperation partners by other suppliers, typically prime contractors or customer consultants. In this case, the recipient of an inquiry who is interested in an order has to deal with the preferences and specifications of the end customer *and* the supplier that has already been contacted. Their scope for selecting cooperation partners themselves, for implementing their own proposal expectations and using their own sales instruments are therefore significantly restricted.

The competition ("competitive intelligence") analysis represents another task as part of the cooperation planning. The analysis of potential competitors and their strengths and weaknesses (especially in their standing with the customer and in their perception) provides information on the opportunities and competitive advantages of certain types of cooperation, as well as the risks that exist with regard to the receipt of the order and its management. In addition, a review regarding the inclusion of certain competitors to defend against their market opportunities should also take place ("If you can't beat them, join them!"). The competition analysis must be accompanied by a review of the internal objectives, the strengths and weaknesses (of particular importance: from the customer's perspective) and the evaluation of the internal opportunities and risks.

For the continued pursuit of the cooperation, the question of the time and the phase in which cooperation contracts and other cooperation decisions can be made more expediently is important. This is explained further in this chapter using the example of the formation of supplier coalitions.

The following provides an outline of a few requirements and influencing factors on which the further course of a project cooperation is predominantly based and which must be included in the decision-making processes. Cooperative project management must primarily be based on the following *preconditions* and *initial data*:

- Project objectives and content specified and predetermined by the customer (specifications, conditions of service and use).
- Location data (construction site) and location-related framework conditions.
- Internal financing options and those of potential partners, especially if the customer requires supplier credits or the arrangement of buyer credit for investment.
- Information on the legal environment (e.g. contract modalities, industrial property rights) and other market-related environmental conditions.
- Information on internal material, personnel and financial capacities and their temporal availability (similar for possible partners).
- Information on the individuals responsible for purchasing and circumstances that influence purchasing for the customer as well as organizations that may be able to influence the purchasing process ("third parties").
- Customer specification and preferences with regard to possible cooperation partners and their deliveries and services.
- Specifications and preferences that the potential inquiry partners may develop with regard to order components, especially the prime contractor (general contractor and consortium leading manager).
- The competition situation.

4.3 Reasons for Cooperation, Project Objectives and Partner Selection

4.3.1 Type of Purchase and Supplier Cooperation

Reasons for the establishment of a project cooperation may originate from the customer's sphere, the considered supplier's internal motives, or from the planning activities of cooperation partners who are looking for a cooperation.

The starting point for the establishment of supplier coalitions is the customer's decision to purchase a total plant package from a supplier association (*system purchase*, cf. Fig. 1) as part of a project instead of the separate purchase of individual components (*component purchase*; cf. Fig. 1). The diagrams should also clarify where the interface problems and risks are in the case of the two purchase types, i.e. who is responsible for ensuring the coordination of the supplies (Günter 1977).

Figures 1 and 2 show the types of purchases as reasons and starting points for cooperation decision-making processes in business-to-business marketing and in technical selling. Table 4 identifies the reasons for cooperation (VDI 1991, p. 1).

4.3.2 Project Objectives and Cooperation

The decision on the pursuit of the project as well as the central determinations of the organizational forms and the partner selection must be linked with the specification of the project objectives. A distinction can be made between the following:

1. Financial outcome objectives of a project (net profit, contribution margin, cash flow, sales margin)
2. Customer-related objectives (establishment or stabilization of a business relationship, receipt of follow-up orders, segment development)
3. Market development objectives, e.g. by designing and delivering a reference plant
4. Suppliers' internal objectives, such as acquisition or expansion of know-how
5. Technology development
6. (Expansion of) experience in project management, potential specialization in certain types of projects

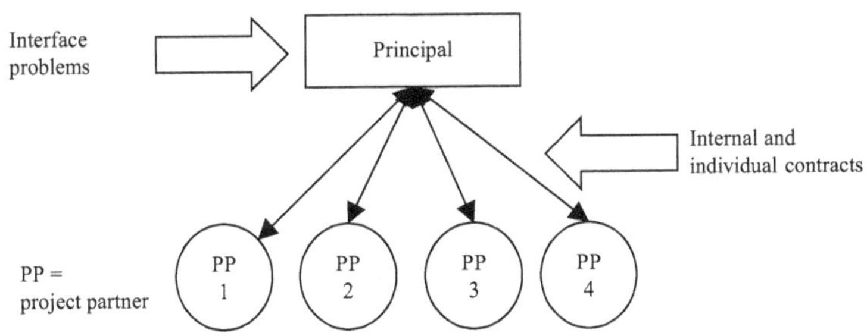

Fig. 1 Purchase type: component purchase

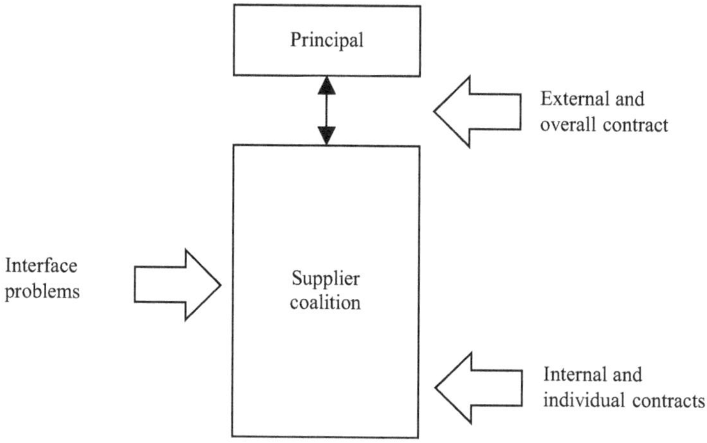

Fig. 2 Purchase type: system purchase

7. Partner-related objectives, e.g. securing a strong market partner for the relevant project or multiple-projects, as well as
8. Risk limitation and diversification

Some of these project objectives can be better achieved through cooperation. This applies for objectives 3, 4, 5 and 6. However, these collide with objectives 1 and 2, at least to the extent that cooperation decisions mean that the outcomes achieved has to be shared with partners and cooperation partners may subsequently become competitors.

4.3.3 Preliminary Considerations on the Division of a Project, Organizational Form and Partner Selection

The cooperation of suppliers in the proposal preparation and order processing in technical sales may take place in various organizational forms and process structures, which are connected with different performance, remuneration and risk distributions. A reciprocal influence exists between this decision on the organizational form of the coalition (e.g. consortium) and the selection of appropriate partners. In specific individual cases, the selection of certain partners and an organizational form is required *before* structuring and allocating the project task; in other cases the decision-making process is reversed or the decisions are reached *simultaneously*. Nevertheless, the problem of partner selection will be discussed first, before the forms of coalition are covered in Sect. 5.

The selection of the most important cooperation partners requires that the supplier under consideration has a rough idea of the breakdown of the service package requested by the customer. This distribution to various suppliers is a key influencing variable for the quality of the proposal and the product or the plant in

Table 4 Reasons for establishing supplier coalitions

1. Impossibility of providing all the requested supplies and services by individual suppliers
2. Lack of internal know-how
3. Lack of industrial property rights
4. Lack of prequalification
5. Better chance of receiving and managing the order with partners
6. Inclusion of local partners in the customer's country (local content, local manufacturing)
7. Support by the partners (financing, acquisition, etc.)
8. Financing/export credit insurance from third countries
9. Cheaper delivery by the partner
10. Possibility of specialization
11. Reduction in project costs
12. Sharing of risk and liability
13. Impossibility of managing the total order volume by a single supplier
14. Neutralizing the competitors
15. Impossibility of appearing under our own brand or nationality
16. Special customer request for a cooperation or for nominated partners

Table 5 Decision-making steps when selecting cooperation partners

1. Rough determination of the form of cooperation and your own position
2. Criteria for determining the cooperation partners
3. List or portfolio of cooperation partners
4. Evaluation of potential cooperation partners
5. Negotiation and selection decisions
6. Mutual specification of the coalition form and the distribution of tasks

the case of more complex capital goods. The approach to the decision-making steps is described in **Fehler! Verweisquelle konnte nicht gefunden werden** (Table 5).

The rough determination of the company's own positions is significantly influenced by the form in which the overall package of a cooperatively managed range of services is broken down. A distinction can generally be made between a horizontal and vertical breakdown of the service bundle (Roth 1977):

- In the case of a *vertical* breakdown, the project is divided into complete subplants, product group and functional units (for example: industrial plant).
- In the case of a *horizontal* breakdown, every subplant is divided into individual sub-functions or processes (e.g. mechanics, construction, electrics, control, etc.) and these services are jointly provided by a specialist, or specialists (for extremely complex capital goods) for all subplants.

The importance of this basic decision, which is made by the customer, their consultant, or even the supplier coalition, is difficult to overstate. Firstly, this defines interfaces at which quality, deadline and other cooperation problems can arise. And, secondly, this also determines the cooperation and coordination requirements that occur when the distributed tasks have to be merged into a marketable and functional whole. In most cases, a vertical breakdown will only be considered for extremely complex and heterogeneous plants. In this case, a horizontal breakdown will generally take place in a second step.

Every more detailed breakdown of a capital good creates additional interfaces. These are risk factors and lead to coordination costs and possibly additional transaction costs. However, on the other hand, occasionally the cost benefits of specialist manufacturers can be exploited, if individual single tasks are separated from a package. These need to be weighed against each other in each individual case: integration quality benefits and the reduction of coordination costs versus specialization benefits and other benefits (e.g. deadline-related benefits in the division of labor).

The following partner selection criteria play a key role when deciding *which* company will take over a certain tasks. Of central importance is the question of who will be responsible for the overall planning of the technical and commercial proposal, the overall acquisition management and the management of the order and project management. The decision on the management, occasionally also referred to as overall control within the supplier association, is reached:

(a) Based on the dominance of certain components as part of the plant (example: the dominance of electrical suppliers for power plants),
(b) Based on the dominance of process know-how (example: the dominance of the supplier who is the process owner in the case of chemical plants),
(c) Based on the quantitative share (volume) of the order and
(d) Based on the dominance of commercial/organizational shares of the overall performance.

Two special features arise in this respect: some companies are specialized in "trading" capital goods and more complex plants. This means: they offer to manage the processing of plant construction orders without having any (significant) manufacturing capacities and often also without capacities for many of the required services. For example, the focus on the planning of the overall design of the plant, the acquisition activities, the process monitoring and the coordination management. Any necessary process know-how is outsourced to specialist providers or purchased.

The second feature is the opportunity of integrating special suppliers for the delivery and service coordination, which is particularly important in competition (material, personnel, deadline-related). For example, these providers may take over the project management tasks. This gives them a key position in a supplier association, which needs to be ensured both organizationally and contractually, so that they have the relevant powers applicable for their overall responsibility. Also essential is the contractual establishment of the partition and breakdown of services and tasks amongst the suppliers with respect to risk aspects and the regulation of possible changes ("claims") as well as conflicts.

4.3.4 The Decision on the Cooperation Partner

Due to the associated risks, the decision on the partner(s) in a project cooperation must be based on a comprehensive and systematic analysis, similar to that of a formal supplier selection and evaluation. This at least requires the preparation of a checklist of the important criteria. The following checklist provides an overview of a few key criteria that should be analyzed in connection with the selection of partners from the group of considered companies. The basic questions that must be asked is: Which partner best meets the requirements for a successful order acquisition and/or management and the requirements for the application of any proposed form of cooperation? This question must be reviewed with regard to the following summarized aspects:

1. Resources and capacities of a potential partner:
   - Technical
   - Organizational
   - Personnel
   - Financial and
   - Know-how-related (including sales/marketing know-how)
   - Reputation/standing

   The following must be clarified: Where and how can a partner help

- in acquisition,
- in financing,
- in local contacts,
- in project management and
- in after-sales services?

2. Customer specifications and preferences:
   The selection of coalition partners often has to consider mandatory customer specifications. In some cases, the customer specifies consortium partners or even subcontractors (in international business this is referred to as "*named subcontractors*", "*nominated subcontractors*"). The reasons for these kinds of specifications from the customer's perspective include existing business relationships or the special capacities of the relevant supplier. This particularly occurs in international marketing, if customers require the fulfillment of *suborders in their own country* (=*Local Content;* if this relates to production: *Local Manufacturing*). A review must also take place to confirm that the considered partners meet the prequalification characteristics specified by the customer. In some cases, certain partners are selected in order to jointly meet prequalification criteria (Engelhardt and Günter 1981, p. 126 et seqq.).
3. Performance and quality criteria:
   - Quality, scope and limitation of supplies and service
   - Local shares of the order/project (local content/local manufacturing)
   - Services, esp. after-sales services

- Financing services
- Standardization (options)
- Rights of use, industrial property rights (patent licenses, etc.)
- Sales capacities (incl. location and branch issues)
- Availability of capacities, delivery deadlines
- Spare parts supply and
- Proposal design and presentation

4. Partner contacts and experiences with the customer, if applicable with their consultants or in the customer country; references and reputation with the customer, in the customer country, in third countries.
5. Additional qualities and expected behavior of a partner, etc.:
   - Risk tolerance; risk distribution (e.g. liability issues)
   - Division and allocation of tasks in acquisition and management
   - Takeover of organizational functions (e.g. management/control)
   - Distribution of costs
   - Credit rating
   - Currency
   - Language and communication
   - Conformity with the corporate policy and culture
   - Compatibility with other partners and
   - The partner's political environment
6. Conditions of cooperation, e.g.:
   - Possible types of contracts
   - Intensity of the cooperation
   - Partner relationship, exclusivity agreements, licensing
   - Term of the agreements and
   - Opportunities for attractive follow-up cooperation
7. Own experience with certain partners (e.g. with regard to the pricing behavior)
8. Competition situation and Competitive strategy perspectives
9. Risk considerations with regard to the considered partner

The result of the review of all the above considerations will allow the group of potential partners to be narrowed down and concentrated. This group can then be further reduced by negotiations. The decision on the cooperation partner then moves to the phase of contractual specification of the cooperation.

4.4 Cooperation Risks and Contracts

Project cooperation and other forms of cooperation enable barriers to access to be overcome and strengths to be bundled; however, they also involve typical risks. Cooperation primarily serves to diversify and limit commercial risks. However, it also introduces additional, new risks. An example is the risk of default of a 'weak' partner in international business.

Table 6 Barriers to cooperation

1. Mentality of "not invented here" or "not produced here"
2. Risks of a know-how leakage and loss
3. Low acceptance and lack of trust in appropriate partners
4. Inadequate contractual clarification of the interests and distribution principles
5. Coordination effort and cost
6. Other subjective perceived risks

The first factor that threatens a cooperation, or makes its success seem uncertain, is the resistance of individuals or entire organizational units against inter-company cooperation ("barriers to cooperation"; Günter 1992, p. 801 et seqq.). On identification of these kinds of barriers, the task is to develop and analyze instruments and strategies that could be suitable for overcoming barriers to cooperation. From a range of various outcomes, a few aspects seem to repeatedly emerge as barriers (cf. Table 6).

The barriers displayed in Table 6 are barriers to entering and/or pursuing a cooperation. Their existence impairs the course as well as the outcome of an already arranged project cooperation. The risks associated with a cooperation, particularly the perceived uncertainties of decision-makers, can also be interpreted as barriers. For procurement decisions in the capital goods sector, the *perceived risk* has been comprehensively discussed as a variable in the purchase decision-making process (synoptic Gemünden 1985). It is therefore prudent to consider both possible "objective risks" as well as the "perceived risk" as a barrier to cooperation in connection with an inter-company cooperation (Günter 1992, p. 802 et seqq.; Molter 1986). In a subjective consideration, a decision-maker's perceived risk can be viewed as a relevant influencing factor on cooperation decisions. These kinds of risk-based decision-making circumstances relate to the partner selection, the restriction of the fields of activity, liability and warranty issues, exclusivity clauses and contractual conditions as well as potential strategic consequences as a result of the cooperation.

In particular, the practical literature on plant and system marketing presents a range of different risk catalogs. This is predominantly due to the fact that the issue of risk limitation for complex capital goods systems with considerable volumes, generally high degree of customization as well as innovation, is of critical economic importance. These risk catalogs (Höffken and Schweitzer 1991, p. 14 et seqq.; otherwise: Verein Deutscher Ingenieure VDI 1991) deal with the risks that arise from marketing these kinds of goods and systems, usually not under the label of perceived risks. However, the following risk assessment clearly shows that, ultimately, both objective as well as perceived risks have an influence on decisions, e.g. as part of the inquiry evaluation and order planning (Backhaus 1980, p. 36; Heger 1988; and Chaps. 1 and 2). In general, the findings from the reappraisal of applicable risk catalogs in the literature show that risks, which (only) arise due to entering/having to enter into a cooperation in the first place—i.e. from the involvement in a consortium to market an industrial plant—are usually underestimated.

Table 7 Types of cooperation risks in horizontal project cooperation

A. Acquisition and proposal preparation risks
Partner-related order receipt risk
Risk of changes to the desired own project share
Cooperation cost risks (interfaces risk)
Risk of default/replacement of partners
B. Risks from processing customer orders after order receipt
Cooperation-based performance risks
Risks from interface changes
Cooperation-based payment risks
Cooperation cost risk (additional cooperation expense)
Risk of default/replacement of partners
Residual risk from risk transfer measures
C. Cross-project risks
Risks from the transfer or leakage of know-how
Risks from the transfer of data and online communication
Image risk as a result of the circumstances of cooperation

These types of risk factors constantly arise in practice; they can be controlled and diversified by carefully planned cooperation contracts (VDI 1991; Chelsom 1989). Table 7 shows a catalog of cooperation risks—compiled from findings in the business—whose consideration is particularly important for project cooperation in the industrial plant construction and engineering sector.

The checklist in Table 7 can be viewed as a "profile grid" that provides information on the various types of cooperation-based risks. It is therefore also the basis for the following development of risk management strategies amongst partners in a horizontal project cooperation (VDI 1991). However, it can also provide indications of how risks can be identified in *other* forms of cooperation, which need to be dealt with in cooperation interactions and which are objects of subjective perceptions and evaluations. For example, it can be assumed that perceived cooperation risks are directly linked to the intensity of the relationship that a company is prepared to enter into. This also creates a link to the incidental stability of a cooperation observed over time.

Project and cooperation risks must be identified and managed in a systematic manner. Forms of risk management include: Risk assumption, risk avoidance, risk reduction, risk sharing and risk transfer. The necessary tool in this respect is the preliminary decision on the company's own order share in the project; this decision results in the assumption of certain risks and the avoidance of others. However, the key risk management tool in a cooperation is contract management (Günter 1995), which secures the cooperation in law (VDI 1991, p. 138 et seqq.).

This "make-safe" is necessary, as the partners invest significant amounts in preparing and developing the proposal (offer). These expenses, including potential tender fees and previously established bid bonds or tender guarantees are lost if the cooperation partner can withdraw so that the company considered here is at risk that their proposal will either not be submitted on time, that it will be incomplete, or that they will also have to withdraw. If the company's own concept is based on a certain technical process or patent of a cooperation partner who is able to withdraw, this may even mean that the company's own proposal will become entirely impossible. Besides the material loss of the project expenses, there may also be a considerable loss of prestige in relation to the customer and potentially the entire market.

It is absolutely essential to contractually commit important cooperation partners to a project at an early stage, unless the strategic option of remaining flexible for as long as possible is considered important. The early specification of cooperation partners can also provide competitive advantages, in that due to their exclusive commitment to your company, they are no longer available for competitors.

Cooperation agreements can be reached through online communication, in writing, verbally or even over the phone. The simplest case only involves the agreement of the cooperation as such, while the further details are subject to subsequent regulation or statutory regulation. Table 8 displays the three options regarding the contractual commitment for a project cooperation (VDI 1991, p. 142 et seqq.).

This leads to the question of how comprehensive a cooperation agreement should be. For a cooperation with intense and complex, i.e. generally association-like relationships between the partners, the cooperation agreement must be adequately extensive in order to prevent future conflicts. If no particular legal form of the cooperation is agreed, the regulations of §§ 705 ff. BGB (German Civil Code) apply in Germany. These regulations on "partnerships under civil law" are general and are included under dispositive law, i.e. they are not mandatory, rather they are at the disposal of the partners (cooperation partners). First of all, this means that they provide the option that the partners can flexibly adapt their cooperation to the relevant project requirements. And, secondly, this does not permit any further reliance on a 'legal background'.

For example, § 706 BGB stipulates that all partners must provide the same contributions, i.e. performances. Pursuant to § 708 BGB, the partners are only liable towards each other to the extent that they would require due care and diligence in their own matters. As the deliveries and services provided by the individual partners, as well as their mutual liability and their liability to external parties, are the two main issues of any major cooperation project, this once again identifies the overwhelming necessity for the contractual specification of the cooperation agreement; in this case, in the form of extensive liability clauses, potentially

Table 8 Three paths to contractual commitment in a project cooperation

The cooperation contract is . . .	
Path A	. . . a bundle of loose, not particularly precise, individual agreements; this "package" is constantly supplemented and adapted during the cooperation
Path B	. . . a general framework agreement that is expanded with flexible annexes and supplements
Path C	. . . a detailed contract with all the necessary regulations that is concluded at an early stage

Table 9 The differing interests in relation to an exclusivity clause

	Case A The partner's capacities can be substituted	Case B The partner's capacities cannot be substituted
From the perspective of the customer (e.g. general contractor)	No interest in exclusivity	Interest in exclusivity
From the perspective of the supplier (e.g. subcontractor)	Interest in exclusivity	No interest in exclusivity

Table 10 Benefits and disadvantages of exclusivity clauses

Benefits of commitment	• Secure an attractive partner
	• Increased planning certainty
	• Risk reduction, e.g. with regard to know-how and data protection
	• Reduction of certain costs
Disadvantages of commitment	• "Suboptimal" selection of cooperation partners
	• Inflexibility

in consortium contracts. The description of the partner deliveries and services often needs to be specified in a separate annex to the contract due to its scope.

Companies are more likely to find themselves in this situation in cooperation projects with foreign partners. The validity of German law can often not be enforced in this case. In many cases the partner's national law or the law of a neutral country, e.g. Swiss law, is agreed. However, these provisions are rarely more appropriate than those provided by §§ 705 ff. BGB. As the particularly strong principle of "good faith", specific to German law, is generally significantly less effective in foreign legislation, this once again reveals the necessity for the contractual specification of cooperation agreements.

Contract management cannot be covered in detail at this point; however, Chap. 5 is dedicated to this topic. The section on the organizational forms of supplier coalitions provides information on the division of performances and risks (Günter 1995). Only the problem of the exclusivity regulation in a project cooperation will now be addressed. On the question of whether a cooperation partner is interested in exclusively committing either themselves or others, the chart in Table 9 shows which differing interests typically arise for specific capacity constellations (VDI 1991, p. 1460). Table 10 compares the arguments for and against exclusive commitment to a certain cooperation constellation.

4.5 Cooperative, Inter-company Project Management

If a supplier or a supplier coalition receives a targeted project order, the main tasks to be managed in *cooperation* are as follows:

- Potential detail negotiations with the customer (technical, commercial)
- Procurement, potentially also the manufacture, transport, installation and commissioning, and
- Providing accompanying services, including financing

In every case there is a high need for cooperation if overall performances are divided and allocated across several suppliers. Performance, deadline and payment coordination must be strictly organized. Project management has proven to be an efficient method of organization in this respect (see Chap. 7 as well as Bea et al. 2011). For larger projects, a cross-company project management, headed by a "*Managing contractor*" has to take over the coordination, management and monitoring tasks in order to reduce the interface risks. In general, the project management is the responsibility of a project manager employed by the technical or commercial manager (principal), if the project is managed within a consortium. However, a *buy* rather than *make* decision is also possible—similar to *outsourcing* (Günter and Kuhl 2000). In this case, project coordination and monitoring is purchased from external service providers. This external project management, particularly common for larger construction or infrastructure projects, may have specialization benefits, may help to prevent capacity bottlenecks and responsibility is easier to assign.

Far-reaching cooperation decisions may frequently also change the cooperation and its structure after receipt of the order. If it proves to be unavoidable, proposal partners may need to be replaced, e.g. if delivery deadlines cannot be complied with. Possible changes to the service to be provided, or in the contract with the customer (which is based on the submitted proposal) must therefore be regulated in a 'change or claim management' clause in the plant contract as a precautionary measure. Accordingly, a change clause in the supplier coalition cooperation contract must allow for smooth adaptations. The necessity of aligning the internal cooperation contract, which regulates the internal relationship in the supplier coalition, to the conditions in the customer contract must be emphasized. For example, if this is not the case, agreements with the customer regarding deadlines or warranties, which are *not* regulated and specified between the consortium partners, can lead to disputes over respective areas of competence, performance gaps, delays in deliveries, liabilities, additional costs and reduced earnings (Molter 1986).

4.6 Termination of a Project Cooperation and Consequences

A cooperation contract ends on fulfillment of all the obligations entered into in the internal relationships between the partners (VDI 1991, p. 252 et seqq.). However, in a marketing cooperation, the fulfillment of the external obligations towards the customer is usually a requirement. Cooperation contracts also permit termination based on premature termination. In addition, certain circumstances, e.g. insolvency of a partner, enable a project cooperation to be terminated.

A termination based on fulfillment is regulated in § 362 (1) BGB (German civil law). When a contract is deemed to be fulfilled depends on the type of contract. The determination of the fulfillment of the contract requires an analysis of the contractual agreements and the type of contract in accordance with the applicable law. Even if a cooperation contract is terminated due to fulfillment, post-contractual obligations may remain or arise, which results in a continuation of a cooperation relationship (warranty claims, ancillary obligations, such as confidentiality obligations or the obligation to maintain and defend a property right). Additional obligations may also be included, such as those relating to environmental protection or product liability law. So, the fulfillment of the contractual tasks is not necessarily the 'natural end' of a cooperation in all cases.

Customer contracts normally contain termination or withdrawal clauses that entitle the customer to either terminate the contract for the future (generally with immediate effect) or, in the case of withdrawal, cancel the contract retrospectively. Internal cooperation regulations generally provide for similar, if not broader agreements, on the premature termination of the cooperation. If the customer prematurely terminates the supply contract with a general contractor, this contractor must be sure that they are also able to terminate the corresponding subcontractor contracts. Consortium contracts usually contain two separate regulations on premature termination of a contract. If the customer terminates the contract with the consortium, this terminates the consortium contract, and the customer contract regulations on the specification of the level of performance with regard to the payments made apply accordingly for internal settlement within the consortium. The other standard regulation provides for the right of members of a consortium to exclude a member of the consortium from the consortium, (for example) if this member seriously breaches their performance obligations.

Beyond the considerations on the termination of a project cooperation, the longer-term consequences from cooperatively provided proposal and order management must also be covered. The successful or less successful sale of a complex capital good also has consequences for a supplier's image. The construction of a plant becomes a reference, which can be used in the communication policy for subsequent projects. The need for cooperation means that image and reference effects are also dependent on the good or poor performance of the cooperation *partner*.

Successful project management increases the opportunities for follow-up orders for a supplier who becomes an *in-supplier* for a certain customer or in a customer country compared to an *out-supplier*.

Ultimately, positive cooperation experiences in a plant project have consequences on subsequent cooperation. In many cases, these experiences, the clarification of interface issues and better information about the proposal partner (=risk reduction) result in known partners receiving preferred treatment for subsequent projects. As a result, cooperation decisions for capital good proposals are not just important on a case-by-case basis, but are also an effective strategic marketing instrument.

5 Project Cooperation in Supplier Coalitions

The previous consideration of the structure and the course of a project cooperation in Sect. 4 identified the topic of the organizational form of a project cooperation; this will be looked at in the following Sect. 5, as the scope and importance of the decisions require certain considerations on the various forms of supplier coalitions (Günter 1977, 1979).

In certain economic sectors, such as the industrial plant business, several suppliers are generally required to receive an order and manage the process, in order to be able to offer the customer's required scope of supplies and manage the order. Two or more suppliers may form a supplier coalition for this reason, in order to submit a joint proposal for a system or a plant and manage the order once it is received. The typical method for organizing project-based cooperation in the plant business and for construction projects are supplier associations, for which the term *supplier coalition* has become established (Günter 1977). These forms of cooperation are based on case by case contractual relationships between the partners, in which the division of the deliveries and services, the customer payment, the liability and other risks are regulated.

Project-based supplier coalitions are predominantly established in four basic organizational forms (Günter 1979; Lemiesz 1978; Hautkappe 1986; Backhaus and Voeth 2010, p. 351 et seqq.):

- As a general contractor with subcontractors
- As consortium
- As a general contractor with an internal consortium (sometimes called "silent consortium" or even "hidden consortium") and
- As a joint venture or syndicate (especially in the construction industry)

The form of a European Economic Interest Grouping (EEIG) and a few others also need to be considered. The decision on one of these forms, if no requirements are specified by a project customer, falls to the considered cooperation partners as a consequence of the desired project structure and distribution. The following roles are available for the individual partner companies:

- General contractor
- Consortium partner, either as the consortium manager (principal) or as a consortium partner (basic member of the consortium)
- Partner in a syndicate, or
- Subcontractor to a general contractor or a consortium partner

This function and role decision also needs to consider the needs and expectations of the project customer and potential cooperation partners.

5.1 General Contractor

In the case of a *general contractor*, a single company takes overall responsibility for the planning, control and management of an industrial project (cf. diagram in Fig. 3). The general contractor, prime contractor or main contractor, is solely responsible towards the customer for the provision of the overall supplies and is solely liable to the customer. The general contractor assigns other suppliers to provide goods and services in the general contractor's name and behalf. This may take place with the knowledge or even at the behest of the principal. The suppliers assigned by the general contractor are in a subcontractor relationship with the general contractor. The term "subcontractor" is used in this respect. However, this is still referred to as a supplier *coalition*, as the general contractor can only carry out their tasks in close cooperation with the subcontractors. Furthermore, in some cases, subcontractors may also be in direct project-based contact with the plant customer, so that a group of suppliers must be considered in this relationship. However, the responsibility for the overall project is centralized to the general contractor at the request of, and in the interests of, the customer ("package from a single source and a single contact").

Out of the group of potential coalition partners, the general contractor is considered to be the company that is in a position

- To prepare the entire project planning and/or
- To take over the acquisition management and project management and/or
- To provide the most important part of the supplies with regard to value/scope, or with regard to the key elements, i.e. which has the "core competence", that characterizes a project. This often excludes construction services; in contrast to

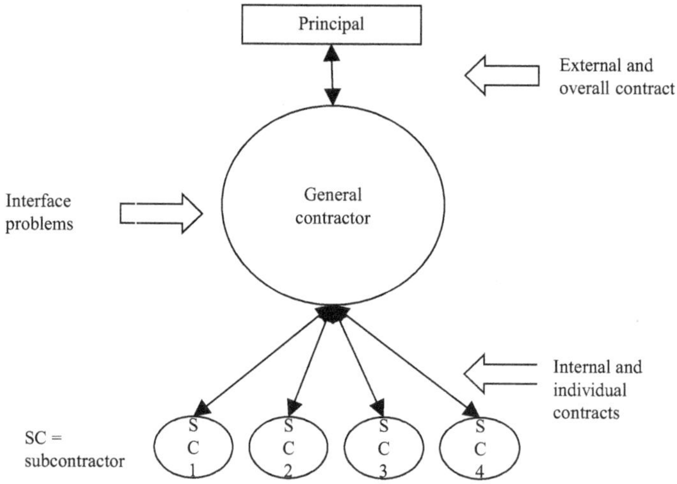

Fig. 3 General contractor with subcontractors (VDI 1991, p. 34)

traffic and construction works, a construction company never takes on the role of general contractor for industrial plants

Of particular importance is the service that integrates all the subservices to a complete major plant. The general contractor's strengths lie more in the necessary process know-how and less in their share of the service. These may be minimal in the case of engineering companies.

Notable benefits of general contractors are that the general contractor has a great deal of freedom in determining their own part of the supplies and performance in a project as well as in the planning and implementation of a technical and economic concept. This is considerably larger than for other forms of supplier coalitions. On the other hand, general contractors are exposed to significant risks, which may sometimes be externally influenced and which cannot always be balanced by additional remuneration or the opportunity to influence the overall project. These kinds of problems generally arise where interfaces between the various subcontractor supplies or between the subcontractors and the tasks of the general contractor arise (difference risks). Gaps generally arise both in the task and performance area as well as in the remuneration and contracting area (contract policy), whose closure is the main task of the general contractor. This requires interface management.

Example 2
The customer requests a warranty period of two years; subcontractor A grants this for their part of the performance, but subcontractor B concedes a maximum of one year. The general contractor may have to take over this warranty to rectify this discrepancy. The general contractor can attempt to transfer these risks to subcontractors who answer to the general contractor. However, this will not always be possible, especially as the general contractor alone is responsible to the customer. Whether the general contractor may have recourse to the subcontractors depends on the contractual relationship between the general contractor and the subcontractor in each individual case.

The general contractor is faced with a variety of decision-making and coordination problems and huge risks in acquisition, proposal planning and management. Their proposal planning must consider possible coordination difficulties in future phases in order to mitigate the risks that arise for the general contractor due to their exclusive responsibility towards the principal. Some of these problem areas are covered here as examples (Nicklisch 1984):

- The general contractor runs into difficulties in project management if individual cooperation partners (subcontractors) do not provide their deliveries on time or in accordance with the requirements. The consequences for the overall project resulting from a potential delay in delivery of individual subcontractors cannot simply be entirely imposed on the responsible party.

- The warranty period for subservices may have expired before the corresponding deadlines for the overall plant even start. In this case the contract policy must kick in and ensure cooperation.
- Problems regarding the coordination of customer payments with the general contractor payments to the subcontractors (assumption or exclusion of the general contractor's del credere liability).
- Agreements on decisions by a court of arbitration and other conflict resolution mechanisms may disintegrate between the parties involved.
- Limitation and assignment of warranty obligations and liability (contractual penalties) often pose the greatest difficulties.
- If a subcontractor damages the overall project while performing their subservices, the general contractor is fundamentally initially liable to the customer. The opportunity for recourse against the party responsible for the damage is often difficult in view of the disproportionate nature of the loss and the delivery, or due to the size of the subcontractor.
- The general contractor also has additional financial burdens, such as bank guarantees, advances for transport costs, custom payments, reimbursement of port fees, etc.
- A general contractor requires a project management that commits highly qualified specialists and which also poses a capacity problem.

The remuneration for taking on the role of general contractor (on average of about 10–15 % of the total order price) may not be able to balance the risks and costs. A general contractor is generally considered for turn-key plants (turn-key projects) and in cases in which the subservices cannot be clearly defined and which can result in significant risks for the customer. A general contractor is generally only assigned at the urgent request of the customer, who lacks the know-how (e.g. developing countries) or who wants clear responsibilities from one source.

The general contractor may attempt to transfer the risks to subcontractors through contractual agreements. As shown by the above examples of problems that may occur, this may be faced with significant difficulties in some cases.

5.2 Open Consortium

A *consortium* is a special form of Joint venture or syndicate. This involves the coming together of a limited number of legally and, generally, also economically independent companies (*consortium partners, members of the consortium*) with similar and/or complementary areas of operation for a specific and temporary cooperation.

In the case of a consortium, the project customer contract is with the consortium and not with the individual suppliers. This means that the *consortium* appears as the contractor (cf. diagram in Fig. 4). Each member of the consortium is jointly and severally liable, unless otherwise explicitly agreed in the contract with the customer. Joint and several liability means that each consortium partner is fully liable

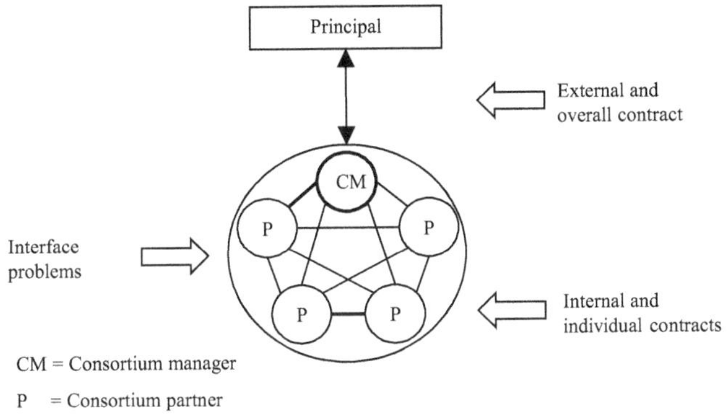

Fig. 4 The open consortium (VDI 1991, p. 37)

for the execution of the overall performance, i.e. not just their section, in their external relationship. The customer can hold each individual member of the consortium liable to fulfill their claims from the contract on the project with regard to warranty, compensation, penalties, etc.

According to German law, a consortium is generally operated in the form of a BGB company in accordance with §§ 705 ff. BGB, in which one of the companies involved acts as the consortium manager (principal) and takes over the technical and administrative management. This company receives compensation from the other members of the consortium for these activities.

The consortium partners conclude a consortium contract between each other, which regulates the rights and duties of every individual supplier (cf. Table 11). The contract also regulates the definition and limitation of the deliveries and services to be provided by each member of the consortium, including any potential change Regulations and claims. A so-called 'completeness clause' must be considered, which defines—in a general form—the process if unforeseen gaps arise in the service descriptions and limitations. Regulations regarding liability and warranties, in the event of customer or third party claims, must also be considered, as well as claims raised by members of the consortium against each other and for unclear cases in which (for example) the party responsible cannot be defined, or at least not directly. Table 11 provides an overview of additional regulation requirements (Horn 1986; VDI 1991).

A consortium is formed either before or, frequently, after the awarding of the contract, potentially also in the preliminary project planning stage for the contractual object. For the acquisition and proposal planning, it seems to be important that contacts take place between potential consortium partners at an early stage, not least to allow them to participate in the endeavors of individual companies to obtain certain major orders and to exercise a certain amount of influence. The distribution of the proposal costs must be regulated in each individual case. It must be regulated in the consortium contract together with the other charges to which the project is exposed and which the consortium partners must deal with.

Table 11 The key content of a consortium contract

1. Consortium objective and partners
2. Definition and limitation of delivery and service sections for every member of the consortium with potential change regulations and claims, incl. completeness clause
3. Liability and warranty for customer claims due to performance by one or more members of the consortium that is not in accordance with the contract due to delay, incorrect or non-performance for third party claims in the event of unclear cases (where the responsible party cannot be defined)
4. Management (principal): Activities, incl. limitations, costs (management fee), liability
5. General duties of the members of the consortium, e.g. information and cooperation obligations
6. Proposal preparation, project organization and management, scheduling
7. Consortium meeting and coordination modalities
8. Financing and the provision of security (bonds, e.g. bid bonds = bid guarantees and performance bonds = performance guarantees)
9. Insurances
10. Financial transaction (payments) and accounting
11. Exclusivity agreement (if necessary)
12. Court of arbitration and applicable law
13. Formal provisions (term of the contract, withdrawal or exclusion of members of the consortium, termination, confidentiality, etc.)

The reasons that induce suppliers to establish a consortium can be diverse and vary significantly for the individual participants:

- The necessary division of labor with regard to the areas of performance due to specialization is an obvious reason. This generally results in the cooperation of companies from the construction, mechanical engineering and electronics as well as IT sectors.
- If the project exceeds a certain volume, this may mean that the involvement of other suppliers is necessary simply for reasons of capacity. In this case, it is often advisable to make these partners fully responsible and involve them in the consortium. The size of the project does not just impact on the scope of service, but also on the manner of risks, which then require liability to be divided between the parties. Similar consequences for consortium cooperation may arise for particularly complex projects and in the case of insufficient know-how of the individual companies in the functional as well as the management area.
- If the customer requests the construction of a plant within a relatively short period, this may also require the formation of a consortium, especially if a capacity expansion is not possible, or seems too risky with regard to long-term employment aspects.
- High costs of acquisition and order attainment may require the bundling of resources. The exploitation of certain sales market know-how and customer relationships may also play a role.

- Financial aspects have an important impact on the formation of a consortium. Firstly, bid bonds may be required, which represent a burden that is easier to bear if it is carried across several shoulders. Furthermore, in some cases, there are significant financial resource requirements for advance payments, investments, building site facilities, etc., for which a distribution is also advisable. Finally, a consortium can provide for the customer's credit requests, especially if export financing and subsidies from other countries can be exploited with the aid of foreign consortium partners. The latter also applies for export credit insurances. In these cases, the involvement of foreign partners in a consortium becomes a tool to secure cheaper financing and credit insurance conditions.
- Another beneficial aspect of a consortium is that it enables every individual member of the consortium to cooperate and participate in the customer negotiations as well as the performance and risk distribution to a much greater extent than would be the case in the role of a subcontractor in the case that a general contractor is assigned.

The selection of suitable partners for a consortium is one of the key issues relating to business cooperation (cf. also Sects. 4.3.3 and 4.3.4; VDI 1991, p. 93 et seqq.). A supplier is much more committed as part of a consortium than in the case of a subcontractor status. The supplier must pay particular attention to the selection of appropriate partners, especially their know-how and reputation, their credit rating and soundness as well as their own and third-party experiences and the assessment of the conflict options. For this reason, certain consortium partners in multiple cases or regularly work together in project cooperation. It is not just important to overcome certain technical interface problems (securing technical compatibility, business in general: the *integration quality*), but previous experiences with the same project management, including the associated difficulties, also play a role.

A reconciliation of interests can be extremely difficult within this kind of supplier coalition, especially if the order situation of the companies involved are different. Accordingly, their interest in obtaining a certain order will also diverge (potentially also due to concessions to the customer), as well as in reserving certain parts of the performance for themselves or in pushing through certain price expectations. Coordinating the time the services are to be provided and the coordination of the pricing (formulation of an overall proposal price for different price strategies amongst the individual partners) can also lead to difficulties. This means that know-how, image/reputation, credit rating, soundness, the minimization of interface problems and the lowest possible conflict potential (corporate cultures, compatibility of the product, price, distribution and other strategies) are important selection criteria for the members of the consortium.

The consortium (without a general contractor) becomes a legal entity towards third parties (external company) so that the customer can raise a warranty, compensation or other claim against *every* individual member of the consortium based on the principle of joint and several liability. For the customer, this has the benefit of distributing the basis for liability. Given that it takes over the joint and several liability for the performance of all the contractual obligations towards the customer, the customer has much better security than in the case of a general contractor or a component purchase. The joint and several liability means that the customer can initially approach any of the consortium partners in order to raise their claims, e.g. regarding warranty.

From the perspective of a project *customer*, the benefit of a consortium project cooperation lies in the distribution of the supplier's basis for liability.

A disadvantage for the customer may be that the consortium has more negotiating power than an individual company. A consortium is generally more able to exercise negotiation pressure than an individual supplier in the position of a component supplier or general contractor. If a large number of suppliers is included in a consortium, there may also be a reduced intensity of competition, as there are fewer competing proposals. Compared to the issuing of individual orders (component purchase), the latter is generally prima facie more cost-effective for customers with adequate know-how than placing the order with a consortium.

5.3 General Contractor with Internal Consortium

Today, a common form of supplier coalition for larger and international projects is the internal consortium with a general contractor. Consortia may appear as "open" or internal ("silent", "hidden") consortia. Both types are not distinguished by the fact of whether the customer is or is not aware of the existence of a consortium. Admittedly, the level of knowledge of the composition and function of the coalition is greater for an open consortium than for an internal consortium. However, for the latter, it is customary that the customer is aware of the companies involved in the consortium, that they are informed of changes and that they may potentially even influence the composition. Rather, the differences lie in the legal structure and consequences.

In the case of an internal consortium (cf. the diagram in Fig. 5), the formal external relationship is that of a general contractor. One supplier (the *internal* consortium manager) concludes an independent contract with the customer, i.e. the project customer, in the *external* relationship. As a result, they alone are initially responsible for the overall performance towards the customer. The customer concludes a project-based contract with a general contractor.

In the *internal* relationship between the cooperation partners, who cluster around the general contractor, or are involved by them, the general contractor concludes a consortium contract with additional suppliers, in which the latter take on the risks from the customer contract. In this case the liability for the overall performance is divided amongst the consortium partners in the internal relationship, resulting in a corresponding risk diversification. Regardless of this, the general contractor can enter into contracts with subcontractors, as is the case for every member of the internal consortium.

The internal consortium differs from a pure general contractor type in the structure of the internal relationship (supplier coalition instead of subcontractor

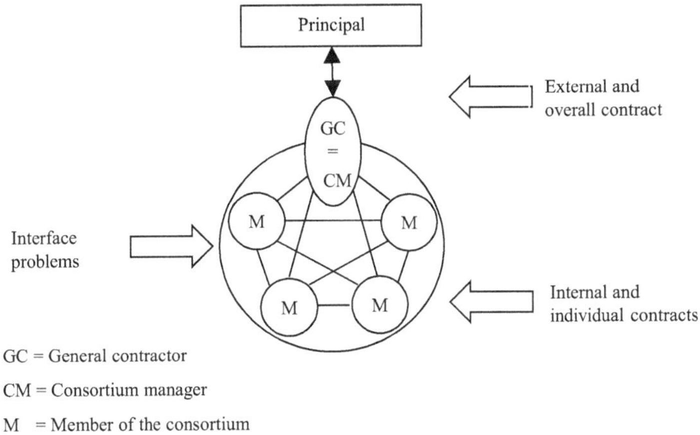

Fig. 5 The hidden consortium (VDI 1991, p. 38)

relationships) and from an open consortium in the structure of the external relationship (*one* contact for liability and warranty issues instead of several contacts for the customer).

The primary benefit of the internal consortium is that the negotiation and responsibility is centralized for the customer, but that an—internal—risk diversification is achieved amongst the suppliers.

5.4 Syndicate

A syndicate also involves the amalgamation of various suppliers in order to provide a certain service for a temporary project period. While a consortium is similar to a supply association of independent partners and the performance takes place independently in the individual companies, a syndicate takes the place of the actual provider of the project. In contrast to a consortium, a syndicate has an independent joint asset, which the partners provide (for example) in the form of machines. The syndicate takes on the role of the employer and assigns orders, such as for the procurement of construction material. A syndicate renders account independently. The partners involved distribute the profit and loss following the conclusion of the project. It has features similar to a temporary company that acts independently and as a separate entity. Project cooperation in the form of a syndicate primarily takes place in the construction industry.

5.5 Decision-Making Criteria for Selecting a Form of Cooperation

The decision on one of the organizational forms described can take place based on different criteria from the perspective of the various parties involved. A few of the most important criteria are:

- Possible customer wishes or requirements
- Targeted scope of tasks or supplies and share of earnings
- Know-how and capacities (capacity objectives)
- Development of certain markets/market segments, potentially with the aid of cooperation
- Profiling and reference
- Consultation and cooperation in the supplier coalition and
- Willingness to take risks

The key benefits and disadvantages of a general contractor or a consortium and the most important decision-making criteria between the two forms are compared in Table 12.

Aside from that, the issue of the time at which a project cooperation is to be contractually established is also important for the structure and the course of a project cooperation in the organizational forms mentioned above.

The *early* establishment of supplier coalitions takes place in the inquiry or proposal (preparation) phase for projects. A *late* commitment can be referred to,

Table 12 Comparison of a general contractor and consortium (Backhaus and Voeth 2010, p. 355)

	General contractor	Consortium
Benefits for the customer	• Only one negotiation partner • Overall risk under one roof	• Performance shares can be negotiated directly • Liability base is enlarged
Benefits for the supplier	• Internal performance can be freely determined for a general contractor • Free selection of subcontractors • Reference benefit	• Share of risk falls for all suppliers • Direct customer contact, not just for the general contractor, but for all members of the consortium (reference) • Financing support may be able to be utilized, if direct customer contact is provided as a requirement
Disadvantages for the customer	• Potentially low liability base for the supplier • If internal know-how is great, services, which may be able to be provided internally, need to be surrendered	• Several negotiating partners • Must be able to assess interface problems
Disadvantages for the supplier	• If the delivery conditions cannot be transferred • Higher risk for the general contractor	• Higher costs due to coordination requirements • Direct liability of all members of the consortium

if a supplier (contractor, general contractor, main contractor) only contractually commits cooperation partners *after* receipt of the order. A cooperation decision and partner selection in the proposal preparation phases is recommended,

- If a supplier is relying on strong market partners, their know-how and capacities
- If the customer has preferences for *specific* proposal partners or supply countries
- If the respective performance has not yet been well-structured and partners are required to structure and specify the proposal
- In contrast, coalitions tend to be formed at later phases
- If the main contractor is in a position to prepare and negotiate the proposal in adequate detail
- If the supplier has a strong market position, possibly even a unique selling point with their products or know-how, or if they enjoy a high preference level with the customer

5.6 Typical Sources of Error When Selecting the Form of Cooperation

Before a decision is made on the form of cooperation, the decision-making parties need to have another look at the following perspectives, which have repeatedly proven to be typical sources of error during the decision-making process (VDI 1991, p. 82 et seqq.).

If a cooperation relationship is to be entered into, special attention must be paid to the following parameters:

- The respective cooperation partner's product range
- The power relationships within the cooperating group
- The willingness of individual cooperation partners to take on risks, especially liability and warranty risks for their own delivery and performance share

Frequently, only the distribution of the deliveries and performances are clarified, while no overall concept that considers all the aspects is drafted for the cooperation. Down the track, this can lead to partners with the strongest interest in the project having to accept the cooperation conditions defined by other partners, which leads to a significant deterioration in the first partner's situation. As a result, all the important aspects of the cooperation must be contractually clarified at an early stage. This is even more important for corporate cooperation.

With respect to a balanced consideration of interests, it is important that all the partners involved make an equal effort to ensure the success of the cooperation. The interests of all partners should be aligned as closely as possible. If this fails, there is the risk that a partner, who has less interest in the transaction, will exploit the other partners with a greater interest for their own benefit, and at the expense of the partners with the stronger interest. This is where a balanced distribution of opportunities and risks is extremely important. In practice, cases sometimes arise that can be used as an example in this respect: a partner with no capacity for additional orders feigns a strong interest, or a partner from a country that grants government-backed credit and favors a competitor from this country, feels too secure in their role as a cooperation partner for these or other reasons. In these cases the partner's true interests are difficult to identify, but it should be attempted in order to prevent incorrect decisions.

Interface Problems

A task that is often neglected is the clear limitation of the areas of responsibility of the individual partners. If this results in gaps in the delivery or performance area, this can lead to significant performance, warranty and liability claims by the customer. This, in turn—especially in consortia—leads to serious disputes between the partners in order to clarify who bears the responsibility and the risk for the claims. The more consortium partners are involved, the more difficult, complicated and protracted the disputes. In the case of a general contractor, they alone bear the risk if the subcontracted deliveries and performances are not assigned properly or in full. However, in the event of disputes, the decision-making options are available to the general contractor alone.

Allocation of Risks

The deliveries and services and the associated areas of responsibility and risks, on the one hand, and the share of the customer price and payment flow, on the other, for the respective partner should align and 'fit'. A partner should take on and potentially calculate the risks that arise from their share, which they can influence and with which they should be familiar based on their experiences. Particular care is required if a partner is happy to take risks, but only has a low liability base (e.g. low share capital). Difficulties can easily arise in the case of risks that are difficult to manage (e.g. for local deliveries and performances, construction and installation). In these cases, the takeover of the respective activities by the customer, or a financial risk involvement by the customer can ease the burden.

Pricing in a Consortium

The cooperation decision should not lead to an unnecessary increase in the proposal and offer price for the project. This risk particularly exists in consortia, and especially if no adequate and clear limitation of responsibility and risk has been defined. Given that each partner bears a part of the other partners' risk in a consortium, due to the joint and several liability, there is the tendency to add these risks together, which can lead to significant price increases. This can only be avoided if all the partners agree to a standard approach to the calculation and openly discuss and jointly assess the risks arising from the cooperation and then agree on a corresponding pricing.

6 Product Development Cooperation

A special form of project cooperation is the cooperation in a project whose purpose is to develop new products or services. This typically relates to the following types of cooperation:

1. Cooperation between a technology supplying or product development company and a production and/or marketing company
2. Cooperation between manufacturers and retailers
3. Cooperation between a company and its suppliers and
4. Cooperation between a company and consultants

The cooperation with suppliers, mentioned in the third point, is used here by way of example. One of the project objectives in these types of cases is the acceleration of the innovation and development cycle. This intends to ensure that a product can enter the second stage of the product life cycle, the market cycle, as quickly as possible based on an accelerated market introduction. The method, which now plays a particular role in reducing the development time, is *Simultaneous Engineering* (Chelsom 1989). This refers to a project-based cooperation of the company in question with suppliers of materials, machines, etc. The aim is to ensure that consecutive steps, such as product development, material ordering, machinery acquisition, etc., overlap and take place in early cooperation with strategic partners on the procurement side (cf. the diagram in Fig. 6). This can be referred to as a vertical project cooperation from the perspective of the developing company. The specific features of simultaneous engineering are summarized in Table 13.

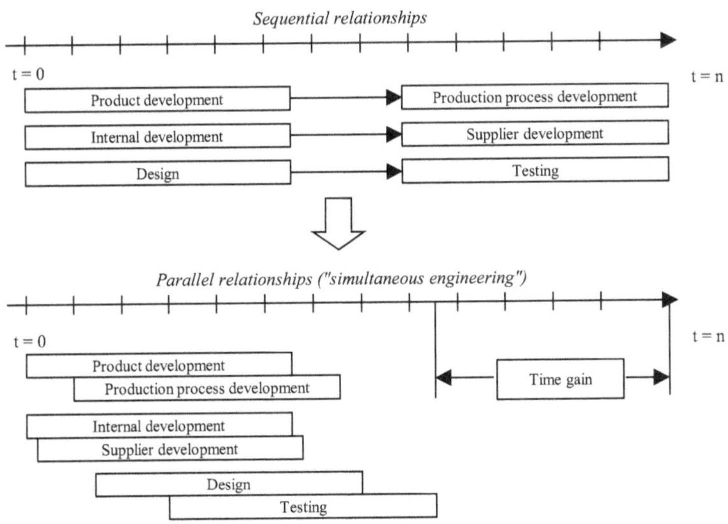

Fig. 6 Diagrammatic representation of planning processes with and without simultaneous engineering (based on Eichler and Steinau 1993, p. 29)

Table 13 Characteristics of simultaneous engineering

Simultaneous engineering
• Is the simultaneous development of products and production facilities with the support of internal project teams and the broad involvement of suppliers and system manufacturers
• Aims to shorten the innovation cycles and improve performance through early coordination
• Is used, for example, in vehicle construction, in the electrotechnical industry and in industrial plant construction
• Requires cross-product, -function and -divisional thoughts and actions, especially cooperation
• Synchronizes sales, production and procurement, etc.
• Must be applied across companies; suppliers, complementary suppliers and customers (users/ downstream processors) must be involved and coordinated
• Uses the opportunities provided by computer assisted design (CAD), engineering (CAE), manufacture (CAM), etc., including with the aid of remote data transmission between the companies involved
• Particularly makes use of the up-to-date methods of project management and project organization
• Opens opportunities in the area of innovation, quality and commitment of suppliers and customers
• Places high demands on partner selection, cooperation and organization
• Involves risks due to mutual dependencies
• Can or will often result in the establishment of long-term business relationships

Particular attention must be paid to the special feature of the decision on the partner selection for this form of project cooperation. The low level of structuring of development projects in early phases means that the early involvement of cooperation partners makes it inflexible and enables the outflow of know-how. It is therefore extremely important to select partners for which it can be identified or assessed that they will support the project and potentially become a permanent supplier for subsequent projects upon successful completion of the initial project. The developing company at least partially forgoes the option of obtaining various proposals in late innovation phases and playing competitors at the supplier level off against each other in favor of faster development times. Instead, the company commits to structuring and managing the project with the partners. This kind of decision requires extensive experience and confidence in the competence of these partners. A contractual safeguard is also required, e.g. with confidentiality and exclusivity clauses.

7 Project Cooperation "Between Market and Hierarchy"

Project cooperation in capital goods marketing is an intermediate form of economic activity between the extremes of "market coordination" (with a decentralized coordination of the decisions on the prices to be paid) and the "hierarchy" form of coordination, i.e. the established form of doing business within an amalgamation or an independent company. More recent economic theory approaches, especially those of New Institutional Economics, provide explanations as to why companies select one of the two extreme forms of coordination of economic activities, or why companies select cooperation as an intermediate form. The transaction cost theory can help to explain and to optimize the selection of an organizational form. It postulates the selection of the organizational form, or cooperation form that is associated with the lowest transaction costs. The transaction costs to be compared include the search costs, initiation costs, contracting costs and control costs (Thommen and Achleitner 2012, p. 861). Information and search costs arise for a project cooperation during partner selection and costs associated with the negotiation of cooperation contracts, while adaptation costs and control costs for these contracts arise as part of the project, configuration and claim management, such as for the industrial plant business. The transaction cost theory can also be used to explain partner changes or the longer-term stability of supplier coalitions in the industrial plant construction business.

A popular representation of the marketing participants is the so-called marketing triangle (supplier-customer-competitor). It is intended to visualize customer and competitor orientation in connection with the "conceptual competitive advantages" (Günter 1997; 2007). However, as discussed above, an extension is required for horizontal and, in a modified form, for vertical marketing cooperation and a "marketing square" has to be assumed (cf. Fig. 7; Günter 1992). This contains the cooperation partner(s) as the fourth element.

The marketing square provides a perspective that is aligned to cooperative strategies for the preparation of corporate decisions in an extended conceptual framework compared to the marketing triangle. It is a different way of thinking, which is based on the consideration of cooperation in marketing. With the increasing importance of vertical cooperation, the traditional perspective of the supplier and consumer/customer as market opponents is becoming less relevant. Admittedly, conflicts of interest between the supplier and the customer will continue to exist, even for this kind of cooperation. However, depending on the intensity of commitment of a business or cooperation relationship, an increasing importance or even dominance of joint, uni-directional objectives is being noticed. For example,

Fig. 7 The marketing square

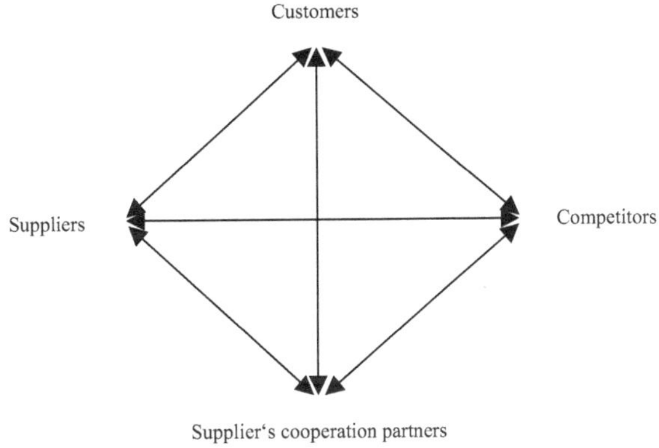

this is ultimately manifested in partial mergers of the participating organizations in project teams or teams for simultaneous engineering as well as in logistics and information chains for just-in-time relationships.

A special form of project cooperation and an example of a combination between a market-based and organizational hierarchy-based coordination is represented by a cooperation for projects in the industrial plant construction business, which is reflected in *BOT contracts* and *BOOT contracts* (cf. also Chap. 3). Build-Operate-Transfer and Build-Operate-Own-Transfer agreements are forms of a proposal and management of plant construction projects between customers and certain constellations of supplier coalitions. The identification of the contract types already provides an indication of the supplier constellation. They are based on the requirement and expectation of the plant customer, to transfer the planning and the construction of a plant ("build") as well as the operation ("operate") and potentially the ownership or joint ownership of the plant ("own") to the supplier. Customers expect a particularly intense commitment from the supplier from these agreements as well as relief in financing, know-how transfer and ultimately also risk reduction. In practice, the implementation of these kinds of requirements means that the supplier coalition also needs to include partners with operation know-how. These, as well as other potential partners, also need to engage in an operating company in the "Own" case. A common financing solution involves the remuneration for the supplier being generated from the income from operating a plant.

The commercial planning and implementation of this form of cooperation involves the following decision-making problems:

The customer specification is at least partially the result of information asymmetries, especially the customer's quality uncertainty regarding the quality of the performance. Suppliers can counteract this by quality signals, such as the submission of information or the establishment of a reputation and communication. However, the key tool and transaction design in terms of information economics is the conclusion of contingent contracts. BOT and BOOT agreements can *also* be interpreted as "contingent contracts" in this sense; at least they contain elements of such contracts. They contain contractual safeguards for the customer and principal in the event that the contractor(s) behave(s) opportunistically and do(es) not provide the desired assistance during or after completion, e.g. when operating the plant and to ensure it fulfills its function. This requires suppliers to reduce the customer's uncertainty by concluding these kinds of contingent contracts. As a result, operator know-how must be integrated during the partner selection and the commitment under commercial law in the case of "own" needs to be economically calculated and defined. The same applies to the financial commitment in the latter case, which suggests the involvement of financially strong partners.

The fundamental question of involvement is posed for every company involved in a supplier coalition, which must be decided based on the strategic positioning and the supplier's self-perception. But, the decision will also have to be considered with respect to competition and risk perspectives, especially for customers with a weak market position. In this case, the personnel and financial resources as well as potential withdrawal opportunities are extremely important.

BOT and BOOT contracts deal with organization options that are also intermediate forms between a pure market-based coordination and an integrated coordination within an individual company. The above shows that this current form of project cooperation is connected with decision-making issues, which are not just not fully resolved in corporate practice, but which are experiencing interesting directions of analysis and activity in light of the New Institutional Economics.

Exercises

1. What are the different phases of proposal planning and order processing?
2. What reasons may lead to cooperation in proposal planning?
3. For what kind of purchases does cooperation with other suppliers seem appropriate? Justify your answer!
4. What is meant by a multi-organizational selling center, and how is it related to inter-company project management?
5. What are the reasons for the early formation of a supplier coalition?
6. What content of a proposal do the key coordination requirements relate to for cooperative proposal planning?
7. What selection criteria for proposal partners are particularly important if a supplier has to cooperate with foreign cooperation partners of which they have almost no knowledge?
8. What reasons may induce a supplier to favor a less well-known foreign supplier as a proposal partner instead of a well-known German supplier?
9. What are the key reasons why company A, who (only) delivers the boilers for a power plant to be constructed, would not take on the role of general contractor?
10. Under what conditions is a supplier in a position to take on the role of a general contractor?
11. Why may cooperation, e.g. in a consortium, also be required between competing suppliers?
12. Customer K requests the installation of control units manufactured by electronics provider E from machine manufacturer M for a new development. What could be the key reasons for these kind of preferences?
13. Why would a plant customer request a supplier coalition
14. in the form of a consortium,
15. in the form of a general contractor?
16. To what extent do the financing requirements of a plant customer influence a plant supplier's cooperation decisions?
17. How important are property rights (licenses) for decisions on and in supplier coalitions?
18. What is the basic reason for a consortium cooperation?
19. What is the specific importance of aligning cooperation and supplier contracts to the plant contract (customer contract)?
20. What are the benefits of a "Build-Own-Operate-Transfer" solution from a project investor's perspective?

Literature

Backhaus, K. (1980). *Auftragsplanung im industriellen Anlagengeschäft*. Stuttgart: Poeschel.
Backhaus, K., Aufderheide, D., & Späth, G.-M. (1994). *Marketing für Systemtechnologien – Entwicklung eines theoretisch-ökonomisch begründeten Geschäftstypenansatzes*. Stuttgart: Schäffer-Poeschel.
Backhaus, K., & Voeth, M. (2010). *Industriegütermarketing* (9th ed.). Munich: Vahlen.
Bea, F. X., Scheurer, S., & Hesselmann, S. (2011). *Projektmanagement* (2nd ed.). Stuttgart: UTB.
Bristor, J. M. (1987). *Buying networks: A model of positional influence in organizational buying*. Ann Arbor: University of Michigan.
Bruhn, M. (2012). *Relationship marketing* (3rd ed.). Munich: Vahlen.
Chelsom, J. V. (1989). Simultaneous engineering in Fallbeispielen. In Verein Deutscher Ingenieure (VDI) (Eds.), *Simultaneous engineering. VDI report* (Vol. 758, pp. 169–180). Düsseldorf.
Eichler, B., & Steinau, S. (1993). Auch Zulieferer müssen immer mehr Flexibilität beweisen. *Handelsblatt, 194*, 29.
Engelhardt, W. H., & Günter, B. (1981). *Investitionsgüter-Marketing*. Stuttgart: Kohlhammer.
Gemünden, H. G. (1985). Wahrgenommenes Risiko und Informationsnachfrage. *Marketing – Zeitschrift für Forschung und Praxis, 7*(1), 27–38.
Günter, B. (1977). Anbieterkoalitionen bei der Vermarktung von Anlagegütern –Organisationsformen und Entscheidungsprobleme. In W. H. Engelhardt & G. Laßmann (Eds.), *Anlagenmarketing, Zeitschrift für betriebswirtschaftliche Forschung* (Vol. 7/77, pp. 155–172). Opladen.
Günter, B. (1979). *Das Marketing von Großanlagen – Strategieprobleme des Systems Selling*. Berlin: Duncker & Humblot.
Günter, B. (1992). Unternehmenskooperation im Investitionsgüter-Marketing –Überlegungen zu einer unterschätzten Strategie. *Zeitschrift für betriebswirtschaftliche Forschung, 44*(9), 792–808.
Günter, B. (1995). Vertragsgestaltung. In M. Kleinaltenkamp & W. Plinke (Eds.), *Technischer Vertrieb – Grundlagen* (pp. 923–945). Berlin: Springer.
Günter, B. (1997). Wettbewerbsvorteile, mehrstufige Kundenanalyse und Kunden-Feedback im Business-to-Business-Marketing. In K. Backhaus, B. Günter, M. Kleinaltenkamp, W. Plinke, & H. Raffée (Eds.), *Marktleistung und Wettbewerb* (pp. 213–231). Wiesbaden: Gabler.
Günter, B. (2007). Verlässlichkeit als Wettbewerbsvorteil im Business-to-Business-Marketing. In J. Büschken, M. Voeth, & R. Weiber (Eds.), *Innovationen für das Industriegütermarketing* (pp. 185–199). Stuttgart: Schäffer-Poeschel.
Günter, B., & Kuhl, M. (2000). Industrielles Beschaffungsmanagement. In M. Kleinaltenkamp & W. Plinke (Eds.), *Technischer Vertrieb. Grundlagen des Business-to-Business Marketing* (2nd ed., pp. 374–450). Berlin: Springer.
Handelsblatt. (2012). Editions 28/29/30. September 2012(189).
Hautkappe, B. (1986). *Unternehmereinsatzformen im Industrieanlagenbau*. Heidelberg: Verlagsgesellschaft Recht und Wissenschaft.
Heger, G. (1988). *Anfragenbewertung im industriellen Anlagengeschäft*. Berlin: Dissertation.
Helm, R., Mehlhorn, A., & Strohmayer, M. (1996). Die Vertrauensproblematik bei zwischenbetrieblichen Kooperationen in der mittelständischen Industrie. *Zeitschrift für Planung, 7*(1), 73–90.
Höffken, E., Schweitzer, M. (1991). Beiträge zur Betriebswirtschaft des Anlagenbaus. *Zeitschrift für betriebswirtschaftliche Forschung*, Special Edition 28/91.
Horn, N. (1986). *Der Konsortialvertrag. Lehrbrief für das Weiterbildende Studium Technischer Vertrieb der Freien Universität Berlin*. Berlin (reprinted 1995).
Klöter, R. (1997). *Opponenten im organisationalen Beschaffungsprozess*. Wiesbaden: Gabler.
Lemiesz, D. (1978). *Abwicklung von Industrialisierungsprojekten. Planung und Errichtung von autonomen, unverbundenen Betriebsstätten in Entwicklungsländern*. Essen: Girardet.

Molter, W. (1986). *Verzugsrisiken im Anlagengeschäft – Risikoverteilung in Anbieterkonsortien*. Berlin: Duncker & Humblot.

Nicklisch, F. (1984). *Bau- und Anlagenverträge – Risiken, Haftung, Streitbeilegung*. Heidelberg: Müller.

Roth, P. (1977). Vergabeformen für die Beschaffung industrieller Anlagen. *Die Betriebswirtschaft, 37*, 193–208.

Söllner, A. (1993). *Commitment in Geschäftsbeziehungen*. Wiesbaden: Gabler.

Thommen, J.-P., & Achleitner, A.-K. (2012). *Allgemeine Betriebswirtschaftslehre* (7th ed.). Wiesbaden: Gabler.

Verein Deutscher Ingenieure (VDI). (1991). *Projektkooperation beim internationalen Vertrieb von Maschinen und Anlagen*. Düsseldorf: VDI.

Weiber, R., & Jacob, F. (2000). Kundenbezogene Informationsgewinnung. In M. Kleinaltenkamp & W. Plinke (Eds.), *Technischer Vertrieb – Grundlagen* (2nd ed., pp. 523–612). Berlin: Springer.

Zentes, J., Swoboda, B., & Morschett, D. (2005). *Kooperationen, Allianzen undNetzwerke* (2nd ed.). Wiesbaden: Gabler.

Index

M. Kleinaltenkamp et al. (eds.), *Business Project Management and Marketing*, Springer Texts in Business and Economics, DOI 10.1007/978-3-662-48507-1

Kolibri 360 GmbH
Ferdinand-Jühlke-Straße 7
99095 Erfurt, Deutschland
produktsicherheit@kolibri360.de